The Prehistory of the Marsh Station Road Site (AZ EE:2:44 [ASM]), Cienega Creek, Southeastern Arizona

Edited by

John C. Ravesloot, Michael J. Boley, and Melanie A. Medeiros

With Contributions by

Karen R. Adams, Chance Copperstone, Brandon M. Gabler,
Gary A. Huckleberry, John A. McClelland, Brian R. McKee,
Barnet Pavao-Zuckerman, Bruce G. Phillips, Paul M. Rawson,
Meaghan A. Trowbridge, and Christine Virden-Lange

Arizona State Museum
THE UNIVERSITY OF ARIZONA.

Arizona State Museum Archaeological Series 202

Arizona State Museum
The University of Arizona
Tucson, Arizona 85721-0026
(c) 2011 by the Arizona Board of Regents
All rights reserved.
Printed in the United States of America

ISBN (paper): 978-1-889747-87-3
Library of Congress Control Number: 2011903184

ARIZONA STATE MUSEUM ARCHAEOLOGICAL SERIES

General Editor: Richard C. Lange
Technical Editors: Lewis S. Borck, Sarah E. Wolff, Laura A. Burghardt

The *Archaeological Series* of the Arizona State Museum, The University of Arizona, publishes the results of research in archaeology and related disciplines conducted in the Greater Southwest. Original, monograph-length manuscripts are considered for publication, provided they deal with appropriate subject matter. Information regarding procedures or manuscript submission and review is given under Research Publications on the Arizona State Museum website: *www.statemuseum.arizona.edu/research/pubs*. Information may be also obtained from the General Editor, *Archaeological Series*, Arizona State Museum, P.O. Box 210026, The University of Arizona, Tucson, Arizona, 85721-0026; Email: langer@email.arizona.edu. Electronic publications and previous volumes in the Arizona State Museum Library or available from the University of Arizona Press are listed on the website noted above.

The Arizona State Museum *Archaeological Series* is grateful to the many donors and supporters who continue to make this publication possible. The cover photograph is Figure 4.11 in the text.

Distributed by The University of Arizona Press, 355 S. Euclid Boulevard, Suite 103, Tucson, Arizona 85719

Contents

vi

Figures

List of Tables

ABSTRACT

This volume describes the archaeological investigations and syntheses of research that William Self Associates, Inc. (WSA), conducted at the Marsh Station Road site (AZ EE:2:44 [ASM]), an extensive, multicomponent, semi-permanent habitation site with occupations spanning from at least 3000 to 550 B.P. (1050 B.C. to A.D. 1400), from the Early Agricultural period through the Hohokam Classic period, located southeast of Tucson. The twelve chapters in this volume include detailed discussions of the cultural setting and environmental context, both past and modern, for the site, as well as of the fieldwork conducted at the site and of specialized analyses of artifacts (ceramics, flaked stone, ground stone, faunal, and shell) and environmental samples, (macrobotanical remains and pollen) recovered from the site. These data are interpreted in order to place the Marsh Station Road site within a local and regional framework in which the site is considered from a heartlands/hinterlands perspective as an important example of how prehistoric farmers in southern Arizona subsisted in a nonriverine landscape.

RESUMEN

En este tomo se sintetizan las investigaciones arqueológicas llevados a cabo por William Self Associates, Inc. (WSA), en el sitio arqueológico Marsh Station Road (AZ EE:2:44 [ASM]), el cual está ubicado al sureste de Tucsón, Arizona. Marsh Station Road es un asentamiento extensivo y semipermanente, de múltiples componentes cronológicos, que abarcaba los años 3000 hasta 550 antes del presente (1050 a.C.–1400 d.C.), o desde los principios del período Agrícola Temprano hasta el fin del período Clásico Hohokam. Los doce capítulos del tomo incluyen discusiones detalladas del contexto cultural y el medioambiente del sitio, tanto prehistóricos como modernos, así como el trabajo de campo llevado a cabo en el sitio, los análisis especializados de artefactos (cerámica, lítica, piedra pulida, hueso, concha), y las muestras macrobotánicas y de polen tomadas para el estudio del medioambiente. Se han interpretado estos datos para situar Marsh Station Road en un esquema local y regional en el cual el sitio es considerado desde una perspectiva centro-periferia, como un ejemplo importante de cómo los agricultores prehistóricos en el sur de Arizona subsistían en un paisaje no ribereño.

Acknowledgments

The archaeological investigation of the Marsh Station Road site (AZ EE:2:44 [ASM]), conducted by William Self Associates, Inc. (WSA), as part of the El Paso to Phoenix Expansion (EPX) project, would not have been possible without the contributions of many people and institutions. We would first like to thank the Kinder Morgan Energy Partners (KMEP) project team: Allan Campbell and Dave Cornman, Project Management (KMEP); Hugo Guerrero, Project Engineer (TRC); Camilla Kahn, Project Engineer (TRC); and Regan Giese, Environmental Compliance (CH2MHill).

All fieldwork was conducted by staff from WSA, whose hard work and dedication was essential to the success of the project. Dr. John Ravesloot served as the principal investigator of the project. Morgan Rieder and Paul Rawson served as field directors and lead monitors for the project, and oversaw all data recovery efforts, while Michael Boley served as an assistant field director for data recovery excavations. Data recovery crew members for the project included Dea Applegate, Pamela Bowler, David Buckley, Janet Clawson, John Curry, Lindsay De Pew, Erica Degelmann, Teodoro (Ted) Eldridge, Natalie Farrell, Reynaldo (Nico) Fuentes, Theodore Gatchell, Damien Huffer, Desrinique Jordan, George Krueger, Jennifer Lippel, Melinda McCrary, Erin McDonald, Melanie Medeiros, Ian Milliken, Connie Moreno, Holley Moyes, Sandra Oh, Matthew Pailes, Sara Parks, Nathan Pike, Meredith Reifschneider, Matt Reynolds, Esther Rivera, Trevor Self, Jason Shields, Jayma Stembridge, Meaghan Trowbridge, Glyceria Tsinas, Tylia Varilek, Brenton Wilcox, Barbara Wold, and Robert (Patrick) Zeller. Field mapping for the project was completed by Trevor Self and Sara Parks. Darling Environmental and Surveying, Ltd., conducted laser mapping of the site, and Skyview Photography provided aerial photography for it. Both John Curry and George Krueger served as archaeological monitors during pipeline construction activities. Dr. John McClelland and Jessica Cerezo-Roman of the Arizona State Museum, University of Arizona, conducted excavations of human remains. Peter Steere and Joseph Joaquin of the Tohono O'odham Nation served as NAGPRA liaisons for the project. Dr. Gary Huckleberry provided geoarchaeological assessments of the site.

The EPX Laboratory was overseen by Lab Manager Olivia Brown Charest and subsequently by Laboratory Director Dr. Brian McKee. Archaeologists/Lab Technicians Dea Applegate, Robert Baker, Katherine Burke, Reynaldo (Nico) Fuentes, Jennifer Hider, Melanie Medeiros, Alicia Retamoza, Robert Sinensky, Kimberly Sonderegger, Tylia Varilek, Rebecca Waugh, Lou Ann Way, and Barbara Wold assisted in the processing and washing of artifacts and environmental samples, preparation of project photographs for archival purposes, and completion of data entry of field and artifact analysis records. Curation of the EPX artifacts was completed by Dea Applegate, Peter Byler, Olivia Brown Charest, Kelly Swartz, Christopher Taylor, and George Vanovich under the direction of Michael Boley and Dr. Brian McKee. Artifact analyses were conducted by numerous WSA staff members and other professional archaeologists in the Tucson area. Ceramic analyses were conducted by Meaghan Trowbridge, with the assistance of Dea Applegate and William Deaver of WestLand Resources, Inc. Flaked stone analyses were overseen by Michael Boley, and conducted by Dea Applegate, John Curry, Reynaldo (Nico) Fuentes, George Krueger, and Dr. Brian McKee. Drs. R. Jane Sliva of Desert Archaeology, Inc., and Jonathan Mabry, the Historic Preservation Officer for the City of Tucson, reviewed the flaked stone projectile point typology in coordination with Michael Boley. Drs. Charles Ferguson, Stephen Richard, and Jon Spencer of the Arizona Geological Society provided valuable guidance regarding raw material identification for the flaked stone analysis. Ground stone analyses were conducted by Dea Applegate, Dr. Jeffrey Baker, and Melanie Medeiros; Dr. Jenny Adams of Desert Archaeology, Inc., assisted in the identification of several unique ground stone artifacts. Zooarchaeological analyses were conducted by Chance Copperstone under the supervision of Dr. Barnet Pavao-Zuckerman of the Arizona State Museum, University of Arizona. Chris Virden-Lange of Tierra Right-of-Way Services conducted the shell analysis. Dr. Karen Adams analyzed all macrobotanical and flotation samples, while Dr. Bruce Phillips of EcoPlan Associates, Inc., conducted the pollen analysis. Dr. John McClelland and Jessica Cerezo-Roman were responsible for all bioarchaeological analyses, which were conducted at the WSA Laboratory in Tucson. Radiocarbon samples were processed by Beta Analytic Radiocarbon Dating Laboratory in Miami, Florida. William Deaver of WestLand Resources, Inc., processed the archaeomagnetic dating samples.

The WSA Cartography/GIS department, including Nazih Fino, Sara Parks, Trevor Self, and Lindsay Wygant, produced all maps and figures for the report. Dr. Brandon Gabler, as database and cartography director, provided oversight of the cartography department as well as data management and statistical analyses for the project. Artifact illustrations were prepared by Sara Parks and Lindsay Wygant; artifact photographs were taken by Sara Parks.

Completion and production of this project report would not have been possible without the help of numerous WSA staff members, including Melanie Medeiros, Peter Byler, Lucy Simpson, Angela Cook, Lindsay De Pew, Rachel Diaz de Valdes, Jay Nordstrom, Stephanie Perez, Whitney Simcik, Tylia Varilek, and Barbara Wold. In addition, Ann Howard of the Arizona State Historic Preservation Office; Jane Childress of the Bureau of Land Management, Las Cruces District Office; and Steve Ross of the Arizona State Land Department visited the WSA excavations at the Marsh Station Road site in June 2007 and provided valuable project guidance. Drs. Paul and Suzanne Fish of the Arizona State Museum, University of Arizona, served as peer reviewers of this report, and their insightful and helpful comments greatly improved the final product. Mr. Scott O'Mack of WSA translated the volume abstract into Spanish. Finally, the editorial staff for the Arizona State Museum's Archaeological Series was responsible for conducting technical and copy editing of the volume as well as formatting, and assisting in bringing this volume to publication.

Chapter 1
Introduction

John C. Ravesloot, Michael J. Boley, and Melanie A. Medeiros

The following report presents the results of archaeological investigations at the Marsh Station Road site (AZ EE:2:44 [ASM]), an extensive, multicomponent, semi-permanent Hohokam habitation site covering approximately 20 acres located near the confluence of Cienega Creek and Mescal Wash, 26 linear miles southeast of Tucson (Figures 1.1 and 1.2). The site was investigated in 2007 as part of the El Paso to Phoenix Expansion (EPX) project (described below), sponsored by SFPP, LP (SFPP), and Kinder Morgan Energy Partners (KMEP). Although William Self Associates, Inc. (WSA), investigated less than four percent of the site as part of the project, during excavations WSA archaeolo-

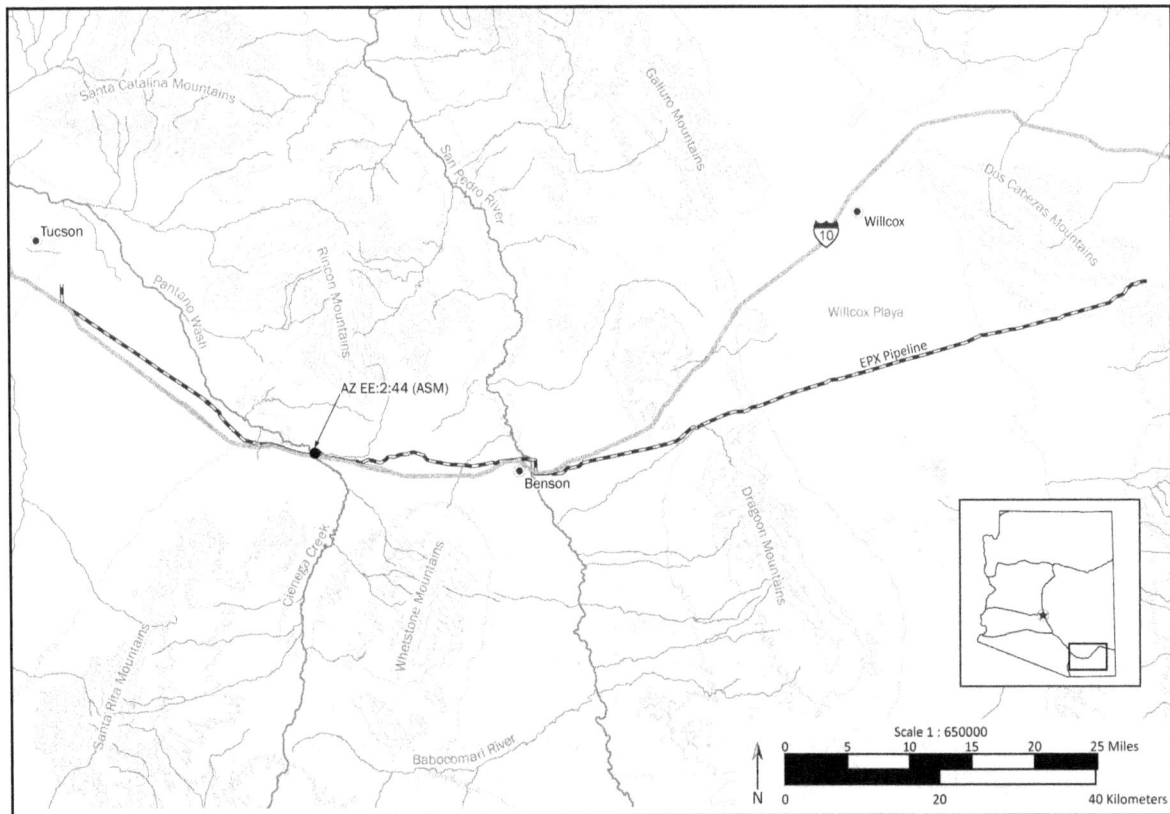

Figure 1.1. Location of the Marsh Station Road site and project area in southeastern Arizona.

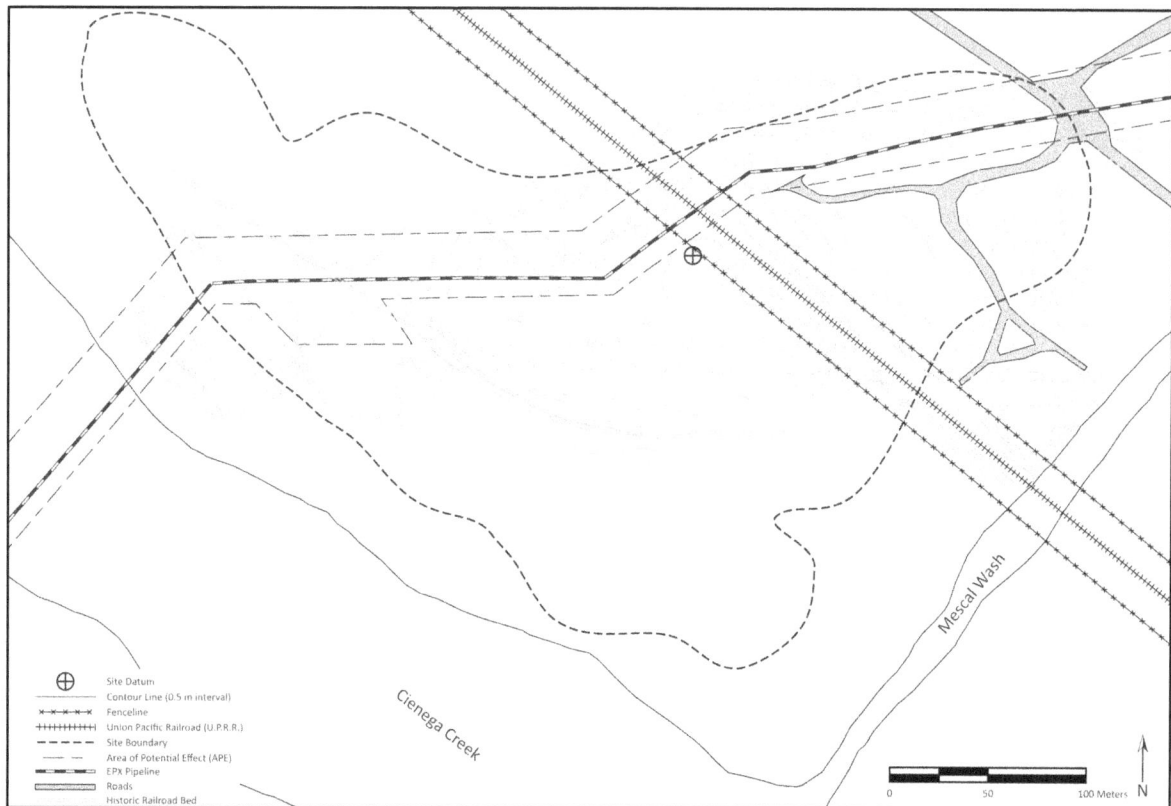

Figure 1.2. Overview of the Marsh Station Road site (AZ EE:2:44 [ASM]) in relation to the EPX project area.

gists documented 192 features, including six pithouses/structures; excavated 138 of these features; and collected over 50,000 artifacts, the majority of which were flaked stone or ceramics. Largely mirroring the occupational history of the nearby Mescal Wash site (AZ EE:2:51 [ASM]; see Vanderpot 2001; Vanderpot and Altschul 2007), the Marsh Station Road site was occupied for over 2,500 years, from at least 3000 to 550 B.P. (1050 B.C. to A.D. 1400). The most intense occupations at the site occurred during the San Pedro phase of the Early Agricultural period and during the late Middle Formative (Rincon phase) period. The San Pedro phase occupation is represented by 37 San Pedro projectile points and two radiocarbon assays (1120–810 B.C. and 1250–1240/1220–980 B.C.), one of which is a maize cob segment containing characteristics similar to other San Pedro phase maize from southern Arizona (Diehl 2005a; L. Huckell

2006; also see Chapter 10), and possibly by 37 aceramic extramural pits and one pithouse. The late Middle Formative (Rincon phase) period is represented by 64 features, including five of the six houses/structures, 10 radiocarbon assays and four archaeomagnetic dates, the presence of decorated ceramic wares dating to this period, and eight projectile points and two maize cob segments indicative of this period. A possible Middle Archaic occupation of the site is also suggested by the presence of Cortaro projectile points, although the excavations produced no absolute dates from this period. In addition, a small Euroamerican historic component dating to the late nineteenth and early twentieth centuries and associated with railroad operations through the region was also documented at the site.

The Marsh Station Road site is important for two interrelated reasons. First, it has been suggested (see Vanderpot and Altschul 2007)

that the Mescal Wash site, just across Mescal Wash from the Marsh Station Road site, is in a "hinterland" between the better known Hohokam, Mogollon, Anasazi, Salado, and Casas Grandes cultural developments. The Mescal Wash site is characterized by elements of what has been labeled "Dragoon," including houses with distinctive recessed hearths, known only from a handful of sites, and a locally made pottery. These characteristics, combined with the lack of ballcourt at such a large site, led Vanderpot and Altschul (2007:63) to conclude that the Mescal Wash site "...was on the fringes of the Hohokam regional system." The Marsh Station Road site, however, presents a different picture. Here, the predominance of Tucson Basin Hohokam red-on-brown pottery and the lack of any "Dragoon" elements indicate a strong tie to the Tucson Basin. Indeed, the Tucson Basin Hohokam may be seen as extending at least as far east as the confluence of Cienega Creek and Mescal Wash. Second, the presence of a substantial Early Agricultural occupation at the site, particularly during the San Pedro phase, complements the emerging picture of how early farmers in southern Arizona used the landscape, a picture that heretofore had been primarily colored by the extensively documented occupations along the Santa Cruz River, and in light of Mabry's (2005b) agricultural niche-filling model (see Chapter 2), highlights the importance of investigating sites located in nonriverine settings, outside of the perceived Hohokam "heartlands" in the Phoenix and Tucson basins. Both reasons indicate that additional archaeological studies in the surrounding region are needed.

This report is divided into 12 chapters. The remainder of this chapter provides an introduction to and background on the EPX project. Chapter 2 provides a cultural context for southern Arizona, spanning from the Paleoindian period through the Classic period, as a backdrop for our interpretation of the Marsh Station Road site. Chapter 3 contains an introduction to the Marsh Station Road site, its prehistoric and modern environmental and geologic setting, a discussion of the previous archaeological research conducted at the site, and the research design applied to the data gathered from the site. Chapter 4 presents the field methods used to investigate the site and the results of excavations. Chapters 5 through 11 describe the results of all analytical investigations for artifacts—ceramics, flaked stone, ground stone, faunal remains, shell, and macrobotanical and pollen remains—recovered from the site. The final chapter presents a synthetic interpretation of the Marsh Station Road site with specific reference to the site research design that guided WSA's studies.

PROJECT DESCRIPTION

The El Paso to Phoenix Expansion project (EPX) consisted of the replacement of approximately 131 miles of pipe, divided into three segments, of the SFPP, LP, El Paso to Phoenix petroleum pipeline in Texas (Segment A), New Mexico (Segment B), and Arizona (Segment C), and the construction of associated facilities. The pipeline is part of SFPP's Pacific operations, a 3,850-mile, common-carrier system delivering gasoline, jet fuel, and diesel fuel to various areas of the western United States. Replacement of the El Paso to Phoenix pipeline was conducted in two phases. The EPX project is the second phase in the larger, overall replacement of the original 8-inch El Paso to Phoenix Pipeline with 12-inch and 16-inch pipes. The first phase of the project, the East Line Expansion (ELX) project, consisted of four segments totaling approximately 243 miles between Texas and Arizona. Cultural resources services and construction of the pipeline and ancillary facilities were completed by WSA and TRC Solutions, Inc. (TRC), between 2005 and 2007 (Goar et al. 2009; Goar, Condon, et al. 2010; Ravesloot et al. 2007).

The Arizona portion (Segment C) of the project consisted of the replacement of approximately 98 miles of 8-inch petroleum pipeline between Apache Pass (Cochise County) and Tucson (Pima County) (see Figure 1.1). For this portion of the project as well as for six alternative routes (Alternates 2–7) ranging from 1,000 feet to 3.4 miles in length, SFPP requested WSA to provide all cultural resources services, including inventory and pedestrian survey (Rawson et al. 2006; Rawson et al. 2007; Rieder et al. 2006), preparation of a treatment plan to guide mitigative efforts, archaeological testing and data recovery, and all other mitigative measures of historic properties that could be affected by this undertaking as well as monitoring during construction. The complete results of mitigative archaeological work, which included data recovery at six prehistoric sites, avoidance of one prehistoric site, mitigative documentation of seven historic linear sites, and the development of an interpretive program for Fort Bowie National Historic site, conducted by WSA for the Arizona portion (Segment C) of the EPX project are presented in the final project report (Ravesloot et al. 2010), on file at the Arizona State Museum (ASM). Cultural resource services for both the Texas (Segment A) and New Mexico (Segment B) portions of the EPX project were provided by TRC; accordingly, the results of archaeological work conducted in those segments are presented in separate reports (Goar, Minjares, et al. 2010a, 2010b).

Chapter 2
Cultural Context

Michael J. Boley

ARCHAEOLOGY OF THE PLEISTOCENE AND EARLY HOLOCENE

The earliest documented Native American occupation of the Americas is the Paleoindian period, which began at least as early as 12,000 years ago—many recent studies place its beginning thousands of years earlier—and lasted until around 10,500 years ago (Meltzer 2009; Figure 2.1). The Paleoindian period was characterized by small, highly mobile bands of people and a hunting-and-gathering way of life adapted to a climate that was generally cooler and wetter than today. Archaeological sites dating to the early part of the Paleoindian period are often associated with the remains of extinct large mammals such as mammoth and bison, which has long been interpreted as reflecting a heavy reliance on hunting big game (Waguespack and Surovell 2003). Paleoindian sites are typically identified by the presence of the distinctive fluted spear points of the Clovis and Folsom traditions. The most notable evidence for the Paleoindian period in southern Arizona comes from the Naco, Lehner, and Murray Springs sites, all located in the upper San Pedro River valley, and all particularly important to the definition and formulation of the Clovis culture (Haury 1953; Haury et al. 1959; Haynes and B. Huckell, eds. 2007). Less Paleoindian material has been recovered near the site (Mabry 1998). Having said that, a Clovis projectile point was recently found on the modern ground surface southeast of Tucson (Hesse 2010), and it is one of only three Clovis points ever found in the greater Tucson area; given their proveniences, all may well have been curated by later Hohokam occupants.

A later (post-Folsom) Paleoindian occupation near Tucson is indicated by the recovery of several Plainview-like points (B. Huckell 1984; Jonathan Mabry, personal communication to WSA 2010). One was recovered at the Pima Canyon site (AZ BB:9:53 [ASM]), one at the Sabino Canyon Ruin (AZ BB:9:32 [ASM[), two from the Lone Hill Site (AZ BB:10:17 [ASM]) in the Catalina Mountains (Agenbroad 1970, cited in B. Huckell 1984), and one at AZ AA:8:14 (ASM) (Hewitt and Stephen 1981, cited in B. Huckell 1984) in the Tortolita Mountains. Available radiocarbon dates associated with Plainview points indicate a widely accepted date range of between 10,200 and 9,800 uncalibrated years B.P. (Bousman et al. 2004; Justice 2002; Holliday 2000; Mabry 1998, 2000).

Date (B.C./A.D)	Tucson Basin Hohokam		Formative Terminology
	Phase	Period	Period
1540-1750	n/a	Protohistoric	Protohistoric
— 1450 —			
	Tucson	Classic	Late Formative
— 1250 —			
	Tanque Verde		
— 1150 —			
	Rincon	Sedentary	late Middle Formative
— 950 —			
	Rillito	Colonial	early Middle Formative
	Cañada del Oro		
— 750 —			
	Tortolita	Pioneer	Early Formative
— 500 —			
	Agua Caliente	Early Ceramic	
— 50 —			
	Cienega	Early Agricultural	Early Agricultural
— 800 —			
	San Pedro		
—1200—			
	Unnamed		
—2100—			
		Middle Archaic	Middle Archaic
— 6000 —			
		Early Archaic	Early Archaic
— 8500 —			
		Paleoindian	Paleoindian
— 9500 —			

Figure 2.1. Chronology of culture history in southern Arizona showing both the Tucson Basin Hohokam and Formative terminology.

ARCHAIC PERIOD

The Archaic period, which began around 10,500 years ago and ended at about 2100 B.C., was also characterized by a hunting-and-gathering way of life, but Archaic peoples exploited a much greater diversity of plant and animal species than their Paleoindian predecessors. The change in emphasis allowed an increasing degree of sedentism, which is reflected in the number and size of Archaic period sites. The Archaic occupation of southern Arizona was originally defined as the Cochise culture by Sayles and Antevs (1941; Sayles 1983) in the San Pedro, Sulphur Springs, and San Simon valleys. Within this tradition, three successive phases were recognized: Sulphur Springs, Chiricahua, and San Pedro. Since the mid-1980s, the long span of Archaic prehistory has typically been subdivided into Early, Middle, and Late periods, replacing earlier, more complicated schemes (B. Huckell 1995). In recent years, the term "Late Archaic" has become reserved for hunting-foraging sites, while contemporary sites with evidence of agriculture are assigned to the Early Agricultural period (see below).

The Early Archaic, which dates from about 8500 to 6000 B.C., is not particularly well-represented in southeastern Arizona. As of 2001, just 19 sites with an Early Archaic component were known in southeastern Arizona (Stevens 2001a). These sites are identified in part by the presence of tapering stemmed projectile points, including Lake Mohave, Jay, and Bajada points (see Justice 2002 and Mabry 1998 for a more detailed discussion of these points' characteristics and their geographic distribution).

Stevens (2001a) notes the absence of radiocarbon dates in southeastern Arizona between 6000 and 3000 B.C. While this may be due to the dearth of alluvial deposits of appropriate age due to erosion, locations that do retain continuous depositional sequences seem to be lacking materials of this age. The most parsimonious interpretation is that there was a significant reduction in the regional population during this particularly hot and dry time.

Evidence of a Middle Archaic (3000 to 2100 B.C.) presence is greatly increased, with 134 identified sites as of 2001 (Stevens 2001a), including some on the east side of the Santa Rita Mountains, not far from Cienega Creek (B. Huckell 1984). Representative projectile point types include Chiricahua, Gypsum, Pinto, San Jose, and Cortaro (see Justice 2002 and Mabry 1998 for a more detailed discussion of these points' characteristics and their geographic distribution). A range of faunal material has been recovered from these sites, and roasting pits, hearths, and middens are not uncommon. Evidence of maize has been noted from at least two sites in the larger region: the Cienega Creek site (AZ W:10:112 [ASM]), on the San Carlos Indian Reservation, Arizona (Haury 1957) and Bat Cave (LA 4935), New Mexico (Wills 1988). While suggestive, the evidence for cultigens in the Middle Archaic is not conclusive, as it is in the subsequent period. This period, referred to as the Late Archaic or, increasingly, as the Early Agricultural period, merits further discussion.

EARLY AGRICULTURAL PERIOD

The end date for the Middle Archaic that is provided above is a recent and possibly provisional development, and is based on the recovery of radiocarbon-dated maize and other annuals from several sites with well-defined agricultural occupations in the middle Santa Cruz Valley (Mabry 2005a). In the Tucson Basin, the period following the Middle Archaic is now generally referred to as the Early Agricultural period, rather than as the Late Archaic, although there is some ambiguity surrounding the distinction between the two terms. Regardless, the earliest beginning of the Early Agricultural period is at 2100 B.C., but the first 900 years of the period are not well known and are unnamed (Mabry 2005a:51). The San Pedro phase begins at about 1200 B.C. and runs to about 800 B.C., at which time the Cienega phase begins and in turn extends to about A.D. 50.

Over the last several years, researchers affiliated with the Center for Desert Archaeology, and especially Jonathan Mabry, have taken the lead in writing about the Early Agricultural period in southern Arizona (Diehl, ed. 1997, 2005; Freeman 1998; Gregory 2001, ed.; Mabry 2005a, 2005b, 2008a, 2008b; Mabry, ed. 1998, 2008; Mabry et al. 1997; Sliva, ed. 2005). Mabry (2005c; 2008b) in particular has synthesized the recently gained information on material culture, hypothesizing on social organization (2008b) and modeling settlement patterns (2005b; 2008b). The following summary of what is known about the Early Agricultural period in the region relies heavily on these sources.

As noted above, the third and most recent phase or stage of the Cochise culture was labeled the San Pedro. At the time of the term's conception, radiocarbon dating had not been developed, so the stage was temporally assigned using geological correlations to between 5,000 and 2,500 years ago (3000 to 550 B.C.; Sayles and Antevs 1941). Based on radiocarbon dates, Antevs (1983) later modified the dates of the stage to 3,500 to 2,000 years ago (1550 B.C. to A.D. 1). But, with the introduction of B. Huckell's classification scheme, referring to this or any other period as the San Pedro fell out of favor. Rather, B. Huckell dated the Middle Archaic from 4300 to 1800 B.C., and the Late Archaic from 1800 B.C. to A.D. 1 to 600. Later, B. Huckell drew a distinction between contemporaneous populations living during the Late Archaic, suggesting that those

groups practicing a hunting-and-gathering lifeway still be referred to as Late Archaic, while those who were practicing a lifestyle that incorporated farming should be called Early Agricultural. He also suggested that the Early Agricultural be divided into two phases, the San Pedro and the Cienega (B. Huckell 1995). So, after a hiatus of a couple decades, the label is once again in common usage, and the Early Agricultural label has effectively replaced the term "Late Archaic." In her dissertation, Stevens (2001a) does not make use of "Late Archaic." Rather, she uses both and Early and Middle Archaic, but refers to the period of time between 1700 B.C. to A.D. 150 as the Early Agricultural. For the rest of this report, the time following the Middle Archaic, which is seen to extend to 2100 B.C., and preceding the advent of formative culture around A.D. 1/50 or thereafter, is referred to as the Early Agricultural; "Late Archaic" will not be used except where it was used by a previous researcher. Following Mabry (2005a) and Stevens (2001a, 2001b), the period from 2100 to 1200 B.C. is referred to as "unnamed." Having made this taxonomic clarification, a summary of the material culture of the Early Agricultural period and particularly of the San Pedro phase, including recent additions noted by Mabry (2008a), is provided below.

As Mabry (2008a) summarizes, a number of changes and additions have been made to the characteristic attributes of the San Pedro phase material culture since 1995, which marks the year B. Huckell suggested the San Pedro phase be separated from the Cienega. Since then a large amount of work has been conducted at sites along the Santa Cruz River in the Tucson Basin that have a San Pedro component. These changes or additions can be seen in the boundaries of the San Pedro complex, cultigens, artifact types (e.g., San Pedro projectile points), feature types, and agricultural technologies and cultivation techniques (Mabry 2008a:7–21).

San Pedro points are distributed in a circle with a 300-mile radius that has its center point at Nogales, Sonora, Mexico, with the exceptions that the points are not known west of the Colorado River or in Baja California (Mabry 2008a:Figure 1.3). As Mabry (2008a:7) points out, however, the core area of the San Pedro complex should probably be restricted to the basins of the desert borderlands, as this is the location of known San Pedro phase settlements. This core area includes southwesternmost New Mexico, northwesternmost Chihuahua, northeastern Sonora, and southeastern Arizona, and is bounded by the Baboquivari Mountains in the west and the Gila River in the north (Mabry 2005a:Figure 3.1; Mabry 2008a:Figure 1.3). Empire projectile points (Stevens and Sliva 2002) may be diagnostic of the earlier portion of the San Pedro phase and are so far restricted to the northwestern half of the core San Pedro complex area as described. Given this concentration, Mabry (2008a:7) "sees the San Pedro complex as representing a primarily lowland adaptation in the Sonoran desert scrub and Chihuahuan desert grasslands zones."

Early Agricultural farmers cultivated a number of tropical plants (Mabry 2005a, 2008a). Primary among these is maize, which is "present at almost every excavated San Pedro site" (Mabry 2008a:9). Other cultigens include pepo squash, cotton, tobacco, common bean, and possibly domesticated amaranth. Whether domesticated or not, amaranth was a part of the diet, as were several other weedy, leafy annuals such as goosefoot, tansy mustard, and dropseed grasses (Mabry 2008a:9). The arrival of other cultigens to the region postdate the earliest dates on maize by at least a millennium (Merrill et al. 2009).

In addition to the appearance of new cultigens, new artifact and feature types were also introduced. San Pedro and Empire dart points are not the only styles recovered from Early Agricultural contexts. Cortaro (Roth and B. Huckell 1992), Cienega, Tallarin (Sliva 2009), and Western Basketmaker-style points have also been recovered (Figures 6.2 and 6.4). Ground stone tools including mortars, pestles, metates, lapstones, proto-palettes, bowls, awls, whorls, disks, rods, pipes, and cruciforms (Adams 2005) were all recovered from Las Capas, as were tools of bone and antler (Mabry 2008a:Table 1.2). Personal adornments made of mica, bone, shell, and fired clay were also recovered from Las Capas. Other fired clay artifacts include small vessels, figurines, pipes, and cornucopia. These latter artifacts may have been used in ritual settings, along with bone tubes, balls, and "dice" as well as pigments and minerals. Features associated with the San Pedro complex include oval to round pit structures; storage structures; various pits for storage, processing and cooking; inhumations and cremations; wells; trash middens; canid burials; and large structures that may have served a communal or ceremonial purpose (Mabry 2008a:9, Table 1.2).

San Pedro phase farmers employed numerous cultivation techniques, including rain-fed farming, dry farming, runoff farming, flood farming, irrigated farming, and water-table farming (Mabry 2005b:Table 5.5). Each of these techniques was characterized by differences in upfront labor and maintenance costs, risk, yield, and energy returns. Looking at these characteristics through the lens of human behavioral ecology, Mabry (2005b) developed a model that seeks to explain how various agricultural niches would have been filled by early agriculturalists in the San Pedro phase. Each niche is conceived of as a:

> [S]pecialized strategy of food production with one or more farming systems, with the optimum location for a specific strategy being that combination of landform, soil, and microclimate in which subsistence goals are most closely and predictably achieved [Mabry 2005b:147].

The technique characterized by the lowest labor investment, lowest risk, highest yield, and highest efficiency is water-table farming, so it is expected that this technique would have been practiced first in any niche. Similarly, overbank flood farming should have been practiced early on. These would have been followed by runoff farming, ak chin farming, and irrigation farming, each characterized by higher labor investments, medium to high yields and energy returns, and low to medium risks. Mabry (2005b:147) hypothesizes that groups would have occupied all the "constantly damp, regularly inundated" niches, then started filling the niches that required more labor and were more risky. Mabry (2005b:147–148) points out that nothing about this model is irreversible; the agricultural niches last occupied would have been those first abandoned, and a resumption of a hunting and gathering would certainly have been possible (see also Stevens 2001a:408).

It has been suggested that San Pedro farmers migrated to the core area described above from Mesoamerica (B. Huckell 1990; Matson 1991), bringing domesticated maize, beans, and squash with them. Others believe that the tropical cultigens reached the area through diffusion (Wills 1988). Merrill and others (2009:21–25) are in the latter camp, and argue that Southern Uto-Aztecan (a subgroup of Proto-Uto-Aztecan) speaking groups, who had come to the southwestern United States and adjacent areas of northwestern Mexico from the Great Basin, "facilitated the diffusion of maize agriculture from Mesoamerica to the US Southwest…through both group-to-group diffusion and relatively short-distance migrations of local farming populations, which frequently repositioned themselves over the landscape to take advantage of damp floodplains and other conditions propitious for cultivating maize." This is not to say that longer-distance migrations did not play a role; the sudden appearance on the Colorado Plateau of Western Basket-

maker points, so similar to San Pedro points, may be the result of long(er)-distance migration (Berry and Berry 1986; Matson 1991, 1999).

Early Agricultural sites have been recorded in a number of ecological zones. In the Tucson Basin, large sites along the Santa Cruz River have garnered deserved attention, but sites have also been documented in the upper bajadas, and fewer numbers are known from the lower bajadas and mountains. Roth (1992) summarized three subsistence-settlement models to account for this distribution. First, she suggested that each of the zones was occupied at different points in time. Second, the occupations may have been coeval, but there were two groups practicing different subsistence strategies (Fish et al. 1990). Third, the sites were left by the same people, who alternately exploited both the floodplains and the upper bajadas (Roth 1989).

Stevens (2001a, 2001b) hypothesized that the distribution of Early Agricultural sites in both the middle San Pedro River valley and the Cienega Valley would be different than in the Tucson Basin due to the environmental structure of the locations. All three places share valley bottom and upland settings, and both of these zones were intensely exploited. The main difference between locations is in the aerial extent and biotic characterization of the bajada settings between valley bottom and upland, and these are the places that Stevens thought would be most different from one valley to another. In the Tucson Basin, the major drainages are close to the bases of surrounding mountains, so the bajada is a "narrow zone on one side of the major drainages and a broad zone with comparatively low species diversity on the other side" (Stevens 2001a:399). In the other two valleys, the major drainages are located centrally between mountain ranges, and the bajada is therefore much larger, but also more biotically uniform. Stevens' (2001a, 2001b) model ended up overestimating the use of the middle bajada in the Tucson Basin and under-estimating it in the Cienega and San Pedro River valleys.

Early Agricultural sites in the Cienega Valley have been recorded from the Santa Rita Mountains (B. Huckell 1984) west of the creek to the valley bottom, where a couple large sites have been excavated. These sites, Don-aldson (AZ EE:2:30 [ASM]) and Los Ojitos (AZ EE:2:137 [ASM]), located along Cienega Creek near its confluence with Matty Canyon, are buried by about 5 m of sediment. Excavations of these sites in the 1950s (Eddy 1958; Eddy and Cooley 1983) and 1980s (B. Huckell 1995) produced evidence of a relatively sedentary population; structures, burials, pits, and diverse artifact assemblages were documented. These occupations date primarily to the Cienega phase, but surface sites document a significant San Pedro phase presence in the valley as well (Stevens 2001a).

Most known Early Agricultural sites in the San Pedro River valley are either clustered on the bajadas along Slaughterhouse Wash and Huachuca Creek, overlook Babocomari River, or are on the lower bajadas (Vanderpot 1997). They are identified largely through the presence of hide-working tools, bifaces, and heavily patinated lithics. At these sites, Cortaro, San Pedro, and Cienega projectile points are well represented. Whalen (1971) specifically addressed the topographical setting of sites in his study between the Whetstone Mountains and the San Pedro. He concluded that the resources pursued were consistent between the hillsides and the river ecozone, although the intensity of occupation was greater on higher ground. Large scale survey of Fort Huachuca, in the San Pedro River valley, used a comparable approach of correlating site function, determined by surface lithic analysis, with topographical location (Vanderpot 1997). Middle Archaic camps were found to be evenly distributed across the landscape, though often on

high spots with a good view; one of the larger sites was on a broad ridge on the upper bajada (Vanderpot 1997:36). Late Archaic or Early Agricultural sites in the Fort Huachuca study area were found to favor the lower elevations along the San Pedro and its tributary washes, and these sites often showed evidence of agave processing (Vanderpot 1997:36–44).

FORMATIVE OR PRE-CLASSIC PERIOD

Use of the term "Formative" in the Tucson Basin is contended (Wallace, ed. 2003). It and its subdivisions are used here to indicate broad, seemingly pan-Southwest changes. Use of the term is not meant to imply that prehistoric cultures in the Southwest were "forming," or that they were on a one-way trajectory toward urbanization. It is used because of the fact that our site is located in a cultural transition zone where three culture areas are thought to intersect. The use of Tucson Basin Hohokam chronological terms is not appropriate when discussing developments in eastern Arizona, and vice-versa. However, the period and phase labels traditionally used to talk about developments among the prehistoric cultures are used where appropriate.

A primary change that marks the beginning of the Formative period (circa A.D. 50–150) in the Tucson Basin is related to innovations in ceramic technology. Ceramic figurines and incipient ceramic vessels were manufactured in the Tucson Basin during the Early Agricultural period (Heidke 2005; Heidke and Ferg 2001; Heidke et al. 1998; Mabry 2008a; Stinson 2005). Beginning in the Agua Caliente phase (circa A.D. 50–500), ceramic vessels began to take on a more utilitarian role, and seed jars were widely manufactured (Heidke 2005). Wallace and Lindeman (2003) refer to this time as the Plain Ware Horizon, and suggest that the Red Ware

Horizon, which is characterized by the inclusion of some vessels with a red slip, began circa A.D. 450–500 and terminated at about A.D. 700, when ceramics began to be manufactured for a variety of domestic uses and were more often decorated. This widespread adoption of a variety of ceramic containers serves as the end of the Early Formative period, which had been largely homogenous across the desert southwest.

This time is also characterized by the development of more formalized and substantial architectural features suggesting more permanent settlements. Differentiation in pithouse styles occurs with pithouses erected inside shallow rectangular or subrectangular pits and supported by post-and-beam frames that were coated with matted grasses and mud (Whittlesey et al. 1994). Larger structures, which may have provided communal or ritual foci, also were constructed. Population increase coincided with more diversified and expanded irrigation agriculture. Archaeological evidence suggests that the importation of shell, turquoise, obsidian, and other materials continued and increased (Whittlesey et al. 1994).

Eventually, distinct cultural patterns began to emerge during the Formative period, expressed in increasingly elaborate material culture and social organization. Two principal cultural traditions are recognized in the Formative period in south-central and southeastern Arizona: the Mogollon and the Hohokam. The Mogollon culture was originally defined by Haury (1936) in southwest New Mexico, but Mogollon sites, artifacts, and influence extended far into Arizona. The Hohokam world would primarily be thought of as extending from Phoenix through central Arizona into the Tucson Basin. Tucson itself has been seen as something of a Hohokam frontier, with ceramic traditions responding to Mogollon influence as well as the Hohokam heartland to the north. There is not a discrete boundary between the cultures, but Mogollon culture is increasingly well represented moving eastward. The mixing of Hohokam and Mogollon artifacts in southeastern Arizona has historically been seen as two different expressions of prehistoric culture: the Dragoon sequence and the San Simon Branch of the Mogollon. Whittlesey and others (1994) note the legacy of two (in a sense competing) southwestern archaeological institutions in defining these terms: the Amerind Foundation and Gila Pueblo.

Dragoon Culture

The concept of a Dragoon sequence originated at the Amerind Foundation, following work in Texas Canyon Fulton 1938), the Sulphur Springs Valley (Fulton and Tuthill 1940), and along the San Pedro (Tuthill 1947). The Amerind researchers believed they had defined a distinct cultural package, although "no attempt has here been made to add Dragoon to the … list of basic cultures of the Southwest … ." (Fulton and Tuthill 1940:64). Rather they proposed that the "basic culture is Hohokam with little more than a veneer of Mogollon influence" (Fulton and Tuthill 1940:55). A four-phase Dragoon chronology was proposed (Tuthill 1947) that tied approximately into the Tucson Basin Hohokam sequence (all dates A.D.; see top of following page).

Ceramic typology was crucial to the Dragoon chronology, because there was no dating by such means as radiocarbon or dendrochronology (Whittlesey et al. 1994). The Dragoon ceramics were seen as distinct, somewhat specialized forms (Fulton and Tuthill 1940). Red-on-brown types were well represented, including Cascabel, Tres Alamos, Deep Well, and Dragoon wares (Tuthill 1947). There were also San Francisco, Dragoon, and Tres Alamos red wares. The plain ware, at least from the Tres Alamos site, was considered to be closely related to Gila Plain. The Tanque

Dragoon Sequence	Approximate Tucson Basin Counterpart
Cascabel phase (700–900)	Rillito phase (Colonial period)
Tres Alamos phase (900–1100)	Rincon phase (Sedentary period)
Tanque Verde phase (1100–1200)	Tanque Verde phase (Classic period)
Tucson phase (1200–1450)	Tucson phase (Classic period)

Verde phase was only represented by ceramics. Phases with a more complete cultural package had other distinctive elements, especially in architectural and burial practice. The occurrence of inhumations rather than cremations in the earlier phases was seen as a strong contrast with the Hohokam and perhaps an example of Mogollon influence.

The Amerind Foundation concept of a liminal Dragoon culture—distinct, yet part of the Hohokam; influenced by the Mogollon, but outside it; discrete, but not a basic culture—is intriguing. Overall, the Dragoon culture has remained something of a footnote, and Gumerman's (1991) contributors were able to explore the Hohokam world without reference to Dragoon, even though they were writing for the Amerind Foundation. Despite the convincing reservations of Whittlesey and others (1994) and the limited use of the term in contemporary papers, there remains a strong sense that Hohokam and Mogollon cultures overlap in this region, producing not only a mixture, but also some specifically local material. A good example of this is provided by the discovery of pithouses with unusual recessed hearths at the Mescal Wash site (AZ EE:2:51 [ASM]; Vanderpot 2001; Vanderpot and Altschul 2007). Without explicitly naming the Dragoon culture, the author(s) found a parallel for this distinctive feature in the sites the Amerind used to define it.

While the Amerind Foundation formulated the Dragoon culture, archaeologists from Gila Pueblo were studying the San Simon and San Pedro River valleys from a different perspective. Whittlesey and others (1994) note the great interest of the Gila Pueblo team in establishing the range, chronology, and indeed the validity of the Mogollon culture that had recently been defined by Haury (1936) in New Mexico. In the San Simon Valley, the San Simon Branch of Mogollon culture was defined by Sayles (1945) as a sequence based on ceramic typology, beginning with the Peñasco phase, continuing through the Dos Cabezas, Pinaleño, Galiuro, and Cerros phases, and ending with the Encinas phase. The San Simon Branch was influenced by surrounding cultural provinces. In the San Simon Valley, this meant close ties with the Mimbres Mogollon on the east; to the west, in the Sulphur Springs and San Pedro River valleys, Hohokam influence was more pronounced (Bronitsky and Merritt 1986). Sayles' original sequence was revised by Franklin (1978) and most recently by Gilman (1997), who has restructured and extended the sequence into five periods (all dates are A.D.):

Early Pit Structure Period	100 to 650
Middle Pit Structure Period	650 to 900
Late Pit Structure Period	900 to 1050
Surface Structure Period	1050 to 1150
Post-1150 Period	1150 to 1450

As a result of her investigations in the San Simon Valley, Gilman (1997:84) found that :

"during the early Pit Structure period, sites were located where the most reliable water was present, allowing access to the densest wild food and the best farmland. More sites and probably more people were present in the later Pit Structure periods, and sites were additionally located on secondary washes and in areas not previously used for habitation."

Hohokam Culture

Hohokam culture was first defined in the Phoenix Basin, the "core" area of the culture (Gladwin 1928; Gladwin and Gladwin 1934; Gladwin et al. 1937). By about A.D. 800, in the Colonial period, the full set of cultural traits had been developed, including public architecture in the form of ballcourts, a large infrastructure of irrigation canals, an extensive trade network with surrounding regions, a mortuary complex based on cremation, and a distinctive material culture of red-on-buff pottery, shell jewelry, and other crafts. The original core-periphery model of the relationship of the Phoenix Basin to the Tucson Basin and other areas (Gladwin and Gladwin 1934; Haury 1976) was later supplanted with the concept of a Hohokam regional system, in which ballcourts served as nodes for social and economic interaction (Abbott et al. 2007; Crown 1991; Doyel 1991; Wilcox 1979; Wilcox and Sternberg 1983). The Phoenix and Tucson Basins share broad developmental similarities over the course of prehistory, but differ in the details. Here, given its proximity to the site, the focus is on the Tucson Basin, and particularly on the Sedentary period.

The Sedentary period, which consists solely of the Rincon phase, is the most studied and well known Hohokam phase in the Tucson Basin, and is the Hohokam phase most relevant to the Marsh Station Road site. Based on differences in ceramic decoration, the Rincon phase has been divided into three subphases: Early, Middle, and Late, each of which lasted 50 to 100 years (Wallace 1985, 1986a, 1986b). Differences among the subphases, however, are not limited to changes in the decorated ceramics; changes in ritual organization and settlement patterns, along with the role of the household, also characterize the three divisions of the Rincon phase (Doelle 1985; Doelle and Wallace 1991; Elson, ed. 1986; Huntington, ed. 1986; Roth 2000; Whittlesey, ed. 2004).

Archaeological work performed by the Institute for American Research (now the Center for Desert Archaeology) in the 1980s provided interpretations of the Rincon phase that informed later work. In addition, excavations at the Valencia (Doelle 1985) and West Branch (Huntington, ed. 1986) sites, Rincon phase villages along the Santa Cruz River, revealed changes in settlement patterns, and, perhaps, subsistence strategies.

The Early Rincon, continuing a trend established in the preceding Rillito phase, witnessed a rapid population increase. In the western Tucson Basin, along the Santa Cruz River, this increase was manifested by the growth of regularly spaced ballcourt villages. In the Middle Rincon subphase, these villages were apparently largely abandoned along with their ballcourts, and a series of smaller hamlets was established along the river. Doelle and Wallace (1991) suggest that this shift may be related to the deep downcutting of the river (Waters 1987), which would have limited the agricultural potential of the area and probably forced the inhabitants to widen their subsistence base. Huntington (1988) argued that this subsistence diversity was also reflected in the variable sizes of houses, in particularly accounting for the larger ones. That is, larger houses would house more people, who would be involved in more tasks relating to various subsistence activities.

People were not only living along the Santa Cruz River during the Rincon phase; there was a significant population living in the eastern portion of the Tucson Basin as well. Indeed, this part of the basin reached its population peak in the Rincon phase (Elson, ed. 1986). Stretches along Tanque Verde Wash and Rincon Creek were particularly densely settled. This expansion even extended as far as the portion of Cienega Creek between Rincon Creek and Mescal Wash. Actually, Elson (ed. 1986:Figure 18.4) limits his discussion of the eastern Tucson Basin to just below the confluence of Cienega Creek and Mescal Wash, and the southeasternmost site he shows, represented as an "Unclassified Large Site," is AZ BB:14:25 (ASM). This site, also known as the New Pantano site, is located less than one mile northwest of the Marsh Station Road site.

Changes in the settlement of the Tucson Basin were mirrored in the San Pedro River valley, where there was a shift during the pre-Classic period to the occupation of secondary drainages rather than major rivers, perhaps due to some unusually wet years in the late eleventh century that drove people away from the surging San Pedro (Altschul 1997:61; Van West and Altschul 1994). Throughout the San Pedro River valley, Rillito and Rincon Red-on-brown ceramics are more abundant than the Mogollon wares, reinforcing the idea of a tighter connection with the Hohokam of the Tucson Basin in general.

The regional system reached its maximum extent during the first half of the Sedentary period, from about A.D. 950 to 1050. New settlements were established and many existing large villages, such as Snaketown on the middle Gila River, attained their greatest size and complexity. Evidence suggests that pottery was being mass-produced by specialists during this time (Abbott 1983, 2000). However, the later part of the period saw major changes: the overall settlement system contracted, populations aggregated along major drainages, and ballcourts were abandoned. By the end of the period, the regional system was collapsing.

CLASSIC PERIOD

The middle of the twelfth century, which marks the beginning of the Classic period, is recognized as a critical turning point in Southwestern prehistory (Cordell and Gumerman 1989; Lekson 1999). The trajectory of Mogollon culture into the Classic period is controversial (Cordell 1997), and it may be that the Mogollon tradition effectively ends at around A.D. 1000 with the introduction of Pueblo-style architecture (Lekson 1999). In the Safford, San Bernardino, Sulphur Springs, and San Pedro River valleys, the period from ca. A.D. 1150 to 1250 or 1300 has been associated with Western Pueblo culture or complex. Originally defined by Reed (1948) and modified by Johnson (1965), this complex "developed in the mountainous region of east-central Arizona and west-central New Mexico about A.D. 1000" and "represents a cultural syncretism of Mogollon features, Pueblo traits, and Hohokam elements" (Johnson and Wasley 1966:249). The period from ca. A.D. 1300 to 1450 throughout southern Arizona is associated with the concept of the Salado, discussed below.

The tumultuous transition from the Sedentary period to the Classic period resulted in numerous changes to the material culture of the Hohokam. In the Classic period, which is composed of the Tanque Verde phase (A.D. 1150–1250) and the Tucson phase (A.D. 1250–1450), semi-subterranean adobe-walled pithouses and above-ground adobe and stone-masonry structures became the principal forms of architecture, and they were typically located inside walled compounds, as at the Marana Platform Mound site (Fish et al. 1992; Fish et al., eds. 1992) and at University Indian Ruin (Hayden 1957). Ball courts were replaced by platform mounds as the dominant form of public architecture, and local examples again include the mounds at the Marana Platform Mound site (Fish et al. 1992; Fish et al., eds.

1992), University Indian Ruin (Hayden 1957), and Jackrabbit Ruin (Scantling 1939, 1940). Red-on-brown ceramics took on a less curvilinear and more rectilinear pattern than in previous periods. Inhumations were added to the burial practices of the Hohokam, and both cremations and inhumations continued through the Classic period. Populations aggregated in larger primary villages, forming along the major drainages throughout the Tucson Basin and beyond. The total population of the region may have peaked in the Tanque Verde phase, but then declined in the Tucson phase.

Explanations of the turbulent Classic period tend to have two broad themes. Environmental change and climatic pressures represent one line of argument. The second emphasizes political (and possibly ideological) developments within the perceived Southwestern regional system. In regards to the first theme, Waters and Ravesloot (2001) have noted that changes to the Gila River occurred between the Sedentary–Classic period transition and that episodes of channel down-cutting and widening were also observed on the Santa Cruz and San Pedro rivers. Down-cutting and widening events would have required extensive reconstruction of canal and field systems associated with these rivers, and may have spurred cultural change.

In regards to the second theme, the beginning of the Tucson phase in the Tucson Basin and the Civano phase in the Phoenix Basin, ca. A.D. 1250, is associated with the advent of what is termed the Salado horizon, defined by the common denominator of Gila Polychrome, the most widely produced and distributed of all ceramic types in the Southwest (Crown 1994; Dean, ed. 2000; Nelson and LeBlanc 1986; Rice 1998). The concept of the Salado (the name comes from the Salt River, or Río Salado) was originally developed to explain the changes that occurred during the Classic period; the Salado were presumed to have been

a mixed Mogollon-Anasazi population that had migrated into the Tonto Basin, and from there into the Phoenix Basin and beyond, "taking with them Pueblo traits such as polychrome ceramics, walled compounds, and inhumation burial practices" (Rice 1998:14).

Lekson (2000) defines what he calls the Chihuahuan Salado as encompassing that portion of the Chihuahuan desert that covers southeastern Arizona, southern New Mexico, and northwest Chihuahua. Within this larger context, he places the valleys of southeastern Arizona in the "Casa–Casas Corridor" (Lekson 2000:286) linking Casas Grandes with Hohokam Casa Grande in the middle Gila Valley. The Casa–Casas Corridor revives a concept suggested previously by Wilcox and Sternberg (1983:255), which conceived of Salado as more an ideology, rather than a basic cultural group, that allowed small-scale regional systems to articulate from the Phoenix Basin to Casas Grandes.

Altschul (1997:65–66) proposed that the differences between sites in the middle and lower San Pedro River valley (i.e., rectangular compounds with interior rooms and Salado polychromes in the lower San Pedro, versus circular compounds with attached rooms on the outside, Babocomari polychrome, and more defensible locations for villages, such as mesas or ridges, in the middle San Pedro) suggests a distinct cultural boundary lying somewhere between Tres Alamos and the Charleston Hills. This program or ideology, however defined, appears to have come to an end in the mid-fifteenth century, when throughout southern Arizona most of the archaeological record itself comes to an end, indicating a massive region-wide depopulation. Recent research by the Center for Desert Archaeology in the lower San Pedro River valley, which is proposed as a regional model for population decline and coalescence, suggests that populations "did not abandon the region en masse at A.D. 1450.

Demographic decline was considerably more complex and involved many of the processes associated with coalescence, including migration and aggregation" (Hill et al. 2004:708).

The lower San Pedro River valley manifests an array of Classic period sites. Doelle and Wallace (1997:Figure 7.3) map a series of major platform mound and walled compound sites spaced along the San Pedro between Benson and Winkelman. They note that sites from the earlier part of the Classic period are less visible, but appear to have been small pithouse villages. This represents a degree of continuity from the pre-Classic (Middle Formative) period. The later Classic settlements are seen to be quite different; they are larger and the structures are predominantly of masonry and adobe construction. Gila Polychrome appears at the later Classic sites, although Doelle and Wallace (1997) avoid being drawn into discussion of the Salado phenomenon. Instead they suggest migration into the San Pedro by Anasazi peoples from the north.

In the same volume, Altschul (1997) presents a study of the upper San Pedro River valley. In this region, larger villages began to aggregate at favorable agricultural locations in the early Classic period. Pithouses remained the favored structure. During the later part of the Classic period, occupation shifted to compact sites in defensible locations. Ceramics associated with these sites included Babocomari Polychrome, but relatively little Gila Polychrome. Altschul interpreted this as a response to increased, invasive settlement farther north in the San Pedro. This correlates well with the pattern suggested by Doelle and Wallace (1997), except Altschul suggests the migrants were part of the "ever-encroaching Salado phenomenon" (1997:67). Further study of the late Classic period in the San Pedro River valley by Altschul and others (1999) reinforced the idea of a cultural boundary between the middle and lower valley zones. The San Pedro River valley was definitely not seen as a conduit for north–south exchange during this period (Altschul et al. 1999:91).

SUMMARY

The foregoing discussion has provided a context that situates the Marsh Station Road site in its larger cultural setting. The general area has witnessed human occupation for millennia, but it is not until the Early Agricultural period and subsequent periods that a denser occupation has been identified in the immediate vicinity of the site. While we expected to recover material from these periods, based on the results of the pedestrian survey of the site (Rieder et al. 2006) as well as the types and ages of other archaeological sites recorded near the Marsh Station Road site (e.g., the Mescal Wash site [AZ EE:2:51 (ASM)], the Old Pantano [AZ EE:2:492 (ASM)], and New Pantano [AZ BB:14:25 (ASM)] sites, as well as numerous smaller sites), we were less sure as to what the character of the material would be, especially that dating to the Middle Formative or later periods. Given the site's location in a sort of 'hinterland,'(sensu Sullivan and Bayman, ed. 2007, and especially Vanderpot and Altschul 2007; also see Chapter 12), Hohokam or Dragoon features and artifacts were considered the leading candidates.

Chapter 3
Project Background

Michael J. Boley, Melanie A. Medeiros, John C. Ravesloot, and Gary A. Huckleberry

The following chapter provides background information related to the investigation of the Marsh Station Road site, including a discussion of both the modern and past environmental setting of the site and its surrounding area, a geomorphic assessment of the site stratigraphy, a summary of previous archaeological research conducted at the site, and the research design for data recovery.

ENVIRONMENTAL SETTING

The Marsh Station Road site is located 26 linear miles southeast of Tucson, Arizona, north of the confluence of Mescal Wash and Cienega Creek, off the south flank of the Rincon Mountains. The site is bounded on the west by Cienega Creek, on the east by Mescal Wash and Marsh Station Road (Pantano Road), on the north by a small, unnamed, ephemeral drainage, and on the south by Cienega Creek and Mescal Wash. As a result of major downcutting of the floodplain, the southern boundary is essentially a bench, falling sharply to Cienega Creek as a low cliff. The Union Pacific Railroad cuts through the eastern portion of the site. The majority of the site is situated on both Pleistocene and Holocene river terraces, although a small portion of the site is located on the Holocene floodplain of Cienega Creek. The Mescal Wash (AZ EE:2:51 [ASM]) site is just across Mescal Wash, approximately 400 meters to the southeast.

Cienega Creek serves as the major drainage channel of the Cienega Valley, which is where the north end the Marsh Station Road site is located. The creek flows north from its source in the Canelo Hills, between the Santa Rita and Empire mountains on the west and the Whetstone Mountains on the east. At its confluence with Mescal Wash, Cienega Creek turns westward. This stretch of the creek, also called Pantano Wash, is fed by tributary canyon streams as it flows into the Tucson Basin where it joins the Rillito River and, eventually, the Santa Cruz River. The Cienega Creek channel adjacent to the site is relatively wide and flat; it is a braided system of active channels cutting between sand bars with dense vegetation and the boughs of fallen trees deposited during periods of high water. Surface water is only occasionally seen in the active channel, although the flow following rain can be impressive. Mescal Wash originates to the east, close to Mescal and the Pima County line, and reaches Cienega Creek along a shallow valley. Today, this wash is more ephemeral than Cienega Creek; water is seen in the channel only after it rains.

The Marsh Station Road site and the surrounding area are in an ecological transition zone (Brown 1982; Brown and Lowe 1980; Eddy and Cooley 1983; Vanderpot and Altschul 2007) where several biotic communities and a varied geology provide an environment of abundant and diverse floral, faunal, and geologic resources. The Tucson Basin (ca. 797 m [2,500 feet]), which is in the Sonoran Desert environment, lies at an elevation lower than and to the west of the site. The site itself is located on the edge of the Chihuahuan Desert grasslands (approx. 1,067–1,524 m [3,500–5,000 feet]). In addition, the flow or high water table of Cienega Creek creates a rich riparian habitat that features a mesquite bosque throughout most of the Cienega Valley. The slopes of the nearby Rincon Mountains (approximately 1,295–2,560 m [4,250–8,400 feet] in elevation) as well as the Santa Rita, Whetstone, and Empire mountains to the south are covered by oak woodlands.

While the Marsh Station Road site, which was recorded at an elevation of approximately 1,097 m (3,600 feet), sits in an ecologically diverse region, most of the site area is occupied by a semidesert grassland community of creosote bush (*Larrea tridentata*), prickly pear (*Opuntia* spp.), barrel cactus (*Ferocactus* spp.), and small mesquites (*Prosopis*). Ocotillo (*Fouquieria splendens*), cholla (*Cylindropuntia* spp.), and yucca (*Yucca* spp.) are found in the higher, eastern, part of the site, while a dense mesquite bosque and a few cottonwoods (*Populus* spp.) grow along Cienega Creek. The tree growth along Mescal Wash is more modest. Local wildlife in the area is diverse and includes, among others, both mule (*Odocoileus hemionus*) and white-tailed deer (*O. virginianus*), pronghorn (*Antilocapra Americana*), coyote (*Canis latrans*), jackrabbits (*Lepus* spp.), cottontails (*Sylvilagus* spp.), skunks (*Mustelidae*), woodrats (*Neotoma* spp.), mice, great horned owls (*Bubo virginianus*), and other raptors.

With regard to climate, rainfall in southeastern Arizona is biannual: monsoon thunderstorms, which are generally localized, short-lived, and accompanied by wind or blowing sand, occur during the summer months while longer, calmer, and more widespread rainfall occurs during the winter months (Sellers and Hill 1974). Temperatures at the University of Arizona weather station, as recorded from 1894 to 2009, range from an average minimum of 3.1° C (37.6° F) in January to an average maximum of 37.9° C (100.1° F) in July; average total precipitation is about 28 cm (11.14 inches; Western Regional Climate Center 2009). The average number of frost free days in the project area varies between 170 and 235 days (Wright 2002).

Although Eddy and Cooley (1983) distinguished between sites located on the floodplain and those located on the surrounding ridges, characterization of the location of the Marsh Station Road site is a bit more complex. As mentioned above, a small portion of the site sits on the Holocene floodplain, but the majority of the site climbs up several terraces along the side of the valley. No features were found in fluvial deposits, and in general, the site contained shallow deposits. These site characteristics are rather unlike Archaic and Early Agricultural sites that have been recorded on the floodplain along Cienega Creek and its tributaries, many of which were buried by several meters of sediment (Eddy and Cooley 1983). Instead, the Marsh Station Road site appears more comparable to the sites along the valley side recorded during the Center for Desert Archaeology's Cienega Valley Survey (Stevens 2001a, 2001b) and WSA's Cienega Access Road Survey (Rawson et al. 2007). However, prior to the entrenchment of Cienega Creek as a result of environmental changes during the late nineteenth and early twentieth century (see below), the majority of the Marsh Station Road site was located on the floodplain, and portions of the site likely experienced significant flooding episodes throughout the site's occupation history.

Geologic and Geomorphic Context

Southeastern Arizona lies within the Basin and Range Physiographic Province (Fenneman 1931; Dohrenwend 1987), a large region defined by geologic structure and topography that extends north-south from Mexico to Oregon and east-west from New Mexico to California. This large region of western North America is characterized by linear mountain ranges bounded by high-angle faults and separated by intervening basins. Most basin and range topography was formed in Arizona during a period of crustal extension 8–15 millions of years ago (Menges and Pearthree 1989). Tectonically, the last five million years have been relatively quiet, particularly in western Arizona, and the dominant geological process has been mountain erosion and basin filling. The Basin and Range Physiographic Province is subdivided based on differences in drainage patterns, elevation, and topographic relief. Most of southeastern Arizona is located within the Mexican Highland Subprovince, an area where mountain ranges tend to align north-to-northwest and rise 500–1300 m above the axes of adjacent basins (Morrison 1985). Basin deposits within this subprovince tend to be highly dissected by streams due to Plio-Quaternary uplift and drainage integration. An exception is the Sulphur Springs Valley where ephemeral streams flow into Willcox Playa, a mostly dry lake bed and remnant of Pluvial Lake Cochise (Waters 1989). Ephemeral streams in the Sulphur Springs Valley are graded to the playa and most of the basin deposits are not dissected, a characteristic that contrasts with the highly dissected San Pedro River valley to the west.

The site area is located just outside of the Sonoran Desert Subprovince, which character-

izes the Tucson Basin. This province covers all of southwestern Arizona and contains north-to-northwest aligned mountain ranges and integrated drainages, but because of greater tectonic stability, mountain ranges are relatively small and highly eroded. Although most of the Sonoran Desert Subprovince is hydrologically connected to the Gila River, basin deposits are only moderately dissected due to a lack of recent uplift.

Several landform types are associated with basin and range topography and located in the region surrounding the site area. Mountain ranges are flanked by gentler slopes or piedmonts that extend from the base of the mountain to the valley axis. Most of these piedmonts are composed of alluvial fan deposits, although individual alluvial fans are seldom recognizable. Most of the alluvial fans have coalesced into a broad apron or bajada, or are highly dissected into a series of drainages and interfluves. Surficial deposits associated with piedmonts are generally Quaternary (1.6 million years ago to present) in age, although older Pliocene (5.2 million–1.6 million years ago) sandstones and mudstones (St. David Formation) are exposed in the upper San Pedro River valley (Johnson et al. 1975; Lindsay et al. 1990). Most piedmonts in the arid to semiarid landscapes of the Southwest are composed of different aged surfaces that can be distinguished based on drained patterns, soil formation, and morphostratigraphic relationships (Bull 1991; Christensen and Purcell 1985; Gile et al. 1981). Older fan deposits are hydrologically disconnected from active fan drainages and undergo a sequence of weathering resulting in rounded, elongated interfluves with mature soils. Pleistocene fan surfaces are relatively stable, experiencing slow denudation and only localized areas of shallow deposition, mainly through slopewash and hillslope colluviation. In southeastern Arizona, soils on relict fan surfaces tend to be very mature (see Holliday 2004:27) with red, clayey and calcareous horizons. Such surfaces are often veneered in cobbles that represent an erosional lag left behind as the fan deposits slowly erode. These landforms tend to be hundreds of thousands of years old (Bull 1991; Gile et al. 1981; Nichols et al. 2006).

Active channels on dissected piedmonts tend to be confined by older, relict fan surfaces on upper valley slopes but become less restricted on the lower piedmont where they may form a more typical bajada composed of coalesced alluvial fans. Where unconfined, streams tend to have distributary channels that interconnect and shift laterally across the piedmont forming bar-and-swale topography and broad zones of periodic flooding (Bull 1991:52–55; Field 2001; Pelletier et al. 2005). Overall alluvial grain sizes decrease downslope on alluvial fans, but the rate of decrease is greatest where fan channels are unconfined and lose stream competence due to reduced flow depths and increased infiltration losses. The distal ends of alluvial fans with distributary stream patterns tend to have young, alluvial soils and are well suited for certain types of indigenous floodwater farming strategies Fish et al. 1992; Muenchrath et al. 2002; Waters and Field 1986).

Principal drainages with externally drained basins usually contain a suite of terraces formed during past episodes of climate change. The upper San Pedro River valley is extensively dissected by piedmont streams such that only small vestiges of earlier Pleistocene terraces are preserved, usually as thin veneers of cobbles on eroded ridges of basin deposits. The San Pedro River is inset into Pliocene-Pleistocene deposits along the axis of the basin and flanked by a Holocene floodplain whose subsurface contains a suite of alluvial deposits, intercalated soils, and paleochannels (Huckleberry et al. 2006). The buried paleochannels record previous episodes of floodplain entrenchment and backfilling (i.e., alluvial cycles) that have

occurred in response to fluctuations in flood regime and climate (Waters and Haynes 2001). The most recent arroyo-cutting event began in the late 1800s, resulting in local lowering of water tables and desiccation of floodplain wetlands. Today the San Pedro River flows with a post-entrenchment channel that inset up to 10 m within the Holocene floodplain (Hereford 1993). Mescal Wash and Cienega Creek, both directly associated with the occupational history of the Marsh Station Road site, also have entrenched floodplains.

Geomorphic Assessment

The Marsh Station Road site, much like the Mescal Wash site, is strategically located next to wetlands and riparian resources associated with Cienega Creek. However, this site extends across three distinct landforms—Pleistocene (T2) and Holocene (T1 and T0) terraces, and the Holocene floodplain (Figure 3.1). Much of the site is located on eroded Pleistocene terrace cut into basin fill deposits with an erosional lag of surface gravels and cobbles (Table 3.1). However, the eastern margin of the site extends onto a low Holocene stream terrace located along Mescal Wash immediately upstream from its confluence with Cienega Creek. Streamcut exposures along Mescal Wash reveal fine-textured, overbank flood deposits and organic soils. It is uncertain to what degree these sediments are derived from Mescal Wash or from Cienega Creek floodwaters that backed up the former channel. Previous archaeological investigations conducted along a fiber optic line revealed the presence of sherds 2 to 3 m below the modern surface of this low terrace (Kearns et al. 2009). The Marsh Station Road site extends southwest across the Union Pacific Railroad onto another Pleistocene stream terrace associated with Cienega Creek. This creosote-covered terrace is situated several meters above the modern channel of Cienega

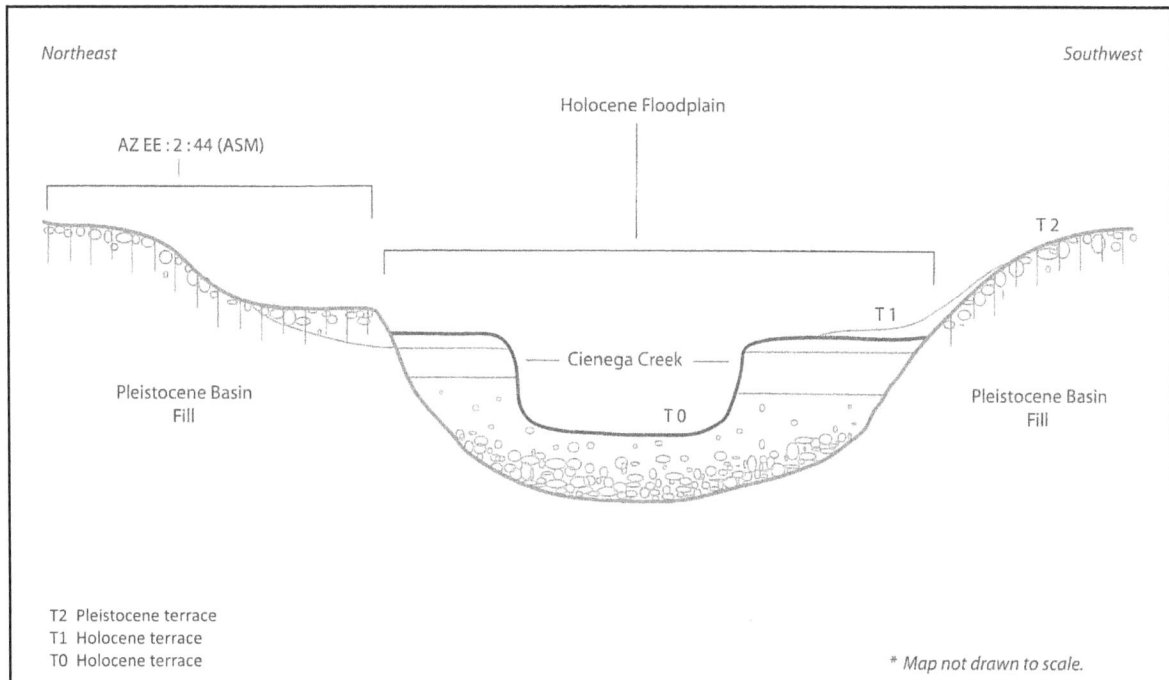

Figure 3.1. Geomorphic setting of the Marsh Station Road site (AZ EE:2:44 [ASM]). Reprinted with permission from Huckleberry 2007:Figure 6.

Creek, which consists of low, mesquite-covered terrace and entrenched channel. Exposures of subsurface deposits associated with this low terrace were not observed on the north bank of Cienega Creek, but stratigraphy is likely similar to that exposed on the south bank where there are over five meters of fine-textured, overbank stream sediments with buried, organic soils.

Given the variety of different aged landforms at the Marsh Station Road site, it is not surprising that there is considerable spatial variability regarding the potential for subsurface cultural deposits. Most of the site occurs on Pleistocene landforms that have little potential for buried archaeology. In contrast, the low inset Holocene stream terraces located along Mescal Wash and Cienega Creek have a high potential for containing buried cultural deposits, as already confirmed by previous test excavations mentioned above. Previous investigations of alluvial stratigraphy exposed in streamcuts along Cienega Creek indicate that fine-textured overbank deposits date to the

late Holocene based on radiocarbon and artifact dating (Eddy and Cooley 1983). Another archaeological site located approximately 2 km downstream from the Marsh Station Road site contains ceramic-bearing, fine-textured alluvial deposits up to 5 m thick (Hemmings et al. 1968). Thus, there has been considerable alluviation along Cienega Creek over the last several thousand years creating favorable conditions for various types of irrigation farming (see B. Huckell 1996). Such conditions combined with low energy, overbank sedimentation creates a situation where buried cultural deposits are likely to occur.

Past Environmental Setting

Although the broad environmental outlines of the late Holocene have remained largely the same, the prehistoric environmental setting of the immediate area was much different than it is now, having changed significantly at the end of the nineteenth century. During prehis-

Table 3.1. Summary of soils in the project area

Location	Temperature/Moisture Regime & Soil Association	Great Groups	Common Landform(s)	Characteristics	Typical Vegetation Cover
Cienega Creek vicinity	Thermic Semiarid 4: White House-Bernardino-Hathaway	Haplargids Calciustolls	nearly level to hilly valley plains and dissected old terraces	deep, well-drained, fine-textured and gravelly, moderately coarse- to moderately fine-textured, nearly level to moderately steep soils	plains lovegrass, beargrass, multiple grama grasses; scattered mesquite and cacti, with some oak trees, grow at higher elevations
	Thermic Semiarid 6: Lithic Torriorthents– Lithic Haplustolls–Rock Outcrop	Torriorthents Haplustolls	mid-elevation hills and mountains	shallow, cobbly and gravelly, well-drained, strongly sloping to very steep soils and rock outcrop	oak, juniper, perennial grasses including Arizona cottontop, cant and Texas bluestem, plains lovegrass, green sprangletop, wolftail, and multiple grama grasses at higher elevations; palo verde, mesquite, whitethorn, catclaw, jojoba, calliandra, saguaro and other cacti, and grasses at lower elevations
	Thermic Semiarid 5: Caralampi-Hathaway	Haplargids Calciustolls	highly dissected old fan surfaces	deep, gravelly, well-drained, moderately coarse- to moderately fine-textured, moderately steep to very steep soils	plains lovegrass, cane and Texas bluestem, calliandra, beargrass, multiple grama grasses, scattered mesquite and cacti, with some oak and juniper at higher elevations

Note: Data obtained from Hendricks (1985)

tory, much of the length of Cienega Creek was indeed a ciénega, "...wetlands characterized by permanently saturated, highly organic reducing soils" (Hendrickson and Minckley 1984:131) that functioned within the ecosystem as self-protecting reservoirs. The rate of flow in the creek was slow, and the surrounding area was a marshland with abundant tall grasses. Surface water was perennial along much of the creek as late as the 1950s (Eddy and Cooley 1983:2), and some localized grassy ciénegas still remain in the upper, southern reaches today (B. Huckell 1995:Figure 2.2). Along most of the channel, this environment was destroyed in the 1880s and 1890s (Bahre 1991) when overgrazing and a cycle of drought followed by heavy rain flowing unimpeded on the bare ground increased the rate of flow of water through the marsh. The increased energy of this flow cut a narrower, deeper channel and much of the original extent of the ciénega became a mostly dry floodplain. The incising of streams was part of a widespread occurrence in southern Arizona, essentially bringing about the degradation of rangeland (Sheridan 1995). Dense mesquite bosque, like that seen today along Cienega Creek and in the site area, rapidly grew along the newly confined channels.

The changes in environmental conditions along Cienega Creek during the late nineteenth century were a dramatic episode in an essentially continuous process. The prehistoric environmental history of the Cienega Valley has been discussed in detail by Eddy and Cooley (1983; also see Huckell 1990). Their work was based upon the correlation of sedimentary episodes in the creek, plant species represented in pollen samples, and faunal (both vertebrate and invertebrate) remains recovered along the length of the creek. Eddy and Cooley (1983:37) suggested that at about 1500 B.C., conditions in the Cienega Valley became relatively stable and wet, allowing the formation of moister ciénega environments that the San Pedro phase

occupants of the area would have been able to exploit (Figure 3.2). These conditions probably persisted until about A.D. 1100 to 1200, at which time increasing aridity reduced the areal extent of the ciénegas (Eddy and Cooley 1983:37). Eddy and Cooley note that the formation of channels partially draining the ciénegas may have created optimum farming conditions, enlarging the accessible alluvial floodplain without creating a shortage of water. There may have been less climatic stability—evidenced by cycles of deposition and erosion in the geologic profile of Cienega Creek—during the (Middle Formative) Colonial and Sedentary periods and into the (Late Formative) Classic period. This process of arroyo cutting and filling may have included events analogous to the nineteenth century episode, but without overgrazing to exacerbate their effects. There was probably drought during this period of arroyo cutting and filling, although Eddy and Cooley thought it likely some water remained available in Cienega Creek. Conditions were thought to have improved in the middle part of the Classic Period, with the reestablishment of grassy ciénegas that lasted into the historic era.

Soils

Soils in the project area are almost entirely Thermic Semiarid soils (Hendricks 1985). Soil classifications delineate specific characteristics of soil groups that provide useful summary information that can help "predict soil behavior under defined use and management or manipulation," (Hendricks 1985:63), as well as regarding potential surface age and soil features that may contribute to archaeological preservation potential and burial characteristics. Table 3.1 contains a summary of soil associations located in the area surrounding the Marsh Station Road site.

Date (B.C./A.D)	Chronology			Sedimentary Environment (from Eddy & Cooley 1983: Fig. 2.16)	Inferred Climatic Conditions (from Eddy & Cooley 1983: Fig. 2.16)
	Tucson Basin Hohokam		Formative Terminology		
	Phase	Period	Period		
1540-1750	n/a	Protohistoric	Protohistoric	Formation of a soil zone; fine-grained deposits; slow runoff.	Stable wet conditions; precipitation slow and steady
— 1450					
— 1250	Tucson	Classic	Late Formative	Arroyo cutting, probably preceded by a period of stripping; fast runoff.	Unstable wet-dry conditions; rapid precipitation; may not have been as intense as the present drought; correlates with the "Great Drought"
	Tanque Verde				
— 1100	Rincon	Sedentary	late Middle Formative	Scour-and-fill deposition; end of deposition in cienegas; fairly fast runoff.	
— 900	Rillito	Colonial	early Middle Formative	Scour-and-fill and quiet deposition; cienegas decrease in areal extent; slow and fast runoff. Shallow integrated channels cut; deposition continued in some cienegas; fast runoff.	Alternating stable wet and unstable wet-dry conditions; unstable wet-dry conditions predominant after A.D. 900.
	Cañada del Oro				
— 700	Tortolita	Pioneer	Early Formative		Unstable wet-dry conditions; probably not as intense as those after A.D. 900.
— 500					
	Agua Caliente	Early Ceramic		Maximum extent of cienegas as little fluvial material was deposited in area; slow runoff.	
— 150					
	Cienega	Early Agricultural	Early Agricultural	Influx of fluvial-laid sediments; no pronounced channeling; slow and fast runoff.	Stable to fairly stable wet conditions; little evidence of strong unstable wet-dry conditions.
— 800					
	San Pedro				
— 1200				Cienega and lacustrine deposits; little fluvial material; slow runoff.	
	Unnamed			?	Probably transitional between wet-dry and stable wet conditions.
— 2100					
	n/a	Middle Archaic	Middle Archaic	Downcutting; fast and sporadic runoff.	Unstable wet-dry conditions.
— 3000					

Figure 3.2. Correlation between past environmental conditions and the chronological sequence of cultural development in the Southwest.

PREVIOUS RESEARCH

The Marsh Station Road site was originally recorded in 1955 by McConville and Holzkamper as part of the Southern Pacific Pipeline project (McConville and Holzkamper 1955; Rieder et al. 2006). The recorders, who referred to the site as Site 4, produced a reasonably representative site map (McConville and Holzkamper 1955:Figure 4) and conducted limited site testing in the northeastern portion of the site. As part of the site testing, McConville and Holzkamper excavated a stone ring, which appears to have been situated south of the Southern Pacific pipeline alignment. They also tested the site area west of the Southern Pacific Railroad (now owned by Union Pacific) where surface artifacts were abundant but buried deposits were limited. In 1958, W. W. Wasley assigned the Marsh Station Road site an Arizona State Museum (ASM) site number—AZ EE:2:44 (ASM)—and entered the file into the ASM site files as a sherd and lithic scatter containing Hohokam and Mogollon ceramics, flakes, and ground stone.

Since 1958, the site record for the Marsh Station Road site has been updated several times, and has generally become less representative of the actual site. In 1993, during a survey of the Marsh Station Road Interchange along Interstate 10, Heidi Roberts of SWCA Environmental Consultants merged the site with two neighboring but distinct sites, AZ EE:2:164 (ASM) and the Mescal Wash site (AZ EE:2:51 [ASM]), although no site card was officially filed with the ASM (see Roberts 1993). In 2001, following their extensive work at the Mescal Wash site, Rein Vanderpot of Statistical Research (SRI) noted that the Marsh Station Road site and the Mescal Wash site are in fact two distinct sites, and indicated that the ASM site record should reflect this separation. However, it was not until Western Cultural Resource Management (WCRM) conducted survey and excavation at the Marsh Station Road site as part of the AT&T NexGen/Core fiber optic project between 2000 and 2007 that the records for the two sites were officially separated (Baker and Jones 2004; Kearns et al. 2001; Kearns 2009).

WCRM's survey and excavation efforts at the Marsh Station Road site marked the first archaeological work conducted at the site since it was originally recorded by McConville and Holzkamper in 1955. The AT&T NexGen/Core right-of-way followed the alignment of a post-war AT&T coaxial cable, which is identified on McConville and Holzkamper's 1955 map of the site and located north of the nearby Union Pacific Railroad. Because the AT&T NexGen/Core project did not cross the railroad tracks, WCRM's recording of the site was limited to the northeastern portion of the site. As a result, the WCRM site map for the Marsh Station Road site effectively limits the site boundary to about one quarter of the site's actual area (Kearns and McVickar 2009:Figure 33.3). During data recovery in 2002, WCRM sampled approximately 5 percent of their recorded site area, and excavated three Rincon phase pithouses, one extramural roasting pit, two extramural pits, eight extramural postholes, and one cremation burial, and recovered over 11,000 artifacts (Kearns and McVickar 2009:335). A small quantity of historic material was also recovered from the site, although no discrete historic period component, other than the presence of the Southern Pacific Railroad and the two AT&T cables, was defined. Diagnostic artifacts (ceramics and projectile points), absolute dates (11 radiocarbon dates on maize cupules and mesquite wood and 1 archaeomagnetic date from a hearth), and architectural comparisons indicate the site was inhabited primarily during the Rincon phase (late Middle Formative/Sedentary period), and possibly into the early Tanque Verde phase (Late Formative/early Classic period); a Cienega phase

(Early Agricultural period) occupation was also suggested by several radiocarbon assays, although the WCRM excavations documented no cultural material clearly associated with the Cienega phase (Kearns and McVickar 2009:335, 411–412). The vast majority of the ceramics recovered from the site consisted of Rincon Red-on-brown sherds and indicate cultural affiliation with Tucson Basin Hohokam, although sherds associated with both the Mogollon and Dragoon cultural traditions were also recovered in much smaller quantities (Kearns and McVickar 2009:378–379, 412).

WSA surveyed the site in 2006 as part of the current project and significantly revised the recorded site boundary (Rieder et al. 2006). The site was recorded on both sides of the Union Pacific Railroad, greatly expanding the mapped site area and, to a degree, restoring the original site boundary mapped by McConville and Holzkamper. The principal difference expressed between the 1955 recording and the 2006 GPS-mapped site boundary is that the site now extends a considerable distance along the eastern bank of Cienega Creek, tapering as it climbs the Pleistocene terrace to the east, resulting in an almost triangular shape. As with previous recordings of the site, an abundant and diverse artifact assemblage was observed during the 2006 survey. Artifacts noted on the surface of the site included primarily Hohokam ceramic sherds dominated by plain wares with only a few pieces of red-on-buff ware observed; significant quantities of flaked stone, including shatter, flakes representing various stages of reduction, and multiple tool types; and small quantities of ground stone and historic trash (Rieder et al. 2006:161). In addition, six features—a rock ring hearth, four rock-filled roasting pits, and a large depression ringed with rocks and dirt—were visible on the surface of the site (Rieder et al. 2006:161).

RESEARCH DESIGN

Research themes for the Marsh Station Road site were developed through consideration of local and regional culture history, the history of archaeological research, and the diverse and rich environmental setting of the site. Five general research themes were initially considered for the Marsh Station Road site—site formation processes, cultural affiliation and interaction, chronology, diet and subsistence, and intrasite activity patterns—as well as more site-specific questions framed within each of these research themes (Table 3.2). However, our excavations produced varying and unexpected results such that few of the specific research questions listed in Table 3.2 were applied to the excavation results as originally envisioned, although each of the five research themes helped, to some degree, to structure our analysis and interpretation of site results as well as the integration of the site data into the regional archaeological discussion. To better interpret our excavation results, we also ultimately incorporated discussions of both a hinterland/ heartland (sensu Sullivan and Bayman 2007; Vanderpot and Altschul 2007) and persistent place (sensu Schlanger 1992; Vanderpot and Altschul 2007) model into our interpretation of the Marsh Station Road site, and considered the importance of the site for investigating Mabry's niche-filling model (2005b) for explaining Early Agricultural period subsistence strategies (see Chapter 12).

Site Formation Processes

Schiffer (1987) has discussed the various natural and cultural processes by which archaeological sites are formed, and the methodologies used to identify, distinguish between, and record these processes. Sites are preserved by certain processes and damaged by others. Schiffer suggests that although the various

Table 3.2. Research questions proposed for the EPX project

Research Theme	Research Question
Site formation processes	1. What kinds of natural site formation processes can be recognized at the Marsh Station Road site?
	2. How have site formation processes affected the contextual integrity of deposits encountered during site treatment?
	3. How do deposits encountered during excavation compare with those predicted on the basis of survey data?
	4. Is there any evidence of material from earlier contexts being reused at the Marsh Station Road site?
	5. What impact has disturbance due to previous construction projects had within the site area?
	6. Is it possible to identify buried cultural deposits outside the site areas identified during survey?
Cultural affiliation and interaction	1. Is there evidence of habitation during the emergence of Formative cultural traditions?
	2. What range of Formative period ceramics are present at the Marsh Station Road site?
	3. Can Dragoon series ceramics be identified at the Marsh Station Road site? Are these distinct from Hohokam and, especially, Mogollon forms?
	4. Do Formative period pit houses at the Marsh Station Road site exhibit distinctive architectural styles?
	5. Are exotic materials like marine shell, obsidian, or trade wares present at the site? To what extent can these be sourced?
	6. Is it possible to determine the phase or periods associated with site structure or arrangement of features within the Marsh Station Road site?
	7. Are integrative features such as ballcourts or compounds present?
	8. Is it possible to assign a cultural affiliation to the Classic period occupations of the Marsh Station Road site, which has yielded Salado and Babocomari/Santa Cruz polychrome ceramics?
	9. Is it possible to identify possible Apache or Sobaipuri associations with features at the Marsh Station Road site?
Chronology	1. When was the Marsh Station Road site occupied?
	2. Is it possible to differentiate the dates of multiple occupations that occurred over time at the Marsh Station Road site?
	3. Is is possible to distinctly date local material, in particular, in contexts with Dragoon series ceramics?
	4. How do the dates of occupation at the Marsh Station Road site compare with our understanding of the culture history of the region?

Table 3.2. Research questions proposed for the EPX project, cont'd

Research Theme	Research Question
Diet and subsistence	1. Are any processing or storage features present that suggest they were used in the exploitation of specific resources?
	2. Is it possible to detect hunting, butchery, plant processing, or cultivating tools amongst the Marsh Station Road site lithic (flaked and ground stone) assemblages?
	3. Is it possible to identify different site activities within the APE?
	4. Does the Marsh Station Road site appear to have been occupied seasonally or year-round?
	5. What food resources were exploited by the Late Archaic/Early Agricultural populations near Cienega Creek and Mescal Wash?
	6. Does subsistence data (floral, pollen, and faunal analyses) provide information concerning the menu of items consumed by people inhabitating the Marsh Station Road site?
	7. Is dietary varibility observed among contemporaneously occupied sites? If so, if this variability due to the occupation of different resource zones?
	8. Does subsistence data from different periods of occupation at the Marsh Station Road site allow us to document dietary change over time?
	9. Does the Marsh Station Road site have evidence of early agricultural development during the Plain Ware Horizon?
	10. To what extent were the Formative period occupants at the Marsh Station Road site dependent on agriculture?
Intrasite activity patterns	1. Can discrete activity areas be identifed within the Marsh Station Road site? If so, do they define site function?
	2. Can activity patterns be discerned, and if so, can the patterning be related to site affiliation?

processes are highly specific to a site location, they are ultimately part of a system of predictable causes and observable effects. Formation processes can be studied systematically, then used to inform our interpretation of sites. In many ways, other analyses are dependent on this first step.

The depositional environment of a site is an important variable in natural formation processes. In a cycle of erosion and deposition, rainwater, wind, and other agents move sediments across the landscape. Some sites are deflated by erosion; others are deeply buried by deposition. By analyzing the topography of a site, wind and water effects can be predicted: material is likely to be blown off exposed locations and deposited in sheltered ones; rainwater flowing downhill gains speed and volume in ephemeral washes. Bioturbation, another critical factor in site formation processes, is subdivided into floralturbation and faunalturbation (Waters 1992). The former defines disturbances caused by plants. Typically this occurs as the result of invasive roots, although in dunal contexts vegetation can trap aeolian sediments and the roots can stabilize the dunes. Faunalturbation defines disturbances caused by burrowing animals; rodents and insects are ubiquitous and remorseless earthmovers.

Cultural behavior also contributes to the site formation process. Artifacts are discarded and features are abandoned within the context of human behavior at the site. Once deposits are created, they are subject to potential disturbance. This may be intentional, as when material is retrieved and recycled, or incidental, as when a pithouse is truncated by a later structure. These processes are essentially ongoing as the site recedes into the past. Rural land-use practices—typically, plowing and livestock grazing—play an important role. In recent times, the construction of linear infrastructure, including railroads, roads, and utilities, has been a major source of disturbance.

Survey observations and the developmental history of the areas adjacent to the site suggest that in the case of the Marsh Station Road site, both cultural behavior associated with the site's occupation and modern development in the form of railroad construction, pipeline construction, and previous archaeological investigations were significant processes in the formation of the site observed during WSA's investigation of the site. In addition, the location of the Marsh Station Road site on an alluvial terrace at the confluence of Cienega Creek and Mescal Wash, in a general area that has been previously shown to contain deeply stratified cultural deposits (e.g., Eddy and Cooley 1983), indicates that environmental factors, such as the flooding of Cienega Creek, may also have made a significant contribution to the formation of the site.

Cultural Affiliation and Interaction

Studies of cultural affiliation and interaction are an important component of archaeological investigations in southern Arizona, where several concurrent cultural traditions—Hohokam, Mogollon, and Dragoon—have been defined (see Chapter 2 of this volume for an in-depth discussion of these three cultural groups and their interactions). As has been suggested for the nearby Mescal Wash site (AZ EE:2:51 [ASM]; see Vanderpot and Altschul 2007), the Marsh Station Road site, located in the Cienega Valley, is in a transitional or boundary zone between the known distributions of these three cultural traditions whose presence in the area waxed and waned from the Middle through Late Formative periods (Rieder et al. 2007:46; also see previous site records by McConville and Holzkamper [1955] and Webb et al. [2000]). Similarly, the Marsh Station Road site, along with the Mescal Wash site, is also located in a geographic area where evidence for the transition from Middle Archaic lifeways to those of the Early Agricultural period (Mabry 2005a, 2005c, 2008a; Stevens 2001a, 2001b) has been previously documented (e.g., B. Huckell 1995; Vanderpot and Altschul 2007). In addition, ethnographic and historic studies have established that protohistoric and historic Native American (Sobaipuri and Apache) populations also utilized the region surrounding the Marsh Station Road site (Basso 1983; Dobyns 1974; Erickson 1994; Sheridan 1995).

Identifying cultural affiliation for the pre-ceramic groups of the region surrounding the site area is not a straightforward business. Essentially, one must rely on equating projectile point types with distinct cultural groups (Shackley 1990; Wiessner 1983), which has its pitfalls. Moving forward in time to the Early Agricultural period, a more diverse material record could ostensibly assist in determining cultural affiliation, but projectile points are still the primary artifact type employed to this end (see Shackley 1996a). This is not to say this avenue should not be explored; on the contrary, the variety of broadly contemporaneous point styles in the Southwest suggests this may be a profitable path to explore.

As mentioned above, the Marsh Station Road site happens to be in an area that has historically been conceived of as a transitional zone or boundary between the Mogollon, Hohokam, and even Dragoon cultures (see, for example, Vanderpot and Altschul 2007), especially during the Formative (Ceramic) period. Different cultures like these can be defined by differences in ceramics, architecture, and even the foods they preferred (Stark et al. 1995). The Mogollon are known for their red-on-brown (Mogollon Red-on-brown, Encinas Red-on-brown) and distinctive white ware ceramics (see Gilman 1997:20–23). Influenced by the Mogollon, the Tucson Basin Hohokam became known for their red-on-brown pottery, rather than adopting a tradition dominated by buff wares from the Phoenix Basin. Sites labeled

as Dragoon are known for houses that contain recessed hearths. Differences such as these, which have previously been documented at sites in the immediate vicinity (McConville and Holzkamper 1955; Vanderpot and Altschul 2007; Webb et al. 2000) of the Marsh Station Road site, may allow for the assessment of the cultural affiliation of the site and its components.

The existence of different cultural groups in southeastern Arizona raises questions about the interactions of those groups. Regional exchange systems, evidenced by marine shell and obsidian artifacts, appear to have been in operation by the Early Agricultural period at the latest (Mabry, ed. 2008). This network continued to develop through the Formative period, evidenced by the movement of a variety of goods, including ceramics, obsidian, shell, turquoise, and other items. Many of the phenomena that characterize the archaeological record for these periods presumably arose from these contacts and can assist in the definition of regional systems. Integrative features such as ballcourts and platform mounds are interpreted as nodes in these networks (e.g., Abbott 2000; Crown 1991; Doelle and Wallace 1991; Doyel 1991; Fish et al., ed. 1992; Gregory and Nials 1985; Wilcox 1983; Wilcox and Sternberg 1983; also see Elson 1998 for an ethnographic perspective). The locations of the project sites are interesting in this context because they are outside the traditionally conceived heartlands of these regional networks, in peripheral areas where participants in different networks may have lived in close proximity. In the concept of the Dragoon culture, there is the suggestion that Hohokam and Mogollon blended in this region, tying the local residents into two extensive networks. In contrast to this, Vanderpot's initial (2001) interpretation of one of the project sites, the Mescal Wash site (AZ EE:2:51 [ASM]), suggests the inhabitants were insular, existing on the fringes of both cultures and only participating in them to a limited extent.

In the succeeding protohistoric or early historic period, two groups are known to have occupied the area through which the project runs: the Sobaipuri (the easternmost of the O'odham) and the Apache. The Sobaipuri presence in the San Pedro River valley has been particularly well studied (e.g., Seymour 1990, 2003), and it is conceivable that a protohistoric occupation could have been identified at the site.

Chronology

Determination of the period(s) of occupation of a site is one of the most fundamental questions for archaeological research and such chronological studies are closely associated with the problem of cultural affiliation (described above). In the Southwest, temporal affiliations for sites are generally established through absolute dating techniques such as dendrochronology, radiocarbon, and archaeomagnetic dating, and/or relatively by the presence of material culture diagnostic to a particular time period. Both optically stimulated (OSL) and thermoluminescence (TL) dating are also becoming more common (e.g., Eiselt and Wells 2003; Ramenofsky and Feathers 2002; Woodson 2002; Woodson et al. 2007). In southern Arizona, radiocarbon dating is the most common, and perhaps the most reliable, technique for obtaining absolute dates, although recent research has suggested that more systematic collection of dendrochronological samples could provide even further refinement of the Hohokam chronological sequence (Dean et al. 1996). Both ceramic seriation and projectile point typologies are well established as relative temporal indicators; in more heavily studied areas, such as the Phoenix and Tucson basins, ceramic and projectile point typological sequences are tied into absolute sequences supported by numerous types of chronometric

dates from excavated sites. Both absolute and relative dating techniques are characterized by varying degrees of reliability that are often tied to the location of the site, formation processes and preservation at the site, limitations related to the science behind absolute dating techniques, and, ironically, the age of the site.

The Marsh Station Road site was occupied over a long period of time, perhaps as early as the Middle Archaic period and possibly as late as the protohistoric and/or historic period, although both survey and previous excavation (Kearns et al. 2009) data indicate that the primary occupation period was likely during the late Middle Formative period (Rincon phase). Constructing a chronology of the occupation of the site is therefore vital for our understanding of the site history and placing the site within a regional context.

Diet and Subsistence

The foods people ate and how they obtained them is a focus of almost any archaeological study. The first step in studying prehistoric diet and subsistence is to reconstruct the natural environment or the setting where the inhabitants of a site pursued their mode of subsistence, whether it was large-game hunting, a mix of hunting and gathering, or an early form of agriculture. Geoarchaeological study of site sediments can provide useful information about the prehistoric environment, including soil type, erosional processes, and climate change, and how these factors may have influenced the availability of plant and animal food sources. Environmental reconstruction can be aided significantly by the interpretation of the pollen profile of soil samples from stratigraphic contexts.

Organic materials recovered from cultural contexts, especially intact features, can be useful in reconstructing both the prehistoric environment and the foodways of site inhabitants. Pollen and flotation samples from food preparation (hearths, roasting pits, etc.), storage features, and middens are particularly important for reconstructing diet at a site. Animal bone found on a site may allow the identification of species present prehistorically. Analysis of the bone and an evaluation of its depositional context may also allow differentiation among the species exploited by site inhabitants and those incidentally present.

Artifacts are also a fundamental source of information about subsistence. Certain components of artifact assemblages of hunters, hunter-gatherers, and early agriculturalists sometimes can be distinguished, a reflection of the specialized nature of the tools required in each subsistence mode. Even a limited number of artifacts recovered at a site may allow a determination of the general mode of subsistence of the inhabitants. If a sufficient number and variety of artifacts are found, finer distinctions in subsistence focus may be possible. Features present similar possibilities, as certain feature types may be associated with specific subsistence activities. For example, many wild plant food sources are seasonal, but a coordinated system of harvest and storage can allow these sources to play an important role in the diet year-round. The form, volume, and positioning of storage features, along with evidence of their former contents, can be important clues to the subsistence focus of site inhabitants. Also, some seasonal plant foods require processing before storage, and specific features and/or artifacts may be associated with this activity.

Intrasite Activity Patterns and Site Structure

Hohokam site structure and household organization has been extensively documented for a variety of site types (e.g., Craig, ed. 2001; Doyel 1987). The pre-Classic model consisted of a group of pithouses clustered around a courtyard (Craig, ed. 2001; Henderson 2001; Henderson and Craig 2008; Wilcox et al. 1981); this model continued in the Classic in the form of the compound (Gregory 1991; Jacobs, ed. 1994; Sires 1987). As Rice (2003:37) states, "these rooms in a courtyard or compound were usually functionally specialized (Doelle and Wallace 1991; Doelle et al. 1987; Henderson 1987, 2001; Henderson, ed. 1987; Rice 1987, 1995), based on distinctions having to do with varying uses of space for storage, tool and craft production, food processing, shelter, and even for accommodating large public gatherings." Extramural activities occurred in the open space around which the rooms were grouped; within this open space were features such as ramadas, hornos, and storage pits.

In contrast to many Hohokam sites, the internal structure of Mogollon sites in southeastern Arizona does not show a similarly consistent pattern, reflecting "a much more informal pattern that suggests a relatively low level of organization" (Whittlesey et al. 1994:81). In the Marsh Station Road site region, an exception to this is the San Pedro River valley, where it appears that population increase during the Classic period resulted in greater social complexity (Altschul and Jones 1990; Altschul et al. 1999; Tuthill 1947).

Although rarer, discrete resource procurement and/or processing loci may also occur within or nearby the Marsh Station Road site. In contrast to residential sites which are expected to contain evidence of diverse activities, resource processing and/or procurement sites are typically considered limited activity sites where only one or two activities generally related to food processing, particularly of native resources, or tool and craft production take place. While these sites are often considered uniformly, they too can yield evidence of intrasite patterning, depending on the resources being exploited (Rice and Ravesloot 2001; Wells et al. 2004).

Identification of a variety of feature types, especially those with clear functions, as well as analysis of artifact patterns within the site and between feature and unit types will help to identify intrasite activity patterns at the Marsh Station Road site.

Chapter 4
Archaeological Investigations at the Marsh Station Road Site, AZ EE:2:44 (ASM)

Melanie A. Medeiros, John C. Ravesloot, Michael J. Boley, Brandon M. Gabler, Paul M. Rawson, John McClelland, and Gary Huckleberry

The Marsh Station Road site (AZ EE:2:44[ASM]) is located north of the confluence of Cienega Creek and Mescal Wash near the Interstate 10–Marsh Station Road Interchange (see Figure 1.1). The site is an extensive, multicomponent, semi-permanent habitation site covering approximately 20 acres (Figure 4.1; also see Figure 1.2), less than 4 percent of which was investigated through subsurface excavation during the EPX project. As a result of excavation, WSA archaeologists documented 192 features, including six pithouses/structures; excavated 138 of these; and collected over 50,000 artifacts, the majority of which were flaked stone or ceramics. Largely mirroring the occupational history of the nearby Mescal Wash site (AZ EE:2:51 [ASM]; see Vanderpot 2001; Vanderpot and Altschul 2007), the Marsh Station Road site was occupied from at least 3000 to 550 B.P. (1050 B.C. to A.D. 1400); the most intense occupation occurred during the late Middle Formative period, with notable hiatuses during the Late Formative (Tanque Verde phase) period and perhaps during the Cienega phase of the Early Agricultural period. A possible Middle Archaic occupation is also suggested by the presence of Cortaro projectile points (but see Boley and Gabler, Chapter 6), although the EPX excavations produced no absolute dates from this period.

Archaeological investigations at the Marsh Station Road site included site mapping, surface collection, preconstruction trenching, mechanical stripping, excavation of test units, and horizontal exposure and full excavation of identified features (Ravesloot et al. 2010). All archaeological materials and records pertaining to the project are curated at the Arizona State Museum, University of Arizona, Tucson.

SITE BOUNDARY AND MAPPING

WSA's pedestrian survey of the Marsh Station Road site resulted in a significant revision of the site boundary over that previously recorded by McConville and Holzkamper (1955:Figure 4). During their survey of the site as part of the Southern Pacific Pipeline Project, McConville and Holzkamper documented the Marsh Station Road site as located "on the northeast bank of Cienega Creek...[running] along the long axis of a gravel ridge which slopes down to a flat area along the Cienega" (McConville and Holzkamper 1955:2), and as measuring "1,100 feet [335 m] in length and 500 feet [152 m] in width at the widest point with deep arroyos on both sides of the ridge" (McConville and Holzkamper 1955:3). However, when WSA archaeologists surveyed the site in 2006, they found a light to dense scatter of artifacts including flaked stone, ceramics, ground stone, and shell as well as several features over a much larger area. As a result, the Marsh Station Road site boundary was significantly enlarged: at its widest point, the site now measures 510 m [1,673 feet] in length and 262 m [859 feet] in width.

AREA OF POTENTIAL EFFECT

During the course of data recovery efforts at the Marsh Station Road site, the APE was modified several times. At the outset, the APE was consistent with the EPX project as a whole, a 100-foot-wide construction corridor centered on the pipeline. However, in order to limit pipeline construction impacts to the Cienega Creek channel and its associated riparian habitat, SFPP, in conjunction with

the Bureau of Land Management and Pima County, determined that the creek channel would be crossed by horizontal directional drilling (HDD). In order to accommodate this additional workspace and staging area required to bore underneath Cienega Creek, the APE was significantly expanded on the east side of the creek. Once the excavation of preconstruction trenches began, however, it became clear that the expanded APE was located in a feature-rich area of the site. After consultation with WSA, SFPP decided to reduce the size of the expanded APE to the extent possible in order to preserve a large portion of the site. This reduced APE, which totaled about four percent of the site area, constituted the area in which the remainder of the data recovery efforts ultimately occurred.

Figure 4.1. Aerial overview of the Marsh Station Road site, post-excavation, showing the site boundary, and the locations of Stripping Areas 1–5, as well as the project right-of-way, Marsh Station Road, and Cienega Creek and Mescal Wash.

SURFACE COLLECTION

A 10-m by 10-m grid consisting of 313 collection units (CUs) was laid over the construction corridor (Figure 4.2).[1] The collection grid covered the full extent of the initial construction corridor, but as a result of several modifications to the corridor that occurred during surface collection and preconstruction trenching, a larger area of the site's surface was collected than that contained within the final construction corridor. Approximately 86 percent or 270 of the 313 collection units contained a total of 9,652 artifacts: 7,329 pieces of debitage, 565 cores, 104 unifaces, 48 bifaces, 12 hammerstones, 22 pieces of ground stone, 1,560 sherds, 267 of which were painted, 3 pieces of worked shell, and 9 pieces of his-

toric glass (Appendix I, Table A). All artifacts collected from the site's surface, except the historic glass, were analyzed. Flaked stone and ceramic diagnostic artifacts were point-provenienced (Figure 4.3).

Artifact density varied within the 270 collection units containing cultural material. Overall, the density was modest, with the majority of the units producing less than 10 artifacts. There were, however, marked increases in artifact density in three areas of the gridded site surface (see Figure 4.3). A small cluster of units with elevated counts in the northeastern corner of the site corresponds with Stripped Area (SA) 1 (see discussion below), where Feature 17, a pithouse, and several other features are located. A significant concentration also was found around the railroad cut, which runs northwest–

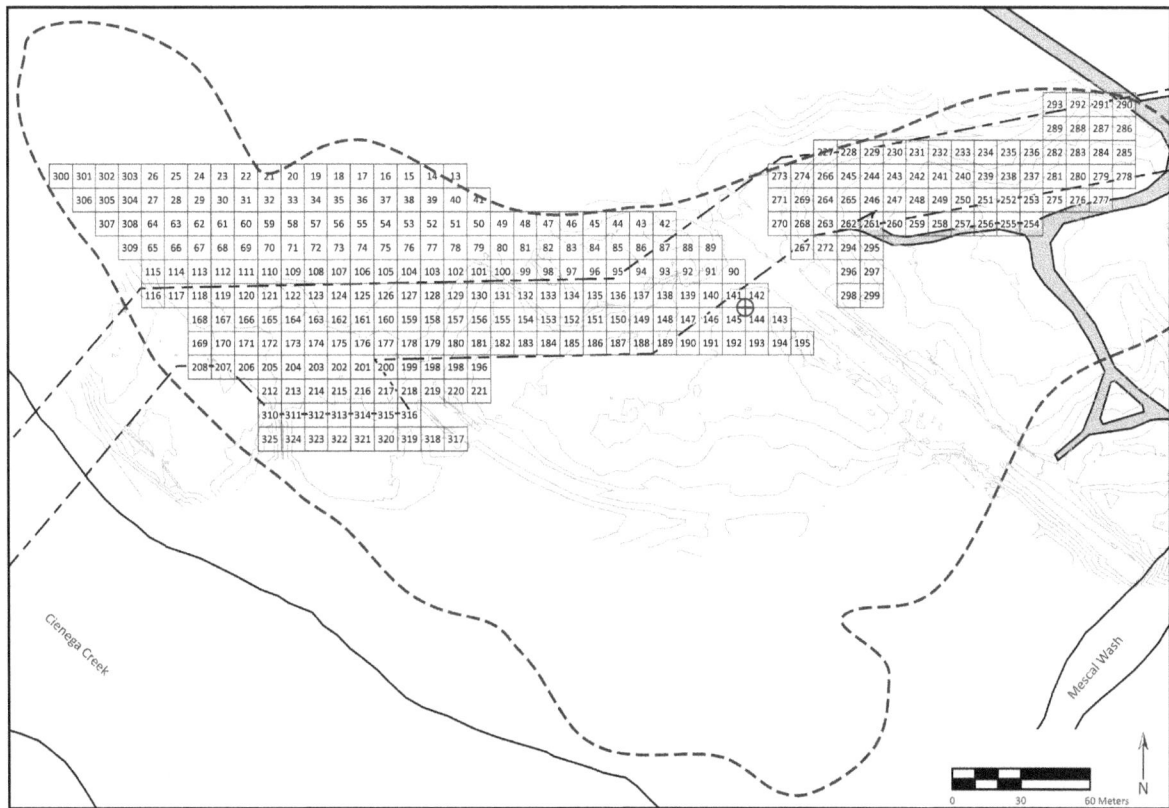

Figure 4.2. Map showing the location of all 313 collection units placed within the project APE at the Marsh Station Road site.

southeast through the east-central portion of the site. McConville and Holzkamper (1955) identified this as an area of trash deposits. No features were found in this area during trenching in 1955 or during the current project, but one roasting pit (Feature 208) was found during construction monitoring. Increased collection densities were also associated with Stripped Areas (SA) 2 through 5 (see discussion below), in the southern portion of the westernmost portion of the construction corridor where the majority of the subsurface cultural features were subsequently found.

The surface diagnostic artifacts from the Marsh Station Road site are found generally within areas of highest surface artifact density (see Figure 4.3), which simply suggests that the diagnostic artifacts were deposited on the surface in relative proportion to the general assemblage. However, of interest is the fact that the majority of diagnostic ceramic artifacts on the surface fall into two major clusters: the area around SA 1, and within SA 4 and 5 (see discussion below). These areas also are the highest concentration of Formative period subsurface artifacts and features.

TRENCHING

The treatment plan stipulated the excavation of 450 meters of trenches, 2 feet wide, placed along both the pipeline alignment and judgmentally within the project area. The placement and length of the trenches was based on site topography and the configuration of the

Figure 4.3. Point provenienced artifacts and the distribution by density of all artifacts recovered from collection units across the surface of the Marsh Station Road site.

pipeline alignment. A series of seven trenches, ranging in length from 18.7 to 64.6 m, was excavated along the pipeline alignment through the site area. An additional 10 trenches, ranging in length from 4.1 to 52.5 m, were placed within the revised expanded construction corridor. Ultimately, 17 backhoe trenches, totaling 570 m in length, were excavated (Table 4.1; Figure 4.4). A total of 44 features and three sub-features were exposed in the profiles of the 17 backhoe trenches (see Table 4.1); these features were drawn and photographed. Stratigraphy was relatively consistent among the 17 trenches (e.g., Figures 4.5–4.7), with five or six strata composed primarily of light brown to brown sandy silt with varying degrees of compaction and types and amounts of inclusions recorded within distinct strata. Stratum 4 was typically

identified as containing a caliche horizon. Cultural features most often originated in Stratum 2 (Pleistocene terrace), approximately 0.20 to 0.40 m below ground surface.

Trenching revealed features concentrated in two areas of the site: a small number of features were present in the upper portion of the site (SA 1), near Marsh Station Road, while a significant number of features were identified on the creek terrace (SAs 2–5), in the lower part of the site near Cienega Creek (Figures 4.8 and 4.9; also see Table 4.1). No features, however, were documented in the central portion of the site, results that are consistent with McConville and Holzkamper's (1955:5) conclusion that there was no depth of cultural material in that area.

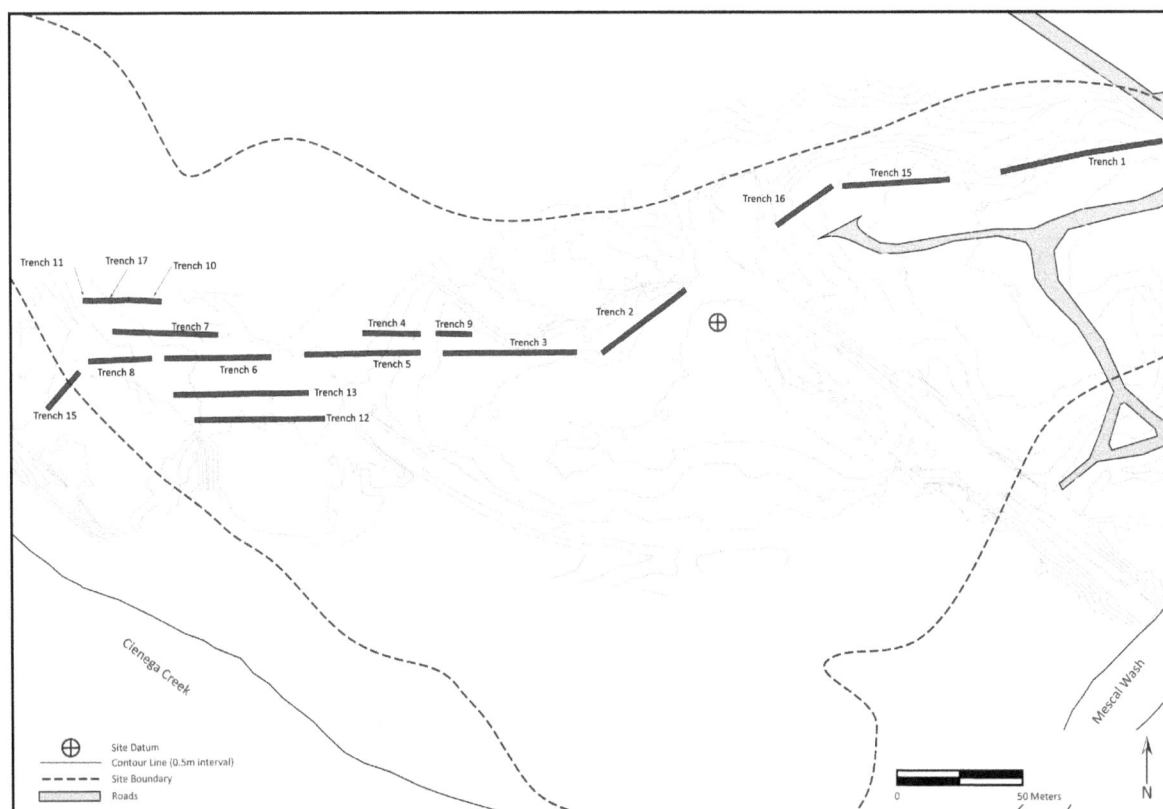

Figure 4.4. Location of the 17 preconstruction trenches excavated at the Marsh Station Road site.

Table 4.1. Characteristics of excavated trenches and the features identified in trench faces

Trench No.	Pipeline Aligment or Judgmental	Length (m)	Orientation	Features Identified
1	Pipeline	64.6	81	F.17, F.17.01, F.18, F.182
2	Pipeline	40.4	57	
3	Pipeline	52.5	91	
4	Judgmental	22.4	94	
5	Pipeline	45.3	91	
6	Pipeline	41.6	91	F.20, F.21, F.22, F.23, F.25, F.74, F.170
7	Judgmental	41.5	93	F.84, F.87, F.120, F.124
8	Pipeline	25.1	91	
9	Judgmental	14.1	95	
10	Judgmental	13.1	93	
11	Judgmental	4.1	94	
12	Judgmental	50.8	91	F.4, F.5, F.6, F.7, F.7.02, F.8, F.39, F. 41, F.41.04, F.64, F.65, F.73, F.75, F.76, F.82, F.83, F.86, F.138
13	Judgmental	52.5	91	F.12, F.13, F.14, F.15, F.16, F.51, F.54, F.58, F.118, F.130, F. 149, F.150, F.157, F.164
14	Pipeline	18.7	43	
15	Pipeline	42.5	80	
16	Pipeline	26.7	60	
17	Judgmental	14.1	90	

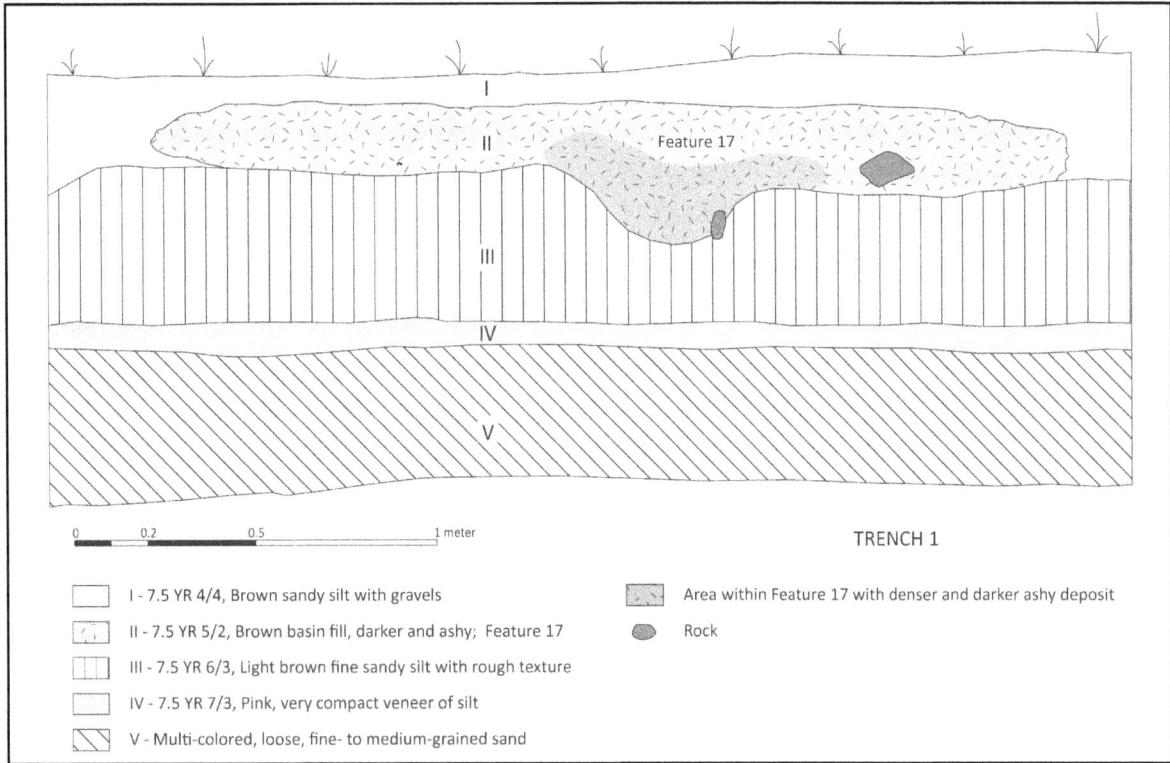

0   0.2   0.5   1 meter   TRENCH 1

I - 7.5 YR 4/4, Brown sandy silt with gravels

II - 7.5 YR 5/2, Brown basin fill, darker and ashy; Feature 17

III - 7.5 YR 6/3, Light brown fine sandy silt with rough texture

IV - 7.5 YR 7/3, Pink, very compact veneer of silt

V - Multi-colored, loose, fine- to medium-grained sand

Area within Feature 17 with denser and darker ashy deposit

Rock

Figure 4.5. Profile of a 3-m segment the north wall of Trench 1, which includes Feature 17.

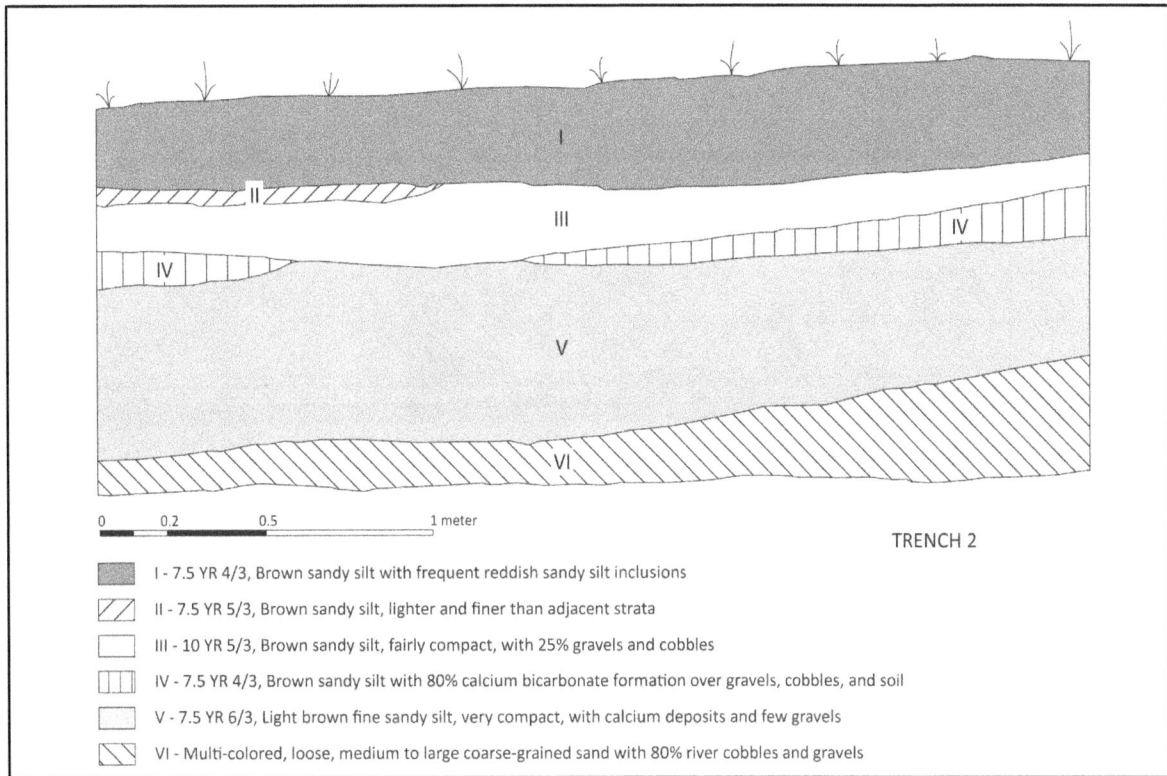

0   0.2   0.5   1 meter   TRENCH 2

I - 7.5 YR 4/3, Brown sandy silt with frequent reddish sandy silt inclusions

II - 7.5 YR 5/3, Brown sandy silt, lighter and finer than adjacent strata

III - 10 YR 5/3, Brown sandy silt, fairly compact, with 25% gravels and cobbles

IV - 7.5 YR 4/3, Brown sandy silt with 80% calcium bicarbonate formation over gravels, cobbles, and soil

V - 7.5 YR 6/3, Light brown fine sandy silt, very compact, with calcium deposits and few gravels

VI - Multi-colored, loose, medium to large coarse-grained sand with 80% river cobbles and gravels

Figure 4.6. Profile of a 3-m segment of the north wall of Trench 2.

Assessment of Geomorphology of Backhoe Trenches

The backhoe trenches were inspected and assessed by Gary Huckleberry, geomorphologist. Backhoe trenches on the dissected, Pleistocene alluvial fan situated north of Cienega Creek and west of Mescal Wash exposed partly eroded, mature soils with advanced degrees of calcification and clay formation. An ancient petrocalcic horizon is truncated and in places capped by a stone line representing erosional lag deposit. In places a red argillic horizon is developed into alluvium that overlies the stone line. All cultural features are intrusive into these ancient soils and buried by more recent, shallow slopewash near the surface.

The Late Pleistocene T2 terrace also contains ancient soils marked by well-developed argillic and petrocalcic horizons. Red argillic horizons tend to be located in the western half of the project corridor whereas the white pet-

rocalcic horizons dominate the eastern half. Because this landform still retains its original terrace morphology and is not significantly dissected, it is uncertain as to the causes of local variability in soil horizonation—i.e., it cannot be attributed to differential preservation like on the higher fan surfaces. Pedogenic variability on the T2 terrace may be attributed to depositional facie resulting in parent material differences that have influenced soil formation: well-sorted sandy alluvium (area of white calcic soils) dominates the eastern half of the corridor whereas cobbly channel deposits (area of red argillic soils) dominate the western half. Cultural features are intrusive into both types of soils and shallowly buried in places by slopewash.

One short trench (Trench 14) was excavated 2.5 m into the Holocene T1 terrace and revealed horizontally bedded, overbank stream deposits associated with Cienega Creek. Sandy sediments are overlain by lower energy over-

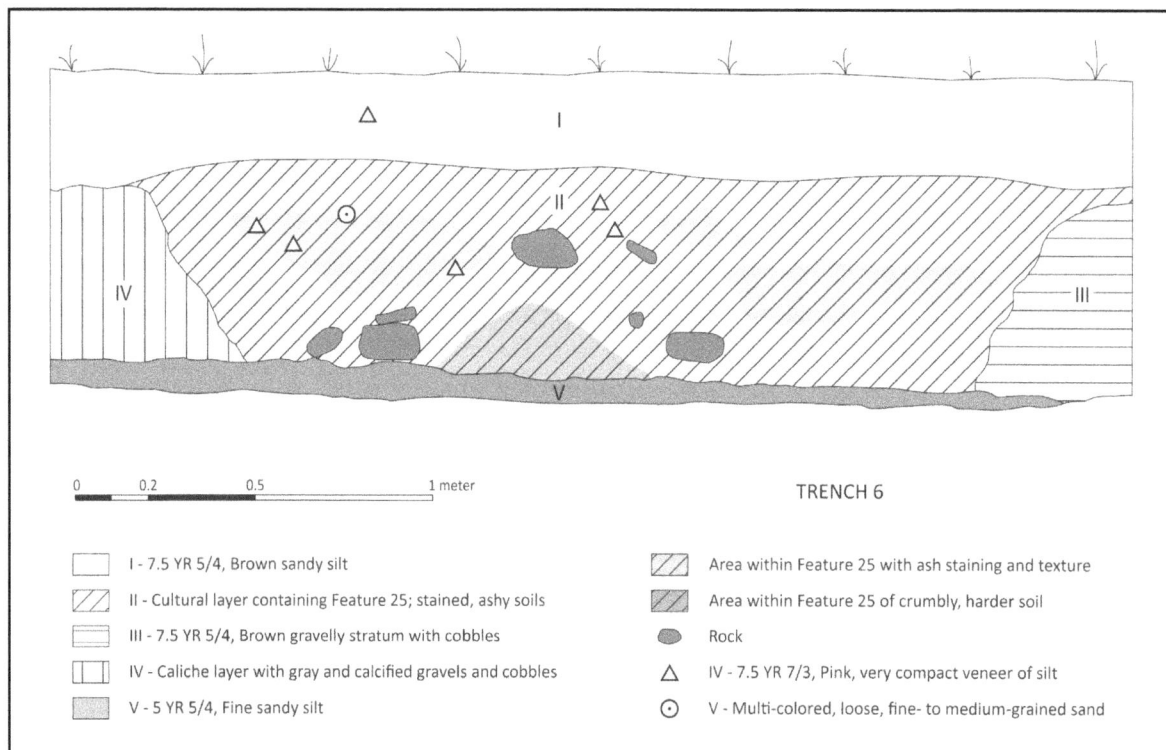

Figure 4.7. Profile of a 3-m segment of the north wall of Trench 6, which includes Feature 25.

bank deposits with greater silt and clay content. There is also a surface wedge of sandy alluvium derived from sheetwash near the T2–T1 terrace boundary. Soil formation is weak and characterized by A over B cambic (weak structure and fine filaments of calcium carbonate) horizonation. Based on pedogenesis and correlation to alluvial chronologies located upstream at the mouth of Matty Wash (Eddy and Cooley 1983) and downstream at the Pantano site (Hemmings et al. 1968), the deposits exposed in Trench 14 are probably less than 1,000 years old and overlie older mid- to late Holocene alluvial deposits. There lower deposits have moderate potential to contain cultural materials.

MECHANICAL STRIPPING

Based upon the results of surface collections and trenching, five areas were targeted for mechanical stripping (see Figures 4.8 and 4.9). These areas were assigned numbers as Stripped Areas (SAs 1–5, Table 4.2), and became de facto loci, although they were smaller and more contiguous than areas traditionally defined as loci and based on arbitrary limits of the construction corridor and mechanical excavation rather than on feature/artifact density. Stripped Area 1 was delineated in the upper portion of the site, where Trench 1 had exposed three features near Marsh Station Road. Stripped Areas 2 through 5 (Figures 4.10 and 4.11) were located in the lower portion of the site, where four trenches had exposed 41 features and two subfeatures (see Table 4.1; also see Figures 4.8 and 4.9). The total area that was mechanically stripped exceeded 1,800 square meters (see Table 4.2).

In the remainder of this chapter (and throughout this report), Stripped Areas 2 and 3 are collectively referred to as one unit, SA 2/3, while Stripped Areas 4 and 5 are also collectively referred to as one unit, SA 4/5. The

Table 4.2. Summary of stripped areas

Stripping Area	Area (m^2)
1	312.68
2	393.18
3	442.46
4	467.13
5	199.63
Total	1815.08

decision to refer to these four stripped areas as two collective units is based on the opinion that each of the strip areas in each of these two units contain similar material culture and features— that is, Stripped Areas 2 and 3 are similar, while Stripped Areas 4 and 5 are similar—and that their separation into four (rather than two) units was an artifact of the placement of two of the judgmental trenches (Trench 7 between SAs 2 and 3, and Trench 13 between SAs 4 and 5) rather than any culturally meaningful distinction.

Before mechanical stripping commenced, 12 2-m by 2-m test units (TUs 1–12) were manually excavated in 10-cm levels from the modern ground surface; their fill was screened through ¼-inch mesh. These units were located in the lower portion of the site, near Cienega Creek, and were excavated in order to obtain controlled samples of artifacts from modern ground surface to sterile before the surface of the site was mechanically stripped. In addition, excavation of these initial TUs confirmed that many of the features at the Marsh Station Road site were shallowly buried approximately 0.20 to 0.40 m below modern ground surface. Once these 12 test units were completed, the five stripped areas were excavated with the backhoe until features were exposed in the stripped surface. Approximately 10 to 20 cm of sediment was removed from each of the

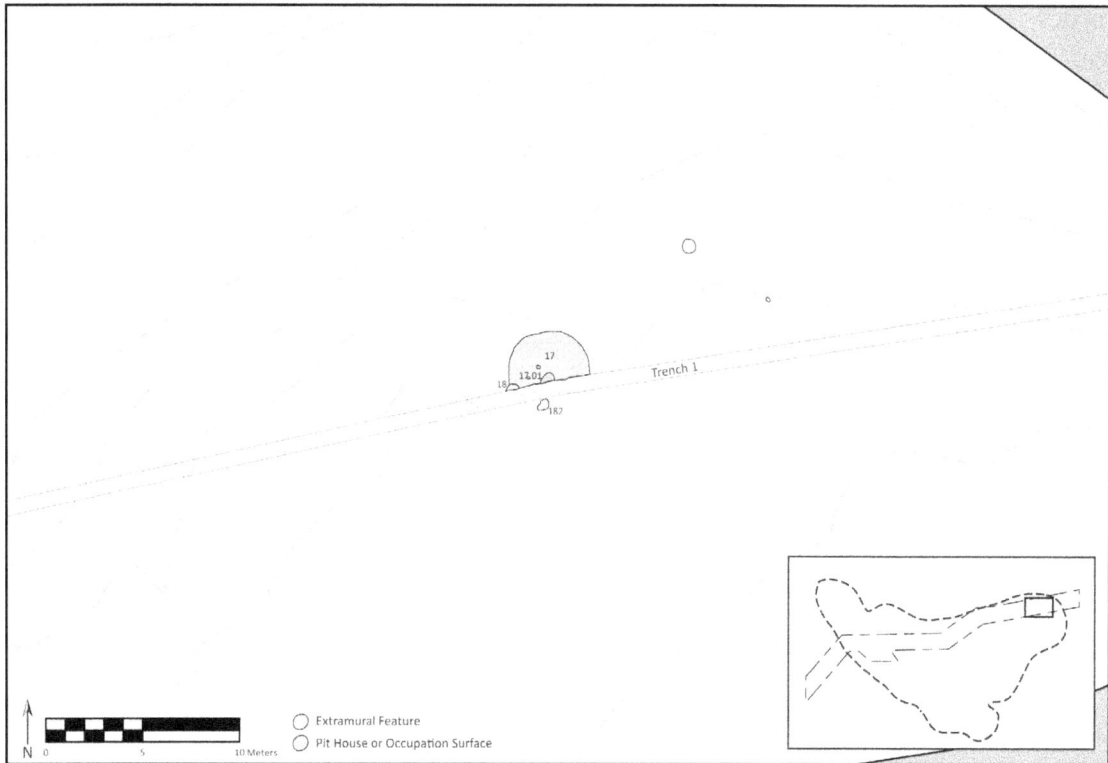

Figure 4.8. Distribution of features discovered during trenching in Stripped Area 1.

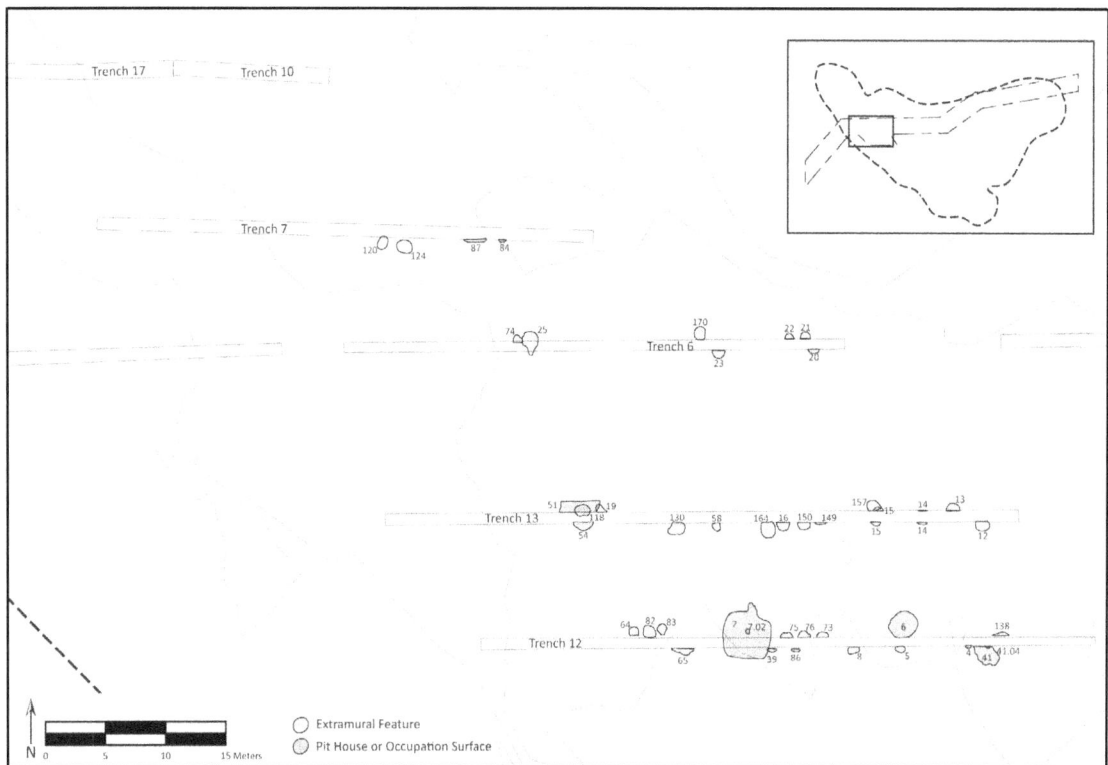

Figure 4.9. Distribution of features discovered during trenching in Stripped Areas 2, 3, 4, and 5.

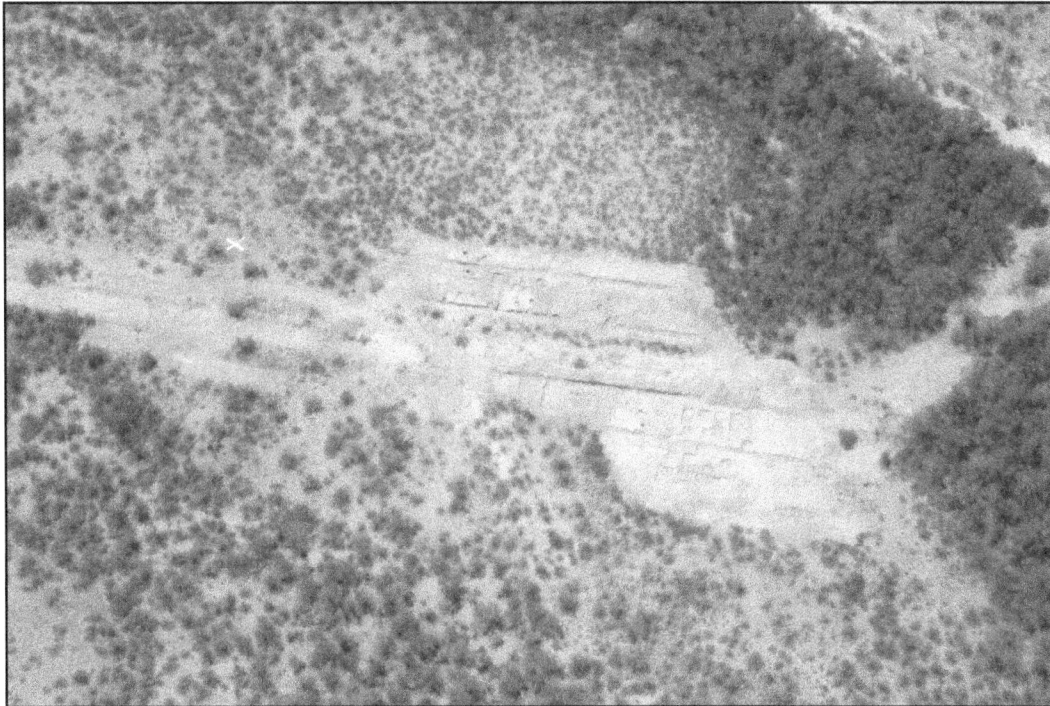

Figure 4.10. Aerial view of Stripped Areas 2/3 and 4/5, post-excavation.

Figure 4.11. Overview of Stripped Area 4/5, view to the northeast, showing multiple layers of features attesting to the lengthy occupation and stratigraphic complexity of the Marsh Station Road site.

stripped areas. Excavation proceeded by hand from this point, with test units, stripped units (SUs), and features excavated within the five stripped areas.

Test Units and Stripped Units

A total of 179 test units were manually excavated in 10-cm levels within the five stripped areas and between trenches (Figures 4.12–4.14). The majority (n = 136) of the test units measured 2 m by 2 m, although other test units ranged in size from 1 m by 1 m to 1 m by 4 m. As mentioned above, the first 12 test units, which were located in SA 2/3 and SA 4/5 (see Figures 4.13 and 4.14), were excavated from the modern ground surface as stratigraphic and artifact controls. Approximately 63 percent of the 179 test units were screened through ¼-inch

mesh; the remaining test units were "grab-sampled." A summary of the distribution and screened-sample of the excavated test units is contained in Table 4.3.

In addition to the test units, a total of 16 stripped units (SUs 1–16) were also manually excavated in the five stripped areas (see Figures 4.13 and 4.14). These SUs were not excavated in levels and they were not screened, but rather were excavated until features were exposed or sterile deposits encountered. The stripped units varied in size, measuring between 0.7 m and 7 m in width, and 2 m and 11 m in length. The stripped units are considered together with the test units in the remainder of this chapter.

Cultural deposits within the test units/stripped units were found to be variable, ranging in depth from the modern ground surface or the stripped surface (i.e., the top of the test/stripped unit) to 1.17 m, but generally occurring

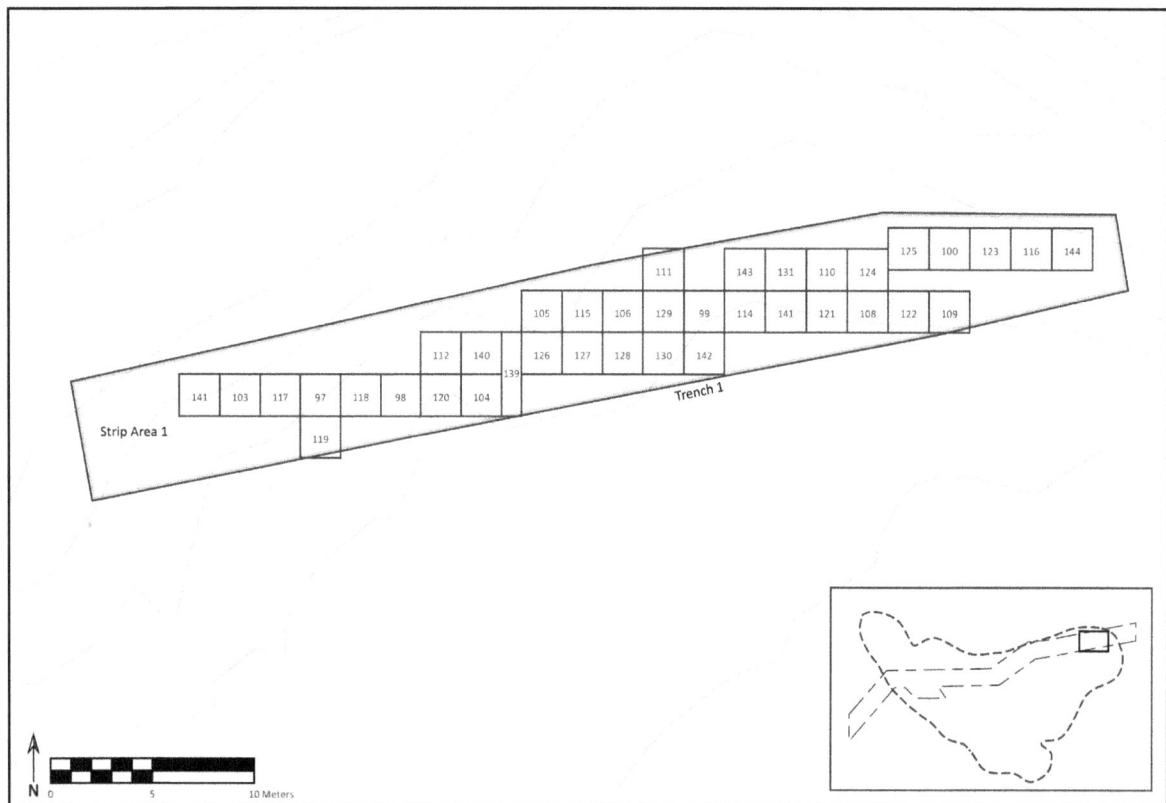

Figure 4.12. Distribution of test units located in Stripped Area 1.

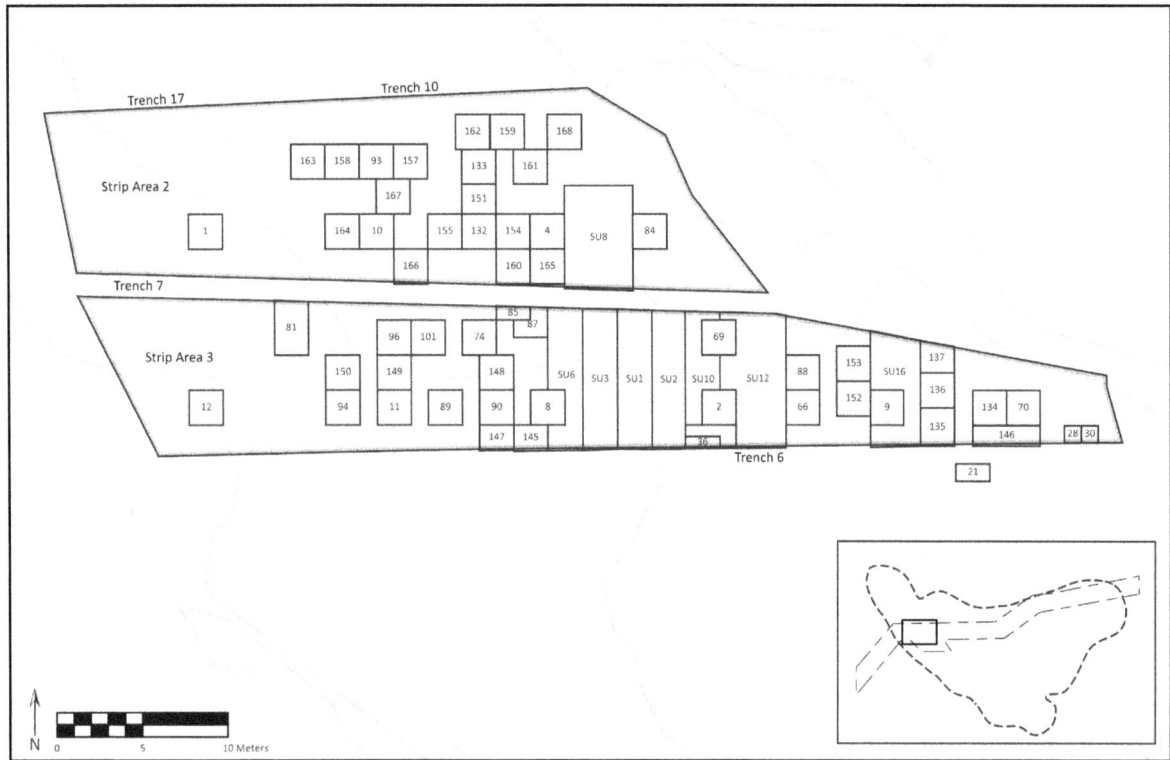

Figure 4.13. Distribution of test units and stripping units located in Stripped Area 2/3.

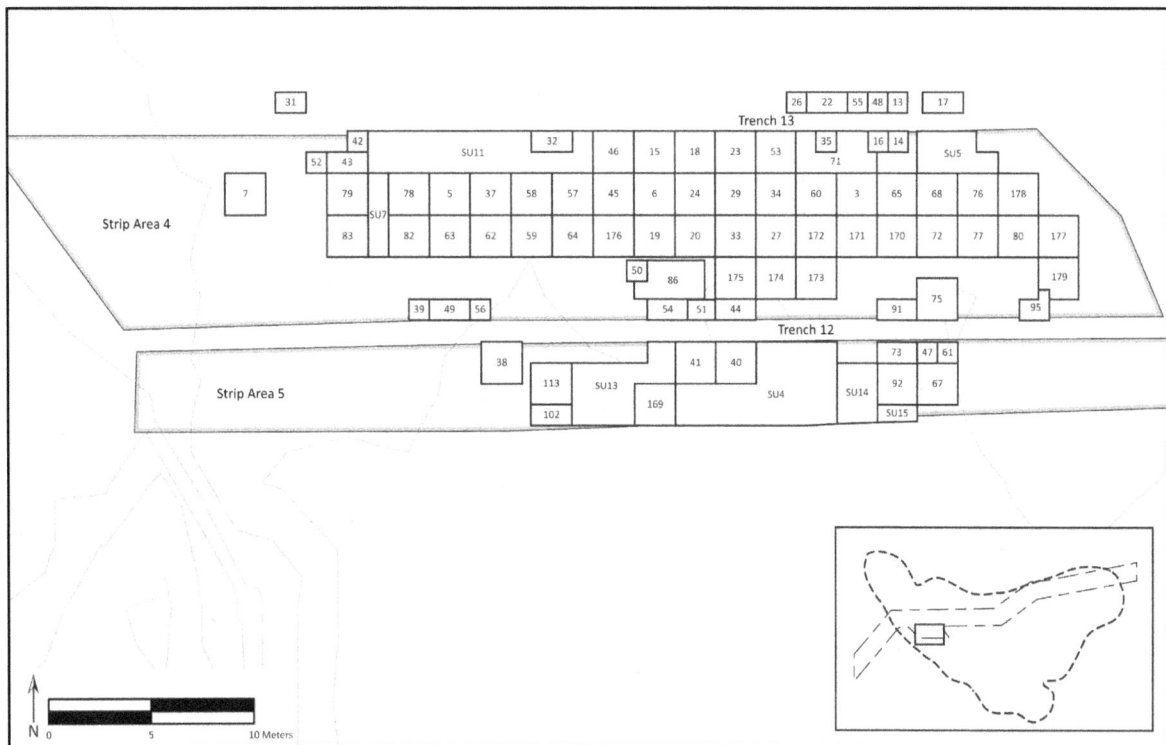

Figure 4.14. Distribution of test units and stripping units located in Stripped Area 4/5.

between 10 and 50 cm. Stratigraphy within the test units was mostly consistent, although variation was present and particularly noticeable trending west-to-east and in SA 4 as compared to other stripped areas. Observed west–east variation was characterized as generally redder, shallower, and rockier in the west, and browner, deeper, and less rocky to the east. This trend was also evident in some of the trenches, and is reported in the geomorphological assessment of the site area (see Chapter 3). Generally, sediment was categorized as low or moderately compacted, brown or yellow-brown sandy and/or silty loam; calcium carbonate deposits, as well as soil containing higher clay content, were also fairly common in the test units, especially in the lower levels. River cobbles ranging in size from 1 to 2 cm to upwards of 30 cm were recorded, as were pieces of charcoal and fire-cracked rock (FCR). The majority of the features documented at the Marsh Station Road site were discovered on the basis of test unit/stripped unit excavation.

A total of 25,308 artifacts was collected from excavated test units/stripped units (Appendix I, Table B and Table 4.4). Artifacts included a wide variety of flaked stone debitage, projectile points, and other flaked stone tools; ground stone artifacts; painted and unpainted sherds as well as several reconstructible vessels and special ceramic artifacts; faunal bone; and worked and unworked shell. Almost every test unit produced artifacts: only seven test units contained no artifacts, while an additional 33 test units contained 20 or fewer artifacts (see Appendix I, Table B). Of the seven TUs that contained no artifacts, three were not screened (they were grab-sampled), which may account for the lack of artifacts recovered from them. Approximately half (n = 7) of the stripped units—all of which were located in SAs 3 or 4—contained artifacts, although only in very low densities.

The density of artifacts recovered from test units varied significantly in different parts of the site. Densities were calculated by dividing the total number of artifacts recovered by the volume of sediment excavated from the unit, thereby allowing for some measure of standardization and comparability between units of different sizes and depths. Stripped Area 1, located at the easternmost edge of the site, contained a generally low density of artifacts (Figure 4.15). Most of the test units in this area contained densities with less than 100 artifacts/m3, and only two contained a density calculated between 101 and 150 artifacts/m3. In SA 2/3, the density of test unit artifacts is considered light to moderate (Figure 4.16). Most test units contain artifact densities between 100 and 200 artifacts/m3; only a few contain densities measuring between 201 and 300 artifacts/m3, and none contain densities greater than 300. Stripped Area 4/5 contains

Table 4.3. Summary of test unit characteristics

Stripping Area	Total Number of Test Units (2 m by 2 m)	Number of units screened through ¼-inch mesh	Percent of units screened through ¼-inch mesh
1	39	19	48.7
2	25	7	28.0
3	51	25	49.0
4	56	23	41.0
5	25	10	40.0

Table 4.4. Distribution of artifacts collected from stripping units

Stripping Unit	Flaked Stone			Ground Stone	Ceramics				Faunal	Total
	Debitage	Core	Biface		Painted	Unpainted	Special	Other		
5	26			2	2	15	2	3		50
6			1							1
9	1									1
11	33		1	3	16	34	2	1		90
13	37					9	2	3		51
14	5					5				10
16	31	1	2		5	19		10	9	77
Total	133	1	4	5	23	82	6	17	9	280

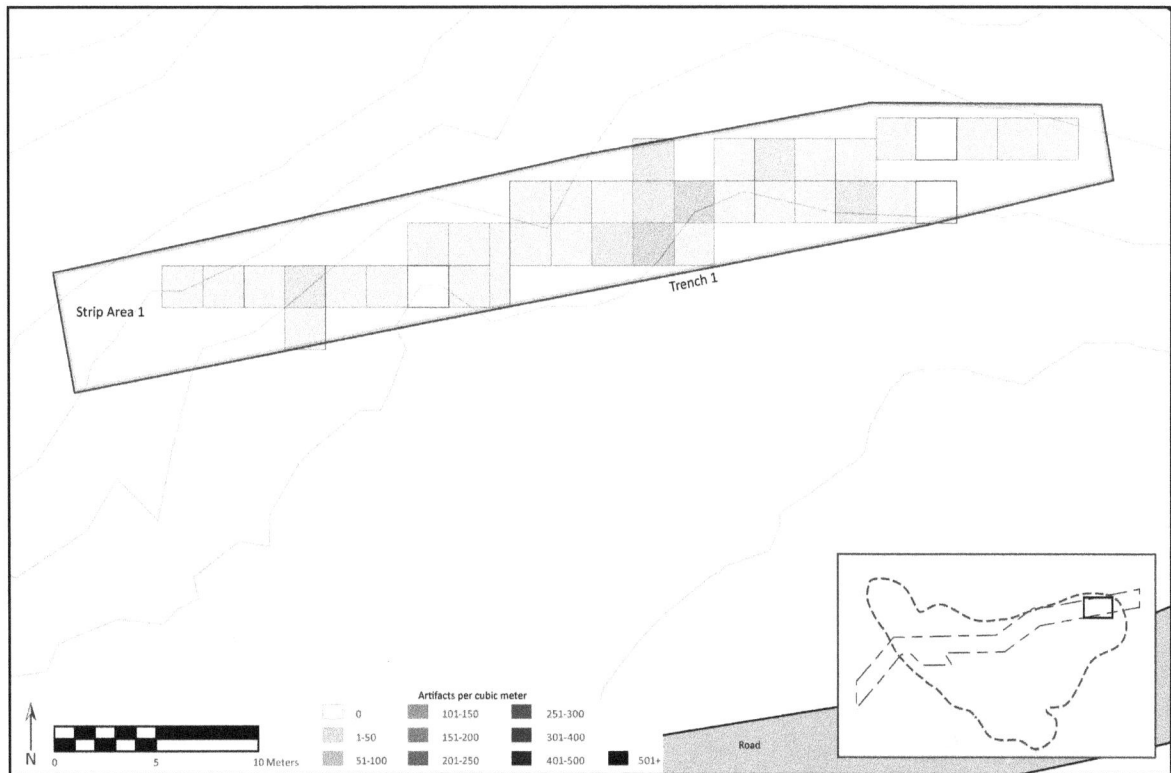

Figure 4.15. The distribution by density of artifacts recovered from test units in Stripped Area 1.

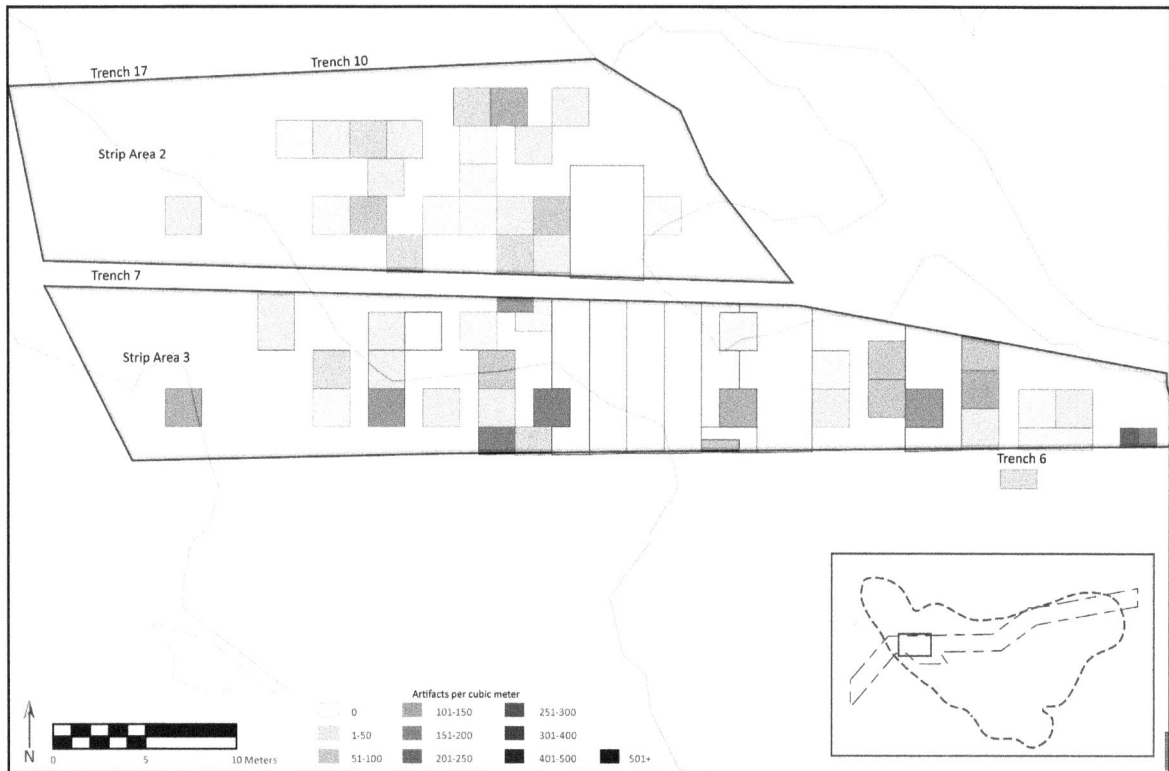

Figure 4.16. The distribution by density of artifacts recovered from test units in Stripped Area 2/3.

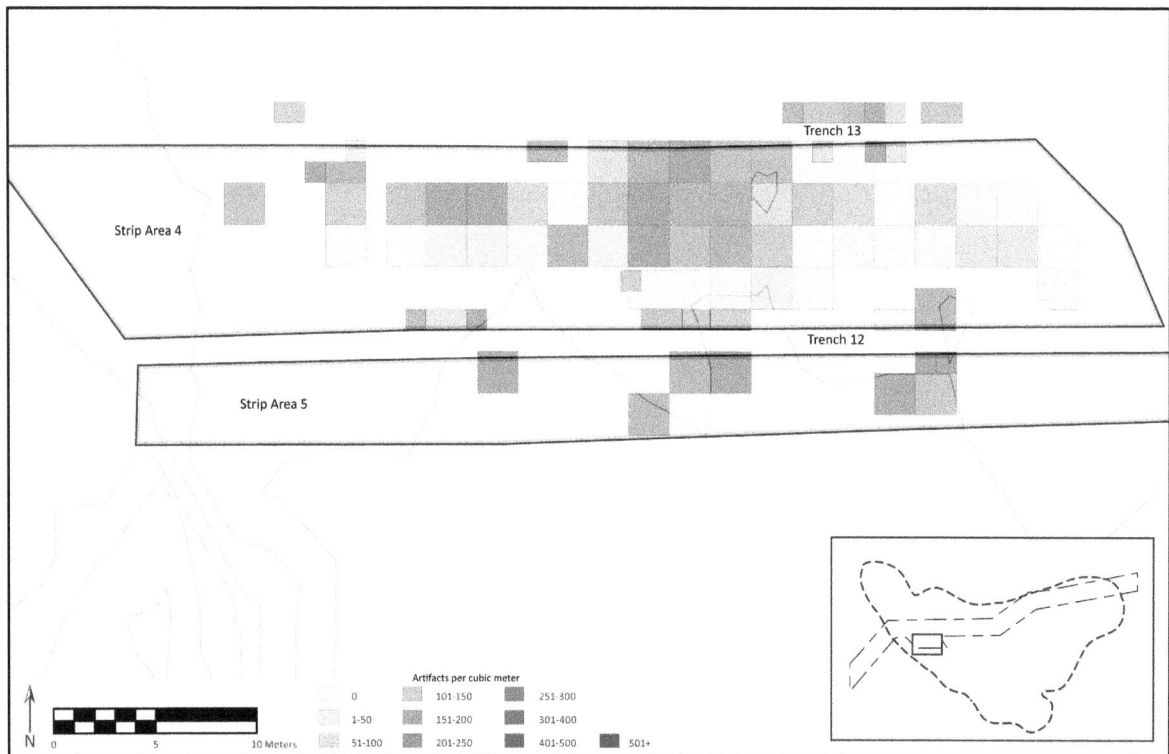

Figure 4.17. The distribution by density of artifacts recovered from test units in Stripped Area 4/5.

by far the densest distribution of artifacts recovered from test units, although the density is differentially distributed throughout the SA area (Figure 4.17). The central portion of SA 4/5 contains the greatest density of artifacts, with most TUs containing more than 300 artifacts/m3. The eastern portion of this SA contains a light density of artifacts, while the western portion contains a moderate density, with some TUs registering a very light density of artifacts, and others containing much higher densities. In general, and especially in SA 4/5, the highest densities occur in those TUs that were placed over features, and in particular over pithouses. It seems likely, then, that the TUs with the lowest densities probably contain artifacts that were distributed across the site over time by general formation processes. The test units with the highest densities probably contain artifacts that are largely associated with the features below.

STATISTICAL COMPARISON OF SURFACE AND SUBSURFACE ARTIFACT ASSEMBLAGES

Downnum and Brown (1998) assessed the reliability of surface assemblages to predict subsurface assemblages in the Hohokam region. They argue that in the Hohokam Southwest, "complex erosional and depositional processes (Brackenridge 1984; Schuster and Katzer 1984; Waters and Field 1986), ephemeral surface architecture (Crown 1983, 1985), and widely dispersed features (Fish et al. 1992) make the interpretation of surface remains especially difficult" (Downum and Brown 1998:111). However, they state—and support with quantitative intersite comparisons of surface and subsurface assemblages—that there is predictive utility in the surface assemblages at Hohokam habitation sites, contrary to Greenwald and Ciolek-Torrello's (1987:137) assertion that surface remains provide "little

clue" to the subsurface assemblage at such sites. Downum and Brown (1998) discovered that the relative proportions of subsurface ceramics and chipped stone are reliably predicted by their surface proportions. Additionally, they found that surface assemblages underestimate subsurface percentages of flaked stone tools and painted ceramics. Further, they conclude that surface assemblages of ground stone and finished flaked stone tools—and for the Marsh Station Road site, faunal, ground stone, and other more sparse remains—are simply less reliable for predicting their respective subsurface assemblages than are the general ceramic and flaked stone categories.

Here we present the results of similar investigations at the Marsh Station Road site, where artifact distributions in three different contexts—surface, initial test units (TUs; those excavated prior to mechanical stripping), and all other test units—are compared through statistical and graphical investigation. These investigations are conducted site-wide, meaning that no comparisons between the different stripped areas are conducted here (the results of analyses of differences between stripped areas are presented later in this chapter). The entire site surface where subsurface investigation occurred is compared with the subsurface investigations, divided into two groups: initial TUs and subsequent TUs. Additionally, we also investigate the potential for differences between these two subsurface groups.

Chi-square tests (supported with Cramer's V) were conducted for these investigations. Although all tests to be discussed were statistically significant at the 95 percent confidence level, they are all weakly significant based on the Cramer's V tests (all Cramer's V tests of strength were 0.13 or lower, indicating very small differences in the distributions between categories). The chi-square tests are primarily driven by large sample size, whereby small differences in number of artifacts amplify the chi-square value to a great degree even though the proportional differences are minimal. Hence, we provide graphical representation of the percentages of artifacts in each category in question to illustrate the insubstantial differences between contexts.

Specifically, there were very weakly statistically significant results exhibited in:

1. the proportion of ceramics and flaked stone relative to each other in CUs and initial TUs (Figure 4.18, includes proportion in all other TUs for comparison);

2. the proportions of specific ceramic and flaked stone artifact types in CUs and initial TUs (Figures 4.19 and 4.20), includes proportion in all other TUs for comparison);

3. the proportions of ceramics and flaked stone relative to each other in initial TUs and all other TUs (see Figure 4.18); and

4. the proportions of ceramics, flaked stone, and faunal bone relative to each other in initial TUs and all other TUs (Figure 4.21).

Therefore, while these results were statistically significant, the Cramer's V tests suggest that all results are very weak; only with much hesitation should there be an interpretation of a difference in the distributions of these artifact classes and types within various depositional contexts. Graphical inspection confirms that there are minimal differences in the proportions of types, and the statistical tests were driven primarily by large sample size. Realis-

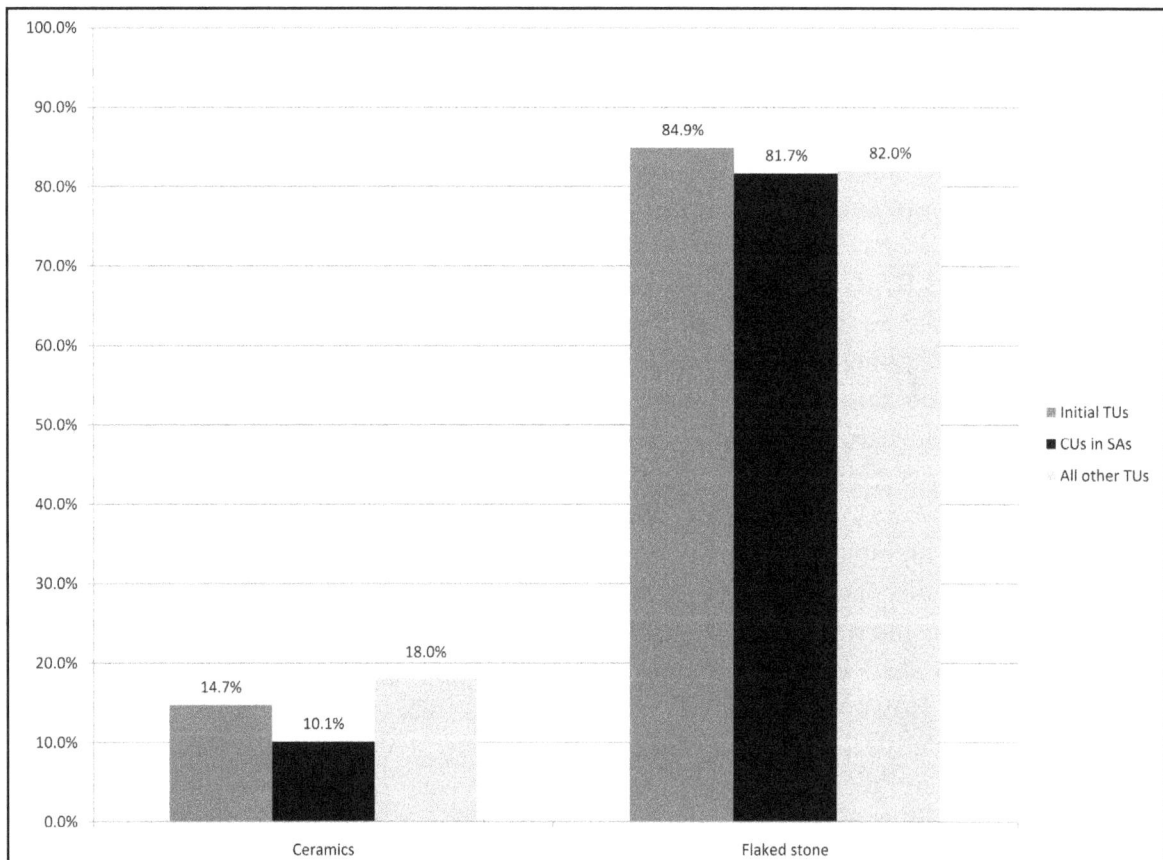

Figure 4.18. The proportion of ceramics and flaked stone relative to each other in CUs and initial TUs (includes proportion in all other TUs for comparison).

tically, there are no substantial differences in the distributions of ceramic, flaked stone, or faunal artifacts between the surface and various subsurface contexts of the Marsh Station Road site. Painted sherds and flaked stone tools are equally represented on the surface and in buried contexts, a surprising result given Downum and Brown's assessment (1998) and the propensity for previous site visits and amateur collection to thin the surface diagnostic assemblage. Additionally, the artifact classes are proportionately represented relative to each other throughout the depositional contexts.

What these results illustrate, confirming some of Downum and Brown's (1998) conclusions, is that surface artifact assemblages of flaked stone and ceramics at Hohokam habitation sites are reliable predictors of general distributions of subsurface artifact patterns. Additionally, we have shown that the artifact assemblage recovered from test units excavated after mechanical stripping of overburden reliably represent the assemblage of artifacts recovered from contexts that were not mechanically stripped—this reaffirms the utility and efficiency of mechanical stripping at this type of Hohokam habitation site.

Contrary to Downum and Brown (1998), however, is our discovery of a higher proportion of flaked stone cores and tools on the surface than in subsurface contexts. To reiterate, this result was very weakly statistically significant, but is *far* different from Downum and Brown's assessment that the "surface assemblages appear to *underestimate grossly* the percentage of chipped-stone tools represented in the

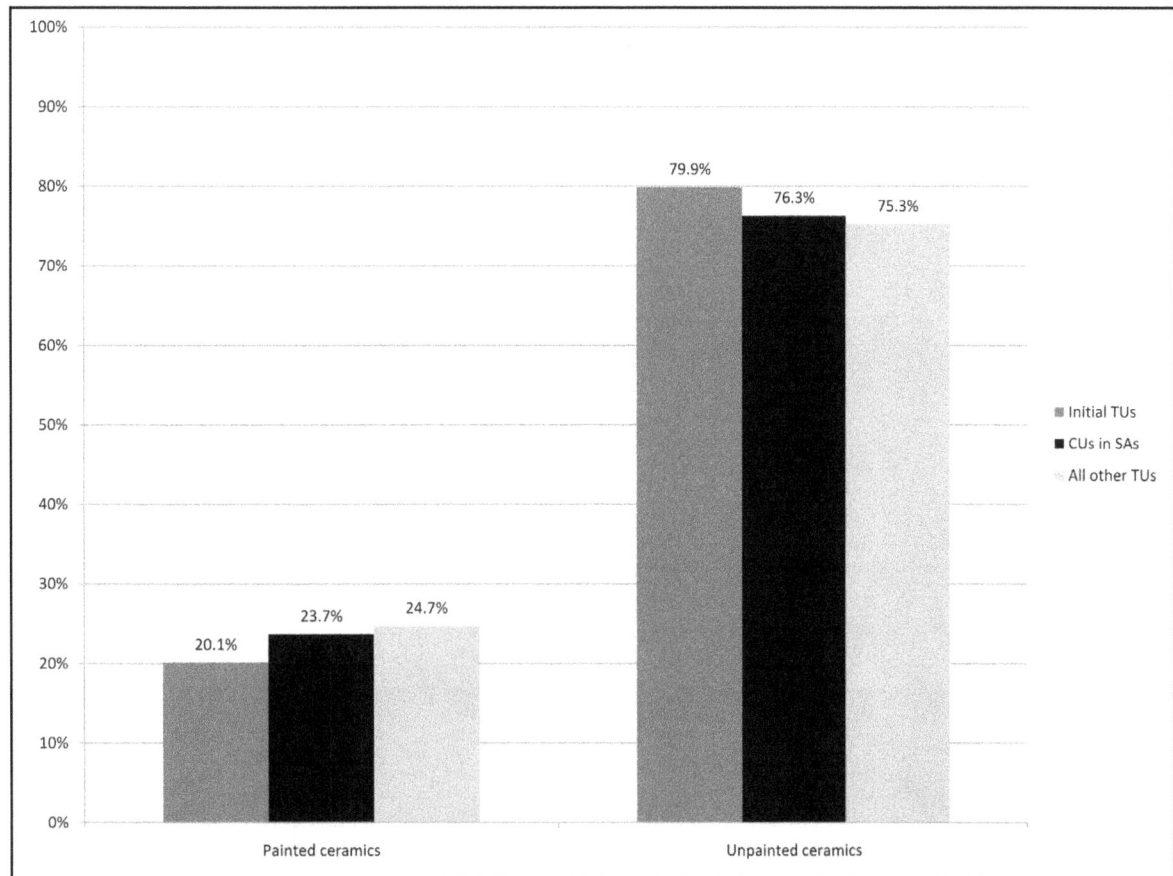

Figure 4.19. The proportions of painted and unpainted ceramics in CUs and initial TUs (includes proportion in all other TUs for comparison).

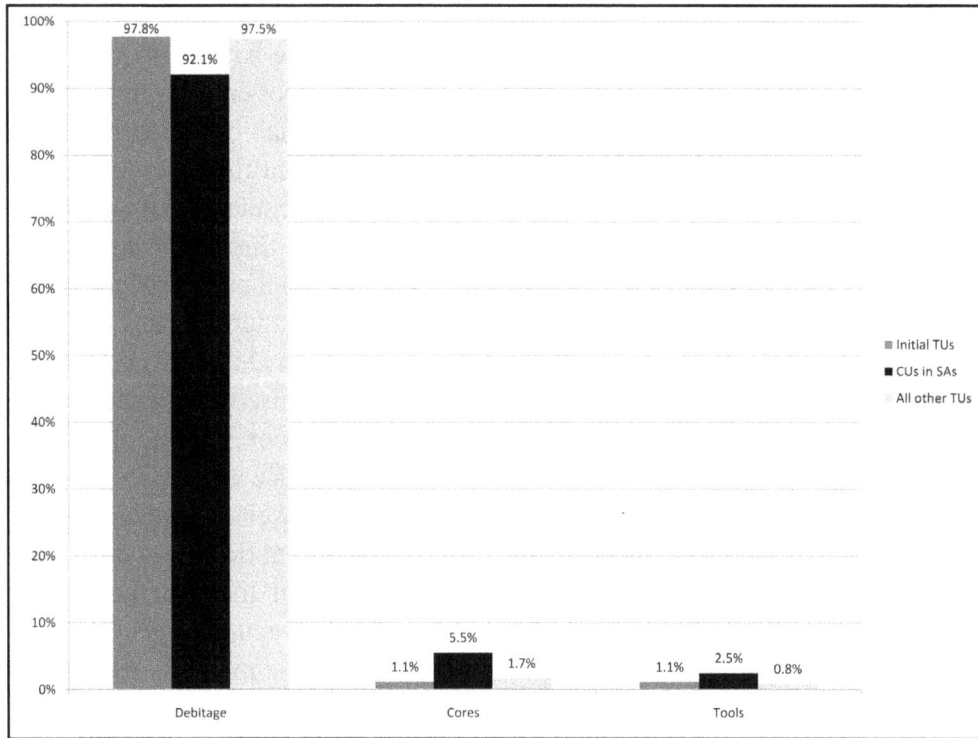

Figure 4.20. The proportions of specific flaked stone artifact types (debitage, cores, and tools) in CUs and initial TUs (includes proportion in all other TUs for comparison).

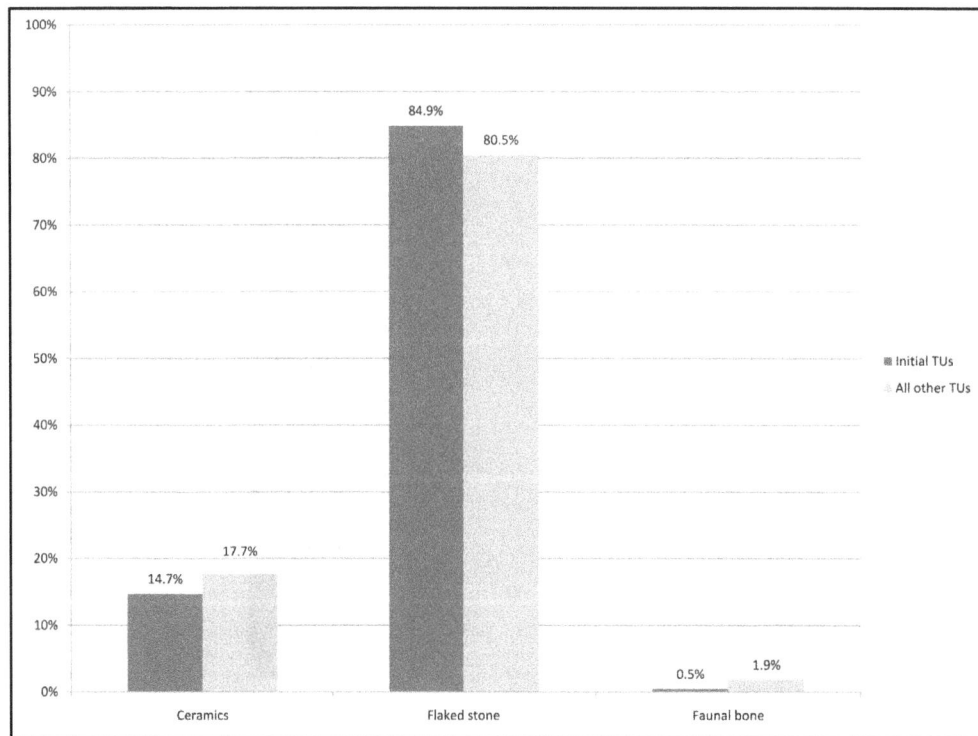

Figure 4.21. The proportions of ceramics, flaked stone, and faunal bone relative to each other in initial TUs and all other TUs.

total assemblage of chipped-stone artifacts" (1998:121, emphasis added). There is not a significant difference in the proportions of cores and tools on the surface and subsurface, so the difference among these classes is more related to debitage. Additionally, we did not discover a significantly lower percentage of decorated ceramic sherds on the surface (23.7 percent compared to 20.1 percent in the 12 initial TUs and 24.7 percent in all other TUs); in fact, the percentages are nearly equal when comparing the surface to all TUs together (24.2 percent, a negligible difference from the 23.7 percent painted ceramics on the surface). As with flaked stone tools, the fact that the surface assemblage of painted ceramics does *not* underestimate the overall painted ceramic percentage is a noteworthy point. Whether these results are due to surface collection methodology (emphasized collection of diagnostics, the visibility of small flakes and plain ware sherds against desert groundcover, the downward migration of debitage, or most likely a combination of these factors) or a reality of the archaeological record is a question that may not be answered with the data from a single site such as Marsh Station Road. However, it should also be noted that the Marsh Station Road site is of a different site type—a large Hohokam habitation site occupied in a semi-permanent nature for at least 2,500 years—than those investigated by Downum and Brown (1998:112)—two large Colonial period habitation villages (Fastimes [AZ AA:12:384 [ASM] and Waterworld [AZ AA:16:94 [ASM]), three seasonally occupied late Pioneer/Colonial period Hohokam farmsteads, and four Hohokam food gathering and processing sites investigated as part of Phase B of the Tucson Aqueduct Project (Czaplicki and Ravesloot, ed. 1988). The differences in site types between the two analyses could be a factor in the results of the current analysis, and should be kept in mind when interpreting these conclusions.

FEATURE EXCAVATIONS

Excavations at the Marsh Station Road site documented a total of 246 features and subfeatures (Appendix I, Table C).[2] Subfeatures, all of which were excavated, account for 54 of this total. Of the remaining 192 features, 138, approximately 72 percent, were at least partially excavated. The remaining 54 features were not excavated as part of these investigations because it was determined that a sufficient number of features, different feature types, and time periods had been investigated, and that excavation of more features was unlikely to add significant new information about the site. The majority of the features were either initially exposed in the faces of trenches or discovered during the excavation of test/stripped units. Stripped Area 1 contained the fewest features; just five features were documented in this northern area of the site (Figure 4.22, Table 4.5). The majority of the features were located in Stripped Areas 2/3 and 4/5, with the highest concentration of features occurring in Stripped Area 4. (Figures 4.23 and 4.24; see Table 4.5). Two features (Features 208 and 209) were documented outside of the five stripped areas, near the existing petroleum pipelines, during construction monitoring.

The majority of the excavated features and subfeatures are prehistoric; only two are historic (see Appendix I, Table C and Table 4.5).[3] Absolute dates—radiocarbon or archaeomagnetic—were obtained for 12 features and five subfeatures (Table 4.6). Subfeatures (e.g., hearths, postholes, etc.) associated with the pit structures and extramural surfaces recorded at the site represent approximately 22 percent of the total features identified; one subfeature (Feature 41.01), a posthole, was determined to be historic in age and therefore not associated with prehistoric Feature 41. Extramural pits—nonthermal and thermal—were by far the most abundant type of feature identified (n = 174;

Table 4.5. Summary of feature types by locus							
	SA 1	SA 2	SA 3	SA 4	SA 4/5	SA 5	Other	Total
Pithouse/Structure	1			3	1	1		6
Occupation Surface				1		1		2
Burial (all excavated)	3		1	2		1		7
Nonthermal Pit								
Excavated		2	26	52		15		95
Not excavated		5	25	9		7		46
Thermal Pit								
Excavated	1	2	1	15		3		22
Not excavated			2	3		2	2	9
Other Prehistoric								
Excavated						1		1
Not excavated			1					1
Historic features								
Excavated				1				1
Not excavated		1					1	2
Total	5	10	56	86	1	31	3	192

Note: Subfeatures are not included in this table

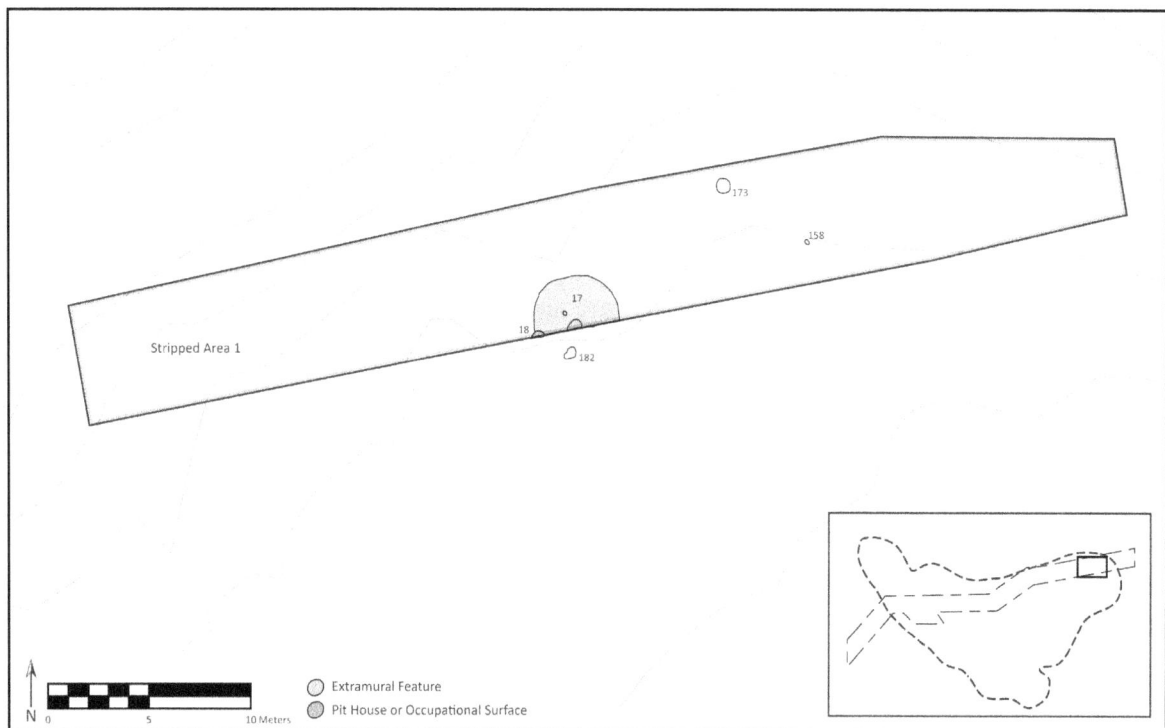

Figure 4.22. Distribution of features in Stripped Area 1.

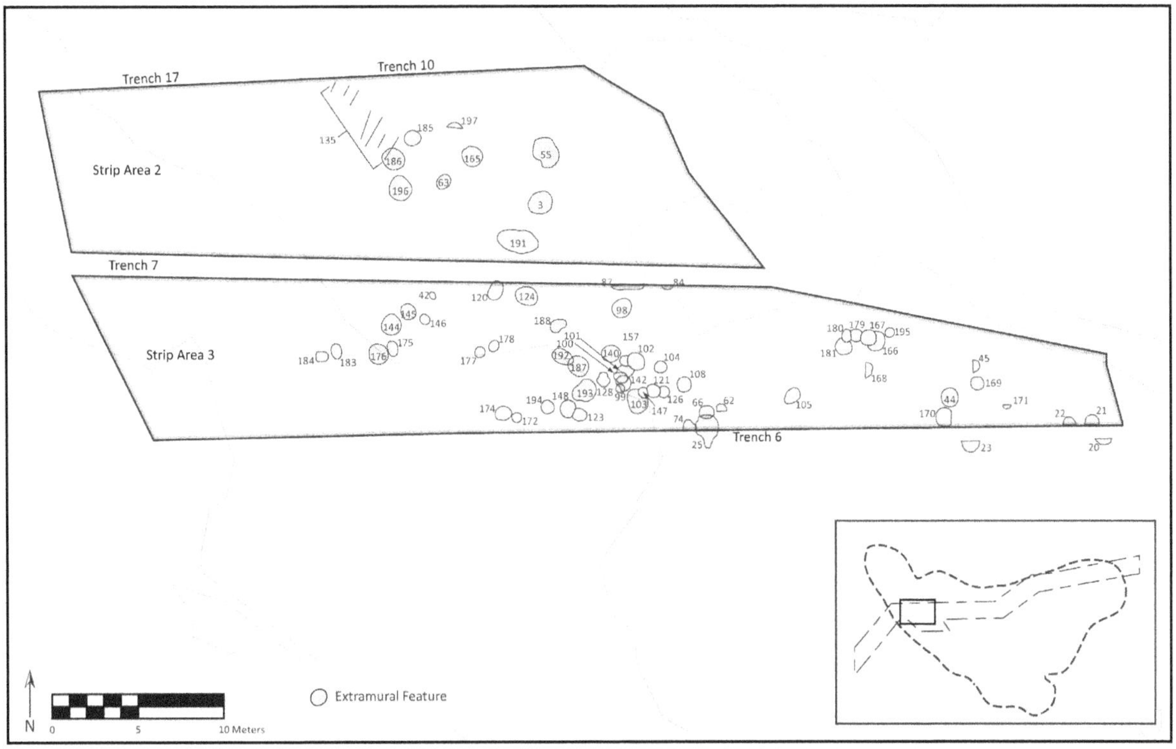

Figure 4.23. Distribution of features in Stripped Area 2/3.

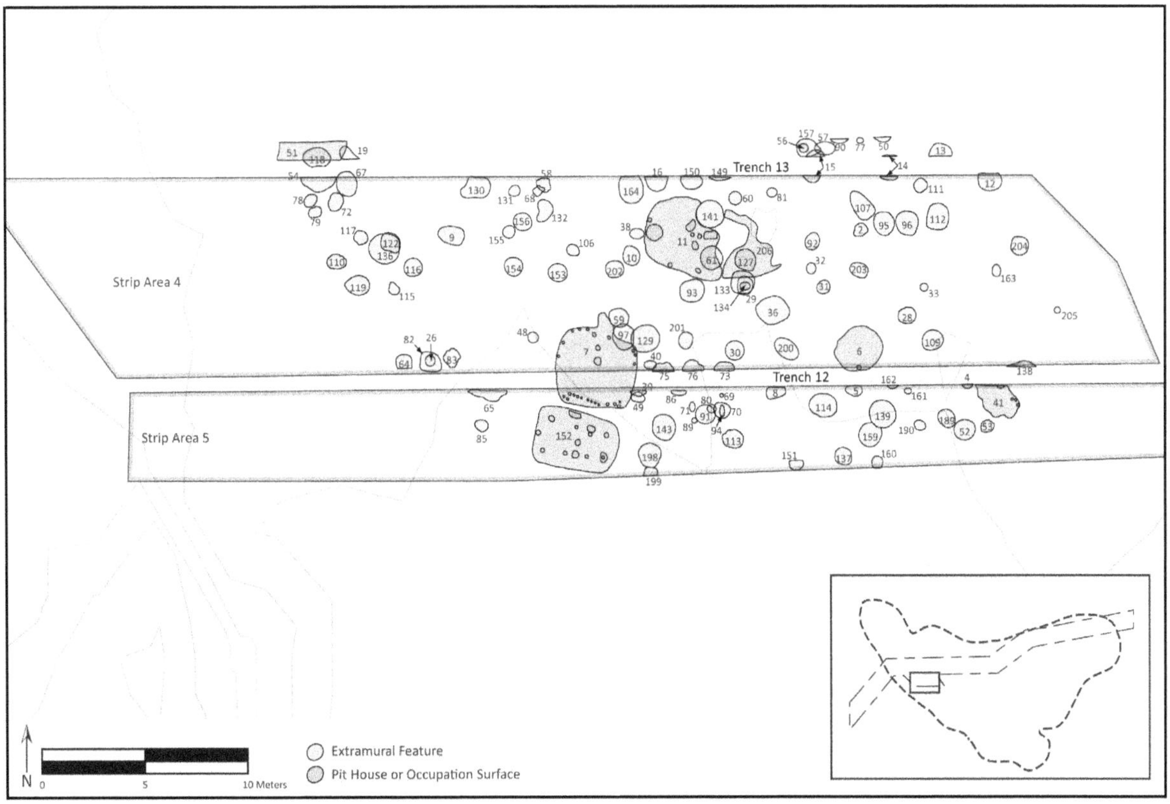

Figure 4.24. Distribution of features in Stripped Area 4/5.

Table 4.6. Radiocarbon and archaeomagnetic dates obtained from features and subfeatures

Site No.	Sample No.	FN	Context	Material	Measured Radiocarbon Age	$^{13}C/^{12}C$ Ratio	Convential Radiocarbon Age	Calibrated Date (2-sigma)
AZ EE:2:44 (ASM)	B-234156	1716.01	Feature 7.02: fill from a central support posthole in a pithouse	Charred maize cupule	770 +/- 40 B.P.	-11.8 o/oo	990 +/- 40 B.P.	A.D. 980 to 1160 (960 to 800 B.P.)
AZ EE:2:44 (ASM)	B-234157	2748.01	Feature 11.09ª fill from a subfloor bell pit within a pithouse	Charred maize cupule	820 +/- 40 B.P.	-14.2 o/oo	1000 +/- 40 B.P.	A.D. 980 to 1060 (970 to 900 B.P.) & A.D. 1080 to 1150 (870 to 800 B.P.)
AZ EE:2:44 (ASM)	B-234158	1181.01	Feature 49: a nonthermal pit	Charred maize cupule	720 +/- 40 B.P.	-10.6 o/oo	960 +/- 40 B.P.	A.D. 1010 to 1170 (940 to 780 B.P.)
AZ EE:2:44 (ASM)	B-234159	1902.01	Feature 61: an indeterminate thermal pit	Charred maize cupule	1220 +/- 40 B.P.	-10.6 o/oo	1460 +/- 40 B.P.	A.D. 540 to 650 (1410 to 1300 B.P.)
AZ EE:2:44 (ASM)	B-234160	2091.01	Feature 72: indeterminate thermal pit	Charred maize cupule fragment	890 +/- 40 B.P.	-12.2 o/oo	1100 +/- 40 B.P.	A.D. 880 to 1020 (1070 to 930 B.P.)
AZ EE:2:44 (ASM)	B-234161	2691	Feature 98: indeterminate thermal bell pit	Charred maize cob segment	2670 +/- 40 B.P.	-10.7 o/oo	2900 +/- 40 B.P.	1250 to 1240 B.C. (3200 to 3190 B.P.) & 1220 to 980 B.C. (3170 to 2930 B.P.)
AZ EE:2:44 (ASM)	B 234162	2372B	Feature 109: nonthermal bell pit	Charred maize cob segment	680 +/- 40 B.P.	-9.7 o/oo	930 +/- 40 B.P.	A.D. 1020 to 1210 (930 to 740 B.P.)
AZ EE:2:44 (ASM)	B-234163	2509.01	Feature 112: nonthermal pit	Charred maize cupule	1270 +/- 40 B.P.	-11.5 o/oo	1490 +/- 40 B.P.	A.D. 450 to 450 (1500 to 1500 B.P.) & A.D. 460 to 480 (1490 to 1470 B.P.); A.D. 530 to 640 (1420 to 1300 B.P.)
AZ EE:2:44 (ASM)	B-234164	2850.01	Feature 136: nonthermal pit	Charred maize cupule	840 +/- 40 B.P.	-10.7 o/oo	1070 +/- 40 B.P.	A.D. 890 to 1030 (1060 to 920 B.P.)
AZ EE:2:44 (ASM)	B-234165	3167.01	Feature 152: floor fill from within a pithouse	Charred material	690 +/- 40 B.P.	-10.7 o/oo	920 +/- 40 B.P.	A.D. 1020 to 1210 (930 to 740 B.P.)
AZ EE:2:44 (ASM)	B-234166	3250.01	Feature 152.03: posthole within a pithouse	Charred material	780 +/- 40 B.P.	-12.5 o/oo	980 +/- 40 B.P.	A.D. 990 to 1160 (960 to 790 B.P.)

Table 4.6. Radiocarbon and archaeomagnetic dates obtained from features and subfeatures, cont'd

Site No.	Sample No.	FN	Context	Material	Measured Radiocarbon Age	$^{13}C/^{12}C$ Ratio	Conventional Radiocarbon Age	Calibrated Date (2-sigma)
AZ EE:2:44 (ASM)	B-234168	1300.01	Feature 7: general fill within a pithouse	Charred maize cupule	820 +/- 40 B.P.	-10.7 o/oo	1050 +/- 40 B.P.	A.D. 900 to 1030 (1050 to 920 B.P.)
AZ EE:2:44 (ASM)	B-234169	2372A	Feature 109: nonthermal bell pit	Charred maize cob segment	780 +/- 40 B.P.	-11.8 o/oo	1000 +/- 40 B.P.	A.D. 980 to 1060 (970 to 900 B.P.) & A.D. 1080 to 1150 (870 to 800 B.P.)
AZ EE:2:44 (ASM)	B-236520	3627.01	Feature 17.01: nonthermal pit within a pithouse	Charred material	820 +/- 40 B.P.	-11.6 o/oo	1040 +/- 40 B.P.	A.D. 900 to 920 (1050 to 1030 B.P.) & A.D. 950 to 1040 (1000 to 920 B.P.)
AZ EE:2:44 (ASM)	B-236521b	1651.01	Feature 44: nonthermal pit	Charred maize cupule	–		2790 +/- 60 B.P.	1120 to 810 B.C. (3060 to 2760 B.P.)
AZ EE:2:44 (ASM)	B-236522	3553.01	Feature 173: bell-shaped roasting pit	Charred maize cupule	700 +/- 40 B.P.	-10.1 o/oo	940 +/- 40 B.P.	A.D. 1020 to 1200 (930 to 750 B.P.)
AZ EE:2:44 (ASM)	WR001		Feature 7.01: plastered hearth in a pithouse	Burned plaster				A.D. 930–1045, A.D. 1080–1145, A.D. 1155–1195, A.D. 1330–1370
AZ EE:2:44 (ASM)	WR002		Feature 152: a pithouse	Pithouse walls				A.D. 930–1025, A.D. 1305–1370, A.D. 1430–1645, A.D. 1755–1870
AZ EE:2:44 (ASM)	WR003		Feature 152: a pithouse	Pithouse floor				A.D. 930–1045, A.D. 1305–1395, A.D. 1430–1325
AZ EE:2:44 (ASM)	WR004		Feature 41: extramural occupation surface	Floor				A.D. 580–725, A.D. 905–1045, A.D. 1305–1625, A.D. 1755–1870

Note: Calibrated by Beta Analytic, Inc. (Beta), Miami, Florida. Archaeomagentic dating performed by William Deaver, WestLand Resources, Inc. (WR), Tucson, Arizona. Raw analysis results for both radiocarbon assays and archaeomagnetic samples can be found in Appendix C, Ravesloot et al. 2010.

[a] Feature 11.09 may be intrusive to Feature 11, rather than an subfeature associated with the feature's occupation.

[b] The original sample was too small for a 13C/12C ratio measurement. However, a ratio including both natural and laboratory effects was measured during the 14C detection to derive a Convential Radiocarbon Age, suitable for applicable calendar calibration.

see Appendix I, Table C). In comparison, relatively few structural features—six pit structures and two occupation surfaces—were exposed. This may be partly explained by the location of the construction corridor, which ran along the northern edge of the site, within the overall site area. Seven of the eight structural features were located in SA 4/5, where the densest distribution of features was encountered; the eighth was in SA 1. It is likely that additional structural features are preserved in this central, lower area of the site. In addition, as discussed below, all but one of the documented structural features appear to date to the Middle Formative period.

Two features were recorded which do not fit the categories outlined above. Feature 69 was a small, basin-shaped, plastered hearth located in SA 5. The feature resembled an intramural hearth from a pithouse, but was apparently an extramural feature. A reconstructible vessel (FN 44-1766) was found just above this feature, in TU 40. Feature 169 was a dense cluster of rocks in SA 3. The rocks, most of which were unmodified and a few of which were fire-cracked, did not appear to be in the fill of a pit, although this feature was not excavated. No artifacts were observed in association with this feature.

WSA recovered 19,376 artifacts from excavated features and subfeatures at the Marsh Station Road site. Artifacts included a wide variety of flaked stone debitage, projectile points, and other flaked stone tools; ground stone artifacts; painted and unpainted sherds as well as several reconstructible vessels and special ceramic artifacts; faunal bone; and worked and unworked shell (Appendix I, Table D). Approximately 79 percent (n = 152) of the excavated features and subfeatures contained artifacts (see Appendix I, Table D).

Finally, while the majority of the recorded features date to the prehistoric period, three historic features, a rock-ring hearth and two previous alignments of the Southern Pacific Railroad, and one historic subfeature, a historic fence posthole (see above), were also recorded.

Pithouses and Structures

Five pithouses and one pit structure were identified at the Marsh Station Road site during the EPX project. Pithouses are those structural features containing architectural elements and subfeatures characteristic of a habitation structure; a structural feature lacking such defining characteristics is referred to as a pit structure. Features 7, 11, 17, 51, and 152 are considered pithouses in the discussion below, while Feature 206 is considered a pit structure. Five of the pit features (Features 7, 11, 51, 152, and 206) were located in SA 4/5, while the sixth (Feature 17) was located in SA 1; no pit features were recorded in SA 2/3. Three of the pit features—Features 7, 17, and 51—were discovered in test trenches; the other three—Features 11, 152, and 206—were found through manual excavation of test units. Five of the pit features were fully excavated. Feature 51 was only partially excavated as it extended closer than ten feet to the active petroleum lines. As discussed below, five of the structures appear to date to the Middle Formative period (Rincon phase; see Table 4.6); however, none appear to be coeval. One pithouse, Feature 11, may date to the Early Agricultural period (see discussion below). Preservation of the features was variable. Features 7, 17, and 152 were quite well preserved, with defined edges, fill material, and subfeatures. Feature 11 was also reasonably preserved, although only as a shallow cut into caliche with a suite of subfeatures. Feature 51 was poorly defined, partly because only a small proportion of the structure could be excavated. Feature 206 was minimally preserved, and its designation even as a pit structure is tentative.

Below, the characteristics of each pit structure, including location, shape, and size; excavation strategy; architectural/structural elements; fill, floor fill, and floor assemblages; diagnostic artifacts and absolute dates; and cultural and temporal affiliation are discussed. In addition, artifact density within the fill of the three most completely excavated pit structures—Features 7, 17, and 152—was calculated based upon a formula devised by Elson (ed., 1986:61). This formula quantifies artifact density by dividing the total number of ceramic sherds by the total volume of pithouse fill (structural and floor fill). This allows for an assessment of the nature of the fill—for example, is it characteristic of intentional trash deposition—and making fill densities broadly comparable. As discussed below, however, application of the formula ultimately did not provide significant insights into prehistoric behavior at the Marsh Station Road site, perhaps in part due to the mixing of artifacts dating to the Early Agricultural and Middle Formative periods in later- dating pit features. The presentation of feature characteristics is followed by a discussion of the pit structures as a whole at the Marsh Station Road site.

Feature 7

This feature was discovered and bisected by mechanical excavation of Trench 12 (Figures 4.25 and 4.26). Following trench excavation, approximately 10 cm of overburden was stripped mechanically, and one 10-cm arbitrary level was manually excavated to expose the edge of the feature. However, following this initial excavation, the entire feature outline was not evident in plan view, and consequently, the feature was dug in a succession of feature excavation units (FEs) until the entire pit structure was visible. FEs 1 through 3, which were located south of Trench 12, were excavated first. Once the familiar shape of a pit structure became apparent, excavations were expanded to the north side of the trench with FEs 4 through 6. All six FEs were excavated in 10-cm arbitrary levels, and all feature fill was screened through ¼-inch mesh. In addition, a seventh feature excavation unit (FE 7) was excavated through the floor of Feature 7 to investigate the possibility of structure remodeling or whether any additional features underlay the pit structure. FE 7 was excavated as one continuous level; the fill was not screened.

Twenty-five subfeatures were identified in the floor of Feature 7 (Table 4.7). These subfeatures were fully excavated in one or two stratigraphic units, and all fill was screened through ⅛-inch mesh.

Structure fill consisted of loosely compacted brown sandy silt, with a small amount (less than 10 percent) of gravel. Only light charcoal flecking was noted, although the flecking increased with depth, and there was no evidence of burning. No roof- or wall-fall debris was present in the excavated fill.

The fill from Feature 7 had 943 artifacts (Table 4.8). Diagnostic artifacts include a San Pedro projectile point, a Cortaro projectile point, and two Rincon Red-on-brown sherds.

The 10 cm of fill immediately above the floor of this pit structure was similar in compaction, texture, and color to the general structural fill, although increased charcoal flecking as well as a small amount of FCR was noted. No roof- or wall-fall debris was present in the excavated floor fill.

A smaller and less diverse artifact assemblage, (see Table 4.8), was recovered from the floor fill. Diagnostic artifacts included a San Pedro projectile point, a Rincon Red-on-brown sherd, and an Early Rincon Red-on-brown sherd.

Feature 7 is a sub-rectangular Hohokam pithouse (see Figures 4.25 and 4.26). The maximum dimensions of the structure were approximately 4 m by 3.70 m (see Table 4.9),

Table 4.7. Subfeatures excavated from Feature 7

Feature No.	Description	Length (m)	Width (m)	Depth (m)	Artifacts/Samples
7.01	Plastered hearth	0.22	0.23	0.08	Flotation sample
7.02	Central support posthole	0.50	0.40	0.12	Pollen & flotation samples; Rincon Red-on-brown sherd
7.03	Posthole	0.17	0.17	0.10	Flaked stone debitage (2)
7.04	Posthole	0.11	0.13	0.07	
7.05	Posthole	0.16	0.14	0.09	Flaked stone debitage (1)
7.06	Posthole	0.08	0.08	0.08	
7.07	Posthole	0.08	0.07	0.06	
7.08	Posthole	0.09	0.08	0.07	
7.09	Posthole	0.08	0.07	0.05	
7.10	Posthole	0.07	0.07	0.06	
7.11	Non-feature				
7.12	Non-feature				
7.13	Non-feature				
7.14	Posthole	0.09	0.09	0.06	Undersized plain ware ceramic
7.15	Posthole	0.08	0.08	0.06	
7.16	Posthole	0.08	0.07	0.07	
7.17	Posthole	0.07	0.07	0.05	
7.18	Non-feature				
7.19	Wall groove	–	–	–	Pollen & flotation samples; flaked stone debitage (5); faunal bone (1)
7.20	Posthole	0.10	0.09	0.10	
7.21	Posthole	0.06	0.07	0.06	Faunal bone (1)
7.22	Posthole	0.08	0.07	0.06	
7.23	Posthole	0.08	0.07	0.06	
7.24	Posthole	0.08	0.08	0.05	
7.25	Posthole	0.08	0.08	0.05	
7.26	Posthole	0.07	0.08	0.05	
7.27	Posthole	0.09	0.07	0.07	
7.28	Posthole	0.08	0.08	0.06	
7.29	Plastered hearth	unk. (0.25 m diameter)	unk.	0.10	Carbonized seed; pollen sample

Table 4.8. Artifacts recovered from the fill, floor fill, and floor of Feature 7

	Fill	Floor Fill	Floor	Subfeatures
Flaked Stone				
Debitage	745	148	2	8
Cores	4			
Projectile point	4	1		
Biface		4		
Uniface	4			
Subtotal	*757*	*153*	*2*	*8*
Ceramics				
Rincon Red-on-brown	2	1		1
Early Rincon Red-on-brown		1		
Indeterminte red-on-brown	32	6	1	
Indeterminate red-on-buff	3			
Brown ware	114			
Brown ware (Red)	3	2	4	
Buff ware	1			
Undersized	21	14		1
Subtotal	*176*	*24*	*5*	*2*
Ground Stone				
Flat mano			1	
Ring fragment		1		
Polishing stone	1			
Shell				
Worked fragment (*L. elatum*)	1			
Freshwater shell	1	1		
Subtotal	*2*	*1*		
Faunal Remains				
Hares and rabbits		11		1
Unidentified mammal	7	42		1
Subtotal	*7*	*53*		*2*
Total	943	232	8	12

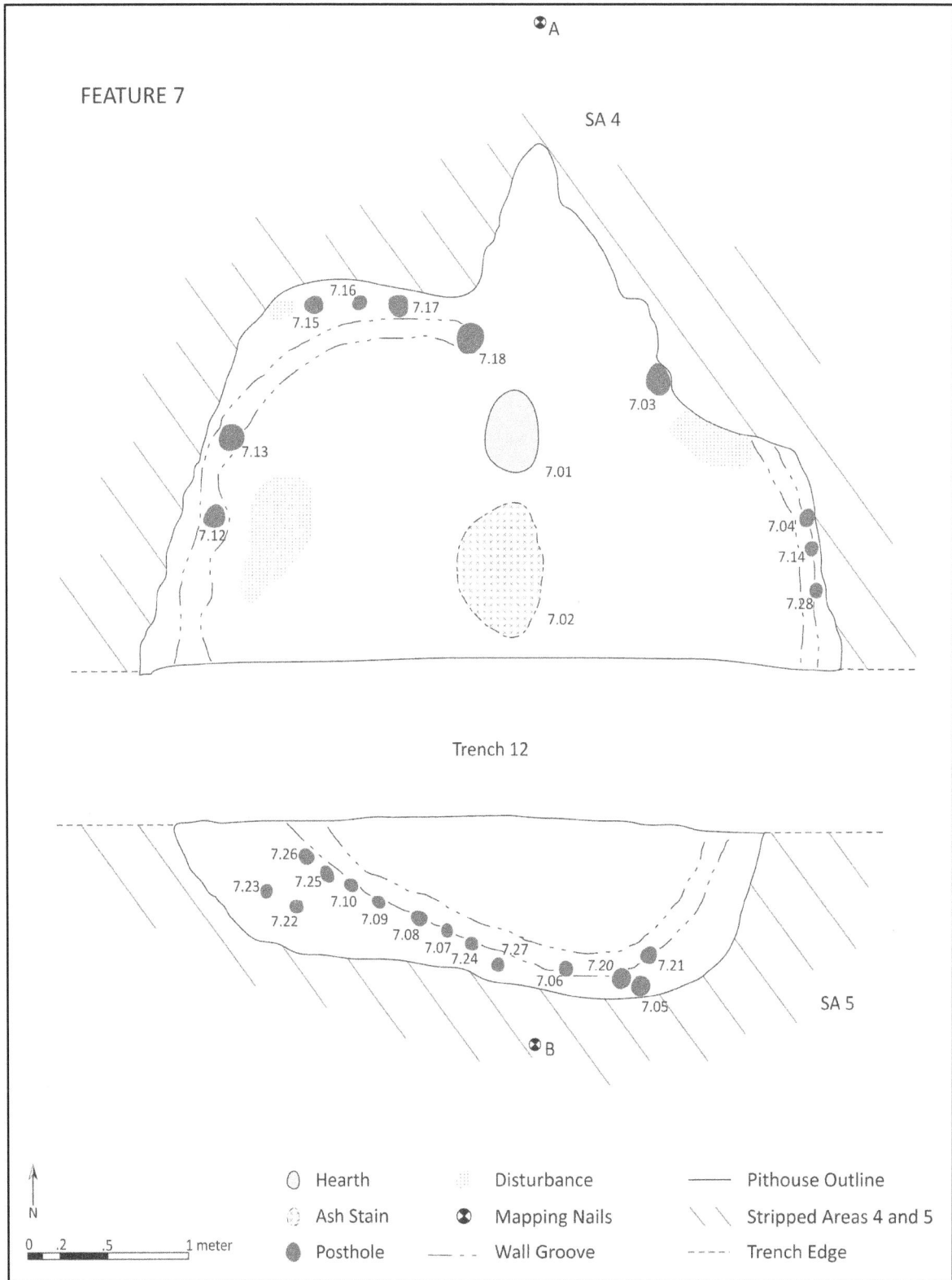

Figure 4.25. Plan and profile view of Feature 7 showing Trench 12, which bisects the feature, and the 25 recorded subfeatures.

while the floor area measured approximately 11.62 square meters. The pit walls, of which approximately 0.08 m were preserved, were unprepared and insloping. At least portions of both the east and west walls were removed in the excavation of Trench 12. The entry way into Feature 7 was a rectangular, unprepared ramp cut into the caliche. The ramp, which measured a maximum of 0.83 m by 0.60 m, is centered on the long axis of the pit structure and is facing due north. The roof was supported by one central post (Feature 7.02).

Twenty-five subfeatures were located and excavated within Feature 7 (see Figure 4.25 and Table 4.7). A plastered hearth (Feature 7.01) with a circular basin measuring 0.08 m deep was located in the "typical" spot near the entrance. Feature 7.01 was a remodel of an earlier plastered hearth (Feature 7.29) discovered beneath it. Feature 7.19 was a wall groove: a continuous trench around the perimeter of

Table 4.9. Characteristics of Feature 7	
Feature Type:	Pithouse
Cultural Affiliation:	Hohokam
Temporal Affiliation:	late Middle Formative (Rincon phase)
Diagnostic Artifacts:	Cortaro point (n=1); San Pedro point (n=2); Rincon Red-on-brown sherds (n=3)
Subfeatures:	Multiple: hearths (n=2), postholes (n=21), wall groove
Provenience:	SA 4/5
Shape:	Subrectangular
Dimensions:	4.00 m x 3.70 m; floor area 11.62 m^2
Depth below datum:	94.84 z–94.70 z
Stratum:	Stratum 2: surface of Pleistocene terrace deposits with modern caliche development

Figure 4.26. Photograph of Feature 7, post-excavation, view to the north.

the structure floor, excluding the entryway. Twenty-one postholes were excavated from within this wall groove; Feature 7.03 appears to ring the entryway. A small assemblage was recovered from several of the subfeatures (see Table 4.7).

The floor of Feature 7 consisted of an unprepared floor surface that appears to have been cut into the natural caliche horizon. The floor, which is patchy in places due to rodent and insect bioturbation, is located approximately 0.34 m below the stripped surface. There was no evidence of burning on the floor except for a small patch of oxidized floor south of the hearth. Very few artifacts were found on the feature floor (see Table 4.7).

Two radiocarbon dates (Beta-234168 and Beta-234156) were obtained from charred maize cupules recovered from Feature 7 (see Table 4.6). The first sample (Beta-234168), collected from the general structural fill, yielded a 2 sigma calibrated date of A.D. 900 to 1030. The second sample (Beta-234156), collected from the central support posthole (Feature 7.02), yielded a 2 sigma calibrated date of A.D. 980 to 1160.

One archaeomagnetic sample consisting of 12 specimens was collected from one of the plastered hearths (Feature 7.01). The sample yielded four date ranges: A.D. 930 to 1045, A.D. 1080 to 1145, A.D. 1155 to 1195, and A.D. 1330 to 1370.

Congruence between both the radiocarbon and archaeomagnetic dates suggests a late Middle Formative (Rincon phase) date for the feature.

Twenty-one environmental samples were collected from the fill, floor, and subfloor features of Feature 7. One macrobotanical sample, collected from the fill of the pithouse, was identified as cottonwood/willow. Of the 18 flotation samples collected, only two contained macrobotanical specimens available for analysis; these were identified as mesquite,

maize, and reedgrass. The two pollen samples, collected from the floor of the feature as well as from the central support posthole, identified a wide variety of floral species including maize, cholla, pinyon pine, oak, mesquite, cheno-ams, low- and high-spine Asteraceae, globemallow, cattail, wild buckwheat, Mormon tea, white mat, creosote bush, and members of the Grass, Lily, and Pea families (see Adams, Chapter 10, and Phillips, Chapter 11).

Feature 7, one of six pit structures discovered and excavated at the Marsh Station Road site, appears to be a house-in-a-pit, with a central support post, a wall groove, at least 21 support posts, and a remodeled plastered hearth. Both the floor and the pit walls were unprepared, having been cut into the natural caliche. The pit walls were insloping and relatively short, which may suggest they are the base of an originally deeper pit, truncated by subsequent features and natural formation processes. The pit structure itself is aligned due north, suggesting that it may have been a seasonal dwelling, as a north-facing entryway would help keep the interior of the house cool during the hot summer months. There was no evidence of burning in the feature, except for oxidation observed on a small patch of floor south of the hearth. No distinct roof- or wall-fall material was detected on the floor of the pit structure or within its fill. An estimated 1.63 cubic meters of fill was excavated from Feature 7.

Feature 7 contained a rather unremarkable floor assemblage consisting of just eight artifacts (see Table 4.9). The sparse floor assemblage, as well as the lack of other subfeatures such as storage pits or activity areas, limits our interpretation of the activities that may have occurred within the structure. However, the small floor assemblage does suggest that this pit structure was cleaned out prior to or at its abandonment. The fill assemblage, which contains a wide variety of artifact types (see

Table 4.9) and is moderately dense, containing 123 ceramic sherds/m3 (following Elson, ed. 1986:61), is likely representative of the gradual post-abandonment filling of the structure with general site deposits, a formation process observed in other units excavated in the area surrounding Feature 7.

Radiocarbon and archaeomagnetic dates, as well as the presence of an Early Rincon Red-on-brown sherd in the floor fill and several Rincon Red-on-brown sherds in the feature fill suggest that Feature 7 was occupied during the Rincon phase/late Middle Formative period. Although several projectile points—two San Pedros and one Cortaro—dating to the Early Agricultural period or earlier were recovered from within the fill of the feature, these artifacts are most likely not associated with the occupation of the pit structure. Rather, they may represent curated artifacts or residues from earlier occupations of the site. The remodeling of the hearth (Feature 7.29/Feature 7.01) indicates that the structure was used at least long enough to require structure maintenance, although no other evidence of maintenance or repair of the structure or of its other subfeatures was evident during excavation.

Feature 7 was one of the smaller houses excavated at the Marsh Station Road site (although larger than Feature 152, see below). A comparison with the dimensions of Rincon-phase houses excavated at the Tanque Verde Wash site (Elson, ed. 1986) shows that Feature 7 would definitely have been one of the smaller features at that site. The general attributes of Feature 7—subrectangular house-in-pit construction, limited plaster confined to the hearth, and a ramp entrance—fit expectations for a Rincon phase Hohokam structure.

Feature 11

Feature 11 was overlain by Stratum 3 overburden, approximately 10 cm of which was stripped mechanically. Following stripping, three 10-cm arbitrary levels were manually excavated to expose the edge of the feature. The western portion of Feature 11 was fairly well preserved and clearly defined, while the eastern portion of the feature was markedly less defined and poorly preserved (Figures 4.27 and 4.28). Following the initial exposure of the feature edge, the feature outline was defined in piecemeal fashion through the excavation of nine FEs. All nine FEs were excavated in 10-cm arbitrary levels; FEs 1–5 and 7–9 were screened through ¼-inch mesh, while FE 6 was screened through ⅛-inch mesh. Ultimately, the poor definition of the eastern portion of the feature prevented the determination of the maximum length of the structure, although an estimated 75 percent of the feature was investigated. In addition, a tenth feature excavation unit (FE 10) was excavated through the floor of Feature 11 to investigate the possibility of structure remodeling or whether any additional features underlay the pit structure. FE 10 was

Table 4.10. Characteristics of Feature 11	
Feature Type:	Pithouse
Cultural Affiliation:	Hohokam
Temporal Affiliation:	late Middle Formative (Rincon phase)
Diagnostic Artifacts:	San Pedro point (n=1)
Subfeatures:	Multiple: firepit, non-thermal pits (n=2), bell-shaped pit, and postholes (n=4)
Provenience:	SA 4
Shape:	Irregular and subrectangular
Dimensions:	Mapped area: 3.50 m x 3.75 m; floor area approximately 13.2 m2
Depth below datum:	94.81 z–94.60 z
Stratum:	Stratum 2: surface of Pleistocene terrace deposits with modern caliche development

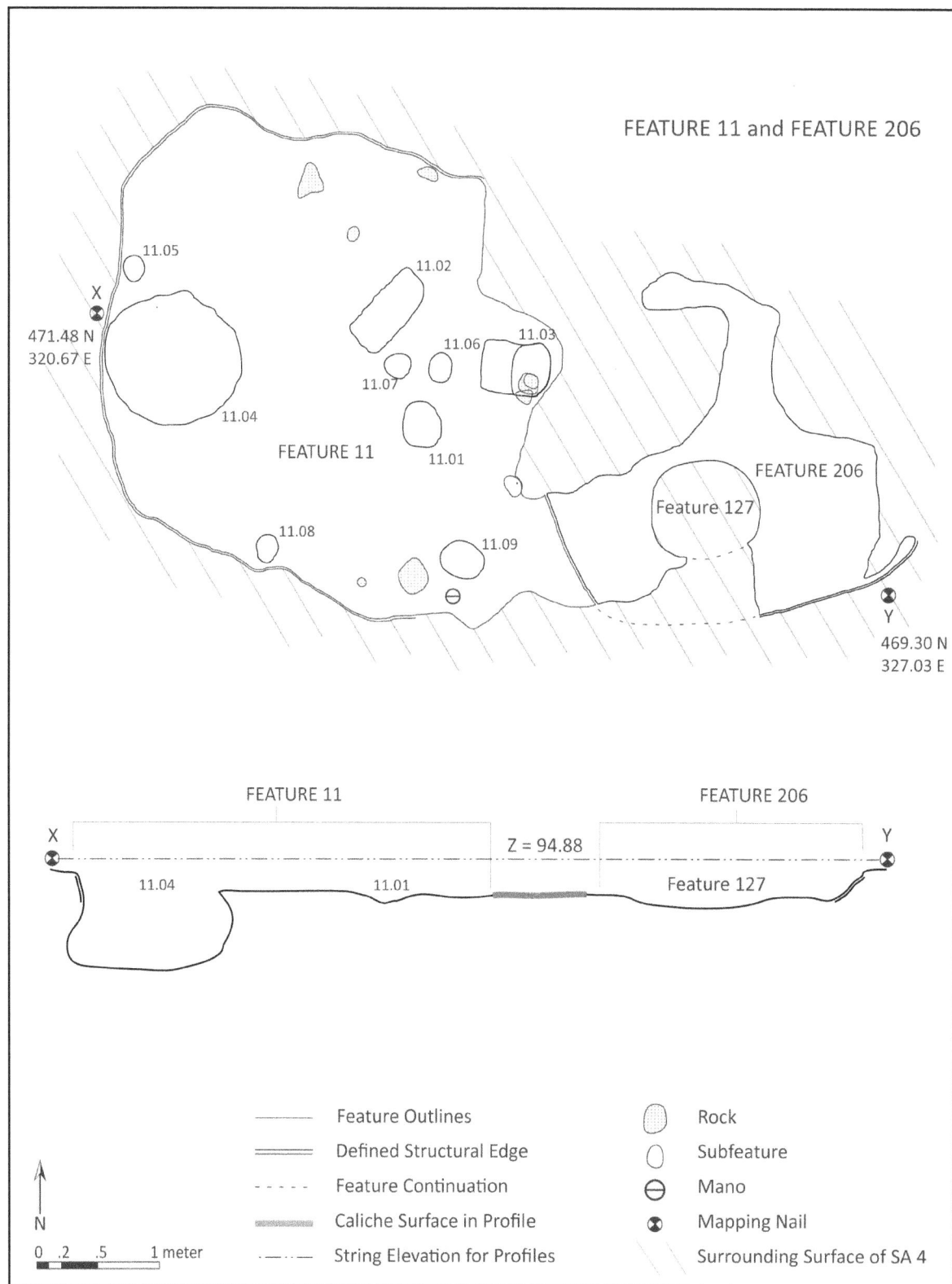

FEATURE 11 and FEATURE 206

11.05

X

471.48 N
320.67 E

11.02

11.06   11.03

11.07

11.04

FEATURE 11

11.01

FEATURE 206

Feature 127

11.08

11.09

Y

469.30 N
327.03 E

FEATURE 11

FEATURE 206

X   Z = 94.88   Y

11.04   11.01   Feature 127

Feature Outlines   Rock

Defined Structural Edge   Subfeature

Feature Continuation   Mano

Caliche Surface in Profile   Mapping Nail

N

String Elevation for Profiles   Surrounding Surface of SA 4

0   .2   .5   1 meter

Figure 4.27. Plan and profile view of Features 11 and 206 showing the features' outlines, their plan and stratigraphic relationships to each other, and the nine subfeatures recorded in Feature 11.

excavated as one continuous level; the fill was not screened.

Nine subfeatures were identified in the floor of Feature 11 (Table 4.11). These subfeatures were fully excavated in one or two stratigraphic units, and fill from eight of the features was screened through ¼-inch mesh; fill from the remaining feature, an informal hearth, was collected as a flotation sample.

Structure fill consisted of loosely compacted brown sandy loam, with a small amount (less than 10 percent) of gravel. Only a few pieces of FCR were noted; there was no evidence of burning. No roof- or wall-fall debris was present in the excavated fill.

A total of 687 artifacts was recovered from the fill of Feature 11, none of which are diagnostic (Table 4.12). It is also worth noting that five shell artifacts were recovered from a unit that was used to investigate this structure, although they were recovered from a depth above that where the structure fill was definitively identified. These artifacts were collected from TU 23, which became FE 9 once the

feature fill was identified. The artifacts, each about 1 cm long, appear to be intentional fragments of a bracelet. That is, the ends of them look to have been incised and then snapped, perhaps to create blanks for shell beads or gaming pieces.

The 10 cm of fill immediately above the floor of this pit structure was virtually identical in compaction, texture, inclusions, and color to the general structural fill. No roof- or wall-fall debris was present in the excavated floor fill.

A slightly larger artifact assemblage (n = 802) was recovered from the floor fill (see Table 4.12). Diagnostic artifacts included a San Pedro projectile point (the other two points were indeterminate to type), an indeterminate Dragoon Red-on-brown sherd, and Snaketown Red-on-buff sherd.

Given Feature 11's state of preservation, it is difficult to assign its shape in plan view, although having said that, it is a more-or-less sub-rectangular pithouse (see Figures 4.27 and 4.28). As mentioned above, the western portion of the pit structure was well preserved, while

Figure 4.28. Photograph of Feature 11, post-excavation, view to the north.

Feature No.	Description	Length (m)	Width (m)	Depth (m)	Artifacts/Samples
		Table 4.11. Subfeatures excavated from Feature 11			
11.01	Firepit (informal)	0.55	0.38	0.09	Flotation
11.02	Non-thermal pit	0.74	0.50	0.10	Pollen & flotation samples; flaked stone debitage (9); indeterminate red-on-brown sherd, brown ware sherds (8), undersized sherd
11.03	Posthole	0.56	0.21	0.41	Flotation sample; brown ware sherd, undersized sherd; flaked stone debitage (3)
11.04	Bell-shaped pit	1.10	1.00	0.65	Pollen & flotation samples; brown ware sherds (5), flaked stone debitage (228), cores (2), faunal bones (2), mica flakes (2)
11.05	Posthole	0.23	0.19	0.06	Flotation sample
11.06	Central support posthole	0.74	0.50	0.10	Flotation sample
11.07	Posthole	0.20	0.18	0.09	Flotation sample
11.08	Posthole	0.25	0.19	0.09	–
11.09	Bell-shaped pit	0.34	0.31	0.25	Flotation sample; flaked stone debitage (15), faunal bones (7)

the eastern portion of the pit structure was poorly defined, and as a result, the feature's eastern extent could not be determined. Excavation revealed approximately 13.2 square meters of floor area; the mapped dimensions of the pit structure measure approximately 3.50 m by 3.75 m (see Table 4.10). The pit walls, which stand approximately 0.21 m high, are unprepared and insloping. No entry way into Feature 11 was observed. The roof was supported by one central post (Feature 11.06).

A total of nine subfeatures were located and excavated within Feature 11, one of which may be intrusive (11.09) (see Figure 4.27 and Table 4.11). An informal, irregularly shaped, unprepared firepit (Feature 11.01) approximately 0.09 m deep was located just south of the central support post (Feature 11.06). The firepit was filled with ashy sand, and its base was oxidized. In addition to the central post, four support posts were identified around

the perimeter of the feature. Three pits—one medium nonthermal pit and two bell pits—were also excavated. One of the bell pits, Feature 11.04, situated along the west wall of the feature, was quite large and contained a substantial artifact assemblage (see Table 4.11), as well as pockets of ash. This feature appeared to have been deliberately capped with a caliche mixture, thereby sealing the bell pit and providing additional floor space in the pit structure. The other two pits contained a small assemblage (see Table 4.11) as well as a small amount of charcoal. It should be noted that the second bell pit (11.09) was assigned to this category based solely on its shape; it is quite small and perhaps not a typical bell pit. No artifacts were recovered from the excavated postholes.

The floor of Feature 11 consisted of an unprepared floor surface that appears to have been cut into the natural caliche horizon. The

Table 4.12. Artifacts recovered from the fill, floor fill, floor, and subfeatures of Feature 11

	Fill	Floor Fill	Floor	Subfeatures
Flaked Stone				
Debitage	499	723		255
Cores	1	2		2
Projectile point		3		
Biface	3			
Uniface				
Subtotal	*503*	*728*		*257*
Ceramics				
Snaketown Red-on-buff		1		
Indeterminate Dragoon Red-on-brown		1		
Indetermiante red-on-brown	4	4		1
Brown (Red)	1	1		
Brown ware	100			14
Undersized	18	18		2
Subtotal	*123*	*25*		*17*
Ground Stone				
Trough mano			1	
Flat Metate			1	
Pecking stone	1			
Subtotal	*1*		*2*	
Faunal Remains				
Hares and Rabbits	6	5		
Small ungulate	25			
Unidentified mammal	29	33		9
Mammal/bird		7		
Subtotal	*60*	*45*		*9*
Mineral				
Mica bead		1	1	
Mica flakes		3		2
Subtotal		*4*	*1*	*2*
Total	687	802	3	285

floor, which is generally well preserved in the western portion but absent in the eastern portion of the structure, is located approximately 0.51 m below the stripped surface. There was no evidence of burning on the floor. Feature 11 contained very few artifacts on its floor (see Table 4.12).

One radiocarbon date (Beta-234157) was obtained from a charred maize cupule recovered from Feature 11.09, a subfloor bell pit (see Table 4.6). The sample yielded a 2 sigma calibrated date of A.D. 980 to 1060 and A.D. 1080 to 1150. It is possible that this sample is intrusive to the pit, or even that the pit is intrusive to the structure, and this is discussed further below.

Seventeen environmental samples were collected from the fill, floor, and subfloor features of Feature 11. One macrobotanical sample, collected from the floor of the pit structure, was identified as mesquite. Of the 15 flotation samples collected, only one—from Feature 11.09—contained macrobotanical specimens available for analysis; these were identified as mesquite, maize, cottonwood/willow, hackberry, creosote bush, and a Monocotyledon. The single pollen sample, collected from the floor of the feature, identified a wide variety of floral species including maize, cattail, willow, cheno-ams, low- and high-spine Asteraceae, globemallow, spiderling, wild buckwheat, white mat, creosote bush, and members of the Grass, Rose, and Pea families (see Adams, Chapter 10, and Phillips, Chapter 11).

Given the lack of external post holes at the floor-wall juncture, Feature 11 may have been a true pithouse with a central support post, several internal pits, perhaps used as storage features, and a hearth, albeit an informal one. Minimal preparation was undertaken in the construction and maintenance of the structure; there is no plaster anywhere in the structure, even in the hearth, and both the walls and the floor are unprepared. In general, Feature 11

was hard to define, although the base of the pit was evidenced by a clear cut into sterile strata. However, the pit walls were insloping and relatively short, which may suggest they are the base of an originally deeper pit. In particular, the eastern portion of Feature 11, which was poorly preserved, may have been truncated by a subsequent pithouse, Feature 206 (see below), discovered during the excavation of Feature 11 (see Figure 4.27). In addition, no entry way was defined for the structure. If there was a formal entry, it may have been located in the poorly preserved eastern portion of the structure, but lacking one makes the orientation of the structure uncertain. Evidence of burning within the structure was present only within the firepit as an oxidized base. No distinct roof- or wall-fall material was detected on the floor of the pit structure or within its fill. Although no volume of excavated fill could be calculated for Feature 11 due to its incomplete nature, an estimated 75 percent of the structure was excavated.

Feature 11 contained an unremarkable floor assemblage consisting of just three artifacts (see Table 4.10). The sparse floor assemblage suggests that this pithouse was cleaned out prior to or at its abandonment. However, the recovery of a perforated mica bead from the floor, as well as another perforated mica bead and several unworked mica flakes from both subfeature and floor fill suggests that bead working may have occurred in the structure. While no meaningful artifact density could be calculated for this partially defined feature (following Elson, ed. 1986), the fill assemblage, which contains primarily flaked stone and ceramics (see Table 4.10), is likely representative of the gradual post-abandonment filling of the structure with general site deposits rather than intentional trash deposition. The floor fill assemblage, however, contains a much higher density of artifacts—primarily flaked stone debitage—in comparison, and may therefore represent intentional trash deposition.

The radiocarbon date from a charred maize cupule recovered from Feature 11.09 suggests that Feature 11 was occupied during the Rincon phase/late Middle Formative period. But this assignment is questionable given that the feature was overlain by Feature 61, which itself produced a charred maize cupule that yielded a 2 sigma calibrated date of A.D. 540 to 650. Given this uncertainty, it is worth pointing out that Feature 11 has some characteristics that are indicative of an Early Agricultural age. The pithouse's somewhat irregular shape, informal hearth, and large bell pit bear resemblance to Early Agricultural structures at Las Capas and Milagro illustrated by Mabry (2008a:Figures 1.13 and 1.14). A San Pedro projectile point was recovered from the fill, but so were some ceramics, including a single Snaketown Red-on-buff sherd and an indeterminate Dragoon Red-on-brown sherd. As with the conflicting dates, it is difficult to know whether the point or the sherds are intrusive. Although the structure may be Middle Formative in age, the possibility that it is Early Agricultural cannot be discounted.

Feature 17

This feature was discovered and bisected by mechanical excavation of Trench 1 (Figures 4.29 and 4.30). Following trench excavation, approximately 10 cm of overburden was stripped mechanically, and one 10-cm arbitrary level was manually excavated to expose the edge of the feature. Unlike both Feature 7 and Feature 11, much of Feature 17 was evident in plan view following the initial stripping of overburden; thus, an outline of Feature 17 was established before excavation of the feature began. Feature 17 was excavated through five FEs. FEs 1 through 4, which were located north of Trench 1, were excavated first; FE 5, located on the south side of Trench 1, was excavated last, after an intrusive cremation burial (Fea-

Table 4.13. Characteristics of Feature 17	
Feature Type:	Pithouse
Cultural Affiliation:	Hohokam
Temporal Affiliation:	late Middle Formative (Rincon phase)
Diagnostic Artifacts:	San Pedro point (n=2); Rincon Red-on-brown sherds (n=2)
Subfeatures:	Multiple: non-thermal pit, postholes (n=2), indeterminate (n=2)
Provenience:	SA 1
Shape:	Subrounded
Dimensions:	4.12 m x 4.62 m; floor area approximately 14.95 m2
Depth below datum:	104.51 z–101.21 z
Stratum:	Stratum 3: Overburden; approximately 20 cm below ground surface

ture 182, see below) was excavated. All five FEs were excavated in 10-cm arbitrary levels. The majority of the feature fill in FEs 1–4 was screened through ¼-inch mesh, although once several small beads were recovered, floor fill in FE 2 was screened through ⅛-inch mesh. All of FE 5 was screened through ⅛-inch mesh. In addition, a sixth feature excavation unit (FE 6) was excavated through the floor of Feature 17 to investigate the possibility of structure remodeling or whether any additional features underlay the pit structure. FE 6 was excavated as one continuous level; the fill was not screened.

Three subfeatures were identified in the floor of Feature 17 (Table 4.14). Two additional subfeatures were later determined to be nonfeatures. These subfeatures were fully excavated in one or two stratigraphic units, and all fill was screened through ⅛-inch mesh.

Structure fill consisted of loosely compacted, soft, brown sandy loam, with a small amount (10 to 20 percent) of gravel. There was

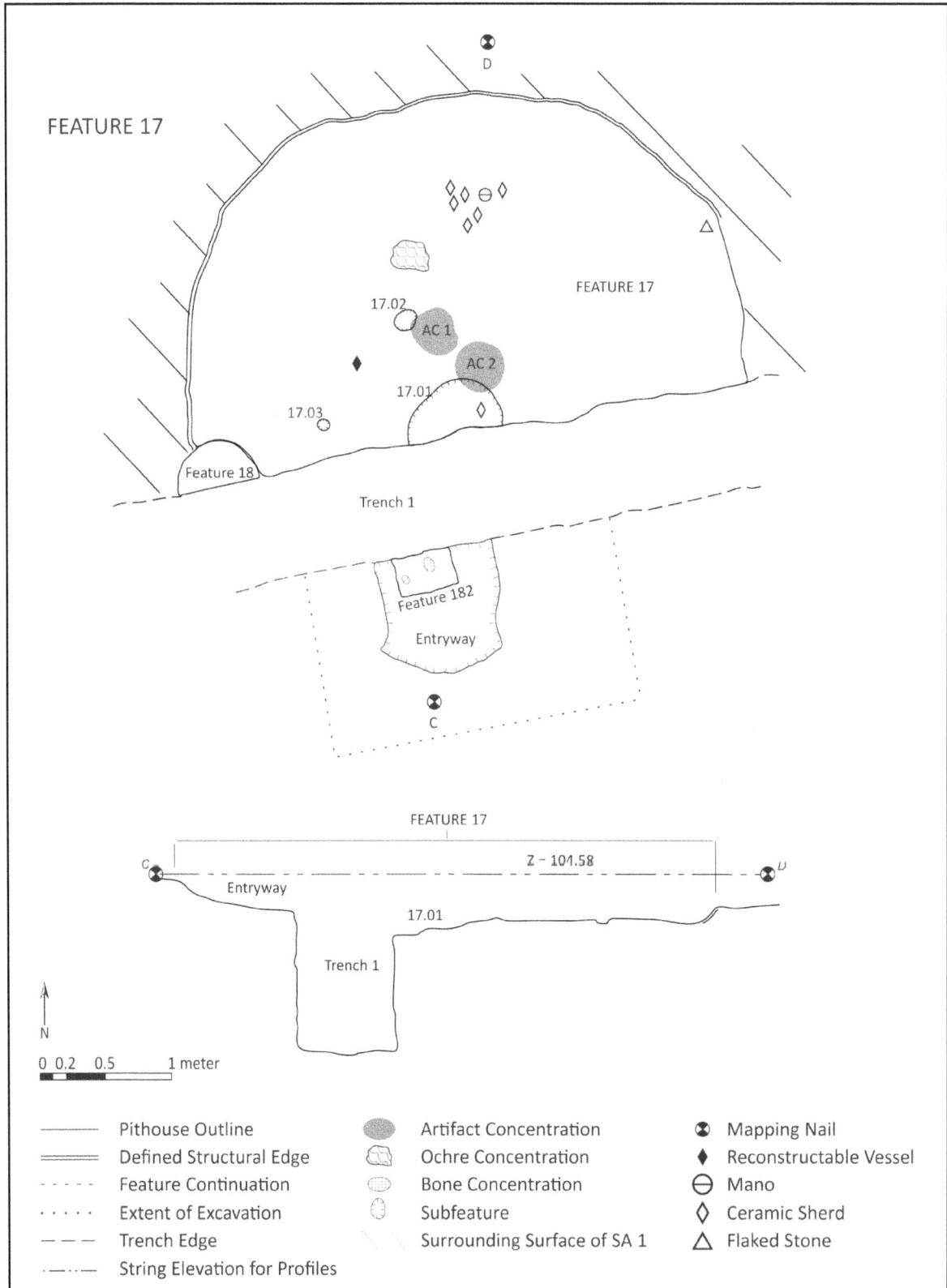

Figure 4.29. Plan and profile view of Feature 17 showing the structure's floor assemblage and subfeatures, the location of Trench 1, and the location of Feature 182, a secondary cremation, located in the entryway.

Table 4.14. Subfeatures excavated from Feature 17

Feature No.	Description	Length (m)	Width (m)	Depth (m)	Artifacts/Samples
17.01	Non-thermal pit	0.57	0.44	0.23	brown ware sherd, undersized sherd, mineral sample
17.02	Posthole	0.17	0.18	0.1	flaked stone debitage
17.03	Indeterminate	0.37	0.28	0.09	flaked stone debitage; undersized sherds (2)
17.04	Indeterminate	0.47	0.3	0.1	–
17.05	Posthole	0.1	0.09	0.04	–

no evidence of burning in the fill, although light charcoal flecking was noted, as well as a few pieces of FCR. No roof- or wall-fall debris was present in the excavated fill. A total of 124 artifacts were recovered from the fill of Feature 11 (Table 4.15). One artifact, a Late Rincon Red-on-brown sherd, is temporally diagnostic.

The 10 cm of fill immediately above the floor of this pit structure was virtually identical in compaction, texture, and color to the general structural fill, although no charcoal and no FCR were noted, and only about 10 percent contained gravel. No roof- or wall-fall debris was present in the excavated floor fill. A slightly larger artifact assemblage was recovered from the floor fill (see Table 4.15). Other than a San Pedro point, the only diagnostic artifact was a Rincon Red-on-brown sherd.

Feature 17 is a sub-rounded house-in-pit (see Figures 4.29 and 4.30). Excavation revealed approximately 14.95 square meters of floor area; the maximum dimensions of the pit structure were estimated at approximately 4.12 m by 4.62 m (see Table 4.13), although the southern wall as well as a portion of the floor near the entrance was removed through excavation of Trench 1. The pit walls, which stand approximately 0.30 m high, are unprepared and insloping. Although two postholes

were recorded, there was no apparent pattern in their placement, and it is unclear how the superstructure was supported. The entry way into Feature 17 is a subrectangular, unprepared ramp. The ramp, which measures a maximum of 0.75 m by 0.93 m, is off-center on the long axis of the pit structure and is facing south. Following abandonment and some in-filling of the structure, a secondary cremation (Feature 182) was placed in the Feature 17 entrance.

Three subfeatures were located and excavated within Feature 17 (see Figure 4.29 and Table 4.14). No hearth was found, and it is likely that the hearth was lost during the excavation of Trench 1. Feature 17.01, a shallow, medium, nonthermal pit, was located in the south half of the structure. Two other subfeatures, both postholes, were also excavated (see Table 4.14). Feature 17.02 was a small interior posthole, while Feature 17.05 was a very small posthole along the edge of the feature. In addition, Features 17.03 and 17.04 were determined to be nonfeatures after excavation.

The floor of Feature 17 consisted of an unprepared floor surface that appears to have been cut into the natural caliche horizon. The floor, which is generally well preserved, is located approximately 0.37 m below the stripped surface. There was no evidence of burning on the floor, although a small burnt patch was observed on the east wall, near the floor.

Feature 17 contained relatively few artifacts on its floor, although significantly more than any other excavated pit structure at the site (see Table 4.15). Diagnostic artifacts included a San Pedro projectile point and an Early Rincon Red-on-brown reconstructible hemispherical bowl. A large stone covered in ochre was recovered from the center of the structure's floor.

One radiocarbon date (Beta-236520) was obtained from a charred maize cupule recovered from Feature 17.01, a subfloor nonthermal pit (see Table 4.6). The sample yielded a 2 sigma calibrated date of A.D. 900 to 920 and A.D. 950 to 1040.

Seven environmental samples were collected from the fill, floor, and subfloor features of Feature 17. Of the six flotation samples collected, two—one from floor fill in Feature 17 and one from Feature 17.01—contained mac-robotanical specimens available for analysis; these were identified as mesquite and maize. The single pollen sample, collected from the floor of the feature, identified a wide variety of floral species including cholla, oak, mesquite, cheno-ams, low- and high-spine Asteraceae, globemallow, wild buckwheat, white mat, creosote bush, and members of the Grass, Mustard, and Nightshade families (see Adams, Chapter 10, and Phillips, Chapter 11).

Feature 17 was located in the upper, northeastern portion of the site (SA 1). It was the only structure found in this area during the EPX project, although three pithouses were excavated in this part of the site by WCRM (Kearns and McVickar 2009). The feature contained very few subfeatures—one medium nonthermal pit, which may have served a processing function, and two postholes were identified; the hearth was probably lost during excavation of Trench 1. Both the floor and the walls, while well defined, were unprepared. Feature 17 had a ramped entryway, located on

Figure 4.30. Photograph of Feature 17, post-excavation, view to the north.

Table 4.15. Artifacts recovered from the fill, floor fill, floor, and subfeatures of Feature 17

	Fill	Floor Fill	Floor	Subfeatures
Flaked Stone				
Debitage	50	45	6	2
Core	1			
Projectile point		1	1	
Subtotal	*51*	*46*	*7*	*2*
Ceramics				
Early Rincon Red-on-brown RV			1	
Rincon Red-on-brown		2		
Late Rincon Red-on-brown	1			
Indeterminte red-on-brown	8	12		
Indeterminate red-on-buff	1			
Brown ware	23		18	1
Undersized	26	38	1	3
Subtotal	*59*	*52*	*20*	*4*
Ground Stone				
Trough mano			1	
Turquoise bead		1		
Axe		2		
Lapstone		1		
Metate fragment (ind.)		1		
Subtotal		*5*	*1*	
Shell				
Whole-shell bead		1		
Disk bead		1		
In-process ring		1		
Ring fragment			1	
Subtotal		*3*	*1*	
Faunal Remains				
Hares and Rabbits	4	21		
Unidentified mammal	8	42	3	
Rodents		4		
Artiodactyls		2		
Mammal/Bird		6		
Subtotal	*12*	*75*	*3*	
Total	124	181	31	6

the south side of the structure and facing south. An intrusive secondary cremation was placed in the entryway of Feature 17, presumably after the feature's abandonment. There was minimal evidence of burning in the feature. No distinct roof- or wall-fall material was detected on the floor of the pit structure or within its fill.

Feature 17 had an estimated floor area of 14.95 square meters, and an excavated volume of 4.49 cubic meters, making it the largest pit structure investigated during EPX project excavations at the Marsh Station Road site, although it still would have been considered relatively small at the Tanque Verde Wash site (Elson, ed. 1986:67). The feature contained a rather small and unremarkable fill assemblage with a calculated ceramic density of 25 sherds/m³—what would be considered low density in Elson's scheme (ed., 1986:61)—suggesting the structure was not used for trash deposition after its abandonment. While the floor fill assemblage was not particularly large, comprised of just 181 artifacts, it contained several interesting artifacts including several stone and shell beads, two axes, a discarded lapstone likely used in the processing of shell (Jenny Adams, personal communication 2009), a San Pedro projectile point, and isolated human remains. The floor assemblage recovered from this feature was also interesting, containing a reconstructible hemispherical bowl, several sherd clusters, another San Pedro projectile point, a shell ring fragment, a trough mano, and an ochre-covered stone. It is unclear whether this floor assemblage was left in situ by design, or by catastrophic abandonment, although there is no evidence to suggest the feature was hastily abandoned due to fire or another natural disaster. Whatever the reason, it seems clear that Feature 17 underwent different abandonment processes than did the other five EPX-excavated pit structures, all of which were cleaned out at abandonment and contained significantly higher artifact densities in their fill.

Radiocarbon dating suggests that Feature 17 was occupied during the late Middle Formative period, or early to middle Rincon phase. Relatively few painted sherds were associated with this structure, although the presence of an Early Rincon Red-on-brown reconstructible hemispherical bowl on the structure's floor provides convincing support for the suggested period of occupation. The presence of two San Pedro projectile points very near or on the structure's floor is likely not indicative of the period of use for the pit structure; rather, they were probably curated by the structure's occupants.

Feature 51

This feature was discovered and partially bisected by mechanical excavation of Trench 13 (Figures 4.31 and 4.32). Following trench excavation, approximately 10 cm of overburden was stripped mechanically, and three 10-cm

Table 4.16. Characteristics of Feature 51	
Feature Type:	Pithouse
Cultural Affiliation:	Hohokam
Temporal Affiliation:	late Middle Formative (Rincon phase)
Diagnostic Artifacts:	Rincon Red-on-brown sherds (n=3)
Subfeatures:	One thermal pit
Provenience:	Trench 13
Shape:	Unclear, but possibly rectangular
Dimensions:	Excavated extent: 3.90 x 2.50 m; excavated floor area approximately 9.75 m2
Depth below datum:	94.66 z–94.44 z
Stratum:	Stratum 2: surface of Pleistocene terrace deposits with modern caliche development; approximately 40 cm below modern ground surface

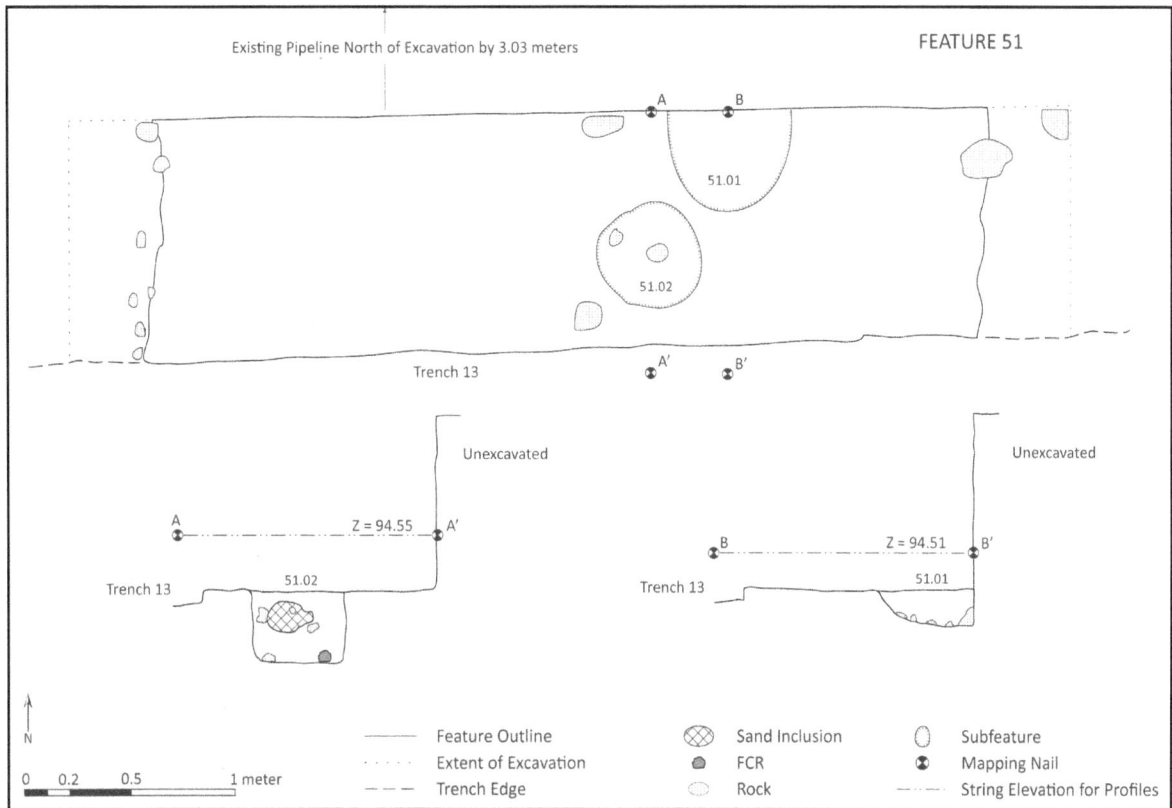

Figure 4.31. Plan and profile view of Feature 51 showing the location of Trench 13, which bisects the feature, and the structure's two subfeatures.

Figure 4.32. Photograph of Feature 51, post-excavation, view to the north.

arbitrary levels were manually excavated to expose the edge of the feature. Less than half of Feature 51 was available for excavation; a large section of the southern portion of this feature was removed by Trench 13, and any remaining portion of the southern extent of the feature was truncated by intrusive pits (Features 54 and 67). In addition, only a small portion of the northern half of the feature could be excavated, as the proximity of existing pipelines to the north of the feature prevented further excavation in that direction. Ultimately, an estimated 25 percent of the feature was excavated through one TU (TU 31) and three FEs, although FE 2, located south of Trench 13, did not actually produce any evidence of Feature 51. All FEs and the single TU were excavated in 10-cm arbitrary levels and their fill screened through ¼-inch mesh. In addition, a fourth feature excavation unit (FE 4) was excavated through the floor of Feature 51 to investigate the possibility of structure remodeling or whether any additional features underlay the pit structure. FE 4 was excavated as one continuous level; the fill was not screened.

Two subfeatures, one of which was later determined to predate Feature 51, were identified in the floor of Feature 51 (Table 4.17). These subfeatures were fully excavated in one or two stratigraphic units, and all fill was screened through ⅛-inch mesh.

Structure fill consisted of variably compact, brown, silty sand with a fair amount of gravel and greater than 10 percent cobbles. There was no evidence of burning in the fill, although a fair amount of charcoal and FCR were recorded. No roof- or wall-fall debris was present in the excavated fill.

Few artifacts (n = 41) were recovered from the fill of Feature 51 (Table 4.18), none of which are diagnostic to culture or period. In part, the very small fill assemblage recovered from Feature 51 may be explained by the small percentage of the feature that was excavated. In addition, 41 artifacts were recovered from Feature 51 fill excavated as part of TU 31.

The 10 cm of fill immediately above the floor of this pit structure was virtually identical in compaction, texture, inclusions, and color to the general structural fill, although less charcoal and FCR was noted. No roof- or wall-fall debris was present in the excavated floor fill.

The floor fill assemblage contained significantly more artifacts—a total of 106—than did the feature fill (see Table 4.18). An additional 68 artifacts were recovered from Feature 51 floor fill excavated as part of TU 31. The only diagnostic artifact recovered from floor fill was a single Rincon Red-on-brown sherd.

Very little can be said regarding the architectural characteristics of Feature 51. The shape of the feature is unclear (see Figures 4.31

Table 4.17. Subfeatures excavated from Feature 51

Feature No.	Description	Length (m)	Width (m)	Depth (m)	Artifacts/Samples
51.01	Thermal pit	0.4	0.5	0.11	brown ware sherd, undersized sherd; flaked stone debitage (7)
51.02[a]	Thermal pit				brown ware sherd, undersized sherd; flaked stone debitage (2)

[a] Later determined to predate Feature 51; subsequently reclassified as Feature 118.

and 4.32), although the excavated portion had parallel pit walls, suggesting the feature was rectangular (see Table 4.16). The pit walls were unprepared, steeply insloping, and measured 0.22 m high. The roof support system could not be determined, as no clear postholes were identified, although several possible postholes were located outside the wall. Feature 51 contained no defined entryway, although it is likely the entryway is either in the portion of the feature located in the pipeline exclusion to the north, or in the portion of the feature destroyed by the excavation of Trench 13. Ultimately, the excavated portion of Feature 51 measured 3.90 m by 2.50 m, with an exposed floor are measuring 9.75 square meters.

Just two subfeatures were identified in the floor of Feature 51 (see Figure 4.31 and Table 4.17). The first, Feature 51.01, was an

unprepared, indeterminate thermal pit with a very shallow (approximately 10 cm) basin-shaped in cross section. The feature was initially observed as an ash stain with charcoal flecks and FCR. Excavation, which extended subfloor, revealed several burnt sherds and a layer of blue-grey river cobbles. It is possible that Feature 51.01 is the hearth of Feature 51, but given the otherwise formal nature of Feature 51's floor, it seems odd that the feature's hearth would be so informal.

Feature 51.02 was initially identified as a second indeterminate thermal pit in the floor of Feature 51. The fill of this pit contained a significant amount of charcoal as well as numerous pieces of bluish-grey FCR. It was subsequently determined that this feature was actually located beneath the floor of Feature 51, and was in fact capped by the plaster floor

Table 4.18. Artifacts recovered from the fill, floor fill, floor, and subfeatures of Feature 51

	Fill	Floor Fill	Floor	Subfeatures
Flaked Stone				
Debitage	5	82	2	9
Cores	1	1		
Biface		1		
Uniface		1		
Subtotal	*6*	*85*	*2*	*9*
Ceramics				
Rincon Red-on-brown		1		
Indeterminate red-on-brown	6	9		
Brown ware	23	10	5	2
Undersized				2
Subtotal	*29*	*20*	*5*	*4*
Shell				
Worked fragment		1		
Faunal Remains				
Hares and Rabbits	4			
Unidentified mammal	2			
Subtotal	*6*			
Total	41	106	7	13

of that structure. Feature 51.02 thus became Feature 118.

Feature 51 contained a prepared floor covered with a thin (< 2 cm thick) layer of plaster. The partially preserved floor, which was located 0.62 m below the stripped surface, was laid on a thin layer of leveling fill over sterile stratum. An earlier pit feature (Feature 118, originally identified as Feature 51.02) was capped by the floor plaster. Feature 51 is one of two pithouses excavated to contain a prepared floor, suggesting it was one of the more formal houses investigated.

The floor assemblage, similar to the fill assemblage, was very small: just seven artifacts were recovered (see Table 4.18). Although more artifacts could be located in the unexcavated portion of the feature, it is likely that this pithouse was cleaned out prior to or at its abandonment.

No radiocarbon or archaeomagnetic samples from Feature 51 or from its subfeature were submitted for analysis as no suitable material was obtained during excavation.

Eight environmental samples—six flotation samples and one pollen sample—were collected from Feature 51. None of the flotation samples contained macrobotanical samples. The pollen samples, one collected from the floor fill and the other collected from the floor of Feature 51, identified a wide variety of floral species including cattail, willow, juniper, cheno-ams, low- and high-spine Asteraceae, wild buckwheat, white mat, creosote bush, and members of the Grass, Mustard, Nightshade, Pea, and Rose families (see Adams, Chapter 10, and Phillips, Chapter 11).

Feature 51 was characterized by a well defined, prepared floor surface, however, very little (< 5 percent) of the pit structure's walls were exposed during excavations, and only an estimated 25 percent of the structure was available for excavation. The feature most likely extended north, towards the pipeline exclusion.

No evidence of the feature was found south of Trench 13. It is possible that the southern portion of the feature was entirely destroyed by Trench 13, although it seems more likely that the feature once continued south of the trench, but was truncated by numerous intrusive pit features located in this area. Apart from the plastered floor and one small thermal pit, there is very little evidence regarding the characteristics and orientation of this pit feature: no entryway, hearth, roof supports, or roof- or wall-fall were documented. The structure contained a fair amount of charcoal and FCR in its fill, but given that no additional evidence of burning was found, this material probably reflects subsequent non-residential activity in the immediate area, rather than burning of the structure itself.

Feature 51 contained a rather unremarkable artifact assemblage. Just seven artifacts were documented on the floor of the structure, and while this may be related to the small percentage of the structure excavated, the structure was most likely cleaned out prior to or at its abandonment. Although the floor fill contained a larger artifact assemblage, it was not particularly dense. The fill assemblage was incredibly sparse, especially when compared to fill assemblages recovered from other excavated pit structures. The paucity of fill artifacts suggests that trash was not intentionally deposited in this feature post-abandonment.

Feature 152

Feature 152 (Figures 4.33 and 4.34) was overlain by Stratum 3 overburden, approximately 10 cm of which was stripped mechanically. Following stripping, the area was shovel-scraped to reveal the outline of Feature 152. The top of the feature was only 10 to 15 cm below the modern ground surface. The feature outline was generally easily discernable from the surrounding fill, and except for a small por-

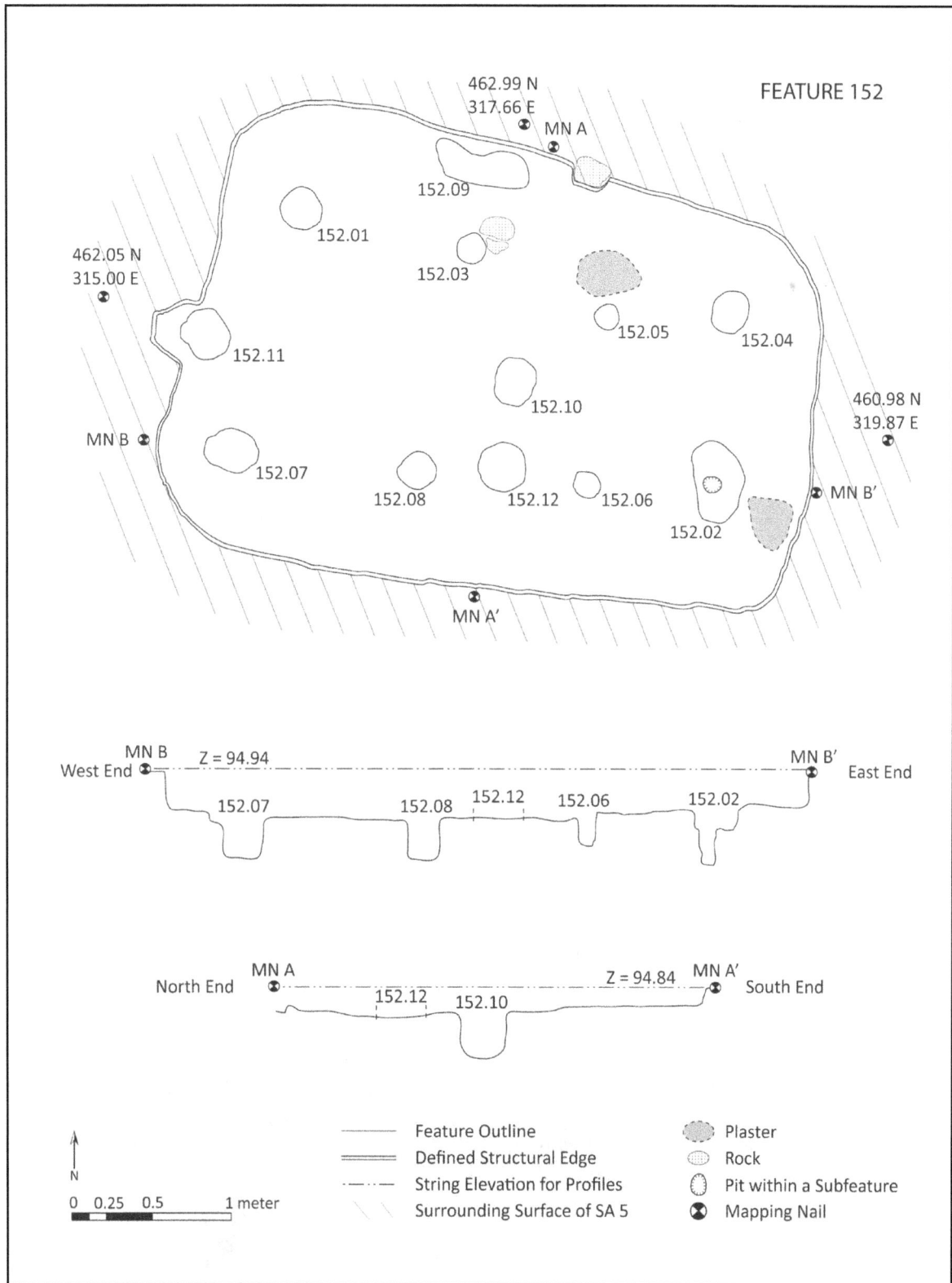

Figure 4.33. Plan and profile view of Feature 152 showing the structure's 12 recorded subfeatures.

Table 4.19. Characteristics of Feature 152

Feature Type:	Pithouse
Cultural Affiliation:	Hohokam
Temporal Affiliation:	late Middle Formative (Rincon phase)
Diagnostic Artifacts:	Rincon Red-on-brown sherds (n=3); San Pedro points (n=2)
Subfeatures:	Multiple: hearth, non-thermal pit, postholes (n=9)
Provenience:	Trench 13
Shape:	Subrectangular
Dimensions:	4.02 x 2.73 m; excavated floor area approximately 10.97 m2
Depth below datum:	94.93 z–94.65 z
Stratum:	Just above Stratum 2: surface of Pleistocene terrace deposits with modern caliche development; approximately 10–15 cm below modern ground surface

tion of the southeast and south-central edges, the pit outline was visible in plan view. The entirety of Feature 152 was excavated through four FEs, all of which were excavated in 10-cm arbitrary levels. FE 1 was screened through ¼-inch mesh; the upper fill of FEs 2–4 was screened through nested ¼-inch and ⅛-inch mesh while the floor fill was screened through ⅛-inch mesh. In addition, a fifth feature excavation unit (FE 5) was excavated through the floor of Feature 152 to investigate the possibility of structure remodeling or whether any additional features underlay the pit structure. FE 5 was excavated as one continuous level; the fill was not screened.

Twelve subfeatures, one of which was subsequently determined to be a nonfeature, were identified in the floor of Feature 152 (Table 4.20). These subfeatures were fully excavated in one or two stratigraphic units, and fill from a nonthermal pit and the hearth were screened through ¼-inch mesh; fill from the remaining features, all postholes, was not screened.

Figure 4.34. Photograph of Feature 152, post-excavation, view to the north.

Structure fill consisted of moderately compact, brown, silty loam with a small amount of gravel, and FCR. There was no evidence of burning in the fill, although a light charcoal flecking was noted. Abundant roof-fall debris, encompassing approximately 60 percent of the structure, was recorded in the feature fill. This roof-fall debris overlaid approximately 10 cm of cultural fill, suggesting the structure was abandoned and was in-filled for a short period of time prior to the roof's collapse.

Fill from Feature 152 contained a significant quantity of diverse artifacts: in all, 1,917 artifacts were recovered from feature fill (Table 4.21). Diagnostic artifacts include a Late Archaic Dart point, a San Pedro projectile point, and one Early and one Late Rincon Red-on-brown sherd.

The 10 cm of fill immediately above the floor of this pit structure was similar in compaction, texture, inclusions, and color to the general structural fill, although less charcoal flecking and fewer pieces of FCR were noted. Very little roof-fall debris was present in the excavated floor fill.

The floor fill also contained a substantial artifact assemblage. A total of 932 artifacts were recovered from the floor fill (see Table 4.21). The only diagnostic artifacts recovered from floor fill were eight Rincon Red-on-brown sherds and a San Pedro projectile point.

Feature 152 is a well-defined, subrectangular Hohokam pithouse (see Figures 4.33 and 4.34). Excavation revealed approximately 10.97 square meters of floor area; the maximum dimensions of the pit structure were estimated

Table 4.20. Subfeatures excavated from Feature 152

Feature No.	Description	Length (m)	Width (m)	Depth (m)	Artifacts/Samples
152.01	Posthole	0.26	0.26	0.24	Flotation sample; flaked stone debitage (2), core
152.02	Posthole	0.5	0.32	0.35	Flaked stone debitage (5); indeterminate red-on-brown sherd, brown ware sherd
153.03	Posthole	0.19	0.19	0.28	Flotation sample; flaked stone debitage (1)
152.04	Posthole	0.23	0.24	0.19	Flotation sample
152.05	Posthole	0.16	0.16	0.19	
152.06	Posthole	0.16	0.17	0.25	Flaked stone debitage (2)
152.07	Posthole	0.19	0.20	0.23	Flotation sample, brown ware sherd
152.08	Posthole	0.22	0.21	0.24	Flaked stone debitage (3)
152.09	Non-feature				Brown ware sherd
152.10	Posthole	0.26	0.23	0.15	Flotation sample; flaked stone debitage (4), uniface, indeterminate red-on-brown sherds (2)
152.11	Non-thermal pit	0.45	0.4	0.48	Flotation sample; flaked stone debitage (7), brown ware sherds (n=2)
152.12	Plastered hearth	0.26	0.26	0.15	Flotation sample; flaked stone debitage (6); faunal bone

Table 4.21. Artifacts recovered from the fill, floor fill, and subfeatures of Feature 152

	Fill	Floor Fill	Subfeatures
Flaked Stone			
Debitage	1188	615	30
Cores	2		1
Projectile points	4	1	
Biface	7	1	
Uniface	3		1
Hammerstones	1		
Subtotal	*1205*	*617*	*32*
Ceramics			
Rincon Red-on-brown		8	
Early Rincon Red-on-brown	1		
Late Rincon Red-on-brown	1		
Indeterminte red-on-brown	67	34	3
Indeterminate red-on-buff	3	2	
Brown ware	246		5
Brown ware (Red)	6	1	
Buff ware	1		
Undersized	243	80	
Subtotal	*568*	*125*	*8*
Ground Stone			
Handstone flat or flat/concave	3		
Trough mano	1		
Mano (other)	1	2	
Polishing stone	1		
Indeterminate fragment	2	7	
Subtotal	*8*	*9*	
Shell			
Whole shell bead		1	
Bracelet fragment	2		
Unworked fragment	1		
Freshwater shell		1	
Subtotal	*3*	*2*	

Table 4.21. Artifacts recovered from the fill, floor fill, and subfeatures of Feature 152, cont'd.

	Fill	Floor Fill	Subfeatures
Faunal Remains			
Lizard		1	
Birds	1		
Hares and Rabbits	25	38	
Unidentified mammal	102	134	1
Rodents	2	3	
Artiodactyl		1	
Small ungulate	3	1	
Mammal/bird		1	
Subtotal	*133*	*179*	*1*
Total	1917	932	41

at approximately 4.02 m by 2.73 m (see Table 4.19); these are the true dimensions and floor area, as 100 percent of the feature was excavated. The pit walls, which are vertical and stand approximately 0.28 m high, are plastered, although the plaster was not well preserved. Nine interior postholes were found within Feature 152. No entryway was defined for Feature 152. Given that the entirety of the feature was excavated, this seems unusual. However, hearth placement implies a south-facing entry, and remnants of the southern wall further imply a stepped entry. Thus, it is possible that evidence of the entryway simply was not preserved.

A total of 12 subfeatures, one of which was determined to be a nonfeature, were located and excavated within Feature 152 (see Figure 4.33 and Table 4.20). A small, formal, plastered hearth (Feature 152.12) approximately 0.15 m deep was centrally located in the southern portion of the feature. Not all of the plaster in the hearth was preserved; however, the patches that were preserved suggested the bowl-shaped hearth was originally plastered all over. Feature 152.11, located near the east wall of the structure, was a small nonthermal pit. In

addition to the hearth and nonthermal pit, nine postholes were excavated from the structure's floor. Features 152.03, 152.05, 152.06, and 152.08 were oriented in a rough square in the center of the structure; Feature 152.10 was located in the center of this square. Features 152.01, 152.02, 152.04, and 152.07, were located roughly in the four corners of the pit structure. A small assemblage was recovered from the subfeatures (see Table 4.21).

Like Feature 51, Feature 152 contained a prepared floor covered with a thin (< 2 cm thick) plaster layer. The floor, located approximately 0.43 m below modern ground surface, was poorly preserved with most of the plaster having deteriorated naturally over time. There was little floor disturbance (< 10 percent), and the preserved floor area was unburned.

Interestingly, Feature 152 did not contain a floor assemblage; only three noncultural rocks were recovered from the floor surface. This complete lack of a floor assemblage implies a planned cessation of structure use.

Two radiocarbon dates (Beta-234165 and Beta-234166) were obtained from charred maize cupules recovered from Features 152 and 152.03 (see Table 4.6). The first sample (Beta-234165), recovered from a flotation sample taken from floor fill, yielded a 2 sigma calibrated date of A.D. 1020 to 1210. The second sample (Beta-234166), collected from an excavated posthole (Feature 152.03), yielded a 2 sigma calibrated date of A.D. 990 to 1160.

Two archaeomagnetic samples, one consisting of 14 specimens and the other consisting of 12 specimens, were collected from the floor and walls, respectively, of Feature 152 (see Table 4.6). The first sample (walls) returned four date ranges: A.D. 930 to 1025, A.D. 1305 to 1370, A.D. 1430 to 1645, and A.D. 1755 to 1870. The second sample (floor) returned three date ranges: A.D. 930 to 1045, A.D. 1305 to 1395, and A.D. 1430 to 1625. Congruence with the radiocarbon dates suggests a Rincon phase/late Middle Formative date for the feature.

Twenty environmental samples were collected from the fill, floor, and subfloor features of Feature 152. Three macrobotanical samples, all collected from general structural fill, were analyzed; specimens were identified as mesquite, maize, and cheno-am. Of the 15 flotation samples collected, three—one each from Feature 152.03, Feature 152.11, and Feature 152.12—contained macrobotanical specimens available for analysis; these were identified as mesquite, maize, Broadleaf yucca, hackberry, reedgrass, grass, and cheno-am. Two pollen samples, one collected from the floor fill and one collected from the floor of the feature, identified a wide variety of floral species including cholla, cattail, willow, pinyon pine, juniper, mesquite, cheno-ams, low- and high-spine Asteraceae, spiderling, wild buckwheat, white mat, creosote bush, and members of the Grass, Mustard, Lily, and Nightshade families (see Adams, Chapter 10, and Phillips, Chapter 11).

Feature 152 is distinctive among the pithouses excavated at the Marsh Station Road site. It was the smallest pithouse of the six excavated, with a floor area of just 10.97 square meters and an excavated volume of 3.07 cubic meters, but the feature had extensive plaster not seen in the other houses. Only one other pithouse, Feature 51 exhibited plaster preparation, but there it was limited to the floor. Although Feature 152 was completely excavated, no entrance for the feature was defined. The lack of an entryway has been viewed as diagnostic of a field house or a small, informal structure (Ferg et al. 1984). However, while Feature 152 is fairly small, it shows considerable surface preparation, and is the most "formal' of the structures excavated at the site. It thus seems unlikely that Feature 152 is a field house or other informal structure, at least by Ferg and others' (1984) definition. Rather, it may be that the entryway to the feature simply did not stand the test of time: the plaster within the feature—on the walls and floor as well as in the hearth—was poorly preserved; various site formation processes may have acted similarly on the entryway, leaving virtually no trace of its existence in the archaeological record.

The artifact density within Feature 152, calculated at 226 sherds/m3, was high for pithouses at the site, and included a wide variety of artifact types (see Table 4.19; also see above). However, no floor assemblage was recovered from this feature, implying a planned abandonment. A significant amount of hard roof-fall debris was observed in the upper fill of the house. The debris rested on an approximately 10-cm layer of cultural fill—the floor fill, which did not contain abundant roof-fall debris. This suggests that after the feature was abandoned some fill accumulated before the roof entirely collapsed. The calculated ceramic sherd density for Feature 152 is just above the minimum density Elson (ed., 1986) would see as clearly indicative of trash fill.

Radiocarbon and archaeomagnetic dates as well as the presence of an Early Rincon Red-on-brown and a Late Rincon Red-on-brown sherd in the feature fill and several Rincon Red-on-brown sherds in the floor fill suggest that Feature 152 was occupied during the late Middle Formative period. Although several San Pedro projectile points were recovered from this structure, they are probably not diagnostic of the structure's period of occupation, as appears to be the case with San Pedro points recovered from the fill of other pithouses.

Feature 206

Feature 206 was overlain by Stratum 3 overburden, approximately 10 cm of which was stripped mechanically. Following stripping, two 10-cm arbitrary levels were manually excavated to expose the edge of the feature. Feature 206 was initially considered an extension of Feature 11 (described above; also see Figure 4.27). However, during excavation of Feature 11, it was tentatively determined that this extension was actually a separate feature. Subsequently, as the feature was not discernible in plan view, it was excavated in piecemeal fashion in a series of three FEs. The three FEs were continuations of TUs 27, 34, and 53, respectively, and were excavated in 10-cm arbitrary levels and were screened through ¼-inch mesh. FEs 7 and 8 from Feature 11 are also considered part of Feature 206. In addition, FE 4 was excavated through the floor of Feature 206 to investigate the possibility of structure remodeling or whether any additional features underlay the pit structure. FE 4 was excavated as one continuous level; the fill was not screened. Ultimately, approximately 25 percent of Feature 206 was available for investigation and excavated.

During excavation of Feature 206, structural fill and floor fill were not differentiated as a result of the ephemeral nature of the feature. Structure fill/floor fill consisted of loosely compacted, brown, silty sand with approximately 20 percent gravel. There was no evidence of

burning in the fill and no charcoal, FCR, or roof- or wall-fall were observed.

Feature 206 contained a few nondescript artifacts: only 40 artifacts were recovered (Table 4.23). No true diagnostic artifacts were recovered, although one humpback biface, tentatively associated with the Early Agricultural period (see Chapter 6), was collected.

Very little can be said regarding the architectural characteristics of Feature 206. This feature was tentatively identified as a subrectangular pit structure: it was poorly defined, contained a poorly preserved unprepared floor, and no evidence of a roof support system, hearth, or entryway (see Figure 4.27 and Table 4.22). The walls of the feature were shallow, measuring just 0.17 m high, unprepared, and insloping. The mapped area of the feature measured 2.60 m by 2.70 m, and the excavated floor area covered just 7 square meters.

Table 4.22. Characteristics of Feature 206

Feature Type:	Pit house
Cultural Affiliation:	Hohokam
Temporal Affiliation:	late Middle Formative (Rincon phase)
Diagnostic Artifacts:	Humpback biface
Subfeatures:	None
Provenience:	SA 4
Shape:	Unclear, tentatively subrectangular
Dimensions:	Mapped area: 2.60 m by 2.70 m; excavated floor area approximately 7.0 m2
Depth below datum:	94.72 z–94.55 z
Stratum:	Stratum 2: surface of Pleistocene terrace deposits with modern caliche development; approximately 20 cm below modern ground surface

Table 4.23. Artifacts recovered from the fill/floor fill of Feature 206

Flaked Stone	
Debitage	33
Cores	2
Biface	1
Subtotal	*36*
Ceramics	
Brown ware	3
Undersized	1
Subtotal	*4*
Total	40

The floor of Feature 206 was a poorly preserved, unprepared sterile stratum. An estimated 75 percent of the floor was disturbed, likely through natural processes. No artifact assemblage was recovered from the floor.

No chronometric (radiocarbon or archaeomagnetic) or environmental (macrobotanical, flotation, or pollen) samples were available for collection from Feature 206.

Feature 206 was tentatively identified as a subrectangular pit structure, although evidence for this feature was limited. No architectural characteristics, other than shallow walls and a poorly preserved floor, were identified. Very little fill was associated with excavation of this feature, which was ultimately identified at the base of test unit excavations and in conjunction with the excavation of Feature 11. Only a small, nondescript artifact assemblage lacking diagnostic artifacts was recovered from the fill of the feature.

Feature 206 overlaps Feature 11, with Feature 206 likely the later feature as its floor surface is lower than that of Feature 11. The structures are comparable, however, in that both are minimally prepared: each is cut into sterile deposits, and lacks floor surface or wall preparation; their projected shapes and dimensions are also comparable (see Figure 4.27).

Although no diagnostic artifacts were recovered from Feature 206, it seems likely the feature dates to the Rincon phase/Middle Formative period. With the possible exception of Feature 11, all other excavated pit structures at the Marsh Station Road site, including those excavated by WCRM (Kearns and McVickar 2009), are also attributed to this phase.

Discussion of Pithouses and Structures

Five definite pithouses as well as one pit structure were excavated by WSA at the Marsh Station Road site. Four of the definite pithouses date to the Rincon phase/late Middle Formative period, and the possible pit structure probably does as well. The fifth definite pithouse may also date to this period, but there is some reason to think it may instead date to the Early Agricultural period. The occupation of the Rincon phase/late Middle Formative structures is established by both radiocarbon and archaeomagnetic samples, as well as by the presence of a variety of decorated ceramic wares dating to this period. Most (n = 5) of the structures were located in SA 4/5, but one was located in SA 1; no pithouses were present in SA 2/3. Variability was evident within this small sample of pit structures. Feature 152 had the most formal attributes—a more rectangular shape, and remnants of plaster on the walls and floor—while Features 7, 11, and 17 were somewhat similar to one another, being more rounded in shape and having little plaster and evidence of formal preparation. Features 11 and 17 were larger than the other structures excavated at the Marsh Station Road site, although they might not be contemporaneous. Given the morphological variability of these structures, it is difficult to compare them as a unit to contemporaneous structures in the Tucson Basin. Having said that, Features 7 and 17 look like they could have been excavated from Rincon contexts at West Branch (Huntington, ed. 1986), Valencia (Doelle 1985), or Tanque Verde Wash (Elson, ed. 1986). Feature 152, however, with its more formal characteristics looks less like the Rincon phase structures at these sites than it does to some structures at Valencia Vieja (Lindeman 2003), an Early Formative period site, even though it produced a Rincon phase/Middle Formative radiocarbon date. Feature 11 has some similarities to other Early Agricultural structures, particularly ones from Milagro and Las Capas (see Mabry 2008a:Figures 1.13 and 1.14). Interestingly, none of the structures possessed recessed hearths, which were documented at the nearby Mescal Wash site (Vanderpot and Altschul 2007) and other sites in southeastern Arizona (Fulton and Tuthill 1940; Tuthill 1947). Similarly, none had adobe cones at the entry ways, as have been documented in Rincon phase structures at sites like Tanque Verde Wash (Elson, ed. 1986), the Hodges Ruin (Kelly et al. 1978), Punta de Agua (Greenleaf 1975), and Sabino Springs (Roth 2000).

Elson's (ed., 1986:61) formula for quantifying the density of artifact assemblages recovered from the fill of features was calculated for the three most completely excavated pithouses at the Marsh Station Road site. Of the three, Feature 17 contained the lowest density of artifacts within its fill, while Feature 152 contained the highest; Feature 7 fell in between the two. Interestingly, however, none of these features contain high enough artifact densities to be characterized as trash fill, according to Elson's formula. Where were the site's occupants throwing the majority of their trash then? There are several possible explanations. It may be that at least one midden exists in another, unexcavated portion of the site. McConville and Holzkamper (1955) recorded two trash mounds, at least one of which appeared to be undisturbed, near the Southern Pacific Railroad. Trash may also have been deposited in other features throughout the site, although

excavated pit features also do not contain significant quantities of trash (see below). Another possibility is that the Marsh Station Road site may have been occupied seasonally/temporarily, which may explain the low(er) degree of trash accumulation at the site. A final possibility is that equating artifact density with ceramic density is not (always) the best way to quantify artifacts in feature fill. While Elson (ed., 1986:61), based on Schiffer's (1976) studies of refuse disposal behavior, believed ceramics were the preferable artifact class to use in calculating artifact density, the formula would not be particularly useful at sites containing a relatively low number of ceramics overall. Although ceramics were the second largest artifact class recovered from the Marsh Station Road site (n = 9,038), significantly more flaked stone was recovered (n = 43,092), suggesting that perhaps flaked stone would be a better artifact class for calculating density at the Marsh Station Road site. However, the situation is even more complicated at the Marsh Station Road site, where we suspect that at least some flaked stone material from the Early Agricultural occupation might be mixed with much of the later feature fill.

In considering the excavated sample of pithouses from the Marsh Station Road site in a more regional perspective, neither the structures' characteristics nor their apparent association with the late Middle Formative period entirely conforms with either our expectations prior to commencing fieldwork or with our initial excavation impressions. Based on the results of excavations at the Mescal Wash site, which documented a wide range of material culture attributable to the Mogollon, Hohokam, and possible Dragoon cultural traditions (see Vanderpot and Altschul 2007), and the presence of numerous Early Agricultural projectile points on the surface of the Marsh Station Road site, we expected to find 1) more variation in the age of the structures, and 2) more similarities to structures previously identified at the Mescal Wash site. As became apparent during excavations, however, cultural material in feature contexts at the site was mixed; Early Agricultural projectile points were routinely recovered with later dating ceramics (e.g., Rincon Red-on-brown), and from the floor or floor fill of pit structures radiocarbon dated to the late Middle Formative period. This mixing of cultural material does not seem to be the result of disturbance, such as bioturbation or pothunting, but rather is likely indicative of either prehistoric behavior that purposefully (e.g., through curation) or accidentally incorporated early dating cultural material into later dating features, or is the result of erosion or sheet wash. The overall picture is that the pithouses from the Marsh Station Road site 1) date to the late Middle Formative period and 2) exhibit a considerable amount of variability, but less than what was observed at the Mescal Wash site.

Occupation Surfaces

Two occupation surfaces—Features 6 and 41—were recorded at the Marsh Station Road site. Both of these were quite limited areas of well defined surface, although there were hints of structural associations with both features: Feature 6 had abundant burned wood and Feature 41 included three posthole subfeatures. It is possible that the presence of a structure concentrated activity in these areas, leading to the definition of a surface, although occupation over most of the site area failed to create such defined surfaces. Similar features have been interpreted as ramadas or windbreaks (Elson, ed. 1986:102–108) at other Hohokam sites in the Tucson Basin, and that is the interpretation followed here.

Feature 6

Feature 6, which originated within Stratum

3, was discovered and bisected by mechanical excavation of Trench 12 (Figure 4.35). In the profile, Feature 6 appeared as a void/dip in the caliche, and was proposed to represent a possible pithouse. Subsequently, approximately 10 cm of overburden was stripped mechanically, and one 5-cm arbitrary level was manually excavated as a test unit (TU 21) to expose feature fill containing distinctive artifacts. Following this initial test unit excavation, the feature was dug in a succession of seven feature excavation units (FEs) (TU 21 became FE 1) although no definitive outline of the feature's extent was ever determined. FEs 1 through 3, which were located north of Trench 12, were excavated first, revealing a poorly preserved occupation surface/floor at their base. Excavation then moved south of Trench 12, where excavation of FEs 4 and 5 revealed very little feature fill and no evidence of an occupation

Table 4.24. Characteristics of Feature 6	
Feature Type:	Extramural occupation surface
Cultural Affiliation:	Hohokam
Temporal Affiliation:	late Middle Formative (Rincon phase)
Diagnostic Artifacts:	Small Contracting Stemmed point (n=2); Cortaro point; Rincon Red-on-brown sherds (n=3)
Subfeatures:	Hearth
Provenience:	SAs 4/5
Shape:	Unclear, tentatively subrectangular
Dimensions:	No defined outline; surface sporadically present across excavated units with total dimensions of 5 m by 4 m
Depth below datum:	94.72 z–94.68 z
Stratum:	Stratum 3: Overburden; approximately 15 cm below modern ground surface

FEATURE 6

Feature 28

Hearth

Trench 12

Feature 5

	Feature 5 and 28 Outlines		— — —	Trench Edge
	Feature 6 Surface Material			Caliche Surface
	Areas of Disturbance		◆	Reconstructable Vessel
	Charcoal; MBOT Samples			Compact Areas
	Extent of Excavation Units			Ash Stain
‡	Historic Fence Post		△	Biface

N

0   .25   .5   .75   1.0 meters

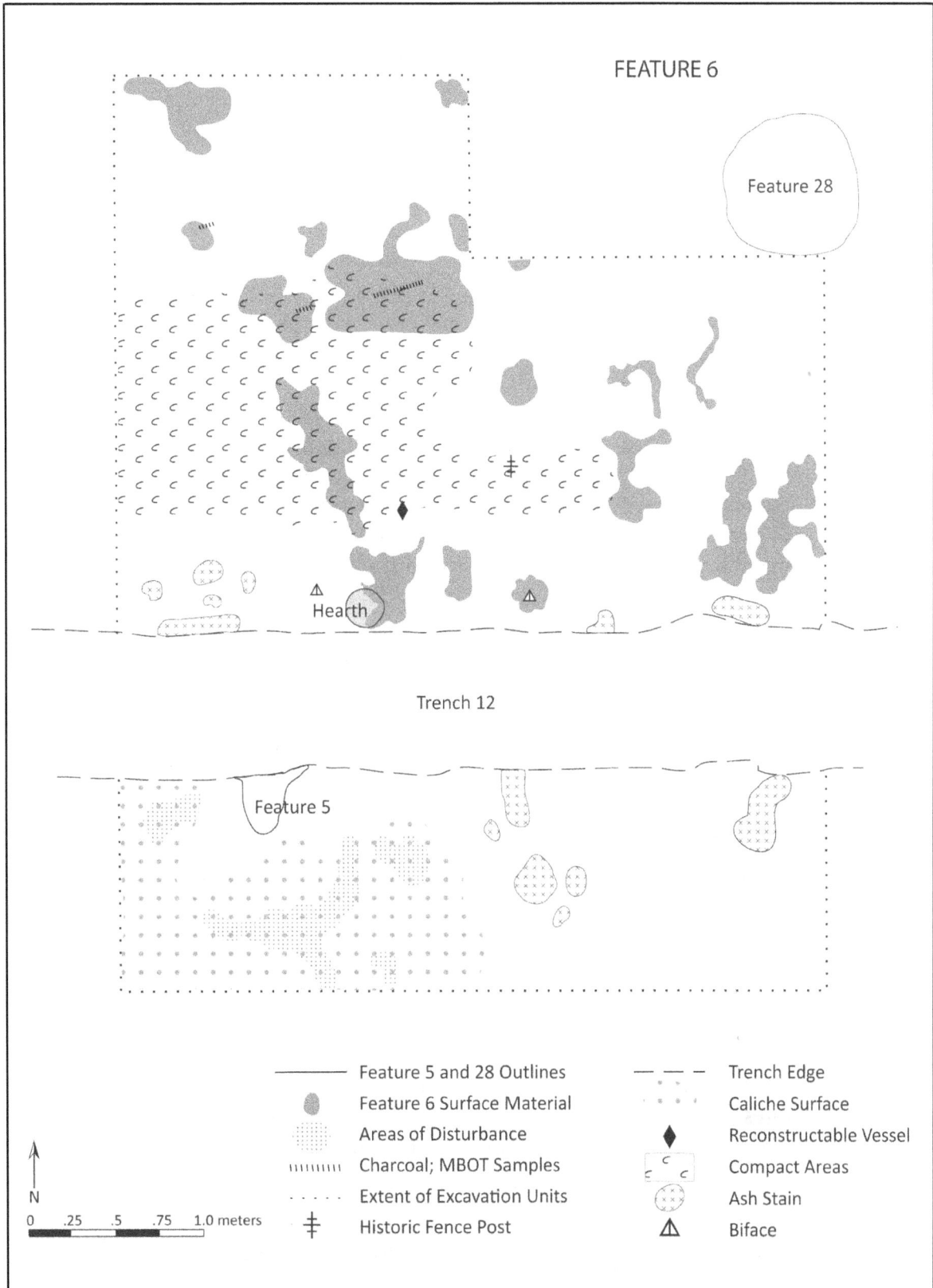

Figure 4.35. Plan view of Feature 6 as well as its single subfeature, an extramural hearth.

surface. Excavation then returned to the north side of Trench 12, with FEs 6 and 7. All seven FEs were excavated in 10-cm arbitrary levels, and all feature fill was screened through ¼-inch mesh; floor fill in FE 3 (a 2-m by 1-m unit) was screened through ⅛-inch mesh to facilitate recovery of small artifacts associated with the occupation surface below.

One subfeature, a hearth, was identified on the occupation surface of Feature 6 (Table 4.25). This subfeature was fully excavated in one stratigraphic unit; the fill was collected as a flotation sample (FN 44-3628) and therefore was not screened.

Fill within Feature 6 was described as variably compact—concrete-like initially, then moderately compact—brown sandy loam containing small gravel inclusions, occasional cobbles of various sizes, and FCR. Light charcoal flecking was present throughout the fill, and localized concentrations of charcoal were also observed. Roof and wall fall in the form of daub was found throughout, although the density of this material varied; greater concentrations were located closer to the occupation surface.

A substantial and diverse artifact assemblage totaling 1,071 artifacts was recovered from the fill of Feature 6 (Table 4.26). However, only a few diagnostic artifacts were recovered. These include a couple of Rincon Red-on-brown sherds and a Small Contracting-stem projectile point.

A significantly smaller artifact assemblage totaling 157 artifacts was recovered from floor fill of Feature 6 (see Table 4.26). The ceramic wares represented are identical, and in relatively similar proportions. Interest-ingly, no flaked stone debitage was recovered, although five projectile points were collected. Three of the projectile points recovered were of indeterminate type, but another Small Contracting-stem point and a Cortaro point were identified in the floor fill assemblage. A shell pendant in the form of a stylized lizard was also recovered.

No walls, wall groove, postholes, or entry-way associated with Feature 6 were observed, and there were no surviving structural elements, if any originally existed (see Figure 4.35). The feature fill included unusual concentrations of roof and/or wall fall material as well as local-ized concentrations of charcoal. This was not typical of the site, and might represent burned, fallen structural material.

One subfeature, Feature 6.01, was exca-vated from the occupation surface of Feature 6 (see Figure 4.35 and Table 4.25). Feature 6.01 was a formal, collared, clay-lined hearth. Some well-preserved plaster was found around the rim of the hearth, and small patches were preserved on the base; no plaster was found on the sides of the pit. Clear patches of oxidation were observed on the north and east rim of the feature. The hearth was bowl-shaped, measured 0.48 m by 0.23 m, and was 0.10 m deep. Fill from the hearth, which was collected as a flota-tion sample, contained loose, brown sandy silt with light charcoal flecking, and was compa-rable to the fill of the feature as a whole.

The occupation surface of Feature 6, located 0.37 m below the modern ground surface, was poorly preserved, patchy, and generally unprepared. The only traces of plas-ter were around the hearth (Feature 6.01, see below). Most of the surface which constituted

Table 4.25. Subfeatures excavated from Feature 6

Feature No.	Description	Length (m)	Width (m)	Depth (m)	Artifacts/Samples
6.01	Plastered hearth	0.48	0.23	0.10	Flotation sample

	Fill	Floor Fill	Surface
Flaked Stone			
Debitage	811		
Cores	5	3	
Projectile points	3	5	
Biface	1	2	1
Uniface	2		
Subtotal	*822*	*10*	*1*
Ceramics			
Rincon Red-on-brown	3	2	
Indeterminte red-on-brown	21	12	
Indeterminate red-on-buff	4	1	
Brown ware	154	82	
Brown ware (Red)	4	2	
Undersized	41	29	
Subtotal	*227*	*128*	
Ground Stone			
Flat Mano	1		
Shell			
Lizard Pendant		1	
Bracelet fragment	1		
Faunal Remains			
Hares and Rabbits	2	8	
Rodents	2		
Unidentified mammal	12	6	
Small ungulate	3	4	
Unknown Class	1		
Subtotal	*20*	*18*	
Total	1071	157	1

Table 4.26. Artifacts recovered from Feature 6

Feature 6 was a defined, compact horizon in the site sediment, traced across excavated units with total dimensions of 5 m by 4 m. The best preservation of the surface was seen in FE 1, near the hearth. With increasing distance from the hearth, the surface gradually became less defined and less continuous. Only one artifact, a biface of silicified sediment, was present on the occupation surface of Feature 6 (see Table 4.26).

No radiocarbon samples were analyzed from Feature 6. Although some patchy clay was preserved on Feature 6.01, a clay-lined hearth, not enough of the clay remained to adequately sample for archaeomagnetic analysis.

Fifteen environmental samples were collected from the fill, occupation surface, and subfeature of Feature 6. All six macrobotanical samples were analyzed; species identified include hackberry, cottonwood/willow, mesquite, and acacia. Two flotation samples from floor fill in FE 1 and in FE 3 contained macrobotanical specimens available for analysis; these were identified as hackberry, reedgrass, cottonwood/willow, mesquite, and maize. One pollen sample, collected from floor fill in FE 1, identified a wide variety of floral species including cholla, cattail, ponderosa pine, cheno-ams, low- and high-spine Asteraceae, wild buckwheat, spurge, white mat, and members of the Grass, Pea, Mustard, and Nightshade families (see Adams, Chapter 10, and Phillips, Chapter 11).

Feature 6 was an occupation surface with a formal hearth. In general, Feature 6 was difficult to excavate and is difficult to interpret. Both the hearth and adjacent floor were well defined, the assemblage of artifacts associated with the surface was quite diverse, and the presence of roof and wall fall in the fill suggested a structure, but no architecture could be defined. Plastered extramural hearths are unusual in the Tucson Basin, but have occasionally been recorded. Two were found at sites excavated in the ANAMAX-Rosemont project, although excavators for this project were also unsure how to interpret them (Ferg et al. 1984:177). Two extramural hearths at the Tanque Verde Wash site also had traces of plaster (Elson, ed. 1986:Table 5.8), although no interpretation of these features is offered. Despite ambiguity in the literature, the plastered hearth associated with Feature 6 implies this area was a focus for cultural activity, and suggests that the feature likely is structural. Artifact density was relatively high in units excavated over the occupation surface of this feature, although relatively few artifacts were in direct contact with the surface, and it is therefore not possible to say what activities were conducted around the hearth. Collection densities on the modern ground surface were high in this part of the site, and this abundance continued through the sediment to the prehistoric occupation surface. Although no chronometric samples were analyzed from Feature 6, the presence of Rincon Red-on-brown ceramic sherds and other non-diagnostic red-on-brown pieces were found close to the surface, and their presence suggests the surface is associated with the most prominent occupation of the site during the late Middle Formative period.

Feature 41

Feature 41 (Figure 4.36) was found at the interface of Stratum 2 and Stratum 3, following mechanical stripping of SA 5, south of Trench 12. Feature fill was identified approximately 0.15 m below the modern ground surface. Following this initial excavation, the feature was dug in a succession of four feature excavation units (FEs). No definitive outline of the feature's extent was ever determined. All four FEs were excavated in 10-cm arbitrary levels, and all feature fill was screened through ¼-inch mesh. In addition, a fifth feature excavation unit (FE 5) was excavated through the occupation

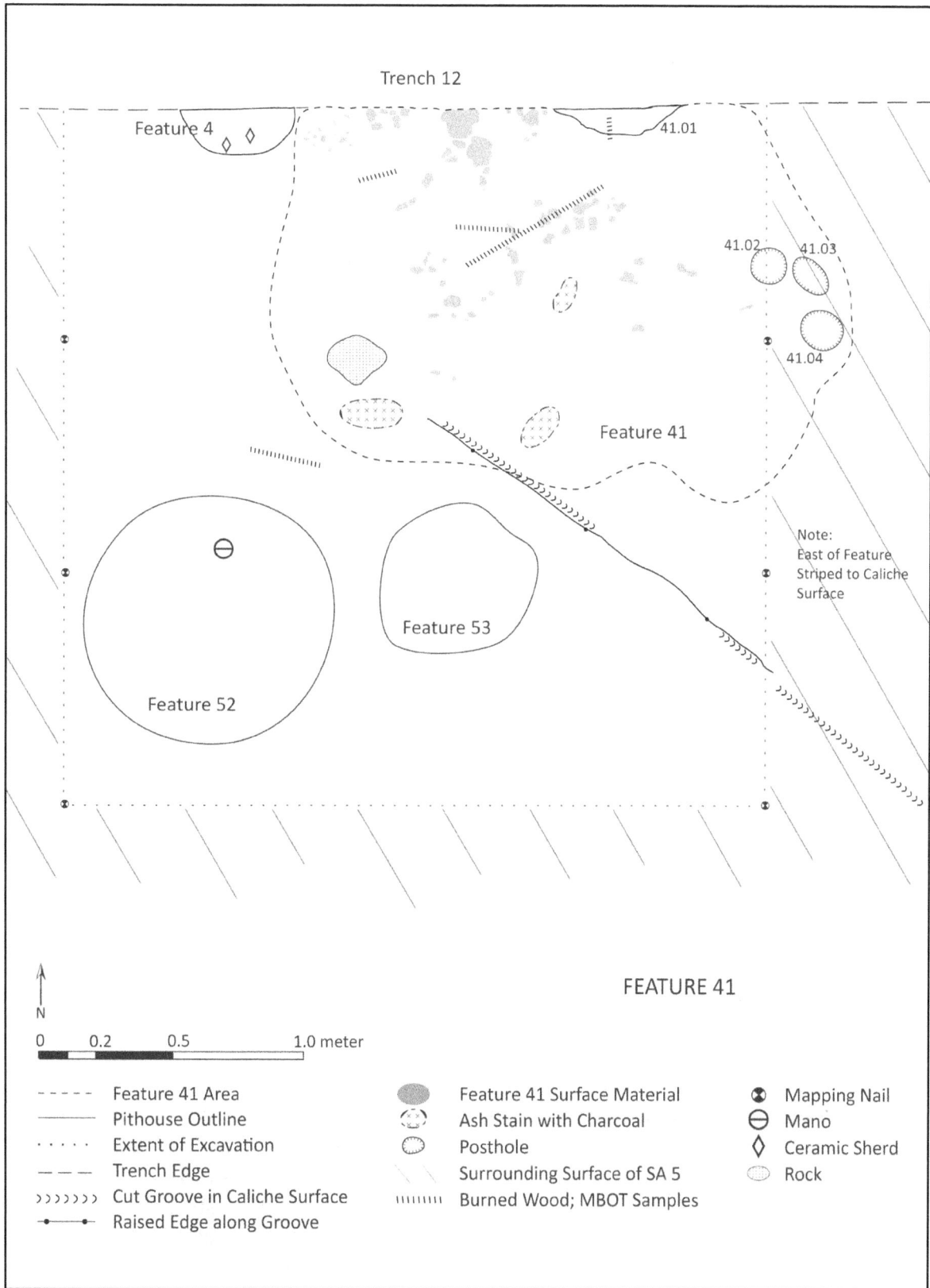

Figure 4.36. Plan view of Feature 41, its subfeatures, and several surrounding features.

Table 4.27. Characteristics of Feature 41

Feature Type:	Extramural occupation surface
Cultural Affiliation:	Hohokam
Temporal Affiliation:	late Middle Formative (Rincon phase)
Diagnostic Artifacts:	Small Contracting Stemmed preform; Rincon Red-on-brown sherd
Subfeatures:	Postholes (n=3)
Provenience:	SA 5
Shape:	Unclear, tentatively subrectangular
Dimensions:	No defined outline; prepared surface measured 1.2 m by 1.8 m; generalized surface traced through four units and measured 16 m²
Depth below datum:	94.82 z–94.71/94.63 z
Stratum:	Interface between Strata 2 (Pleistocene terrace deposits) & 3 (Overburden); approximately 15 cm below modern ground surface

surface of Feature 41 to investigate the possibility of previous surfaces and identify any additional subfeatures. FE 5 was excavated as one continuous level; the fill was screened through ⅛-inch mesh.

Four subfeatures, all postholes, including one that was subsequently determined to be historic in age and therefore not associated with Feature 41, were excavated from the east side of the occupation surface uncovered in FE 1 (Table 4.28). All four subfeatures were fully excavated as one level; their fill was not screened.

Only fill from FEs 1 and 2 was considered associated with Feature 41; fill from FEs 3 and 4 was considered overburden or associated with other nearby features (Features 4, 52, and 53).

Fill excavated from Feature 41 was identified as floor fill, rather than feature fill, because just 10 to 20 cm of fill was excavated before the occupation surface was reached.

Floor fill from Feature 41 was characterized as very compact, brown sandy silt with a small amount of gravel (< 3 percent). Very light charcoal flecking was noted throughout the fill, and there were localized, dense concentrations of horizontal, burned, linear wood fragments and one burned vertical beam in a posthole. Small amounts of roof and wall fall (daub) were also recorded. The fill of Feature 41 was comparable with the fill of Feature 6.

A relatively small assemblage, only 267 artifacts, was recovered from the floor fill of Feature 41. No diagnostic artifacts were present in the assemblage (Table 4.29).

No defined outline was identified for Feature 41, and no walls, wall groove, or entryway were observed, although there were small amounts of roof and/or wall fall present in the feature fill (see Figure 4.36).

Three postholes were found associated with this feature (see Figure 4.36 and Table 4.28). A fourth posthole was discounted as a prehistoric feature when traces of unburned wood were found. This post was probably part of a right-of-way fence associated with the Southern Pacific Railroad grade (Feature 135) near the feature. The three posts associated with Feature 41 were quite close together, and could be seen as an alignment. All three postholes were small (see Table 4.28) and it is likely they represent the remains of a light structure, perhaps a windbreak, rather than a more substantial structure such as a ramada.

In addition, three extramural pits were excavated near Feature 41. All three originated at the same level as Feature 41. They were recorded as features, rather than subfeatures, but may have been associated with activity on the occupation surface. Feature 4, bisected by Trench 12, was a thermal pit with excavated dimensions measuring 0.45 m long, 0.20 m wide, and 0.15 m deep. The fill was described as ashy with charcoal flecks and small amount of FCR. Feature 52 was a bell pit measuring 1.08 m long, 1.05 m wide, and 0.78 m deep. The fill of the pit contained moderate amounts of charcoal and FCR, possibly trash fill. Feature 53 was a relatively broad and shallow non-thermal pit with dimensions measuring 0.55 m long, 0.65 m wide, and 0.15 m deep. It was filled with sandy loam and lightly flecked with charcoal but lacked FCR.

The occupation surface of Feature 41, located between 0.26 m and 0.34 m below the modern ground surface, was poorly preserved and patchy. Portions of the exposed surface were unmodified natural deposits: caliche and reddish gravel. Other parts of the surface were informal floor: compact, smooth, and ash-stained. A small portion of the surface near Trench 12 was plastered. The prepared surface was rather limited in extent, occurring in an area measuring 1.2 m by 1.8 m and present only in FEs 1 and 2. However, the more generalized surface representing the top of sterile deposits on which Feature 41 rested was traced through all four FEs, with a total area of 4 square meters. No artifacts were recovered in direct contact with the occupation surface.

One archaeomagnetic sample, consisting of 12 specimens, was collected from the occupation surface of Feature 41 (see Table 4.6). The sample returned four date ranges: A.D. 580 to 725, A.D. 905 to 1045, A.D. 1305 to 1625, and A.D. 1755 to 1870.

Twelve environmental samples were collected from the floor fill and occupation surface and subfeatures of Feature 41. All six macrobotanical samples were analyzed; species identified include hackberry, mesquite, and juniper. Of the four flotation samples collected, two—from floor fill in FE 2 and from subfloor FE 5—contained macrobotanical specimens available for analysis; these were identified as mesquite and juniper. Two pollen samples, collected from floor fill and the occupation surface in FE 1, identified a wide variety of floral species including cattail, juniper, cheno-ams, low- and high-spine Asteraceae, globemallow, wild buckwheat, spiderling, white mat, creosote bush and members of the Grass, Pea, Mustard, Lily, and Nightshade families (see Adams, Chapter 10, and Phillips, Chapter 11).

Feature 41 was an occupation surface associated with a cluster of three small postholes. The feature included an area of well-defined, ash-stained floor which faded into a less clearly defined surface. The three postholes may be the remains of a light structure, possibly a windbreak. The presence of a small number of non-diagnostic red-on-brown sherds and one diagnostic Rincon Red-on-brown sherd suggested Feature 41 was associated with the late Middle Formative/Rincon phase Hohokam

Table 4.28. Subfeatures excavated from Feature 41

Feature No.	Description	Length (m)	Width (m)	Depth (m)	Artifacts/Samples
41.01	Fence post (Historic & not associated with Feature 41)	0.08	0.08	0.40	Preserved late historic/ modern wood
41.02	Posthole	0.10	0.10	0.22	–
41.03	Posthole	0.10	0.08	0.18	–
41.04	Posthole	0.10	0.10	0.16	–

Table 4.29. Artifacts recovered from Feature 41	
	Floor Fill
Flaked Stone	
Debitage	238
Cores	3
Uniface	1
Subtotal	*242*
Ceramics	
Indeterminte red-on-brown	2
Brown ware	16
Undersized	3
Subtotal	*21*
Ground Stone	
Flat Mano	1
Trough Mano	1
Lapstone (pigment processing)	1
Subtotal	*3*
Shell	
Freshwater shell	1
Total	267

occupation of the site. Feature 41 is comparable with Feature 51 at the Tanque Verde Wash site (Elson, ed. 1986:107). Both features had burned wood, small postholes and a floor surface which was primarily unprepared, sterile stratum. Very limited interpretation of these features is possible, but Feature 41 may be related to Feature 6 (described above). Both features were located at similar elevations, were relatively close to one another, and were overlain by fill that contained fragments of daub and burned beams.

Extramural Pits

Extramural pits were the most numerous feature recorded at the Marsh Station Road site. During this investigation, 173 pits were recorded—approximately two thirds (n = 117, 67 percent) of which were excavated. The pre-

historic inhabitants of sites in southern Arizona lived mostly outdoors, and as such, pit features have been seen as the key to understanding their use of extramural space (Whittlesey 2004a:56; Wöcherl 2005). At least some of our knowledge about pit function derives from eth-nographic analogy (e.g., see Gasser et al. 1990; Halbirt et al. 1993), although archaeological studies have become increasingly interested in investigating pit function in recent years (e.g., Craig and Walsh-Anduze 2001; Wöcherl 2005). Pits have been associated with a variety of cooking and processing activities and were not necessarily limited to one use, but rather might have had multiple uses throughout their use-life, possibly in a functional cycle. Thus, the contents of an archaeologically excavated pit do not necessarily represent its original func-tion or purpose (Halbirt et al. 1993; Schiffer 1976). In the Southwest, pits of all types are often found to contain trash, although it has been suggested that pits were never dug with the express purpose of trash disposal (Archer 1998:79). Rather, it may be that trash disposal was the last use of a pit exhausted for other purposes (e.g., an infested storage pit). As with the excavated pithouses, the pits at the Marsh Station Road site were not generally characterized by dense trash fills.

Chronological Development of Pits

Extramural pits are one of the most common feature types recorded at archaeological sites in the Southwest, and they have a long developmental history. In Arizona, extramural pits have sometimes been associated with Paleoindian occupations, although these associations are often equivocal (Mabry 1998:107). The association of many pit forms—slab-lined and unlined pits, trash-filled pits, rock-filled roasting pits—with Early Archaic settlements seems to be more secure, however. It seems that almost the full repertoire of pit forms were developed during the Archaic period, and the range of pits has remained fairly consistent since this time. No innovative pit forms are associated with significant changes in subsistence activity, such as the adoption of agriculture, although the number and types of pits in use at any given time appears to have increased as reliance on agricultural produce developed (e.g., see Wöcherl 2005). Even at Classic period sites (e.g., see Craig and Walsh-Anduze 2001), the range of reported pit types is consistent with earlier sites, possibly excepting the prevalence of puddling pits used in architectural adobe production.

What this long-term consistency in pit type means is that the age of pit features must be drawn from the study of their contents, rather than from the form of the pits themselves. An individual pit feature is therefore difficult, although not impossible, to evaluate,

especially if it is unexcavated. Wöcherl (2005) was able to suggest chronological trends related to subsistence changes in pits and their contents at specific sites through the Early Agricultural and Early Ceramic periods in southern Arizona. Even within this patterning, however, it was clear that individual sites in the study area had distinctive trajectories, probably reflecting adaptation to their unique environment; pit use evolved differently at Los Pozos and Las Capas (Wöcherl 2005:46), despite their relative spatial proximity and approximately coeval occupations.

Classification of Pit Forms

Extramural and subfeature pits excavated at the Marsh Station Road site were categorized by type based upon in-field determinations of feature type using a system of feature codes widely used throughout southern Arizona. Occasionally pit features were reclassified post-excavation based on a review of the excavation data and/or material and environmental analysis data. Unexcavated pit features were assigned a type based on their visible morphology and condition, although it should be understood that these designations are tentative without excavation evidence. In the field, all excavated pit features were initially divided into thermal and nonthermal features, and then classified more specifically by type, for example as a roasting pit or a bell pit. Attributes used to classify pits include morphology, preparation (e.g., lining, plaster, etc.), evidence of thermal activity, and artifact and/or environmental data.

In addition to the in-field pit type feature coding, pits at the Marsh Station Road site were also categorized using Wöcherl's (2005) classification scheme. Wöcherl's scheme is derived from her study of primarily Early Agricultural (San Pedro and Cienega phase) period pit features, and therefore seemed applicable to the pit features at the Marsh Station Road site, which we initially believed contained a significant Early Agricultural component (see discussion, above). Although the results of the radiocarbon and archaeomagnetic dating later revealed that most of the pits probably dated to the late Middle Formative period rather than to the Early Agricultural period, we retained the pit classification scheme, as there is no overt reason why the scheme, which is based on pit morphology, would not be applicable to pits dating to other periods given that overall pit morphology seems to have changed very little through time.

Wöcherl's (2005) classification scheme distinguishes seven types of pits (Table 4.30), although in practice, the distinction between circular and oval pits did not seem appropriate for the assemblage of pits excavated at the Marsh Station Road site. The populations of basin-shaped and straight-sided pits are each considered as a whole; merging Classes 1 and 3, and Classes 2 and 4. No conical pits were recorded at the Marsh Station Road site, affirming Wöcherl's (2005:20) note that they are rare. In contrast, irregular pits were well represented in the excavated sample.

Thermal and Nonthermal Pits

Pit features may be divided into thermal and nonthermal features. This binary distinction cuts across the morphological distinctions

Table 4.30. Wöcherl Pit Classification Scheme

Class 1	Basin-shaped, circular
Class 2	Straight-sided, circular
Class 3	Basin-shaped, oval
Class 4	Straight-sided, oval
Class 5	Bell-shaped
Class 6	Conical
Class 7	Irregular

Note: from Wöcherl (2005)

of the Wöcherl classification, as pits within one class may exhibit thermal or nonthermal characteristics. Halbirt and others (1993) made an extensive study of thermal pits and their likely components. They noted that the properties of thermal pits could be varied, and that this was related to context and ultimately function. For example, ash results from the complete combustion of wood, while charcoal results from a more limited oxygen supply. Ash might therefore be expected in shallow, open pits, whereas charcoal would be likely in deeper, more confined pits. Thus, a shallow hearth might contain ash, while a deep roasting pit would more likely contain charcoal.

The determination of thermal versus nonthermal pits may be subjective. Thermally generated material—ash and charcoal—would be present in the general cultural debris of a site and could be incorporated into nonthermal pits fairly easily. The evaluation of whether the presence of ash and/or charcoal is related to the function of the pit is really a judgment of the density of material present, the type of material (e.g., FCR, burned artifacts) present, and other characteristics of the pits, such as oxidation/reduction on the pit walls. The same is true of fire-cracked (or fire-affected) rock, which has a functional role in roasting pits, but also has other uses, such as heating water. Residual FCR from previously used features would also be present on the site and might be, and often is, incorporated in nonthermal pit fill. It has been suggested that rock was deliberately cached at some sites, for future reuse. The Archaic occupants of the Coffee Camp site studied by Halbirt and others (1993:131) would have had to import rock desired for pits, and might be expected to have curated it for reuse. The occupants of the Marsh Station Road site, however, would not have faced this problem, and might be expected to have been more concerned with clearing away inconvenient material.

In addition to the presence (or absence)

of ash, charcoal, and FCR, the color of the sediment within, near, and at the base of the pit is also considered in assessing whether the feature should be considered thermal or nonthermal. Intense heat within a feature, combined with an adequate supply of oxygen, might oxidize the sediment around the edge of the pit, creating red colors. Deep thermal pits at the Marsh Station Road site, however, tended to show a bluish-grey discoloration of terrace gravel rocks around their edges and at their base, which was interpreted as a reduction effect, the result of heat on the caliche coating the rocks in an oxygen-deprived environment. Thermal effects such as this are really the best indicator of a thermal feature. Note, however, that Wöcherl (2005:22) suggests many storage pits would be fired as part of the process of preparing the pit for use.

The Population of Pits at the Marsh Station Road Site

As indicated above, the project identified 173 extramural pit features at the Marsh Station Road site. Approximately two thirds of these features were excavated (n = 117; 67 percent). Most (n = 144) of these pits were exposed in their entirety in mechanically or manually stripped units. These features were typically bisected, with the entire feature fill excavated in two feature excavation units. Pits were also discovered during mechanical trenching (n = 28). The remaining, in-situ fill of these pits was manually excavated. Samples and artifacts were collected from pits discovered during mechanical trenching, and their dimensions and cross sections were inferred. Two pits (Features 207 and 208), both rock-filled roasting pits, were discovered during monitoring. The locations and profiles of these pits were recorded, but they were excluded from the analysis of excavated pits. Recording of the unexcavated features (n = 55) was limited to measuring their surface extent and mapping their location. All unexcavated pit features were tentatively designated as thermal or nonthermal, and only a few could be assigned more specific provisional types (e.g., roasting pit). The unexcavated pits contribute to the understanding of the total distribution of features within the site, but are excluded from the discussion and tables which follow due to the limited information regarding their morphology and contents (but see Appendix I, Table C and Table 4.5).

A detailed description of each pit from the Marsh Station Road site would be redundant. Instead, general remarks are made about each class of pit, the excavated pit features are summarized in tables, and a few representative examples are described for each class. Generally two examples of each class were judged sufficient to represent the sample, with preference given to features associated with radiocarbon dates. Material suitable for carbon dating was not abundant at the Marsh Station Road site, but samples were obtained from two basin, one straight-sided, three bell, and three irregular pits. Each of these features was therefore described in order to place the samples in context.

Basin Pits

Basin pits were the most common class of excavated pit feature (n = 43), representing 37 percent of the excavated pits (Table 4.31). Ten of the basin pits were thermal features. As this category encompasses Wöcherl's Classes 1 and 3 in both thermal and nonthermal forms, it is likely that a range of functions are represented. There was considerable variation in the sizes and depths of these pits, and in the ratios of width-to-depth. None of the pits was really deep relative to width; the deeper pits were about twice as wide as they were deep, while the shallowest ones were up to seven times as wide as they were deep. Saucer-shaped (shal-

Table 4.31. Summary of basin pit characteristics

Feature No.	Pit Type[a]	Locus	Excavated	Wöcherl Pit Class	Dimensions (m) Length	Width	Depth	Fill Inclusions	Artifacts	Samples
5	TP	SA 5	Partial	3	0.79	0.60	0.30	Charcoal & FCR (abundant)	Ceramics, flaked stone	Flotation, pollen, macrobotanical
10	NTP	SA 4	100%	1	0.92	0.84	0.30	Charcoal (moderate), FCR (minor)	Flaked stone debitage, biface, & core; ground stone, faunal bone	Flotation, pollen
23	NTP	S TR 6	Partial	3	0.90	0.70	0.44		Ceramics, flaked stone debitage & core	Flotation, pollen
28	TP	SA 4	100%	1	0.20	0.73	0.28	Ash (moderate), Charcoal (fair), FCR (abundant)	Ceramics, ground stone, faunal bone, mineral	Flotation, pollen, macrobotanical
29	TP	SA 4	100%	1	0.86	0.85	0.50	Charcoal & FCR (abundant)	Ceramics	Flotation, pollen
30	TP	SA 4	100%	1	0.87	1.00	0.45	Charcoal (moderate), FCR (abundant)	Ceramics	Flotation, pollen
31	NTP	SA 4	100%	1	0.61	0.61	0.28	Charcoal (minor)	Flaked stone, mineral, faunal bone	Flotation, pollen, macrobotanical
33	TP	SA 4	100%	1	0.43	0.43	0.20	Ash (fair), FCR (moderate)	Ceramics, flaked stone debitage and core	Flotation, pollen
39	TP	SA 5	Partial	3	0.66	0.19	0.26	FCR (moderate)	Ceramics, flaked stone	Flotation, pollen
49	NTP	SA 5	100%	1	0.77	0.62	0.11	Ash & Charcoal (minor)	Ceramics, flaked stone	Flotation
53	NTP	SA 5	100%	1	0.55	0.65	0.15	Charcoal and FCR (minor)	Ceramics, flaked stone debitage & cores, faunal bone	Flotation, pollen
60	TP	SA 4	100%	3	0.58	0.48	0.14	Charcoal (minor), FCR (abundant)	Ceramics, flaked stone debitage & biface; ground stone	

Table 4.31. Summary of basin pit characteristics, cont'd.

Feature No.	Pit Type[a]	Locus	Excavated	Wöcherl Pit Class	Dimensions (m)			Fill Inclusions	Artifacts	Samples
					Length	Width	Depth			
61	TP	SA 4	100%	1	1.10	1.00	0.18	Ash & Charcoal (minor), FCR (moderate)	Ceramics, flaked stone debitage, cores, & uniface; faunal bone	Flotation
64	NTP	SA 4	100%	1	0.58	0.86	0.10	Charcoal (minor), FCR (abundant)	Ceramics, flaked stone	Flotation, pollen
73	NTP	SA 4	100%	3	1.16	0.39	0.41		Flaked stone debitage & uniface; ground stone	Flotation, pollen
78	NTP	SA 4	100%	3	0.62	0.60	0.17	FCR (minor)	Ceramics, flaked stone debitage & biface	Flotation, pollen
81	TP	SA 4	100%	1	0.58	0.56	0.34	Ash, Charcoal, & FCR (moderate)	Ceramics, flaked stone, ground stone, glass	Flotation, pollen
85	NTP	SA 5	100%	1	0.59	0.58	0.10	Charcoal & FCR (minor)	Flaked stone	Flotation, pollen
89	NTP	SA 5	100%	1	0.22	0.20	0.15		Flaked stone	Flotation
90	NTP	N TR 13	Partial	1	0.22	0.85	0.42	Charcoal & FCR (minor)	Ceramics, flaked stone, ground stone	Flotation, pollen
94	NTP	SA 5	100%	1	0.80	0.72	0.11	FCR (minor)	Flaked stone, ground stone	Flotation, pollen
96	NTP	SA 4	100%	1	1.02	1.05	0.18	FCR (minor)	Flaked stone debitage & biface; mineral	Flotation
99	NTP	SA 3	100%	1	0.43	0.55	0.17		Flaked stone	Flotation, pollen
101	NTP	SA 3	100%	1	0.83	0.75	0.14		Flaked stone	Flotation, pollen
103	NTP	SA 3	100%	3	1.36	1.18	0.14		Ceramic, flaked stone	Flotation, pollen
104	NTP	SA 3	100%	3	0.75	0.61	0.24		Flaked stone debitage & biface	Flotation, pollen
106	NTP	SA 4	100%	1	0.57	0.50	0.16	Charcoal & FCR (minor)	Flaked stone	Flotation, pollen

Table 4.31. Summary of basin pit characteristics, cont'd.

Feature	Pit type	SA	Completeness	Count				Thermal evidence	Artifacts	Samples
107	NTP	SA 4	100%	3	1.70	0.90	0.57		Ceramics, flaked stone, ground stone, faunal bone	Flotation, pollen, radiocarbon
111	NTP	SA 4	100%	1	0.69	0.60	0.17	Charcoal & FCR (minor)	Flaked stone, faunal bone	Flotation, pollen
114	NTP	SA 5	100%	3	1.40	0.90	0.22	FCR (minor)	Flaked stone debitage & biface	Flotation, pollen
115	NTP	SA 4	100%	1	0.62	0.50	0.09	Charcoal (minor)	Flaked stone	Flotation, pollen
116	NTP	SA 4	100%	1	0.75	0.70	0.19	Charcoal & FCR (minor)	Flaked stone	Flotation, pollen
117	NTP	SA 4	100%	1	0.67	0.66	0.27		Ceramics, flaked stone debitage, core, & biface; faunal bone	Flotation, pollen
118	TP	SA 4	100%	1	0.95	0.88	0.45	Ash (fair), FCR (minor)	Ceramics, flaked stone debitage & uniface, faunal bone	Flotation, pollen, macrobotanical
120	NTP	SA 3	100%	3	0.80	1.20	0.32	FCR (minor)	Flaked stone debitage, core, & biface	Flotation, pollen
123	NTP	SA 3	100%	1	1.22	1.12	0.12	FCR (minor)	Flaked stone	Flotation, pollen
124	NTP	SA 3	100%	1	0.97	1.17	0.90	Ash (minor), FCR (abundant)	Flaked stone, ground stone	Flotation, pollen
127	NTP	SA 4	100%	1	0.89	0.85	0.10		Flaked stone debitage & biface	
130	NTP	SA 4	100%	3	1.25	0.85	0.23	Ash (minor)	Ceramics, flaked stone debitage & core	Flotation, pollen, macrobotanical
131	NTP	SA 4	100%	1	0.56	0.50	0.06	Ash (fair)	Ceramic	Flotation
142	NTP	SA 3	100%	3	0.95	0.88	0.28	Ash & FCR (minor)	Flaked stone	Flotation, pollen
145	NTP	SA 3	100%	1	0.81	0.85	0.12	FCR (minor)	Ceramic, flaked stone	Flotation, pollen
149	NTP	SA 4	Partial	1	1.15	0.25	0.63	FCR (minor)	Ceramics, flaked stone, ground stone, faunal bone	Flotation, pollen

[a]NTP: Non-thermal pit; TP: Thermal pit; FCR: Fire-cracked rock

low basin) pits analyzed by Halbirt and others (1993) tended to be associated with thermal attributes, and were interpreted as hearths or open cooking pits, uses suggested for non-thermal basin pits include as basket rests and for food processing. Hull (1984) attempted to correlate different plant species with processing pits of different sizes excavated at Hohokam sites along the Salt-Gila Aqueduct. Different average pit sizes did emerge (Hull 1984:Figure III.3.3.), but all features appeared to have been used for processing more than one plant. Other than as general roasting pits or nonthermal pits, specific functions for the basin pits at the Marsh Station Road site were not determined.

Feature 49

Feature 49 originated in Stratum 3 over-burden, and less than 10 cm of overburden was mechanically stripped to expose this feature in plan view. The feature was excavated in two units, each in one stratigraphic level. All fill was screened through ¼-inch mesh. Feature 49 originated at a higher elevation than, and was intrusive to, Feature 7.

Fill from Feature 49 consisted of moderately compacted brown sand and silt with numerous pea-sized gravel inclusions and small amounts of charcoal and ash. Fifteen cobbles were present at the top of the exposed feature fill, but no FCR was observed in the feature fill. No artifacts were recovered from the fill of Feature 49.

Feature 49 was identified as a small, circular, nonthermal, basin pit (see Table 4.32). The feature's walls were insloping and unlined. As no other evidence of thermal activity, such as oxidized walls/basin or FCR, were noted in the feature fill, the small amount of ash and charcoal observed in the fill probably derived from general on-site occupation debris.

One radiocarbon date (Beta-234158) was obtained from a charred maize cupule recovered from Feature 49 (see Table 4.6). The sample yielded a 2 sigma calibrated date of A.D. 1010 to 1170.

Only one environmental sample, a flotation sample, was collected and analyzed from Feature 49. Analysis of macrobotanical remains recovered from the flotation sample identified mesquite and maize (see Adams, Chapter 10, and Phillips, Chapter 11).

Feature 49, a small nonthermal pit, was located in Stripped Area 4. No artifacts were recovered from Feature 49, suggesting that it was completely cleaned out after its use life, and likely was in-filled rather quickly, most likely with sediment from the general site area. Its stratigraphic relationship to other nearby features, in particular to Feature 7, to which Feature 49 was intrusive, indicates that this nonthermal pit postdates Feature 7, but not by much given the close correspondence in radiocarbon dates between the two features. The single radiocarbon date obtained from pit fill indicates that the feature probably dates to the Rincon phase/late Middle Formative period.

Table 4.32. Characteristics of Feature 49

Feature Type:	Nonthermal pit
Cultural Affiliation:	Unknown
Temporal Affiliation:	late Middle Formative (middle–late Rincon phase)
Diagnostic Artifacts:	None
Subfeatures:	–
Provenience:	SA 4
Shape:	Basin, circular
Dimensions:	0.77 m by 0.62 m; 0.11 m deep; estimated volume: 0.04 m³
Depth below datum:	95.02 z–94.91 z
Stratum:	Stratum 3: Overburden; less than 10 cm below modern ground surface

Feature 61

Feature 61 originated in Stratum 3 over-burden, and less than 10 cm of overburden was mechanically stripped to expose this feature. The feature was excavated in two units, in one stratigraphic level. All fill was screened through ¼-inch mesh. Feature 61 appeared to be superimposed over the edge of Feature 11, thereby stratigraphically overlying that feature.

Fill from Feature 61 consisted of slightly compacted brown sand and silt with numerous hardened, reddish inclusions and small amounts of charcoal and ash. The fill included a moderate amount of rock, about half of which (n = 15) was identified as fire-cracked. Eighty artifacts were recovered from the fill of Feature 61 (Table 4.34), although none were diagnostic.

Feature 61 was identified as a broad, shallow indeterminate thermal pit (Figure 4.37; also see Table 4.33). No clearly defined walls were visible, and the feature's boundaries were determined based on the extent of FCR, associated rock pile, and artifact distribution. The base, however, was clearly defined as an exposure of sterile caliche.

One radiocarbon date (Beta-234159) was obtained from a charred maize cupule recovered from Feature 61 (see Table 4.6). The sample yielded a 2 sigma calibrated date of A.D. 540 to 650.

One environmental sample, a flotation sample, was collected and analyzed from Feature 61. Analysis of macrobotanical remains recovered from the flotation sample identified mesquite, juniper, and maize (see Adams, Chapter 10, and Phillips, Chapter 11).

Feature 61, an indeterminate thermal pit, was located in Stripped Area 4. A small artifact assemblage was recovered from Feature 61. Its stratigraphic relationship to other nearby features, in particular to Feature 11, which it overlays, indicates that this thermal

Table 4.33. Characteristics of Feature 61

Feature Type:	Thermal pit
Cultural Affiliation:	Unknown
Temporal Affiliation:	late Early Formative? (Tortolita phase?)
Diagnostic Artifacts:	None
Subfeatures:	–
Provenience:	SA 5
Shape:	Basin, circular
Dimensions:	1.10 m by 0.62 m; 1.00 m deep; estimated volume: 0.15 m³
Depth below datum:	94.81 z–94.63 z
Stratum:	Stratum 3: Overburden; less than 10 cm below modern ground surface

Table 4.34. Artifacts recovered from the fill of Feature 61

Flaked Stone	
Debitage	58
Cores	3
Uniface	1
Subtotal	*62*
Ceramics	
Brown ware	15
Faunal Remains	
Hares and Rabbits	1
Unidentified mammal	1
Mammal/bird	1
Subtotal	*3*
Total	80

FEATURE 61

MN B
469.41 N
324.01 E

MN A
470.73 N
323.99 E

MN B

MN A

Z=94.82

N →

0   0.1   0.25   0.5 meters

	Feature Outline		Rock
	Feature Outline at Base		Mapping Nail
	String Elevation for Profiles		Flaked Stone
	Caliche		Ceramic Sherd

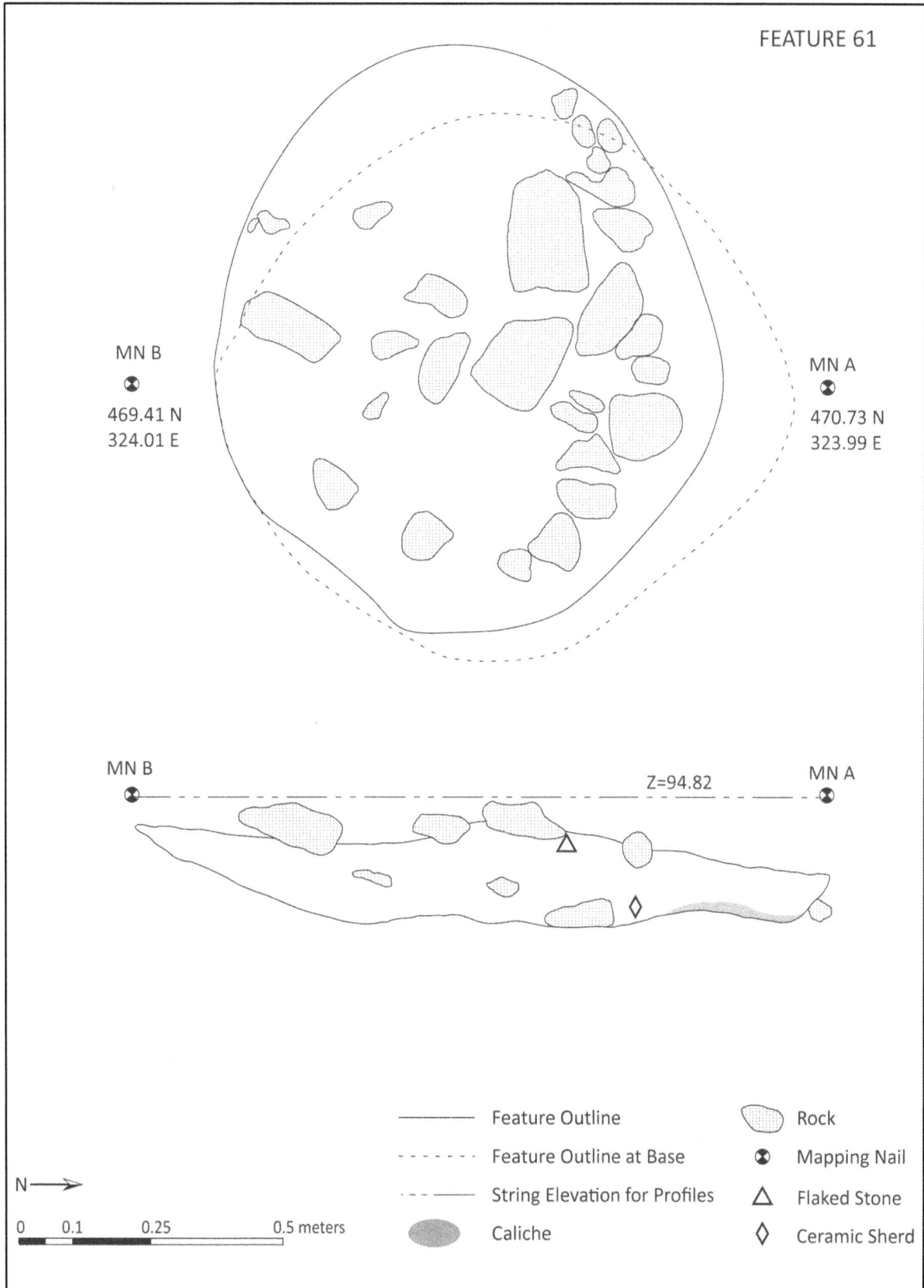

Figure 4.37. Plan and profile view of Feature 61.

pit postdates the pit structure. However, the single radiocarbon date obtained from pit fill indicates that the Feature 61 probably dates to the Tortolita or late Snaketown phase/late Early Formative period, while radiocarbon dates suggest that Feature 11 dates to the Rincon phase/late Middle Formative period. As discussed above, it is possible that the subfeature from which the Feature 11 radiocarbon date is associated is actually intrusive to Feature 11, and that the pithouse itself is Early Agricultural in age. This interpretation seems bolstered by the stratigraphic position and radiocarbon age of Feature 61.

Straight-sided Pits

A total of 21 straight-sided pits were recorded at the Marsh Station Road site (Table 4.35). This category of pit represented approximately 18 percent of the total number of excavated pits. Straight-sided pits were split between Wöcherl's Class 2 (n = 7) and Class 4 (n = 14). None of the straight-sided pits were thermal features. As with the basin pits, the straight-sided pits were not very deep relative to their width; the deepest features were twice as wide as they were deep. The shallowest feature (Feature 113) was twelve times as wide as it was deep, although this feature may have been truncated by a stripped unit. Straight-sided pits have been repeatedly interpreted as storage features (Craig and Walsh-Anduze 2001; Hackbarth 1993; Halbirt et al. 1993), and this is probably true for some of the Marsh Station Road pits. Others, however, seem rather shallow for storage pits. The straight-sided storage pit shown by Wöcherl (2005:Figure 218), for example, appears to be quite deep. At the Early Agricultural site of Los Pozos, straight-sided pits were seen to be closely related to bell pits, and might have been paired in some instances (Wöcherl 2005:44–45). Other than as general nonthermal pits, or as discussed above, specific

functions for the straight-sided pits at the Marsh Station Road site were not determined.

Feature 44

Feature 44 originated in Stratum 3 overburden, and less than 10 cm of overburden was mechanically stripped to expose this feature. The feature was excavated in two units, in one stratigraphic level. All fill was screened through ¼-inch mesh.

Fill from Feature 44 consisted of variably compact brown sandy loam, with small amounts of charcoal. Fill near the top of the feature was very hard and compact, but quickly became soft and loosely compacted. Thirty small pieces of FCR and charcoal flecking were recorded, but no oxidation was observed in this feature. The pit also included three large, rounded, caliche-coated rocks. These did not appear to be fire-cracked.

A total of 195 artifacts were recovered from the fill of Feature 44 (Table 4.37). A complete San Pedro projectile point was the only diagnostic artifact recovered from Feature 44.

Feature 44 was identified as a large, oval, shallow nonthermal pit (Figure 4.38; also see Table 4.36). The walls were straight-sided and unprepared; the base was fairly flat and composed of a sterile caliche horizon. Although numerous rocks, including some FCR, were recovered primarily from the western half of this feature, it is unclear how they were incorporated in the feature fill. The rocks may represent roasting or boiling stones and may have been dumped into the feature at some point in the past.

One sample (Beta-236521)—a charred maize cupule—was submitted for radiocarbon dating, but the sample was too small for $13C/12C$ ratio measurement and AMS analysis (see Table 4.6). However, Beta Analytic combined both natural and laboratory techniques (chemical and detector induced fractionation)

Table 4.35. Summary of straight-sided pit characteristics

Feature No.	Pit Type	Locus	Excavated	Wöcherl Pit Class	Dimensions (m)			Fill Inclusions	Artifacts	Samples
					Length	Width	Depth			
9	NTP	SA 4	100%	4	1.00	1.50	0.17		Ceramics, flaked stone, faunal bone	Flotation, pollen
13	NTP	N TR 13	Partial	2	0.98	0.60	0.21	Charcoal & FCR (minor)	Ceramics, flaked stone, faunal bone, glass	Flotation, pollen
14	NTP	TR 13	Partial	2	0.60	0.97	0.12	Charcoal & FCR (minor)		Flotation
21	NTP	SA 3	100%	2	0.67	0.82	0.30	Charcoal (minor)	Flaked stone, faunal bone, metal	Flotation, pollen
22	NTP	SA 3	100%	4	0.59	0.90	0.15	Charcoal (minor)	Flaked stone	Flotation, pollen
38	NTP	SA 3	100%	4	0.67	0.55	0.10	Charcoal & FCR (minor)	Ceramics, flaked stone	Flotation, pollen
44	NTP	SA 3	100%	4	1.10	0.95	0.56	Charcoal & FCR (minor)	Ceramics, flaked stone debitage, cores, & biface; faunal bone	Flotation, pollen
54	NTP	SA 4	Partial	2	1.80	0.65	0.24	Charcoal (minor)	Ceramics, flaked stone debitage, cores, & bifaces	Flotation, pollen
57	NTP	TR 13	Partial	2	1.05	0.90	0.35	FCR (moderate)	Ceramics, flaked stone debitage, tools, & cores; ground stone, faunal bone	Macrobotanical, pollen
74	NTP	SA 3	Partial	4	0.96+	0.64+	0.43	Charcoal (minor)	Flaked stone debitage, cores, & uniface	Flotation, pollen

Table 4.35. Summary of straight-sided pit characteristics, cont'd.

Feature No.	Pit Type	Locus	Excavated	Wöcherl Pit Class	Dimensions (m)			Fill Inclusions	Artifacts	Samples
					Length	Width	Depth			
75	NTP	SA 4	100%	2	1.04	0.33	0.37		Ceramics, flaked stone debitage & core	Flotation
79	NTP	SA 4	100%	4	0.62	0.50	0.24	FCR (minor)	Ceramic, faunal bone	Flotation, pollen
93	NTP	SA 4	100%	4	1.80	1.07	0.26	FCR (minor)	Flaked stone debitage, cores, & biface; faunal bone	Flotation, pollen
97	NTP	SA 4	100%	2	1.21	0.85	0.36		Ceramics, flaked stone debitage & bifaces	Flotation, pollen
100	NTP	SA 3	Partial	2	0.78	0.55	0.16			Flotation
108	NTP	SA 3	100%	2	0.80	0.70	0.42	Charcoal & FCR (minor)	Flaked stone	Flotation
1101	NTP	SA 4	100%	2	0.75	0.94	0.19	Charcoal (minor)	Ceramics, flaked stone, worked shell	Flotation, pollen
113	NTP	SA 5	100%	2	1.01	0.86	0.08	Charcoal & FCR (minor)	Flake stone debitage & core, faunal bone	Flotation, pollen
126	NTP	SA 3	100%	2	0.60	0.66	0.24	Charcoal (minor)	Flaked stone	Flotation, pollen
140	NTP	SA 3	100%	2	1.13	0.93	0.17		Ceramics, flaked stone	
141	NTP	SA 4	100%	2	1.26	1.31	0.35	FCR (minor)	Ceramics, flaked stone debitage & bifaces	Flotation, pollen

MN B
489.73N
314.95E

MN A
491.10N
314.97E

MN A
491.10N
314.97E

Z=94.92

MN B
489.73N
314.95E

94.36

FEATURE 44

N

0   0.1   0.25   0.5 meters

Feature Outline   Mapping Nail

String Elevation for Profile   Rock

Top of Caliche Stratum   Rodent Burrow

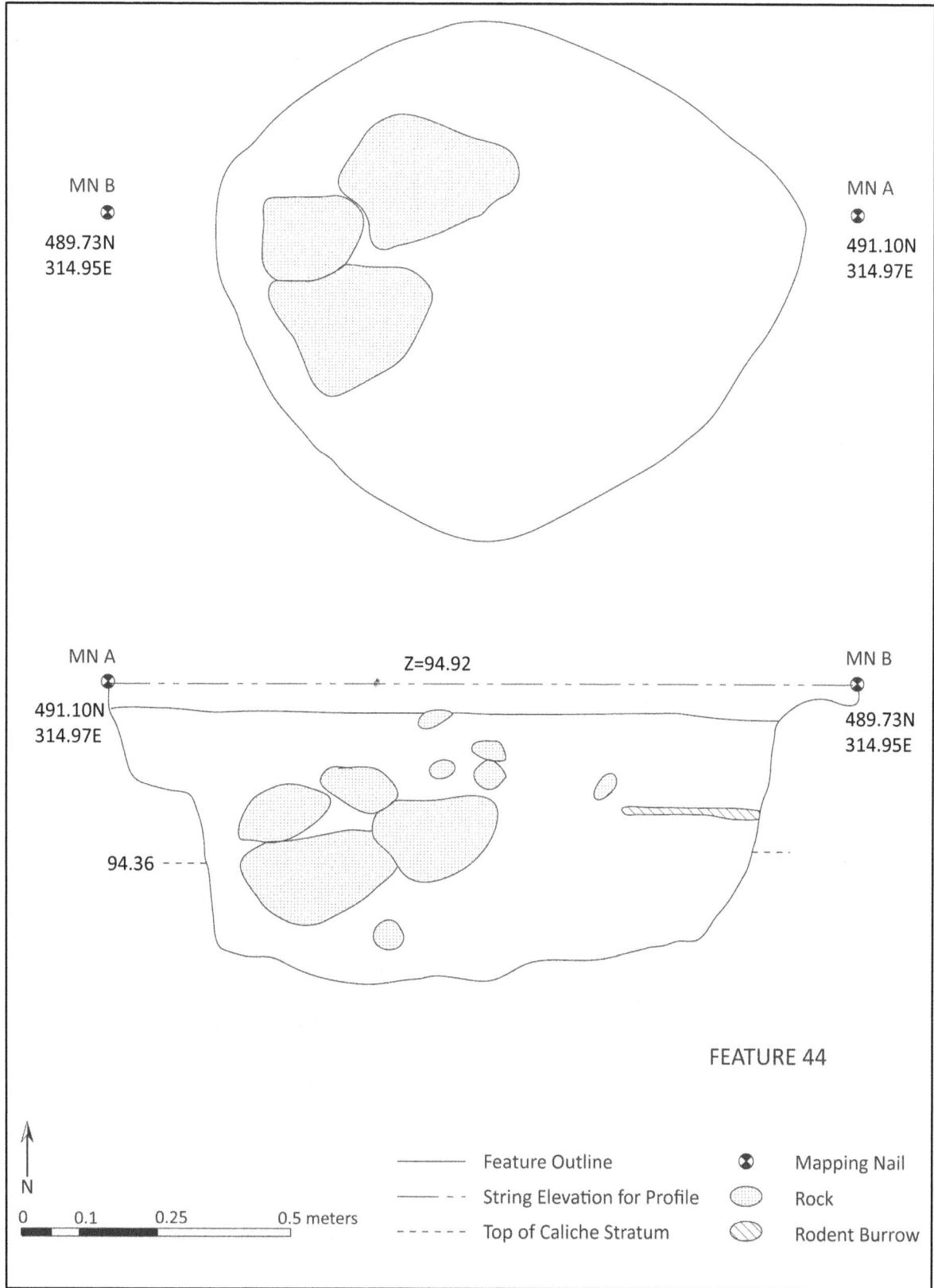

Figure 4.38. Plan and profile view of Feature 44.

Table 4.36. Characteristics of Feature 44

Feature Type:	Nonthermal pit
Cultural Affiliation:	Unknown
Temporal Affiliation:	Early Agricultural (San Pedro phase)
Diagnostic Artifacts:	San Pedro point
Subfeatures:	–
Provenience:	SA 3
Shape:	Straight-sided, oval
Dimensions:	1.10 m by 0.95 m; 0.56 m deep; estimated volume: 0.46 m³
Depth below datum:	94.66 z–94.10 z
Stratum:	Stratum 3: Overburden; less than 10 cm below modern ground surface

Table 4.37. Artifacts recovered from the fill of Feature 44

Flaked Stone	
Debitage	146
Cores	3
Projectile point	1
Subtotal	*150*
Ceramics	
Indeterminate red-on-brown	1
Brown ware	9
Undersized	7
Subtotal	*17*
Shell	
Freshwater shell	1
Faunal Remains	
Ungulate	21
Artiodactyl	5
Unidentified mammal	1
Subtotal	*27*
Total	195

to measure a ratio during 14C detection to derive a Conventional Radiocarbon Age, suitable for applicable calendar calibration. The sample yielded a 2 sigma calibrated date of 1120 to 810 B.C.

One environmental sample, a flotation sample, was collected and analyzed from Feature 44. Analysis of macrobotanical remains recovered from the flotation sample identified mesquite, saltbush, and maize (see Adams, Chapter 10). Feature 44, a large, oval, shallow nonthermal pit excavated in SA 3, was one of two features (the other being Feature 98, discussed below) at the site radiocarbon dated to the Early Agricultural period. Within SA 3, Feature 44 is located near several other identified features (see Figure 4.23); however, none of these other features were excavated, and as a result, it is not possible to discuss its stratigraphic relationship to these other features.

Feature 97

Feature 97, which originated at the surface of sterile Stratum 2 deposits, was identified during the excavation of FE 5 of Feature 7, to which it was intrusive. Test Unit 86 was then excavated immediately west of Feature 97 in order to determine its extent. What was thought to be Feature 97 was discovered at the bottom of Level 1 in TU 86, at which point FE 1 of Feature 97 was excavated. However, it was later determined that FE 1 actually corresponded to another nonthermal pit, Feature 129, which was intrusive to Feature 97; the western boundary of Feature 97 only slightly overlapped with Feature 129 (Figure 4.39). Following this initial excavation, what was believed to be Feature 97, represented by reddish-brown fill distinct from the surrounding fill in Features 7 and 129, was divided into two units, FE 2 and FE 3, which were excavated in one stratigraphic level; all fill was screened through ¼-inch mesh.

Fill within Feature 97 was moderately compact, brown, silty sand, with small amounts of charcoal. Although the fill corresponded with a solid brown categorization, it appeared reddish-brown relative to the surrounding fill. Rock was abundant in the pit, accounting for about half the volume of the fill. Some of the rock appeared to be fire-affected, but most did not. No oxidation was observed in this pit. Just 24 artifacts were recovered from the fill of Feature 97 (Table 4.39). None of the artifacts were diagnostic.

Feature 97 was identified as a medium, circular, shallow, nonthermal pit (see Figure

Table 4.38. Characteristics of Feature 97

Feature Type:	Nonthermal pit
Cultural Affiliation:	Unknown
Temporal Affiliation:	late Middle Formative (Rincon phase)
Diagnostic Artifacts:	None
Subfeatures:	–
Provenience:	SA 4
Shape:	Straight-sided, circular
Dimensions:	1.21 m by 0.85 m; 0.36 m deep; estimated volume: 0.31 m³
Depth below datum:	94.74 z–94.38 z
Stratum:	Stratum 2: surface of Pleistocene terrace deposits with modern caliche development; more than 10 cm below modern ground surface

Table 4.39. Artifacts recovered from the fill of Feature 97

Flaked Stone	
Debitage	22
Projectile point	1
Subtotal	23
Faunal Remains	
Hares and Rabbits	1
Total	24

4.39). The walls were straight-sided and unprepared; the base was fairly flat and composed of a sterile caliche horizon (see Table 4.38). Although numerous pieces of FCR were observed in the fill of this feature, it is unclear how they came to be incorporated into the fill. The rocks may represent roasting or boiling stones and may have been dumped into the feature at some point in prehistory.

No suitable chronometric (radiocarbon or archaeomagnetic) samples were collected from Feature 97.

Two environmental samples, one macrobotanical sample and one flotation sample, were collected from Feature 97. The single macrobotanical sample was identified as mesquite. The flotation sample did not contain any macrobotanical material suitable for analysis (see Adams, Chapter 10).

Feature 97, a medium nonthermal pit, was identified in SA 4 as one in a cluster of three (the other two being Feature 129 and Feature 59; see Figure 4.39) nonthermal pits. Stratigraphic observations suggested that Feature 97 was the earliest of the three pits, although no radiocarbon samples and no diagnostic artifacts were recovered from the fill of this pit. However, Feature 97 was also identified as intrusive to Feature 7, which was determined to date to the Rincon phase/late Middle Formative period. It stands to reason that Feature 97 also dates to or postdates this phase.

Bell Pits

Sixteen bell pits were excavated at the Marsh Station Road site, representing 14 percent of the total number of excavated extramural pits (Table 4.40). There was considerable variation in the dimensions of these features: aperture diameters ranged from 0.70 m to 1.35 m, and depths ranged from 0.25 m to 0.86 m. Despite this variety, bell pits are seen to represent a distinctive class of pit feature and are fairly consistently interpreted as storage facilities (Archer 1998:66; Craig and Walsh-Anduze 2001:132; Hackbarth 1993:514), and more specifically as associated with plant-derived food storage. This is often discussed in terms of storage of agricultural surplus, but bell storage pits are fairly common in pre-agricultural Archaic sites (Halbirt et al 1993). Other functions have occasionally been suggested for bell pits. Gasser and others (1990) interpreted the bell pits at Va-pak, on the Ak-Chin Indian Community, as cooking or roasting pits. Three of the bell pits excavated at the Marsh Station Road site were interpreted as thermal features and may be roasting pits. These features include Feature 173 (described below), which had a dark, charcoal-stained fill and was densely packed with FCR. According to Wöcherl (2005), bell pits are an intentional form; the larger pits represent a considerable investment of effort. Wöcherl

(2005:38) estimates that a "good sized" bell pit would have taken at least a day to excavate, with additional preparation time before use. Set against this investment, she also notes that a suite of bell pits would have the potential to store a remarkable amount of food. The 130 bell pits excavated at Las Capas had an estimated total capacity of 41,600 quarts (Wöcherl 2005:37). Their use is widespread in space and time, not only in the American Southwest but essentially around the world (for example, the frequent excavation of bell pits in Iron Age sites in England lead Coles (1973:39–45) to conduct replication experiments and draw analogies from pits excavated in Guatemala, Mexico, Zambia, and Zimbabwe). This ubiquity demonstrates that they were an effective technology for their intended purpose, whether for storage or something else. Bell pits at the Marsh Station Road site are considered storage

Figure 4.39. Photograph of Feature 97, post-excavation, showing its relationship to Features 59 and 129; view to the north.

Table 4.40. Summary of bell pit characteristics

Feature No.	Pit Type	Locus	Excavated	Dimensions (m) Aperture Length	Aperture Width	Maximum Length	Maximum Width	Depth	Fill Inclusions	Artifacts	Samples
16	NTP	SA 4	Partial	0.96	0.80+	1.02	0.80+	0.42	Charcoal & FCR (minor)	Ceramics, flaked stone debitage, cores, & biface	Flotation
20	NTP	SA 3	Partial	0.15+	0.85	0.35+	1.13	0.29	Charcoal & FCR (minor)	Flaked stone debitage, core, & tools; faunal bone	
52	NTP	SA 5	100%	0.82	0.93	1.20	1.10	0.78	Charcoal (fair), FCR (minor)	Ceramics, flaked stone debitage, cores, & tools; ground stone	Flotation, pollen, macrobotanical
58	NTP	SA 4	100%	0.76	1.10	1.20	1.40	0.70	Charcoal (minor), FCR (moderate)	Flaked stone debitage, core, & tools; faunal bone	Flotation, pollen
59	TP	SA 4	100%	0.70	0.76	0.90	1.20	0.58	Charcoal & FCR (moderate)	Ceramics, flaked stone debitage, core, & tools; faunal bone, mineral	Flotation, pollen
67	NTP	SA 4	Partial	1.10	1.00	1.20	1.12	0.56	Charcoal & FCR (minor)	Ceramics, flaked stone debitage, cores, & uniface; faunal bone	Flotation, pollen
76	NTP	SA 4	Partial	0.83	0.42	0.90	0.54	0.38	Charcoal (minor)	Flaked stone debitage, core, & tool; faunal bone	Flotation, pollen
98	TP	SA 3	100%	0.95	1.10	1.23	1.25	0.63	Charcoal (minor), FCR (moderate)	Flaked stone debitage, cores, & tools; ground stone; mineral; faunal bone	Flotation, pollen, macrobotanical
102	NTP	SA 3	Partial	0.88	0.83	0.93	0.98	0.54	Charcoal & FCR (minor)	Flaked stone debitage & cores, faunal bone	Flotation, pollen
109	NTP	SA 4	100%	0.96	0.88	1.40	1.38	0.86	Charcoal (moderate), FCR (minor)	Ceramics, flaked stone debitage & biface, gournd stone, faunal bone, worked shell	Flotation, pollen, macrobotanical
129	NTP	SA 4	100%	1.20	1.30	1.50	1.45	0.53	Charcoal & FCR (moderate)	Ceramics, flaked stone debitage, cores, & tools, faunal bone, worked bone	Flotation, pollen, macrobotanical
134	NTP	SA 4	Partial	0.44	0.35	0.57	0.43	0.21		Flaked stone	
139	NTP	SA 5	100%	1.35	1.32	1.52	1.42	0.42	Charcoal (minor), FCR (moderate)	Ceramics, flaked stone debitage, core & tools; ground stone, faunal bone	Flotation, pollen
157	NTP	SA 3	Partial	0.50+	0.54+	0.55+	0.60+	0.42		Flaked stone debitage & biface	Flotation
165	NTP	SA 2	100%	1.05	1.05	1.12	1.12	0.25	Charcoal & FCR (moderate)	Flaked stone debitage & uniface	Flotation, pollen
173	TP	SA 1	100%	0.92	0.91	1.25	1.29	0.63	Charcoal & FCR (abundant)	Ceramics, flaked stone, ground stone, faunal bone	Flotation, pollen

pits, except for the three thermal bell pits that are likely roasting pits.

Feature 98

Feature 98 originated at the surface of Stratum 2, sterile deposits with caliche inclusions. Between 10 cm and 20 cm of overburden was mechanically and manually stripped to expose this feature. The feature was excavated in two units: FE 1 was excavated in one stratigraphic level, while FE 2 was excavated in three 20-cm arbitrary levels. All fill was screened through ¼-inch mesh.

Fill from Feature 98 was soft, dark gray, silty loam with caliche and sand inclusions. A moderate density of FCR and a minor amount of charcoal was found throughout the fill. Natural rock in the terrace gravels underlying the feature and along the feature walls were observed to have been heated to a bluish-gray color.

A total of 459 artifacts were recovered from Feature 98 (Table 4.42). Notably, no ceramics were recovered from the fill of Feature 98. The only diagnostic artifact in the Feature 98 assemblage was a San Pedro projectile point.

Feature 98 was identified as an indeterminate, thermal, bell pit (Figures 4.40 and 4.41; also see Table 4.41). The pit was oval in plan view, and both its walls and base were unlined. Although terrace cobbles at the base of the pit and along its walls were tinted bluish from heating, little evidence of thermal activity was found within the fill of the pit, which contained minor charcoal flecking, unburned faunal remains, and a high density of flaked stone. The pit's contents suggest it was used as a trash pit following its original use as roasting pit. In addition, the concentrated distribution of artifacts within the pit fill suggested one or more discrete deposition episodes, rather than more-or-less continuous trash disposal.

One radiocarbon date (Beta-234161) was

Table 4.41. Characteristics of Feature 98

Feature Type:	Thermal pit
Cultural Affiliation:	Unknown
Temporal Affiliation:	Early Agricultural (San Pedro phase)
Diagnostic Artifacts:	San Pedro point
Subfeatures:	–
Provenience:	SA 3
Shape:	Bell
Dimensions:	Aperture: 0.95 m by 1.10 m; Maximum Extent: 1.23 m by 1.25 m; Base: 1.15 m by 0.95 m; Depth: 0.63 m; estimated volume: 0.67 m³
Depth below datum:	94.30 z–93.67 z
Stratum:	Stratum 2: surface of Pleistocene terrace deposits with modern caliche development; between 10 and 20 cm below modern ground surface

Table 4.42. Artifacts recovered from the fill of Feature 98

Flaked Stone	
Debitage	364
Cores	5
Projectile point	5
Biface	2
Unifaces	2
Subtotal	*378*
Ground stone	
Flat/concave mano	1
Flat handstone	1
Subtotal	*2*
Shell	
Freshwater shell	2
Faunal Remains	
Hares and Rabbits	6
Ungulate	10
Unidentified mammal	61
Subtotal	*77*
Total	459

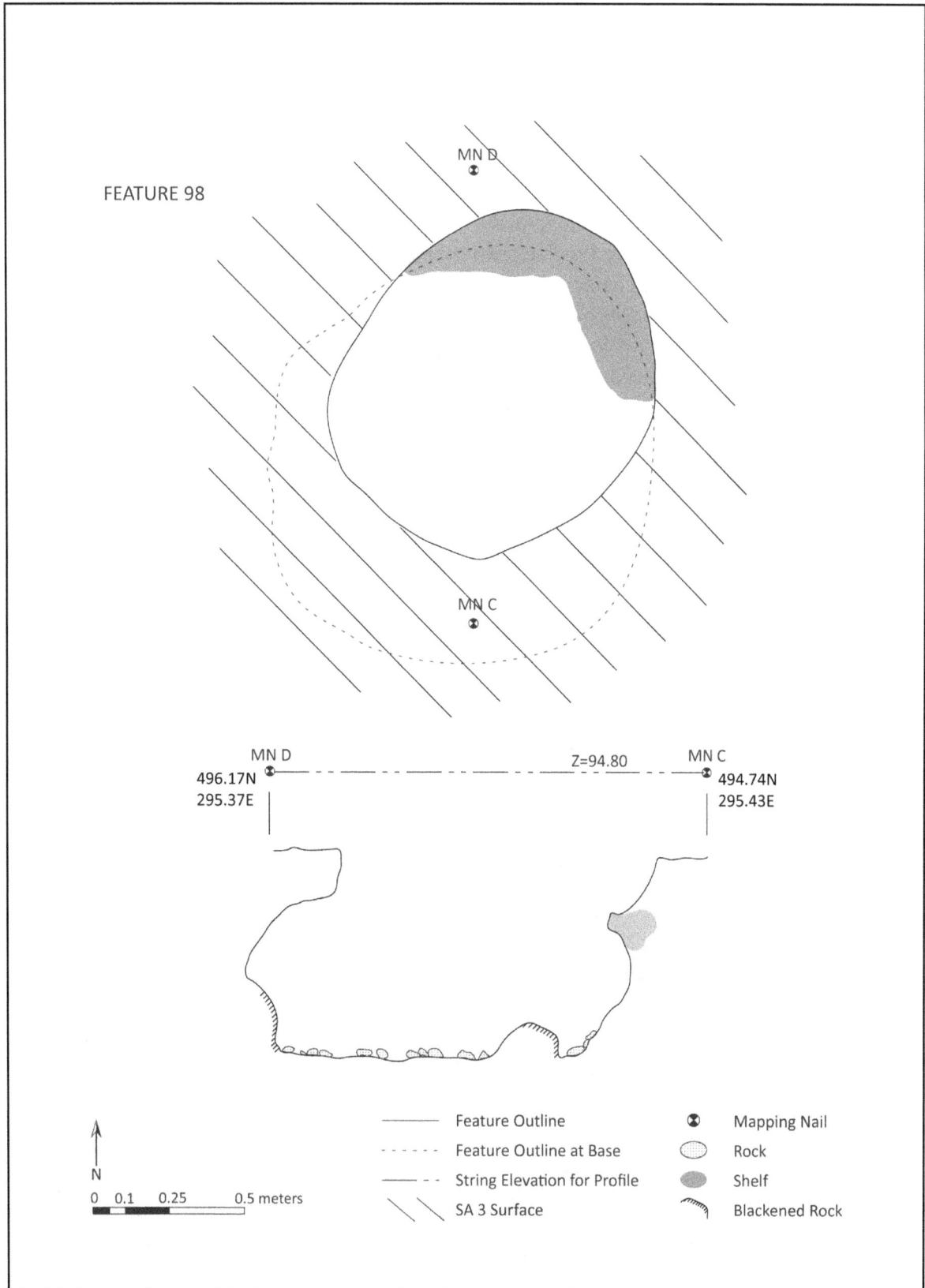

Figure 4.40. Plan and profile view of Feature 98.

obtained from charred maize recovered from Feature 98 (see Table 4.6). The sample yielded a 2 sigma calibrated date of 1250 to 1240 B.C. and 1220 to 980 B.C.

Six environmental samples—one macrobotanical sample, three flotation samples, and two pollen samples—were collected from the fill of Feature 98. Analysis of the macrobotanical sample identified a charred maize cob segment most similar to maize characteristic of the San Pedro and Cienega phases of the Early Agricultural period (see Adams, Chapter 10, for a full discussion of this cob segment). Two of the three flotation samples contained macrobotanical material suitable for analysis; plants identified include saltbush, grasses, cheno-ams, and mesquite. The two pollen samples identified a wide range of species including cholla, cattail, willow, cheno-ams, low- and high-spine

Asteraceae, globemallow, wild buckwheat, white mat, juniper, creosote bush, plantain, and members of the Grass, Mustard, Pea, and Rose families (see Adams, Chapter 10, and Phillips, Chapter 11).

Feature 98, a bell pit interpreted as a roasting pit and then a trash pit, likely dates to the San Pedro phase of the Early Agricultural period, as indicated by the radiocarbon date, the recovery of a San Pedro projectile point, the lack of ceramics in the pit's fill, and the Early Agricultural period characteristics of the maize cob segment recovered from the pit.

Feature 109

Feature 109, which originated within the Stratum 3 cultural deposits approximately 0.20 m below the modern ground surface, was discovered through excavation of TU 75. The

Figure 4.41. Photograph of Feature 98, post-excavation, view to the west.

feature was excavated in two units, each as one stratigraphic level. All fill was screened through ¼-inch mesh.

The fill of Feature 109 was characterized as soft, brown sandy silt with moderate gravel inclusions and occasional larger rocks. Four of the rocks were identified as fire-cracked. A moderate density of charcoal was noted throughout the fill.

A rather large (n = 551) and unusual artifact assemblage was recovered from the fill of Feature 109, and primarily from the fill of FE 1, the northern of the two feature excavation units from this feature (Table 4.44). In particular, 44 bones identified as belonging to a either a coyote or a dog were present in the feature fill. Although these remains were not articulated, they likely represent intentional burial or disposal of a domestic dog (see Pavao-Zuckerman and Copperstone, Chapter 8, for a full discussion of these remains). Several diagnostic ceramic sherds were recovered from the feature fill: 21 Late Rincon Red-on-brown sherds and one Sahuarita Polychrome sherd. The presence of these sherds suggests that the feature dates to the late Rincon phase/Middle Formative period.

Feature 109 was identified as a nonthermal bell pit (Figures 4.42 and 4.43). This feature had a slightly irregular shape and profile, a typical attribute of bell pits at the site (see Table 4.43). The aperture of the feature was circular; the sides and base of the pit were somewhat uneven, and did not seem to have been prepared. No plaster or oxidation was noted.

Table 4.43. Characteristics of Feature 109

Feature Type:	Nonthermal pit
Cultural Affiliation:	Unknown
Temporal Affiliation:	late Middle Formative (late Rincon phase)
Diagnostic Artifacts:	Rincon Red-on-brown sherds (n=21), Sahuarita Polychrome sherd (n=1)
Subfeatures:	–
Provenience:	SA 4
Shape:	Bell, basin base
Dimensions:	Aperture: 0.96 m by 0.88 m; Maximum Extent: 1.40 m by 1.38 m; Depth: 0.86 m; estimated volume: 1.16 m³
Depth below datum:	94.68 z–93.82 z
Stratum:	Stratum 3: Overburden; 20–25 cm below modern ground surface

Table 4.44. Artifacts recovered from the fill of Feature 109

Flaked Stone	
Debitage	265
Biface	1
Subtotal	*266*
Ceramics	
Late Rincon Red-on-brown	21
Sahuarita Polychrome	1
Indeterminate Red-on-brown	25
Indeterminate Red-on-buff	9
Brown ware	49
Brown (red) ware	1
Undersized	37
Subtotal	*143*
Ground stone	
Flat metate	1
Shell	
Bracelet fragment	1
Freshwater shell	1
Subtotal	*2*
Faunal Remains	
Hares and Rabbits	4
Carnivore	44
Unidentified mammal	90
Unidentified bird	1
Subtotal	*139*
Total	551

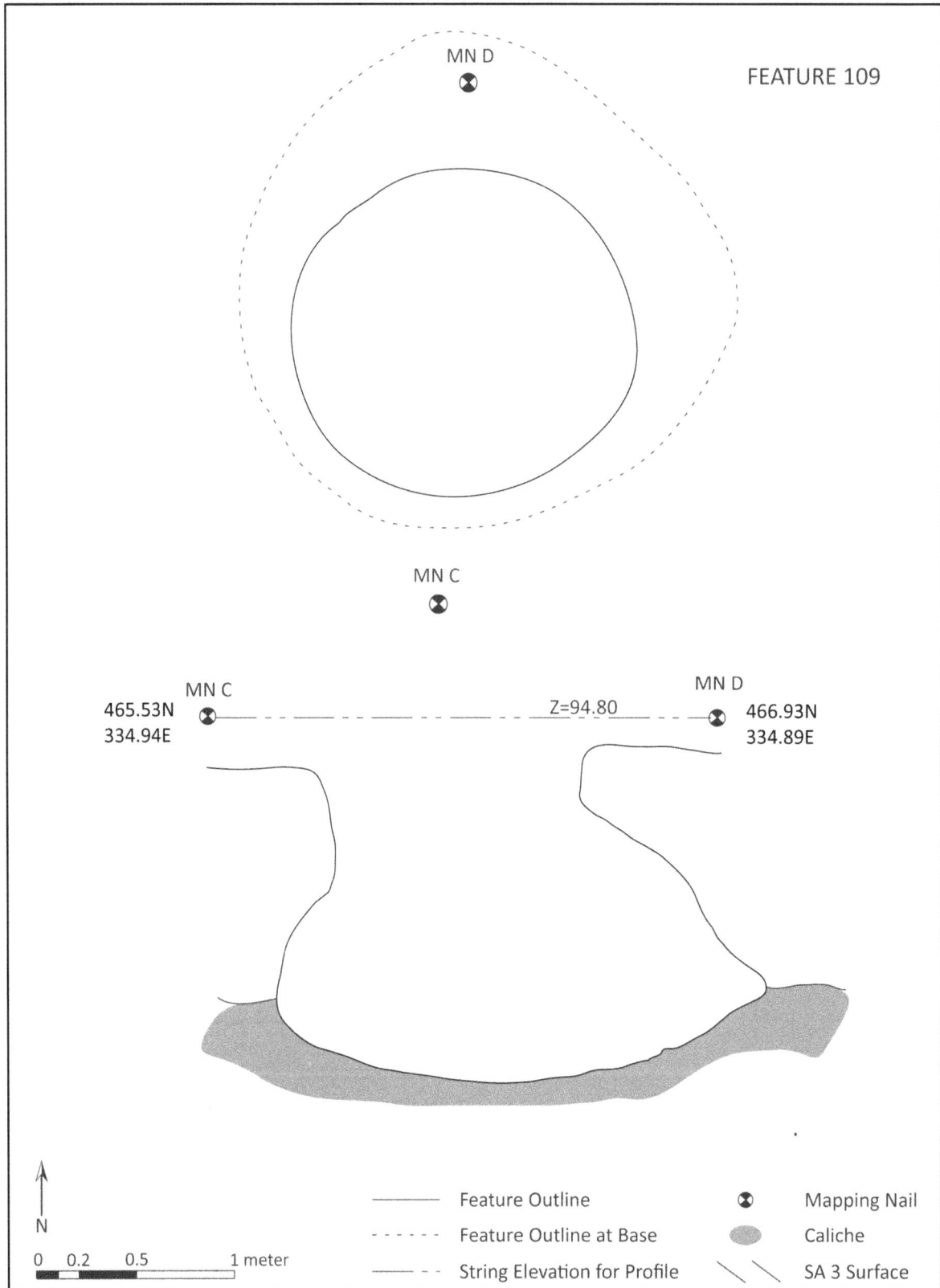

Figure 4.42. Plan and profile view of Feature 109.

Two radiocarbon dates (Beta-234162 and Beta-234169) were obtained from charred maize cupules recovered from Feature 109 (see Table 4.6). The first sample (Beta-234162) yielded a 2 sigma calibrated date of A.D. 1020 to 1210. The second sample (Beta-234169) yielded a 2 sigma calibrated date of A.D. 980 to 1060 and A.D. 1080 to 1150.

Eight environmental samples—two macrobotanical samples, five flotation samples, and one pollen sample—were collected from Feature 109. One macrobotanical sample contained two charred maize cob segments identified as containing physical attributes characteristic of later dating (post-Early Agricultural) maize varieties (see Adams, Chapter 10 for a full discussion of this). The other macrobotanical sample was identified as mesquite. Two of the five flotation samples contained macrobotanical material suitable for analysis; plants identified include cheno-ams, reedgrass, maize, saltbush, and mesquite. The single pollen sample identified cholla, cattail, cheno-ams,

low- and high-spine Asteraceae, globemallow, spiderling, wild buckwheat, white mat, and members of the Grass, Mustard, Rose, and Lily families (see Adams, Chapter 10, and Phillips, Chapter 11).

Feature 109, identified as a nonthermal bell-shaped pit, contained a large and diverse artifact assemblage, most of which were presumably deposited in the feature as trash following the end of its use-life. However, the discovery of a probable canid burial (see above) as well as a possible Late Rincon Red-on-brown reconstructible vessel, suggests that some of the artifacts may be related to the canid burial, rather than deposited as trash.

Feature 173

Feature 173, which originated within the Stratum 3 cultural deposits approximately 0.40 m below the modern ground surface, was discovered through excavation of TUs 142 and 143. Approximately 10 cm of overburden was mechanically stripped, followed by the manual

Figure 4.43. Photograph of Feature 109, post-excavation, view to the south.

excavation of three 10-cm arbitrary levels in TUs 142 and 143. Upon discovery of Feature 173, two units were excavated; FE 1 was excavated as one stratigraphic level, while FE 2 was excavated in three 20-cm arbitrary levels. All fill was screened through ¼-inch mesh.

Fill in Feature 173 was characterized as moderately compact, dark gray, fine-grained sand with abundant charcoal and a significant amount of FCR. Most of the rocks recovered from Feature 173 were burned a bluish-grey color.

The feature contained a modest assemblage, divided almost evenly between ceramic sherds, flaked stone debitage, and faunal bone (Table 4.46). Three pieces of ground stone, two manos and a netherstone, all of which were complete and burned, were also recovered.

The manos were fire-cracked, while the netherstone burning appears to be unrelated to its presence in Feature 173. The only diagnostic artifacts were one Late Rincon Red-on-brown sherd, one Rincon Red-on-brown sherd, and one Mimbres Black-on-white sherd that was too small to identify as to style.

Feature 173 was a rather large bell pit interpreted as a roasting pit (Figures 4.44 and 4.45). The feature aperture, which measured 0.92 m by 0.91 m, was circular (see Table 4.45). Both the walls and the basin-shaped base were unlined, although both were burned.

One radiocarbon date (Beta-236522) was obtained from a charred maize cupule recovered from Feature 173 (see Table 4.6).

Table 4.45. Characteristics of Feature 173

Feature Type:	Thermal
Cultural Affiliation:	Unknown
Temporal Affiliation:	late Middle Formative (late Rincon phase)
Diagnostic Artifacts:	Rincon Red-on-brown sherds (n=1), Rillito Red-on-brown sherd (n=1), Mimbres Black-on-white sherd (n=1)
Subfeatures:	–
Provenience:	SA 1
Shape:	Bell; basin base
Dimensions:	Aperture: 0.92 m by 0.91 m; Maximum Extent: 1.25 m
Depth below datum:	104.38 z–103.75 z
Stratum:	Stratum 3: Overburden; 40 cm below modern ground surface

Table 4.46. Artifacts recovered from the fill of Feature 173

Flaked Stone	
Debitage	21
Ceramics	
Late Rincon Red-on-brown	1
Rincon Red-on-brown	1
Mimbres Black-on-white	1
Indeterminate Red-on-brown	12
Brown ware	17
Buff ware	1
Undersized	3
Subtotal	*36*
Ground stone	
Flat mano	1
Trough mano	1
Flat netherstone	1
Subtotal	*3*
Faunal Remains	
Hares and Rabbits	7
Ungulate	2
Unidentified mammal	17
Mammal/bird	4
Subtotal	*30*
Total	90

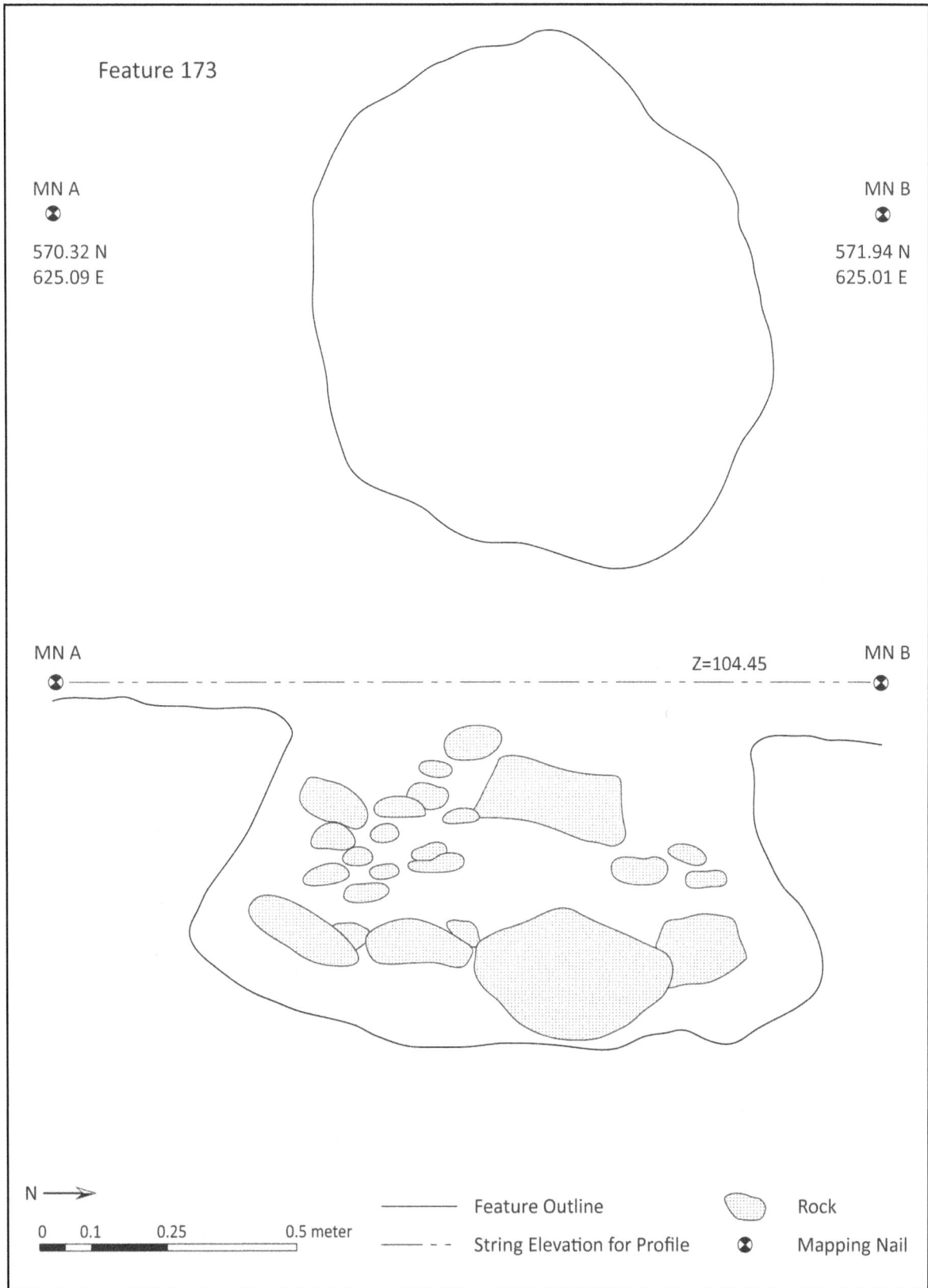

Feature 173

MN A

570.32 N
625.09 E

MN B

571.94 N
625.01 E

MN A

Z=104.45

MN B

N →

0   0.1   0.25   0.5 meter

———— Feature Outline

– – – String Elevation for Profile

Rock

Mapping Nail

Figure 4.44. Plan and profile view of Feature 173.

The sample yielded a 2 sigma calibrated date of A.D. 1020 to 1200.

Two environmental samples, both flotation samples, were collected from the fill of Feature 173. One sample contained macrobotanical material suitable for analysis; species identified included hackberry, maize, and mesquite (see Adams, Chapter 10).

Feature 173, a large bell-shaped roasting pit, was an isolated extramural pit excavated in SA 1. In addition, of the five features identified in SA 1, it was the only extramural pit; the other four features consisted of a pithouse (Feature 17) and three secondary cremations (Features 18, 158, and 182). None of the burials were absolutely dated, but the pithouse, like Feature 173, also dates to the late Middle Formative period.

Irregular Pits

Irregular pits were well represented among the features at the Marsh Station Road Site. The 37 irregular pits recorded represent 31 percent of the excavated extramural pits (Table 4.47), only a slightly smaller percentage than basin pits. This percentage seems unusually high, and may be inflated by the inclusion of partial pit remnants, truncated by later features, and trenching. The total may also reflect a willingness to assign this category; irregularity is subjective and some pits could have been shoe-horned into other categories. It might also be explained, in part, by the gravels and caliche the pits were excavated into, which did not make for very good and clean cuts. By comparison, only 12 percent of the pits

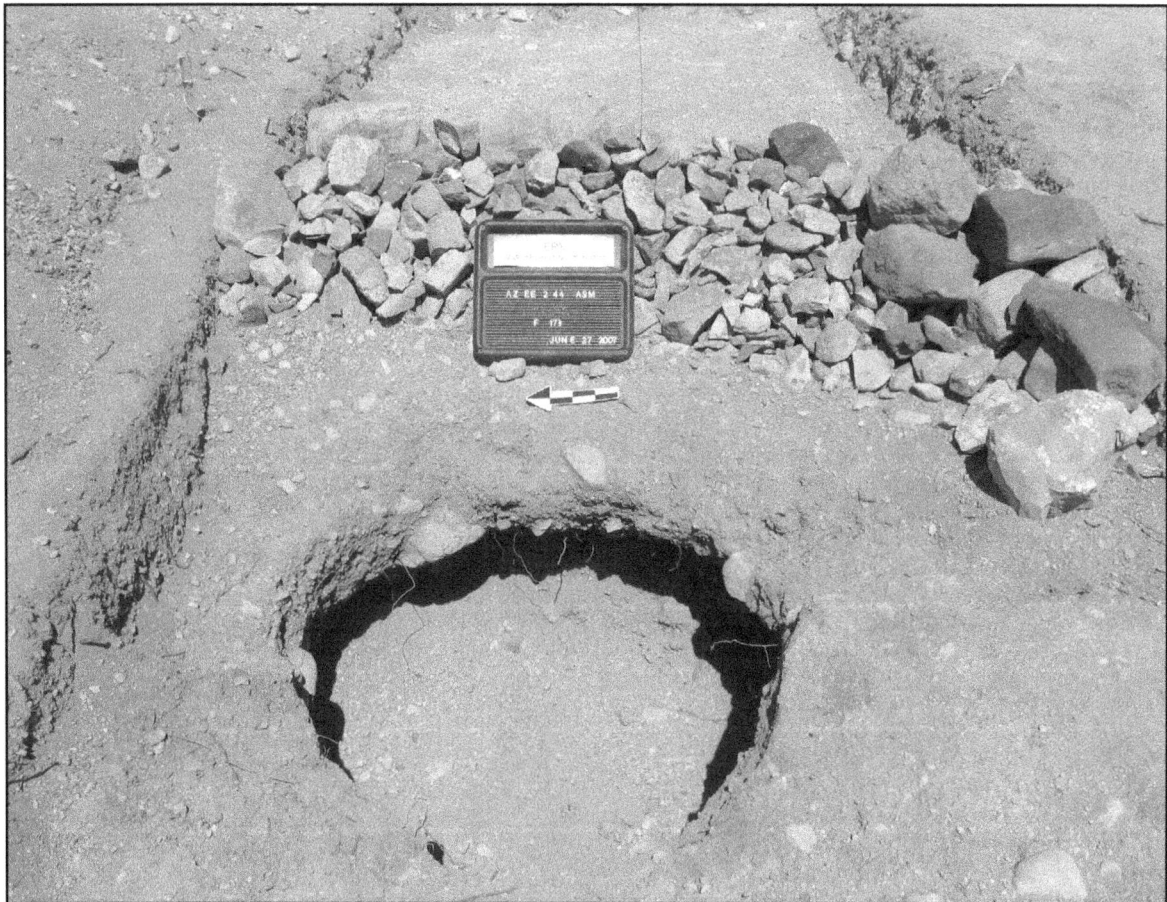

Figure 4.45. Photograph of Feature 173, post-excavation, view to the east.

Table 4.47. Summary of irregularly shaped pit characteristics

Feature No.	Pit Type	Locus	Excavated	Wöcherl Pit Class	Length	Width	Depth	Fill Inclusions	Artifacts	Samples
						Dimensions (m)				
3	TP	SA 2	100%	7	1.39	1.31	0.24	Charcoal & FCR (moderate)	Flaked stone debitage & biface	Flotation, pollen
4	TP	SA 5	Partial	7	0.45+	0.20+	0.15	Ash & Charcoal (moderate)	Ceramics, flaked stone, faunal bone	Flotation
12	NTP	SA 4	Partial	7	1.10	0.90	0.46	Charcoal (minor), FCR (fair)	Ceramics; flaked stone debitage, cores, & tools; faunal bone	Flotation, pollen
15	NTP	SA 4	100%	7	1.35	1.10	0.21	FCR (minor)	Ceramics, flaked stone	Flotation
19	TP	SA 4	Partial	7	0.80	0.86	0.63	Ash & Charcoal (minor), FCR (abundant)	Ceramics; flaked stone debitage, core, & bifaces; worked shell	Flotation, pollen
25	NTP	SA 3	100%	7	1.60	1.22	0.45	Charcoal (minor)	Ceramics; flaked stone debitage, tools, & cores; faunal bone	Flotation, pollen
26	NTP	SA 4	100%	7	1.20	1.10	0.33	Charcoal (minor), FCR (moderate)	Ceramics, flaked stone debitage, cores, & biface	Flotation
40	TP	SA 4	Partial	7	0.44	0.30	0.21	Charcoal (minor), FCR (moderate)	Ceramics, flaked stone	Flotation, pollen
42	NTP	SA 3	100%	7	0.95	0.80	0.24	Charcoal & FCR (minor)	Flaked stone, ground stone	Flotation, pollen
48	NTP	SA 4	100%	7	2.80	2.10	0.10		Ceramics, flaked stone debitage & core	
50	NTP	N TR 13	Partial	7	0.25	0.86	0.51	Charcoal (minor), FCR (moderate)	Ceramics, flaked stone	Flotation, pollen
55	TP	SA 2	100%	7	1.40	1.25	0.18	FCR (moderate)	Flaked stone	Flotation
56	TP	SA 4	Partial	7	0.62	0.55	0.16	Charcoal (minor)	Ceramics, flaked stone	Flotation
62	NTP	SA 2	100%	7	0.66	0.53	0.21	Charcoal (minor), FCR (moderate)	Flaked stone	Flotation, pollen
63	NTP	SA 2	100%	7	0.85	0.83	0.24	Ash & FCR (minor)	Flaked stone debitage & core	Flotation, pollen
65	NTP	SA 5	100%	7	1.95	0.55	0.27	Charcoal & FCR (minor)	Ceramics, flaked stone, ground stone	Flotation, pollen
66	NTP	SA 3	100%	7	1.46	1.04	0.24	Charcoal (minor)	Flaked stone debitage, core, & tools; faunal bone	Flotation, pollen
68	NTP	SA 4	Partial	7	0.54+	0.43+	0.13	Charcoal (minor)	Ceramics, flaked stone	
70	NTP	SA 5	100%	7	0.60	0.24	0.12	FCR (minor)	Ceramics, flaked stone, ground stone	Flotation

Table 4.47. Summary of irregularly shaped pit characteristics, cont'd.

Feature No.	Pit Type	Locus	Excavated	Wöcherl Pit Class	Dimensions (m) Length	Width	Depth	Fill Inclusions	Artifacts	Samples
71	NTP	SA 5	100%	7	0.46	0.28	0.09	FCR (minor)	Faunal bone	Flotation
72	TP	SA 4	100%	7	1.03	0.97	0.40	Charcoal & FCR (minor)	Ceramics, flaked stone debitage & bifaces, ground stone, faunal bone	Flotation, pollen
80	NTP	SA 5	100%	7	0.42	0.46	0.13		Ground stone	
82	NTP	SA 4	100%	7	0.61	0.59	0.16	Charcoal (fair), FCR (minor)	Flaked stone	Flotation, pollen
83	NTP	SA 4	100%	7	0.86	0.60	0.25	Charcoal (moderate), FCR (minor)	Ceramics, flaked stone	Flotation, pollen
84	NTP	SA 3	Partial	7	0.68	0.22	0.16		Flaked stone	Flotation, pollen
86	NTP	SA 5	Partial	7	0.76	0.24	0.38	Charcoal (minor)	Ceramics, flaked stone	Flotation, pollen
91	NTP	SA 5	100%	7	0.85	0.86	0.18	Charcoal & FCR (minor)	Ceramics, flaked stone	Flotation, pollen
95	TP	SA 4	100%	7	1.00	1.04	0.36	Ash (fair), FCR (moderate)	Ceramics, flaked stone debitage & biface, faunal bone	Flotation, pollen
105	NTP	SA 3	100%	7	0.94	0.84	0.27		Flaked stone debitage & bifaces, faunal bone	Flotation, pollen
112	NTP	SA 4	100%	7	1.50	1.00	0.42	Ash (minor), Charcoal & FCR (moderate)	Ceramics, flaked stone debitage, cores, & hammerstone; ground stone, faunal bone	Flotation, pollen
119	NTP	SA 4	100%	7	1.15	0.88	0.33		Ceramics, flaked stone debitage & cores, ground stone, faunal bone	Flotation, pollen
122	NTP	SA 4	100%	7	0.96	0.85	0.64	FCR (abundant)	Ceramics, flaked stone, ground stone, faunal bone	
128	NTP	SA 4	100%	7	0.70	0.84	0.09			Flotation
132	NTP	SA 4	100%	7	1.01	0.71	0.15	Charcoal (minor)	Ceramics, flaked stone debitage & unifaces	Flotation, pollen
133	NTP	SA 4	100%	7	1.16	1.02	0.06	Charcoal (minor)		
136	NTP	SA 4	100%	7	1.35	1.25	0.52	FCR (abundant), Charcoal (moderate)	Ceramics; flaked stone debitage, core, & biface; faunal bone	Flotation, pollen
137	NTP	SA 5	100%	7	0.76	0.74	0.29	Charcoal (minor)	Flaked stone	Flotation, pollen

from the Early Agricultural Wetlands Site, on the middle Santa Cruz River, were classed as irregular (Archer 1998). The sediment at this site was composed of clay, silt, and fine sand, which may have allowed for more-regular feature digging. Similarly, Wöcherl (2005) reported that irregular pits composed between 2 percent and 18 percent of a site's pit features in her sample of five Early Agricultural sites in the Tucson Basin. As might be expected, the irregular pits excavated at Marsh Station Road were varied. They included nine thermal features (see Table 4.47).

Feature 72

Feature 72 originated within Stratum 3, cultural overburden. Approximately 10 cm of overburden was mechanically stripped, and a further 10 cm manually excavated to expose this feature. The feature was bisected and excavated as one stratigraphic level. All feature fill was screened through ¼-inch mesh.

Fill from Feature 72 was characterized as soft, brown, sandy loam containing small amounts of charcoal and FCR. A total of 195 artifacts were recovered from the fill of Feature 72 (Table 4.49). One diagnostic artifact, a San Pedro projectile point, was recovered from this feature.

Feature 72 was an irregularly shaped pit that appeared asymmetric in plan view, and had unlined walls that varied from insloping to vertical to undercutting. The base of the pit was excavated into sterile gravels and caliche that demonstrated bluish-grey discoloring as a result of heating. The north-northeastern portion of the feature was intruded upon by Feature 67.

One radiocarbon date (Beta-234160) was obtained from a charred maize cupule recovered from Feature 72 (see Table 4.6). The sample yielded a 2 sigma calibrated date of A.D. 880 to 1020.

Table 4.48. Characteristics of Feature 72

Feature Type:	Thermal
Cultural Affiliation:	Unknown
Temporal Affiliation:	late Middle Formative (Rillito–middle Rincon phase)
Diagnostic Artifacts:	San Pedro point
Subfeatures:	–
Provenience:	SA 4
Shape:	Irregular
Dimensions:	1.03 m by 0.97 m; 0.40 deep; estimated volume: 0.32 m³
Depth below datum:	94.77 z–94.37 z
Stratum:	Stratum 3: Overburden; 20 cm below modern ground surface

Table 4.49. Artifacts recovered from the fill of Feature 72

Flaked Stone	
Debitage	165
Projectile point	2
Subtotal	*167*
Ceramics	
Indeterminate Red-on-brown	5
Brown ware	14
Subtotal	*19*
Ground stone	
Flat handstone	1
Faunal Remains	
Rodents	4
Unidentified mammal	4
Subtotal	*8*
Total	195

Two environmental samples, one flotation sample and one pollen sample, were collected from the fill of Feature 72. Analysis of the macrobotanical material recovered from the flotation sample identified maize and mesquite. Analysis of the pollen sample identified cattail, willow, low- and high-spine Asteraceae, cheno-ams, globemallow, Arizona poppy, wild buck-wheat, spurge, white mat, and members of the Grass, Pea, and Parsley families (see Adams, Chapter 10, and Phillips, Chapter 11).

Feature 72, and irregularly shaped extra-mural pit with evidence of thermal activity, was excavated in SA 4, near several other extramural pits and a pithouse (Feature 51) (see Figure 4.24). The feature, which dates to the late Middle Formative period, was intruded upon by Feature 67, a bell pit. While it seems clear, based on the stratigraphic relationship between the two features, that Feature 72 pre-dates Feature 67, the latter feature was not absolutely dated, nor were any other features in the immediate vicinity of Feature 72.

Feature 112

Feature 112 originated within Stratum 3, cultural overburden. Approximately 10 cm of overburden was mechanically stripped, and a further 10 cm manually excavated to expose this feature. The feature was bisected and exca-vated as one stratigraphic level. All feature fill was screened through ¼-inch mesh.

Fill from Feature 112 was characterized as soft, brown, silty sand. A moderate density of FCR, charcoal, and small amounts of ash were also found in the fill. Both FCR and natu-ral rock in the terrace gravels underlying the feature were heated to a bluish color. In addi-tion, the excavator noted that burned artifacts, such as faunal bone and ground stone, were recovered from the fill of FE 2, while mostly unburned artifacts were recovered from FE 1.

This project recovered 188 artifacts from the fill of Feature 112 (Table 4.51). As noted

by the excavator, some of these, particularly the ground stone and faunal bone fragments, were burned. No diagnostic artifacts were recovered.

Feature 112 was identified as a medium nonthermal pit, but this feature was difficult to categorize. The pit was irregular, with edges varying from undercut to basin-shaped, and was broad and relatively shallow (Figure 4.46; also see Table 4.50). While the general shape suggested it was bell-shaped, the irregulari-ties in the walls and its depth were uncharacteris-tic of typical bell pits. In addition, fill within the pit and discoloration of the natural rocks underlying the pit suggested that the feature may have been used for thermal activities, but the evidence was not convincing enough to warrant classification of the pit as thermal.

One radiocarbon date (Beta-234163) was obtained from a charred maize cupule recovered from Feature 112 (see Table 4.6). The sample yielded a 2 sigma calibrated date of A.D. 450 to 450, A.D. 460 to 480, and A.D. 530 to 640.

Two environmental samples, one flota-tion sample and one pollen sample, were col-lected from the fill of Feature 112. Analysis of the macrobotanical material recovered from the flotation sample identified cheno-ams, juniper, maize, and mesquite. Analysis of the pollen sample identified relatively few spe-cies, including willow, cheno-ams, low- and high-spine Asteraceae, wild buckwheat, white mat, and members of the Grass, Pea, and Rose families (see Adams, Chapter 10, and Phillips, Chapter 11).

Feature 112, an irregularly shaped pit with some evidence of thermal activities, was excavated in SA 4, near several other extramu-ral pits (see Figure 4.24). Radiocarbon dating identified Feature 112 as one of the few features excavated at the Marsh Station Road site that dates to the Early Formative period. The other Early Formative feature, Feature 61, is also

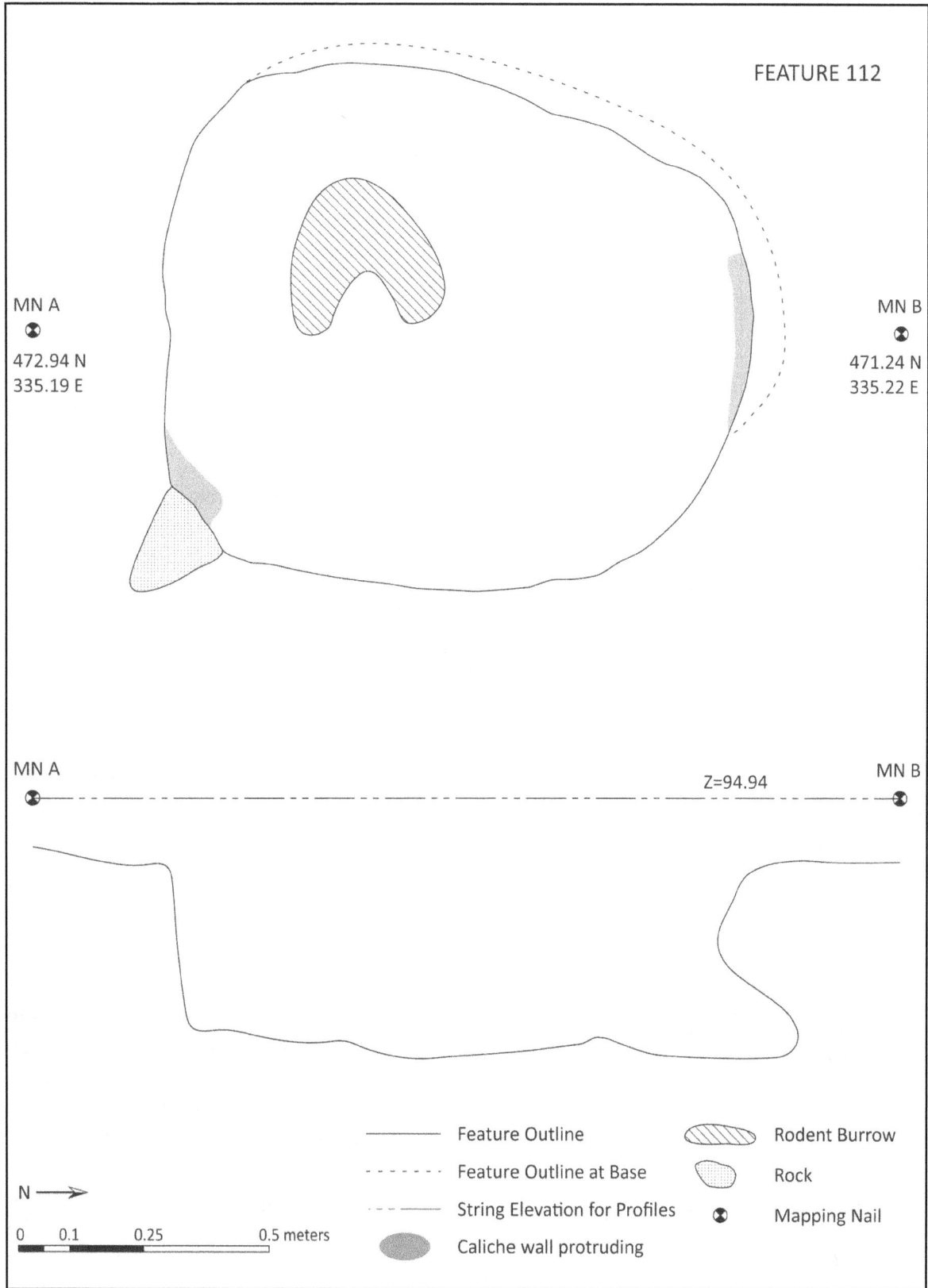

Figure 4.46. Plan and profile view of Feature 112.

Table 4.50. Characteristics of Feature 112

Feature Type:	Nonthermal
Cultural Affiliation:	Unknown
Temporal Affiliation:	Early Formative (late Agua Caliente–Tortolita phase)
Diagnostic Artifacts:	None
Subfeatures:	–
Provenience:	SA 4
Shape:	Irregular
Dimensions:	1.50 m by 1.00 m; 0.42 deep; estimated volume: 0.54 m³
Depth below datum:	94.79 z–94.37 z
Stratum:	Stratum 3: Overburden; 10 cm above Stratum 2 (Pleistocene terrace deposits)

Table 4.51. Artifacts recovered from the fill of Feature 112

Flaked Stone	
Debitage	147
Cores	4
Hammerstone	1
Subtotal	*152*
Ceramics	
Brown ware	4
Undersized	7
Subtotal	*11*
Ground stone	
Flat/concave mano	1
Mano (multiple)	1
Flat metate	1
Subtotal	*3*
Faunal Remains	
Hares and Rabbits	3
Ungulate	1
Rodent	1
Unidentified mammal	17
Subtotal	*22*
Total	188

an extramural pit located about 10 m west of Feature 112, near Feature 11, a pithouse.

Feature 136

Feature 136 originated at the surface of sterile Stratum 2. Less than 10 cm of overburden was manually stripped to expose this feature. Once exposed, the feature was bisected and excavated as one stratigraphic level in two feature excavation units. However, it later became apparent that Feature 122, another nonthermal and possibly bell pit, was intrusive to Feature 136 and had actually removed a significant percentage of the north-northeast portion of Feature 136. Thus, fill from Feature 136 is actually represented by FE 2, while most of the fill from FE 1 (approximately 80 percent) is associated with Feature 122. Regardless of feature designations, all fill was screened through ¼-inch mesh.

Fill from Feature 136 was described as slightly hard, sandy loam containing abundant FCR, and a small quantity of charcoal. Observations made during excavation indicate that FCR and flaked stone artifacts were differentially distributed within the fill, with FE 1 containing more rocks and flaked stone, and FE 2 containing fewer rocks and flaked stone. As mentioned above, this differential distribution can probably be explained by the presence of Feature 122. Ninety-nine pieces of flaked stone debitage were the only artifacts associated with Feature 136.

Feature 136 was classified as a medium nonthermal pit. This feature had quite steep sides and a flat base (see Table 4.52). In plan view it was irregular, but somewhat circular. As mentioned above, the fill contained abundant FCR, but Feature 136 generally lacked other evidence of burning. It seems likely Feature 136 was in fact a nonthermal pit and that the FCR was redeposited from other features, most likely from Feature 122 and possibly as trash fill.

One radiocarbon date (Beta-234164) was obtained from a charred maize cupule recovered from Feature 136 (see Table 4.6). The sample yielded a 2 sigma calibrated date of A.D. 890 to 1030.

Two environmental samples, one flotation sample and one pollen sample, were collected from the fill of Feature 136. Analysis of the macrobotanical material recovered from the flotation sample identified maize and mesquite. Analysis of the pollen sample revealed a wide variety of species including oak, cheno-ams, low- and high-spine Asteraceae, liguliflorae, spiderling, globemallow, white mat, creosote bush, and members of the Grass, Mustard, Nightshade, and Lily families (see Adams, Chapter 10, and Phillips, Chapter 11).

Feature 136, a large irregularly shaped nonthermal pit, was located in SA 4 near several other nonthermal pits (see Figure 4.24). The pit, which dates to the late Middle Formative period, was the only pit in this group that

---

Table 4.52. Characteristics of Feature 136

Feature Type:	Nonthermal pit
Cultural Affiliation:	Unknown
Temporal Affiliation:	Middle Formative (Rillito–middle Rincon phase)
Diagnostic Artifacts:	Cortaro point
Subfeatures:	–
Provenience:	SA 4
Shape:	Irregular
Dimensions:	1.35 m by 1.25 m; 0.52 deep; estimated volume: 0.69 m³
Depth below datum:	94.84 z–94.32 z
Stratum:	Stratum 2: surface of Pleistocene terrace deposits with modern caliche development; less than 10 cm below modern ground surface

---

was absolutely dated. However, Feature 122 is intrusive to Feature 136, and therefore likely post-dates it.

Human Burials

Seven burials—four secondary cremations and three primary inhumations—were recorded and excavated at the Marsh Station Road site. In addition, seven isolated occurrences of human remains were also recovered from the site. Three burials were located in SA 1, one burial was located in SA 3, and three burials were located in SA 4. Human remains from all seven burials were generally poorly preserved, and thus the data gathered from analysis of the remains is somewhat limited. None of the remains were securely dated; only one burial, Feature 8 (Burial 1) contained a diagnostic artifact—a San Pedro projectile point. However, given the location of the feature, in SA 4/5 near other features dated to the late Middle Formative period, and the general site pattern of finding Early Agricultural period projectile points in later dating features, it seems more likely that this San Pedro projectile point was also curated with the remains, and should not be seen as temporally diagnostic of the burial itself.

The human remains recovered from the Marsh Station Road site were analyzed in the field and in the WSA laboratory during June and July 2007, by Jessica Roman-Cerezo and Dr. John McClelland of the Arizona State Museum. Observations were limited to non-destructive methods. Inventory, assessment of age and sex, and documentation of pathologies was conducted in accord with procedures outlined in Buikstra and Ubelaker (1994). Following analysis, the remains were repatriated to the Tohono O'odham Nation.

The seven burial features are described below, and the results of the osteological analysis, prepared by Dr. John McClelland, are presented. Characteristics of the burial features are summarized in Table 4.53.

Feature 8 (Burial 1): Secondary Cremation

Feature 8 (Burial 1), a secondary cremation pit of indeterminate morphology, was disturbed during mechanical excavation of Trench 12. A portion of the feature remained in situ on the south side of the trench, within an unexcavated, gridded, test unit. Rather than excavating the entire test unit, a 0.50 m by 0.30 m unit was excavated to reveal Feature 8 in plan view. The pit itself was steep-sided, and dug from cultural/slopewash deposits into sterile caliche. There was no evidence of burning visible in the pit itself. The pit contained a significant, consolidated block of fill with abundant human bone, which appeared to be the displaced fill of a reconstructible vessel (FN 44-664.003) of Tucson Basin brown ware. Although the vessel was not reconstructed, it was identified as a medium-sized jar with a slightly flared rim, and estimated to be approximately 50 percent complete. Along with this vessel, 15 brown ware sherds, 5 decorated sherds, a flaked stone drill, a discoid, a San Pedro projectile point, and a bone awl were recovered with this burial.

This feature contained 694 grams of thoroughly incinerated bone from an adult individual. The quantity of bone is approximately half of the minimum expected from a complete cremated adult skeleton. All body regions are represented with the exception of the dentition and to the extent that elements could be identified as to side, bones from both sides of the body appear to be present. Average fragment size is about 2 centimeters, but some larger fragments are present.

Long bone fragments are mostly white in color, while cranial and axial fragments tend to be gray or blue-gray. The bone exhibits moderate to heavy cracking and mild to moderate warping. These characteristics are consistent with burning while the bone retained significant moisture content, suggesting cremation of a fleshed body.

The individual was likely to have been a mature adult, possibly in the range of 40 to 45 years, based on the morphology of the auricular surface of the left ilium, the presence of vertebral osteophytosis, and evidence of arthritis. A fragment of the body of a thoracic vertebra has a large osteophyte on one margin. A fragment of the proximal epiphysis of the ulna exhibits marginal lipping, suggesting arthritis of the elbow. No other pathologies were observed. There are no diagnostic characteristics to permit an assessment of sex.

Feature 18 (Burial 2): Secondary Cremation

Feature 18 (Burial 2), a secondary cremation pit with steep walls and an uneven, basin-shaped base, was disturbed during mechanical excavation of Trench 1. A portion of the feature remained in situ on the north side of the trench, within unexcavated fill of Feature 17, a pithouse. The pit contained cremated human remains dispersed throughout its fill; no evidence of burning within the pit itself was observed. The burial contained no clear grave goods, although some flaked stone debitage, a few ceramics sherds, and two pieces of faunal bone were recovered from the fill.

This feature contained 93 grams of well-fragmented calcined human bone. The color of the bone fragments ranges from gray to white with smaller long bone fragments mostly white and fragments from major long bones showing a mixture of black, gray, and white. There is a moderate amount of cracking and warping, indicative of firing while moist or in the flesh.

Identified elements included bones from the cranial, appendicular, and extremity regions. The individual was most likely an adult, based on the thickness and overall size

Table 4.53. Characteristics summary of seven burials excavated at the Marsh Station Road site

Feature (Burial)	Burial Type	Age	Sex	Elements Recovered	Pathologies	Burial Characteristics	Associated Artifacts
8 (1)	Secondary Cremation	Adult, 40–45 yrs.	Unk.	All body regions are represented with the exception of the dentition and to the extent that elements could be identified as to side, bones from both sides of the body appear to be present	Vertebral osteophytosis, arthritis of the elbow	*Measurements:* 0.65 m L, 0.35 m W, 0.28 D; *Characteristics:* cremation likely displaced fill f rom Vessel 1; no evidence of burning in the pit itself	Vessel 1: Tucson Basin Brown ware RV, medium-sized jar with a slighly flared rim; 15 brown ware sherds, 5 decorated sherds (ind. red-on-brown and red-on-buff), a flaked stone drill, a discoid, a San Pedro projectile point, a bone awl, and 8 faunal bones were all associated with the cremation
18 (2)	Secondary Cremation	Adult, younger than 50 yrs.	Unk.	Bones from the cranial, appendicular, and extremity regions	None observed	*Measurements:* 0.30 m L, 0.12 m W, 0.32 D; *Characteristics:* dispersed remains; pit has straight-sided walls, basin-shaped base; no evidence of burning in the pit itself	No clear grave goods, although some flaked stone debitage, a few brown ware ceramic sherds were collected from the cremation
87 (3)	Primary Inhumation	Child, 3–6 yrs.	Unk.	A few unburned fragments from the cranium and several loose deciduous and permanent teeth	Talon cusp	*Measurements:* 1.86 m L, 0.45 m W, 0.50 D; *Characteristics:* large, irregular earthen pit, oriented E-W; cranium was probably laid on its side, approximately 15–20 cm of fill beneath remains	No clear grave goods, and only a light density of flaked stone was recovered
92 (4)	Primary Inhumation	Adult, 18–50 yrs.	F	Most of the bones of the cranial vault, manible, a sphenoid fragment, an unsided maxilla fragment, and two mandibular premolars; all the long bones from the right side (except the ulna), as well as some long bones from the left side; axial remains	Enamel hypoplasia	*Measurements:* 0.93 m L, 0.88 m W, 0.23 D; *Characteristics:* indeterminate circular/oval earthen pit demarcated by large cobbles located directly over the remains; significant root disturbance; remains were oriented N-S, lying face-up with the legs flexed; position of the arms was indeterminate	No clear grave goods, although 123 pieces of flaked stone debitage, a biface, eight brown, brown(red) ware and undersized ceramic sherds, and two faunal bones were recovered
	Secondary Cremation	Child, 12+ yrs.	Unk.	Long bone shaft fragments; no diagnostic characteristics	None observed		

Table 4.53. Characteristics summary of seven burials excavated at the Marsh Station Road site, cont'd.

Feature	Burial Type	Age	Sex	Elements Recovered	Pathologies	Burial Characteristics	Associated Artifacts
158 (5)	Secondary Cremation	Adult, 18–50 yrs.	M	There are identified elements from all body regions except for the extremities, although the majority (2/3) derive from the l ong bones	None observed	*Measurements:* 0.33 m L, 0.33 m W, 0.19 D; *Characteristics:* shallow, earthen pit with no clear boundaries; remains were clustered, and perhaps were originally contained within a basket or a bag	No clear grave goods, one piece of flaked stone debitage
182 (6)	Secondary Cremation	Adult, 12+ yrs.[a]	Unk.	*Concentration A:* mandibular fragments, a tooth root fragment, a tibia shaft fragment, an ilium fragment, a few major long bone shaft fragments; *Concentration B:* fragments from the left and right temporals, a parietal fragment, a few unidentified cranial vault frag-ments, an ulna fragment, a few major and minor long bone shaft fragments, one metatarsal or metacarpal shaft fragment, and one small rib fragment	None observed	*Measurements:* 0.40 m L, 0.30 m W, 0.10 D; *Characteristics:* shallow undefined pit; minor root disturb-ance; cremated remains were recovered from two distinct concentrations collected separately as one burial	No clear grave goods; one flake was recovered, and probably was not actually associated with the burial
200 (7)	Primary Inhumation	Adult, 30–45 yrs.	Male	All regions of the skeleton are represented: vertebral column and pelvic girdle by a few frag-ments, portions of all the long bone shafts with the exception of the right ulna, both right and left ribs, largely intact skull, dentition	None observed	*Measurements:* 1.37 m L, 081 m W, 0.19 D; *Characteristics:* poorly defined, shallow, earthen pit, with minor root disturbance; remains were in a mixed position, but the arms were extended and the legs the flexed	108 pieces of flaked stone debitage and nine ceramic brown ware and undersized sherds were recovered from the burial; however, their association with the burial is questionable

[a] One small cranial fragment likely belonging to a juvenille (2–12 yrs.) was also recovered

of long bone fragments. An open lambdoid suture was evident on one occipital fragment, suggesting that the individual was younger than 50 years old. There are no diagnostic criteria to permit an assessment of sex. No pathologies are evident.

Feature 87 (Burial 3): Primary Inhumation

Feature 87 (Burial 3), a primary inhumation containing cranial fragments and teeth belonging to a single individual, was observed in the south face of Trench 7 in SA 2/3. Cultural overburden was manually excavated until the burial was visible in plan view, at which point it was excavated in two units. Human remains were recovered only from the western unit (FE 2). In addition, no clear grave goods were present, and only a light density of flaked stone debitage was recovered from the burial fill. While the excavated burial was large enough to contain a complete skeleton, only cranial fragments and dentition were recovered, leading excavators to suspect this could be a secondary rather than a primary inhumation. However, the east–west orientation of the burial as well as the location of the recovered remains in the western end of the burial was more indicative of primary inhumation. It is likely that the rest of the skeleton was once present, but that it disintegrated over time. The designation of these remains as belonging to a child (see below and Table 4.53), which generally do not preserve well, supports this interpretation. It is still curious, though, that the fragile cranial elements preserved while more robust elements, such as the femoral head, did not.

The remains from this feature consist of a few unburned fragments from the cranium and several loose deciduous and permanent teeth. The cranial remains are very fragmentary and the teeth are poorly preserved. The enamel has a chalky and eroded appearance while the dentin has the appearance of woven bone.

Dental development indicates that this individual was a child between three and six years of age. The permanent teeth have no occlusal wear and show only the initial stages of root development. They probably had not yet erupted. Deciduous molars show moderate to heavy wear, consistent with a prehistoric diet. The thin cranial vault fragments are consistent with this age estimate.

No pathologies are present on the few cranial vault fragments, but observability is extremely limited. There are no carious lesions on the deciduous teeth, but no other dental pathologies are observable due to the degraded condition of the enamel.

One partially formed permanent maxillary incisor possesses a rare morphological trait, described as a talon cusp. This is an accessory lingual cusp that reaches nearly to the occlusal surface and is continuous with the marginal ridge.

Feature 92 (Burial 4): Primary Inhumation and Secondary Cremation

Feature 92 (Burial 4), a primary inhumation of a single individual and a secondary cremation of another individual, was discovered during the excavation of TU 60 in SA 4. The feature was identified by a quasi-circle of large, non-fire-cracked rocks, ranging from 50 to 60 cm in size. The feature, generally circular to oval in shape, was bisected along a north–south line and excavated in two units. Large cobbles were located directly over the remains within the burial, separated by only a few centimeters of fill. A large rock/slab was also located directly over the cranium, again separated by only a few centimeters of fill. The recovered skeletal remains were generally poorly preserved, having been crushed by the weight of the cobbles and stone slab, and affected by significant root disturbance and other post-depositional processes. The presence of a secondary cremation along with the primary inhumation in Feature 92 was not recorded in the field, but rather was only identified during post-excavation osteological analysis of the fill recovered from within the burial. No clear grave goods were associated with the burial, although some flaked stone and a few ceramic sherds were recovered from the feature fill. In addition, the base and midsection of a preform was recovered from directly underneath the large slab located over the cranium.

This burial consisted of a poorly preserved adult inhumation. Most of the bones of the cranial vault are represented, along with the mandible, a sphenoid fragment, and an unsided maxilla fragment. There are two mandibular premolars, but the crown is preserved on only one tooth. All of the long bones from the right side are present with the exception of the ulna. Fragments from the left leg bones were also identified. None of the long bone epiphyses are preserved.

Axial remains are limited to fragments from two cervical vertebrae and a rib fragment. The only extremity fragments are a few metacarpal shaft pieces. The cortical surfaces of the bone fragments are highly degraded.

Dental wear and the size and thickness of the postcranial elements indicate that the individual was an adult, probably in the young to mature adult range (18–50 years). The individual is possibly female, based on the morphology of the supraorbital margin and the overall gracility of the skeletal elements.

The first mandibular premolar has a horizontal hypoplastic groove on the buccal aspect of the crown indicative of an episode of interrupted growth during development. The position of the defect suggests that this disruption most likely occurred between the fourth and sixth years. Enamel hypoplasia has been attributed to either a short period of nutritional deficiency or an acute disease episode (Goodman and Rose 1990).

No skeletal pathologies are present, but observability was very limited due to degradation of the cortical surfaces. Due to the absence of long bone articular surfaces, the presence or absence of arthritis cannot be determined. Vertebral remains are too fragmentary to assess the presence or absence of osteophytosis.

Included with the miscellaneous bone fragments from this inhumation are approximately 20 small burned long bone shaft fragments. The total weight of cremated bone is about 10 grams and the average fragment length is 2 centimeters. The bone is white with some gray on the internal surfaces. Cracking is very evident in addition to a little warping of the fragments, indicating firing while moisture was retained. These bone fragments are consistent in appearance with human bone, but no diagnostic characteristics are present.

If human, the bone fragments are most likely representative of a subadult or older individual (12 years or older) based on the thickness of the cortical bone and the inferred diameter of the long bone shafts. They almost certainly represent a different individual than the principal set of remains in Burial 4.

Feature 158 (Burial 5): Secondary Cremation

Feature 158 (Burial 5), a secondary cremation pit with poorly defined boundaries, was encountered while excavating TU 121. The burial was located approximately 20 cm below the modern ground surface, in SA 1 near Marsh Station Road. The pit contained concentrated, cremated human remains in its fill; however, no associated cremation vessel was present, and it is possible the cremated remains were originally contained within a basket or a bag of some sort. The burial was in good condition, with no evidence of root or insect disturbance. Little variation between the feature fill and the surrounding fill as well as the poor definition of the burial itself suggests that the burial was likely excavated and quickly refilled with the excavated sediment. The burial contained no clear grave goods, although a light density of flaked stone debitage was recovered from the feature fill.

This feature contained the partial cremated remains of an adult individual. A total of 561 grams of well-fragmented bone is present. There are identified elements from all body regions except for the extremities. More than two-thirds of the fragments appear to derive from the long bones.

The bone is mostly gray in color with some white pieces and a few that are charred (black). The latter are limited to one major long bone shaft fragment and a few cranial vault fragments. The white long bone fragments have many transverse cracks. There is little evidence of warping, although there is evidence of shrinkage of one molar root fragment. These characteristics suggest that the bone was not very highly fired—either a fire of relatively short duration or one of a relatively low temperature. The charred fragments also may have rolled out of the cremation fire prematurely.

Age is assessed as young to mature adult (18 to 50 years). This is based on fusion of the head of a rib, full development of a permanent molar root, cortical thickness of long bone shaft fragments, general inferred size of the elements, and a lack of any signs of osteoporosis. The individual was possibly male, as indicated by the size of the proximal epiphysis of an ulna, general robusticity of the skeletal elements, and the thickness of the occipital fragment. No pathologies are evident.

Feature 182 (Burial 6): Secondary Cremation

Feature 182 (Burial 6), a shallow, undefined secondary cremation pit, was observed in the profile of Trench 1 while searching for the outline of Feature 17, a pithouse. The cremation was located approximately 0.25 m below modern ground surface, in the partially filled entryway of Feature 17, and contained only minor root and rodent disturbance. The pit contained two distinct concentrations of cremated human remains. The concentrations were collected separately, but are assumed to be components of a single burial, a supposition supported by the osteological analysis (see below). The burial contained no clear grave goods; one piece of flaked stone debitage, probably not associated with the burial, was recovered from the feature fill.

The remains consist of cremated human bone fragments primarily from two concentrations. The total weight of burned bone is 195 grams. Concentration A held mandibular fragments, a tooth root fragment, a tibia shaft fragment, an ilium fragment, and a few major long bone shaft fragments. Concentration B held fragments from the left and right temporals, a parietal fragment, a few unidentified cranial vault fragments, an ulna fragment, a few major and minor long bone shaft fragments, and one metatarsal or metacarpal shaft fragment. One small rib fragment is also present. Overall, about three-quarters of the bone fragments by weight derive from long bones.

A majority of the bone is white in color and the rest is gray. The white fragments exhibit much cracking and some warping. The bone is highly fragmented.

All of the bone from both concentrations are consistent with a single subadult or older individual, except for one thin cranial vault fragment which appears to belong to a juvenile (2–12 years old). The age estimate for the rest of the remains is based on thickness of bone, size of the ulna shaft, mandible, and ilium. This indicates an individual of adult size, but there are no diagnostic criteria to narrow down the estimate further. No pathologies are present, but observability is extremely limited.

Feature 200 (Burial 7): Primary Inhumation

Feature 200 (Burial 7), a primary inhumation of a single individual, was discovered during the excavation of TU 174 in SA 4, approximately 40 cm below modern ground surface. The earthen pit was poorly defined, its outline barely visible in plan view. Root disturbance appears to have fractured all the long bones present. The burial was oriented southeast–northwest, and the body was interred on its back. The arms appeared extended alongside the skeleton, while the legs were flexed. No clear grave goods were associated with the burial. Some flaked stone and a few ceramic plain ware sherds were recovered from the burial, but their association with the burial is questionable.

This feature contained the partial, unburned remains of a single adult individual. The remains are poorly preserved. Long bone epiphyses are not present and the cortical surfaces are degraded. All regions of the skeleton are represented, although the vertebral column and pelvic girdle is represented only by a few fragments. Portions of all the long bone shafts with the exception of the right ulna could be identified in the lab. Both right and left ribs were identified in situ, but counts could not be verified in the lab due to fragmentation and poor preservation of the heads. There are prominent gnaw marks on the proximal portion of the shaft of the left humerus.

The skull is largely intact and was removed from the burial pit in a block of sediment. Some of the sediment was cleaned off in the lab, but this effort was limited in order to preserve the integrity of the skull out of respect for the wishes of the descendants.

The individual was assessed as likely in the range of 30 to 45 years. This is based on evidence that all the major cranial sutures were at least partly open, very heavy tooth wear, and an absence of osteoporosis of the long bone shafts. The individual was very likely male, as indicated by a large and robust cranium and a square chin.

Two anterior maxillary teeth exhibit non-carious exposure of the pulp chamber. This condition indicates an extremely rapid rate of wear. Normally, a tooth responds to heavy wear through the deposition of secondary dentin to maintain closure of the pulp chamber. The condition is likely to lead to an abscess, but missing alveolar bone prevented assessment in this case. No carious lesions were evident, although interproximal surfaces could not be fully assessed.

Antemortem tooth loss is indicated at the position of the left first mandibular molar and possibly the occluding left first maxillary molar. The left third mandibular molar was possibly congenitally absent. Enamel surfaces were not sufficiently preserved to permit assessment of calculus, enamel hypoplasia, or hypocalcification.

There is a large perforation on the left side of the mandible in the area of the mandibular foramen. There is no evidence of remodeled or reactive bone at this location and the root tips of the mandibular teeth are not exposed. This defect is likely taphonomic in nature.

The cranium and face were distorted by soil pressure. However, the broad face and projection of the malar region are consistent with Native American ancestry.

No skeletal pathologies are observed, although observability is minimal. Milder expressions of periosteal reactions would not be visible due to degradation of the cortical surfaces. The long bone shafts have thick and dense cortical bone. There is no evidence of joint disease on the few epiphyses of the carpal phalanges that are observable.

Isolated Occurrences of Human Remains

In addition to the remains from the numbered burials, there are a few isolated burned bone fragments from several locations (Table 4.54). Each represents the remains of a single individual. The color of the fragments is mostly white, with some gray portions. Cracking is present on most pieces.

Historic Features

Some historic use of the site area was documented by WSA at the Marsh Station Road site. The Class III report noted that the Southern Pacific Railroad (now Union Pacific) crossed the site; this railroad alignment had previously been assigned a site number AZ Z:2:40 (ASM). Small amounts of historic trash also were recorded during survey (Rieder et al. 2006) of the Marsh Station Road site, and some historic trash consisting mostly of glass shards and various pieces of metal were recovered primarily from the site surface. Aside from the current alignment of the Southern/Union Pacific Railroad, two additional historic alignments of the railroad were identified during mitigation.

Feature 135 was exposed while cleaning the stripped surface of SA 2. It consisted of the impressions of seven railroad ties. Traces of railroad-associated earthworks were found in dense vegetation at the site boundary, and could be followed northwest towards Cienega Creek. These earthworks, in conjunction with the railroad tie impression, were identified as the original alignment of the Southern Pacific railroad, built along Cienega Creek in 1880 (Myrick 1975). Occasional pieces of coal found in the stripped areas were probably associated with this railroad. The railroad ties were laid directly on the compact ground surface, without ballast, seemingly keeping with the expedient construction of the original track.

The original alignment was prone to flood damage, and lead Southern Pacific to relocate their track up the side of the Cienega Valley in 1887 (Myrick 1975; Rieder et al. 2006). This second alignment also crossed the site area. The grade was preserved as a linear earthwork, lacking ballast or other distinctive features. It was built from site sediment, and included prehistoric artifacts. During survey the abandoned railroad was misinterpreted as an erosion control feature, and was subsequently identified while reviewing aerial photographs of the proposed Cienega Creek HDD bore. It was possible to trace the grade for a distance through dense vegetation north, eventually into the modern track (see Figure 1.2). During monitoring of the most recent pipeline construction it was possible to draw a profile of the grade.

NATURE OF SITE SAMPLE

The site encompasses some 78,990 square meters. As mentioned above, 325 collection units, each 10 meters square, were laid over the portion of the site to be impacted by construction. Surface artifact density and subsurface testing with backhoe trenches guided the lateral stripping of a small portion of the construction corridor by mechanical means. This project mechanically stripped 1,815 square meters (see Table 4.2), representing just about 2.3 percent of the site area. Knowing to what extent this is representative of the unexamined portion of the site is difficult to ascertain, although both surface and subsurface data collected during excavation suggests that additional features are likely present south of Stripped Area 4/5. Excavations conducted by WCRM in the northeastern part of the site, near Stripped Area 1, suggest that additional features may be located in this area of the site as well (Kearns and McVickar 2009). Our interpretations of the site are necessarily limited by the small portion of

Table 4.54. Isolated human bone recovered from the Marsh Station Road site

Unit	Location	Designation	Age	Weight (g)	Elements Represented
TU 3	SA 4	IO1	Adult	1	Occipital
TU 27	SA 4	IO2	Adult	2	Parietal, minor long bone
TU 29	SA 4	IO3	Adult	2	Major long bone
Feature 6	SA 5	IO4	Adult	3	Occipital, frontal
TU 53	SA 4	IO5	Adult	4	Parietal or frontal
na	SA 4/5 spoil	IO6	unk.	unk.	unk.
na	Monitoring	IO7	Subadult (12+ yrs)	unk.	Major long bone, possible minor long bone

the site investigated during the EPX project.

Despite these uncertainties, the recovered artifacts and documented features provide a comprehensive sample of the site within the construction corridor. It is also clear that WSA was successful in targeting the feature-rich portions of the site within the corridor as evidenced by the fact that during construction monitoring just two features were found in previously unexamined portions of the site.

Spatial Distribution

Several statistical investigations were conducted using chi-square analysis to assess differences in the spatial distribution of flaked stone and ceramics at the Marsh Station Road site. Such analyses were not performed with other material classes because sample sizes were not large enough to yield reliable statistical results. The analysis of the flaked stone and ceramic spatial distribution revealed several interesting, if not necessarily interpretively useful, patterns. First, it was determined that there is a statistically significant difference, although one that is not likely meaningful, in the distribution of ceramics and flaked stone between the surface and subsurface. Further investigation shows that the chi-square test was

driven by the large number of flaked stone artifacts. Ceramics constitute 16.2 percent of the surface artifacts at the site, and 17.8 percent of the subsurface artifacts. The surface ceramics constitute 17.3 percent of the total site ceramic assemblage, while the surface flaked stone constitutes 19 percent of all flaked stone at the site. Therefore, the extremely high number of flaked stone artifacts and the low number of ceramic artifacts results in a significant test ($\chi2 = 12.35$, df $= 1$, p $< .001$) even though, again, the actual differences in percentages between surface and subsurface for each material class are minimal.

A second test sought to differentiate between the two major stripped areas—SA 2/3 and SA 4/5—counting all artifacts, from surface and subsurface contexts within each stripped area. The results of this test ($\chi2 = 790.7$, df $= 1$, p $< .001$) show that the data suggest a major difference in the proportion of ceramics in SA 2/3 versus in SA 4/5. The ceramics in SA 2/3 make up nine percent of all ceramics, while the flaked stone in SA 2/3 constitutes 24 percent of all flaked stone. Additionally, the ceramics are only six percent of the combined flaked stone and ceramic total for SA 2/3, while the ceramics constitute 18 percent of this total for SA 4/5. There is an unquestioned distinction between

Table 4.55. Distribution of raw material types in collection units, test units, and excavated features

Raw Material	Raw Material Group[1]	CU (%)	TU (%)	Feature (%)	Totals
Silicified sediment	3	2120 (26.24)	640 (26.47)	3228 (22.37)	5988
Chert	9–11	932 (11.53)	572 (23.66)	3680 (25.5)	5184
Silicified sediment/ limestone with speckles	1 & 2	1708 (21.14)	287 (11.87)	1491 (10.33)	3486
Silicified sediment/ limestone without speckles	1 & 2	1087 (13.45)	318 (13.15)	1907 (13.21)	3312
Quartzite	4	955 (11.82)	178 (7.36)	1780 (12.33)	2913
Bisbee chert	5 & 19	476 (5.89)	190 (7.86)	891 (6.17)	1557
Chalcedony	9–11	205 (2.54)	91 (3.76)	733 (5.08)	1029
Rhyolite	6–8	228 (2.82)	37 (1.53)	205 (1.42)	470
Sandstone	3	196 (2.43)	35 (1.45)	145 (1.00)	376
Maroon rhyolite/andesite	6–8	39 (0.48)	12 (0.50)	141 (0.98)	192
Jasper	9–11	13 (0.16)	7 (0.29)	80 (0.55)	100
Igneous other	na	19 (0.24)	20 (0.82)	34 (0.24)	73
Quartz	4	14 (0.17)	13 (0.54)	40 (0.28)	67
Gray quartzite	4	48 (0.59)			48
Andesite	6–8	12 (0.15)	4 (0.17)	19 (0.13)	35
Metamorphic other	na	5 (0.62)	10 (0.41)	18 (0.12)	33
Porphyritic igeneous	na	14 (0.17)	1 (0.04)	12 (0.08)	27
Granite	na	1 (0.01)	2 (0.08)	5 (0.03)	8
Obsidian	na	1 (0.01)		5 (0.03)	6
Sedimentary other	na	6 (0.07)			6
Bisbee quartzite	5 & 19		1 (0.04)	2 (0.01)	3
Basalt	6–8	1 (0.01)		1 (0.007)	2
Slate	na			1 (0.007)	1
Turquoise	na			1 (0.007)	1
Unknown/indeterminate				12 (0.08)	12
Total		8080	2418	14331	24929

Note: Raw material types were coded as "na" if they were 1) only identified in the ground stone assemblage, which was not subdivided into raw material groups, or 2) they were represented by few enough artifacts to prohibit statistical analyses

SA 2/3 and SA 4/5 for the two most abundant artifact classes recovered at the Marsh Station Road site. However, it is unclear whether the observed differences in the distribution of ceramics and flaked stone between SA 2/3 and SA 4/5 are indicative of distinctive behavior between the two areas, or whether they are more a function of temporal differences in the occupation of the site.

Finally, the data suggest no significant difference ($\chi2 = 0.5$, df = 1, $0.2 < p < 0.5$) in the distribution of ceramics and flaked stone within subsurface contexts (test units versus features) at the Marsh Station Road site. This test served the purpose of assessing differences in discard practices between what we as archaeologists identify as features and the areas outside of the features, showing that there is no such difference at this site.

Raw Material Distribution

Twenty-four different raw materials, as well as one unknown raw material type, were identified in the flaked and ground stone assemblages at the Marsh Station Road site; their distribution across collection units, test units, and features is shown in Table 4.55. Silicified sediments and chert, followed by silicified sediment/limestone and quartzite, were by far the most common raw material types. Quantities of the remaining raw materials types drop off quickly, with only a few pieces of nonlocal (i.e., not available within the immediate site area) raw material types, such as obsidian, slate, and turquoise, having been recovered.

Chi-squared analyses were also performed on the spatial distribution of raw material types between surface (collection units) and subsurface (test units and features) deposits, and between stripped areas. The analyses only investigated the distribution of raw material types in the flaked stone assemblage. Given that flaked stone represents approximately 99 percent of the raw material counts (Table 4.55), inclusion of the raw material types represented by ground stone artifacts, and other artifacts, is unlikely to alter the results.

The chi-squared analyses indicated that generally, the distribution of raw material types between surface and subsurface contexts is not significantly different. That is, they remain basically the same whether comparing all surface artifacts to all subsurface artifacts, or looking at restricted subsets of both assemblages. However, there were two conspicuous results. First, raw materials in groups 1 & 2—silicified sediments/limestone with and without speckles (see Table 4.55)—occur in higher-than-expected numbers on the surface and in lower-than-expected numbers in subsurface contexts. Second, cryptocrystalline silicates (groups 9–11; see Table 4.55) occur in higher-than-expected numbers subsurface and in lower-than-expected numbers on the surface. While this difference is interesting, it is difficult to assign behavioral meaning to the differential distribution of these raw material types.

The chi-squared analyses also revealed several statistically significant differences in the distribution of raw materials across stripped units. Raw materials in groups 1 & 2 and 9–11 occur in lower-than-expected numbers in SA 2/3, and higher-than-expected numbers in SA 4/5; but the opposite is true for raw materials in groups 3, 4, 6–8, and 5 & 19. While there is, thus far, no behaviorally meaningful explanation for these differences, it is curious that raw materials in groups 1 & 2 and 5 & 19 display a reverse-relationship distribution, even though raw materials in both groups are locally available, and that raw material groups 1 & 2 and 9–11 display the same relationship, even though their proximity to the site, and therefore their availability, are distinctly different (see Boley and Gabler, Chapter 6). These relationships are largely mirrored when chi-squared analyses of raw material distributions across features are performed, suggesting that there may be temporal differences driving the significant results of the chi-squared tests, given that SA 2/3 is generally considered to be Early Agricultural, while SA 4/5 is generally considered more representative of the late Middle Formative occupation.

Chronological Distribution

The majority of artifacts recovered from the Marsh Station Road site are not chronologically diagnostic, and thus this discussion focuses on those chronological indicators present in the ceramic and flaked stone assemblages (Figure 4.47), as well as absolute dates for features obtained through radiocarbon and archaeomagnetic dating.

Interestingly, the general chronological pictures presented by the ceramic and flaked stone assemblages are somewhat contradictory. As mentioned briefly above, the vast majority of the chronologically diagnostic ceramic sherds date to the Middle Formative period, and in particular to the Rincon phase, although the Rillito and possibly the Tanque Verde and Tucson phases are also minimally represented. While a small number of sherds were recovered from features dated to the Early Agricultural period, these were almost certainly intrusive, and no ceramic wares characteristic of the early ceramics horizons were identified Although a strict reliance on only the ceramic assemblage for temporal resolution of site occupation could prove misleading, in this case, the ceramic data point primarily towards an occupation during the Middle Formative period.

The flaked stone assemblage also provides a somewhat misleading chronological picture of the site. The vast majority of the diagnostic

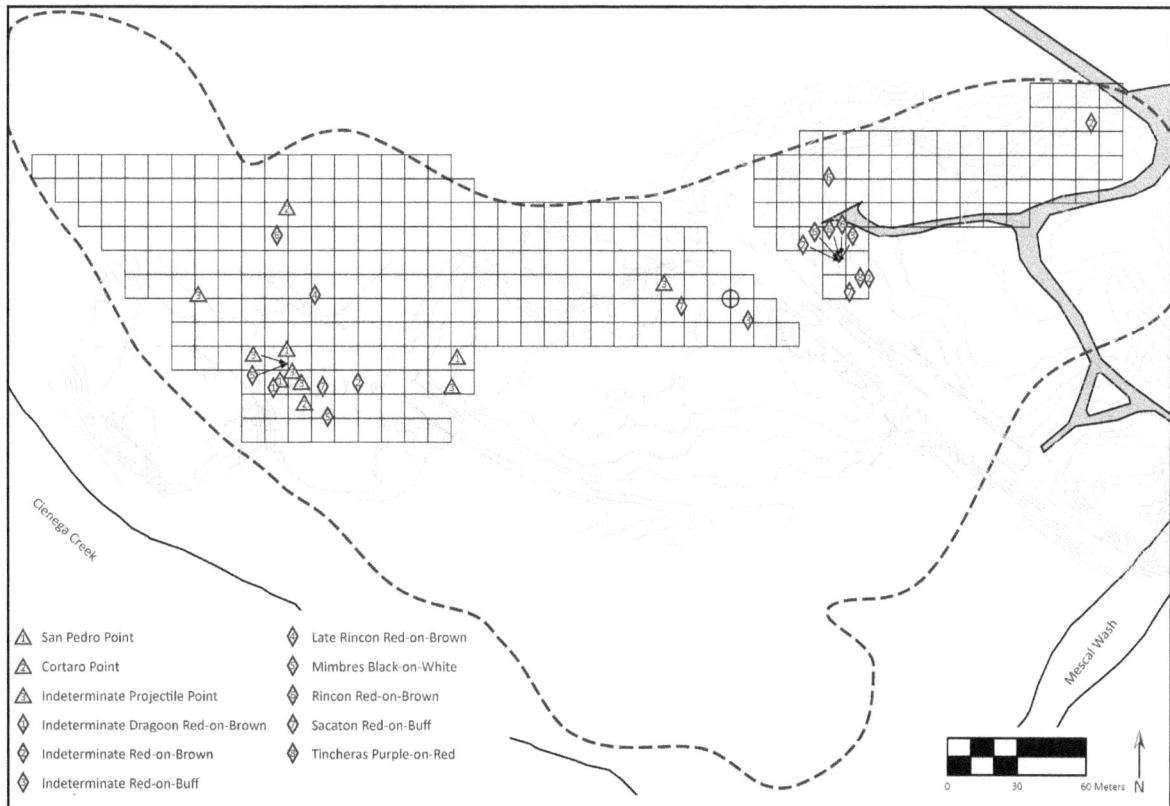

Figure 4.47. Distribution of diagnostic projectile points and ceramics recovered from the surface of the Marsh Station Road site.

projectile points recovered from the site date to the Early Agricultural period, while very few date to the Middle Formative period. At first glance, the presence of so many Early Agricultural points suggests that the Marsh Station Road site primarily dates to that period. However, as previously discussed in this chapter, many of these Early Agricultural points were recovered from features, and in particular from pithouses, that have been radiocarbon and/or archaeomagnetic dated to the Rincon phase/ late Middle Formative period, and that have painted ceramics dating to the same period. Thus, one is left wondering why so many Early Agricultural period points were recovered in later-dating features, and why a paucity of later-dating projectile points was recovered from the site.

Analysis of the debitage characteristics and raw material distributions within the flaked stone assemblage also suggests some behavioral differences in flaked stone manufacture between the Early Agricultural and Middle Formative periods. It appears that the manufacture of bifaces may have been more common during the Early Agricultural period than during the Middle Formative period. In addition, cryptocrystalline silicates are overrepresented in SA 2/3, which has been tentatively characterized as containing features predominantly associated with the Early Agricultural period, and underrepresented in SA 4/5, which contains features primarily dating to the Middle Formative period. However, while there appear to be rather clear chronological, and in fact, spatial differences in the distribution of these raw material types, there is little evidence to suggest why these differences exist in the first place. Perhaps they can be attributed to general changes in flaked stone technology, observed by Parry and Kelly (1987), and discussed further in Chapter 6.

SUMMARY

The Marsh Station Road site (AZ EE:2:44[ASM]) is an extensive, multicomponent, semi-permanent habitation site covering approximately 20 acres (see Figures 1.2 and 4.1). As described above, only a small percentage of the site was investigated through site mapping, surface collection, preconstruction trenching, mechanical stripping, excavation of test units, and horizontal exposure and full excavation of identified features during the EPX project. During these investigations, WSA archaeologists documented 192 features, including six pithouses/structures; excavated 138 of these; and collected over 50,000 artifacts. Sixteen radiocarbon assays and four archaeomagentic analyses, as well as a number of diagnostic projectile points and ceramic artifacts, indicate that the site was occupied from at least the San Pedro phase of the Early Agricultural period through the late Classic period, with notable hiatuses during the Late Formative (Tanque Verde phase) period and perhaps during the Cienega phase of the Early Agricultural period.

In the following chapters, detailed analyses of each artifact class (ceramics, flaked stone, ground stone, faunal, and shell) as well as of the environmental samples (macrobotanical and pollen) are presented. In the final chapter of the volume, data from the current chapter is used in conjunction with data from the artifact and environmental sample analyses to interpret the occupation history of the site and to place the site within a regional framework.

Endnotes for Chapter 4

[1] A total of 325 collection units was orginally laid out over the site's surface. Prior to surface collection, the first 12 of these units fell out of the APE, and therefore were not collected. However, the original numbering of the collection units (CUs 1–325) was retained for archival purposes. Thus, on Figure 4.2, only CUs 13–325 are depicted, for a total of 313 collection units.

[2] A total of 269 features, subfeatures, and what were ultimately determined to be nonfeatures was documented at the Marsh State Road site; four feature numbers were voided prior to excavation, and an additional 19 features and subfeatures were determined to be nonfeatures following their excavation (see Appendix I, Table C and Table 4.5).

[3] While most of the unexcavated features are likely prehistoric, unless clearly associated with the historic period (e.g., Features 135 and 209), temporal designations were not assigned to unexcavated features.

Chapter 5
Ceramic Analysis

Brian R. McKee, Meaghan Trowbridge, and Brandon M. Gabler

The ceramics recovered from the Marsh Station Road site provide critical information relevant to a variety of research questions relating to site formation processes, reuse, and chronology. In Arizona, ceramics have been produced for at least the last 2,000 years, and many decorated types can relatively date archaeological deposits to within 100 and 200 year intervals. Ceramics also can provide important information relevant to subsistence, production technology, social organization, interaction, and exchange.

WSA archaeologists collected 9,038 ceramics from the Marsh Station Road site (AZ EE:2:44 [ASM]). Tables 5.1 and 5.2 show the distribution of artifact type and ceramic ware, respectively. Of the 9,038 total ceramics, 5 were reconstructible whole or partial vessels, 1 was a ceramic figurine, 8,992 were sherds, 1 was a fired-clay bead, and 39 were ceramic artifacts that had been modified by prehistoric inhabitants. It should be noted that the reconstructible vessels and reworked vessels comprise many individual sherds that are counted only once in the totals above; the total number of individual sherds for the Marsh Station Road site is 9,198 ceramic sherds. For the remainder of this chapter, except for the discussion of reconstructible vessels themselves, these vessels are counted as one artifact rather than many sherds of the same type or ware.

This chapter begins with a discussion of the objectives of the Marsh Station Road site ceramics analysis. A summary of the methods utilized in the analysis and descriptions of the ceramic types follow. We then present the analysis results, compare the site results with those of other projects conducted in the area, and examine the implications of this study for more general research questions.

RESEARCH GOALS

The analysis of the Marsh Station Road site ceramic assemblage was conducted with several objectives in mind. The first is largely descriptive, to characterize the nature and diversity of the assemblage recovered during the project. That characterization includes classifying the ceramics in existing typologies based on paste, decoration, temper, and the examination of the vessel forms represented by the sherds. Descriptive data include the counts, sizes and any evidence of post-breakage modification of the sherds recovered.

The second objective involves the exploration of changes in the assemblage through time. Were there differences in types/wares, vessel forms, or temper? Are there changes in the frequencies of plain wares over time, particularly during the difficult-to-date early

Table 5.1. Ceramic artifacts by artifact type

General Sherds	Modified Artifacts	Figurines & Beads	RVs (counted in total)	Count of Sherds in RVs* (not counted in total)	Total
8992	39	2	5	62, 49, 18, 5, 11	9038

*RV=reconstructible vessel

portion of the sequence? We also used previously established ceramic chronologies to independently date features.

A third objective is to explore possible connections between the people inhabiting this site and other people living to the east and north living in the regions surrounding the site. Intrusive ceramics have the potential to shed light on that issue by indicating peoples' long-distance transport or exchange of pots across the landscape. Based on survey data (Rieder et al. 2006), and on data from other sites in the immediate vicinity of the Marsh Station Road site, the current analysis focused on connections with groups living in the mountainous region to the east andand north in the Phoenix Basin to the north of the site. Connections with the Tucson Basin, to the west of the site, were not explicitly considered as evidence of interaction here because, as is discussed in Chapters 4 and 12 as well as in the conclusions of the current chapter, the Marsh Station Road site is interpreted as more-or-less within the Tucson Basin. In addition, although the Hohokam had definite interaction with groups to the south, neither our initial survey data nor data from sites in the immediate vicinity suggested contact with groups to the south. This inference is supported by our analysis data (see below).

The final set of objectives relates to the examination of formation processes of the archaeological record, those processes by which the dynamic behaviors of past peoples are translated into the static material forming the

archaeological record (Schiffer 1987:14–18). Formation processes can result in information loss through the degradation of materials, but also can introduce patterning of their own (Schiffer 1987:10). Formation processes act at a variety of scales, including those of artifacts, features, sites, and regions (Schiffer 1987). In this chapter, we concentrate on their effects on artifacts. We consider general themes related to formation processes including vessel reuse as well as discard processes and post-depositional impacts on discarded materials.

METHODS

Methods employed in the ceramic analysis were designed to recover as much pertinent information as possible and to answer the specific research questions posed for the site.

Attribute Analysis

Ceramic sherd analysis was conducted in two stages. The first consisted of the bulk identification of types, which was completed for all sherds from the site by Meaghan Trowbridge, who was coached by William Deaver of West-Land Resources. The second stage recorded morphometric attributes. This stage recorded several attributes regarding the forms of rim sherds, as well as metric attributes such as rim diameter, sherd thickness, and two-dimensional sherd size. No design attribute inventory was conducted, as too few whole and reconstructible vessels (three decorated, one red-slipped, and one unknown) were recovered to permit a meaningful study.

During the first analytical stage, sherds were separated into bulk categories of painted and unpainted. From that point, all sherds were classified by ware and type. Plain ware (unpainted) sherds were identified by ware only (e.g., brown ware, red ware, unpainted buff ware). Those wares were subdivided based on temper, to examine possible changes in unpainted ceramics through time and space (see below). Painted sherds were classified by types defined within each ware category (e.g., Rincon Red-on-brown, Sacaton Red-on-buff). When a specific painted type could not be definitively identified, sherds were classified by a general painted ware (e.g., indeterminate red-on-brown). The types identified by the analysis are discussed in further detail below. Sherd counts of each ware and type were recorded for each context. Ceramic counts from both stages of analysis were entered into a Microsoft Access database from which pertinent tables were generated.

During the morphometric analysis, all ceramics recovered from features, all painted ceramics, and 25 percent of the remaining plain ware sherds were analyzed. Rim sherds were examined to determine rim form, rim lip finish, and rim diameter. Sherds were sorted by size and placed in ordinal categories. Average thickness was measured using metric calipers, and temper was identified and described for each. Rim diameter was determined using the curve-fitting method (Egloff 1973; Plog 1985).

The goal of temper analysis is to record attributes related to clay paste and temper. Temper is any nonplastic inclusion purposefully added to clay to improve or alter certain performance characteristics of the clay during manufacture and use (Schiffer and Skibo 1987; Shepard 1976). Sometimes naturally occurring inclusions in the clay can resemble temper. Temper was examined using a 10x hand lens and a 10x to 50x Nikon stereozoom binocular microscope. The three most abundant temper materials in each sherd were qualitatively identified, along with the relative size and texture of temper fragments. No petrographic analyses were conducted as assemblage variation appeared to be minimal.

Whole and Reconstructible Vessels

In all, five reconstructible vessels were recovered. Unbroken and complete vessels are considered to be whole, while reconstructible vessels were broken but at least 20 percent complete. Often there is a distinction made between reconstructible vessels and partial vessels based on the degree of completeness (e.g., Smith et al. 2004:158). However, the number of whole and reconstructible vessels recovered is small enough that they were lumped into a single category. All reconstructible vessels were reassembled (other than FN 44-664.03, from the Marsh Station Road site, which was associated with a cremation) to interpret the original vessel form and acquire all relevant measurements.

Measurements recorded for whole and reconstructible vessels include maximum vessel height, orifice diameter, maximum diameter, average wall thickness, mass, and volume. Measurements were in centimeters with the exception of wall thickness, which was measured in millimeters with digital calipers. Volume in liters was measured by filling the vessels with Styrofoam packing peanuts, which were then measured in graduated vessels. Volume could only be measured for those vessels that were either complete or nearly complete.

Vessel forms for whole and reconstructible vessels were classified based on previous descriptions provided by Deaver (1984:269–276, Figures 4.12 and 4.14). Wares and types were assigned based on the same criteria as those used for the bulk sherd analysis. When applicable, surface treatment was described, including abbreviated analyses of painted designs. Basic components of stylistic attributes were recorded, such as general symmetry and design layout, and both form and design of whole and reconstructible vessels were illustrated.

Use wear and post-firing modifications were described when applicable and include normal wear from everyday use as well as deliberate modifications such as repair holes and refurbishing of broken vessels. All recorded modifications occurred while vessels were still in systemic context (Schiffer 1987). Use wear was described in purely qualitative terms, and no attempt was made to seriate vessels based on use or modification. To the extent possible, temper was identified for each vessel. Temper identifications consist of dominant material type and, when visible, the texture and relative size of temper inclusions. These observations were made using a 10x hand lens.

Other Ceramic Analyses

Thirty-nine worked ceramics, one ceramic figurine, and one spherical, fired-clay bead were also recovered from the Marsh Station Road site. Worked sherds vary greatly in both shape and size, and include disks (both perforated and unperforated), utilized sherds, reworked vessels (such as scoops crafted from large sherds), and indeterminate worked sherds. Some of the perforated sherd disks analyzed were likely used prehistorically as spindle whorls, although the formal category of disk was used to avoid possible functional misidentifications. All worked sherds and nonvessel ceramic artifacts (e.g., beads and figurines) from the project were analyzed separately from the bulk sherds, as were the whole and reconstructible vessels.

Detailed discussion of modified and reworked ceramics is presented below.

Further Investigation of Plain Wares

Some researchers have noted that the classification of plain ware pottery in the Tucson Basin defies the archaeologist and is often a futile pursuit (e.g., Doyel 1977:26; Greenleaf 1975:55). While there have been studies arguing for temporal variation in plain ware at Tucson Basin sites (Deaver 1984; Heidke 1986; Kelly et al. 1978; Whittlesey 1986), the relevant characteristics have yet to be thoroughly and systematically described.

The Tucson Basin plain brown ware ceramics from the Marsh Station Road site were analyzed to determine whether there are any significant identifiable diachronic or synchronic patterns of variability. The distinction of plain ware "types" during the bulk analysis of ceramics was based on primarily qualitative and relative observations of temper inclusions and surface treatments (see Deaver 1984 for the conceptual basis). The types created were based on the relative proportions of mica and sand in the temper as well as the presence or absence of surface polishing or smoothing.

The distributions of these types were charted for all dated features at the Marsh Station Road site. Features were independently dated based on decorated ceramics, the presence of temporally diagnostic projectile points, and radiocarbon assays. Only features containing more than 10 plain ware sherds were assessed in this part of the analysis. Although the relative frequencies of mica-tempered to sand-tempered undecorated ceramics do differ between features, neither spatial nor temporal patterns are evident. Overall, it appears that the occurrence of sand- versus mica-tempered sherds at the Marsh Station Road site is unpredictable and, for the most part, random.

We also studied the thickness of plain

ware sherds from features at the Marsh Station Road site. Whalen (1996) found decreasing thickness of ceramic utility vessels as a correlate to the increasing reliance on agriculture in the Southwest. Given the great time depth of occupation at the Marsh Station Road site, we were interested to see whether trends in vessel thickness over time could be detected. In the features investigated, the thicknesses of individual sherds varied from 3.4 to 12.3 mm, but the mean thicknesses were very similar between features, ranging between 5.7 and 6.7 mm. The distribution of sherd thickness within individual features was also investigated, and although a few very thick or very thin sherds were present, these extremes were always outliers to the general distributions of the sherds within the features. This small study indicates that there is no significant spatial or temporal variation in the thicknesses of plain ware sherds from features at the Marsh Station Road site.

DESCRIPTION OF WARES AND TYPES IDENTIFIED

Of the 9,038 ceramic artifacts, 27.8 percent are undersized or unidentifiable, and could not be classified to ware (undersized sherds are smaller than 2 cm in maximum dimension, and unidentifiable sherds are too eroded, burned, or otherwise indefinite to be assigned to a ware category). Most of the 6,524 classified sherds are unpainted (76.9 percent) and include plain brown ware, plain buff ware, and red ware. Is it also possible that some of the sherds classified as unpainted are in fact unpainted portions of decorated wares, rather than true plain wares. However, in the absence of any evidence of decoration, sherds were classified as unpainted. The 1,507 painted ceramics are dominated by indeterminate red-on-brown (81.5 percent), Rincon Red-on-brown (10.4 percent), and a small percentage were classified as uncom-

mon local types or intrusive, nonlocal types (8 percent). All types recovered and described here have been recorded elsewhere; we did not designate any new types. Because they have been well documented in other publications (see Heckman et al. 2000; Wallace 1986c; Whittlesey 1986; Whittlesey 2004, ed.), we provide only summary type descriptions, and reference more detailed descriptions and illustrations published elsewhere in the discussion that follows.

Plain Ware

Plain ware sherds from this collection consisted mostly of plain brown wares (not to be confused with Tucson Basin brown wares, which are largely painted types). During the first stages of analysis, we attempted to separate plain wares into different categories to investigate potential temporal and spatial patterning. Based on surface finish and temper inclusions, those categories were assigned arbitrary numbers, and analysts classified each plain ware sherd into one of these groups. A few scholars have argued that there is indeed variation in plain brown ware over time in the Tucson Basin (Deaver 1984; Kelly et al. 1978; Whittlesey 1986), although the differences have not yet been described in a systematic manner. In the end, it appears that the distinctions we made were largely insignificant. Without clearer stratigraphic separation and stronger corroborating chronological indicators, such as a detailed corresponding painted ceramic chronology, it is risky to posit that the slight differences among them are temporally significant. For the purposes of this report, plain brown wares are considered as one broad ceramic category (see above).

Of the 6,521 sherds analyzed that were identified at least to the level of ware, 4,874 (74.7 percent) were classified as plain brown ware. Every feature excavated contained primarily plain, unpainted sherds. Within the plain ware ceramics, a number of worked sherds were identified as well as two nonvessel ceramic artifacts (one fired-clay bead and one female figurine). Of the plain brown ware sherds, 358 were rim sherds, 36 percent of which were from unrestricted vessels (bowls) and 55 percent from restricted vessels (jars or incurved bowls). The remaining rim sherds were too small to confidently assign a vessel form. In addition, one partial plain ware vessel was associated with a human cremation.

Red Ware

Like plain brown wares in the Tucson Basin, there are few typological classifications for red wares. Red ware ceramics are typically technologically similar to plain wares, with the addition of a red slip on one or both surfaces. No painted red ware sherds were identified at the Marsh Station Road site. A total of 120 unpainted red ware sherds was identified (1.8 percent of classified ceramics), including 12 rim sherds and 1 worked sherd. Red ware sherds were primarily tempered with sand with slight variations in paste color from brown to a darker, grayish brown. One whole, reconstructed vessel was classified as red ware, and based on vessel form and construction technique, it can be placed in the late Classic period (William Deaver, personal communication 2007).

Tucson Basin Brown Ware

Of the 1,507 painted sherds, 92.1 percent (n=1,388) were typed as Tucson Basin brown wares and included Rincon Red-on-brown, Rincon Black-on-brown, Rillito Red-on-brown, and Sahuarita Polychrome, a variant of Rincon Polychrome. The large category of indeterminate red-on-brown is also included under the heading of Tucson Basin brown

ware. Indeterminate red-on-brown ceramics could not be classified as a particular design type, mostly due to their small size. Of the total Tucson Basin brown ware ceramics identified, 88.4 percent (n=1,227) are indeterminate red-on-brown.

The painted Tucson Basin brown ware ceramics include 230 rim sherds, 7 worked sherds, 1 reworked plate, and 2 partially reconstructed vessels. Most Tucson Basin brown ware classifications are derived from sequences and types defined at Snaketown by Gladwin (Gladwin et al. 1937; Kelly et al. 1978) and Haury (1937a). Alterations to the sequence have been made over the years, but the basic types and definitions have remained largely the same. Heckman (2000a) provides a comprehensive overview of currently accepted and utilized type classifications for Tucson Basin brown ware, most of which were used as the basis for type classification in this project.

Rillito Red-on-Brown

Only one Rillito Red-on-brown sherd (< 0.1 percent of Tucson Basin red-on-brown ceramics) was positively identified. Rillito is the earliest Tucson Basin brown ware identified at the Marsh Station Road site. Rillito temper tends to have high mica content due to the addition of schist to the typical sand temper. Pottery was usually decorated with only one or two design motifs, unlike the later more detailed Rincon style. Heckman (2000a:89–90, Figure 43) describes and illustrates Rillito Red-on-brown ceramics.

Rincon Red-on-Brown

Rincon Red-on-brown is typically characterized by diverse designs. Deaver (1984) defined three Rincon Red-on-brown styles (A, B, and C) based on design, although he more recently revisited the Rincon styles and classified them in a more chronological fashion as fitting into Colonial and Sedentary styles (Deaver 2004). Wallace (1986c) divided Rincon Red-on-brown into three subtypes: Early, Middle, and Late. Heckman (2000a:89, 91–92, Figures 44 and 45) provides a detailed discussion and illustrations of Rincon Red-on-brown. A total of 157 Rincon Red-on-brown sherds (11.3 percent of the Tucson Basin red-on-brown ceramics) was recovered. It is likely that many of the 1,228 indeterminate red-on-brown artifacts date to the Rincon phase but lack defining characteristics to allow temporal assignment.

Due to the few large diagnostic Rincon Red-on-brown ceramics collected, it was difficult to confidently assign them to subtypes or styles. Only a few sherds were characterized as Early (n=3) and Late (n=26) Rincon, and one reworked vessel was classified as Middle Rincon (William Deaver, personal communication 2007). These classifications were based loosely on earlier types/styles defined by Deaver (1984) and Wallace (1986c) and are simply used to imply that particular sherds clearly belong to either the beginning or the ending of the Rincon stylistic phase. Without a large enough comparative assemblage, we could not confidently fit all Rincon sherds into subtypes.

Rincon Black-on-Brown

Rincon Black-on-brown was defined as a new pottery type directly stemming from Rincon Red-on-brown (Deaver 1984:322). This variant is sometimes referred to as Rincon Black-on-white due to its white slip. Aside from the black pigment and white slip, this type is indistinguishable from its red-on-brown counterpart. Five (0.4 percent of Tucson Basin red-on-brown artifacts) Rincon Black-on-brown sherds were identified from the Marsh Station Road site.

Sahuarita Polychrome

Sahuarita Polychrome pottery has been recorded only minimally from projects in the Tucson Basin. Deaver (1984:328) first identified Sahuarita Polychrome as "a hybrid of Rincon Polychrome and Río Rico Polychrome." Most Sahuarita Polychrome vessels are bowls, and the type is proposed to have been produced near the Santa Cruz River (Deaver 1984; Frick 1954). Typical vessels have red-slipped interiors with red or black painted exteriors, usually on a white slip. Two sherds (0.1 percent of Tucson Basin red-on-brown artifacts) identified as Sahuarita Polychrome (William Deaver, personal communication 2007) were recovered from the Marsh Station Road site.

Dragoon Brown Ware

Dragoon pottery was first defined by the Amerind Foundation as a part of the Dragoon complex, and originally included painted types such as Cascabel, Tres Alamos, Dragoon, Deep Well, and Benson Red-on-brown (Tuthill 1947:50–64). Dragoon designs typically exhibit a less-skillfully executed combination of style elements from both Mogollon and Hohokam ceramics, and are predominantly found throughout the San Pedro River valley. As mentioned by Heckman (2000b:43), the Dragoon type descriptions are rather ambiguous and overlapping, and the chronological sequence is not clearly defined. Taking this into account, only one broad type, indeterminate Dragoon Red-on-brown, was identified at the Marsh Station Road site, and just two sherds (0.1 percent of painted ceramics) were recovered. Heckman (2000b:43–62, Figures 19–28) describes and illustrates the Dragoon brown ware tradition.

Trincheras Purple-on-Red

Sometimes referred to as Trincheras Purple-on-brown (Whittlesey 1992:41), this type is presumed to have been produced near the Altar Valley in Sonora, Mexico (Gladwin and Gladwin 1929), but it occurs over a large geographic area (Heckman 2000c:76). Trincheras pottery exhibits both technological and stylistic variability, although one of its major defining characteristics is the purple-tinted paint, most likely the result of specular hematite-based pigments (Heckman 2000c:77). One (< 0.1 percent of painted ceramics) Trincheras Purple-on-red sherd was identified from the Marsh Station Road site. Heckman (2000c:75–81, Figures 36–40) provides detailed descriptions and illustrations of Trincheras Purple-on-red ceramics.

Hohokam Buff Ware

Despite the numerous large-scale excavations of Hohokam sites in recent decades, the original Snaketown volumes describing Hohokam buff wares (Gladwin et al. 1937; Haury 1976) remain the basis for defining all Hohokam design types used today, as well as the general chronological sequence for Hohokam ceramics. Buff wares were produced primarily in the Gila and the Salt river valleys, near the Phoenix Basin, but were distributed across a wide geographic region. These types are often encountered in the Tucson Basin, and it is debated whether they indicate exchange networks or potential migration and colonization by Hohokam peoples (Whittlesey 1998).

The Hohokam red-on-buff types all correspond directly with cultural phases (Whittlesey and Heckman 2000:95–106). In total, 103 (6.8 percent of painted ceramics) Hohokam red-on-buff sherds were identified during this project, most from the Marsh Station Road site. Of those, only 14 could be positively identi-

fied as belonging to specific design types; the remaining 89 sherds were classified as indeterminate red-on-buff. Twelve (11.7 percent of red-on-buff ceramics) were designated Sacaton Red-on-buff, which dates to the Sedentary period. At the Marsh Station Road site, Sacaton Red-on-buff was almost always found in direct association with Rincon Red-on-brown (also see Heckman 2000a:83). The two other sherds identified as Hohokam are Sweetwater Red-on-gray (n=1; 1 percent) and Snaketown Red-on-buff (n=1; 1 percent), both of which date to the Pioneer period (Haury 1937a).

Mimbres White Ware

Mimbres Black-on-white is a well-known type originating in the Mogollon culture region of southwestern New Mexico and southeastern Arizona. Mimbres styles were first described by Haury (1936), and have come to be easily recognizable due to their depictions of everyday activities and lifelike animal images as well as distinctive geometric designs (Whittlesey and Heckman 2000:106–110). In the Tucson Basin, Mogollon ceramics are classified as intrusive wares and are likely the result of interregional exchange and trade. Though not necessarily found in high numbers, Mimbres Black-on-white is a rather consistent inclusion in ceramic assemblages from the San Pedro region. Eight (0.5 percent of painted ceramics) Mimbres Black-on-white sherds were recovered from the Marsh Station Road site. All are small, and it is not possible to determine the style of the sherds or a chronological distinction based on design elements.

ANALYSIS RESULTS

The following discussion provides the results of our ceramic investigations. The results of the sherd analysis are presented first and are followed by those of the whole and reconstructible vessel analysis and the analysis of the worked sherds.

Sherd Analysis

A total of 9,038 ceramics were recovered from the Marsh Station Road site, and included 5 reconstructible vessels, 8,992 sherds, 2 non-vessel ceramics, and 39 instances of ceramic reuse. The sherds are from a variety of recovery contexts including surface collection units, test units, trenches, stripping units, stripping areas, and features (Table 5.2), with most coming from test units (47 percent), feature excavation units (32 percent), and collection units (17 percent).

At the Marsh Station Road site painted ceramics are the minority of the total ceramic artifacts recovered (17 percent). Undersized and unidentified sherds constitute 28 percent of the total, while unpainted ceramics constitute 55 percent. Body sherds make up the majority of the total general sherds, numbering 8,375 of 8,983 sherds (93 percent), with 603 rim sherds (7 percent), 1 handle, and 4 other vessel portions.

Most of the painted ceramics site-wide are indeterminate red-on-brown (n=1,228 of 1,507 painted ceramics, 81 percent). Of the remaining painted ceramics, 89 (5.9 percent) are indeterminate red-on-buff. Of the 190 painted ceramics that can be identified to the level of type, 157 (83 percent) are identified as Rincon Red-on-brown. The remaining 33 sherds include Sacaton Red-on-buff (6 percent), Mimbres Black-on-white (4 percent), Rincon Black-on-brown (3 percent), indeterminate Dragoon Red-on-brown (1 percent), Sahuarita Polychrome (1 percent), and one each of Rillito Red-on-brown, Snaketown Red-on-buff, Sweetwater Red-on-gray, and Trincheras Purple-on-red.

Feature versus Nonfeature Contexts

The relative frequencies of painted and unpainted ceramics did not differ much between feature and nonfeature contexts. Undersized and unidentified sherds constitute 28.3 percent (n=2,517) of the overall assemblage and 28 percent (n=854 of 3,060) of the assemblage recovered from features, while unpainted sherds make up 55 and 57 percent, respectively, of each (n=5,014 of 9,038 total, n = 1,758 of 3,060 from features). Painted sherds constitute 16.7 percent (n=1,507) of the overall assemblage and 15.8 percent (n=485) of the sherds recovered from features.

Table 5.3 shows the relative frequencies of painted ceramic types between feature and nonfeature contexts. Based on the associated table, there are apparently no significant differences between the distributions of ceramic types in feature and nonfeature contexts. Clearly Rincon Red-on-brown dominates the typed painted assemblage across the entire site. More Early and Late Rincon sherds were identified in feature contexts, but that likely is the result of formation processes differentially preserving larger sherds (which are more likely to be classified into finer divisions) in features. The frequency differences for the rare ceramic types likely result from the extremely small sample sizes.

Vessel form frequencies also did not differ significantly between feature and nonfeature contexts. Table 5.4 indicates the relative proportion of rim sherds from bowls versus jars from feature and nonfeature contexts at the Marsh Station Road site. The general distribution throughout the site is strongly weighted towards jars over bowls, although it should be noted that a large percentage of sherds could not be classified into either category. Also important to note is that the large majority of sherds from the site were plain ware, and plain

Table 5.2. Ceramic type frequencies (sherd counts) by broad contextual categories

Unit	Other		Unpainted			Painted															Total Unpainted	Total Painted	Total Sherds
	Undersized	No Type or Ware Specified	Unpainted Brown Ware	Red Slipped Brown Ware	Unpainted Buff Ware	Early Rincon Red-on-brown	Middle Rincon Red-on-brown	Late Rincon Red-on-brown	Rincon Red-on-brown	Indeterminate Dragoon Red-on-brown	Indeterminate Red-on-brown	Indeterminate Red-on-buff	Rillito Red-on-brown	Sacaton Red-on-buff	Snaketown Red-on-buff	Sweetwater Red-on-gray	Rincon Black-on-Brown	Sahuarita Polychrome	Trincheras Purple-on-red	Mimbres Black-on-white			
Collection unit	401	2	863	22	5			1	31	1	205	25		3			1		1	2	890	270	1563
Test unit	1247	1	2210	60	11		1		54	1	627	28	1	7	1		4			5	2281	729	4258
Trench	6		2	1							4	1									3	5	14
Stripping unit	17		85						2		20			1							85	23	125
Stripping area			59	2				1	5		12					1					61	19	80
Feature excavation unit	812		1616	34	4	3		24	33		352	31		1				2		1	1654	447	2913
No unit	31		39	1					2		8	4									40	14	85
Total	2514	3	4874	120	20	3	1	26	127	2	1228	89	1	12	1	1	5	2	1	8	5014	1507	9038

Table 5.3. Painted ceramic type frequencies (sherd counts) comparing feature and nonfeature contexts

	Indeterminate Red-on-brown	Indeterminate Red-on-buff	Early Rincon Red-on-brown	Middle Rincon Red-on-brown	Late Rincon Red-on-brown	Rincon Red-on-brown	Rincon Black-on-brown	Rillito Red-on-brown	Sacaton Red-on-buff	Snaketown Red-on-buff	Mimbres Black-on-white	Indeterminate Dragoon Red-on-brown	Sweetwater Red-on-gray	Sahuarita Polychrome	Trincheras Purple-on-red	Total
All non-features	841	56		1	2	92	5	1	11	1	7	2	1		1	1021
All features	386	33	3		24	35			1			1		2		485

ware ceramics tend to be predominantly jars rather than bowls.

Feature Types

Similar patterns apply when the ceramic assemblage is broken down by feature type. Table 5.5 shows counts of sherds of different ceramic types at the Marsh Station Road site in pit structures, extramural surfaces, thermal pits, nonthermal pits, postholes, and burials. The painted sherds make up 11 to 27 percent of the total ceramic assemblages for the various feature types. The highest percentage of painted sherds is for bell pits. The lowest figure comes from burials. However, burials also had the highest percentage of undersized and unidentifiable sherds (n=42 of 81; 52 percent), which deflates the percentages of both painted and unpainted ceramics.

Among the painted ceramics, indeterminate red-on-brown sherds dominate the assemblages for all feature types. The frequencies of individual painted types, other than indeterminate red-on-brown, are low enough that comparisons between feature types are not meaningful.

Vessel form frequencies also do not appear to differ significantly between feature types. Table 5.6 shows the proportions of sherds identified as coming from bowls and jars from the different feature types. Bowls comprise 23.5 percent to 28.8 percent of the assemblages, and jars 39.4 percent to 57.1 percent. The values for both bowls and jars are lower in cases where more indeterminate forms are represented, which likely increases the differences in vessel forms between feature types.

Table 5.4. Proportions of vessel forms (rim sherd counts) comparing feature and nonfeature contexts

	Bowls	Jars	Indeterminate
Features	24.1	48.0	27.9
Non-features	21.6	48.6	29.8

Table 5.5. Ceramic type frequencies (sherd counts) by feature type

Feature Type	Undersized	No Type or Ware Specified	Unpainted Brown Ware	Red Slipped Brown Ware	Unpainted Buff Ware	Early Rincon Red-on-brown	Late Rincon Red-on-brown	Rincon Red-on-brown	Indeterminate Red-on-brown	Indeterminate Red-on-buff	Sacaton Red-on-buff	Sahuarita Poly-chrome	Mimbres Black-on-white	Total Unpainted	Total Painted	Total Sherds
Bell pits	144		140	4	1		22	3	66	12		2	1	145	106	395
Extramural surfaces	76		268	6	1			6	41	5				275	52	403
Thermal pits	25		102	3		1		3	17					105	21	151
Non-thermal pits	72		142	3				6	29	3	1			145	39	256
Postholes	1		6						1	1				6	2	9
Pit structures	494		1013	18	2	2	2	17	225	14				1033	260	1787
Burials	42		29	1					8	1				30	9	81
Totals	854	0	1700	35	4	3	24	36	387	35	1	2	1	1739	489	3082

Table 5.6. Proportions of vessel forms (rim sherd counts) comparing different feature types

	Bowls	Jars	Indeterminate
Pit structures	23.5	50.8	25.7
Extramural surfaces	28.8	51.6	19.5
Thermal pits	27.8	57.1	15.1
Nonthermal pits (minus postholes)	24.1	39.4	36.4

Table 5.7. Whole and reconstructible vessels recovered from the Marsh Station Road site

FN	Type	Form	Number of Sherds	Mass (g)	Max. Height (cm)	Max. Diameter (cm)	Orifice Diameter (cm)	Volume (liters)
44-0664.03	unknown	flared-rim jar	62	594.1	unk.	unk.	18 to 24	unk.
44-1540.01	red-slipped	stovepipe neck jar	49	848.6	19.4	16	9.4	1.75
44-1766	Middle Rincon Red-on-brown	bowl modified into plate	18	523.2	2.0	unk.	unk.	
44-2976	Early Rincon Red-on-brown	hemispherical bowl	5	131.0	8.5	16	16.0	unk.
44-3333	Rincon Red-on-brown	cauldon-shaped jar	11	263.9	unk.	20	18.0	unk.
212-0333	Dragoon red-on-brown	sub-hemispherical bowl	99		14.0	36	36.0	4.00

The majority of the datable decorated ceramics recovered pertain to the Middle Formative period/Rincon phase. Several dozen sherds came from San Pedro and general Early Agricultural contexts. The frequencies of non-Rincon phase datable ceramics are low enough that ceramic-based chronological assessments should be limited to presence/absence, and meaningful comparisons of types and vessel forms between phases are not possible.

Reconstructible Vessels

In addition to the fragmentary ceramic remains, five complete or partially reconstructible ceramic vessels were recovered (Table 5.7). Whole or partial vessels provide additional information beyond that provided by sherds. Vessel forms, which often correlate with their functions, generally can be better understood, and whole or partial vessels can be measured, indicating their overall size, and other dimensions, such as the orifice diameter (Braun 1980, 1983), provide clues to vessel use. Of course,

all sherds represent portions of ceramic vessels, and the division between sherds and partial vessels is somewhat arbitrary; for the purposes of this project, sherds or groups of matching sherds were treated as partial vessels if enough were present to estimate the form and dimensions of the complete vessel. One ceramic artifact whose original dimensions could not be estimated (FN 44-1766) was recorded as a reconstructible vessel. This vessel was a portion of a bowl that was reused as a plate. Although the dimensions of the original bowl could not be reconstructed, the dimensions of the reused form could (see below). The partial vessels discussed below contain 20 to 98 percent of the original vessels.

FN 44-0664.03 is a medium-sized jar with a slightly flared rim. The vessel was associated with a cremation; repatriation protocols dictated that it was neither washed nor reconstructed. Apparently, about half of the vessel was represented by the 62 recovered sherds. Their mass measured 594.1 g. Because washing was not permitted, it was difficult to ascertain the type with confidence, but it appeared unpainted. The paste is typical of Tucson Basin sand-tempered brown plain wares. The rim diameter was estimated at between 18 and 24 cm, and the wall thickness averaged 0.56 cm. No obvious use wear was visible.

FN 44-1540.01 (Figure 5.1) came from Test Unit (TU) 24, directly above the fill of a pit house (Feature 11). However, the vessel was recovered from sediments that are stratigraphically distinct from the pit house fill, the vessel postdates the structure by at least several centuries, and there are no indications that the vessel was associated with the structure. About 80 percent of the vessel, an unpainted red-slipped jar, was represented by the 49 recovered sherds. The portion recovered weighed 848.6 g. The vessel stands 19.4 cm high, with a maximum diameter of 16 cm and a 9.4- cm wide orifice. The volume was measured at 1.75 liters and the walls average 0.66 cm thick. The jar has a

stovepipe-style neck. William Deaver (personal communication, 2007) notes that this form is characteristic of the late Classic period. The vessel construction is irregular and the interior has not been smoothed, probably indicating hand modeling. The base shows some use wear, and heavy wear is present along one side of the vessel body, extending onto the neck. There is no apparent scratching or post-firing burning.

FN 44-1766 (Figure 5.2) is also discussed below, in the section on reuse. The vessel was recovered from above an extramural hearth (Feature 69) from TU 40, but the vessel not directly associated with that feature. The original vessel was a large Middle Rincon Red-on-brown bowl. The design is quartered with small spiral motifs and hatching. After its original use and breakage, it was modified by edge grinding and recycled as a plate. None of the rim was preserved or identified, so the size and form of the original vessel remain

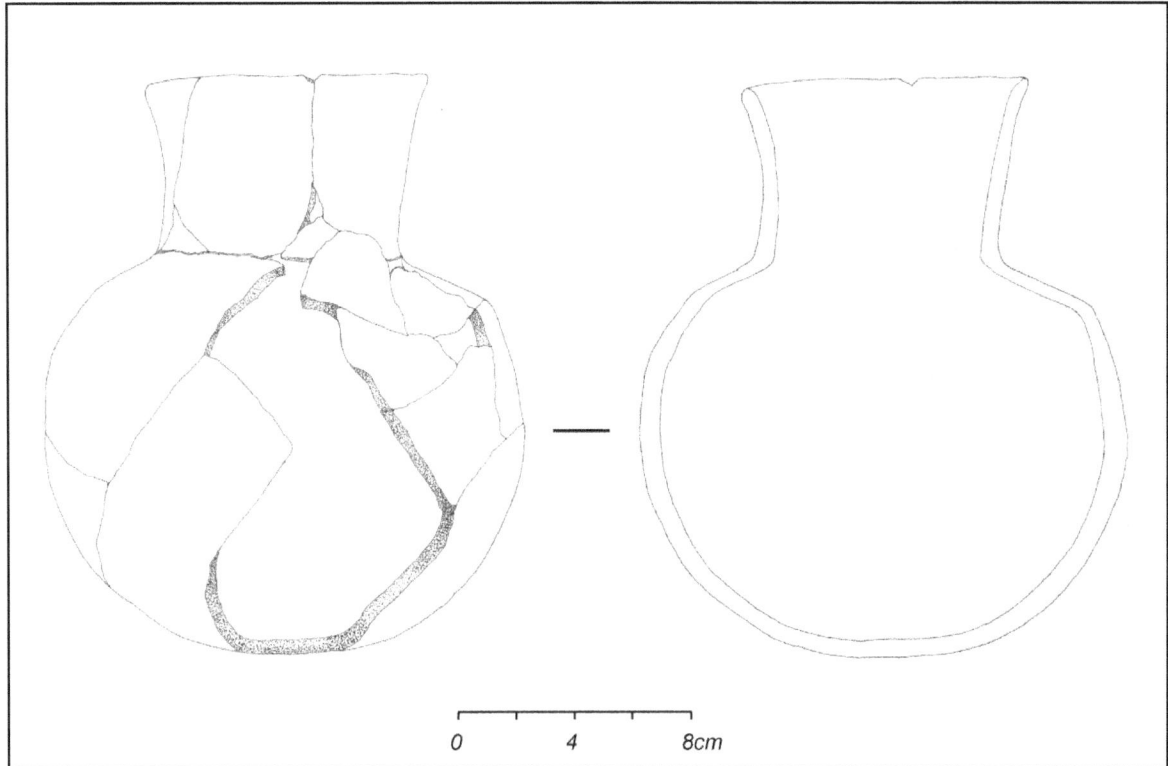

0   4   8cm

Figure 5.1. FN 44-1540.01, a stovepipe-necked jar.

unknown. Approximately 95 percent of the reworked plate was recovered as 18 sherds weighing 523.2 g. The plate is roughly circular but somewhat irregular. Its diameter is 23 cm and its thickness averages 0.79 cm. There is little curvature, and the total height is only about 2 cm. The near flatness across that large area indicates that the original bowl was quite large.

FN 44-2976 (Figure 5.3) came from a pit house, Feature 17. It consists of about 20 percent of a small hemispherical bowl. The vessel, classified as Early Rincon Red-on-brown, was recovered as five sherds from near the structure floor. The mass of those sherds is 131 g. The interior is painted in a quartered design. The complete vessel had a maximum height of 8.5 cm, a maximum diameter (and orifice

diameter) of 16 cm, and the walls averaged 0.55 cm thick.

FN 44-3333 (Figure 5.4) came from TU 142 and was not associated with any feature. About 30 percent of the vessel, typed as a small Rincon Red-on-brown cauldron-shaped jar, was recovered. The design consists of horizontally sectioned bands. The interior is slightly polished but not smudged. The partial vessel was recovered as 11 sherds with a total mass of 263.9 g. Original dimensions include an orifice diameter of 18 cm, a maximum diameter of 20 cm, and an average thickness of 0.77 cm. The portion recovered was not sufficient to estimate the height of the original vessel. Use wear is relatively light, and no areas of heavy use or burning were noted.

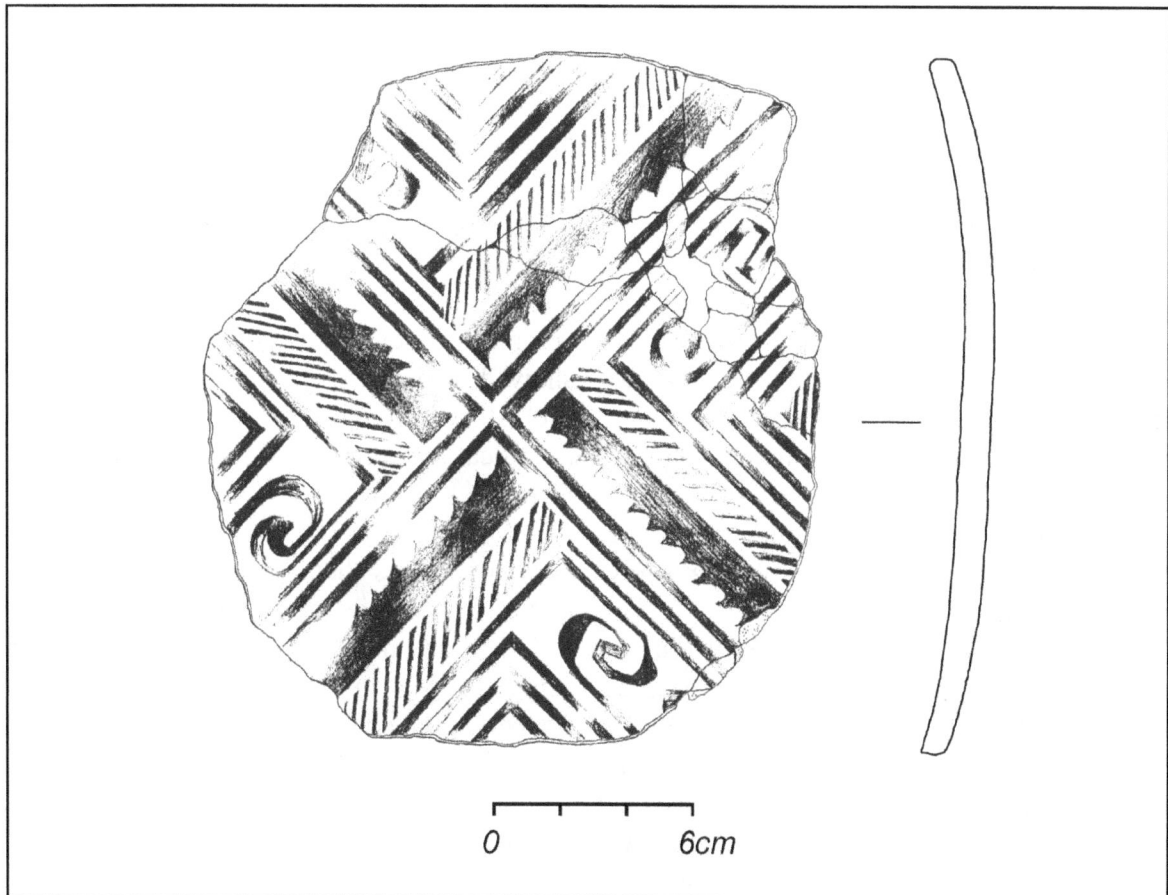

Figure 5.2. FN 44-1766, a large Middle Rincon Red-on-brown bowl reused as a parching plate.

Modified Vessels: Reuse and Maintenance Processes

An interesting aspect of the ceramic assemblage recovered at the Marsh Station Road site involves vessels and portions thereof that had been modified during prehistoric times either to continue to fulfill their original functions or to perform new ones. Formation process studies (Schiffer 1987) provide a useful framework for the study of the reuse and maintenance of ceramic vessels, as well as other artifact classes. Formation processes are the means, both cultural and noncultural, by which the dynamic behaviors of past societies are transformed into the static material recovered as the archaeological record.

Formation Processes

The distinction between systemic and archaeological context is crucial to understanding formation processes. Systemic context refers to artifacts and locations participating in a behavioral system. While archaeological context refers to materials that were previously used in a cultural system, but are now elements of the static entity known as the archaeological record (Schiffer 1972:157). In other words, items in systemic context are still undergoing use and manipulation by humans. Items in archaeological context have, at some point, been in systemic context, but are now isolated from active cultural processes and are only modified by noncultural factors.

The life history approach is useful in exploring the effects of formation processes on artifacts (LaMotta and Schiffer 1999). Each artifact has a unique life history in some respects, but recurrent activities and processes cross-cut most life histories allowing12 for generalization (Schiffer 1972, 1987:13, 1992:8). The first stage of any artifact's life history is procurement, in which raw materials are extracted from the natural environment. Manufacture, the second stage, involves changing the raw materials into an artifact, which then enters the use stage. Wear and deterioration occur during use, and maintenance may be necessary to keep artifacts functioning. At some point, artifacts no longer function for their original purpose. They may be reused with remanufacture, a change in use, or a change in user. At the end of an artifact's use life, it is discarded and deposited to enter the archaeological record. Discarded artifacts still deteriorate due to noncultural formation processes and may even re-enter systemic context if recovered by people (Schiffer 1972:8–9).

Reuse Processes

Reuse processes keep items in systemic context that otherwise would pass to archaeological context (Schiffer 1987:27). Reuse can readily be observed among living societies (Deal 1998; Deal and Hagstrum 1995; Kramer 1997), but its recognition archaeologically is often more difficult. Reused artifacts in archaeological settings can be identified by their condition, their context, or both (McKee 2007). Thirty-nine ceramic artifacts recovered during this project showed evidence of reuse or maintenance in prehistory. All were recognized because of modification from the original ceramic vessel forms.

Schiffer (1987:27–32) describes several reuse processes that can keep items in systemic context that might otherwise be transferred to archaeological context or that can bring items from archeological context into systemic context. The first is lateral cycling, which involves a change in the user of an item without modification or change in the item's use. Lateral cycling tends to be archaeologically invisible.

Recycling involves the modification and use of an artifact for a purpose other than its

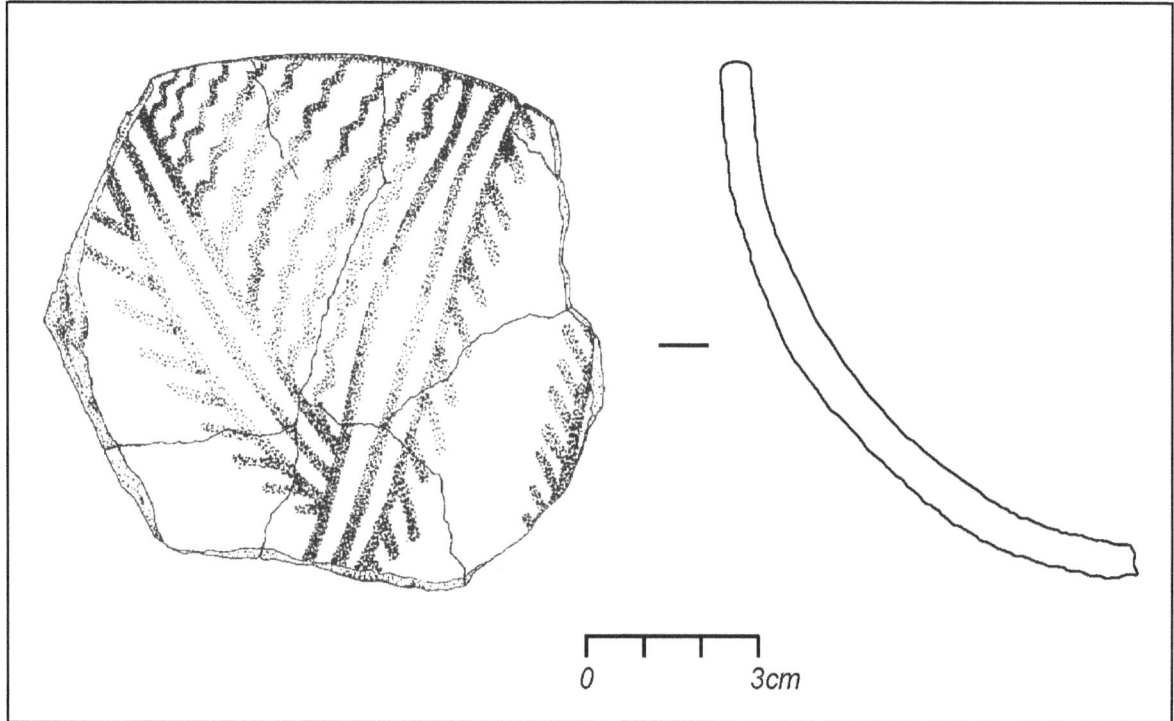

Figure 5.3. FN 44-2976, an Early Rincon Red-on-brown hemispherical bowl fragment..

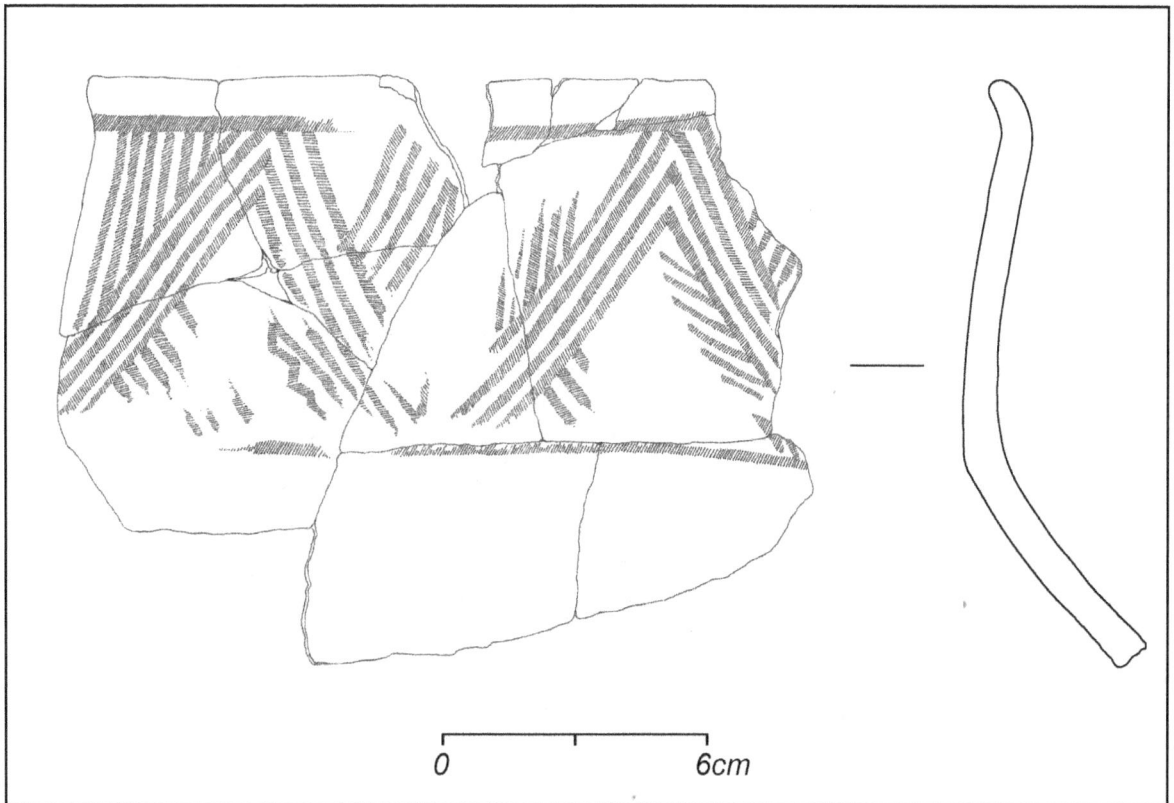

Figure 5.4. FN 44-3333, a Rincon Red-on-brown cauldron-shaped jar fragment..

original intended use. Kramer (1997:42–43) noted that people in Rajasthan frequently recycled sherds for a variety of purposes. They could be used in building construction or as ladles, scoops, or paint palettes. Potters recycled ceramics at higher frequencies than did the general population, and often used them in the ceramic manufacturing process as molds, palettes, rotary devices for pots being decorated, or as rests (Kramer 1997:73).

Deaver (1984:374–376) distinguished several instances of recycling, which he called secondary vessels or shaped sherds, in the Santa Rita Mountains. Secondary vessels are large sherds or partial vessels that have been modified and used for a different purpose than the original vessel. Deaver (1984:374–375) identified bowls that had been worked into shallow plates or scoops, jars modified into bowls or scoops, and large sherds used as palettes or scoops. Deaver (1984:375–376) also identified sherds that had been modified to produce disks or other geometric shapes. Disks were by far the most common shapes (Deaver 1984:376), and ranged from 16 mm to 123 mm in diameter. About half of those disks had been perforated (Deaver 1984:376). Whittlesey (2004b:317–318) also noted the recycling of broken vessels at the West Branch site in the Tucson Basin. She found that recycling was a common way to obtain informal parching plates.

Secondary use involves the use of an object for a purpose other than its original intent, without modification (Schiffer 1987). The archaeological recognition of secondary use relies heavily on context (McKee 2007). Secondary use was undoubtedly common in prehistoric Arizona, but is difficult to recognize archaeologically. Whittlesey (2004b:317–318) noted that at the West Branch site, incomplete vessels were likely used for storage of non-liquid items, although there was no direct evidence of such uses. She also indicated that fragmentary containers were used to line stor-

age pits and hearths, and that large sherds were used to cap storage containers (2004b:318).

Vessel maintenance is distinct from reuse, but can also result in changes in form that are sometimes archaeologically visible. Schiffer (1987:29–30) notes that maintenance changes are apt to be fairly minor, and that artifacts continue to be used for their original functions. Mend holes, in which holes are drilled on either side of a crack in a vessel and are then lashed with string to prevent further propagation of the crack, are probably the most common archaeologically visible form of ceramic maintenance (Deaver 1984:374; Herr 1993:353).

The 39 instances of vessel modification identified at the Marsh Station Road site all fall into the categories of recycling and maintenance. Contextual information was not sufficient to recognize secondary use or lateral cycling. Three basic processes were used in prehistory to modify the ceramics we recovered: flaking and breaking, abrasion, and drilling. Flaking and breaking involves chipping or snapping the sherd into a rough shape (Oppelt 1984:1). In some cases, sherds are flaked to form a sharp cutting or scraping edge. Also used is abrasion through both grinding and polishing. Drilling is the third technique identified in the assemblage. Oppelt (1984) noted that most holes in worked sherds are biconical, involving drilling from one side and then the other, although conical drilling from only one side was also practiced. Oppelt (1984) also noted that sherds can be incised with a sharp instrument, but there was no evidence of incision among these 39 ceramics.

Mend Holes

Two sherds from the Marsh Station Road site showed evidence of maintenance in the form of drilled holes, which likely are mend holes for string lashing. FN 44-2602 is a rim sherd from a jar that has one mend hole centered 2.2

cm below the rim. That hole was biconically drilled, with outside diameters of 7 mm on each side. The minimum diameter is approximately 4 mm. FN 44-1704.01 is a body sherd with a biconical drill hole. Only about one-fourth of the hole is present, precluding its accurate measurement. It is uncertain whether the drill hole relates to mending a vessel or if the sherd is part of a perforated sherd disk.

Sherd Disks

Sherd disks are broken pottery fragments that have been shaped into a roughly circular form through flaking and/or grinding. The disks recovered at the site can be divided into two broad categories: perforated and unperforated (Table 5.8). The project recovered eight unperforated (Figure 5.5) and seven perforated disks (Figure 5.6).

Two of the unperforated sherd disks were recovered from the surface, and consequently, information regarding their relationships to features is lacking. These disks include FN 44-16.01, about half of an originally 2.65 cm-diameter disk that was only roughly shaped by flaking, and FN 44-709.01, which originally measured about 3.5 cm in diameter, and was not carefully shaped. Both disks are incomplete. A third disk, FN 44-2330.01, was recovered from a stripping unit, with no discernable feature associations. This third disk is complete, measures 2.8 cm in diameter, and had been flaked; portions of the perimeter also had been lightly ground.

The remaining unperforated sherd disks came from pit houses. Two of them, FN 44-2309.01 and FN 44-2456, were from Feature 11. The former was complete and measured 3.15 cm in diameter. Its perimeter had been ground following its initial shaping by flaking. FN 44-2456 was slightly larger, about 3.9 cm in diameter. Only about 40 percent of the original disk was recovered. The

initial shaping was by flaking, but most of the perimeter was subsequently ground. Two other unperforated sherd disks, FN 44-3155.01 and FN 44-3014.01, came from Feature 152. Both were incomplete. Only about 25 percent of FN 44-3155.01 was recovered. The diameter was estimated at 3.8 cm, and the margin was ground. About 40 percent of FN 44-3014.01 was present. Its diameter is estimated at 3.0 cm. This disk may have been drilled, but breakage obscures clear evidence to resolve that question. It is quite irregular, and the identification as a disk is somewhat tentative. The final unperforated sherd disk, FN 1267.01, came from Feature 51. This complete 4.3-cm diameter disk was only roughly shaped by flaking.

One of the perforated sherd disks, FN 44-2648, came from a stripping unit; its associations with features are unknown. About half of this 5.5-cm diameter disk was recovered. It was biconically drilled, and appears to have been ground after its original shaping by flaking. The artifact is not particularly rounded, arguing against its use as a spindle whorl. Two other perforated sherd disks, FN 44-1557 and FN 44-2111, came from test units, and therefore contextual associations are uncertain. FN 44-1557 represents only about one-fourth of the original artifact. We estimate its original outside diameter at 2.3 cm. The conical hole is quite large, about 1.2 cm in diameter. The margin was apparently ground to some degree after initial shaping by flaking, but the shaping is still fairly rough. FN 44-2111 is a complete 4.8-cm diameter disk. It is nicely rounded and the 0.77- cm biconical hole is centered. Most of the perimeter has been ground.

Two perforated sherd disks, FN 44-1690.01 and FN 44-1692, came from Feature 6, a hearth with an associated surface. The former is about one-third of an originally 4.3-cm diameter irregularly-shaped disk. The biconical hole is about 1 cm in diameter. The overall shape is far from round. FN 44-1692

Table 5.8. Sherd disks recovered from the Marsh Station Road site

FN	Perforated	Ceramic Ware/Type	Outside Diameter (mm)	Minimum Hole Diameter (mm)	Mass (g)
44-16.01	No	unpainted	26.5		2.63
44-709.01	No	indeterminate red-on-brown	>32		5.00
44-1267.01	No	unpainted	43.4		13.10
44-2309.01	No	unpainted	31.5		9.06
44-2330.01	No	unpainted	28.1		4.97
44-2456	No	red-slipped brown ware	38.9		5.33
44-3155.01	No	indeterminate red-on-brown	unk. (est. 38)		1.82
44-1557	Yes	unpainted	est. 23	est. 12	1.35
44-1690.01	Yes	unpainted	est. 32	est. 10	2.84
44-1692	Yes	unpainted	est. 43	est. 18	7.06
44-2111	Yes	unpainted	47.7	7.65	21.26
44-2313	Yes	unpainted	est. 24	est. 8	2.08
44-2648	Yes	unpainted	55.3	6.60	14.29
44-3014.01	No	unpainted	29.9		4.46
44-3237	Yes	indeterminate red-on-brown	45.0	8.10	14.71

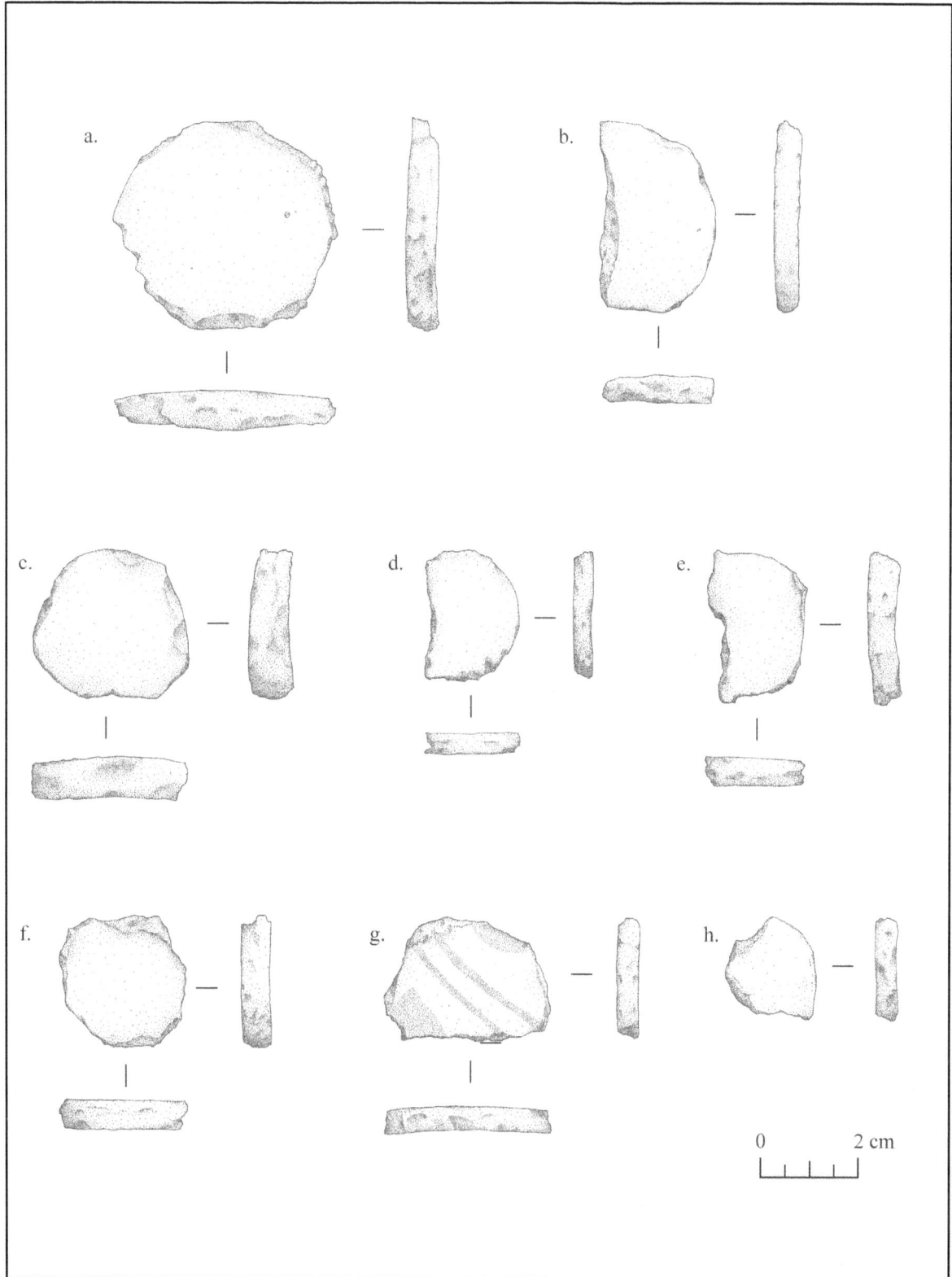

Figure 5.5. Unperforated sherd disks recovered from the Marsh Station Road site: a. FN 1267.01, b. FN 2456, c. FN2309.01, d. FN 1601, e. FN 3104.01, f. FN 2330.01, g. FN 709.01, h. 3155.01.

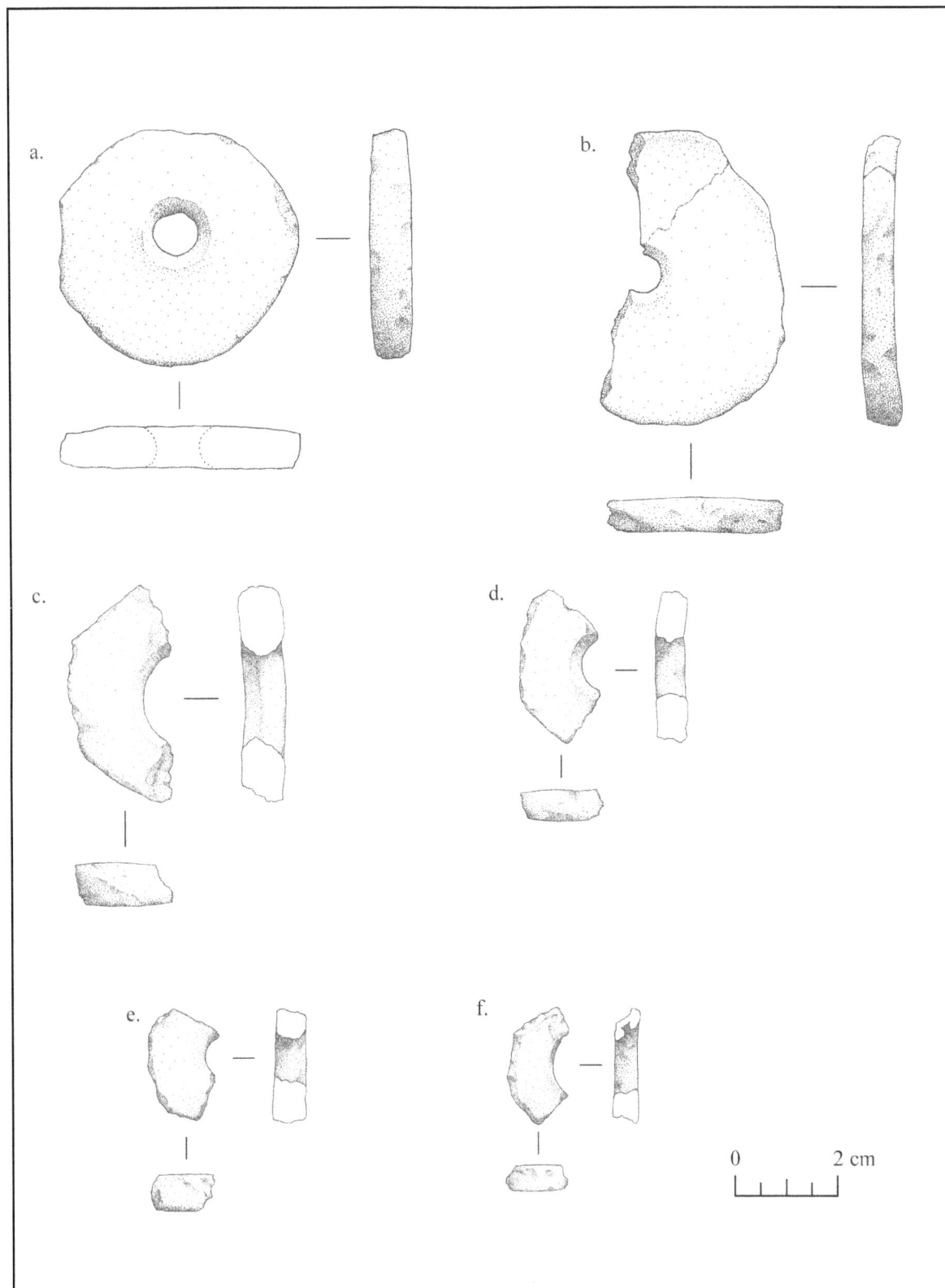

Figure 5.6. Perforated sherd disks recovered from the Marsh Station Road site: a. FN 2111, b. FN 2648, c. FN 1692, d. FN 1690.01, e. FN 2313, f. FN 1557.

is much rounder, but the flaked perimeter was not extensively ground. About one-third of the original disk was recovered. The biconical hole is quite large, with a 1.8-cm estimated diameter. FN 44-2313 came from Feature 4, an indeterminate thermal feature. It is quite small, with its outside diameter estimated at 2.4 cm. The disk was only roughly shaped by flaking and is not particularly rounded. The conical hole is estimated at 8 mm in diameter. The final perforated sherd disk recovered is FN 44-3237 (Figure 5.7), which came from a pit house (Feature 152). The 4.5-cm diameter disk was nicely rounded by flaking, but little grinding is apparent. The 8-mm hole was conically drilled.

The sherd disk assemblage recovered at the Marsh Station Road site allows some inferences regarding the manufacturing process. All were apparently initially shaped by flaking, and several were subsequently further modified by grinding along the perimeter, processes described by Oppelt (1984:1). About half were perforated. All the perforated sherds had either conical or biconical holes, indicating a flaring drill used from one or both sides.

Five of the seven perforated disks were broken, and in all cases, the break passed through the hole. That is a likely location for breakage during use or after discard, but it also is possible that the disks broke during the manufacturing process. Most of the broken perforated disks were crudely shaped, with minimal perimeter grinding. Drilling the hole was likely risky, and the sherd was likely to break during the process. Because of that risk, we hypothesize that a likely manufacturing sequence was to roughly shape the disk by flaking, drill the hole, and only expend the time involved in the final shaping by grinding for those sherds that survive the drilling process.

Several interpretations have been advanced for the use of sherd disks. Oppelt (1984:3) cites Hodge (1950), who reported that a Zuñi informant described the use of pottery disks in deer hunting; they were placed in hoof prints to prevent the deer from backtracking. Haury (1976) noted the presence of small pottery disks at the bases of the main roof supports of the great kiva at Point of Pines and interpreted them as having religious significance. Small worked sherds also have been ethnographically documented as counters or gaming pieces (Culin 1992:45 [1907]; Oppelt 1984:3).

Other possible interpretations have been posited for perforated disks. The most frequent one is that they were used as whorls for spindles or drills. In her survey of Southwestern spinning tools, Kent (1957:472–473) discussed wooden and fired-clay spindle whorls. She also noted that perforated sherds often had been proposed as spindle whorls, but did not find ethnographic evidence for that interpretation in publications on the Southwest. She cautioned against the uncritical acceptance of that interpretation, noting that while round sherd disks with well-centered holes functioned well experimentally as spindle whorls, less regular ones did not (Kent 1957:473).

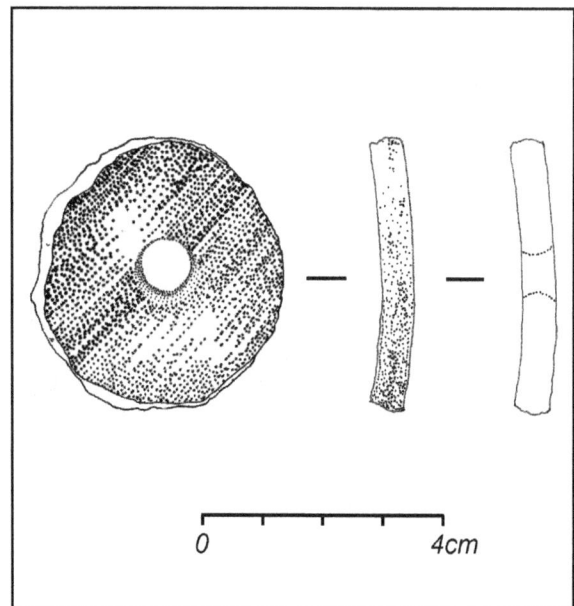

Figure 5.7. FN 44-3237, a perforated sherd disk.

Additional proposed uses for perforated sherd disks include as buttons or toggles for clothing (Oppelt 1984:3). They could also have served as beads or pendants, and all the uses proposed for unperforated disks also could be valid for the perforated ones. The perforated disks recovered by likely had a variety of uses. Only three of them, FN 44-2111, FN 44-1692, and FN 44-3237, approximate roundness and have centered holes; the other four would not have functioned well as flywheels. The well-shaped disks could have been used as whorls to spin any of the various agave and yucca fibers present in southern Arizona or as flywheels for drills or other rotating tools.

Indeterminate Worked Sherds

This is a residual category that comprises those modified sherds that do not fit into any of the categories above (Table 5.9). Eighteen were recovered from the Marsh Station Road site. FN 44-20 may be a disk fragment, but if so, only about 20 percent is present. One margin is flaked in a roughly circular shape; grinding, if present, is minimal. This artifact was recovered from the surface in Collection Unit (CU) 145. FN 44-502 is a small sherd with one margin exhibiting some polish, likely due to its use as a scraper. It also came from the surface in CU 296. FN 44-853.01 is a longer sherd with one margin exhibiting considerable grinding that came from Stripped Area 4/5. FN 44-869 is a sherd with one heavily utilized margin that also came from Stripped Area 4/5. This is probably what Herr (1993:349–352; see also Waterworth and Blinman 1986:4–6) defines as a beveled-edge item. These are scoops or scrapers that have acquired a beveled edge from prolonged use. FN 44-963 is another indeterminate, possibly reworked sherd. It is irregular in shape, with rounding on one margin. That rounding could result from scraping something irregular—such as processing agave fibers—or it could simply

result from differential weathering while part of the sherd was buried. This artifact came from Stripped Area 2/3.

FN 44-1667.01 came from Feature 6, a hearth with an associated surface. One margin is rounded and exhibits some smoothing and polish. It may be a portion of a large sherd disk, or may have been used to scrape an indeterminate material. If it is part of a disk, the disk was considerably larger than the other disks recovered by the project and may have served as a lid. FN 44-1896.01, from an indeterminate thermal pit (Feature 61), contained three modified sherds. Two are discussed here and the third below. The first is a small, thin sherd with some rounding along one margin, likely from scraping. The second is larger with a heavily used 5.5-cm long margin. The wear is heavy enough to qualify this as a beveled-edge item. FN 44-2409.01 came from the same thermal feature. It is larger than most of the other reworked sherds, and appears to have been refired. One margin is somewhat rounded, likely from scraping use. FN 44-2739.01, from TU 60, is a small sherd with one rounded margin exhibiting heavy polish, likely from scraping use. FN 44-2828.01, which came from a nonthermal pit (Feature 136), is more highly modified than most other reworked sherds. This small sherd is apparently a fragment of a larger oval-shaped piece. The edge is quite regular and finely ground. FN-3014.01 is another small sherd showing some rounding along one margin, possibly from scraping use. It came from a pit house (Feature 152). FN 44-3069.01 is a very small sherd exhibiting light to moderate grinding and possible use along one margin. It also came from Feature 152 and could be a disk fragment. FN 44-3230.01 is another very small sherd showing heavy use. Again, this was found in the same pit house (Feature 152) and is classified as a beveled-edge item. FN 44-3122.01 is a very heavily weathered plain brown ware sherd. One margin has been heav-

Table 5.9. Indeterminate worked sherds recovered from the Marsh Station Road site

FN	Morphological Type	Possible Function	Ceramic Ware/Type	Max. Dimension (mm)	Mass (g)
44-20	indeterminate reworked sherd		unpainted	29.91	3.56
44-502	indeterminate reworked sherd		indeterminate red-on-brown	37.50	10.07
44-853.01	indeterminate reworked sherd		unpainted	54.70	11.14
44-869	indeterminate reworked sherd beveled edge item		indeterminate red-on-brown	42.30	7.72
44-963	indeterminate reworked sherd		unpainted	63.50	20.74
44-1667.01	indeterminate reworked sherd	scraping	indeterminate red-on-brown	33.40	4.26
44-1896.01a	indeterminate reworked sherd beveled edge item		unpainted	55.80	18.00
44-1896.01b	indeterminate reworked sherd		unpainted	30.20	4.10
44-2409.01	indeterminate reworked sherd		indeterminate red-on-brown	11.47	59.20
44-2739.01	indeterminate reworked sherd		unpainted	37.80	7.60
44-2828.01	indeterminate reworked sherd		unpainted	45.30	6.32
44-3014.01	indeterminate reworked sherd		unpainted	32.10	5.34
44-3069.01	indeterminate reworked sherd		unpainted	26.90	2.43
44-3122.01	indeterminate reworked sherd beveled edge item	scraping	unpainted	46.00	14.25
44-3230.01	indeterminate reworked sherd beveled edge item	scraping	unpainted	26.20	2.92
44-3542.02	indeterminate reworked sherd		Mibres black–on–white	34.70	5.72
44-3550.01	indeterminate reworked sherd		unpainted	46.50	10.42
44-1304	oval reworked sherd	scraping	red-slipped brown ware	75.60	36.06
44-1719.01	indeterminate reworked sherd	scoop	unpainted	88.40	47.21
44-1267.02	indeterminate reworked sherd	scoop	unpainted	129.90	66.90
44-3192.01	reworked partial vessel	plate	indeterminate red-on-brown	166.00	198.20
44-3254.01	indeterminate reworked sherd	scoop	indeterminate red-on-brown	155.00	133.20
44-1896.01c	indeterminate reworked sherd	scoop	unpainted	120.10	99.60
44-1766	plate	parching plate	Middle Rincon Red-on-brown	523.20	23.00

ily utilized to the point that we classified it as a beveled-edge item (Herr 1993:349–352). It came from Stripping Unit 11.

FN 44-3542.02 came from a roasting pit (Feature 173). It is a small Mimbres Black-on-white sherd that shows moderate abrasion on one margin. The sherd appears to have been refired. FN 44-3550.01 also came from this roasting pit. It is apparently part of a larger, oval-shaped sherd tool. One margin exhibits moderate use-polishing. FN 44-1304, made on a rim sherd from a large (32-cm to 34-cm diameter) red-slipped bowl, is a complete, well-preserved scraper. It is oval-shaped and similar in form to several of the blade-shaped scrapers illustrated by Herr (1993:350–351). Herr uses the Tewa term kajepe to refer to this form.

Six larger reworked sherds were recovered from the site. Four are interpreted as having been reused as scoops (Figure 5.8), and two as plates. The functional assignment of the sherds to the scoop category was based on both their form, as they are somewhat elongate and appropriately shaped for that purpose, and have wear on one or more margins that apparently resulted from abrasion in extracting items from a container. FN 44-1267.02 consists of three sherds comprising a portion of an originally larger artifact. It was recovered from inside a pit house (Feature 51). The recovered portion is about 13.5 cm long and the worn edge is about 7.4 cm wide. That edge is quite rounded, with most wear on what was originally the exterior surface of the vessel consistent with the inferred scooping use.

FN 44-1719.01 came from a bell pit (Feature 52). It was recovered as a single sherd that had apparently been refired. One margin exhibits some rounding, although far less than is present on FN 44-1267.02. That margin is about 8.3 cm long, and the perpendicular length is 7.8 cm. The rounding is unifacial, occurring on what was originally the outside of the vessel, consistent with the scooping interpretation.

The third worked sherd recovered as part of FN 44-1896.01 from the thermal pit (Feature 61) was in three pieces. A rounded edge is 12.0 cm long, and the perpendicular dimension is 8.3 cm. The rounding is moderate but consistent with scooping.

The final large sherd interpreted to have been reused as a scoop is FN 44-3254.01. This sherd, which was recovered in three fragments, came from TU 131. The complete artifact is 16.5 cm long. Heavy rounding is present along a 7.5-cm long margin, and lighter rounding is present along a 4.9-cm long area on the opposite side of the artifact. The wear on both margins is on what would have been the exterior portion of the original vessel, consistent with the scooping interpretation.

Two additional large ceramics apparently were reused as plates. FN 44-3192.01 came from TU 114 and was recovered as 10 individual sherds that were refit. The complete item represented is a 14.1-cm by 13.1-cm sherd. It was relatively square in form, with considerable rounding on one margin. That rounding could have resulted from use as a scoop, as is the case for the artifacts described above, or it could be due to grinding when the plate was prepared. This artifact does not exhibit the heavy refiring that was present for FN 44-1766 (below).

One of the most interesting examples of modified ceramics is FN 44-1766 (see Figure 5.2), which was also discussed above in the section on reconstructible vessels. It came from TU 40 and was recovered from above a hearth (Feature 69), but was not directly associated with that feature. The original vessel was a large Middle Rincon Red-on-brown bowl. After it broke, it was modified by edge grinding and recycled as a plate. None of the rim was preserved and identified, so the size and form of the original vessel remain unknown. Approximately 95 percent of the reworked plate was recovered as 18 sherds that weighed

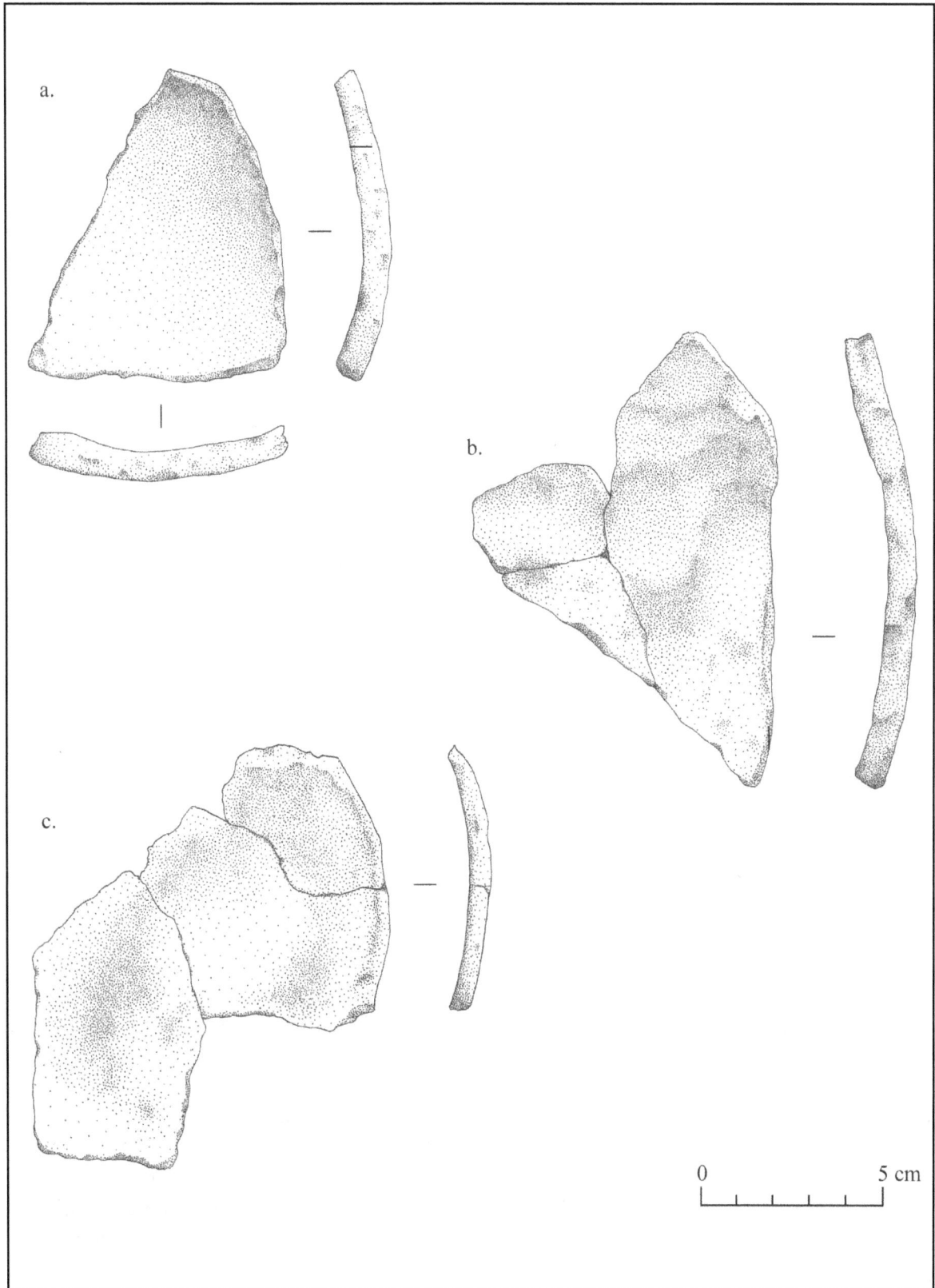

Figure 5.8. Reused sherds interpreted as scoops: a. FN 1719.01, b. FN 1896.01, c. FN 1267.02.

523.2 g. The plate is roughly circular but somewhat irregular. Its diameter is 23 cm and the thickness averages 0.79 cm. There is little curvature, and the total height is only about 2 cm. The plate was heavily refired following its modification from the original bowl, as evidenced by sooting and discoloration, causing the red paint to appear white and the brown to appear dark gray and black.

Whittlesey (2004b:317) notes that parching plates were commonly obtained from both unpainted and painted vessels originally used for other purposes at the West Branch site, and that appears to be the best interpretation of this artifact. Whittlesey (2004b:285) observes that parching vessels tend to be large shallow plates or griddles. She also mentions (2004b:315) that at the West Branch site, archaeologists recovered numerous recycled containers that were likely parching plates, and that they were frequently found on pit structure floors. Whittlesey (2004b:316) bases her interpretations on Castetter and Underhill (1935:45–46), who describe the production of gruel by the Akimel O'odham and Tohono O'odham. Mesquite, corn, and pumpkin seeds were parched, finely ground, and stored in sealed jars. The meal could later be mixed with water to form a gruel that could be eaten without cooking or could be formed into tortillas that could then be cooked on a grill or in ashes (Whittlesey 2004b:316).

The 39 reworked sherds represent approximately 0.4 percent of the total ceramic assemblage recovered at the Marsh Station Road site. Oppelt (1984:4–5) reviewed published reports representing 17 Anasazi, 13 Hohokam, and 10 Mogollon sites. His study indicated that worked sherds represented 0.27 percent of the total sherds reported at Anasazi sites, 0.15 percent of those reported at Mogollon sites, and 0.04 percent of those reported at Hohokam sites. His sampling was not systematic and did not account for differences in data recovery and analysis at those sites. Nonetheless, it is interesting that WSA recorded 10 times the relative frequency of worked sherds at this site as Oppelt did for his Hohokam sample, more than twice as many as the Mogollon sample, and nearly twice as many as the Anasazi sample. The inhabitants of the Marsh Station Road site apparently were potentially reusing a higher proportion of the discarded ceramic material than the people who lived in the sampled sites. That difference could relate to the semi-permanent nature of the site occupation (see Chapter 4), which may have resulted in fewer vessels being discarded and therefore there was less "raw material" for the production of modified sherds. That interpretation is highly speculative, but could serve as an avenue for future research.

Oppelt (1984) also examined sherd disks as a percentage of the worked sherds among the three groups. He found that disks represented 78 percent of the worked sherds among the Hohokam, 65 percent among the Mogollon, and 38 percent among the Anasazi, compared to 38 percent for the Marsh Station Road site. Perforated disks were 38 percent of the worked sherd assemblage for the Mogollon, 34 percent for the Hohokam, and 8 percent for the Anasazi. One possible interpretation relates to the production of cotton textiles in the Hohokam region. Perforated disks are 18 percent of this worked sherd assemblage. The apparent underrepresentation relative to neighboring groups could relate to different activities being conducted or differences in data recovery or analysis.

Nonvessel Ceramic Artifacts

Most of the ceramic artifacts recovered, and discussed above, were ceramic vessels or portions of vessels, but two additional nonvessel ceramic artifacts were recovered from the Marsh Station Road site. FN 2336 (Figure 5.9) is a spherical fired-clay bead that measures 1.8

cm in diameter. No paint is preserved on the bead, which has a cylindrical hole approximately 1.5 mm in diameter. One side of the hole exhibits post-depositional damage, but string wear is present on the other. The bead came from TU 80 and is not associated with any features.

The second nonvessel ceramic artifact, FN-3238, is the torso of a small human female figurine (Figure 5.10); the head is absent. The figurine came from a mixed stratum containing structural remains in a Rincon phase pit house (Feature 152). It is possible that the figurine came from an elevated context inside the structure, but that interpretation is somewhat speculative as the stratum was highly mixed. The surviving portion is 4.0 cm long, 1.4 cm wide, and 1.2 cm thick; it weighs 7.19 g. The figurine is made from a single clay coil and the overall shape is roughly cylindrical. The right shoulder is missing and likely broke at the same time as the head detached. The left shoulder has a protruding section that may represent an arm, which was pinched from the body coil; the figurine's breasts and short cone-shaped legs were also formed directly from the main body

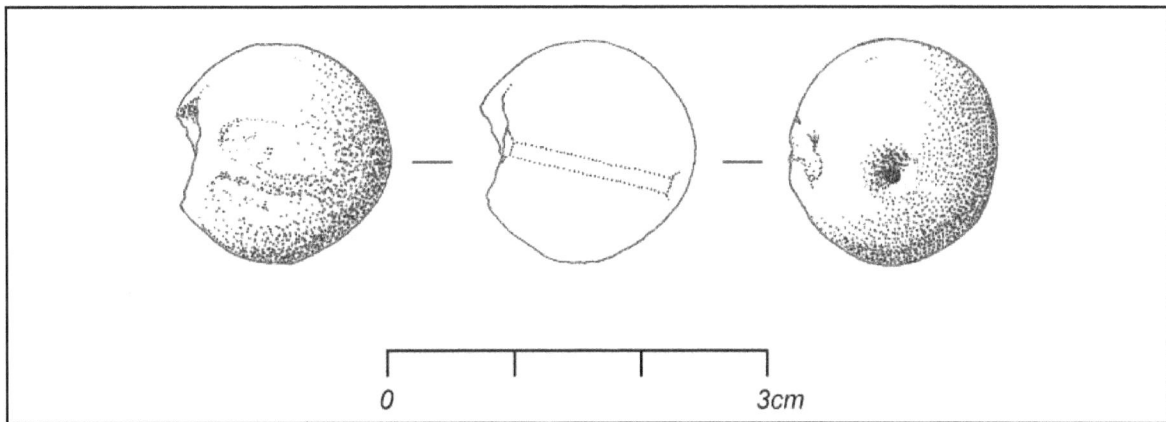

Figure 5.9. FN 44-2336, a fired clay bead.

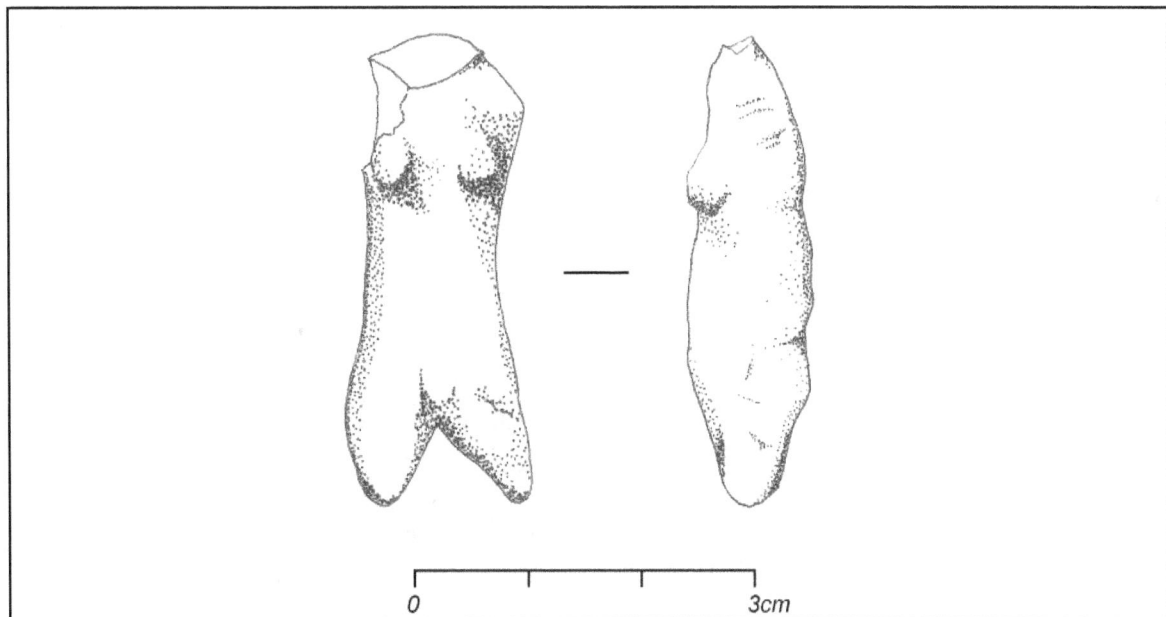

Figure 5.10. FN 44-3238, a fired clay figurine.

coil, rather than added as separate bits of clay. The figurine closely resembles some of those illustrated by Whittlesey (2004c:324) that came from the West Branch site. She notes that those figurines are similar to many previously recovered from various Hohokam Rincon phase sites in the Tucson Basin, including Hodges Ruin (Kelly et al. 1978), the Punta de Agua sites (Greenleaf 1975), Julian Wash (Mabry 1996), Los Morteros (Heidke 1995), and Tanque Verde Wash (Elson, ed. 1986).

SPATIAL DISTRIBUTION OF CERAMIC ARTIFACTS

Chi-square analyses were performed on the ceramics assemblage from the Marsh Station Road site with multiple goals in mind. First, we were interested to discover any influences of site formation processes on the distribution of identifiable ceramics on the surface and below the surface. Specifically, we wanted to test whether there were differences in the ratios of painted to unpainted artifacts between the two data recovery contexts. This information would serve to inform our knowledge of site disturbance such as amateur collection of artifacts from the site (if it occurred, we would expect to find a smaller percentage of painted artifacts on the surface than in buried contexts). Second, we wanted to assess the difference, if any, in distribution of broad ceramic types between various spatial contexts across the site to attempt to identify different use areas.

In comparing surface to subsurface contexts, the proportion of painted ceramics remains nearly equal, at 23 percent of the surface ceramics compared to 24 percent of the subsurface ceramics, whether the surface ceramics are limited to those in the stripped areas only ($\chi^2=0.03$, p > 0.5), or the entire surface collection ($\chi^2=0.08$, df = 1, p > 0.5) of the Marsh Station Road site. There is also no difference in the distribution of painted

and unpainted ceramics when comparing the surface to just the test units ($\chi^2=0.4$, df=1, p > 0.5), or just the features ($\chi^2=1.08$, df = 1, 0.2 < p < 0.5).

Across the site, we investigated the distribution of ceramics with respect to the stripped areas (Stripped Areas 2 and 3 [SA 2/3] are combined because of their proximity, as are Stripped Areas 4 and 5 [SA 4/5]) and with respect to various feature types. While there were not nearly as many ceramics found in SA 2/3 as there were in SA 4/5, the differences in distribution of the existing ceramics between these stripped areas are not statistically significant except for the surface artifacts when considered alone. On the surface, there are more painted ceramics than expected in SA 2/3 ($\chi^2=6.57$, df=1, 0.01 < p < 0.02; painted ceramics constitute 43 percent of the total, compared to only 22 percent of the total surface ceramics in SA 4/5). Sample size is quite low on the surface at SA 2/3, with only 30 total ceramics recovered. The significance of this test result is more suspicious when combined with the insignificant test results comparing ceramic distributions from test units ($\chi^2=0.31$, df=1, p > 0.5), features ($\chi^2=0.48$, df=1, 0.2 < p < 0.5), and all ceramics combined ($\chi^2=2.01$, df=1, 0.1 < p < 0.2) between SA 2/3 and SA 4/5. Therefore, while there is a dramatic difference in the total number of ceramics recovered from the two general areas (353 in SA 2/3; 4,616 in SA 4/5), the distribution of those ceramics does not reflect a difference in site formation processes or general uses of the areas (much higher proportions of painted wares could indicate a ritual or ceremonial use of the area). The number of painted ceramics in SA 2/3 (90 total, 59 of which are indeterminate red-on-brown) renders a comparison with respect to individual types highly suspect, so we do not discuss that here.

Finally, we wanted to compare the distribution of ceramics in different feature types, first at the broad level of painted versus unpainted artifacts, then refining into a few of the more common categories of each type, with the remaining grouped together into "other." The first test (χ^2=64.92, df=6, p < 0.001) revealed a higher than expected percentage of painted ceramics in features falling into the class of bell pits, with fewer than expected painted artifacts in pit structures and extramural surfaces. The second test (χ^2=85.06, df=12, p < 0.001) was also significant, reinforcing the same basic patterns as the first test but focusing some detail on the plain brown wares and Tucson Basin red-on-brown wares. The ceramics were divided into four broad type categories: plain brown, other plain, Tucson Basin red-on-brown, and other painted. Bell pits again drove the chi-square, with much higher percentages of both painted categories than expected, and fewer plain brown ceramics than expected. Extramural surfaces and pit structures had higher percentages of plain brown artifacts, with fewer painted artifacts (fewer other painted in structures, fewer Tucson Basin red-on-brown in extramural surfaces) than expected. When examining just the painted types, comparing the distribution of Tucson Basin red-on-brown ceramics with the other painted types (χ^2=11.94, df=4, 0.01 < p < 0.02) yields a significant result, whereby the data suggest there are more "other painted" artifacts than expected in the bell pits, and fewer of them than expected in structures.

Due to the low counts of ceramics in features ascribed to the Early Agricultural (San Pedro phase) period, and the lack of our ability to refine the dates of Formative period features, statistical investigation of temporal change in ceramic distributions proved futile. Additionally, since the Early Agricultural features were largely ascribed such status due to the relative lack of ceramics, the statistics would involve circular logic and produce misleading, if not incorrect, results.

REGIONAL COMPARISON OF THE MARSH STATION ROAD SITE CERAMIC ASSEMBLAGES

Here we provide a brief comparison of the Marsh Station Road site's ceramic assemblage to other areas of the Tucson Basin, and specifically within the Cienega Valley.

The Marsh Station Road site was likely reoccupied during the Rincon phase expansion and population increase (Stevens 2001a:169–171) of Tucson Basin peoples, as reflected in Stevens' (2001a) Cienega Valley survey during which she recorded dozens of Sedentary period (A.D. 950–1150) archaeological sites. The ceramic assemblage at the Marsh Station Road site resembles most closely sites like AZ EE:2:11 (ASM), another Cienega Valley site discussed by Eddy and Cooley (1983:23–30), and the Valencia site (AZ BB:13:15 [ASM]), in the Santa Cruz River drainage. Rincon Red-on-brown wares, with some Dragoon trade wares at Marsh Station Road and AZ EE:2:11 (ASM), dominate the identified painted assemblages at these sites. However, the presence of buff wares (Sacaton and Snaketown Red-on-buff, Sweetwater Red-on-gray) and Rillito Red-on-brown provides support for multiple occupations at the Marsh Station Road site, and therefore distinguishes it from other Cienega Valley sites discussed by Eddy and Cooley (1983). The distribution of surface ceramics at the Valencia site, a large Hohokam habitation site (Doelle and Wallace 1991:313–315), also resembles that of the Marsh Station Road site assemblage, with the majority of painted wares dating to the Rincon phase. However, the Valencia site decorated ceramics totaled 40 percent of the ceramics on the surface of the site (where the Rincon phase ceramics were found), and 42 percent of the decorated sherds were assigned to a specific ceramic group. In contrast, decorated sherds were only 16 percent of the Marsh Station Road site assemblage, and only 13 percent of those were identified to specific ceramic types (see Table 5.2). This is a significant difference in the proportion of ceramics identified to dated types, and this may reflect the difference in site type in addition to differing post-depositional disturbance between the two sites. The Valencia site was a more permanently occupied habitation site, whereas the Marsh Station Road site appears to have occupied on a semi-permanent basis.

Vanderpot and Altschul (2007:56–61) briefly discuss the ceramic assemblage at the Mescal Wash site (AZ EE:2:51 [ASM]), and pending further publication of the full site report the Marsh Station Road assemblage is similar. Red-on-brown wares, especially Rincon phase, with some Sacaton (though less abundant at the Marsh Station Road site), make up the majority of identified painted wares. There is a higher proportion of Phoenix Basin buff wares and Dragoon brown wares at the Mescal Wash site (Vanderpot 2001) than at the Marsh Station Road site, perhaps indicating more regional exchange, or a more intense occupation, at the former site. Additionally, a few Mimbres Black-on-white sherds were found at the Mescal Wash site in association with features dated to the Rincon phase (A.D. 950–1150; Vanderpot and Altschul 2007:57); eight Mimbres Black-on-white sherds were recovered from the Marsh Station Road site, though lacking in chronological context.

SUMMARY AND CONCLUSIONS

Excavations at the Marsh Station Road site recovered 9,038 ceramic artifacts, including 5 complete or reconstructible vessels, 39 reworked, and 2 nonvessel ceramic artifacts. The ceramics recovered at the site provide important information relevant to the chronology of the site, cultural contacts of the people living there, and formation processes. Some information was also recovered that helps in the interpretation of various activities conducted at the site.

Temporally diagnostic projectile points and radiocarbon dates indicate that the site was occupied for more than 2,000 years, from the Early Agricultural period (1200 B.C.–A.D. 50) to the Tanque Verde phase (A.D. 1150–1300) of the late Classic period, with a few historic features present as well. However, most of the ceramics were plain wares and could not be dated beyond very broad chronological periods. The majority of the datable ones belong to the Rincon phase. Many of the radiocarbon dates also pertain to that phase (see Chapter 4, Table 4.9), but others indicate Rillito and possible Tanque Verde phases, intervals that are only sparsely represented in the ceramics assemblage. A small percentage of the plain ware and indeterminate red-on-brown sherds likely belong to the Rillito phase, and a very few could represent the Tanque Verde phase, though this is unlikely due to the lack of additional evidence (other than a radiocarbon assay) of a Tanque Verde phase occupation at the Marsh Station Road site. Some ceramics were recovered from Early Agricultural San Pedro phase features, but those are almost certainly intrusive.

Nearly all the ceramics recovered by the project are brown wares (n=6,471 of 6,606 identified ceramics; 98 percent), and most types are associated with the Tucson Basin sequence, indicating affiliations with that area. Far smaller numbers of buff ware ceramics indicative of the Salt and Gila river basins were recovered, as were a very few Mimbres sherds. Though only a few Mimbres sherds were recovered (eight, all at the Marsh Station Road site, and all too small to be confidently classified into a Mimbres period), they indicate a connection to the mountainous Mimbres region to the east and north. No ceramics associated with groups living to the south, in northern

Mexico, were recovered from the Marsh Station Road site.

Vessel forms can provide some indications of activities conducted at sites. The Marsh Station Road site excavations recovered only five whole or partial reconstructible vessels, however. Those vessels represent a variety of forms of both bowls and jars, but the small sample size limits interpretation. The rim sherd assemblage provides a larger sample for the interpretation of vessel form frequencies. From all contexts, about twice as many rim sherds from jars were recovered as from bowls. It is not clear, however, whether the difference between the two forms reflects differences in vessel frequencies during the site occupation, or jars wearing out and being discarded more frequently than bowls. The number of sherds recovered is a product of both the number of vessels present on the site and the average use-life of those vessels (McKee 2007; Schiffer 1987). Ethnographic studies indicate that serving vessels and cooking jars tend to be discarded more frequently than most other vessel forms (Mills 1989) due to both thermal and mechanical stresses. Determining the reasons for differences in frequency of the different vessel forms should be a goal of future research.

The modified sherds recovered from the site provide some of the most interesting behavioral information of the project. Several vessels showed signs of repair in prehistory, such as mend holes drilled to lash cracks in vessels. A number of sherds had also been ground to form disks, some of which had been perforated. Ethnographic examples discussed above indicate a number of possible behaviors associated with those disks. The project also recovered other modified sherds of a variety of forms. Several appear to have been used as scoops, and one (FN 44-1766) apparently was used as a parching plate.

The two nonvessel artifacts provide information regarding other aspects of life in southeastern Arizona. The fired-clay bead suggests that personal adornment was important to the inhabitants of the Marsh Station Road site, while the clay figurine may indicate religious activities, the play of children, art for art's sake, or other unknown purposes.

In summary, the ceramics recovered from the Marsh Station Road site provide considerable information regarding the prehistoric inhabitants of southeastern Arizona. They help to build the chronology of the occupations of the site, as well as provide a number of insights into the behaviors of site inhabitants.

Chapter 6
Flaked Stone Analysis
Michael J. Boley and Brandon M. Gabler

This chapter describes the flaked stone artifact assemblage from the Marsh Station Road site (AZ EE:2:44 [ASM]). It also presents the goals of the analysis and the methods used in the analysis, and a research framework that provides a focus for the inquiry and interpretation of the assemblage.

This analysis had two goals. The first was to describe the flaked stone assemblage quantitatively and qualitatively. The second goal was to look at characteristics of the assemblage through the lens of an investigative framework referred to as the organization of technology in order to explore the hypothesis that mobility strategies changed from the Early Agricultural period to the Formative period, and that flaked stone assemblages reflect this change. The assemblage from the Marsh Station Road site is broken down in a number of ways, including by recovery context, spatial distribution, and chronological distribution.

SAMPLING AND METHODS

The flaked stone assemblage from the Marsh Station Road site consists of 43,092 artifacts, including 41,526 pieces of debitage, 1,035 cores, 340 bifaces, 174 unifaces, and 17 hammerstones (Table 6.1). Of the total, 28,142 artifacts recovered from the Marsh Station Road site were subjected to detailed coding (Table 6.2). The coded sample includes all bifaces and unifaces, and all artifacts recovered from the surface and from feature excavations. It also includes 5,425 pieces of debitage and 88 cores recovered during the excavation of test units, which account for approximately 27 percent of the debitage and cores from test units. The primary target of the test unit coding was what are referred to as the "initial test units." These 12 test units are the only ones that were excavated from the modern surface; all the other test units were excavated from a surface that had been mechanically or manually stripped. The initial test units were spread out 10 m apart in SAs 2, 3, and 4. The entire test unit assemblage was subject to a rough sort, which ensured that no non-artifacts would be curated and no bifaces or unifaces would be left unidentified. About 87 percent (n = 3,241) of the debitage and 83 percent of the cores (n = 36) from the initial test units were coded in detail. The remaining 2,184 pieces of test unit debitage were subjectively selected from test units so that at least 25 percent of the debitage from each stripped area would be coded. The debitage, cores, and hammerstones that remained, while not fully coded, were counted individually and weighed collectively by the contexts from which they were recovered.

Table 6.1. Total counts by artifact class

Artifact Class	Quantity
Debitage	41,526
Cores	1035
Hammers	17
Biface	340
Uniface	174
Total	43,092

The use of different analytical systems is well known as a major obstacle in the ability to conduct intersite comparisons of flaked stone assemblages (B. Huckell 1998:111; Sullivan and Rozen 1985). At the outset of this analysis, knowing that the majority of projectile points recovered from the Marsh Station Road site (AZ EE:2:44 [ASM]) dated to the Early Agricultural period, it was decided to design the analysis to produce data comparable to other sites with Early Agricultural components recently excavated in the Tucson Basin (Diehl, ed. 2005; Mabry, ed. 1998; Sliva, ed. 2005; Wallace, ed. 2003). Relied upon quite heavily was the work of R. Jane Sliva (1998, 2003, 2005), as well as the work by Andrefsky (1998), B. Huckell (1998), and Whittaker (1994). As the overall analytical effort progressed, however, it became apparent that the flaked stone assemblage from the Marsh Station Road site was not "purely" Early Agricultural. Indeed, only two features produced both dates and projectile points from the Early Agricultural period, although other features that either produced Early Agricultural points and/or were aceramic may date to this period as well. Regardless, the attribute-based system that was employed produces results that are comparable for assemblages of any age.

Process

Artifacts were sorted into one of five primary categories whose definitions were drawn largely from Sliva (1998). Debitage is any flaked stone artifact struck from some parent material that is not subsequently worked. Cores are cobbles or tablets showing one or more flake scars. Bifaces are any artifact that has been worked on two sides of an edge, and unifaces are those that have been worked on one side. Hammerstones are cobble or cobble fragments that display various degrees of battering. Artifacts in each of these types were coded for four basic attributes: maximum dimension, mass, grain, and raw material type. For debitage, maximum dimension and mass were used to distinguish potential retouch flakes from other flakes, and this is elaborated upon in detail below. Grain and raw material type are discussed further in the next section. Beyond these four attributes, the analysis

Table 6.2. Coded sample by site, artifact type, and context

	Surface	Feature	Test Unit	Other Subsurface	Total
Biface	64	112	142	22	340
Core	566	126	88	4	784
Debitage	7329	14,075	5425		26,829
Hammer	12	3			15
Uniface	104	34	35	1	174
Total	8075	14,350	5690	27	28,142

became more specifically oriented to the artifact type. Debitage was coded for completeness, portion present, dorsal scar count, amount of dorsal cortex, whether it macroscopically appeared to have been utilized or not, and for characteristics of both the platform and termination. Cores were coded as to type (reflecting the nature and extent of flake removal), and to use as a tool, if at all. Unifaces were coded for the nature, reach, and extent of their retouch and like bifaces, were coded as to "intuitive type" (see Sliva 1998 for a relevant discussion). Hammerstones were examined for the type and extent of apparent use.

All of the coding was done in WSA's laboratory in Tucson. The senior author coded artifacts and directly supervised four other coders, who worked in close concert with one another. To ensure consistency, all coders were trained to the extent necessary to identify technological and morphological characteristics of individual artifacts. Their work was checked until it became evident that all coders were making like observations. To ensure consistency, ready access was provided to specimens representing the different material types and the range of variation in grain. Maximum dimension was recorded to the nearest hundredth of a millimeter using digital calipers, and mass was recorded to the nearest tenth of a gram using a digital scale. Data was entered from the hard copies into a Microsoft Access database. Each line of data was then checked against the hard copies by a different person. Where discrepancies were found, the appropriate corrections were made.

Raw Material Type and Grain

While determining the metric attributes was relatively straightforward, attributing each piece to a raw material type (Table 6.3) was less so. Heeding Sliva's (1998:307) and Stevens' (2001a:229) admonitions about being overly confident in assigning raw material types, WSA consulted three geologists (Drs. Charles Ferguson, Stephen Richard, and Jon Spencer) from the Arizona Geological Survey, all of whom had spent time in the field mapping the geology near the project area (Ferguson et al. 2001; Richard et al. 2002; Spencer et al. 2002). Presenting them with a representative sample of raw material types recovered from the site permitted a significant conclusion to be drawn: it is very difficult to macroscopically determine rock types. Even for those with extensive experience in looking at rocks, sole reliance on macroscopic observations allows for considerable variation in attribution of type. No thin-sections of any rocks were made, and despite knowledge of the various warnings, raw material types were attributed to all the coded flaked stone artifacts as best as possible.

A review of the relevant archaeological literature (B. Huckell 1998; Sliva 1998, 2003, 2005; Stevens 2001a), geologic maps, and the flaked stone assemblage itself resulted in 21 raw material categories being established, although it is likely that more raw material types are actually represented in the assemblage. It is also likely that some debitage was assigned to incorrect types. This misattribution most likely occurred with the "silicified sediment" types, which account for just over half of the coded sample.

There are six reasons to assume that the bulk of what was recovered at the Marsh Station Road site is local in provenance. First, the aforementioned geologists saw only one artifact they felt might not have been of local origin. Second, the underlying geology is quite varied (Dickinson 1991; Richard and Harris 1996). The site is underlain by the Pantano formation, which in the area of the Marsh Station Road site is "extremely varied in composition ... ranging from conglomerates to very fine grained sandstones and mudstones, to gypsum evaporates, to rock slide avalanche

Table 6.3. Raw material types identified in the flaked stone assemblage

Codes	Raw Material Types
1	silicified sandstone/limestone (with speckles)
2	silicified sandstone/limestone (without speckles)
3	silicified sediments (sandstones, siltstones, mudstones, limestones)
4	quartzite
5	Bisbee chert
6	rhyolite
7	andesite
8	basalt
9	chert
10	jasper
11	chalcedony
12	quartz
13	obsidian
14	porphyritic igneous
15	metamorphic other
16	sedimentary other
17	igneous other
18	sandstone
19	Bisbee quartzite
20	gray quartzite
21	maroon rhyolite/andesite
22	glass
99	unknown/indeterminate

breccias, and andesitic volcanic rocks" (Pima Association of Governments 2003). Third, a perusal of the literature discussing prehistoric procurement of stone from the Early Agricultural into the Formative suggests that groups in the Tucson Basin overwhelmingly used local stone (see Sliva 2005:74; also see Sliva 2003:238 [citing Eppley 1990:128–131]; Eppley 1986:279). Fourth, the site's location at the confluence of two significant washes provided a varied bedload from which to pick and choose, and, as was the case further up Cienega Creek, the nearby older terraces and pediments provided a second source of material (B. Huck-

ell 1995:60–61). Fifth, recognized stone types from sources not distant from the Marsh Station Road site, like the "Saguaro rhyolite" and "Saguaro jasper" described by Eppley (1986), were recovered in negligible qualities, if at all. Lastly, just eight obsidian artifacts were recovered. While it is still possible that the site inhabitants were traveling some distance to obtain non-obsidian raw material, it is more likely that they were procuring the majority of their material locally.

In lieu of being able to really iron out the raw material types, the analysis emphasized the artifacts' texture, or "grain." This attribute was certainly more important to the knappers than was the geologic rock type. Therefore grain was coded on a scale of 1 to 5, from very fine to very coarse. The category of very fine was reserved for obsidian and cryptocrystalline silicates. While not as smooth or glassy as the very fines, fines are also of a high quality from a knapping standpoint. The very coarse and coarse categories included those artifacts of a grain that would be difficult to fashion into a formal flaked stone tool. Medium-grained artifacts included the rest. While this was a subjective effort, an attempt was made to ensure that individual investigators coded grain consistently. That this was successful is suggested by the fact that the average mass and maximum dimension steadily increase as the grain becomes coarser. On average, the finer the material, the more it was worked.

Investigative Framework

A framework referred to as the organization of technology (Andrefsky 1994; Binford 1979; Kelly 1988, 2001; Shott 1986) has dominated research on flaked stone assemblages for years. Kelly (1988) defines organization as the "spatial and temporal juxtaposition of the manufacture of different tools within a cultural system, their use, reuse, and discard, and their relation not only to tool function and raw-material type and distribution, but also to behavioral variables which mediate the spatial and temporal relations among activity, manufacturing, and raw-material loci" (Kelly 1988:717). One important behavioral variable is a group's degree of residential mobility. Greater settlement mobility may affect technology whereby "tools should become less specialized and more multifunctional in character ... and designed to enhance their portability" (Shott 1986:20).

Parry and Kelly (1987) noted the widespread evidence for the increase of a more expedient and non-standardized reduction technology through time and relate this change to an increase in low residential mobility or even year-round sedentism. Applied to southern Arizona, Sliva (2003, 2005) has used changes in the proportions of formal bifaces, along with certain other assemblage-level characteristics, to make statements about behavioral changes over time from the Middle Archaic to the Formative period in the Tucson Basin. She (Sliva 2003, 2005) has also used other assemblage-level attributes to bolster Parry and Kelly's (1987) initial observation linking increased sedentism to changes in core technology.

Assemblage Description

The first goal of this analysis was simply to describe the assemblage. While a necessary and useful step in the analysis of any site's flaked stone, it is of particular importance here because very little work in the immediate vicinity has been published. With this goal in mind, the basic characteristics of the assemblage as a whole will be offered. This description begins by summarizing all artifacts by their type, and then turns to site-specific assemblages.

Artifact Types

Flaked stone artifacts from the Marsh Station Road site were placed into one of five categories: bifaces, unifaces, cores, hammerstones, and debitage. All together, 28,142 (65 percent) of 43,092 artifacts were coded (see Tables 6.1 and 6.2).

Bifaces

A total of 340 bifaces (0.79 percent of all flaked stone) was recovered from this site. The plurality of bifaces are projectile points or projectile point fragments (n = 145). The remaining types are projectile point preforms (n = 69), drills (n = 17), humpback bifaces (n = 13; see Sliva 2005:67), alternate retouches (n = 4; see Sliva 1998:309), discoids (n = 3; see Sliva 1998:314a–b), and those that were less formally modified but that displayed flaking on two faces (n = 89).

Unifaces

A total of 174 unifaces (0.40 percent of all flaked stone) was recovered from this site. Unifaces were coded for the nature, reach, and extent of their retouch (B. Huckell 1998; Sliva 1998). The nature of the retouch refers to whether the scars are contiguous or irregularly situated on the piece. Reach describes how far into the piece the scars extend from the margin. If more than 10 percent of the maximum dimension of the artifact, the reach is described as invasive; otherwise as marginal. Finally, extent refers to how much of the perimeter of the uniface has been worked. If greater than 20 percent, the retouch is extensive and if less it is nonextensive. In addition to these objective characteristics, the unifaces were also coded as to their intuitive type, which include endscrapers, sidescrapers, composite scrapers, perforators, notches, denticulates, and those for which no determination was possible.

Cores

A total of 1,035 cores (2.4 percent of all flaked stone) was recovered from this site, 784 (75.7 percent) of which were coded, including all cores from the surface and from feature excavations and cores from non-feature subsurface excavations.

Hammerstones

A total of 17 hammerstones (0.04 percent of all flaked stone) was recovered from this site.

Debitage

Debitage was of course the most common flaked stone artifact type recovered from the site. Collected were 41,526 pieces of debitage (96.4 percent of all flaked stone), of which 26,829 (64.6 percent) were fully coded (see Tables 6.1 and 6.2).

Marsh Station Road Site Assemblage

All of the tools and all of the flaked stone from surface and feature contexts were coded, as was approximately 27 percent of the material from nonfeature subsurface contexts (mostly test units) (see Table 6.2). This coded sample of 28,142 is approximately 65 percent of the entire site assemblage. As large as the coded assemblage is, it suffers from some deficiencies that limit its interpretive potential. The primary issue is a veritable lack of vertical stratigraphy. Given that the flaked stone artifacts represent over 2,000 years of occupation at the site and span from the Late Archaic or Early Agricultural into the Formative period, this is a problem. This problem is dealt with in two ways. First, the assemblage is analyzed spatially. Second, almost all features were assigned a temporal designation, albeit with varying degrees of resolution and certainty (see Table 4.7). Still, this allows for the possibility of speaking to changes in flaked stone technology over time, some of which have been previously identified in the Tucson Basin (Sliva 2003, 2005). After providing some basic spatial and temporal information on the assemblage, brief summaries of each artifact type recovered from the site are offered. The discussion of debitage from the site includes sections on potential retouch flakes (sensu Sliva 2005) and utilized flakes. Following that, the site assemblage is analyzed spatially and chronologically. The technological profile (sensu Sliva 2005) of the Marsh Station Road site is then discussed.

Contextual Notes

The following spatial and temporal discussions of the Marsh Station lithics use various sub-assemblages by necessity. As mentioned above, all artifacts from the surface and from features were coded (see Table 6.2), so they can be used in comparisons of both artifact type and raw material type. From the test units, all bifaces and unifaces were coded, but not all debitage, cores, and hammerstones. About 27 percent of the debitage and cores from test units were fully coded (hammerstones count so few that they are rarely used in these comparisons). This means that not all debitage and cores from the test units can be used in comparisons of raw material type, but because they were rough-sorted, they can be used in comparisons of artifact type.

Test units and features were excavated in one of five stripped areas (SAs) (see Chapter 4). SA 1 is located in the northeastern part of the site, while SAs 2 through 5 are in the northwestern part of the site, along Cienega Creek (see Figure 4.2). SAs 2 and 3 and SAs 4 and 5 are here considered each as a single unit, as they are each separated only by a backhoe trench. The distance between SA 2/3 and SA 4/5 is only about 15 m, but during excavation the impression was developed that there might be meaningful behavioral and/or chronological differences between the two groups of SAs. Specifically, it seemed as though artifact density was much higher in SA 4/5 (see below), that there was much less Formative material in SA 2/3 (see Chapters 4 and 5), and that there was an evenly spread but thin Early Agricultural component across both SAs (Figure 6.1).

Much more of the site was surface-collected than ultimately opened for excavation (see Chapter 4), so surface and subsurface materials that are compared are not of the same areal extents. This obtains for even the surface-subsurface comparisons of just the areas that were excavated (SAs). This is because the mechanically stripped areas were not stripped on the same 10-m by 10- m gridlines that the surface collection units were set on.

The raw material types used in this analysis are discussed above (see Table 6.3). For the purposes of the comparisons given below, raw material types were either assigned to one of several groups or dropped altogether (Table 6.4).

Temporal Assignment of Features

Numbers were assigned to 209 features. Four were voided, and 13 were determined not to be features. An attempt was made to give a temporal assignment to the remaining 192 features and subfeatures (see Table 4.7). Fifty-four features were assigned to an Unknown category, in most instances because they were not excavated. Sixty-two features could not be assigned any more specifically than to the entire span of the site occupation, Early Agricultural–Formative. Three features were assigned to the historic period. These 119 features are not included in the analyses that follow. Thirty-six features (and 30 subfeatures associated with them) were assigned with varying degrees of resolution to the Formative period. Assigning features to the Early Agricultural period was generally not so straightforward. Features 98 and 44 were the only two that were radiocarbon dated to the Early Agricultural period (see Chapter 4). These two pits, located in SA 3 about 20 m apart, were both dated to the San Pedro phase, and each contained one San Pedro point (both of which are "typical" San Pedro points, FN 44-2687 in Feature 98 and FN 44-1642 in Feature 44) in their fill. Thirty-five other features were assigned as being possibly Early Agricultural either because they were aceramic and/or because they contained diagnostic artifacts. Of course, aceramic is not

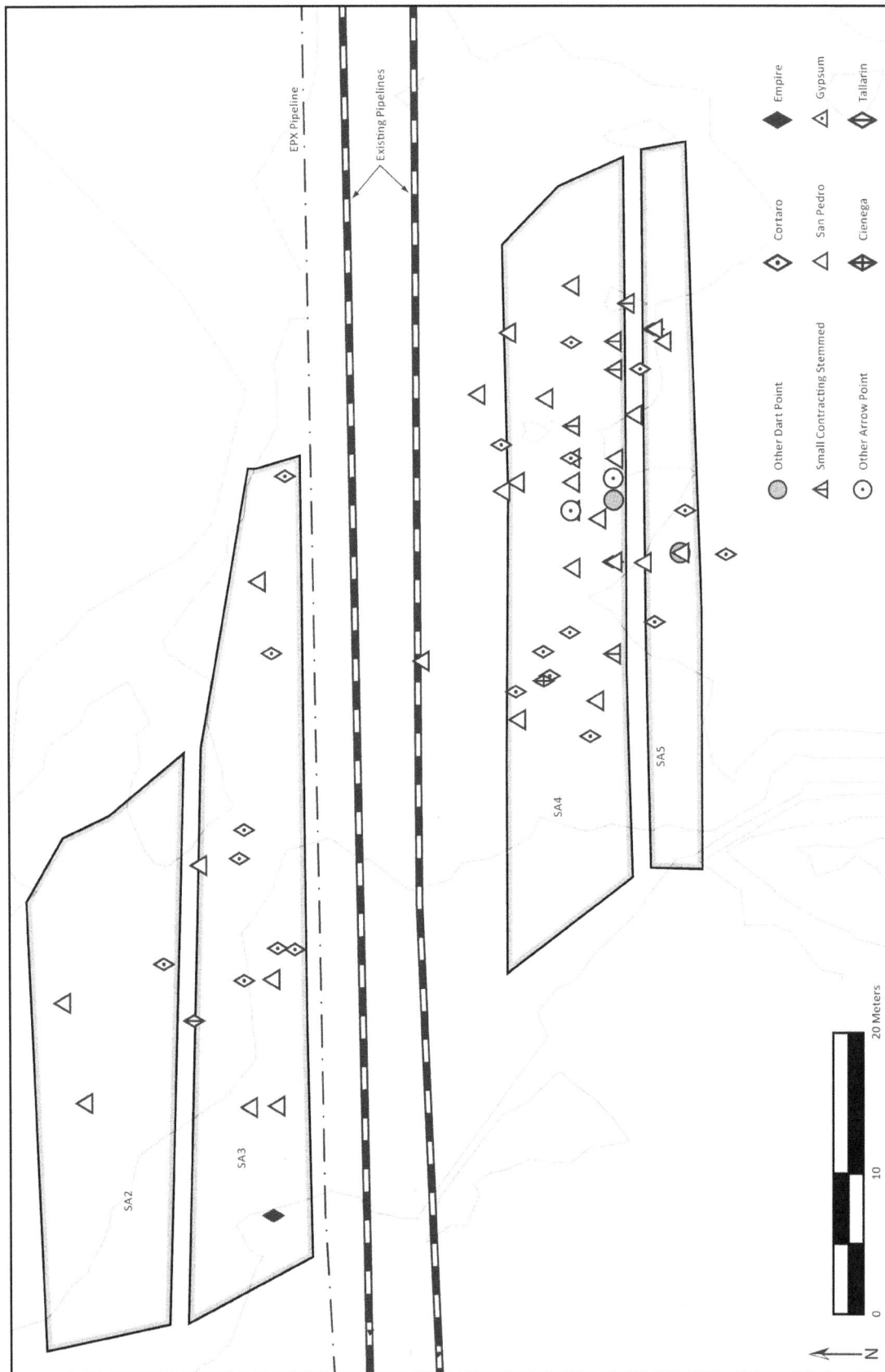

Figure 6.1. Spatial distribution of temporally diagnostic projectile points recovered from Stripped Areas 2–5.

Table 6.4. Assignation of raw material types to categorical groups

Group	Raw Material Codes	Raw Materials
1	1 & 2	silicified sandstone/limestone (with speckles); silicified sandstone/limestone (without speckles)
2	3	silicified sediments (sandstones, siltstones, mudstones, limestones)
3	4	quartzite
4	5 & 19	Bisbee chert; Bisbee quartzite
5	6–8	rhyolite; andesite; basalt
6	9–11	chert; jasper; chalcedony

necessarily the same as preceramic, but they are nonetheless considered as a group.

In an attempt to support this attribution, there was a hope, probably a naïve one, that the flaked stone assemblages from Features 98 and 44 would be similar enough to one another, and different enough from other features, to allow for the creation of an Early Agricultural flaked stone "signature" that could be extended to other features, particularly the possible Early Agricultural ones. As it turned out, the assemblages from these two features are not very similar. This dissimilarity can be seen in five attributes of the debitage (metrics, debitage completeness, platform type, amount of dorsal cortex, and types of raw material) as well as in the cores. The Feature 98 debitage has on average a greater maximum dimension (24.5 mm versus 19.9 mm) and mass (3.5 g versus 2.5 g), and has a much greater percentage of complete flakes (60 percent versus 41 percent). Of debitage with a platform, Feature 98 has more cortical (10 percent versus 5 percent) and crushed (18 percent versus 5 percent) platforms than does Feature 44. Feature 98 has a greater number of flakes with dorsal cortex (27 percent versus 14 percent). A significant chi-square shows that the raw material type distributions

from the features are statistically different. In addition, the Feature 98 cores are quite a bit larger (52.7 mm versus 46.3 mm) and heavier (55.5 g versus 34.7 g), and while none of the cores from Feature 44 retain any cortex, all the cores from Feature 98 do.

Taken all together, these attributes suggest that these two approximately coeval assemblages resulted from different circumstances and may represent different subsets of the flaked stone technological system of this period. It appears that the Feature 98 assemblage was formed by knappers focusing on a hard-hammer core reduction with the goal of producing fairly large flakes. On the other hand, the Feature 44 assemblage contains more flakes thought to be the result of tool manufacture and also displays a greater working of the debitage, as indicated by the smaller average size of and less dorsal cortex on flakes. The implications of this are clear. First, these differences will not permit the combining of the two assemblages into a homogenous assemblage which one could extend to other similar assemblages of unknown age. Second, that these two San Pedro phase assemblages can be so different plants a seed of doubt about finding meaningful patterns over time.

Bifaces

A total of 340 bifaces was recovered from this site. This number includes projectile points and non-projectile point bifaces.

Projectile Points

Seventy-four projectile points (21.8 percent of bifaces) from the Marsh Station Road site were identified to type by the senior author with the assistance of R. Jane Sliva and Jonathan Mabry. The points provide a definite, but slightly complicated, chronological picture of the occupation of the site. Of the 74 points from this site identifiable to a recognized type, about 90 percent are Early Agricultural. Of these, over half can be classified as San Pedro points. Others (Sliva 2005:95; Shackley 1996b) have noted a great deal of morphological variation in what archaeologists call San Pedro points, and this is borne out in the present sample. Figure 6.2 (a–e) shows some of the variation in notch shape and neck width of identified San Pedro points. In fact, some of these points are morphologically more similar to Basketmaker Corner-notched points than the archetypal San Pedro point, as Sliva (2001:93) notes with regard to similar points recovered from Los Pozos. According to Sliva (2005:95), at present this variation does not seriate temporally and neither does it occur in discrete spatial concentrations. Rather, it reflects the choices of individual populations. This variation within the San Pedro type, combined with two other broadly contemporaneous point styles, the Empire (Stevens and Sliva 2002) and the Tallarin (R. Jane Sliva, 2007, personal communication to Michael Boley), both of which were recovered from the Marsh Station Road site (Figure 6.2f–g), hint at a potentially interesting demographic situation at the site during the San Pedro phase, although this is not addressed here. The Cienega phase, however, is less well represented, with just a single Cienega Flared point (Figure 6.2h).

In addition to the Early Agricultural points, a single Gypsum point and eight arrow points were also recovered (Figure 6.3a–c). The Gypsum point suggests a pre-San Pedro phase use of the area, though this style overlaps with the Early Agricultural as well (Justice 2002:191; B. Huckell 1996). The eight arrow points are of two types, both of which have been recovered from sites in the Tucson Basin. Six are very similar to points recovered from Valencia Vieja (Wallace, ed. 2003), illustrated and described by Sliva (2003:243–4) as Small Contracting Stemmed points. These were recovered from Tortolita phase contexts and, as Sliva notes, likely "represent the earliest manifestation" of a style that continued into later periods. Indeed, the Hodges Contracting Stem points illustrated in both Justice (2002:280) and Kelly and others (1978:90) bear a strong resemblance and suggest that these points recovered from the Marsh Station Road site may date to the Tortolita or Rillito phases or, presumably, the intervening phases as well. The other two arrow points are also akin to points illustrated in Justice (2002) and Kelly and others (1978). Straight- to incurvate-bladed and concave-based, they look like Justice's (2002:279–80) Snaketown Triangular Concave Base type. From the Hodges Ruin, points from both the Rincon and Cañada del Oro phases resemble mistaken for this type (Kelly et al. 1978:90).

Twenty-seven Cortaro points (36.5 percent of the 74 projectile points) were recovered from the Marsh Station Road site (for examples, see Figure 6.4). This point type was named after the predominant type of finished biface recovered from the Cortaro Fan site (Roth and B. Huckell 1992). Described as a Middle to Late Archaic projectile point at the time, both the chronological and functional inferences have been questioned since. Noting the "morphological irregularities" of the type and the "low quality raw materials" (Sliva

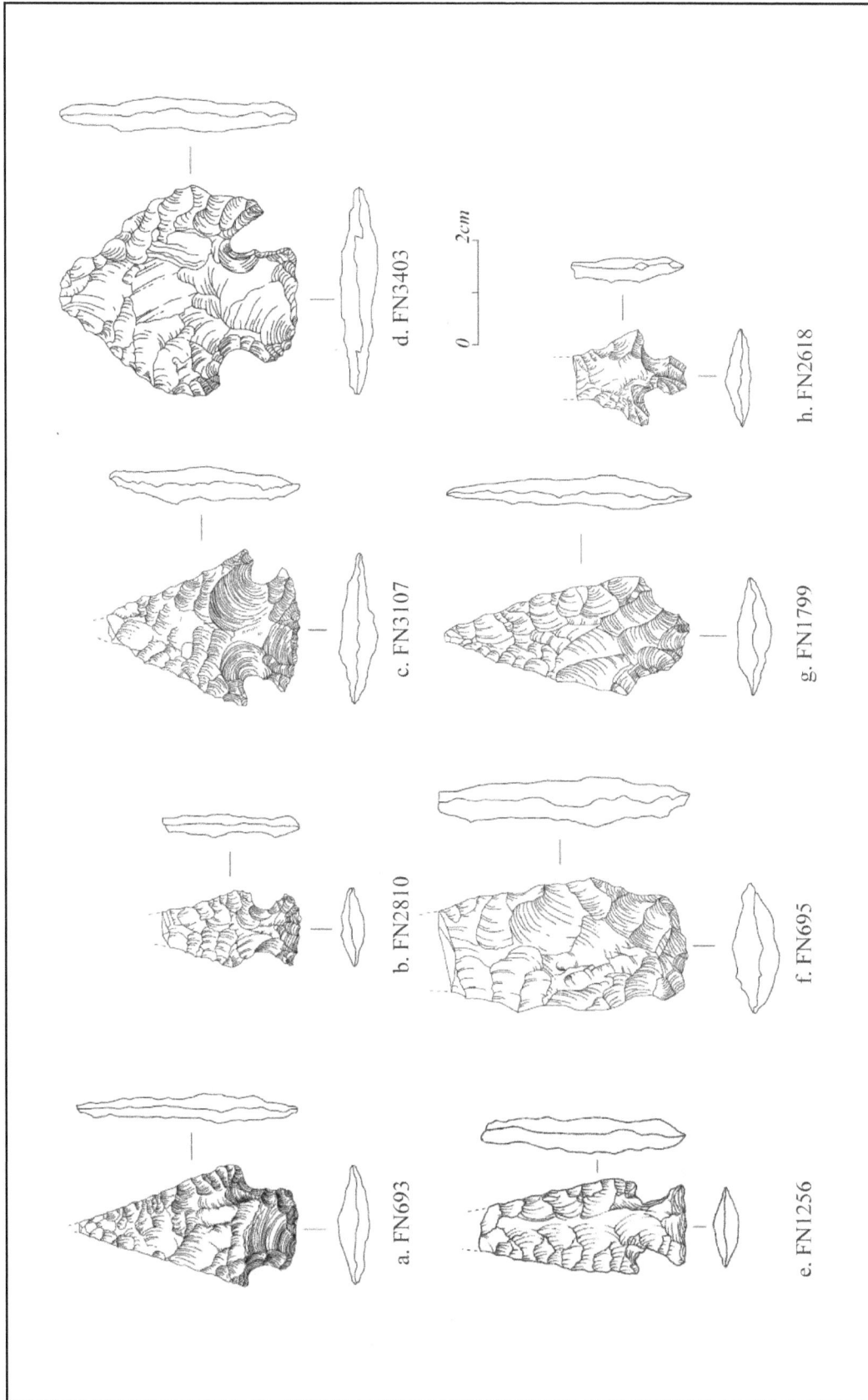

Figure 6.2. Early Agricultural period projectile points: a–e) San Pedro projectile points, f) Empire projectile point, g) Tallarin projectile point, and h) Cienega Flared projectile point.

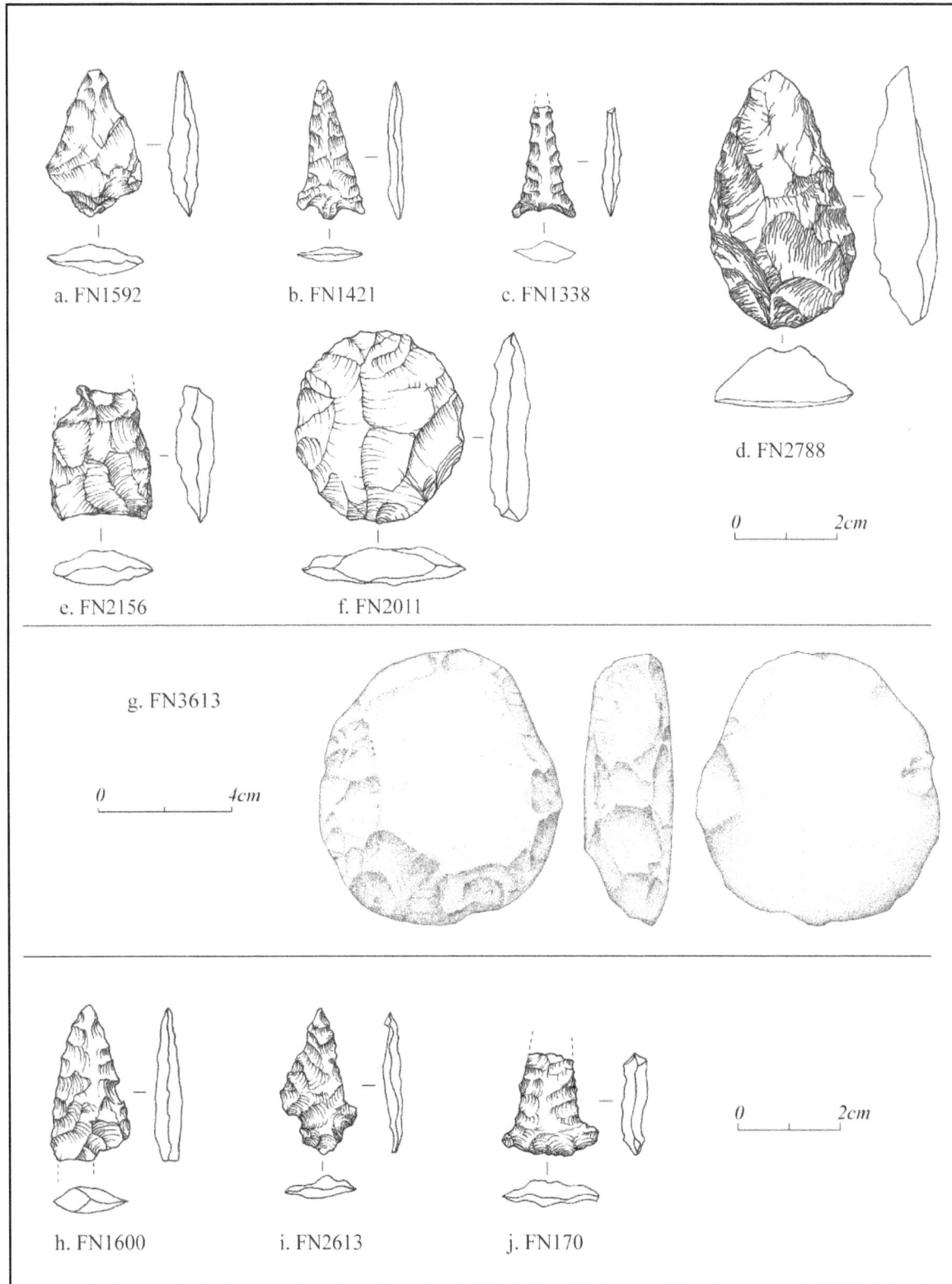

Figure 6.3. Various flaked stone artifacts from the Marsh Station Road site: a) Gypsum projectile point; b) Hohokam Small Contracting Stemmed arrow point; c) Unidentified Hohokam-style arrow point; d) Humpback biface; e) unnotched biface with concave base; f–g) discoids; h–i) hafted knives; and j) drill.

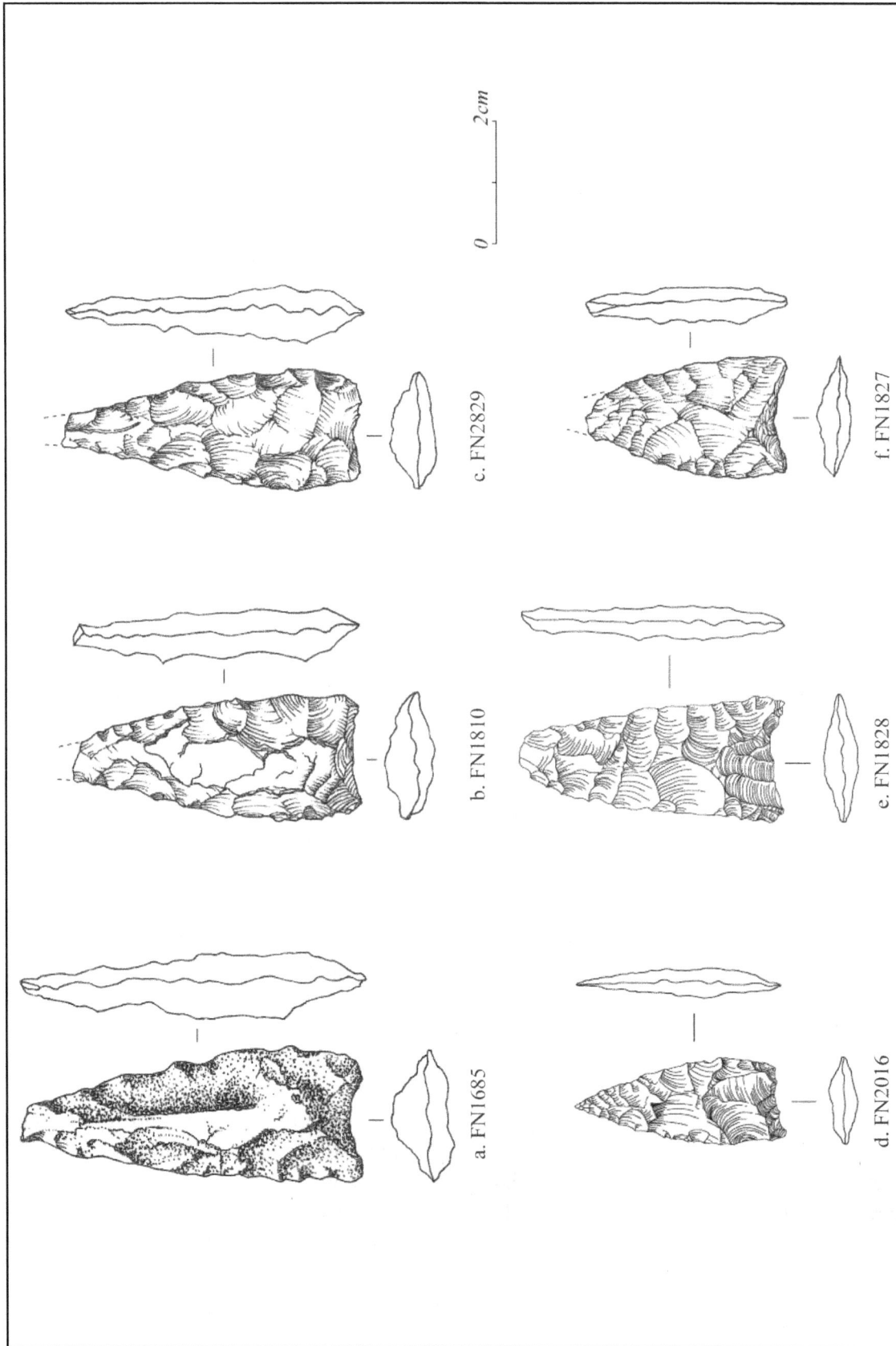

Figure 6.4. Variation in Cortaro projectile points recovered from the Marsh Station Road site.

2005:93, 1999:41) out of which these tools were manufactured, Sliva questions whether all Cortaro points were actually used as projectile points. With regard to chronology, most researchers have concurred with the Middle to Late Archaic assignment. In a surface survey of the Cienega Valley, Stevens considered Cortaro points to be diagnostic of the Chiricahua phase of the Middle Archaic period, in part based on Cortaro points that were recovered from the Middle Archaic component at Los Pozos (Sliva 1999). Justice (2002:179), citing Gladwin and others (1937), however, notes that similarly shaped bifaces were recovered from Hohokam contexts at Snaketown. It seems likely that the Cortaro point style extended beyond the Chiricahua phase and that they should not be used as a diagnostic of that phase.

As with Cortaro assemblages from other sites, the Marsh Station Road site produced some thin, smaller, well-made Cortaro points that almost certainly did function as projectile points. At the other end of the spectrum are those that are thick, larger, and more crudely made. Indeed, some of these latter examples might be seen to trend into another group of bifaces, those that Sliva calls "humpback bifaces" (Sliva 2005; see also Jeske 1992), 13 of which were recovered from the Marsh Station Road site (Figure 6.3d). Also recovered from Las Capas, Sliva describes these thick bifaces, particularly noting the "humps on one aspect that are the result of stacked stepped flake terminations" that might strengthen them against "torque-induced breakage" (Sliva 2005:67, 69). Approximately 10 bifaces recovered from the Marsh Station Road site that were coded as Cortaro points share this characteristic, but they are smaller and, like Cortaro points, have concave bases. It might be that these bifaces, strengthened by their humps, are hafted tools used to drill other materials, a conclusion also reached by Sliva (2005:93; see also Eppley 1986:274).

Other artifacts lend credence to this idea. One is an unnotched biface with a concave base and parallel sides up to about 2.5 cm above the base, at which point there is an abrupt shoulder on one of the margins (Figure 6.3e). The biface is broken just above this shoulder, but the distal portion looks as if it would have been narrow and drill-like. The biface's asymmetry suggests it was not a projectile. At least two other bifaces, practically identical to this one, have been presented in the literature (Roth and B. Huckell 1992:359g; Windmiller 1973:141e), and both of these are broken in approximately the same spot, perhaps suggesting a common use. Further, another complete biface in the assemblage shares the characteristics of the proximal parallel-sidedness and abrupt shoulder on one margin, but this one does not have a concave base. It seems likely that these artifacts are more similar functionally to one another than are all bifaces with concave bases. At any rate, it is probable that not all bifaces now typed as Cortaro points are actually Cortaros points as defined by Roth and B. Huckell (1992). Rather, this category of artifact likely comprises a range of morphological and functional types.

With respect to the quality of raw material used to manufacture the San Pedro and Cortaro points, there is no practical difference. Fine-grained materials are the most common at about 50 percent for each, followed by very fine-grained materials at about 40 percent, with the remainder made of medium-grained materials. That the San Pedro points collected from the Marsh Station Road site were made from the same range of materials and in the same proportions is interesting given the suggestion presented above that Cortaros are more often made of lower quality materials. The eight arrow points provide a different picture in that six of the eight were made of cherts or chalcedonies, and the other two on fine-grained silicified sediments. Though the sample is small it suggests that these later knappers desired finer textured material than earlier inhabitants.

Other Bifaces

In addition to projectile points and humpback bifaces, other biface types recovered include discoids, alternate retouched pieces, knives, a variety of drills, and 87 (25.6 percent of bifaces) informally but intentionally modified artifacts. The three discoids are probably best considered as two different artifact types. The first type, of which one discoid was recovered, is a well-knapped, thin biface made on a flake blank where the platform is still visible (Figure 6.3f). Almost perfectly circular, it may have functioned as a handheld cutting instrument. The other two are more akin to the two discoids of unknown function recovered from the Santa Cruz Bend site and photographed by Sliva (1998:314a–b) (Figure 6.3g). The four artifacts coded as alternate retouched pieces share few characteristics other than that they all have "flakes struck from a common margin but with staggered impact points, forming a sinuous edge" (Sliva 1998:309). Two bifaces were probably hafted knives (Figures 6.3h and i). Seventeen bifaces were coded as drills. Three of them merit brief elaboration due to their morphological similarities with one another (Figure 6.3j). Made on very fine-grained flake blanks, their bases are crescent-shaped with a narrow, tapering blade extending from it. They were presumably hafted at the junction of the base and blade. All three are missing their distal-most portions.

Unifaces

The 174 unifaces from the Marsh Station Road site encompass a great range of morphological variability. The possible combinations of the codable retouch attributes result in a total of seven different categories into which a uniface could be placed (Figure 6.5). Unifaces char-

acterized by both contiguous and extensive retouch, as described above, account for nearly three-quarters of the total, which seems to indicate that the manufacture of these artifacts was planned and not haphazard. Interestingly, however, this seemingly planned reduction does not correspond to any particular artifact type. Indeed, these unifaces include sidescrapers, endscrapers, composite scrapers, indeterminate unifaces, a perforator, and a denticulate. It should be noted that unifaces of a type do not necessarily adhere to a single morphology. That is, for example, not all the sidescrapers in the assemblage look like one another. So while many of the knappers knew they wanted a piece with certain edge characteristics, they were apparently not held to any mental image of precisely how such a piece should look morphologically.

Unifaces were made on very fine-grained material only 17 percent of the time, noticeably less than the 27 percent of all debitage that was very fine-grained, and much less than the 47 percent of bifaces that were flaked on very fine material. It would seem that the site occupants were deliberately not choosing the finest material when they were making unifaces, presumably for reasons related to the intended functions of these artifacts.

Cores

A total of 1,035 cores was recovered from the Marsh Station Road site, 784 (75.7 percent) of which were coded. More than 42 percent were coded as having multiple platforms, suggesting "little planning, little concern for the conservation of raw material, and little control over the morphology of the resultant flakes" (Sliva 1998:322). Single platform cores (19 percent), bidirectional cores (7 percent), and tested pieces (6 percent) demonstrate a similar lack of concern over the results of core reduction. Another type, the opposed platform core (4 per-

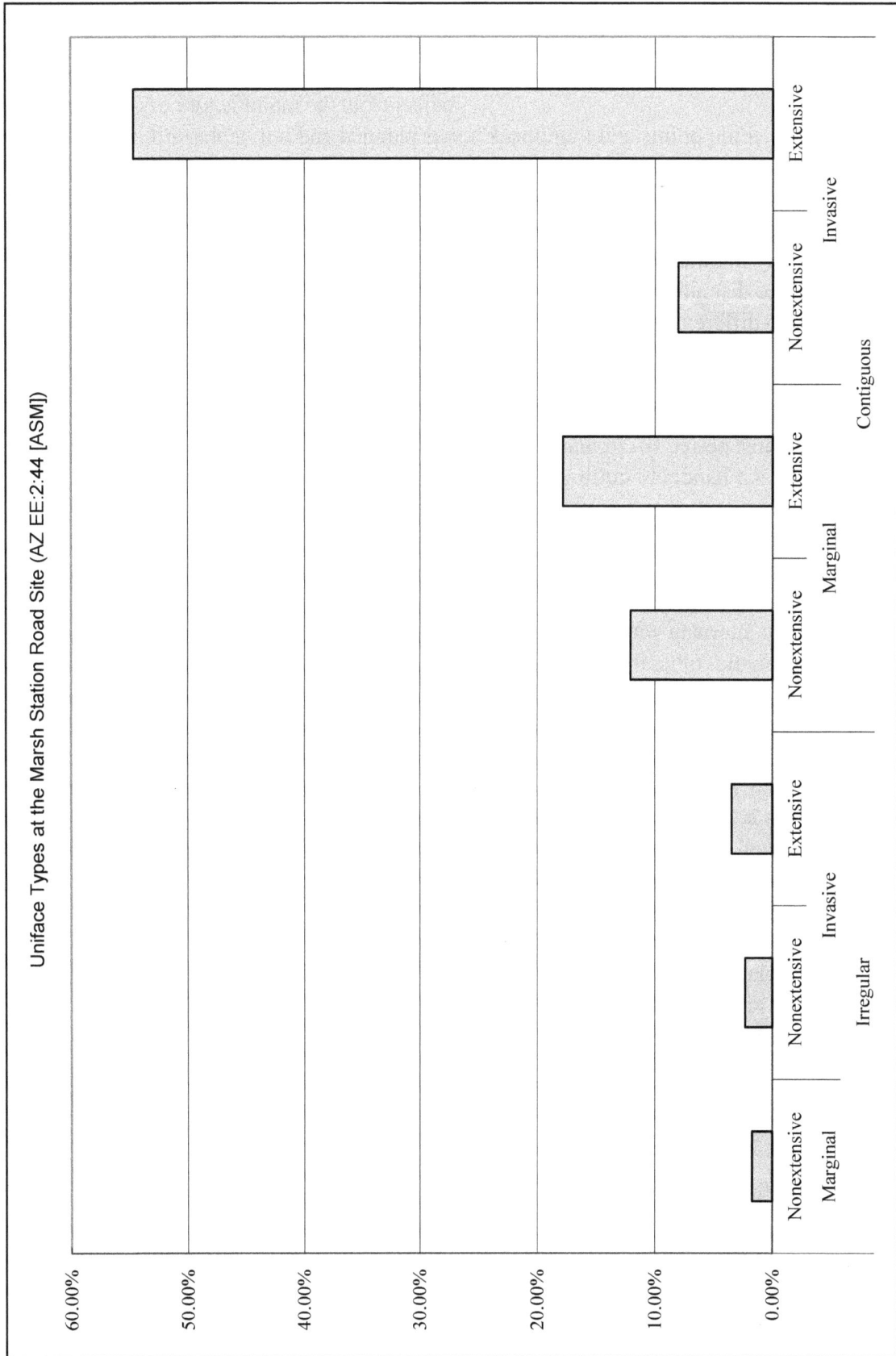

Figure 6.5. Percentages of unifaces with different types of retouch.

cent) might suggest a more planned reduction, but it is just as likely that these cores are simply bidirectional and that the platforms happen to be on opposite sides from one another. One core type, the bifacial core, does indicate a planned reduction. Only 14 of these were recovered from features at the site and, suggestively, both of the well-dated Early Agricultural features are represented. Core fragments make up 5 percent of the assemblage. Only one bipolar core was identified. This dearth is probably a reflection of the abundance of local cobbles large enough to render a bipolar technology unnecessary. Sixty-four of the cores were coded as also having been used as tools, including scrapers/planes, choppers, and hammerstones, as discussed below.

The plurality of cores was medium-grained (42 percent). Fine-grained cores account for 35 percent, and very fine-grained cores make up about 11 percent of the total. Coarse- and very coarse-grained materials make up the rest, accounting for 10 percent and 2 percent, respectively. These percentages are interesting when compared to the percentages of the grains of debitage. While the percents for cores and debitage are nearly equal for the fine, coarse and very coarse categories, the very fine and medium percentages are quite a bit different. Twenty-seven percent of the debitage was coded as very fine, and 30 percent as medium-grained. The question is, why is very fine-grained debitage so much better represented than very fine-grained cores?

Core fragments are the core type best represented by very fine-grained material, at 21 percent. This might suggest that very fine-grained cores were, more often than other core types, reduced to a greater extent, perhaps in some instances to almost nothing, and they simply were not recovered. The core type second best represented by very fine-grained material, however, is the tested piece, which is directly contrary to the expectation of work-

ing the best material to dust. Perhaps, then, excavations failed to recover very fine-grained cores because they were not onsite. It is possible that the inhabitants were reducing these cores onsite, then taking them when they left, implying fairly short stays at the site.

Hammerstones and Core Tools

Twenty-six of the 64 core tools mentioned above were coded as core hammerstones. In addition to these 26, 17 additional hammerstones were recorded. Characteristics indicating use as a hammerstone included one or more of the following: battering, step fracturing along the margin used to do the hitting, and flake scars due to removals that occurred at the time of impact(s). Given the counts of other artifact types in the flaked stone assemblage, this is a very small number. This paucity of hammerstones, combined with the great variety in expedient tools, particularly in the morphological variability of the unifaces as discussed above, may suggest a "short-term seasonal occupation geared towards specific tasks" (Sliva 2003:241).

Debitage

Debitage is of course the most common flaked stone artifact class, and in many ways the most informative. Of the 41,526 pieces of debitage recovered from the Marsh Station Road site, 26,842 were analyzed and coded. This total includes 100 percent of the debitage from feature and surface contexts, as well as about 27 percent of the material that was recovered from test units and other miscellaneous excavations. The debitage assemblage is here explored in two ways, through potential retouch flakes and utilized flakes.

Potential Retouch Flakes
R. Jane Sliva (2005) has developed a category

of debitage she refers to as potential retouch flakes (PRF). PRFs "represent the set of debitage falling within the metrical parameters exhibited by bifacial thinning flakes (BTF)," which include all the "identified BTF across all Desert Archaeology assemblages" (Sliva 2005:48). The metrical parameters include flakes that have a mass index (MI) within a standard deviation of the mean of all the BTFs. The MI is obtained by dividing a flake's mass by its maximum dimension and is a "proxy used to express relative flake thickness" (Sliva 2005:48), whereby lower values indicate thinner flakes and include most of the observed BTF. Examining the complete and fragmentary subsets of BTF separately, Sliva (2005:48) found that the MI of whole BTFs was <.076, and <.050 for incomplete BTFs.

While BTFs were not specifically sought in the present analysis, 247 were nonetheless noted during the coding of debitage from the Marsh Station Road site. Certainly there were more flakes in the assemblage that were produced during the manufacture of bifaces, but the 247 noted display archetypal attributes of a BTF. These BTFs, like some of the other artifact types discussed above, match an "intuitive type." In this case, these artifacts are thin and acortical; they have platforms both lipped and uncrushed, a ridge on the dorsal surface, and a slightly concave ventral surface when viewed laterally. The 181 complete BTFs from the Marsh Station Road site have a mean MI of 0.032 and a standard deviation of .021, meaning that PRF for complete flakes includes all those with an MI <.054. The 66 incomplete BTFs from the site have a mean MI of 0.030 and a standard deviation of .016, meaning that PRF for incomplete flakes includes all those with an MI <.046.

These MIs are noticeably less than those that Sliva (2005:48) obtained. It might be that only BTFs from a later stage of biface manufacture were identified, or it might be that the knappers at the site were generally manufacturing smaller bifaces. Whatever the reason, the differences have implications for interpretation, and this will be discussed further below.

More in accord with Sliva's findings, however, PRFs from this site include over 88 percent of all observed BTFs, whether complete or fragmentary, while her PRF included 91 percent of all observed BTFs. These numbers suggest that the category of PRF is useful in separating flakes resulting from tool manufacture, as opposed to those created from core reduction.

The PRF established from the Marsh Station Road site BTFs provides a different picture than the PRF established with the BTFs from

Table 6.5. Percent of potential retouch flakes in project assemblages

	AZ EE:2:44 (ASM) PRF	Desert Archaeology PRF
All flakes	44.43	52.59
All flakes from features	57.67	66.04
All flakes from late Middle Formative features	56.99	65.38
Early Agricultural features	57.63	66.83
Possible Early Agricultural features	61.50	69.82
Feature 44	72.22	77.78
Feature 98	56.35	67.49

all Desert Archaeology assemblages. Table 6.5 provides the percentages of PRF in a number of subassemblages from the site, figured with the MIs from the present assemblage and all of Desert Archaeology's. Of all the flakes coded, regardless of context, the percentage of PRFs as determined by the present analysis and by Sliva (2005) with the Desert Archaeology assemblages is 44 percent and 53 percent, respectively. Narrowing the scope to just those flakes recovered from features, the numbers change to 58 percent and 66 percent. This increase is likely due to the exclusion of the surface assemblage, which was composed of fewer smaller-sized flakes. Further restricting the scope and looking just at late Middle Formative features gives 57 percent and 65 percent PRFs. Definite Early Agricultural features, albeit only two in number, have 57 percent and 67 percent (and as mentioned above, these two features are quite different from one another). The last subset examined Marsh Station Road site features includes those that might be Early Agricultural in age. These have PRFs of 62 percent and 70 percent, noticeably higher than PRF assemblages from other subsets of features.

The general picture provided by PRFs, whether figured using BTFs from the present study or from Desert Archaeology, is not one of change over time. The PRFs from the well-dated features are very similar to one another, whether late Middle Formative or Early Agricultural. The exception is the group of features that might be Early Agricultural in age. The 70 percent PRFs (using Desert's metrics) from this assemblage falls right between the 68 percent and 72 percent PRFs Sliva found for late and early San Pedro contexts, respectively, from Las Capas (Sliva 2005:54). While this similarity is suggestive, the fact that the definite Early Agricultural features have fewer PRFs indicates that caution is warranted. Perhaps percentage of PRFs is of more utility when

considered as just one of many characteristics of an assemblage (see section on Technological Profiles below).

Utilized Flakes

While every coded piece of debitage was examined for evidence of use-wear, concerns about the accuracy and reliability with which it could be identified led to a cautious conservatism— about one half of one percent was coded as being utilized. Our caution may well have been warranted given that over 42 percent (n = 104) of the debitage coded as utilized was collected from surface contexts, despite surface debitage accounting for only about 27 percent of the coded assemblage. This suggests that some artifacts that appeared utilized were actually modified by any number of post-depositional factors, including the building of railroad alignments and two previous pipelines through the portion of the site investigated during the present project.

Twenty years ago Bruce Huckell (1989) suggested that meaningful information could be derived from Hohokam assemblages of utilized flakes and accordingly called on researchers to incorporate them into their studies. Huckell (1989), however, did not glean too much from the utilized flakes he examined from the sites Fasttimes and Waterworld. His most significant finding was that the average sizes of the utilized flakes from the two sites were very similar. Whether or not the average size of all flakes from the sites is also similar is unclear, and B. Huckell (1989) does not address the range of sizes of the utilized flakes. This is an important point in that any variation in the size of utilized flakes may speak to larger technological issues.

Teltser (1991) addressed this issue. She argued that utilized flakes produced within a technology not characterized by standardized core reduction should not themselves be standardized. Looking at an assemblage from a sedentary village site along the Mississippi River, she found that the evidence of use wear on a flake did not correlate with other attributes of the flake, such as platform type or dorsal cortex. Teltser (1991) used this information to argue that these knappers were not producing specific types of flakes with the intent of using them. Rather, any flake produced during core reduction was as likely to be used as any other.

One way to approach determining the sort of flaked stone reduction strategy employed at a site is to compare the utilized flakes to the larger debitage assemblage. If the utilized flakes appear to form a restricted subset of the debitage, it could be argued that the knappers were deliberately creating flakes standardized to some extent. Conversely, if the utilized flakes seem to mirror attributes of the larger assemblage, and if the larger assemblage lacks any characteristics of standardization, it could be argued that the technology was not standardized.

Two differences in the utilized versus larger assemblages are of note. First, utilized flakes are more often complete than are flakes in the larger assemblage (63 percent to 55 percent). Second, the utilized flakes are quite a bit more likely to still retain some amount of dorsal cortex (45 percent to 23 percent). Together, these attributes suggest that there was a preference for flakes created early in the reduction process. If so, it might also be expected that utilized flakes would be larger, on average, than the larger debitage assemblage. Indeed, the utilized flakes have an average maximum dimension nearly double that of the rest of the debitage. These attributes make it clear that there was a preference for a certain type of flake, but do not speak directly to the question of standardization. The standard deviation of the maximum dimension for each assemblage is quite different (σ=25.3 for the utilized flakes, σ=14.2 for the larger assemblage), which indi-

cates that the utilized flakes are more dispersed in size than the rest of the debitage, suggesting that utilized flakes were neither chosen nor manufactured in any standardized way.

Spatial and Temporal Distributions at the Marsh Station Road Site

We now turn toward an examination of any spatial or temporal patterning in the assemblage from the Marsh Station Road site, and to the "technological profiles" of the site.

Surface and Subsurface Assemblages

Chi-square tests indicate that cores and unifaces occur in higher-than-expected numbers on the surface, irrespective of the exact contexts investigated (Tables 6.6–6.9). The relationships hold true whether all surface artifacts are compared to all subsurface artifacts, or for example, just the features or test units are compared to the surface artifacts that overlay them. It is difficult to interpret this as indicative of meaningful prehistoric behavior. Rather, it seems more likely that this relationship is a reflection of post-depositional factors, both natural and cultural. Perhaps cobbles and flakes that were on the surface got nicked during railroad or previous pipeline construction, and were misidentified during coding.

As with artifact types, the surface to subsurface relationships of raw material types do not change with the contexts examined. They remain basically the same whether comparing all surface artifacts to all subsurface artifacts, or looking at restricted subsets of both assemblages. Two of these relationships are conspicuous. First, the number of artifacts made from silicified sandstone/limestone with and without speckles (raw materials 1 & 2; see Table 6.4) is higher than expected on the surface and lower than expected subsurface. Second, the number of cryptocrystalline silicates (raw materials

Table 6.6. Distribution of raw material type by collection unit (CU)

	Debitage	Cores	Unifaces	Bifaces	Hammerstones	Total
All Collection Unit Totals	*7329*	*565*	*104*	*48*	*12*	*8058*
1 Silicified sandstone/limestone (with speckles)	1553	124	24	2	5	1708
2 Silicified sandstone/limestone (without speckles)	1009	61	9	5	2	1086
3 Silicified sediments (sandstones, siltstones, mudstones, limestones)	1934	146	30	8	2	2120
4 Quartzite	836	104	10	5		955
5 Bisbee chert	426	36	11	3		476
6 Rhyolite	192	24	8	1	2	227
7 Andesite	7	3	1	1		12
9 Chert	865	43	6	18		932
10 Jasper	13					13
11 Chalcedony	196	5		3	1	205
12 Quartz	13	1				14
13 Obsidian	1					1
14 Porphyritic igneous	11	1	2			14
16 Sedimentary other	2					2
17 Igneous other	8	3				11
18 Sandstone	184	7	3	1		195
20 Gray quartzite	43	5				48
21 Maroon rhyolite/andesite	36	2		1		39

b.

Raw Material Groups	CU Raw Material Group Totals
1 & 2	2794
3	2120
9, 10, & 11	1150
5 & 19	476
4	955
6, 7, & 8	239

Table 6.7. Distribution of raw material type by artifact type recovered from features

	Debitage	Cores	Unifaces	Bifaces	Hammerstones	Total	b.	Raw Material Groups	Feature Raw Material Group Totals
All Features	14,075	126	34	112	3	14,350			
1 Silicified sandstone/limestone (with speckles)	1471	13	6			1490		1 & 2	3397
2 Silicified sandstone/limestone (without speckles)	1875	18	5	8	1	1907		3	3223
3 Silicified sediments (sandstones, siltstones, mudstones, limestones)	3160	26	8	26	2	3223		9, 10, & 11	4493
4 Quartzite	1716	26	5	16		1763		5 & 19	891
5 Bisbee chert	871	16		4		891		4	1763
6 Rhyolite	195	4	2	4		205		6, 7, & 8	223
7 Andesite	17	1				18			
9 Chert	3616	19	7	37		3680			
10 Jasper	77			3		80			
11 Chalcedony	720		1	12		733			
12 Quartz	39	1				40			
13 Obsidian	5					5			
14 Porphyritic igneous	12					12			
17 Igneous other	7					7			
18 Sandstone	144	1				145			
21 Maroon rhyolite/andesite	138	1		2		141			
99 Unknown/indeterminate	12					12			

Table 6.8. Distribution of raw material type by artifact type recovered from the initial 12 test units (TUs)

Initial Test Units: Totals for Coded Artifacts	Debitage	Cores	Unifaces	Bifaces	Totals		Raw Material Groups	Initial TUs Raw Material Group Totals
	3241	36	20	22	3318	b.		
1 Silicified sandstone/limestone (with speckles)	452	6	3	2	463		1 & 2	791
2 Silicified sandstone/limestone (without speckles)	321	4	1	2	328		3	944
3 Silicified sediments (sandstones, siltstones, mudstones, limestones)	926	12	6		944		9, 10, & 11	922
4 Quartzite	230	5	1	1	237		5 & 19	277
5 Bisbee chert	268	2	1	2	273		4	237
6 Rhyolite	56	1		1	58		6, 7, & 8	79
7 Andesite	9		1		10			
8 Basalt	11				11			
9 Chert	751	4	3	11	769			
10 Jasper	32				32			
11 Chalcedony	116		3	2	121			
12 Quartz	11				11			
13 Obsidian	1				1			
14 Porphyritic igneous	1	1			2			
15 Metamorphic other	1				1			
16 Sedimentary other	2			1	3			
17 Igneous other	3				3			
18 Sandstone	36	1	1		38			
19 Bisbee quartzite	4				4			
21 Maroon rhyolite/andesite	10				10			
Initial Test Units - Noncoded Artifacts	416	6			422			
Total Initial Test Units	3657	42	20	22	3740			

Table 6.9. Distribution of raw material type by artifact type recovered from non-initial test units (TUs)

	Debitage	Cores	Unifaces	Bifaces	Hammerstones	Totals	b. Raw Material Groups	Non-initial TU Raw Material Group Totals
Subsurface Non-feature Units, no initial Test Units Totals	*2184*	*52*	*15*	*122*		*2373*		
1 Silicified sandstone/limestone (with speckles)	272	9	2	4		287	1 & 2	605
2 Silicified sandstone/limestone (without speckles)	297	12	2	7		318	3	635
3 Silicified sediments (sandstones, siltstones, mudstones, limestones)	602	10	1	22		635	9, 10, & 11	670
4 Quartzite	158	7	2	7		174	5 & 19	190
5 Bisbee chert	177	2	1	10		190	4	174
6 Rhyolite	34	0	0	3		37	6, 7, & 8	41
7 Andesite	3	0	1	0		4		
8 Basalt	0	0	0	0		0		
9 Chert	499	10	6	57		572		
10 Jasper	7	0	0	0		7		
11 Chalcedony	78	2	0	11		91		
12 Quartz	13	0	0	0		13		
14 Porphyritic igneous	1	0	0	0		1		
18 Sandstone	32	0	0	0		32		
21 Maroon rhyolite/andesite	11	0	0	1		12		
Non-initial Test Units - Noncoded Artifacts	*13,824*	*221*	*0*	*0*	*1*	*14,046*		
Total Subsurface Non-initial Test Units	16,008	273	15	122	1	16,419		

9–11; see Table 6.4) is higher than expected subsurface and lower than expected on the surface. As with differences in artifact types, this is difficult to interpret as behaviorally meaningful, although it is interesting.

Turning to a comparison of all features versus all test units, cores are again the conspicuous artifact class, overrepresented in test units and underrepresented in features. This difference is driven by the material in SA 4/5, as the chi-square for SA 2/3 is not significant. What this indicates with regard to prehistoric behavior, if anything, is not clear. The distributions of raw material types are statistically different, but, again, this is difficult to interpret.

Stripped Area Comparisons

The SA comparisons are limited to those between SA 2/3 and SA 4/5, due to their proximity to one another and to perceived possible temporal differences. Comparison of artifact types between SA 2/3 and SA 4/5 with chi-square tests reveals that cores are the only type category that departs from the expected counts, but not in every comparison. It is true when all units are compared, as well as when collection units are compared. The test of test units across these SAs is still significant, but no relationship is particularly conspicuous. When features across these SAs are compared, the chi-square test is no longer significant. So how to explain higher-than-expected counts of cores on the surface of SA 2/3, and lower-than-expected counts in SA 4/5? As with differences in the surface to subsurface comparisons, it is difficult to ascribe this to meaningful prehistoric behavior. Having said that, feature and artifact density is greater in SA 4/5, so it is possible that the prehistoric inhabitants were removing themselves some slight distance and isolating core reduction from other loci of activity. If true, however, one might also expect to see more debitage in SA 2/3. Since these differences are not maintained below the surface, it is more likely that the surface cores in SA 2/3 are a result of post-depositional factors, as suggested above. Additionally, a Student's t-test reveals that the density of debitage ($t = 2.164$, $p = 0.034$) and the total flaked stone density ($t = 2.202$, $p = 0.031$) within features in SA 2/3 is significantly lower than the respective densities in SA 4/5.

Turning to a comparison of raw material types between all recovery contexts in SA 2/3 and SA 4/5, there are a number of conspicuous differences. Raw material types 1 & 2 and 9–11 (see Table 6.4) occur in lower-than-expected numbers in SA 2/3 and higher-than-expected numbers in SA 4/5. The reverse of this is true for raw material types 3, 4, 6–8, and 5 & 19. Given the presumed proximity of the site to sources for raw material groups 1 & 2 and 5 & 19, it might have been expected that they would demonstrate the same relationship, and probably the opposite relationship as raw material group 9–11. That this is not the case is interesting, but again, difficult to explain. Perhaps a word of caution about relying too heavily on the significance of chi-squares is warranted. Looking at the percentages of material types shows that the greatest difference between SAs is less than 3.5 percent (for raw material group 1 & 2). The difference in raw material group 9–11 across SAs is less than 3 percent.

Most of these differences can be attributed to differences that are apparent in the feature assemblages across SAs, as opposed to the assemblages from collection units and test units. The differences in raw material groups 6–8 and 5 & 19 are not conspicuous in the feature assemblage, but the rest of the relationships are the same as when examining all contexts. Why are there differences across SA 2/3 and SA 4/5 in the counts of different raw material types? Specifically, why do groups 1 & 2 and 9–11 have the same relationship, and why do groups 1 & 2 and 5 & 19 not have the same relationship?

Chronological Comparison of Feature Groups

As discussed above, features (with their associated flaked stone and raw material counts in Tables 6.10 and 6.11, respectively) were assigned to a group reflecting their presumed chronological association. Many were assigned to either a group likely belonging to the Early Agricultural period or to the Middle Formative period. These two groups were compared against each other with chi-square tests for both artifact type and raw material type. The test for distributions of artifact types is not significant. That is, there is no meaningful difference in the distribution of artifact types through time, suggesting that the occupants had similar needs and goals with regard to flaked stone. However, certain characteristics of the debitage assemblage contradict this. In features assigned to the Early Agricultural period, a significant chi-square test shows that the number of cortical platforms is lower than expected, while lipped platforms are overrepresented. Related to this, flakes with no dorsal cortex are overrepresented in features assigned to the earlier period, while flakes with some dorsal cortex are overrepresented in features assigned to the later period. Together, these characteristics suggest that the debitage in the assemblage assigned to the earlier group was reduced further than that in the later group, and that the manufacture of bifaces may have been more common in the earlier group than the later.

Turning to raw material, however, the chi-square test is significant and it is worth noting that the more conspicuous differences largely mirror differences in raw materials between SAs 2/3 and SAs 4/5. That is, the relationships between SAs 2/3 and SAs 4/5 are largely the same as the relationships between features assigned to the possible Early Agricultural period and the Middle Formative period, respectively. This suggests that SAs 2/3 may be "weighted" more to the Early Agricultural period while SAs 4/5 are more reflective of the Middle Formative period, notwithstanding the lack of differences with regard to artifact type.

Technological Profiles

Sliva (2005) has compiled the technological profiles for flaked stone assemblages from a number of sites in an attempt to discern meaningful differences across functional or temporal assignment. These profiles include information about the assemblage such as the relative percentages of tools, size of debitage and cores, percent of noncortical debitage and PRFs, and the ratio of flakes to cores. While Sliva (2005) found that no single characteristic from the profiles is temporally or functionally diagnostic, she states that certain suites of attributes are. She argues, for example, that sites can be grouped together based on their tool class distributions. Middle and Late Archaic hunting camps and some Early Agricultural agricultural sites are characterized by having more bifaces than formal or expedient unifaces. Archaic base camps and foraging camps, some Early Agricultural agricultural sites (Los Pozos), and Formative agricultural sites (including Hohokam villages) have more formal unifaces than either bifaces or expedient unifaces.

Table 6.12 shows the technological profiles for the site and site components and allows for temporal and functional comparisons with the sites provided by Sliva (2005:88–89). In light of Sliva's (2005) discussion, of particular interest here are the high relative percentages of bifaces in the tool assemblages. These numbers place the Marsh Station Road site as a whole, as well as its temporally assigned subassemblages, into a group with Middle and Late Archaic hunting camps and some Early Agricultural agricultural sites. On the surface, this makes sense. The Marsh Station Road site produced little in the way of evidence for significant agricultural activity (see Chapters

Table 6.10. Distribution of artifact type by feature

Feature Number	Debitage	Cores	Unifaces	Bifaces	Hammerstones	Totals
2	2					2
3	14			1		15
4	5					5
5	11					11
6	1447	8	2	12		1469
7	897	4	4	9		914
7.03	2					2
7.05	1					1
7.19	5					5
8	0			3		3
9	25					25
10	105	1		1		107
11	1348	5	1	7		1361
11.02	9					9
11.03	3					3
11.04	228	2				230
11.09	15					15
12	191	3	2	2		198
13	53					53
15	11					11
16	201	2		1		204
17	101	1		2		104
17.02	1					1
17.03	1					1
19	111	1		2		114
20	48	1	1	1		51
21	40					40
22	18					18
23	107	1				108
25	61	3		2	1	67
26	126	4		1		131
31	12					12
32	2					2
33	1	1				2
34	1					1
36	34		1	2		37
38	15					15
39	2					2

Feature Number	Debitage	Cores	Unifaces	Bifaces	Hammerstones	Totals
Table 6.10. Distribution of artifact type by feature, cont'd.						
40	1					1
41	451	6	2	1	1	461
41.01	3					3
42	26					26
43	7					7
44	146	3		1		150
45	27	1				28
46	6					6
47	3					3
48	108	1				109
50	16					16
51	549	7	1	4		561
51.01	7					7
51.02	2					2
52	504	10	2	2		518
53	31	2				33
54	68	2		2		72
55	17					17
56	7					7
57	149	10	2	2		163
58	94	1	1	1		97
59	379	1	1	2		383
60	28			1		29
61	58	3	1			62
62	1					1
63	11	1				12
64	37					37
65	48					48
66	20	1	1	1		23
67	26	2	1			29
68	3					3
70	9					9
72	165			2		167
73	28		1			29
74	30	2		1		33
75	30	1				31

Feature Number	Debitage	Cores	Unifaces	Bifaces	Hammerstones	Totals
76	37	1		1		39
77	2					2
78	4			1		5
81	36					36
82	1					1
83	20					20
84	2					2
85	21					21
86	10					10
87	18					18
90	27					27
91	20					20
92	123			1		124
93	109	5		1		115
94	10					10
95	128			1		129
96	37			1		38
97	74			3		77
98	364	5	2	7		378
99	3					3
101	22					22
102	152	3				155
103	40					40
104	7			1		8
105	94			2		96
106	16					16
107	110					110
108	84					84
109	265			1		266
110	7					7
111	15					15
112	147	4			1	152
113	12	1				13
114	67			1		68
115	3					3
116	8					8
117	11	1		1		13
118	25		1			26

Table 6.10. Distribution of artifact type by feature, cont'd.

Feature Number	Debitage	Cores	Unifaces	Bifaces	Hammerstones	Totals
			Table 6.10. Distribution of artifact type by feature, cont'd.			
119	45	2				47
120	52	1		1		54
122	36					36
123	17					17
124	35					35
126	13					13
127	8			1		9
129	607	4		3		614
130	5	1				6
132	15		3			18
134	2					2
136	99	1		1		101
137	10					10
138	7					7
139	166	1		2		169
140	12					12
141	132			2		134
142	10					10
145	15					15
149	55					55
151	18					18
152	1809	2	2	12		1825
152.01	2	1				3
152.02	5					5
152.03	1					1
152.06	2					2
152.08	3					3
152.1	4		1			5
152.11	7					7
152.12	6					6
157	24			1		25
158	1					1
165	209		1			210
173	21					21
182	1					1
200	108					108
206	33	2		1		36
Total	14,075	126	34	112	3	14,350

Table 6.11. Distribution of raw material type by feature

Feature Number	1 Silicified Sandstone/Limestone (with speckles)	2 Silicified Sandstone/Limestone (without speckles)	3 Silicified Sediments	4 Quartzite	5 Bisbee Chert	6 Rhyolite	7 Andesite	9 Chert	10 Jasper	11 Chalcedony	12 Quartz	13 Obsidian	14 Porphyritic Igneous	17 Igneous Other	18 Sandstone	21 Maroon Rhyolite/Andesite	99 Unknown/Indeterminate	Totals
2								1		1								2
3	1	1	6	3				4										15
4	1	1	1		1			1										5
5	1	3	1	2				3	1									11
6	171	254	301	181	77	20	1	318	10	107	6			1	16	6		1469
7	93	107	206	122	37	9	1	251	3	56	3		2		6	18		914
7.03								2										2
7.05	1																	1
7.19				1				4										5
8			1	2														3
9	4	6	1	3	1	2		7		1								25
10	15	7	40	13	3	4		20		4					1			107
11	146	196	289	157	92	21		368	7	55	3			1	15	11		1361
11.02	1		1	3				3		1								9
11.03		1		1	1													3
11.04	16	52	32	30	12	3		58	2	17	2				2	4		230
11.09	1	3		1	4			5							1			15
12	12	22	55	32	6	1	2	62		6								198
13	3	3	15	16	3	4		7		2								53
15	2	2	1	1	2			2								1		11
16	13	24	16	28	31	5		64		16					4	3		204
17	4	12	21	17	4			34	3	7	1			1				104
17.02			1															1
17.03				1														1
19	19	7	47	8	4			22		5					1	1		114
20	5	1	19	13				13										51
21		1	10	11	3			11		3						1		40
22	2	2	1	4	2			5		2								18
23	8	14	17	27	7	1		24		7						3		108
25	14	7	22	12	2	1		7	1	1								67

Table 6.11. Distribution of raw material type by feature, cont'd.

Feature Number	1 Silicified Sandstone/Limestone (with speckles)	2 Silicified Sandstone/Limestone (without speckles)	3 Silicified Sediments	4 Quartzite	5 Bisbee Chert	6 Rhyolite	7 Andesite	9 Chert	10 Jasper	11 Chalcedony	12 Quartz	13 Obsidian	14 Porphyritic Igneous	17 Igneous Other	18 Sandstone	21 Maroon Rhyolite/Andesite	99 Unknown/Indeterminate	Totals
26	9	30	20	9	5			47	1	9	1							131
31	1	2	1					7		1								12
32				1						1								2
33								2										2
34	1																	1
36	5		12	3	2			10		3	1					1		37
38		2	4	2	1			2		4								15
39								2										2
40				1														1
41	59	88	119	70	12	4	2	78		23			1	1	3	1		461
41.01		1	1	1														3
42	4	5	1	10		1	1	3				1						26
43		1	1		1	1		2							1			7
44	20	17	31	24	10			38	1	4					2	3		150
45	3	1	11	3				9		1								28
46	1		1	1	1			1	1									6
47	1	1						1										3
48	8	4	44	4	6			36		6					1			109
50	4	1		7	1			3										16
51	90	50	106	79	34	1	2	151	1	30				1	6		10	561
51.01				2		1		3		1								7
51.02	2																	2
52	18	57	182	68	36	4		111	2	31	1				6	2		518
53	1	7	8	4	3			8		1	1							33
54	11	17	5	7		1		25	1	2	3							72
55			3	5	1		1	6		1								17
56		3	4															7
57	10	35	27	35	13	5		31	2	4						1		163
58	5	17	50	6	4			13	1						1			97
59	68	50	72	45	17	7		96	8	13					6		1	383

Table 6.11. Distribution of raw material type by feature, cont'd.

Feature Number	1 Silicified Sandstone/Limestone (with speckles)	2 Silicified Sandstone/Limestone (without speckles)	3 Silicified Sediments	4 Quartzite	5 Bisbee Chert	6 Rhyolite	7 Andesite	9 Chert	10 Jasper	11 Chalcedony	12 Quartz	13 Obsidian	14 Porphyritic Igneous	17 Igneous Other	18 Sandstone	21 Maroon Rhyolite/Andesite	99 Unknown/Indeterminate	Totals
60	2	2	17	1	1			5		1								29
61	8	14	14	5	6	1		9		3					2			62
62										1								1
63	2	1	1	3		1	1	1		1	1							12
64	10	1	3	4	6			10		1				1		1		37
65	5	11	7		4			15		6								48
66	5	1	1	4	1	1		7	2							1		23
67		2	4	1	2	2	1	13		4								29
68	1		1					1										3
70	1		2		1			5										9
72	23	17	71	9	10	3		29		5								167
73		10	4	7	1	1		3		1					1	1		29
74	3	1	2	5	4	1		15	1	1								33
75	6	1	4	3	3	2		12										31
76	6	4	8	2	4		1	12	1						1			39
77					1			1										2
78	3	1	1															5
81	3	8	5	11	4			5										36
82		1																1
83	5	3	2		1		1	8										20
84	1							1										2
85	3	1	3	2				11		1								21
86	2	2	1	3	1			1										10
87	1	6	1	1				5		1							3	18
90	5	3	5	6		1		7										27
91	4	3	5	1				5		1					1			20
92	5	28	15	8	9	1		38		14						5	1	124
93	4	16	27	10	6	1		41		4						6		115
94	1			4				4		1								10
95	16	15	36	20	11	2		22	1	2	1				1	1		128

Table 6.11. Distribution of raw material type by feature, cont'd.

Feature Number	1 Silicified Sandstone/Limestone (with speckles)	2 Silicified Sandstone/Limestone (without speckles)	3 Silicified Sediments	4 Quartzite	5 Bisbee Chert	6 Rhyolite	7 Andesite	9 Chert	10 Jasper	11 Chalcedony	12 Quartz	13 Obsidian	14 Porphyritic Igneous	17 Igneous Other	18 Sandstone	21 Maroon Rhyolite/Andesite	99 Unknown/Indeterminate	Totals
96	1	2	2	8	4	2		18		1								38
97	17	3	12	6	4	10		24		1								77
98	7	28	194	42	26	4	1	58	2	9		3			3	1		378
99	1	1		1														3
101	7		5		3			5		2								22
102	25	16	25	24	11	3		47		2					1		1	155
103	9	3	10	1	1			11		3		1			1			40
104	3	1	2		1		1											8
105	16	5	17	8	6			37		4					3			96
106	1	1	3	4	2			4		1								16
107	8	17	27	11	9	3		26		5				1		3		110
108	10	10	8	11	4			32		5						4		84
109	17	26	101	26	22	2		35		18			2		12	5		266
110	2			2				3										7
111	3	1	2	4	3	1		1										15
112	28	12	20	22	7	8	1	43	2	5	1		1		2			152
113	2	4	2	2	1			2										13
114	8	3	17	3	5	1		19	6	2					3		1	68
115				1				2										3
116	1	1	2	1				2							1			8
117	1	2	2	3	1			4										13
118	2	1	5	1	2			15										26
119	11	6	4	8	3			8		5					1		1	47
120	6	5	17	3	3	4		14	1								1	54
122	5	2	2	3	4			18	1	1								36
123	3	3	4		2			2	1						2			17
124	2	2	4	2	6	1		13		4	1							35
126	1			3	1	1		3								4		13
127	1		2	1	2			2	1									9
129	56	96	144	56	41	6		160	4	18	2	1			16	14		614

Table 6.11. Distribution of raw material type by feature, cont'd.

Feature Number	1 Silicified Sandstone/Limestone (with speckles)	2 Silicified Sandstone/Limestone (without speckles)	3 Silicified Sediments	4 Quartzite	5 Bisbee Chert	6 Rhyolite	7 Andesite	9 Chert	10 Jasper	11 Chalcedony	12 Quartz	13 Obsidian	14 Porphyritic Igneous	17 Igneous Other	18 Sandstone	21 Maroon Rhyolite/Andesite	99 Unknown/Indeterminate	Totals
130	1	1			1			1								2		6
132	2	3	3	7	1	1		1										18
134		1						1										2
136	33	2	9	10	6	5	1	25	3	4			1		2			101
137		2	1		4			3										10
138	1	1	1		2			2										7
139	27	24	27	26	9	2		43	1	6	1		1	1	1			169
140	2	1		2		1		5		1								12
141	18	13	15	22	8	5		42		8					2	1		134
142	3	4	1					2										10
145	2	1	3		3			3							3			15
149	8	4	9	2	5			24		3								55
151		1	7	1	4	1		2							2			18
152	128	253	370	175	125	21	1	568	8	136	8	1	2		12	17		1825
152.01			1	1				1										3
152.02	1		2					2										5
152.03				1														1
152.06			2															2
152.08		1			2													3
152.1	1	1		2				1										5
152.11		3						2		1		1						7
152.12		1	3		1			1										6
157		1	2	3	5			11		3								25
158																	1	1
165	7	42	64	54	15	4		20		3						1		210
173	2	2	2	4	1	1		9										21
182		1																1
200	15	22	17	7	7			25		8							7	108
206	6	5	2	4	2	4		9		1						3		36
Total	1490	1907	3222	1763	891	205	18	3679	80	733	40	5	12	7	145	141	12	14,350

Table 6.12. Technological profiles of the Marsh Station Road site assemblage

Component	n	Tool (%)	Debitage				Cores			% Tools	
			Avg Size	Avg MI	NC[a] (%)	PRF (%)	% Flakes: Core	Avg Size		Unifaces	Bifaces
AZ EE:2:44 (ASM)	41,526	1	25.77	0.129	77	44/53	2.5	39	66.06	34	66
AZ EE:2:44 (ASM)– San Pedro phase	510	2	23.14	0.085	76	58/67	1.6	64	50.32	20	80
AZ EE:2:44 (ASM)– late Middle Formative period	8,425	1	21.9	0.081	82	57/65	0.6	159	61.04	20	80
AZ EE:2:44 (ASM)– possible San Pedro phase	2,774	1	22.26	0.076	85	62/70	0.8	121	62.99	21	79

[a] NC= Not Coded; % NC is flakes only, not shatter

10 and 11), so it is not surprising that the site would not look very much like the agricultural sites summarized by Sliva (2005). Judging by this one ratio, the Marsh Station Road site was occupied temporarily or semi-permanently, perhaps by groups targeting a limited number of seasonally available resources (see Chapter 12).

But is this single ratio of formal bifaces to unifaces powerful enough to permit such conclusions to be drawn? Sliva, noting a difference in the number of bifaces relative to unifaces at about 400 B.C., states that this change is due to "an increasing commitment to agriculture and an accompanying decrease in the proportion of large animal food in the diet" (Sliva 2005:90). It is noteworthy that the flaked stone data signaled this transition at 400 B.C, as opposed to the appearance of cultigens at the beginning of the San Pedro phase (or even earlier), or with the introduction of ceramics. Indeed, it calls into question the utility and sensitivity of flaked stone assemblages in this context. Even if it is ultimately shown that flaked stone assemblages lack the sensitivity to discern larger technological shifts across time, they are still useful for comparative purposes.

DISCUSSION AND CONCLUSIONS

This chapter described the flaked stone assemblages from the Marsh Station Road site (AZ EE:2:44 [ASM]). Over 43,000 artifacts were collected, and over 28,000 were analyzed. Debitage was by far the most numerous artifact type, and bifaces, unifaces, cores, and hammerstones were also recovered. The chapter provided the following: background on how the analysis was conducted, assemblage-wide summaries of the different artifact types, an assemblage description, and more-detailed explorations of certain components of the Marsh Station Road site assemblage.

Analysis of the distribution of artifact types and raw material types from different recovery contexts and across space at the Marsh Station Road site was not too illuminating. In short, surface contexts produced higher-than-expected numbers of cores and unifaces, while subsurface contexts produced lower-than-expected numbers of those same artifact types. It is difficult to ascribe meaningful prehistoric behavior to those differences. Similarly, when looking at just the test unit assemblage versus the feature assemblage, cores are overrepresented in the former, but again this is difficult to explain.

Looking at comparisons across space, specifically SA 2/3 to SA 4/5, meaningful differences are again hard to come by. With regard to artifact type, there is not a significant difference between the features from these two groups, although there is between the surface and test unit assemblages (and again, this is a difference in the expectations of cores). The similarity in feature assemblages would seem to indicate that the goals of the knappers in these different locations changed very little, if at all. Turning to raw material types, there are some statistically significant differences, but they are again very difficult to explain. For example, why would cryptocrystalline silicates (raw material group 9–11) be overrepresented in SA 4/5 and underrepresented in SA 2/3? Why would material from groups 1 & 2 and 5 & 19, all of which is thought to be locally available, be differentially distributed within and across the two groups of SAs?

Perhaps the answer is related to temporal differences in the occupation of the site. During fieldwork, an impression was developed that SA 2/3 was perhaps more Early Agricultural in age while SA 4/5 was more Formative. This was primarily due to the veritable lack of ceramics recovered from SA 2/3, and it was strengthened by radiocarbon dating two features in SA 3 to the Early Agricultural period (both of which also contained San Pedro points). While assigning many of the aceramic features in SA 2/3 to the Early Agricultural period for means of comparison is admittedly tenuous, it was nonetheless deemed worthwhile to do. Comparing these features against the Formative features with a chi-square test reveals no difference with regard to the distribution of artifact types. Certain characteristics of the debitage assemblage, however, contradict this homogeneity and suggest the debitage resulted from different goals in reduction. Specifically, it appears that the manufacture of bifaces may have been more common in the putative Early Agricultural assemblage than the Formative assemblage. Turning to the comparison of raw material types, the distributions of the possible Early Agricultural assemblage to the Middle Formative assemblage largely mirrors that of the distributions of SA 2/3 to SA 4/5. This is not surprising given that virtually all of the features assigned to the Early Agricultural are located in SA 2/3, and it does little to explain the differential distributions of raw material types.

Another way of attempting to look at changes over time was by examining both the PRFs and the technological profiles of the assemblages (Sliva 2005). This was unsuccessful, due to one or more of the following reasons. First, the Early Agricultural sample was too small and too internally variable to permit a meaningful and informative comparison with Middle Formative materials. Second, the degree of sedentism did not change much from the Early Agricultural to the Middle Formative. That is, perhaps a more noticeable change along these lines occurred before the Early Agricultural. Third, while sedentism may have increased during the time from the Early Agricultural to the Middle Formative in some areas of the larger region, it did not happen locally at the Marsh Station Road site, perhaps due to the nature of site occupation. Fourth, flaked stone assemblages are not particularly sensitive in detecting this larger change.

During the time the Marsh Station Road site was occupied, it appears that the site occupants consistently employed a rather haphazard reduction technology. Unpatterned core reduction, a marked paucity of hammerstones, and nonstandardization in unifaces and utilized flakes all point to a largely unplanned technology focused on the immediate task at hand. These characteristics of the flaked stone assemblage, combined with both a dearth of nonlocal material, and a wealth of knappable stone in the immediate vicinity, suggest that the site inhabitants, whether in the Early Agricultural or Middle Formative, occupied the site in the same semi-permanent manner, and likely for the same reasons.

Most interesting are the numerous Early Agricultural points and the possibly earlier Cortaro points. It was suggested, following other researchers, that not all Cortaro points are projectile points. The present sample of these bifaces could help to explore the variation currently subsumed by this single type.

Chapter 7
Ground Stone Artifacts

Melanie A. Medeiros

The following chapter discusses the results of the analysis of the ground stone assemblage from the Marsh Station Road site. The assemblage collected and analyzed from the site is relatively small, with 173 artifacts, the majority of which are food processing tools. Despite the small assemblage size, the ground stone provides a unique and important line of evidence from which proposed research questions (see Chapter 3 and Table 3.2) as well as questions related to larger regional and artifact-specific issues can be addressed. In particular, this chapter explores questions pertaining to site formation processes, site occupation strategies, diet and subsistence, and intrasite activity patterns. The assemblage is considered within a technological framework that utilizes a life-history approach to understand the role of ground stone artifacts in the social and economic lives of their owners and users (J. Adams 2002).

A TECHNOLOGICAL FRAMEWORK FOR ANALYSIS

Following J. Adams 2002, the ground stone analysis was conducted within a technological framework, which not only considers the morphology and associated function of an artifact, but also the knowledge, ideas, and behavior associated with the manufacture, use, and discard of an artifact (see also J. Adams 2005; Dobres and Hoffman, ed. 1999; Nelson 1990; Nelson and Lippmeier 1993). Artifacts are therefore considered not as random, individual artifacts occurring within a site, but as comprising part of a technological system through which various crafts and foods are produced, distributed, consumed, and discarded. The usefulness of a technological framework lies in its ability to connect basic artifact analysis—measuring, describing, and classifying—with "patterns in the data that can be used to discuss the behavioral constructs expressed in the socio-material practices of groups and individuals" (J. Adams 2002:17) and from which inferences related to specific research questions can be made.

Within a technological framework, certain characteristics of an artifact's life history (sensu Schiffer 1987; also see J. Adams 2002)—design and manufacture, use, wear, kinetics, and disuse—are considered and analyzed in order to conceptualize and understand the knowledge, choices, and actions behind artifact manufacture, use, and discard. Questions considered as part of the design and manufacture stage include "how an item was designed and manufactured, why the material was selected, and what features were made to fit the chosen material with the planned function of the object" (J. Adams 2002:18). Characteristics examined may include raw material granularity, durability, and availability; the use of comfort features; and purpose and intentionality (in the form of expedient or strategic design) (J. Adams 2002:18–21; Bostwick and Burton 1993; Fratt and Biancaniello 1993; Horsfall 1987; Nelson and Lippmeir 1993; Stone 1994).

The analysis of the use of an artifact considers both primary and secondary uses of an artifact, and the categorization of each use—sequential versus concomitant as well as whether an artifact had only a single use, usually the one for which it was designed, or in the case of secondary uses, whether it was reused, redesigned, used for multiple purposes, or recycled (J. Adams 2002:21–22). Considerations of artifact wear include assessments of the type of wear (fatigue, abrasive, or tribochemical) and contact surface, and the amount of wear (unused, light, moderate, heavy, and worn out) as well as indications of wear management strategies, such as using multiple surfaces of a single artifact, maintaining even use of surfaces, and replacing worn-out tools (J. Adams 2002:25–26). Data derived from the analysis of artifact wear and wear management strategies can also be used to make inferences regarding artifact use intensity (intensive or extensive) and artifact efficiency (J. Adams 2002:26–27, 2005). The analysis of the kinetics of ground stone artifacts determines the type and force of motions related to tool operation (J. Adams 2002:41), which include stroke (reciprocal vs. circular, flat vs. rocking) and impact fractures (crushing, pounding, pecking, and chopping). Finally, artifacts eventually fall into disuse and enter the archaeological record. Disuse can occur through several different processes, including discard, loss, caching, and abandonment, and for different, perhaps culturally significant, reasons (J. Adams 2002:42–43).

Analysis of the archaeological context as well as the condition of the artifact can yield data that inform about the behavioral actions behind the disuse of artifacts.

ANALYSIS METHODS

The ground stone assemblage was analyzed by Dr. Jeffrey Baker and Dea Applegate, with contributions by Melanie Medeiros. Each artifact was viewed at various magnifications ranging from 10x to 50x using a Nikon zoom stereomicroscope. Descriptive and use-wear characteristics were recorded for the entire assemblage; artifacts were classed by type and subtype (following J. Adams 2002), and examined for a variety of attributes including material type, condition (completeness), the type and level of use, number of use surfaces, design and manufacturing processes, the presence of burning and/or residue, and artifact compatibility. Material types followed those used in the flaked stone analysis (see Chapter 6) with additional categories added where necessary. Metric measurements of the length, width, thickness, and weight of each artifact were also made. For small- and medium-sized artifacts, length, width, and thickness measurements were made using digital calipers and recorded to the nearest hundredth of a centimeter, while for larger artifacts, the same measurements were made using a measuring tape and recorded to the nearest centimeter; all artifacts were weighed using a digital scale and the weights were recorded to the nearest gram.

DESCRIPTION OF ARTIFACT TYPES AND SUBTYPES

Several typological categories of ground stone artifacts were recovered from the Marsh Station Road site, including food processing tools, general processing tools, manufacturing tools, and paraphernalia. In the following section, each artifact category is briefly discussed and artifacts belonging to each category are identified.

Food Processing Tools

Food processing tools are those artifacts that were used in the procurement, preparation, and cooking of foodstuffs, and often represent one of the most common categories of ground stone artifacts recovered from a site. Food processing tools can include "manos and metates, mortars and pestles, cooking slabs, pikistones, griddles, [comals], firedogs, fire-cracked rocks, hoes, axes, and tchamahias" (J. Adams 2002:49–50). However, not all types of food processing tools are found at every site, and the same type of tool can serve similar or different functions within and between sites.

Manos and metates are tools used together as food processing implements, especially in the production of corn flour, although other foods, such as amaranth or mesquite pods, are also processed with these tools (J. Adams 1979, 1999, 2002; Euler and Dobyns 1983; Wright 1994). The metate serves as the netherstone (bottom stone) upon which materials are ground, while the mano is a hand-held stone that is rubbed in a reciprocal (back-and-forth) or circular motion over the metate surface. There are four distinct types of manos and metates—basin, flat/concave, trough, and flat; the configuration of which is determined by use, upkeep, and the original shape (J. Adams 2002:99–112). All four types of manos and metates were recovered from the site. Recent research has suggested that the development of the mano and metate types are a technological change associated with an increase in grinding intensity and efficiency over time rather than an evolutionary development associated with

the transitions to agriculture (J. Adams 1993, 2002:120–127).

Mortars and pestles are another type of netherstone/handstone combination of food processing tools. Unlike manos and metates, however, food resources are not ground using mortars and pestles, but rather are processed through crushing, stirring, or pounding strokes (J. Adams 2002:127). There are also several distinct types of mortars including pebble mortars, rock mortars, boulder mortars, and stationary mortars; types are distinguished by portability and basin size (J. Adams 2002: 128). Pestles, which can be made from either stone or wood, sometimes exhibit secondary use not associated with their corresponding mortar, for example as a straightener or abrader, or as a handstone used to grind other food resources or materials.

General Processing Tools

Tools are categorized as general processing tools when their primary use cannot be attributed to either food processing or manufacturing activities. Tools placed within this category include handstones, lapstones, and netherstones; polishers, smoothers, and abraders; mortars and pestles; axes, hoes, picks, crushers/fergoliths, and choppers; reamers, saws and files, planes, and tabular tools; fire-drill hearths; and whorls. General processing tools are used to process a wide variety of materials, including pigment, bone, wood, clay, and other organic materials, and are used in many different types of activities. They are typically recovered in smaller quantities than food processing tools, yet because their uses are so diverse, they represent a larger percentage of activities that occurred at a site (J. Adams 2002, 2005).

Manufacturing Tools

Manufacturing tools are tools used to produce

other artifacts, including other ground stone tools, pottery, bone and wooden artifacts, architectural features, and various types of paraphernalia, and may include hammerstones, pecking stones, pottery and lithic anvils, choppers, abraders, and chisels. Manufacturing tools are not necessarily ground themselves (e.g., hammer- and/or pecking stones), but are considered an important aspect of a ground stone assemblage nonetheless because of their role in the manufacture and maintenance of ground stone artifacts.

Paraphernalia

Following J. Adams (2002:191), artifacts identified as paraphernalia include "personal and group ritual equipment, gaming devices, weights, ornaments, representations (morphic, geometric, and abstract), and items whose specific functions are unknown," many of which have numerous subtypes based on distinctive morphological attributes (e.g., type of perforation). Artifact functions associated with paraphernalia are usually classified as symbolic, ritualistic, or decorative/identity-oriented. Such uses have been primarily identified through the ethnographic record, rather than through archaeological context. As J. Adams (2002:191) suggests, though archaeology may not provide data about the specific meanings behind artifacts classed as paraphernalia, their analysis, at the very least, can indicate something about "the tools and techniques used in their manufacture."

ANALYSIS RESULTS

A total of 173 ground stone artifacts was recovered from the Marsh Station Road site (AZ EE:2:44 [ASM]) (Table 7.1). The ground stone artifacts comprise a wide variety of artifact types and subtypes. Approximately 57 percent of the assemblage was fragmentary, while about 37 percent of the assemblage was comprised of whole artifacts (Table 7.2). Most of the artifacts (78.6 percent) were only used in one task; however, of the artifacts that exhibited secondary use (21.4 percent), almost all (73 percent) were less than half complete (Table 7.3). The majority of the artifacts (54.9 percent) were recovered from nonfeature (CUs, TUs, SAs, trenches, and the non-feature Feature 36) contexts, while the rest were distributed among identified feature types (Table 7.4).

Raw Materials

Within the ground stone assemblage at the Marsh Station Road site, igneous other, which consists of primarily plutonic igneous rocks other than granite, is the most common material type (Table 7.5). The second most common material type is metamorphic other, followed by quartzite. These material types, along with most of the other material recovered from the site were probably collected from the bed or terraces of Mescal Wash or Cienega Creek. The Rincon Mountains (the source of Mescal Wash) consists of a granite core surrounded by a mass of metamorphic and sedimentary rocks (Chronic 1983). The Empire and Whetstone mountains, which supply tributaries of Cienega Creek, have a similar composition. In all three ranges, the sedimentary rocks include a variety of breccias and conglomerates, while the metamorphic rocks include quartzite and gneiss (Chronic 1983). Although it is possible that some of the raw material may have been collected from the mountains themselves, most of the raw material appears to be water worn, probably an indication that the material was carried downstream from its original source.

Two small fragments of vesicular basalt (from disturbed locations), a piece of turquoise, and a piece of slate are the only rocks present in the collection that are not available in the area

Table 7.1. Summary of the ground stone assemblage

	Quantity	Percent of Assemblage
Mano	77	44.25
Metate	23	13.22
Pestle	1	0.57
Handstone	24	13.79
Netherstone	8	4.60
Polishing stone	4	2.30
Hammerstone	1	0.57
Pecking stone	3	1.72
Lapstone	2	1.15
Finger ring	1	0.57
Barrel bead	1	0.57
Spindle base	1	0.57
3/4-grooved axe	2	1.15
Abrader	1	0.57
Indeterminate	25	14.37
Total	174	100.00

Table 7.2. Completeness of ground stone artifacts

	Whole	More than Half	Less than Half	Conjoined Fragments	Indeterminate	Total
Mano	33	3	39	2		77
Metate	6		14	3		23
Pestle	1					1
Handstone	11		8	4	1	24
Netherstone	2		6			8
Polishing stone	3	1				4
Hammerstone			1			1
Pecking stone	3					3
Lapstone	1	1				2
Finger ring			1			1
Barrel bead	1					1
Spindle base	1					1
3/4-grooved axe	2					2
Abrader		1				1
Indeterminate			25			25
Total	64	6	94	9	1	174

Table 7.3. Number of uses by artifact condition

	Single	Reused	Multiple	Total
Whole	56	3	5	64
More than half	5	1		6
Less than half	67	26	1	94
Conjoined fragments	8		1	9
Indeterminate	1			1
Total	137	30	7	174

immediately surrounding the site. However, all three of these materials are generally available from multiple sources within the Tucson Basin (Miksa and Tompkins 1998).

Food Processing Tools

Food processing tools, which include 77 whole and fragmentary manos, 23 whole and fragmentary metates, and 1 pestle, comprise the largest percentage (58.4 percent) of ground stone artifacts in the Marsh Station Road site assemblage. Manos and metates from all subtypes were identified, although flat (28 percent) and flat/concave (24 percent) manos and metates are the most common subtypes (Tables 7.6a and 7.6b); trough (14 percent) and basin (11 percent) manos and metates are less common, while those manos and metates that fall into multiple categories or for which a subtype could not be identified comprise 23 percent of the total number of manos and metates. Two of the basin manos are likely compatible with the basin metates, although neither was recovered as a set, while a number of the flat and flat/concave manos seem to match up fairly well with the flat or flat/concave metates. This, however, may be attributable to the relatively uniform surfaces of the manos and metates rather than any clearly articulated use relationship between them. In addition, none of the trough manos are compatible with the single trough metate.

The pestle (FN 44-3642) is a long, narrow granitic rock with some evidence of battering (stone-on-stone contact) on one end (Figure 7.1). However, the wear is fairly light, and this particular artifact was probably only used briefly in that manner.

The majority (73 percent) of the food processing tools—55 manos and 18 metates—exhibit moderate to heavy wear on at least one use surface; 30 (54.5 percent) of these manos were used on at least two surfaces. Only 10 manos (and no metates) exhibited secondary use (Table 7.7). Of these, seven mano fragments were recycled as fire-cracked rock; three whole flat manos were reused as hammerstones. The majority of the manos (79.22 percent) and the metates (78.26 percent) were expediently designed; only nine manos (11.69 percent) and two metates (8.7 percent) exhibited evidence, which includes various comfort features (finger and hand grips), of strategic design (Table 7.8). Given that few manos have comfort features, and the ones that do have comfort features were all moderately to heavily worn, wear on the majority of the food processing tool assemblage is probably the result of extensive use.

One food processing tool, a broken basin metate (FN 44-1769) recovered from Feature 65 (nonthermal pit), deserves special mention. This metate was intentionally brought to the end of its use-life, despite the fact that it only

Table 7.4. Distribution of ground stone artifacts by unit type (CUs, TUs, and Features)

	Mano	Metate	Pestle	Hand-stone	Nether-stone	Polishing Stone	Hammer-stone	Pecking Stone	Lap-stone	Finger Ring	Barrell Bead	Spindle Base	Axe	Abrader	Ind.	Total
FEATURES																
Early Agricultural Period																
Feature 42 Nonthermal pit	3			1												4
Feature 98 Bell pit	1			1												2
Feature 124 Nonthermal pit		3														3
Feature 139 Bell pit		1		1											1	3
Early Formative Period																
Feature 112 Nonthermal pit	2	1														3
Middle Formative Period																
Feature 119 Nonthermal pit	1															1
Feature 122 Nonthermal pit		2														2
Feature 136 Nonthermal pit	1															1

Table 7.4. Distribution of ground stone artifacts by unit type (CUs, TUs, and Features), cont'd.

	Mano	Metate	Pestle	Hand-stone	Nether-stone	Polishing Stone	Hammer-stone	Pecking Stone	Lap-stone	Finger Ring	Barrell Bead	Spindle Base	Axe	Abrader	Ind.	Total
Late Middle Formative Period																
Feature 6 Extramural Surface	1															1
Feature 7 pit Structure	1					1				1						3
Feature 11 pit Structure	1	1						1								3
Feature 17 pit Structure	1	1							1		1		2			6
Feature 41 Extramural Surface	2								1							3
Feature 52 Bell pit				1												1
Feature 72 Thermal pit				1												1
Feature 109 Bell pit		1														1
Feature 152 pit Structure	4			3		1	1								9	18
Feature 173 Bell pit	2				1											3

Table 7.4. Distribution of ground stone artifacts by unit type (CUs, TUs, and Features), cont'd.

	Mano	Metate	Pestle	Hand-stone	Nether-stone	Polishing Stone	Hammer-stone	Pecking Stone	Lap-stone	Finger Ring	Barrell Bead	Spindle Base	Axe	Abrader	Ind.	Total
Early Agricultural–Formative Periods																
Feature 10 Nonthermal pit		1														1
Feature 28 Thermal pit	1															1
Feature 57 Nonthermal pit				1												1
Feature 60 Thermal pit	1															1
Feature 65 Nonthermal pit		1														1
Feature 70 Nonthermal pit															1	1
Feature 73 Nonthermal pit	1															1
Feature 80 Nonthermal pit					1											1
Feature 81 Thermal pit	1															1
Feature 90 Nonthermal pit	1														1	2
Feature 94 Nonthermal pit	1															1
Feature 107 Nonthermal pit	2	1														3
Feature 149 Nonthermal pit	2															2

Table 7.4. Distribution of ground stone artifacts by unit type (CUs, TUs, and Features), cont'd.

	Mano	Metate	Pestle	Hand-stone	Nether-stone	Polishing Stone	Hammer-stone	Pecking Stone	Lap-stone	Finger Ring	Barrell Bead	Spindle Base	Axe	Abrader	Ind.	Total
Feature 202 Nonthermal pit	1															1
Subtotal	*31*	*13*		*9*	*2*	*2*	*1*	*1*	*2*	*1*	*1*		*2*		*12*	*77*
NONFEATURE																
Feature 36				2												2
Subtotal				*2*												*2*
COLLECTION UNITS																
CU 91				1												1
CU 124	1															1
CU 143				1												1
CU 145		1														1
CU 149														1		1
CU 161	1															1
CU 169	1															1
CU 202	1															1
CU 212	1															1
CU 241															1	1
CU 296	5	3		1	1											10
CU 308				1												1
CU 323	1															1
Subtotal	*11*	*4*		*4*	*1*									*1*	*1*	*21*

Table 7.4. Distribution of ground stone artifacts by unit type (CUs, TUs, and Features), cont'd.

	Mano	Metate	Pestle	Hand-stone	Nether-stone	Polishing Stone	Hammer-stone	Pecking Stone	Lap-stone	Finger Ring	Barrell Bead	Spindle Base	Axe	Abrader	Ind.	Total
STRIPPED AREAS																
SA 3					1											1
SA 4	6	2			1											9
SA 4/5					1										1	2
SA 5	1	1				1						1				4
Subtotal	*7*	*3*			*3*	*1*						*1*			*1*	*16*
TRENCHES																
Trench 3	1															1
Trench 13		1														1
Subtotal	*1*	*1*														*2*
TEST UNITS																
TU 2				1												1
TU 9				1												1
TU 11				2												2
TU 19				1												1
TU 27	2							1								3
TU 29				1												1
TU 33	4			1											1	6
TU 34	1															1
TU 40								1							1	2
TU 41	1					1									2	4
TU 55				1												1
TU 64															3	3

Table 7.4. Distribution of ground stone artifacts by unit type (CUs, TUs, and Features), cont'd.

TEST UNITS	Mano	Metate	Pestle	Hand-stone	Nether-stone	Polishing Stone	Hammer-stone	Pecking Stone	Lap-stone	Finger Ring	Barrell Bead	Spindle Base	Axe	Abrader	Ind.	Total
TU 67					1											1
TU 68	1															1
TU 71		1														1
TU 72	2															2
TU 76	1															1
TU 83	1															1
TU 92	1														2	3
TU 93	2			1												3
TU 111	1															1
TU 136	3				1											4
TU 137	2															2
TU 148	1															1
TU 152	1															1
TU 155	1															1
TU 158	1		1												1	3
TU 169	1															1
TU 172		1														1
Subtotal	*27*	*2*	*1*	*9*	*2*	*1*		*2*							*10*	*54*

Table 7.5. Artifact types by raw material

	Speckled Silicified Limestone	Silicified Limestone	Silicified Sediments	Quartzite	Rhyolite	Andesite	Basalt	Metamorphic Other	Sedimentary Other	Igneous Other	Sandstone	Bisbee Quartzite	Granite	Turquoise	Slate	Total
Mano		1	3	17			1	22	2	27		1	3			77
Metate		1		2	1	1	1	6	8				3			23
Pestle													1			1
Handstone			3	3				4	1	10	2		1			24
Netherstone				1				2		3	2					8
Polishing stone				4												4
Hammerstone	1															1
Pecking stone				2							1					3
Lapstone										1					1	2
Finger ring										1						1
Barrel bead														1		1
Spindle base											1					1
3/4-grooved axe												2				2
Abrader									1							1
Indeterminate			3	3				5		13			1			25
Total	1	1	10	32	1	1	2	39	12	55	6	3	9	1	1	174

Table 7.6a. Artifact subtypes for manos and handstones

	Basin	Trough	Flat	Multiple	Flat/Concave	Other	Total
Mano	6	13	21	3	20	14	77
Handstone			15		5	4	24
Total	6	13	36	3	25	18	101

Table 7.6b. Artifact subtypes for metates and netherstones

	Basin	Trough-Open	Flat	Flat/Concave	Indeterminate	Total
Metate	5	1	7	4	6	23
Netherstone			6		2	8
Total	5	1	13	4	8	31

has moderate wear, through the manufacture of a hole in its basin (Figure 7.2). This hole was clearly manufactured, rather than created through heavy use: the basin of the metate, even at its thinnest point, is still approximately 5 cm (2 inches) thick and the metate is still functional. In addition, there are flakes and impact fractures in the basin and on the base of the metate around the edge of the hole.

In the archaeological literature, artifacts that have been intentionally destroyed in this manner are referred to as "killed" (J. Adams 2008, 2002; Chapman 2000; Haury 1985:231,

244; Martin et al. 1956:72; Schelberg 1997). Holes punched in the bottom of intentionally destroyed pots or metates are called kill holes. J. Adams (2008) has suggested, based on an extensive survey of the ethnographic literature of the Southwest, that the intentional breaking and destruction of such artifacts occurs for many reasons—to release the life-force or spirit of the artifact, as part of mortuary or other ritual ceremony, as the result of the death of the artifact's owner, to end the use-life of a worn out or obsolete artifact, or simply to prevent use of the artifact by others—and that the act itself is

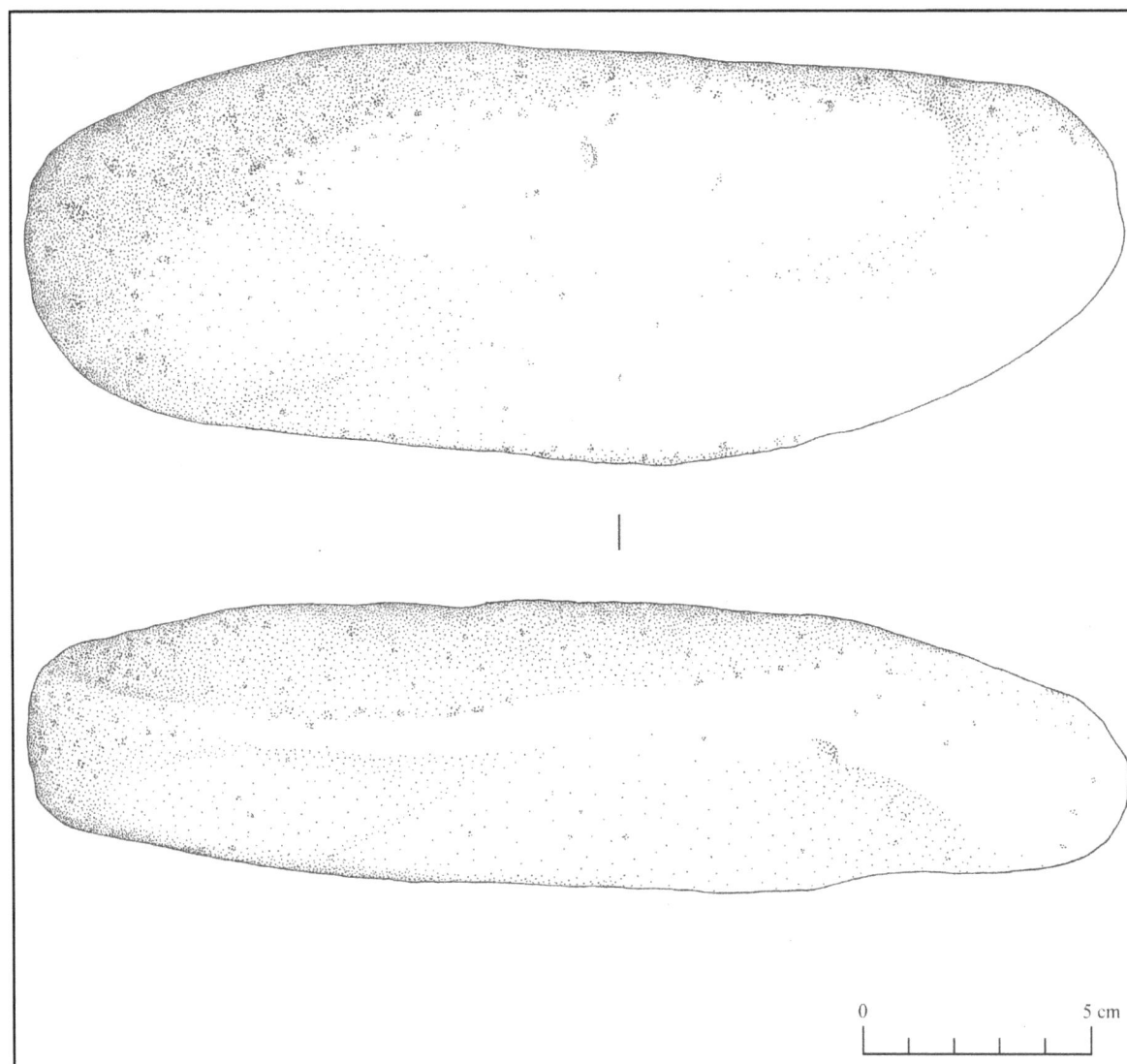

Figure 7.1. Illustration of the only pestle (FN 44-3642) recovered from the Marsh Station Road site.

"...complex...invoking power, meaning, and social action" (J. Adams 2008:213; also see Chapman 2000; Hoffman 1999). Metates in particular are considered valuable household tools, and were likely used by multiple women in a household over several generations (J. Adams 2008:225). J. Adams (2008:225) posits that their intentional destruction may have been to release the life-force of the metate, vested with parts of all of its users over the generations, and was an important act necessary to secure the well-being of the household (also see Chapman 2000). Although as archaeologists we cannot know exactly why the killed metate recovered from the Marsh Station Road site was intentionally destroyed, its presence at this site provides a glimpse into the lives of the site's occupants beyond their simple everyday tasks.

General Processing Tools

General processing tools (24.3 percent) comprise the second largest category of ground stone artifacts recovered from the Marsh Station Road site. A variety of general processing tools including handstones, netherstones, polishing stones, ¾-grooved axes, lapstones, an abrader, and a spindle base are represented in the ground stone assemblage. The majority (47.6 percent) of these tools are whole (see Table 7.2), and exhibit only one use (88.1 percent) (see Table 7.7). Just under half (45.24 percent) of the general processing tools were moderately to heavily worn; most (38.1 percent) of these were handstones, netherstones, or lapstones. Approximately one-third (n = 12) of the tools had at least two use surfaces; nine of these were moderately to heavily worn. Only five general processing tools—two axes, two lapstones, and the spindle base—were strategically designed (see Table 7.8).

The majority (57.1 percent) of handstones and netherstones as well as the abrader were used against a hard/stone surface in general processing tasks. Seven handstones contained pigment residue on their surface, and were most likely used to process pigment; another handstone was used to process clay. The first lapstone (FN 44-3214), recovered from Feature 17, was likely used to process shell, as determined through use-wear analysis (Jenny Adams, 2009, personal communication to Melanie Medeiros; see also Virden-Lange, Chapter 9, for a discussion of the evidence for shell manufacture at the Marsh Station Road site). The edges of the lapstone had been ground for comfort as well as worn smooth and polished by oils in the hand. No shell residue was noted on the surface of the artifact during analysis; however, the artifact was washed before the analysis was undertaken, and no field notes exist documenting the condition of the artifact prior to its washing. Both surfaces of the artifact had been heavily used.

The second lapstone (FN 44-1154), recovered from Feature 41, was used for mixing black, and possibly red, pigment rather than for grinding minerals to produce powdered pigment (Figure 7.3). The lapstone, which fits easily in the hand, was strategically designed: both faces and all four edges have been ground smooth and polished; the lapstone does not have an articulated border, either flat or designed, typical of Hohokam palettes (J. Adams 2002:146; Haury 1975, 1976; Hawley 1947; White 2004). Although pigment processing lapstones, such as the one recovered from the Marsh Station Road site, are sometimes referred to as "proto-palettes," there are inherent problems with this classification, which mistakenly links pigment processing lapstones with the specialized and often ritualized palettes characteristic of the Hohokam (Jenny Adams, 2009, personal communication to Melanie Medeiros; also see J. Adams 2002:146–148).

Table 7.7 Number of uses by artifact type

	Single	Reused	Multiple	Total
Mano	67	7	3	77
Metate	22		1	23
Pestle	1			1
Handstone	21	3		24
Netherstone	8			8
Polishing stone	4			4
Hammerstone	1			1
Pecking stone	3			3
Lapstone	2			2
Finger ring	1			1
Barrel Bead	1			1
Spindle base	1			1
3/4-grooved axe			2	2
Abrader	1			1
Indeterminate	8	17		25
Total	141	27	6	174

Table 7.8. Artifact design

	Expedient	Strategic	Indeterminate	Total
Mano	61	9	7	77
Metate	18	2	3	23
Pestle	1			1
Handstone	22		2	24
Netherstone	7		1	8
Polishing stone	4			4
Hammerstone	1			1
Pecking stone	3			3
Lapstone		2		2
Finger ring		1		1
Barrel bead		1		1
Spindle base		1		1
3/4-grooved axe		2		2
Abrader	1			1
Indeterminate	25			25
Total	143	18	13	174

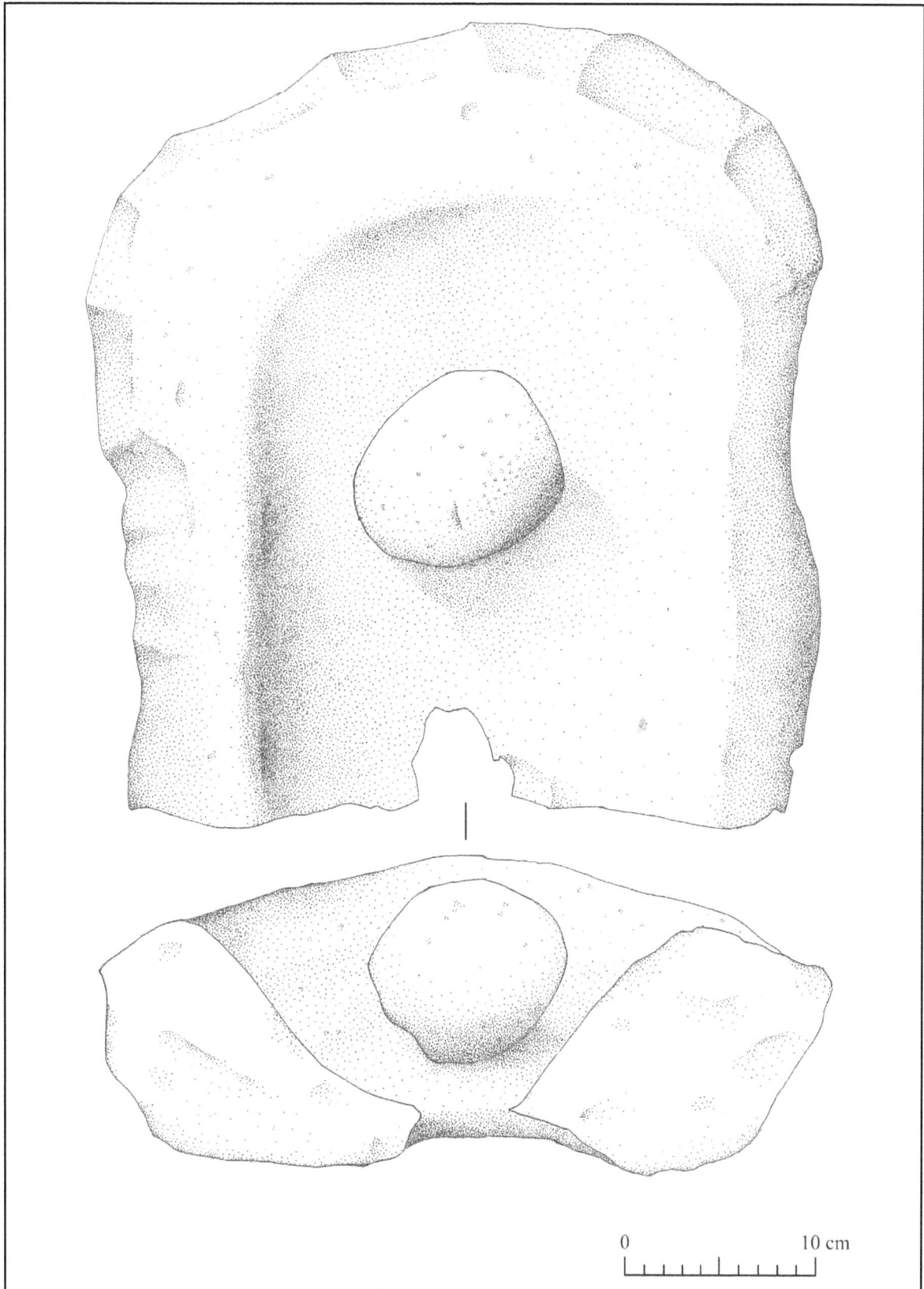

Figure 7.2. A killed basin metate (FN 44-1769) recovered from Feature 65, a nonthermal pit.

Two of the four polishing stones were used against a hard/stone surface in general processing tasks; their specific use could not be determined. The other two polishers were used against a softer surface, possibly against wood; again, their specific use could not be determined. Three of the four polishers had light wear; the other was only moderately worn. The fact that no pottery polishers were recovered supports the conclusion that pottery manufacture did not occur at the Marsh Station Road site (see Chapter 4), although the lack of pottery polishers could also be the result of the small area of the overall site area that was investigated.

The two axes (FN 44-3105 and FN 44-3106) are both ¾-grooved axes made from Bisbee quartzite. Both artifacts, which were recovered whole from the floor fill of Feature 17, were used for multiple purposes. The first axe (FN 44-3105) is small and was strategically designed, having been pecked, ground, and polished during the manufacturing process (Figure 7.4a). The bit edge is still sharp with only minor evidence of use. The ¾-groove is deep with ridges on both the bit and poll ends; however, there is no evidence of hafting. Given these characteristics, it is likely this axe was minimally used as a chopper, and then retired from its primary function. This axe was a multi-use tool: the poll sides and poll end, as well as both sides of the bit exhibit concomitant secondary use as a handstone/abrader in general processing tasks. The second axe (FN 44-3106), which is also small, is characterized by a strategic design, heavy wear, and a shallow groove with evidence of hafting (Figure 7.4b). The bit edge, which is still somewhat sharp, has been resharpened. The faces and sides of the axe are rough with impact fractures remaining from the manufacturing process; only the bit edge and the groove appear smooth and polished. The entire surface of the axe, except for the bit edge, is covered in clay, suggesting the axe may have been used to process clay or as an agricultural tool. Both poll faces have been worn flat through secondary concomitant use as an abrader; red pigment is present on both poll faces. Small quantities of red pigment are also present on the poll end, which displays secondary wear from battering, probably from use as a hammerstone.

The spindle base (FN 44-1595) is a small, semi-circular concretion with one small cupule in the center (Figure 7.5). The face of the tool has been ground smooth; the underside of the tool is rounded, although the base has been worked so that it sits relatively flat. However, the tool is still fairly unstable; to facilitate use, additional working to further flatten the base further would have been necessary. The cupule is relatively shallow, approximately 0.25 cm deep, and does not have wear indicative of use. Most likely, this tool was never used, and may still have been in a production state.

Manufacturing Tools

Twenty manufacturing tools, 17 hammerstones and 3 pecking stones, were recovered from the Marsh Station Road site; an additional 26 core hammers were also identified. Only the pecking stones (n = 3), which were analyzed as ground stone artifacts, are presented in the tables in this chapter. All hammerstones were analyzed as part of the flaked stone assemblage, and are therefore contained in tables and discussed in the flaked stone chapter (Chapter 6). Both these tool types are used in the manufacture of other stone tools (both flaked and ground stone), although hammerstones tend to be used more often with flaked stone and in initial quarrying activities, while pecking stones tend to be used to shape and maintain ground stone tools. The hammerstones, therefore, were analyzed as flaked stone tools. All of the hammerstones show evidence of battering on at least on end; four have wear indicative of crushing, suggest-

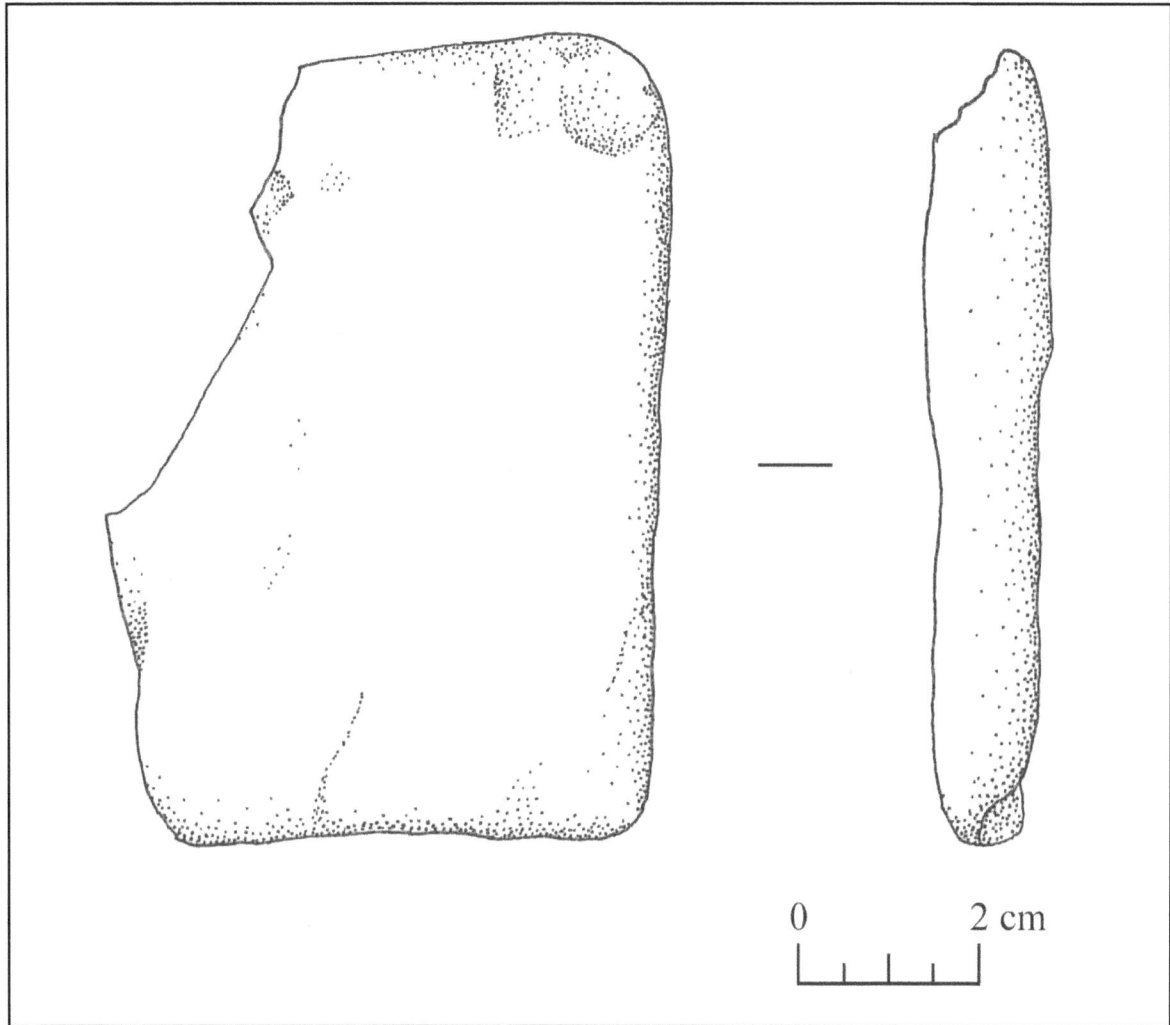

Figure 7.3. A lapstone (FN 44-1154) used to process black and possibly red pigment recovered from Feature 41, an occupation surface.

ing they may have been used concomitantly as pestles (although no mortars were recovered from the site), while one shows evidence of abrasion. Two of the pecking stones show only light wear; the other has moderate wear. All manufacturing tools were expediently designed.

Following Sliva (2003:241), Boley and Gabler (Chapter 6), have suggested that the paucity of hammerstones recovered from the Marsh Station Road site, in relation to other tool types, may indicate that the site was occupied on a short-term and seasonal basis. The general lack of pecking stones recovered from

the site also supports this interpretation. The WCRM excavations recovered an additional 5 hammerstones and 1 pecking stone. Kearns and McVickar (2009) also note that this is an unusually low number of these tools relative to other tool types.

Paraphernalia

Two ornamental items—a finger ring and a barrel bead—were recovered from two different pit houses at the Marsh Station Road site. The finger ring (FN 44-1494), which was manufactured from igneous rock and pecked,

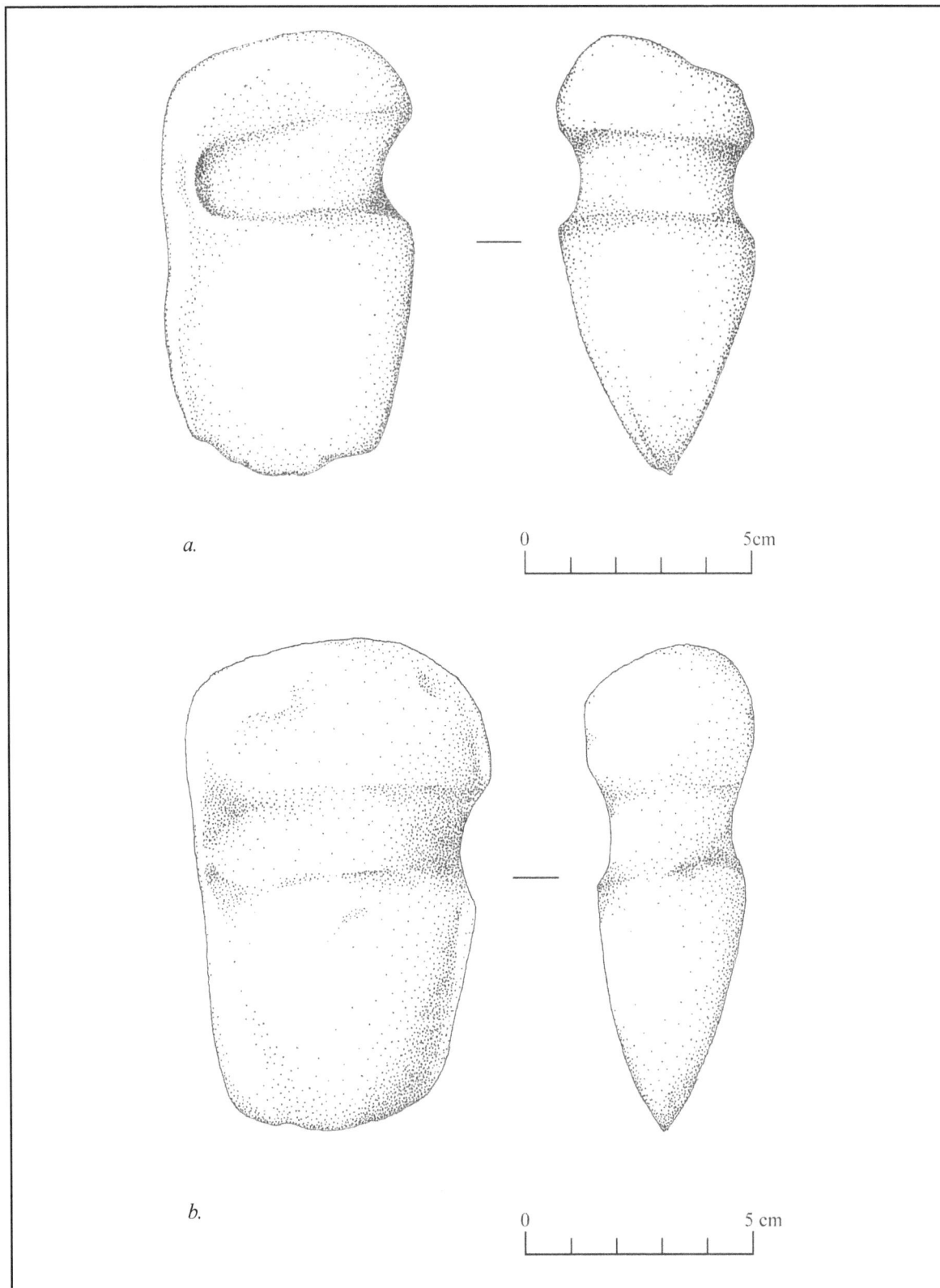

Figure 7.4. Illustration of two axes recovered from floor fill of Feature 17 at the Marsh Station Road site: (a) Axe #1 (FN 44-3105) and (b) Axe #2 (FN 44-3106).

ground, and polished smooth, was just under half complete (Figure 7.6a). It was recovered from the floor fill of Feature 7. The barrel bead (FN 44-3104), which was made from a light greenish-blue turquoise (Figure 7.6b), was recovered whole next to the two axes from the floor fill of Feature 17. The bead is very small and roundish. Its edges have been ground smooth; its perforation is cylindrical, and may have been drilled with a cactus spine (J. Adams 2002:213–214; Haury 1931:86–87).

Chronological Distribution

As stated previously, ground stone artifacts are not generally considered temporally diagnostic. Many artifact types occur over a broad period of time, without any significant differences in their morphology or function over time. While broad generalizations can sometimes be made based on a few temporal trends (e.g., there are temporal variations in the appearance, most common type, and function of different mano and metate subtypes; J. Adams 2002), temporal trends evident in ground stone assemblages are usually assessed using indirect dating techniques (i.e., ceramic seriation, other temporally diagnostic artifacts, radiocarbon dating of features, etc.).

At the Marsh Station Road site, 75 ground stone artifacts were recovered from 32 features. Approximately 57 percent of these artifacts were recovered from features that date to the Rincon phase of the Sedentary (Middle Formative) period (Table 7.9a). Another 16 percent came from features that date to the San Pedro phase of the Early Agricultural period, while just 4 percent came from features that date to the Agua Caliente phase of the Early Formative period. Sixteen artifacts (21.3 percent) were recovered from features indeterminately dating from the Early Agricultural through Formative periods; one artifact was recovered from a feature of unknown age.

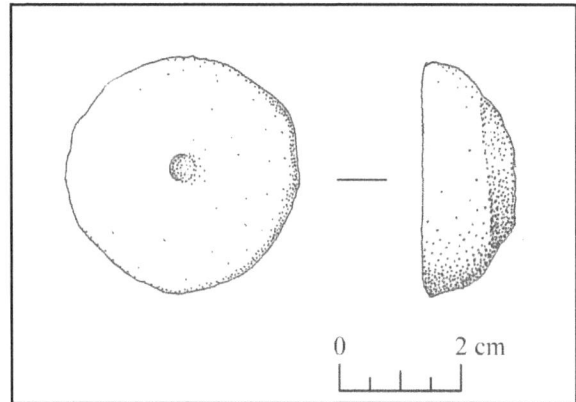

Figure 7.5. Illustration of an unused spindle base (FN 44-1595) recovered from the Marsh Station Road site.

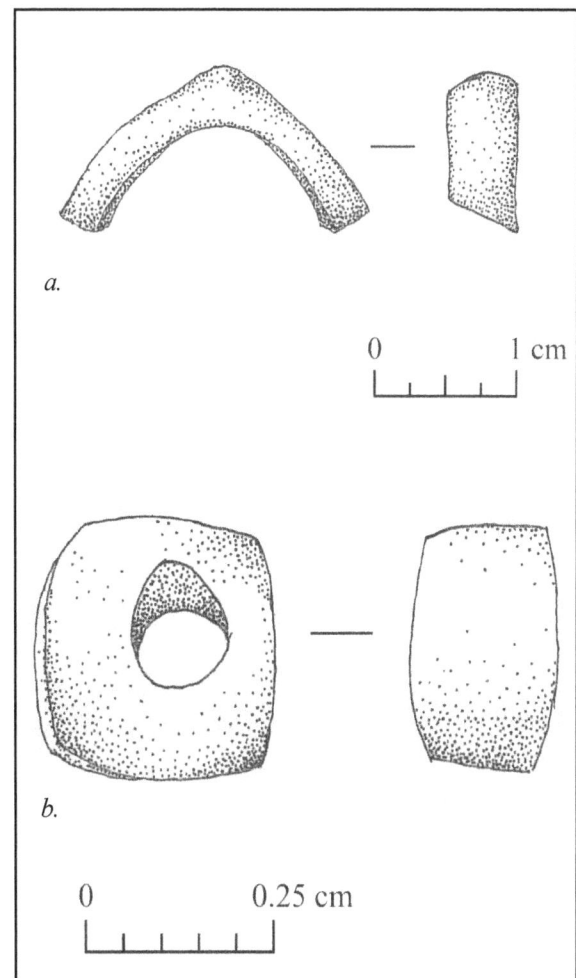

Figure 7.6. Stone paraphernalia recovered from the Marsh Station Road site: a) ring fragment (FN 44-1494) recovered from the floor fill of Feature 7; b) turquoise barrel bead (FN 44-3104) recovered from the floor fill of Feature 17 (below).

Early Agricultural Period

The small sample of ground stone (n=12) associated with features dating to the Early Agricultural period inhibits understanding of the use of ground stone during the earliest occupation at the Marsh Station Road site. Food processing tools consisting of four manos and four metate fragments comprise the majority of the Early Agricultural assemblage. In addition, three handstones, one of which was used to process pigment, and one indeterminate fragment are also associated with featrures dating to this period.

Both basin and flat and flat/concave subtypes of food processing tools are represented in the Early Agricultural assemblage by three basin metate fragments and two flat and two flat/concave manos (Table 7.9b). While earlier researchers have suggested that the presence of basin and flat manos and metates, or more noticeably, the lack of trough manos and metates, indicates a reliance on wild food stuffs rather than on agricultural products (e.g., Haury 1950, 1976; Martin 1943; Rinaldo 1952; Sayles 1983; Sayles and Antevs 1941), more recent research has shown that these subtypes were also used to grind agricultural products, including corn (J. Adams 2002:120–121). J. Adams (1999; 2002:121) has suggested that the different subtypes of food processing tools are not representative of "how foods were acquired but were instead sensitive to changes in recipes and the ways foods were processed." Basin and flat/concave subtypes may have been more typical of wet grinding, whether of wild or domesticated seeds, whereas trough designs may have been introduced as more efficient tools for the processing of dried seeds.

Use wear analysis on the manos and metates dating to the Early Agricultural period at the Marsh Station Road site indicates that these tools were used to process maize as well as other wild plant seeds. Macrobotanical evidence in the form of a charred cob segment and flotation samples confirm that domesticated maize was present at the site during this early period (see Chapter 10; also see Chapter 11, for a different perspective based on pollen evidence).

Early Formative Period

Only three artifacts—one flat/concave mano, one multiple-type mano, and one flat metate—are associated with features that date to the Early Formative period (see Table 7.9b). The small assemblage dating to this period is most likely directly tied to the small sample of features (n = 2, only 1 of which contained ground stone) excavated dating to the Early Formative period. Use-wear indicates that these three artifacts were used to process maize, however, the sample is not robust enough to make further inferences regarding the role of ground stone during this period.

Middle Formative Period

The largest number and widest variety of ground stone artifacts recovered at the Marsh Station Road site date to the Middle Formative (n=4) and late Middle Formative (n=39) periods (see Table 7.9a). Food processing tools (44.2 percent) still comprise the majority of the ground stone assemblage. Every subtype of manos and metates is present. Tools of the trough subtype make their first appearance during the late Middle Formative period, and during this period, few tools of the basin subtype were recovered compared with the number recovered dating to the Early Agricultural period. As discussed previously, while the trend towards the appearance and increasing numbers of trough manos and metates and the apparent decline of basin manos and metates between the Early Agricultural and Middle Formative periods is representative of a general

Table 7.9a. Temporal distribution of ground stone artifacts from dated features

	Early Agricultural San Pedro Phase	Early Formative Agua Caliente Phase	Middle Formative Rincon Phase	Early Agricultural through Formative	Unknown	Total
Mano	4	2	14	10	1	31
Metate	4	1	5	2		12
Pestle						
Handstone	3		5	1		9
Netherstone			1	1		2
Polishing stone			2			2
Pecking stone			1			1
Abrader			1			1
Finger ring			1			1
Barrel bead			1			1
Spindle base						
Lapstone			1			1
3/4-grooved axe			2			2
Indeterminate	1		9	2		12
Total	12	3	43	16	1	75

Note: Only ground stone artifacts recovered from features for which a temporal designation was assigned are included in this table

Table 7.9b. Temporal distribution of manos and metates from dated features

	Early Agricultural San Pedro Phase	Early Formative Agua Caliente Phase	Middle Formative Rincon Phase	Early Agricultural through Formative Periods	Unknown	Total
Basin mano			1	1		2
Flat mano	2		4	4		10
Flat/concave mano	2	1	1	3	1	8
Trough mano			5			5
Mano, multiple		1				1
Mano, other			3	2		5
Basin metate	3			1		4
Flat metate		1	2			3
Flat/concave metate			2	1		3
Metate, unk.	1		2			3
Total	8	3	20	12	1	44

Note: Only ground stone artifacts recovered from features for which a temporal designation was assigned are included in this table clinal distribution of mano and metate subtypes through time (J. Adams 2002:121), it is not indicative of a transition from a subsistence strategy based on hunting and gathering to a reliance on agriculture. Rather, the presence of the trough subtype more likely suggests a change in the way seeds were processed, with the focus shifting to more efficient production of flour from dried seeds (J. Adams 1999, 2002). What is unclear is whether this change in the way flour was produced was brought about by practical reasons related to the storage and type of foods produced, by social reasons, or by some combination of the two (J. Adams 2002:121).

Except for four handstones and one netherstone dating to other periods, all other general processing and manufacturing tools, as well as both ornaments date to the late Middle Formative period (see Table 7.9a). It appears that a wide variety of activities relating to craft production, including shell and pigment processing and ornament production, as well as tool manufacture occurred at the site during this period. However, the relatively low number of general processing and manufacturing tools recovered suggests that 1) craft production and tool manufacture were being performed for primarily local consumption, and 2) that these activities, while performed at the site, were not of primary importance; rather, food processing and production was the dominant activity associated with ground stone use at the Marsh Station Road site.

Discussion

There is relatively little obvious chronological patterning within the ground stone assemblage at the Marsh Station Road site. With the evidence available, it is unclear whether this lack of chronological patterning is the result of a bias in the excavated feature sample towards features that date to the Middle Formative period (approximately 60 percent; see Chapter 4; also see Table 7.9a), or whether it is representative of different behavior related to the manufacture, use, and discard of ground stone artifacts in different periods in southern Arizona, or some combination of the two. There are, however, several important inferences that can be made regarding the temporal distribution of ground stone at the Marsh Station Road site.

First, the presence of manos and metates with use wear indicative of maize processing during all periods of occupation at the site indicates that agricultural products, in particular corn, were an important aspect of the diet throughout the history of the site (also see Chapter 10; but see Chapter 11 for a different perspective). Similarly, wild plant products, such as amaranth, various grasses, and mustard seeds, were also likely processed with ground stone during all periods of occupation. Although flat and flat/concave manos and metates were present in consistent proportions at the site during all periods, there appears to be a trend in distribution of both basin and trough subtypes in which basin subtypes decrease and trough subtypes first appear at the site between the Early Agricultural and late Middle Formative periods. However, as argued by J. Adams (1999, 2002:120–121), this trend is not indicative of a subsistence system transitioning from hunting and gathering to agriculture-based; rather, it is representative of a transition to a more efficient grinding technology and a change in the way foods were prepared.

Second, J. Adams (2005) has suggested that both artifact density, in terms of the ratio of whole to broken items, and the richness of the assemblage , in terms of the number of distinct artifact types present in the assemblage, can be used to assess intensity of occupation of a site. All things being equal, a more intensely occupied site should have a higher density of broken artifacts as well as a richer artifact assemblage than a site that was less intensely occupied (J. Adams 2005:101). In the case of the Marsh Station Road site, whole to broken artifact ratios and assemblage richness values were calculated for both the Early Agricultural and Middle Formative periods. Whole to broken artifact ratios were obtained by dividing the number of whole artifacts by the number of broken artifacts in the assemblage. The assemblage richness was calculated by dividing the number of distinct artifact types associated with features dating to either the Early Agricultural or Middle Formative periods by the total number of distinct artifact types identified for all periods at the site. The richness values for the Marsh Station Road site were also compared to richness values calculated by J. Adams (2005) for several other Early Agricultural period sites in the Tucson Basin. Interestingly, the two analyses provide divergent interpretations of differences in the intensity of site occupation during these periods.

The ratio of whole to broken artifacts during both the Early Agricultural and the Middle Formative periods was virtually the same (1:1 and 0.83:1, respectively), suggesting that the intensity of site occupation did not differ significantly between the two periods. Assemblage richness, on the other hand, differed significantly between the Early Agricultural and Middle Formative periods. The Early Agricultural ground stone assemblage had a richness value of just 0.1875; only 3 of a possible 16 artifact classes1 date to this period. The Middle Formative period ground stone assemblage, however, has a significantly higher richness value—0.8125, with 13 of the 16 artifact classes dating to this period. The richness values suggest that occupation of the Marsh Station Road site during the Early Agricultural period was not particularly intense, whereas by the Middle Formative period, occupation intensity had increased dramatically.

While it seems likely that the site experienced different occupation intensities through time, the discrepancies between the artifact density ratios and the richness values calls for a more thorough examination of the data. There are several explanations for the discrepancies between the two calculations. First, calculation of the artifact density ratio assumes that both whole and broken artifacts entered the archaeological record in the same way. However, archaeological and ethnographic research indicates that whole and broken artifacts are not treated in the same way nor do they enter the archaeological record in a similar manner (J. Adams 2005:101; Schiffer 1987). The artifact density ratios calculated for the Marsh Station Road site may therefore not be indicative of site occupation intensity, but rather may reflect similar behavior regarding the disposal of whole and broken artifacts through time.

Second, the discrepancies between the artifact density ratios and the richness values may be related to the sample of excavated features as well as the excavated sample of the overall site area rather than a reflection of site occupation intensity. More features dating to the Middle Formative period (n=64) were excavated than were features dating to the Early Agricultural period (n = 38). In addition, a wider variety of feature types, including pit structures, extramural areas, and nonthermal, thermal, and bell pits at the site date to the Middle Formative period; the only feature types dating to the Early Agricultural period that were excavated are nonthermal and thermal pits and possibly one pit house. The sample of excavated features dating to the Middle Formative period, both in terms of numbers and types, provides a more comprehensive and robust assemblage from which activities involving the use of ground stone at the site can be assessed.

Despite the sampling bias in favor of the Middle Formative period, however, the low diversity in artifact types of the Early

Agricultural assemblage is interesting in and of itself. The richness value is extremely low when compared to richness values calculated for other similar sites dating to the same period (see J. Adams 2005; e.g., Las Capas has a richness value of 0.76, compared to 0.1875 at the Marsh Station Road site). The low richness value at the Marsh Station Road site may therefore have been significantly impacted by the sample of excavated structures and/or the overall site area. However, it also suggests that the occupation of the site might have been less continuous and less intense during the Early Agricultural period in comparison to the nature of the occupation of the site during the Middle Formative period, and with occupations at other Early Agricultural sites, such as Las Capas and Los Pozos, in the Tucson Basin.

Spatial Distribution

Of the 173 ground stone artifacts recovered from the Marsh Station Road site, 95 (54.9 percent) were recovered from non-feature excavations—collection and test units, stripped areas, trenches, and one non-feature, Feature 36—while 72 (41.6 percent) were recovered from structures or pits, and another 4 (2.3 percent) came from extramural areas (see Table 7.4). Very few artifacts were recovered from the floor of features (n = 4); the majority of artifacts were found in structural or feature fill (n = 56), in natural deposits with cultural artifacts (n = 68), or on the surface of the site (n = 23); an additional 23 artifacts were recovered from the last 10 to 15 cm above structure floors.

Collection and Test Unit Distribution

Only one collection unit (representing ground stone present on the surface of the site), CU 296, contained more than one ground stone artifact. Ten fragmentary artifacts, including five manos, three metates, one handstone,

and one netherstone, were collected from this unit. While such a clustering of ground stone artifacts might indicate an activity area, this particular collection unit is located immediately outside of the Union Pacific Railroad right-of-way, and the clustering is more likely representative of disturbance to the surface of the site related to construction, use, and/or maintenance of the railroad than it is of any prehistoric activity. Eight test units (TUs 27, 33, 41, 64, 92, 93, 136, and 158) contained between three and six artifacts each; the remaining test units contained fewer than two artifacts each. One test unit in particular, TU 33, contained six artifacts—four manos, one handstone, and one indeterminate fragment—only one of which was whole. This test unit was located over a bell pit, Feature 58, and a nonthermal pit, Feature 68, and the artifacts contained in the test unit may in fact be related to either of these features.

Feature Distribution

Seventy-six artifacts were recovered from features (see Table 7.4). Both pit structures and nonthermal pits contained the majority of the ground stone. Smaller quantities were collected from bell pits, thermal pits, and extramural areas. As previously mentioned, most of the features date to the late Middle Formative period, and consequently, the feature assemblage is most representative of ground stone use during that time.

Forty-three artifacts representing just four artifact types (manos, metates, handstones, and netherstones) were recovered from nonthermal, thermal, or bell pits. Both whole and broken artifacts were recovered from pits in fairly even proportions (whole to broken ratio is 1:0.875); only minimal differences in the whole to broken artifact ratio between different pit types (nonthermal pits, 1:0.72; thermal pits, 1:1; and bell pits, 0.66:1) were observed. The majority

(79 percent) of the whole artifacts recovered from pits were either moderately or heavily worn, indicating that these artifacts were likely discarded into the pits near or at the end of their use lives. Only five whole, lightly used artifacts were recovered, most likely from storage, from nonthermal and bell pits; no lightly used artifacts were recovered from thermal pits. Thermal pits did not contain any metate fragments, but otherwise, there was virtually no difference in the distribution of the four artifact types recovered from nonthermal pits. Interestingly, however, no ground stone fragments recycled as fire-cracked rock were present in thermal pits. Rather, they were recovered from the fill of three nonthermal pits (Features 70, 73, and 90) and one bell pit (Feature 139), and from the floor fill of one pit structure (Feature 152). The similarity between the ground stone assemblages recovered from the three pit types suggests that the pits were not treated significantly different in regards to the storage and discard of ground stone artifacts.

The widest variety of ground stone artifact classes was recovered from pit structures, all of which date to the late Middle Formative period (see Table 7.4). Thirty-three artifacts representing 9 artifact types were recovered from 4 pit houses (Features 7, 11, 17, and 152) and 2 occupational surfaces (Features 6 and 41). Four of these artifacts—three manos and a lapstone used to process pigment—came from the two occupational surface; however, none of the artifacts were recovered from the occupation surfaces of these areas. It is therefore difficult to infer whether ground stone manufacture or use occurred in either of the extramural areas. Two of the pit houses, Features 7 and 11, only contained three artifacts each. Feature 7 had a flat mano on its floor; a broken finger ring was recovered from floor fill and a pebble polisher was in the general structural fill. The presence of the flat mano on the floor of Feature 7 suggests that this artifact may have been used in

the structure; however, because no compatible metate was recovered from this feature, it is possible the mano was simply in storage (also see Chapters 10 and 11 for a discussion of the macrobotanical and pollen remains from this feature). Feature 11 contained a flat mano (originally used as a trough mano) and metate set on its floor, suggesting that corn grinding/food processing occurred in this structure (also see Chapters 10 and 11 for a discussion of the macrobotanical and pollen remains from this feature). A pecking stone was also recovered from the general fill of the structure.

Feature 17, another pit structure, contained six ground stone artifacts, all but one of which were recovered from floor fill. The ground stone assemblage from this structure is interesting—the assemblage contained two food processing tools: a trough mano was recovered from the floor of the pit structure, while an indeterminate metate fragment came from floor fill. In addition to the metate fragment, two ¾-grooved axes, a lapstone likely used to process shell, and a turquoise barrel bead were also recovered from the floor fill. No other feature excavated at the site contained more than one unique ground stone artifact, and most contained none. In fact, both the floor and the floor fill within Feature 17 contained numerous unique artifacts other than ground stone, including a reconstructible vessel, four ornamental shell artifacts, mica flakes, ochre, two San Pedro projectile point fragments, and several flaked stone tools, as well as non-burial human remains. The artifact assemblage in Feature 17 suggests that the abandonment/post-abandonment depositional processes this feature underwent are unique and distinct from those the other excavated pit structures dating to the same time period underwent. However, based on the current excavated site sample (approximately 4 percent), it is difficult to make any behavioral inferences regarding Feature 17's artifact assemblage. The assemblage may be unique at the site, suggesting that Feature 17 held some special significance or status for the occupants of the site, and/or that the discard of these items into the pit structure may have been related to the structure's function during its use and/or played an important role in the structure's abandonment. On the other hand, this "unique assemblage" might be explained by the fact that features containing similar assemblages were not excavated during the current project. While the location of Feature 17 in SA 1, near the railroad and some distance from the other pit houses excavated by WSA, which were across the railroad down by Cienega Creek, as well as the size of the feature, which was larger than any of the other excavated pit houses, supports the idea that this feature may be somewhat unique at the site, we know that other pit houses dating to the late Middle Formative were located in the same area as Feature 17 (Kearns and McVickar 2009). Unfortunately, detailed information regarding these pit houses and their artifact assemblages was unavailable at the writing of this chapter.

Feature 152, the final pit structure, contained the largest ground stone assemblage at the Marsh Station Road site: 17 artifacts were recovered from this structure. While the assemblage from Feature 152 is three times larger than the assemblage recovered from Feature 17, half the artifacts recovered are indeterminate fragments, many of which were recycled as fire-cracked rock; all of these fragments were recovered from the floor fill. It is possible that the fragments were dumped into the structure as part of a hearth or roasting pit cleaning; regardless, they are likely not related to the use of Feature 152. All other artifacts, which include four manos, three handstones, and a pecking stone, were recovered from the general fill within the structure.

Discussion

The overall spatial distribution of the ground stone assemblage at the Marsh Station Road site is more informative about discard behavior than it is about use behavior. The overwhelming majority of artifacts were found either on the surface of the site or in excavated test units with no apparent association with any feature (exception TU 33; see above discussion) and no contextual data. There was no recognizable clustering of artifacts on the surface, in the test units, in pit houses, or on occupational surfaces that would suggest the presence of an activity area in which ground stone was manufactured and/or used. Of the artifacts recovered from features, most were found in general fill, whether in nonthermal, thermal, or bell pits, or in pit structures or above occupation surfaces. More artifacts of fewer subtypes were recovered from all pit types. While approximately half of these artifacts were whole, the majority of the artifacts were moderately to heavily used, suggesting that food processing and general processing tools were often discarded into pits towards or at the end of their use lives. Very few artifacts were recovered in situ. Four whole, lightly used manos may have been in storage in several nonthermal and bell pits; one mano on the floor of both Feature 7 and Feature 17 as well as the mano and metate set on the floor Feature 11 are the only other artifacts from which primary use behavior can be inferred. Every other ground stone artifact recovered from the Marsh Station Road site was likely discarded, either when the artifact was used up or broken, or when the site was abandoned. Feature 17 contained an interesting ground stone assemblage, which as suggested above, indicates that this structure underwent different abandonment/post-abandonment depositional processes than did the other excavated pit structures; with the available evidence, it is difficult to make further behavioral inferences. In addition, because only one piece of ground stone was recovered from the floor of this structure, it is difficult to assess whether ground stone was actually utilized in this structure, or whether special ground stone items were simply deposited in the structure's fill at or after its abandonment.

INTERPRETATION

The ground stone assemblage from the Marsh Station Road site contained items from all four artifact categories—food processing, general processing, and manufacturing tools, and paraphernalia—suggesting that a variety of activities including food and pigment processing, craft and ornament production, and tool manufacture and maintenance occurred there. However, the assemblage provides little information concerning activity areas where ground stone manufacture and/or use may have occurred as very few artifacts were recovered from an occupation surface. The mano and metate set found on the floor of Feature 11 suggests that food—most likely a wide variety of wild and domesticated plants (see Chapters 10 and 11)—was probably processed in the pit structure. The other two artifacts—a flat and a trough mano—recovered from an occupation surface were not found with compatible metates; while these tools may have been utilized in the structures, they could also have been in storage. The majority of the remaining ground stone assemblage was recovered from storage or general discard contexts in the feature fill of nonthermal, thermal, and bell pits, pit structures, or above the two occupation surfaces. The paucity of ground stone artifacts recovered from use surfaces or the floors of pit structures or from storage contexts suggests that occupants took still-viable artifacts with them when they left the site, that artifacts were either reused by the site's occupants

during subsequent occupations and/or were scavenged from the site, or that artifacts were stored or discarded in unexcavated portions of the site. However, the unique ground stone items recovered from the floor fill of Feature 17, in conjunction with the presence of unique assemblages of other material classes on the floor and in the floor and general fill of the feature, suggests that these items were not simply discarded at the end of their use lives, but rather that their discard into the pit structure may have been related to the structure's function during its use and/or played an important role in the structure's abandonment. The presence of a killed metate, the intentional destruction of which was a socially and/or ritually meaningful act (J. Adams 2008), also provides a unique perspective on the variety of cultural behavior resulting in the disuse and discard of ground stone artifacts at the Marsh Station Road site.

While the temporal distribution of ground stone at the Marsh Station Road site may, at least in part, be an artifact of site sampling, there is a distinct difference in both the type and variety of artifacts recovered between the earliest and latest periods of occupation. Ground stone dating to the Early Agricultural period consisted of only 12 artifacts representing just 3 artifact types of food processing and general processing tools. The Middle Formative period assemblage, however, contains many more artifacts (n = 44) as well as a wider variety of artifact types representing all three tool classes—food processing, general processing, and manufacturing—as well as paraphernalia. This difference, as suggested above, could be an artifact of site sampling related to the number and types of features excavated dating to each respective period. A greater number and wider variety of features were excavated which date to the Middle Formative period; consequently, a larger and more diverse ground stone assemblage is expected. However, the categorical differences in the Early Agricultural and Middle

Formative period assemblages also suggest that there are actual differences in the nature of occupation of the Marsh Station Road site during these periods. In particular, the ground stone assemblages dating to these two periods indicate that the site was less intensely occupied during the Early Agricultural period, whereas the site was more intensely occupied, probably by a larger population, during the Middle Formative, and especially during the late Middle Formative period. While some artifacts (n = 16) were recovered from features indeterminately dating between the Early Agricultural and Middle Formative periods, they only consist of food processing and general processing tools. If these tools could be definitively attributed to the Early Agricultural period, it would increase the assemblage size, but the variety of activities represented would probably remain similar, and therefore the interpretation would most likely not change significantly.

Chapter 8
Faunal Remains
Barnet Pavao-Zuckerman and Chance Copperstone

The following chapter presents the results of zooarchaeological analysis of faunal specimens recovered during excavations at the Marsh Station Road site. The fieldwork that produced the faunal samples reported here was conducted in 2007. All excavated materials were sieved through a ¼-inch mesh. Additional soil samples were taken and subject to fine-screening through ⅛-inch mesh. The Marsh Station Road site produced a total of 2,407 faunal specimens. All zooarchaeological remains from the Marsh Station Road site were analyzed according to standard zooarchaeological methods as described below.

ANALYTIC METHODS: PRIMARY DATA

Vertebrate remains were identified using standard zooarchaeological methods (Reitz and Wing 2008). All identifications of the materials reported here were made by Chance Copperstone under the direction of Dr. Barnet Pavao-Zuckerman using the comparative skeletal collections housed at the Stanley J. Olsen Laboratory of Zooarchaeology, Arizona State Museum, University of Arizona. A number of primary data classes are recorded, including taxonomic identification, skeletal element, element portion, and symmetry. The Number

of Identified Specimens (NISP), or bone count, is determined for every taxonomic identification. Specimens that cross-mend with other specimens in the same minimum analytical unit (Field Number [FN]) are counted as single specimens. No attempt was made to cross-mend specimens from separate FN's, except when noted below. All specimens were weighed to provide additional information about the relative abundance of identified taxa. Indicators for sex, age at death, and modifications are noted where observed.

ANALYTIC METHODS: SECONDARY DATA

MNI, the Minimum Number of Individuals, was estimated for the assemblage based on paired elements (lefts and rights) and age. While MNI is a standard zooarchaeological quantification method, the measure has several well-known biases. MNI emphasizes small-bodied over larger-bodied taxa. For example, the presence of ten cottontails indicates emphasis on the exploitation of lagomorphs; however, one deer likely supplies more meat. Further, some elements are more readily identifiable than others, resulting in the inflation of dietary contribution as estimated by MNI. Cattle teeth, which are often readily identifiable from very small fragments, exemplify this situation. Basic to MNI is the assumption that the entire individual was utilized at the site. From ethnographic evidence, it is known that this is not always true (Perkins and Daly 1968:96–106). This is particularly the case for larger individuals, animals used for special purposes, and where food exchange is an important economic activity (Thomas 1971:366–371; White 1953:396–398).

On occasion, the MNI for an organism is smaller than the MNI for a corresponding higher taxonomic level. For instance, it is possible that the MNI for cottontails (*Sylvilagus* sp.) could be four while the MNI for desert cottontail (*Sylvilagus audubonii*) is only one. In these cases the MNI for the lower, more specific, taxonomic category (*Sylvilagus audubonii*) is written in parentheses in the species list to indicate that a higher MNI was determined for a higher taxonomic level. The parenthetical number is not used in subsequent calculations.

MNI is also subject to bias introduced by the way samples are aggregated during analysis. The aggregation of archaeological samples into large analytical units (Grayson 1973:432–439) allows for a conservative estimate of MNI, while the "maximum distinction" method, applied when analysis discerns discrete sampling units, results in a much larger MNI. In estimating MNI for the Marsh Station Road site assemblage, all faunal remains were combined for analysis in order to maximize the sample size.

Biomass, an estimate of the amount of meat tissue contributed by different taxa, can compensate, in part, for some of the problems encountered with MNI. Predictions of biomass are based on the allometric principle that the proportions of body mass, skeletal mass, and skeletal dimensions change with increasing body size. The relationship between body weight and skeletal weight is described by the allometric equation (Simpson et al. 1960):

$$Y = aX^b$$

In this equation, X is specimen weight, Y is the biomass, b is the constant of allometry (the slope of the line), and a is the Y intercept for a log itz and Cordier 1983:237–252; Reitz et al. 1987:304–317; Wing and Brown 1979). Values for a and b are derived from calculations based on data at the Florida Museum of Natural History, University of Florida, and the University of Georgia Museum of Natural History. Allometric formulae for biomass estimates are not currently available for amphibians or lizards so biomass is not estimated for these groups.

The utility of derived quantitative measures such as MNI and biomass is heavily influenced by sample size (Casteel 1978:71–77; Grayson 1979:199–237, 1981:77–88; Wing and Brown 1979). In general, samples of at least 200 individuals or 1400 specimens are needed for reliable interpretations. Smaller samples frequently will generate a short species list with undue emphasis on one species in relation to others.

The species identified from the Marsh Station Road site are summarized in faunal categories based on vertebrate class to facilitate comparisons of relative dietary contribution. These categories include: Reptiles, Wild Birds, Wild Mammals, Domestic Birds, Domestic Mammals, and Commensals. In order to permit comparison of MNI and biomass, the summary tables include biomass calculations only for those taxa for which MNI is estimated.

Several taxa are tentatively classified as commensal. These include kangaroo rats (*Dipodomys* sp.) and white-throated woodrats (*Neotoma albigula*). While commensal animals might be consumed, these animals are commonly found in close association with humans and their built environment. They are animals whose presence people either do not encourage or actively discourage. Coyote/domestic dog (*Canis latrans/familiaris*) might also be commensal but is not put into this category because of evidence of butchery and burning. Other animals identified here as consumed might also, at other times, be commensal.

The presence or absence of elements in an archaeological assemblage can shed light on animal use strategies such as butchering practices and transportation costs. The artiodactyl and canid elements identified from the site are summarized into categories based on body portion. The Head category includes skull fragments, including antler, horn core, and teeth. The atlas and axis, along with other vertebrae and ribs, are placed into the Vertebra/Rib category. It is likely the Head and Vertebra/Rib categories are under-represented because of recovery and identification difficulties. The vertebrae and ribs of pronghorn (*Antilocapra americana*), mule deer (*Odocoileus hemionus*), white-tailed deer (*Odocoileus virginianus*), and bighorn sheep (*Ovis canadensis*) are difficult to distinguish when fragmentary, or in the absence of key morphological features. Further, other similarly sized, nonungulate species may also be present in the sample. In the absence of diagnostic features, vertebrae and rib specimens are identified only as "ungulate-sized mammal" and are not reported in these body portion categories. The Forequarter category includes the scapula, humerus, radius, and ulna. Carpal and metacarpal specimens are presented in the Forefoot category. The Hindfoot category includes tarsal and metatarsal specimens. The Hindquarter category includes the innominate, sacrum, femur, and tibia. Metapodiae and podiae which could not be assigned to one of the other categories, as well as sesamoids and phalanges, are assigned to the Foot category.

Relative ages of the artiodactyls and canids identified are estimated based on observations of the degree of epiphyseal fusion for diagnostic elements and tooth eruption data, when available (Severinghaus 1949:195–216; Silver 1969:283–302). When animals are young their elements are not fully formed. The epiphysis, the area of growth along the shaft and the end of the element is not fused. When growth is complete, the shaft and the epiphysis fuse. While environmental factors influence the actual age at which fusion is complete (Watson 1978:97–102), elements fuse in a regular temporal sequence (Gilbert 1973; Purdue 1983:1207–1213; Schmid 1972). During analysis, specimens are recorded as either fused or unfused and placed into one of three categories based on the age in which fusion generally occurs. Unfused elements in the early-fusing category are interpreted as evidence for juveniles; unfused elements in the middle-fusing and late-fusing categories are usually interpreted as evidence for subadults, though sometimes characteristics of the specimen may suggest a juvenile. Fused specimens in the late-fusing group provide evidence for adults. Fused specimens in the early- and middle-fusing groups are indeterminate. Modifications can indicate butchering methods as well as site formation processes. Modifications are classified as rodent-gnawed, burned, calcined, cut, hacked, abraded (polished or ground), eroded, and red-stained. Gnawing by rodents indicates that specimens were not immediately buried after disposal and can result in loss of an unknown quantity of zooarchaeological material. Burned specimens may result from exposure to fire when meat is cooked. Burn marks may also occur if specimens are burned intentionally or unintentionally after discard. Burning at extreme temperatures can cause calcination and is usually indicated by blue-gray discoloration. Cuts are small incisions across the surface of specimens. These marks were probably made by knives as meat was removed before or after cooking. Cuts may also be left on specimens if attempts are made to disarticulate the carcass at joints. Hack marks are evidence that some larger instrument, such as a cleaver, was used. Presumably, a cleaver, hatchet, or ax would have been employed as the carcass was dismembered rather than after the meat was cooked. Worked specimens, such as those with abrading, grinding, or polish, include those which show evidence of human modification for reasons probably not associated with butchery. Many of these worked specimens are modified into identifiable bone tools. Stained specimens exhibit coloration possibly due to the application of pigments prior to burial.

RESULTS

A total of 26 individuals were identified from 2,407 specimens within the faunal assemblage (Table 8.1). The combined sample size of the Marsh Station Site zooarchaeological assemblage is large and adequate to interpretation of human behavior at the site. Because of the large size of the assemblage, further subdivisions by time period and feature type are possible and presented below. With a few exceptions, noted below, preservation of faunal remains from the Marsh Station site was excellent. Evidence for post-depositional taphonomic modifications, such as rodent-gnawing and superficial erosion, are noted and discussed below.

Species Diversity

Cottontails (*Sylvilagus* spp.) (MNI = 6) and black-tailed jackrabbits (*Lepus californicus*) (MNI = 4) represent the majority of the assemblage's MNI, contributing a minimum of 10 individuals. Wild birds, including a band-tailed pigeon (*Columba fasciata*), a greater roadrunner (*Geococcyx californianus*), and an indeterminate perching bird (Passeriformes), account for three individuals. Wild mammals, including the above lagomorphs, in addition to coyote/

domestic dog (*Canis latrans/ familiaris*), bobcat (*Felis rufus*), mule deer (*Odocoileus hemionus*), and bighorn (*Ovis canadensis*), contribute 69.2 percent of the total MNI and 73.8 percent of the total biomass for the assemblage (Table 8.2). No distinction could be made between coyote and similarly sized domestic dogs based on the available faunal material in the assemblage. While a number of specimens were present, the remains were highly eroded, hindering observation of fine-scale diagnostic features. The kangaroo rat (*Dipodomys* sp.) and white-throated woodrat (*Neotoma albigula*), both identified as commensal species make a minimal contribution to the total MNI. Domestic cattle (*Bos taurus*) and chicken (*Gallus gallus*) also contribute minimally to the assemblage, and likely result from nineteenth and twentieth century activities at the site. One lizard (*Sauria*) cranium and an indeterminate invertebrate (shell) were also identified.

Effect of Fine Screening

Soil samples from Marsh Station Road features were also subject to fine screening. Table 8.1 includes zooarchaeological remains recovered using ¼-inch mesh plus those samples recovered using fine screening (⅛-inch mesh). Analysis of fine-screened materials from the site only slightly increased the diversity of the assemblage, adding one unique taxa to the assemblage: eastern cottontail (*Sylvilagus floridanus*) (Table 8.3). The vast majority of the fine-screen sample (96 percent) was not identifiable below the taxonomic level of Class. Given time and budget constraints, only a portion of the fine-screened materials from Marsh Station were fully analyzed. Based on the results of analysis of this small fine-screened sample, and cursory examination of the remaining fine-screened materials, it was determined that completion of the fine-screen analysis would not sufficiently add to the interpreta-

	NISP	MNI		Weight	Biomass
Taxa		#	%	(g)	(kg)
Sauria	1	1	3.8	0.30	na
Lizards					
Aves	1			0.20	0.005
Medium bird					
Aves	1			0.20	0.005
Small bird					
Gallus gallus	1	1	3.8	0.70	0.015
Domestic chicken					
Columbidae	1			0.10	0.003
Pigeons and doves					
Columba fasciata	1	1	3.8	0.10	0.003
Band-tailed pigeon					
Geococcyx californicus	1	1	3.8	0.30	0.007
Greater roadrunner					
Passeriformes	1	1	3.8	0.00	0.000
Perching birds					
Mammalia	717			55.97	0.984
Indeterminate mammal					
Mammalia	741			1722.90	21.510
Small mammal					
Mammalia	25			20.30	0.395
Medium mammal					
Mammalia	277			387.90	5.622
Ungulate-sized mammal					
Leporidae	22			4.30	0.098
Hares and rabbits					
Sylvilagus sp.	66	6	23.1	14.90	0.299
Cottontails					

Table 8.1. Species list, all fauna

Table 8.1. Species list, all fauna, cont'd.

Taxa	NISP	MNI #	MNI %	Weight (g)	Biomass (kg)
Sylvilagus audubonii Desert cottontail	1	(1)		1.70	0.042
Sylvilagus floridanus Eastern cottontail	2	(1)		0.10	0.003
Lepus sp. Hares and jackrabbits	48			21.20	0.411
Lepus californicus Black-tailed jackrabbit	121	4	15.4	49.60	0.883
Lepus alleni Antelope jackrabbit	15	1	3.8	13.30	0.270
Rodentia Rodent	17			1.11	0.029
Sciuridae Squirrels	6			0.70	0.019
Ammospermophilus harrisi Yuma antelope squirrel	4	1	3.8	0.30	0.009
Spermophilus sp. Ground squirrels	1	1	3.8	0.30	0.009
Dipodomys sp. Kangaroo rat	2	1	3.8	0.10	0.003
Sigmodontinae New World rats and mice	2			0.10	0.003
Neotoma albigula White-throated woodrat	2	1	3.8	0.40	0.012
Canis latrans/familiaris Coyote/ domestic dog	50	2	7.7	67.60	1.167
Felis rufus Bobcat	1	1	3.8	0.30	0.009

Taxa	NISP	MNI #	MNI %	Weight (g)	Biomass (kg)
Table 8.1. Species list, all fauna, cont'd.					
Artiodactyla Even-toed ungulate	5			32.50	0.604
Odocoileus sp. Mule deer/White-tailed deer	27			49.30	0.878
Odocoileus hemionus Mule deer	2	1	3.8	19.60	0.383
Bos taurus Domestic cattle	14	1	3.8	57.70	1.012
Ovis canadensis Bighorn sheep	4	1	3.8	24.40	0.466
Vertebrata Indeterminate class	156			6.90	
Vertebrata Mammal/Bird	70			4.30	
Invertebrata Invertebrate	1			0.70	
Total	2407	26	100	2560.38	35.156

tion of human behavior at the site to justify the significant time investment needed.

Skeletal Portion Recoveries

Coyote/domestic dog is well represented within the assemblage, with elements from all skeletal regions recovered (Table 8.4). Given the highly eroded nature of the specimens and the absence of a complete cranium, species identification was not possible. The 11 elements found within the Head category are limited strictly to teeth from both the upper and lower jaw. The majority (n = 44) of these specimens are from a single feature (Feature 109), a Formative period bell pit. Given the degree of skeletal completeness represented in this assemblage, it is likely that these remains represent an intentional burial or disposal of a domesticated dog. However, a cut mark on the humerus of the animal in Feature 109 suggests some post-mortem processing. Domestic cattle portions included a rib shaft, a phalanx, and miscellaneous tooth fragments. Two metatarsal fragments account for the mule deer within the assemblage. The recovery of bighorn sheep was restricted to a single innominate. Unfortunately, this specimen was not found within a feature and is therefore not attributable to a specific time period.

Demographic Observations

While sample size is a factor in determining demographic patterns for the Marsh Station Road site, there is a noticeable lack of evidence of juveniles within the deer (*Odocoileus* sp.) specimens (Table 8.5). Fusion was observed in the early, middle, and late categories, suggesting that adult animals were processed. Similarly, the lack of unfused coyote/domestic dog elements suggests that the individuals had reached the adult stage at the time of death. However, no elements in the late fusing category were recovered to provide decisive evidence that the canids represented here were indeed adults.

Bone Modifications

Modification occurred almost exclusively within the mammal and invertebrate categories; only one small bird specimen and no lizard specimens exhibited modification. Erosion of bone was the most common taphonomic modification observed (n = 471). This erosion was likely caused by in situ chemical erosion or solar exposure prior to burial. The poor preservation of the eroded specimens suggests that some portion of the assemblage was destroyed

	MNI		Biomass	
	#	%	kg	%
Reptiles	1	3.8	na	na
Wild birds	3	11.5	0.009	0.2
Domestic birds	1	3.8	0.015	0.4
Wild mammals	18	69.2	2.961	73.8
Domestic mammals	1	3.8	1.012	25.2
Commensals	2	7.7	0.014	0.3
Total	26		4.011	

Table 8.2. Summary table, all fauna

Table 8.3. Species list, fine screen only

Taxa	NISP
Aves Small bird	1
Mammalia Indeterminate mammal	5
Mammalia Small mammal	25
Mammalia Large mammal	1
Sylvilagus floridanus Eastern cottontail	2
Lepus alleni Antelope jackrabbit	4
Rodentia Rodents	2
Vertebrata Indeterminate vertebrate	156
Vertebrata Mammal/bird	24
Total	220

by taphonomic factors prior to recovery. Burning was the most common human-caused modification within the assemblage (n = 196) (Table 8.6). Burning at high heat, as indicated by calcination, was evident in 119 specimens, including on the single modified bird bone. Eight cut marks were observed, including four cuts on a single ungulate-sized shaft fragment. One hacked cottontail vertebra was also recorded. Evidence of bone tool production, specifically awls and beads, was exhibited among the indeterminate, small, medium, and ungulate-sized mammals. A section of a bivalve shell bracelet represented the lone invertebrate specimen in the assemblage.[1] One medium-sized mammal long bone fragment was stained with red pigment. Rodent gnawing was noted on less than one percent (NISP = 14) of the Marsh Station specimens, suggesting that this destructive activity was minimal. Given the slight representation of rodents in the assemblage as a whole, this result is not surprising.

Intrasite Variability

The Marsh Station Road Site assemblage boasts a fairly robust sample size that permits some further division of the assemblage and examination of patterns of intrasite variability

Table 8.4. Element distribution, all fauna

	Mule Deer	Bighorn Sheep	Domestic Cow	Domestic Dog/Coyote
Head			6	11
Vertebra/Rib			2	4
Forequarter				4
Hindquarter		1		2
Forefoot				1
Hindfoot	2			10
Foot			1	17
Total	2	1	9	49

Table 8.5. Epiphyseal fusion (NISP), all fauna			
	Unfused	Fused	Age at Fusion
Deer:			
Early Fusing:			
Humerus, distal		1	12-20 months
Metapodials, proximal		3	Before birth
1st/2nd phalanx, proximal		6	11-20 months
Middle Fusing:			
Calcaneus, proximal		1	26-29 months
Metapodials, distal		3	26-29 months
Late Fusing:			
Humerus, proximal		1	42 months
Dog/Coyote:			
Early Fusing:			
Acetabulum		1	Unknown
1st/2nd phalanx, proximal		3	Unknown
Middle Fusing:			
Calcaneus, proximal		1	Unknown

including observations of subsistence strategies by time period and patterns in faunal recovery as they relate to feature functionality.

Temporal Variability

Faunal remains from the Marsh Station Road site are attributable to several mostly overlapping time periods. While the assemblage itself is large, the sample sizes of the assemblages that can be assigned to given time periods is much smaller, limiting our ability to make observations of change over time during this important time period in southern Arizona prehistory. In particular, the Early Agricultural component is small, including only a total of 102 bone fragments. A total of 1,404 specimens are affiliated with the Formative period. Some

of these materials can be further identified as belonging to subdivisions within this broader time period. Twenty-five specimens date to the Early Formative period, the smallest sample size from the larger Formative assemblage. A single pit house is identified as belonging to the Rillito or Rincon phase and yielded 128 animal bone specimens. An additional 715 specimens from a number of feature types are more specifically attributed to the Rincon phase/Middle Formative. The remaining Formative period specimens (n = 536) could not be identified to a more specific cultural phase or time period.

Early Agricultural Subsistence
The small size of the Early Agricultural assemblage (N = 102) makes interpretation of subsistence behavior problematic (Table 8.7).

Table 8.6. Bone modifications, all fauna

Taxa	Rodent-gnawed	Burned	Calcined	Cut	Hacked	Abraded	Eroded	Red-stained
Indeterminate mammal	1	20	34	1		4	274	
Small bird			1					
Small mammal	2	44	39			4	43	
Medium mammal						1	16	
Ungulate-size mammal	3	18	24	5		5	45	1
Hares/rabbits	1	3	1				7	
Cottontail		6	1		1		1	
Desert cottontail	1							
Eastern cottontail		1	1					
Jackrabbit		1	3					
Black-tailed jackrabbit	1	15	5	1			15	
Antelope jackrabbit		2	1				1	
Dog/Coyote	3		1	1			42	
Bobcat			1					
Deer							6	
Domestic cow	1						5	
Indeterminate class		79	3					
Mammal/Bird	1	7	4				16	
Invertebrate						1		
Total	14	196	119	8	1	15	471	1

The assemblage includes both lagomorphs (*Lepus californicus* and *Sylvilagus* sp.) and deer (*Odocoileus* sp.). Deer remains contribute slightly more to the biomass of the assemblage. Unfortunately, this sample is not large enough to serve as an Early Agricultural baseline for reconstructing shifts in faunal resource exploitation and landscape use strategies that occurred concomitant with agricultural intensification in the region.

Early Formative Subsistence
Likewise, the small sample size of the Early Formative assemblage (N = 25) makes it difficult to reconstruct changes in faunal exploitation strategies over time within the Formative period (Table 8.8). Jackrabbit (*Lepus* sp. and *Lepus californicus*) and squirrel (Sciuridae) are the only identifiable taxa in the assemblage. No deer were identified, although the

single ungulate-sized specimen, while lacking diagnostic features, is consistent with the body size of deer. Given the small sample size, the lack of ungulates should not be interpreted as reflecting past human decision making strategies. The presence of black-tailed jackrabbit (*Lepus californicus*) may indicate brush clearing around the site for agricultural purposes, as these animals prefer more open grassland areas (Hoffmeister 1986). Alternatively, the presence of this animal could reflect the presence of abundant natural grasslands during the Early Formative occupation.

Middle Formative Subsistence
By combining materials from features identified to the Rillito and/or Rincon phases, we can derive a description of faunal resource exploitation strategies during the Middle Formative period (Table 8.9). The Middle Forma-

Table 8.7. List of identified taxa for the Early Agricultural period

Taxa	NISP	MNI #	MNI %	Weight (g)	Biomass kg	Biomass %
Mammalia Indeterminate mammal	5			0.80	0.022	2.6
Mammalia Small mammal	60			9.70	0.203	24.9
Mammalia Ungulate-sized mammal	30			25.60	0.487	59.7
Lepus californicus Black-tailed jackrabbit	4	1	33.3	0.90	0.024	2.9
Sylvilagus sp. Cottontail	2	1	33.3	0.30	0.009	1.1
Odocoileus sp. Deer	1	1	33.3	3.00	0.071	8.7
Total	102	3	100.0	40.30	0.816	99.9

tive sample includes most of the Formative period materials (N = 843). The assemblage contains a diversity of species including lizards, small birds, lagomorphs, other small mammals, and deer as well as a probable dog burial. Most of the species represented could have been obtained locally without extensive long-distance hunting forays. An exception is bighorn sheep, the closest modern population of which is located some 50 km away in the Santa Catalina Mountains (B. Huckell 1995). Band-tailed pigeons (*Columba fasciata*) are larger than domestic pigeons, and live in woodland habitats including oak canyons, foothills, and chaparral (Peterson 1990). Woodpeckers would also have been common in the riparian woodland environment near the site.

The proportional representation of the two species of jackrabbit may provide an indication of the vegetation cover at the site during the Middle Formative period. Antelope jackrabbits (*Lepus alleni*) are, on average, larger-boided than black-tailed jackrabbits (*Lepus californicus*) and are more often found in groups (Hoffmeister 1986). While these characteristics make this species an attractive prey resource, antelope jackrabbits also tend to prefer shrubby habitat with creosote bushes, mesquite thickets, and fewer grasses. Black-tailed jackrabbits tend to be more abundant where mesquite brush is cleared, and where there is more availability of grassland habitat. The greater representation of black-tailed jackrabbit in the Middle Formative assemblage may indicate that the area around

Taxa	NISP	MNI #	MNI %	Weight (g)	Biomass kg	Biomass %
Mammalia	1			0.5	0.014	10.7
Indeterminate mammal						
Mammalia	17					50.3
Small mammal				2.8	0.066	
Mammalia	1					14.5
Ungulate-sized mammal				0.7		
Lepus sp.	3			0.7	0.019	14.5
Jackrabbit						
Lepus californicus	1	1	50	1.1	0.029	21.7
Black-tailed jackrabbit						
Sciuridae	1	1	50	0.1	0.003	2.5
Squirrels						
Vertebrata	1			0.2		
Mammal or bird						
Total	25	2	100	6.1	0.131	114.2

Table 8.8. List of identified taxa for the Early Formative period

the site was cleared of shrubs for agricultural purposes, creating a habitat that was less preferable to antelope jackrabbit.

Both mule deer (*Odocoileus hemionus*) and white-tailed deer (*Odocoileus virginianus*) occur in southern Arizona; however, where the two species live in the same region, white-tailed deer tend to be restricted to higher elevations, while mule deer will keep to the chaparral (Hoffmeister 1986:547). The identification of mule deer in the assemblage may indicate greater usage of lower altitude habitats to hunt game, although the number of specimens is too small to permit further interpretation.

Formative Period Subsistence
In order to depict an overall pattern of vertebrate exploitation strategies in the Formative period, all materials from Early, Middle, and other Formative period features are combined in accompanying tables. Because the majority of materials from the Formative period are from Middle Formative features, interpretation of Middle Formative and overall Formative exploitation strategies are quite similar.

Dietary practices during the Formative period encompassed a wide range of taxa, including small birds, lagomorphs, other small mammals, and deer (Tables 8.10 and 8.11). As observed above, the Middle Formative canid (dog or coyote) burial also exhibits postmortem modification that may indicate that the carcass was processed for meat. However, given the high degree of skeletal completeness (Table 8.12), interpretation of these remains with regard to their incorporation into human subsistence strategies is inconclusive.

The larger Formative assemblage reveals a similar pattern of the relative representation of black-tailed jackrabbit versus antelope jackrabbit. This may indicate human modification of the local environment for agricultural purposes by the removal of mesquite and other shrubs preferred by antelope jackrabbit.

The relative representation of cottontail (*Sylvilagus* sp.) versus jackrabbit (*Lepus* sp.) remains may also indicate localized land clearing for agriculture, as cottontails tend to prefer areas with adequate shrub and ground cover for protection from predators. The presence of eastern cottontail (*Sylvilagus floridanus*) in the Marsh Station assemblage suggests that human hunters brought game to the site some distance from upland areas, including mountains and mountain slopes.

Three small mammal species were identified in the assemblage: kangaroo rat (*Dipodomys* sp.), ground squirrel (*Spermophilus* sp.), and white-throated woodrat (*Neotoma albigula*). Because of their small body size, kangaroo rat and woodrat are assumed to be commensal taxa, although it is entirely possible that both of these species were exploited as a food resource. Likewise, the larger-bodied ground squirrel is assumed to have contributed as a food resource, but may represent an accidental inclusion in the archaeological record.

While the majority of deer specimens could not be identified to a particular species, the presence of two mule deer (*Odocoileus hemionus*) specimens suggests that large-game hunting was not focused exclusively in upland areas. Mule deer tend to inhabit lower elevation chaparral environments where their ranges overlap with white-tailed deer (*Odocoileus virginianus*). The skeletal portion recovery pattern for deer is unusual (see Table 8.12). With the exception of a single humerus specimen, the deer assemblage is dominated by low-utility foot elements. The absence of head elements suggests that the carcasses were dressed in the field before being brought to the site, but the high frequency of elements from the feet suggests that field dressing was minimal. The pattern of skeletal portion recovery likely has less to do with human behavior than with identifiability. A large sample of ungulate-sized mammal specimens (n = 108) could not be more

Taxa	NISP	MNI		Weight	Biomass	
		#	%	(g)	kg	%
Lacertilia Lizards	1	1	5.9	0.30		
Aves Medium-sized bird	1	1	5.9	0.20	0.005	0.09
Columbidae Doves and pigeons	1			0.10	0.003	0.05
Columba fasciata Band-tailed pigeon	1	1	5.9	0.10	0.003	0.05
Picidae Woodpeckers	1	1	5.9	0.20	0.005	0.09
Mammalia Indeterminate mammal	124			31.40	0.585	11.20
Mammalia Small mammal	403			53.10	0.939	17.97
Mammalia Medium mammal	23			11.60	0.239	4.57
Mammalia Ungulate-sized mammal	46			42.20	0.816	15.61
Leporidae Rabbits and hares	15			1.80	0.045	0.85
Lepus sp. Jackrabbit	16			10.30	0.215	4.11
Lepus californicus Black-tailed jackrabbit	71	3	17.6	30.70	0.573	10.97
Lepus alleni Antelope jackrabbit	2	1	5.9	0.50	0.014	0.27

Table 8.9. List of identified taxa for the Middle Formative period

Table 8.9. List of identified taxa for the Middle Formative period, cont'd.

Taxa	NISP	MNI #	MNI %	Weight (g)	Biomass kg	Biomass %
Sylvilagus sp. Cottontail	47	5	29.4	10.20	0.213	4.07
Rodentia	4			0.80	0.022	0.41
Sciuridae Squirrels	4			0.50	0.014	0.27
Spermophilus sp. Ground squirrel	1	1	5.9	0.30	0.009	0.17
Neotoma albigula White-throated woodrat	2	1	5.9	0.40	0.012	0.22
Canis familiaris/latrans Dog or coyote	44	1	5.9	63.40	1.101	21.07
Odocoileus sp. Deer	4			5.60	0.124	2.37
Odocoileus hemionus Mule deer	1	1	5.9	14.50	0.292	5.59
Vertebrata Mammal or bird	31			3.80		
Total	843	17	100.0	282.00	5.226	100.00

specifically identified, and this unidentified assemblage is dominated by long bone shaft fragments, the very element category types that are missing from the deer element distribution worksheet. Further, skeletal elements of the foot, which dominate the deer assemblage, tend to be the most diagnostic elements in distinguishing between ungulate species (i.e., deer, pronghorn, and bighorn sheep).

There is some evidence for age at death in the assemblage—the deer individual identified in the assemblage was at least 26 months old at death (Table 8.13). As observed above, the dog/coyote individual recovered in Feature 109 was fully mature at the time of death.

Burning and calcining are the most common modifications in the assemblage (Table 8.14). Heat-modified specimens could have been burned during food preparation or disposal. Many of the specimens were also highly eroded, possibly from in situ chemical erosion. It is likely that this taphonomic process negatively affected preservation in the zooarchaeological assemblage. A single medium-mammal specimen was modified (abraded) into a possible bone awl, and an ungulate-sized mammal specimen from within a pit house (Feature 11) was colored red, perhaps with ochre. Faunal material recovered from Feature 11, a pit house radiocarbon dated to the Middle Formative period, is considered to be part of the Middle Formative assemblage in this chapter. However, please see Chapter 4, where discussion of this feature suggests that it may actually be more characteristic of an Early Agricultural pit house.

Feature Type Variability

A number of feature types are represented in the faunal assemblage, including pit houses and other structures; thermal pits, including hearths, roasting pits, and other thermal pits; nonthermal pits; bell pits; and burials (Table 8.15). Not surprisingly, the pit house assemblages contained the widest variety of taxa. Small rodents are not common in the pit house or other structure assemblages, suggesting either that structures were not occupied for a very long period of time, or that features located external to structures were used for the storage of foodstuffs. Small rodents, however, are uncommon throughout the site assemblage, so this pattern may reflect broader characteristics of the local environment (that small rodents were not common in the area). The zooarchaeological remains recovered from within structures is consistent with small fragment-size food refuse left behind after meal consumption. The assemblage does not indicate that these structures were used for disposal following the occupation life of the feature.

Thermal pits contained assemblages dominated by small mammal and unidentifiable remains. Very few of these specimens were modified by heat, suggesting that these features were used for disposal after the final burning episode.

Most nonthermal pits contained small quantities of unidentified mammal remains, although a few nonthermal pits contained what appears to be food refuse, including the remains of lagomorphs, rodents, and deer.

While bell pits may have been used for storage, most of these features do not appear to have been used for the storage of meat or animal carcasses. Most bell pits contained remains that likely represent small-bodied animals that became trapped in the pit features. A few bell pits contain specimens of larger-sized animals such as ungulates, but these features are the minority. As observed above, Feature 109, a bell pit, contained the remains of a nearly complete dog or coyote, suggesting that bell pits may have been used for more than just storage. While a single cut mark was noted on the skeleton, the skeletal completeness of the animal suggests that the pit contained the intentional burial or disposal of a domestic dog. The high degree of superficial erosion and the presence of some gnaw marks on the dog/coyote skeleton indicates that the animal's carcass was exposed to the elements and scavenging animals for some period of time before burial. This taphonomic evidence suggests that some portion of the skeleton did not survive the ravages of time. Zooarchaeological materials from burials are suggestive of accidental inclusion of isolated animal bone rather than burial accompaniments.

Discussion

The zooarchaeological assemblage from the Marsh Station Road site is large, but the sample sizes of the assemblages that can be assigned to given time periods is much smaller, limiting our ability to make observations of change over time during this important time period in southern Arizona prehistory.

However, when all assemblages from the Early, Middle, and indeterminate Forma-

Taxa	NISP	MNI		Weight	Biomass	
		#	%	(g)	kg	%
Lacertilia Lizards	1	1	5.6	0.3		
Aves Small-sized bird	1			0.2	0.005	0.1
Aves Medium-sized bird	1			0.2	0.005	0.1
Columbidae Doves and pigeons	1			0.1	0.003	0.0
Columba fasciata Band-tailed pigeon	1	1	5.6	0.1	0.003	0.0
Picidae Woodpeckers	1	1	5.6	0.2	0.005	0.1
Mammalia Indeterminate mammal	334			35.0	0.645	7.4
Mammalia Small mammal	525			69.3	1.193	13.7
Mammalia Medium mammal	25			20.3	0.395	4.5
Mammalia Ungulate-sized mammal	108			161.7	2.558	29.3
Leporidae Rabbits and hares	17			2.4	0.058	0.7
Lepus sp. Jackrabbit	27			13.7	0.277	3.2
Lepus californicus Black-tailed jackrabbit	87	4	22.2	38.6	0.705	8.1
Lepus alleni Antelope jackrabbit	3	1	5.6	3.6	0.083	1.0

Table 8.10. List of identified taxa for the Formative period

Taxa	NISP	MNI #	MNI %	Weight (g)	Biomass kg	Biomass %
Sylvilagus sp. Cottontail	52	5	27.8	11.0	0.228	2.6
Sylvilagus floridanus Eastern cottontail	2	(1)		0.1	0.003	0.0
Rodentia	11			1.0	0.026	0.3
Dipodomys sp. Kangaroo rat	2	1	5.6	0.1	0.003	0.0
Sciuridae Squirrels	5			0.6	0.017	0.2
Spermophilus sp. Ground squirrel	1	1	5.6	0.3	0.009	0.1
Neotoma albigula White-throated woodrat	2	1	5.6	0.4	0.012	0.1
Canis familiaris/latrans Dog or coyote	44	1	5.6	63.4	1.101	12.6
Artiodactyla Even-toed ungulates	2			15.5	0.310	3.6
Odocoileus sp. Deer	19			40.4	0.734	8.4
Odocoileus hemionus Mule deer	2	1	5.6	19.6	0.383	4.4
Vertebrata Indeterminate class	75			3.2		
Vertebrata Mammal or bird	55			6.1		
Total	1404	18	100.0	507.4	8.759	100.5

Table 8.10. List of identified taxa for the Formative period, cont'd.

Table 8.11. Summary table for the Formative period

	MNI		Biomass	
	#	%	kg	%
Reptiles	1	5.6		
Wild birds	2	11.1	0.010	0.3
Wild mammals	13	72.2	3.578	99.3
Commensals	2	11.1	0.015	0.4
Total	18	100.0	3.603	100.0

Table 8.12. Element distribution (NISP) for the Formative period

	Dog	Deer
Head	10	
Vertebra/Rib	3	
Forequarter	4	1
Hindquarter	1	
Forefoot	1	5
Hindfoot	14	5
Foot	11	10
Total	44	21

Note: this table includes all cf. and sp. identifications.

Table 8.13. Epiphyseal fusion (NISP) for deer for the Formative period

Element	Unfused	Fused	Age at Fusion
Distal humerus		1	12-20 months
Proximal first phalanx		2	17-20 months
Proximal second phalanx		1	11-17 months
Proximal calcaneus		1	26-29 months
Distal metapodials		3	26-29 months

Note: this table includes all specimens with cf. or sp. identifications.

Table 8.14. Bone modifications for the Formative period

Taxa	Rodent-gnawed	Burned	Calcined	Cut	Abraded	Hacked	Eroded	Red-stained
Small-sized bird								
Woodpecker			1				1	
Indeterminate mammal		14	17	1			121	
Ungulate-sized mammal		16	3				29	1
Medium-sized mammal					1		16	
Small-sized mammal		59	34				34	
Cottontail or jackrabbit		1	1				6	
Jackrabbit		2	2					
Antelope jackrabbit		1	1				1	
Black-tailed jackrabbit		6	5				10	
Cottontail			1			1		
Eastern cottontail		1	1					
Rodent							1	
Deer							4	
Dog or coyote	1			1			41	
Indeterminate class		54						
Mammal or bird		5	5				16	
Total	1	159	71	2	1	1	280	1

tive period features are combined, a reasonable depiction of Formative period vertebrate exploitation strategies can be gleaned from the archaeological record. The zooarchaeological assemblage from the Formative period assemblage suggests exploitation of a diverse variety of local habitat types including stream, riparian forest, and desert grassland environments. Human agricultural activities at the site may also have modified existing local vegetation regimes to the benefit of certain prey species, such as black-tailed jackrabbit, and to the detriment of other lagomorph species.

The Formative period was a time of increased agricultural intensification and human sedentism in the region. However, while humans may have become more sedentary, foraging ranges to exploit large wild game may have increased as animal resources immediately surrounding sedentary communities were depleted (Stevens 2001b:3–5). The skeletal element distribution pattern for deer, as well the unidentified ungulate-sized mammal assemblage suggests that while field dressing of carcasses involved removing the head, lower-utility foot elements were returned to the place of consumption. This may indicate that large-game hunting did not take place far distances from the occupation site. However, foot bones are useful as raw materials for the manufacture of bone tools, including fishhooks and awls. Although no fishhooks were noted in the assemblage, a possible awl was excavated from Feature 59 (a bell pit), suggesting that bone tool manufacture took place at the site. Additional bone awls were identified in contexts that could not be firmly associated with the Formative time period.

Some evidence for zooarchaeological patterning in feature types is also noted. A lack of small mammal remains within structures suggests that food storage may have taken place outside of structures. Bell pits and non-thermal pits frequently contain the remains of small mammals and rodents, an indication that these features were used for storing foodstuffs such as agricultural products. The absence of other zooarchaeological remains suggests that the animal bone remains represent accidental inclusion of pest species, rather than storage of meat or animal carcasses within these features. Bell pits may also have been used for disposal or intentional burial of canids.

Concluding Thoughts

The zooarchaeological assemblage from the Marsh Station Road site reflects the diversity of natural environments that are accessible within a relatively short distance from the site. However, Formative period subsistence strategies appear to be primarily focused on the riparian forest and desert grassland habitats for the exploitation of birds, lagomorphs, other small mammals, and deer. The size of the Early Agricultural and Early Formative assemblages are not large enough to permit observation of diachronic changes in subsistence strategies during a time period of increased agricultural intensification and sedentism; however, the Middle Formative and overall Formative assemblages suggest that humans did not travel long distances to acquire large game. During the Middle Formative period, animal resource exploitation strategies were focused on locally available animal resources. These assemblages may also indicate that humans modified local environments through agricultural activities, thus influencing the locally available suite of small wild game species.

Table 8.15. Species lists by unit and feature

Unit No.	Type	Affiliation	Taxonomic Name	Common Name	NISP
F.2	hearth	historic	Vertebrata	indeterminate class	8
F.5	roasting pit	Formative	Aves	small bird	1
			Rodentia	rodent	2
			Mammalia/Aves	mammal or bird	2
			Total		**5**
F.6	other structure	Formative	unknown mammal		11
			small mammal		60
			ungulate-size mammal		7
			Lepus sp.	jackrabbit	7
			Lepus californicus	black-tailed jackrabbit	1
			Total		**86**
F.7	pit house	Formative	Mammalia/Aves	mammal or bird	3
			unknown mammal		5
			small mammal		43
			medium mammal		3
			Lepus sp.	jackrabbit	8
			Sylvilagus sp.	cottontail	3
			Sylvilagus floridanus	eastern cottontail	1
			Total		**66**
F.7.19	floor groove	Formative	Leporidae	jackrabbit or cottontail	**1**
F.7.21	posthole	Formative	Mammalia/Aves	mammal or bird	1
			unknown mammal		1
			small mammal		1
			Ungulate-size mammal		2
			Total		**5**
F.8	burial	Formative	Mammalia/Aves	mammal or bird	3
			Lepus alleni	antelope jackrabbit	4
			Total		**7**
F.9	nonthermal pit	Formative	ungulate-size mammal		**1**
F.10	nonthermal pit	Formative	Mammalia/Aves	mammal or bird	**2**

Table 8.15. Species lists by unit and feature, cont'd.

Unit No.	Type	Affiliation	Taxonomic Name	Common Name	NISP
F.11	pit house	Formative	Mammalia/Aves	mammal or bird	7
			Lepus alleni	antelope jackrabbit	1
			Lepus californicus	black-tailed jackrabbit	11
			small mammal		50
			Sylvilagus sp.	cottontail	1
			unknown mammal		49
			ungulate-size mammal		27
			Total		**146**
F.11.04	nonthermal pit	Formative	unknown mammal		2
F.11.09	bell pit	Formative	small mammal		7
F.12	nonthermal pit	Formative	small mammal		9
			ungulate-size mammal		9
			Lepus sp.	jackrabbit	3
			Sylvilagus sp.	cottontail	2
			Total		**23**
F.13	nonthermal pit	Formative	unknown mammal		2
F.14	nonthermal pit	unknown	unknown mammal		1
			Mammalia/Aves	mammal or bird	8
			Total		**9**
F.16	bell pit	unknown	small mammal		1
F.17	pit house	Formative	Mammalia/Aves	mammal or bird	6
			unknown mammal		8
			small mammal		44
			Lepus sp.	jackrabbit	2
			Lepus californicus	black-tailed jackrabbit	17
			Rodentia	rodent	1
			Sciuridae	squirrels and chipmunks	3
			Odocoileus sp.	deer	2
			Sylvilagus sp.	cottontail	6
			Total		**89**
F.18	burial	Formative	Mammalia/Aves	mammal or bird	5
			small mammal		1
			Total		**6**

Table 8.15. Species lists by unit and feature, cont'd.

Unit No.	Type	Affiliation	Taxonomic Name	Common Name	NISP
F.19	roasting pit	Formative	small mammal		3
			Lepus californicus	black-tailed jackrabbit	1
			Sylvilagus sp.	cottontail	1
			Mammalia/Aves	mammal or bird	1
			Total		**6**
F.20	bell pit	Formative	ungulate-size mammal		1
F.21	nonthermal pit	unknown	ungulate-size mammal		1
			Bos taurus	cattle	1
			Total		**2**
F.23	nonthermal pit	unknown	Small mammal		2
F.25	nonthermal pit	Formative	Mammalia/Aves	mammal or bird	1
			unknown mammal		172
			small mammal		2
			medium mammal		1
			ungulate-size mammal		25
			Leporidae	jackrabbit or cottontail	1
			Lepus californicus	black-tailed jackrabbit	4
			Sylvilagus sp.	cottontail	4
			Rodentia	rodent	2
			Artiodactyla	even-toed ungulate	2
			Odocoileus sp.	deer	15
			Total		**229**
F.28	roasting pit	Formative	small mammal		2
			indeterminate class		59
			Total		**61**
F.29	roasting pit	Formative	unknown mammal		3
			small mammal		3
			Sylvilagus floridanus	eastern cottontail	1
			indeterminate class		7
			Total		**14**
F.30	roasting pit	unknown	small mammal		1
			indeterminate class		20
			Total		**21**
F.31	nonthermal pit	unknown	indeterminate class		53

Table 8.15. Species lists by unit and feature, cont'd.

Unit No.	Type	Affiliation	Taxonomic Name	Common Name	NISP
F.39	roasting pit	Formative	Mammalia/Aves	mammal or bird	2
F.41	other structure	Formative	unknown mammal		2
			small mammal		8
	(ramada?)		ungulate-size mammal		1
			indeterminate class		9
			Total		**20**
F.44	nonthermal pit	Early	unknown mammal		1
		Agricultural	ungulate-size mammal		21
			Odocoileus sp.	deer	5
			Total		**27**
F.51	pit house	Formative	Mammalia/Aves	mammal or bird	10
			Columba fasciata	band-tailed pigeon	1
			Picidae	woodpecker	1
			unknown mammal		5
			small mammal		15
			ungulate-size mammal		9
			Leporidae	jackrabbit or cottontail	3
			Lepus alleni	antelope jackrabbit	1
			Lepus californicus	black-tailed jackrabbit	23
			Sylvilagus sp.	cottontail	1
			Spermophilus sp.	ground squirrel	1
			Odocoileus sp.	deer	3
			Total		**73**
F.51.01	thermal pit	Formative	Mammalia/Aves	mammal or bird	1
			Rodentia	rodent	1
			Total		**2**
F.52	bell pit	Formative	*Lepus californicus*	black-tailed jackrabbit	1
F.53	nonthermal pit	Formative	Mammalia/Aves	mammal or bird	5
F.54	nonthermal pit	Formative	small mammal		5
			ungulate-size mammal		5
			Leporidae	jackrabbit or cottontail	6
			Lepus californicus	black-tailed jackrabbit	2
			Total		**18**
F.57	nonthermal pit	Formative	small mammal		3
			ungulate-size mammal		7
			Lepus californicus	black-tailed jackrabbit	2
			Total		**12**

Table 8.15. Species lists by unit and feature, cont'd.

Unit No.	Type	Affiliation	Taxonomic Name	Common Name	NISP
F.58	bell pit	unknown	small mammal		8
			ungulate-size mammal		3
			Sylvilagus sp.	cottontail	1
			Total		**12**
F.59	bell pit	Formative	small mammal		2
			medium mammal		1
			Lepus californicus	black-tailed jackrabbit	3
			Total		**6**
F.60	roasting pit	unknown	Mammalia/Aves	mammal or bird	1
			unknown mammal		1
			Total		**2**
F.61	thermal pit	Early Formative	Mammalia/Aves	mammal or bird	1
			unknown mammal		1
			Lepus californicus	black-tailed jackrabbit	1
			Total		**3**
F.66	thermal pit	Formative	*Lepus californicus*	black-tailed jackrabbit	1
F.67	bell pit	Formative	ungulate-size mammal		4
			Lepus californicus	black-tailed jackrabbit	2
			Total		**6**
F.71	nonthermal pit	Formative	unknown mammal		1
F.72	thermal pit	Formative	unknown mammal		2
			small mammal		2
			Rodentia	rodent	2
			Dipodomys sp.	kangaroo rat	1
			Total		**7**
F.76	bell pit	unknown	unknown mammal		133
			small mammal		6
			ungulate-size mammal		13
			Lepus alleni	antelope jackrabbit	1
			Canis latrans/ familiaris	coyote or dog	1
			Total		**154**
F.79	nonthermal pit	unknown	unknown mammal		22
			Leporidae	jackrabbit or cottontail	1
			Canis latrans/ familiaris	coyote or dog	2
			Total		**25**

Table 8.15. Species lists by unit and feature, cont'd.

Unit No.	Type	Affiliation	Taxonomic Name	Common Name	NISP
F.87	burial	unknown	*Ammospermophilus harrisi*	Harris' antelope squirrel	1
F.92	burial	Formative	small mammal		1
F.93	nonthermal pit	Formative	unknown mammal		7
			small mammal		1
			ungulate-size mammal		2
			Total		**10**
F.95	roasting pit	unknown	unknown mammal		14
			small mammal		1
			ungulate-size mammal		6
			Lepus alleni	antelope jackrabbit	1
			Lepus californicus	black-tailed jackrabbit	1
			Rodentia	rodent	2
			Artiodactyla	even-toed ungulate	2
			Total		**27**
F.97	nonthermal pit	Formative	*Lepus californicus*	black-tailed jackrabbit	3
F.98	bell pit	Early Agricultural	unknown mammal		1
			small mammal		60
			ungulate-size mammal		10
			Lepus californicus	black-tailed jackrabbit	4
			Sylvilagus sp.	cottontail	2
			Total		**77**
F.102	bell pit	unknown	Mammalia/Aves	mammal or bird	1
			unknown mammal		2
			small mammal		13
			Ungulate-size mammal		1
			Leporidae	jackrabbit or cottontail	1
			Lepus californicus	black-tailed jackrabbit	10
			Sylvilagus sp.	cottontail	3
			Total		**31**
F.105	nonthermal pit	Early Agricultural	unknown mammal		3
F.107	nonthermal pit	Formative	unknown mammal		4
			small mammal		2
			ungulate-size mammal		5
			Total		**11**

Table 8.15. Species lists by unit and feature, cont'd.

Unit No.	Type	Affiliation	Taxonomic Name	Common Name	NISP
F.109	bell pit	Formative	medium bird		1
			unknown mammal		70
			medium mammal		20
			Lepus californicus	black-tailed jackrabbit	4
			Canis latrans/familiaris	coyote or dog	44
			Total		**139**
F.111	nonthermal pit	unknown	ungulate-size mammal		1
F.112	nonthermal pit	Early Formative	small mammal		17
			ungulate-size mammal		1
			Sciuridae	squirrels and chipmunks	1
			Lepus sp.	jackrabbit	3
			Total		**22**
F.113	nonthermal pit	unknown	Small mammal		1
F.117	nonthermal pit	Formative	unknown mammal		3
			small mammal		2
			Total		**5**
F.118	thermal pit	Formative	small mammal		5
			small mammal		2
			Leporidae	jackrabbit or cottontail	1
			Total		**8**
F.119	nonthermal pit	Formative	unknown mammal		2
			ungulate-size mammal		1
			Rodentia	rodent	3
			Odocoileus hemionus	mule deer	1
			Odocoileus sp.	deer	1
			Total		**8**
F.129	bell pit	unknown	unknown mammal		9
			small mammal		10
			ungulate-size mammal		3
			Total		**22**
F.136	nonthermal pit	Formative	unknown mammal		1
			ungulate-size mammal		2
			Total		**3**

Table 8.15. Species lists by unit and feature, cont'd.

Unit No.	Type	Affiliation	Taxonomic Name	Common Name	NISP
F.139	bell pit	unknown	unknown mammal		17
			small mammal		26
			ungulate-size mammal		1
			Lepus sp.	jackrabbit	4
			Lepus alleni	antelope jackrabbit	5
			Lepus californicus	black-tailed jackrabbit	4
			Sylvilagus sp.	cottontail	1
			Total		**58**
F.141	nonthermal pit	Formative	unknown mammal		1
F.149	nonthermal pit	unknown	ungulate-size mammal		4
F.152	pit house	Formative	Lacertilia	lizard	1
			Mammalia/Aves	mammal or bird	1
			Columbidae	dove or pigeon	1
			unknown mammal		5
			small mammal		233
			ungulate-size mammal		4
			Leporidae	jackrabbit or cottontail	4
			Lepus sp.	jackrabbit	12
			Lepus californicus	black-tailed jackrabbit	13
			Sylvilagus sp.	cottontail	34
			Rodentia	rodent	2
			Sciuridae	squirrels and chipmunks	1
			Neotoma albigula	white-throated woodrat	2
			Odocoileus hemionus	mule deer	1
			Total		**314**
F.152.12	hearth	Formative	small mammal		1
F.165	bell pit	unknown	Mammalia/Aves	mammal or bird	2
F.173	bell pit	Formative	Mammalia/Aves	mammal or bird	4
			unknown mammal		10
			small mammal		7
			ungulate-size mammal		2
			Leporidae	jackrabbit or cottontail	1
			Lepus californicus	black-tailed jackrabbit	4
			Sylvilagus sp.	cottontail	2
			Total		**30**

Table 8.15. Species lists by unit and feature, cont'd.

Unit No.	Type	Affiliation	Taxonomic Name	Common Name	NISP
TU 3			small mammal		4
			unknown mammal		5
			Total		**9**
TU 6			small mammal		2
			ungulate-size mammal		3
			unknown mammal		5
			Total		**10**
TU 15			small mammal		1
TU 18			*Lepus californicus*	black-tailed jackrabbit	1
			small mammal		1
			Total		**2**
TU 19			ungulate-size mammal		1
TU 20			small mammal		1
			unknown mammal		1
			Total		**2**
TU 23			unknown mammal		14
			Lepus sp.	jackrabbit	1
			small mammal		5
			ungulate-size mammal		1
			Total		**21**
TU 24			ungulate-size mammal		2
			unknown mammal		1
			Total		**3**
TU 27			ungulate-size mammal		4
TU 34			ungulate-size mammal		9
TU 35			ungulate-size mammal		5
TU 36			*Lepus alleni*	antelope jackrabbit	2
			Lepus sp.	jackrabbit	3
			Sciuridae	squirrels and chipmunks	1
			small mammal		21
			Ovis canadensis	bighorn sheep	4
			unknown mammal		7
			Total		**38**
TU 40			small mammal		7
			ungulate-size mammal		1
			unknown mammal		1
			Total		**9**

Table 8.15. Species lists by unit and feature, cont'd.

Unit No.	Type	Affiliation	Taxonomic Name	Common Name	NISP
TU 41			ungulate-size mammal		3
			unknown mammal		18
			small mammal		2
			Lepus californicus	black-tailed jackrabbit	1
			Sylvilagus sp.	cottontail	1
			Total		**25**
TU 43			small mammal		1
TU 45			*Lepus californicus*	black-tailed jackrabbit	1
TU 47			ungulate-size mammal		4
			Leporidae	jackrabbit or cottontail	1
			small mammal		1
			unknown mammal		29
			Total		**35**
TU 50			unknown mammal		9
TU 51			*Lepus californicus*	black-tailed jackrabbit	1
TU 52			*Felis rufus*	bobcat	1
			small mammal		1
			Total		**2**
TU 53			ungulate-size mammal		4
			unknown mammal		13
			Bos taurus	cattle	1
			Rodentia	rodent	1
			Sylvilagus sp.	cottontail	3
			Total		**22**
TU 55			small mammal		1
TU 59			Leporidae	jackrabbit or cottontail	1
			Odocoileus sp.	deer	1
			unknown mammal		11
			Total		**13**
TU 60			*Odocoileus* sp.	deer	1
			Lepus sp.	jackrabbit	1
			Total		**2**
TU 61			Leporidae	jackrabbit or cottontail	1
TU 62			Mammalia/Aves	mammal or bird	2

Table 8.15. Species lists by unit and feature, cont'd.

Unit No.	Type	Affiliation	Taxonomic Name	Common Name	NISP
TU 64			ungulate-size mammal		8
			unknown mammal		17
			Lepus sp.	jackrabbit	1
			small mammal		1
			Total		**27**
TU 67			*Lepus californicus*	black-tailed jackrabbit	2
TU 68			unknown mammal		5
			small mammal		5
			ungulate-size mammal		1
			Total		**11**
TU 72			*Ammospermophilus harrisi*	Harris' antelope squirrel	3
			Rodentia	rodent	1
			Total		**4**
TU 73			small mammal		1
			unknown mammal		1
			Total		**2**
TU 75			ungulate-size mammal		5
			unknown mammal		3
			Canis latrans/ familiaris	coyote or dog	1
			Lepus sp.	jackrabbit	1
			small mammal		2
			Total		**12**
TU 78			unknown mammal		1
			ungulate-size mammal		2
			small mammal		2
			Total		**5**
TU 79			small mammal		1
			unknown mammal		2
			Total		**3**
TU 92			*Lepus californicus*	black-tailed jackrabbit	2
			small mammal		2
			ungulate-size mammal		1
			unknown mammal		4
			Total		**9**
TU 97			Invertebrata	invertebrate	1

Table 8.15. Species lists by unit and feature, cont'd.

Unit No.	Type	Affiliation	Taxonomic Name	Common Name	NISP
TU 106			small mammal		1
TU 111			ungulate-size mammal		3
TU 112			*Geococcyx californianus*	roadrunner	1
TU 127			ungulate-size mammal		1
TU 128			*Canis latrans/ familiaris*	coyote or dog	1
			unknown mammal		3
			Total		**4**
TU 129			unknown mammal		1
			small mammal		1
			Total		**2**
TU 130			small mammal		4
			unknown mammal		1
			Total		**5**
TU 131			ungulate-size mammal		3
TU 137			small mammal		2
			ungulate-size mammal		1
			Total		**3**
TU 142			ungulate-size mammal		4
TU 143			ungulate-size mammal		4
			unknown mammal		9
			Total		**13**
TU 147			ungulate-size mammal		4
			unknown mammal		2
			Total		**6**
TU 152			unknown mammal		1
TU 153			ungulate-size mammal		1
TU 156			*Canis latrans/ familiaris*	coyote or dog	1
TU 158			*Bos taurus*	cattle	3
			ungulate-size mammal		3
			Sylvilagus sp.	cottontail	1
			Sigmodontinae	New World mice and rats	2
			Sylvilagus audubonii	desert cottontail	1
			Total		**10**
TU 162			*Gallus gallus*	chicken	1

Table 8.15. Species lists by unit and feature, cont'd.

Unit No.	Type	Affiliation	Taxonomic Name	Common Name	NISP
TU 163			*Bos taurus*	cattle	2
			unknown mammal		1
			Total		**3**
TU 169			small mammal		1
TU 171			*Lepus californicus*	black-tailed jackrabbit	1
			small mammal		3
			Mammalia/Aves	mammal or bird	1
			Total		**5**
SA 3			*Bos taurus*	cattle	2
			small mammal		3
			Total		**5**
SA 4			ungulate-size mammal		20
			Bos taurus	cattle	5
			Total		**25**
SU 16			Passeriformes	perching bird	1
			unknown mammal		8
			Total		**9**

ENDNOTE FOR CHAPTER 8

[1] Fifty pieces of worked and unworked shell were recovered from the Marsh Station Road site; however, this bracelet fragment was inadvertently not separated from the faunal bone material recovered in a flotation sample, and therefore was initially analyzed as faunal material. This bracelet fragment, as well as all other shell recovered from the Marsh Station Road site, is discussed in Chapter 9 of this volume.

Chapter 9
Shell Artifacts

Christine H. Virden-Lange

Shell artifacts were recovered during excavations at the Marsh Station Road site (AZ EE:2:44 [ASM]), located near the confluence of Cienega Creek and Mescal Wash. Forty marine shell artifacts and three intrusive freshwater snails were recovered from collection units, test units, and features, and twelve specimens of freshwater shell were recovered from the heavy fractions of flotation samples. The freshwater shell includes *Anodonta californiensis, Succinea luteola, Succinea* sp., *Rumina decollate, Pisidium, Hawaiia,* and *Helisoma,* all of which are present in the local environment. Only *Anodonta* has been utilized in prehistoric contexts, therefore the remaining specimens probably are not culturally significant. Although the collections recovered from the site is small, there are several unique items of personal adornment in the assemblage, described below.

METHODOLOGY

Each specimen was examined visually using a 10x (power) hand lens, and a detailed record was developed that included a written description of the artifacts, photographs or illustrations where appropriate, and a set of linear measurements. Attributes recorded included condition, shape, decorative motifs and technological features, and diameters of perforations. The measurements were obtained through the use of a digital vernier caliper, and were recorded to the nearest hundredth of a millimeter. When possible, the relative completeness of the artifact was estimated. For ornaments, if a full set of linear measurements could be obtained, it was considered to be complete. For fragmented material, the completeness estimate represents the percentage of the original valve that is present. Fragments that could be re-fitted were considered to be a single occurrence with the number of fragments recorded. In some cases, shell fragments that did not re-fit but displayed similar morphological characteristics were considered as probably coming from the same shell. This occurred frequently in the case of *A. californiensis*, a freshwater clam that is extremely brittle when the shell is dried out and tends to fracture into many small pieces. For all ornament types, the use of the artifact was evaluated where appropriate by determining if it was the primary use (the original or first use of the artifact), or the secondary use. In other words, was it designed for a particular use but then reused or redesigned for a different task (Adams 1997)? For example, occasionally a broken *Glycymeris* bracelet will be reworked into another form, such as a needle or pendant.

The classification structure used is largely based upon that developed by Gladwin and Haury for the shell material from Snaketown (Haury 1937b; 1976). Shell identifications to genus and, if possible, to species for the marine shell were made in accordance with Keen (1971), while the freshwater specimens were identified using Bequaert and Miller (1973), Cheatum and Fullington (1971), and Drake (1959). Definitions of the terminology used in the descriptions relating to the structural elements of the shell that were employed during the analysis as well as useful descriptive illustrations can be found in glossaries available in books by Keen (1971) and Brusca (1980).

SOURCES OF MARINE SHELL

Marine shell obtained by the prehistoric people of southern Arizona derived mainly from the Gulf of California, a northern finger of the tropical Panamic province, with a few specimens originating off the coast of southern California. The Gulf of California is a unique area where, from the south, the warm waters of the southern Panamic California current meet cooler waters from the north off the western coast of the Baja Peninsula, near Magdalena Bay, converging before they turn out to sea. These contrasting currents form two distinct biotic communities or zones, both of which have been utilized as sources of shell by the Hohokam. However, many species of shell occur in only one of these zones or may have a restricted distribution and relative frequency in the other (Brusca 1980:18; Keen 1971:55). As summarized by Howard (1993:336) in her discussion of the Hohokam shell assemblage at Shelltown and the Hind site, many researchers have suggested that the Hohokam acquired their Panamic shell specimens from along the northern Sonoran Coast, particularly from Adair Bay, and within it the smaller Cholla Bay, near Puerto Peñasco (Rocky Point), within the northern Gulf region (Haury 1976; Hayden 1972). Hayden (1972:78, 81) also identified this area, as well as the coastal regions to the south of Puerto Penasco, as a probable source of Hohokam shell. Trails and petroglyphs of shells in the area, especially around the Sierra Pinacate, support this proposal (Hayden 1972:78).

The *Glycymeris* (da Costa 1778), often used by the Hohokam, is a type of clam with a shell that is sturdy and porcelaneous in texture and is usually fairly symmetrical in shape. They usually occur offshore, with single valves of white, dead shells fairly common in beach drift. The species are differentiated by brown patterns on the shell exterior and by size, with *G. gigantea* being larger than *G. maculata*. *G. gigantea* seems to be confined to the Gulf of California area from Bahia Magdalena, Baja California, to Acapulco, Mexico (Reeve 1843), while *G. maculata* is found from the northern part of the Gulf of California and Bahia Magdalena, Baja California, to Zorritos, Peru (Broderip 1832). The Hohokam appeared to have collected beach-drift *Glycymeris* shells, selected by size, for particular ornaments such as bracelets, ring/pendants, and small whole-shell beads.

While most of the marine shell recovered from Hohokam sites seemingly originates from the Gulf of California, one marine shell, *Haliotis* spp., only lives in the coastal waters off the coast of California. *Haliotis,* a nacreous mollusk commonly known as abalone, was one of two shell types (the other being *Pteria sterna,* which is found in the Gulf of California) that were favored by the Hohokam for the manufacturing of special ornaments.

SOURCES OF NON-MARINE SHELL

In southern Arizona, local rivers, such as the San Pedro, Santa Cruz, and Gila rivers, would have provided a secondary, non-marine source for procuring shell, whether for ornament manufacture or as a source of protein. The freshwater pelecypod or bivalve known as *A. californiensis* is one of the most commonly occurring freshwater shell species in Hohokam assemblages. Although this species was once native to most of the permanent rivers and streams in Arizona prior to the development of water retention devices (dams) that occurred during the early part of the twentieth century, *A. californiensis* is now restricted to the upper Black River and other streams in the White Mountains as it survives only in association with a certain species of host fish, which over time is being lost (Bequaert and Miller 1973:220–223). Based on the frequencies of shell recovered from prehistoric sites in the Phoenix Basin and Salt River drainage area, as well as from the Tucson Basin, archaeologists believe that mollusks such as *A. californiensis* were harvested from the rivers and canals as a food source in prehistoric times and served as a raw material for ornament manufacture (Bequaert and Miller 1973:221; Haury 1976:306; Schroeder and Virden 1994:189; Vokes 1988:373). *A. californiensis* is very nacreous on the interior of the valve, which made it popular among consumers of shell ornaments who did not have access to *Haliotis*. However, the shell becomes particularly fragile and brittle when dried; in order to reduce breakage, local artisans would have collected fresh specimens for ornament manufacture so that the shell could be cut when it was still green and pliable. According to Haury (1976:308), *A. californiensis* is more frequently recovered at Hohokam sites than either *Haliotis* or *P. sterna*, probably due to the difficulty in obtaining adequate supplies of raw material

for ornament manufacturing from more distant environments.

SHELL MATERIAL FROM THE MARSH STATION ROAD SITE (AZ EE:2:44[ASM])

The shell material recovered during excavations at the Marsh Station Road site (AZ EE:2:44 [ASM]) includes 35 artifacts representing 22 identifiable, finished, formal ornaments (62.9 percent); 3 pieces that were in the process of production when they broke (8.6 percent); 2 bracelets reworked into another form (5.7 percent); 5 worked fragments (14.3 percent); and 3 unmodified fragments (8.6 percent) (Table 9.1). Eight shell species and five ornament forms were identified in the assemblage (see Table 9.1). Bracelets, fragments or in-process, manufactured from *G. sp.* valves dominate the collection with 57.1 percent of the artifacts. The remaining artifacts were distributed between a cut-shell pendant (2.9 percent), beads (8.6 percent), ring/pendants (5.7 percent), and an in-process ring (2.9 percent) manufactured from several different shell species. All of the shell artifacts were recovered from non-mortuary contexts including test units, feature excavations, and heavy fraction flotation samples from feature excavations.

Identified Shell Species in the Artifact Assemblage

As mentioned above, eight shell species—seven marine species and one freshwater species—were identified in the Marsh Station Road assemblage (see Table 9.1). The marine shell species are all available from the Gulf of California and include six marine pelecypods—juvenile *Glycymeris* sp., *G. gigantea, L. elatum, Pecten vogdesi, and Argopecten circularis*—and one marine gastropod—*Nassarius* as well as an indeterminate gastropod. In addition, a

Table 9.1. Shell artifacts summarized by artifact form and genus.

Genus	Cut Pendant	Disk Bead	Whole Shell Bead	Bracelet	In-process	Re-worked	Ring/Pendant	In-process	Worked	Un-worked	Total (%)
Marine Shell											
Anodonta californiensis	1								1		2 (4)
Glycymeris sp.				16	2	2	2	1			23(46)
Glycymeris gigantea										1	1 (2)
Laevicardium elatum	1	1							2	1	5 (10)
Nassarius			1								1 (2)
Pecten vogdesi										1	1 (2)
Argopecten circularis									1		1 (2)
Indeterminate gastropod			1								1 (2)
Freshwater Shell											
Succinea luteola										2	2 (4)
Succinea sp.										3	3 (6)
Pisidium										2	2 (4)
Rumina decollata										1	1 (2)
Hawaiia										1	1 (2)
Heliosoma										1	1 (2)
Indeterminate											
Gastropod										2	2 (4)
Fragment										3	3 (6)
Total	2	1	2	16	2	2	2	1	4	18	50
(%)	(4)	(2)	(4)	(32)	(4)	(4)	(4)	(2)	(8)	(36)	(100)

single cut-shell ornament was manufactured from *A. californiensis*, a locally available freshwater bivalve.

Glycymeris is the most abundant marine genera in the assemblage, which is primarily a reflection of its use in the manufacture of bracelets: the thicker, more robust *Glycymeris* held up better when used for bracelet manufacturing than did other shell types. In the Marsh Station Road assemblage, this genus is represented by specimens identified as *G.* sp and *G. gigantea*. Both *G.* sp. and *G. gigantea* derive from and are restricted to the warmer waters of the Gulf of California, and both common on the beach today, as they likely would have been prehistorically. Specimens, which include white beach-drift shells (i.e., dead shells) as well as those retaining some of their natural brownish coloration, were selected by size for the manufacturing of bracelets and ring/pendants.

L. elatum is another bivalve that is present in larger numbers in the collection. This shell is a large Pacific cockle which can attain lengths exceeding 150 mm, and is a light yellow color when fresh. It has morphological characteristics—a thin shell with flattened side panels and distinctive vertical ribs that are flat and relatively evenly spaced across the broad back of the shell—that aid in identifying the shell when present in a collection as smaller fragments. This valve is frequently used for carved shell ornaments such as pendants and beads, although it has also been used as a container (Nelson 1991). The northern range of this species extends along the west coast of California and Baja California (Keen 1971:160), although it does not appear to be as common in these colder waters as it is in the Panamic province in the Gulf of California, where the *Laevicardium* valves present in the current artifact assemblage most likely originated.

P. vogdesi and *A. circularis* are bivalves that are represented as single occurrences in the collection. They are both members of the *Pectinidae* family (scallops), and prefer the warm waters of the Gulf of California (Keen 1971). They are found at the extreme low tide zone and in offshore sand. Both of these species are thin-walled valves that have distinct ribs on the exterior of the shell as well as remarkable coloration when fresh. The identification of the various *Pecten* species is frequently based on the colored patterns on the exterior of the shell; thus, if the specimen is fragmented, very small, or is bleached/beach drift, the colored patterns will be missing, making it difficult to assign the shell to a particular species. In prehistoric times, these particular mollusks were utilized as whole shell beads and pendants by simply abrading or drilling a perforation near the hinge area. Smaller shells would be employed as beads, while larger shells were used as pendants.

Nassarius, or basket shells, have a distinctive sculpture which is apt to be cancellate with a tapering spire and rounded aperture. This gastropod tends to be small, and was typically employed as a whole shell bead. *Nassarius* coloration is usually pale brown to white, with some displaying banding. Some species also display axial and spiral ribs with beading.

Non-Artifact Shell Species in the Assemblage

A total of 13 freshwater snails and 2 clam shells were recovered during excavations and from the heavy fractions of processed flotation samples from features including the fill of nonthermal pits, bell pits, pit house structural and floor fill, and from overburden. The shell identified includes *Succinea luteola, Rumina decollate, Pisidium, Hawaiia, and Helisoma* as well as indeterminate fragmented shell (see Table 9.1). All but the *Pisidium* are land and terrestrial snails; *Pisidium* is a small aquatic bivalve. These mollusks require particular environments: grassland and/or moderate vegetation cover or shallow water such as ponds, marsh land, and/or a slow moving stream habitat (Drake 1959:146), and as a result, are often used as environmental indicators. Their occurrence at the Marsh Station Road site is probably the result of flooding of Cienega Creek or of ponding due to heavy rains. One specimen of *Succinea* was collected from floor fill while two others were recovered from disturbed contexts, but these are probably incidental occurrences. These particular freshwater snails and clams are not usually of cultural importance, and their presence in the prehistoric features is probably fortuitous and not a result of cultural activity. Therefore, these freshwater noncultural shells will not be discussed further in this report.

Finished Artifacts

The bulk of the Marsh Station Road assemblage was comprised of finished ornaments of personal adornment or worked fragments, with only 8.6 percent identified as unworked fragments. These ornaments fell into five categories: pendants, bracelets, ring/pendants, and beads (two types). Two other artifacts had been reworked from bracelets for a secondary function. One reworked bracelet became a carved pendant, while another had been seg-

mented for an indeterminate function (possibly gaming pieces).

Beads

Three beads representing two different styles of bead were recovered during excavations. Whole shell beads are probably the simplest bead form to manufacture, as all an artisan needs to do is perforate the shell by simply grinding it on something abrasive until the shell has a hole worn through it, punching a hole through the outer lip of the aperture, or drilling a small perforation using a stone drill. A whole shell bead (FN 44-3399.01) was manufactured from a *Nassarius* shell by punching a perforation in the outer lip, opposite the aperture, for stringing (Figure 9.1a). The valve measures 6.55 mm in length; the diameter of the perforation measures 1.76 mm. The apex of the spire on this small gastropod had broken off. A second whole shell bead was manufactured from an unidentifiable small gastropod that measured 4.5 mm in length. The apex of the spire was missing, and there were natural holes in the outer lip that were utilized for stringing.

The second style of bead is a disk bead, manufactured from an unidentifiable white

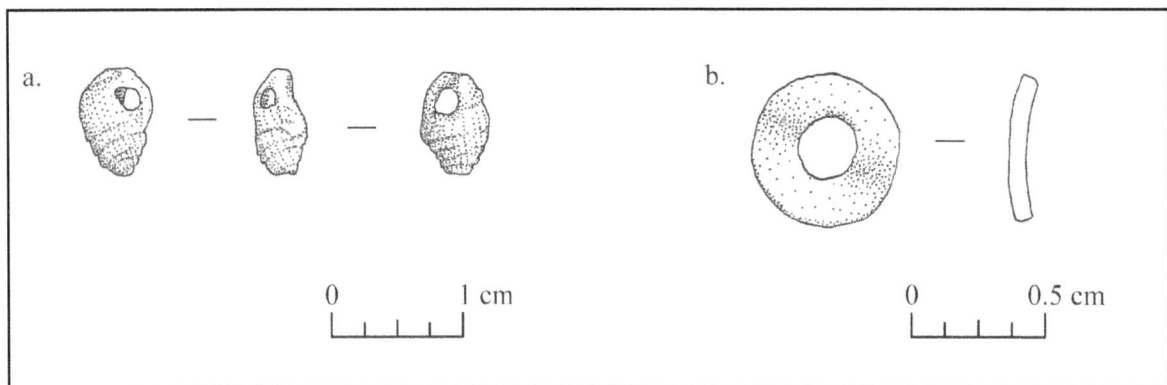

Figure 9.1. Two shell beads recovered from the Marsh Station Road site: (a) a whole shell bead manufactured from Nassarius *shell (FN 44-3399.01), and (b) a disk bead manufactured from an unidentifiable shell species (FN 44-3103).*

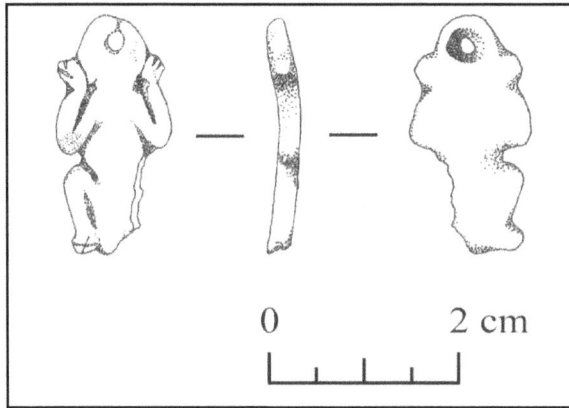

Figure 9.2. The only identifiable pendant—a stylized lizard cut-shell pendant (FN 44-1433)—recovered from the Marsh Station Road site.

marine shell species. During the manufacturing process of disk beads, most of the morphological characteristics used to identify shell to genus are lost. However, most of the white shell beads in the prehistoric archaeological record were made from marine bivalve shells such as *Glycymeris* or *L. elatum*, although *Dosinia* was also sometimes used. The disk bead (FN 44-3103) is a donut-style bead, where the sides are wide in plan view but thin in profile (Figure 9.1b). The perforation for suspension is also larger than what is seen in the smaller disk beads, the outer diameter measuring 5.69 mm and the inner diameter measuring 0.58 mm.

Pendants

Only one identifiable pendant—a cut-shell pendant (FN 44-1433) manufactured from *L. elatum*—was present in the assemblage (Figure 9.2). The motif on the pendant is that of a stylized lizard about three-quarters complete; a portion of the pendant broke away sometime in the past. The lizard measures 26.81 mm in length, 12.85 mm in width, and 2.71 mm in thickness. The pendant was cut from the back of the valve and has a slight curvature on the interior side. The exterior growth ribs of the valve run horizontally across the lizard's back. The lizard body is elongated, with a rounded

head. All four legs are bent and close to the body, and the toes and legs have been incised to show relief. Due to the pendant breakage, both the tail and the right back leg are missing. Detail is shown on the interior surface only, suggesting it was worn with the exterior of the valve next to the body. The belly is slightly diamond-shaped due to the incising of the front and back legs. The perforation was conically drilled from the exterior side of the shell and is slightly off-set in the head end of the pendant so that the lizard hangs tail-down. All edges of the pendant have been ground and smoothed, with some grinding striations still visible on the interior edges.

A fragment of *A. californiensis* that has been worked and exhibits part of a perforated edge may represent a pendant as well, but is discussed with the fragmented material as not enough shell remains to make a positive identification.

Bracelets

Bracelets manufactured from *Glycymeris* sp. valves were the most abundant ornament type of the collection (n = 20). Of this total, only one band had been decorated, two were in the process of manufacture, and two pieces had been reworked into other forms. Band treatment was similar for most of the fragments, and consisted of grinding down the back of the valve to create a facet along one edge. For the most part, the natural outer margins were retained, creating band cross-sections that were low-triangular to triangular (from the natural outer margin), with an occasional vertical rectangular profile. Inner edge treatment, which consisted of grinding and smoothing of the edge, was similar for most pieces. Only two dorsal fragments have umbones present, one of which was perforated by means of oblique grinding on the back of the umbo, producing a circular perforation with irregular inner edges. Haury (1976:313) suggested that the purpose of the perforated umbo may have been to attach small objects such as feathers that would be suspended from the band. Others feel they may have been sewn onto clothing or suspended as pendants.

Band widths were slightly variable, ranging from 2.4 to 7.68 mm, with a mean value of 4.86 mm. Band thickness ranged from 3.56 to 8.06 mm, with a mean value of 4.65 mm. For a band diameter to be measurable, approximately 25 percent of the band needs to be present. The band diameters were fairly consistent, ranging from 44 to 60 mm, with a mean value of 45.12 mm. Only one band fragment had been burned and one exhibited worm damage; a few fragments exhibited weathering, with the remaining specimens in good condition. The band widths at the Marsh Station Road site fall into the three bracelet styles as defined by Haury (1937b:142; 1976:313). The majority of the bands (n = 14) were between 4 and 6 mm in width, which would place them within Haury's Type 2 style or medium-width band, while one is smaller (Type 1 band) and one fragment is larger, placing it in the Type 3 or wide-band category. Chronologically, the Marsh Station Road bracelets are characteristic of those found in the Sedentary and possibly into the early Classic periods (Haury 1976:313).

Two band fragments had umbones present that exhibited different styles of treatment. The first band fragment (FN 44-2841) is a dorsal-margin fragment with one side margin, including the umbo, attached (Figure 9.3a). The umbo had been reduced by grinding to a rounded tab and was not perforated. The band is small, thin, and well-polished, with the hinge teeth ground down and a horizontal rectangular cross section. The band diameter is projected to measure 52 mm in diameter. A second band fragment (FN 44-3335) is a dorsal-margin with an umbo present that is natural except for the ground back of the band (Figure 9.3b). A small hole was created as a result of oblique grinding.

The exterior treatment consisted of grinding and polishing, with no facets visible. The inner edge was ground smooth and polished, creating a double-faceted triangular cross section of the band. The fragment was too small to try to determine band diameter.

All of the band fragments were of the plain variety except for one (FN 44-1235; Figure 9.3c) from Feature 19, a roasting pit. It was a side- and ventral-margin fragment that had the exterior of the band ground flat, with the outer margin reduced to almost vertical to create a flat surface. The inner edge had been ground to vertical, smoothed, and polished, creating a squared cross section for the band. The design was incised on the outer flat surface of the band, and when worn, would have been visible on the band surface. The design consisted of a series of nine groups of incised lines that were crossed like Xs to create a pattern. It probably took several strokes of a sharp stone tool to create each incised line, as there is visible evidence of slippage. The distance between the Xs was slightly variable. It is not known how far around the band this pattern extended, but almost 50 percent of the band is represented, with a probable diameter of 52 mm. The incised design may have represented segments of a snake, which was a common motif utilized by the Hohokam.

Reworked Bracelets

A ventral- and side-margin fragment of a bracelet (FN 44-3621) was remodeled into a pendant with a snake motif (Figure 9.3d). The natural crenulations had been ground smooth but were still visible, while the inner edge was smooth and polished. There was a break at the ventral-margin end which had been smoothed but was still slightly irregular. The broken end of the side margin had been ground down to taper, creating a tip or a tail. Seven lines were incised across the margin of the band to create a segmented tail of a snake. A perforation for suspension, measuring 1.95 mm in diameter, was drilled at the ventral-margin end so that it represents the head of the snake; thus the tail would have hung down. The piece represents about 40 percent of a band, with a projected diameter of 52 mm. The pendant would have been suspended with the exterior side to the body as the incised tail is on the interior of the valve.

A *Glycymeris* bracelet fragment (FN 44-2780) had been reworked after breakage.

The fragment, consisting of a ventral-, dorsal-, and side-margin piece, had been segmented into five pieces using the groove, cut, and snap method of manufacturing. The ends had been partially smoothed on the edges, leaving a "lip" in the center that had not been totally removed. The segments resemble small pegs and may have been used as gaming pieces or bead blanks of some sort. The lengths are slightly variable, ranging from 11.43 to 14.07 mm, with a mean of 12.76 mm. Grinding striations and facets are still visible on the pieces.

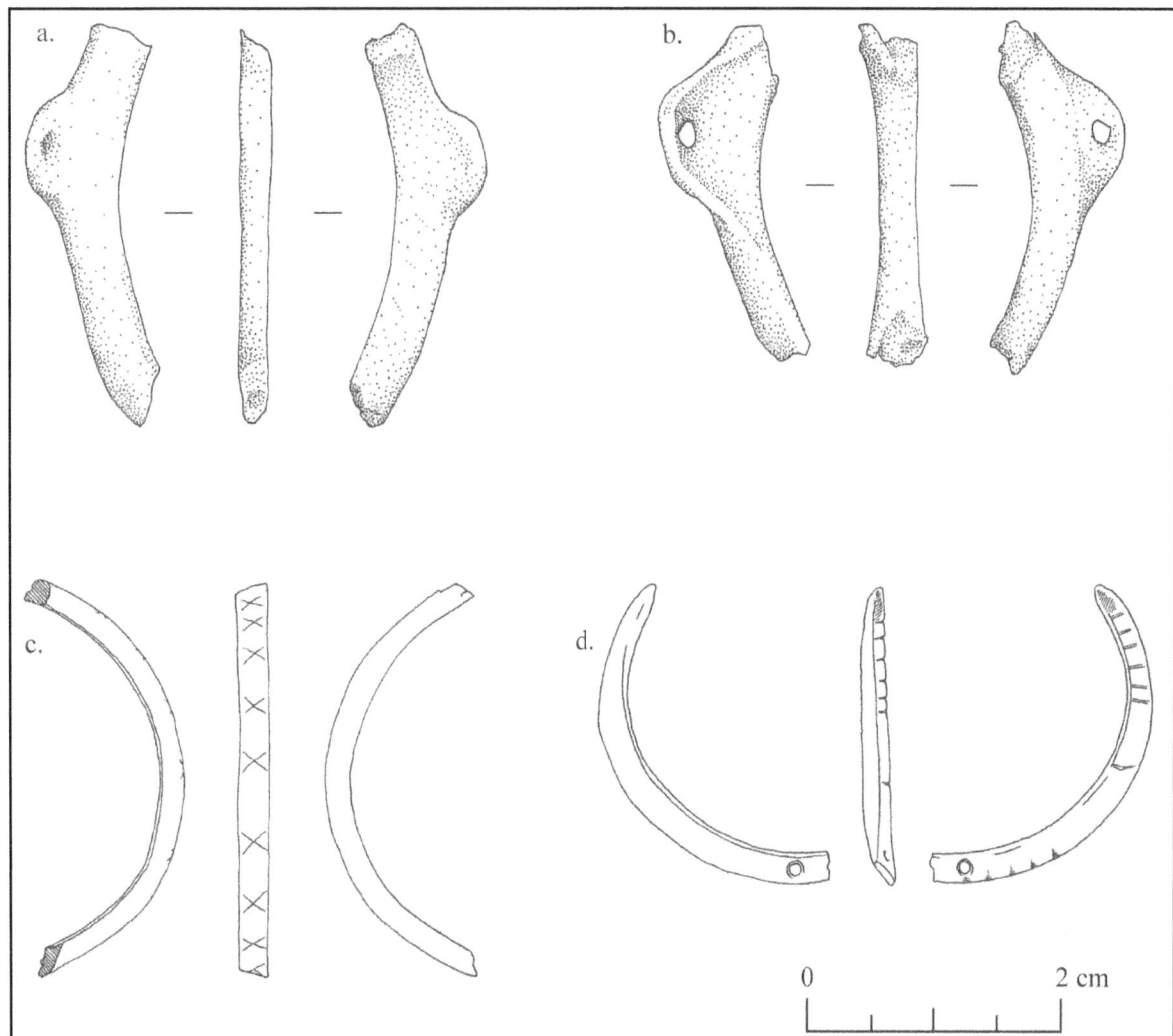

Figure 9.3. Four bracelet fragments in the Marsh Station Road site assemblage: (a) FN 44-2841, (b) FN 44-3335, (c) 44-1235, and (d) 44-3621. Both (a) and (b) have umbones exhibiting different styles of treatment. The bracelet illustrated in (c) is the only decorated bracelet in the assemblage, and the bracelet illustrated in (d) was remodeled into a pendant with a snake motif.

Ring/Pendant

Two ring/pendant fragments manufactured from juvenile *Glycymeris* valves were collected during excavations. The first (FN 44-2557) is a side/dorsal-margin fragment with an umbo included, and the second (FN 44-3391) is a side-margin fragment. The band treatment for both specimens is similar to that of bracelets, but was different for both. The umbo of FN 44-2557 is natural, except for flat grinding on the back of the band which resulted in a small perforation (Figure 9.4a). Some natural coloring is still present on the back of the umbo. The inner edge and exterior treatment for this specimen created a faceted triangular cross section for the band. About 25 percent of the band is represented, with a projected diameter of 18 mm.

The band treatment for FN 44-3391 was different in that the exterior of the valve was reduced by grinding to nearly vertical with the inner edge ground smooth and polished (Figure 9.4b). This treatment created a narrow, thin, flat band with a projected diameter of 18 mm.

Manufacturing Evidence

There is limited evidence present reflecting the efforts by the local craftspeople to supply some of the demands for shell ornaments, even though the sample size is small. Two in-process *Glycymeris* bracelet fragments (FN 44-21 and FN 44-2591) were collected from the site. Both fragments exhibited grinding on the back of the valve to reduce it while the outer margin was left in its natural state, thereby creating a low-faceted triangular cross section for the bands. The inner edge had been chipped and some initial grinding had taken place on both specimens; however, the grinding was not finished.

An in-process ring/pendant (FN 44-3399) was also present in the collection (Figure 9.5).

This was an almost whole juvenile *Glycymeris* valve. The back of the valve was partially reduced by grinding until perforated, leaving an incomplete platform and the inner edge was still irregular. The valve broke at the umbo during the reduction process, and was discarded.

Fragmentary Material

Shell fragments that are worked but are too incomplete to be classified, or fragments that lack any evidence of being worked, are not uncommon in Hohokam assemblages. These remnants may be the result of the fragmentation of finished artifacts, local manufacturing activities, or the accidental breakage of whole, unworked valves. There is some evidence for on-site production of ornaments at the Marsh Station Road site: several partially completed artifacts were recovered from the site (see above discussion), as was a lapstone that may have been used in the manufacture of shell ornaments (see Chapter 7). While this evidence suggests that shell manufacturing did occur at the site, the evidence is limited. It seems more likely that most of the fragmented material recovered from the Marsh Station Road site derived from accidental breakage of finished artifacts. Eight fragments of shell were collected from non-mortuary contexts, five of which exhibit worked edges and may be ornaments that fragmented. Unfortunately, not enough of the artifacts remain in order to make a positive determination.

Worked Shell Fragments

In most shell assemblages, there are worked fragments present that, due to a lack of diagnostic features, cannot be assigned to a specific artifact category. These fragments generally have one or two worked facets or edges suggesting they originally may have been part of a finished ornament.

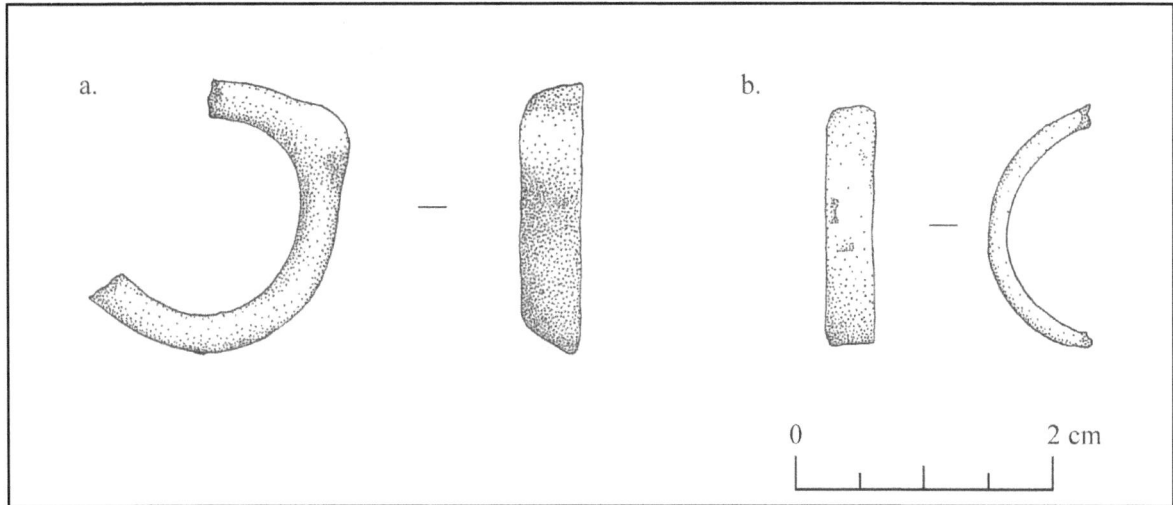

Figure 9.4. Two ring/pendant fragments recovered from the Marsh Station Road site: (a) FN 44-2557, and (b) FN 44-3391; both were manufactured from juvenile Glycymeris valves.

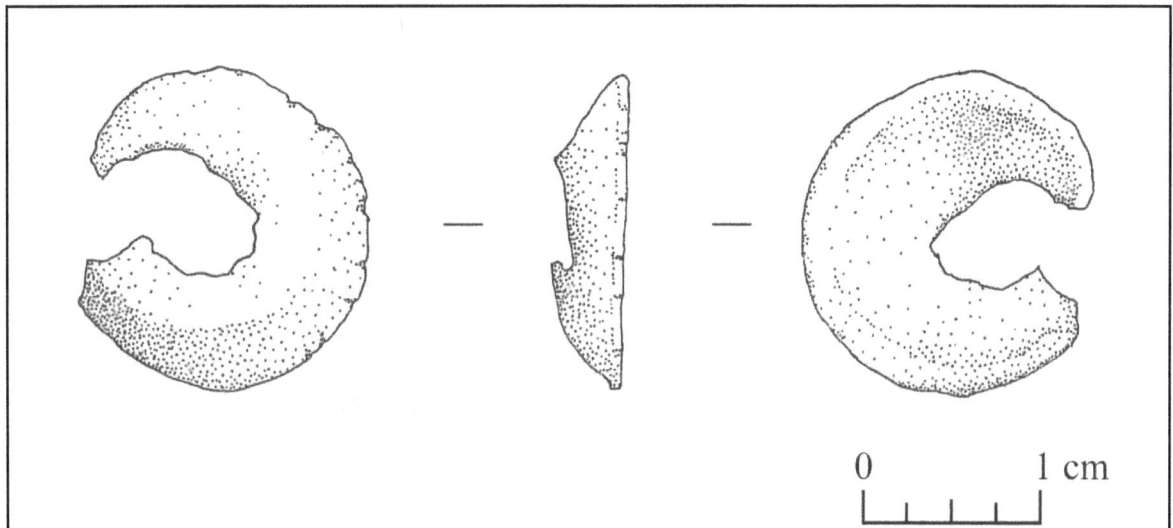

Figure 9.5. A partially completed ring/pendant (FN 44-3399) recovered from the Marsh Station Road site. This artifact is one of a handful of shell artifacts in the assemblage that provide evidence for shell ornament manufacture at the site. FN 44-3391; both were manufactured from juvenile Glycymeris valves.

FN 44-2159 consists of two fragments of *A. californiensis* that refit. The upper edge has been cut and ground smooth, and a partial perforation is also present. The fragments may have been a cut-shell geometric pendant that broke, but not enough is present to make a positive determination. FN 44-3587.01 is another fragment of *A. californiensis* with one edge that has been cut and ground smooth and has cortex on the exterior. The form and function of the fragment is indeterminate. FN 44-1383.1 is a badly burned fragment of *L. elatum* with one edge that appears to have been cut and snapped along a rib line. Another worked fragment (FN 44-735.01) of *L. elatum* had two edges ground smooth that formed a 90 degree angle; the remaining edges were irregular from breakage. The form and function of this fragment is unknown, but it may have been a corner of a geometric pendant. FN 44-1622 is a fragment of *A. circularis* that may have been a wing fragment from a flying bird motif cut from the valve. The growth ribs extend vertically across the width of the possible wing, which has cut edges that have been ground smooth. It may have been a pendant, but that is uncertain.

Unworked Shell Fragments

Unworked fragments were collected from several features and represent valves of *G. gigantea* and *L. elatum,* and the left-hand valve of a *P. vogdesi* shell. None of the fragments exhibited modification, thus it is not known what form or function they may have had. However, the left-hand valve of the *P. vogdesi* shell has been found at other sites as whole shell pendants with perforations for suspension usually drilled in the hinge area of the dorsal margin.

Discussion

The prehistoric shell assemblage recovered during excavations at the Marsh Station Road site is small but diverse, representing both finished ornaments of personal adornment as well as examples of possible ornament production at an unknown scale. Five ornament types—bracelets, ring/pendants, cut-shell pendants, and whole and disk beads—are represented in the collection. These five types are fairly evenly distributed among the features with all of the artifacts recovered from the fill of pit structures, nonthermal and thermal pits, or sampling units (Table 9.2). This suggests that most of the shell material represents discarded by-products of shell production activities, the breakage of finished ornaments, and in some cases is indicative of post-abandonment use of the structure or domestic feature for trash disposal.

Bracelet fragments dominate the collection, representing 40 percent of the total recovered shell artifacts. The bracelet fragments were recovered from non-mortuary contexts including collection units, test units, and pit houses, as well as thermal and nonthermal pits (see Table 9.2). Bracelets with perforated umbones and a decorated band, one each of which are present in the Marsh Station Road assemblage, are typically assigned to the Sedentary period (Haury 1976:313). In the overall assemblage, there were single occurrences of Type 1 (thinner, narrow) and Type 3 (wide) bands, with the bulk of the assemblage in the Type 2 medium-band category according to Haury's (1976) bracelet chronology, which correlates with the Sedentary into the early Classic period. Nine of the bands, representing roughly half of the total finished bracelet fragments, had enough of the band present to project a band diameter. The diameters ranged from a minimum of 44 mm to a maximum of 60 mm, with a mean value of 45.12 mm. However, four of these bands measured 52 mm in diameter, which suggests some standardization of band diameters. Howard (1993) also found bracelet band standardization at Shelltown and at the Hind Site, two large shell ornament production loci in the Papagueria west of the Tucson Basin. At these sites there was an abundance of similarly sized bracelets and raw valves, which suggests that the local crafts people were purposefully choosing valves of similar size. Based on the data from Shelltown and Hind site, Howard (1993) has suggested that sites strictly manufacturing for large scale exchange or redistribution, rather than for primarily local consumption, should have fewer finished bracelets than the number of in-process bracelets (also see Griffith 1989:784) present at the site due to the exportation of the finished product. Conversely, a higher number of finished ornaments would suggest that the inhabitants of the site(s) were either importing finished products or were producing bracelets primarily for local consumption. At the Marsh Station Road site, the majority of the shell bracelets were finished artifacts rather than in-process pieces (see Table 9.2). This could suggest that the bracelets in the current assemblage were made by the local crafts people for local consumption, as they are stylistically similar to the in-process specimens. Small-scale exchange and re-distribution of the artifacts, similar to a cottage industry, could also have been occurring.

Roughly half of the bracelets exhibited a facet or grinding platform on the back of the valve, a result of the reduction of the back of the valve (core area) by grinding during the manufacturing process, which obliterates the core but produces shell flakes or debitage. The scant data from the examples in the assemblage suggests that the local crafts people were manufacturing bracelets by reducing the backs of the valves or core area by a series of grinding and chipping episodes in order to thin the shell and provide an edge that made continued chipping easier. This technique—numerous episodes of flat grinding—produces a flat platform or facet on the back of the shell. The artisans also used chipping on the outer margins to reduce the diameter of the valve and/or steepen the outer face as well as chipping on the interior surfaces that were then reamed smooth. The subsequent grinding and chipping would reduce the valve to produce the size of band desired. This method of valve reduction has been recorded from sites in the Gila Bend area such as the Painted Rocks (L. Huckell 1981:65; Wasley and Johnson 1965:33) and in the Papaguería at Shelltown and the Hind Site (Howard 1993:358), and is like the method employed at Snaketown (Haury 1976:306).

Studies of other shell bracelet manufacturing loci as described for the Trincheras culture by Johnson (1960) as well as in the Papaguería (Ferg 1980:389; B. Huckell and L. Huckell 1979:159) demonstrate that the reduction techniques used in these locales are different than those observed at the Marsh Station Road site. There are three important characteristics of these other reduction techniques: 1) leaving a core (the top back of the valve) behind as part of the manufacturing debris; 2) chipping and reaming of the interior edge of the valve to the desired size; and 3) performing a final smoothing and polishing of the band. In this reduction technique, the band is most vulnerable and tends to break, especially if it has damage from worm boring which weakens the shell, during the second step. The bracelet assemblage at the Marsh Station Road site differs from this reduction technique, as described, at almost every step. The bands exhibit platforms and facets on the back of the valves from grinding, with no flakes or cores present in the collection, suggesting that the core was obliterated through grinding on an abrasive surface. In addition, none of the in-process bands have been polished, and most of the interiors have not been reamed smooth but are unfinished, exhibiting chipping or flaking scars.

Feature 17, a pit house dating to the late Middle Formative period, produced four shell ornamnents, which is the greatest and most diverse occurrence of shell from any of the features. The assemblage from this structure includes the *Laevicardium* disk bead and *Nassarius* whole shell bead from structure fill, an in-process *Glycymeris* ring from the floor fill, and a finished *Glycymeris* ring fragment from the floor of the structure. The types of shell artifacts recovered from Feature 17 suggest that the household may have participated in the manufacture of shell ornaments on a limited scale. However, evidence for a manufacturing locus, which would include an abundance of shell waste material, caches of raw material, a multitude of reamers and abraders, and shell dust on the structure floor, appear to be missing from this locus. The paucity of tools

Table 9.2. Shell material summarized by context.

Context	Cut Pendant	Disk Bead	Whole Shell Bead	Bracelet	In-process	Re-worked	Ring/Pendant	In-process	Worked	Un-worked	Intrusive	Indeterminate	Total
Collection Unit 124				1									1
Collection Unit 145					1								1
Collection Unit 322									1				1
Collection Unit Subtotal				*1*	*1*				*1*				*3*
Test Unit 7				1									1
Test Unit 12				1									1
Test Unit 23						1							1
Test Unit 41				1									1
Test Unit 47				1									1
Test Unit 53				1									1
Test Unit 59	1												1
Test Unit 60										1			1
Test Unit 67					1								1
Test Unit 72				1									1
Test Unit 77				1									1
Test Unit 97				1									1
Test Unit 128				1									1
Test Unit 158										1			1
Test Unit 162										1			1
Test Unit 169									1				1
Test Unit 178						1							1
Test Unit Subtotal	*1*			*9*	*1*	*2*			*1*	*3*			*17*

Table 9.2. Shell material summarized by context, con'd.

Context	Cut Pendant	Disk Bead	Whole Shell	Bracelet	In-process	Re-worked	Ring/Pendant	In-process	Worked	Un-worked	Intrusive	Indeter-minate	Total
Feature 6, Occupation surface	1			1									2
Feature 7, Pit house				1					1		2		4
Feature 17, Pit house		1	1				1	1					4
Feature 14, Nonthermal pit											1	1	2
Feature 19, Roasting pit				1									1
Feature 21, Nonthermal pit											1		1
Feature 29, Roasting pit												1	1
Feature 41, Occupation surface											1		1
Feature 42, Nonthermal pit											1		1
Feature 44, Nonthermal pit										1			1
Feature 51, Pit house									1	1			2
Feature 98, Thermal pit											1	1	2
Feature 109, Bell pit				1							1		2
Feature 110, Nonthermal pit							1						1
Feature 152, Pit house			1	2						2			5
Feature Subtotal	*1*	*1*	*2*	*6*			*2*	*1*	*2*	*4*	*8*	*3*	*30*
Total	2	1	2	16	2	2	2	1	4	7	8	3	50
(%)													(100)

associated with Feature 17 could be a result of pre-abandonment floor cleaning.

Rings such as those found in Feature 17 have been found in other shell assemblages at sites that date as early as the late Early Formative (Pioneer) period at the Yuma Wash site (Vokes 2001a). The form became increasing popular during the early Middle Formative (late Colonial) period, with their popularity continuing through much of the Late Formative (Classic) period (Vokes 1987:259, 2001b:388–389). The attractiveness of this ornament form is found in the multiple roles to which it has been assigned, including occurrences of inhumations with bands encircling the fingers of an individual (Fewkes 1896:362; Vokes 2001b:389). Di Peso (1956:92) cited a few cases where multiple ring-pendants had been placed in the region of the neck suggesting that they may have been strung as beads or pendants. Shell bands recovered during the Tonto Creek Archaeological project were found alongside the heads of buried individuals, suggesting they may have been worn as earrings (Vokes 2001b:389).

The overall composition of the shell assemblage is consistent with what one would find at a Hohokam site dating to the Middle Formative (Sedentary) period, although some characteristic ornament types, such as *Olivella* beads and etched or painted shell (Haury 1976:315; Nelson 1991:18), are missing. Temporally sensitive ornament forms such as the ring/pendants and the whole shell pendants from *Argopecten* and *P. vogdesi* all occur in higher frequencies during the Sedentary into the Classic periods (Nelson 1991:45, 49). At the Marsh Station Road site, these shell species and ornament types occur in limited numbers; instead, the assemblage of finished ornaments is dominated by the presence of *Glycymeris* bracelets (n = 16), which represents 70 percent of the finished ornaments. However, the size of the bands, umbo treatment, and band

decorations are within the parameters of those assigned to the Middle Formative (Sedentary) period, according to Haury's (1976:313) bracelet chronology based on his work at Snaketown.

Evidence for manufacturing, in the form of in-process ornaments and raw material, were associated with the structural fill of two of the pit houses and several of the sampling units (see Table 9.2). A similar circumstance occurred at Snaketown (Haury 1976:306) which suggests that the presence of the shell material may not be associated with the occupation of the structures, but that it might possibly represent secondary trash.

Intersite Comparisons

A lack of comparable material from excavated sites in this region makes comparisons in this direction difficult, thus a few sites from the Tucson Basin to the west were selected for their proximity to the area and their temporal association. The Marsh Station Road shell assemblage is similar to those at Sedentary period sites in the nearby Tucson Basin. In general, the assemblage is dominated by plain bracelets, which represent about 40 percent of the finished ornaments in the collection. The relative abundance of *Glycymeris* bracelets present has also been reported at other sites located in the Tucson Basin, such as at the Julian Wash site, where they comprise between 50 and 70 percent of the finished artifacts (Vokes 2006a:27). This figure actually reflects a decline in the relative presence of *Glycymeris* bracelets from the 70 to 90 percent of finished artifacts found in assemblages in the early Middle Formative (Colonial) period at sites such as Fastimes (AZ AA:12:384 [ASM]; Vokes 1989). The presence of perforated umbones and medium-width bands is comparable to Sedentary period sites in the Tucson Basin such as ShellMan (Vokes 2006b:4.7), the West Branch site (Vokes

2004:291), and Hodges Ruin (Kanakoff and Hill 1978:117–118). Similarly, the treatment of a bracelet dorsal margin re-worked into a pendant with a snake motif is also seen at the West Branch site (Vokes 2004:290) and at AZ AA:12:674 (ASM) (Virden-Lange 2005:2). The incised or decorated bracelet band present in the current shell assemblage is stylistically similar to other decorated bands with snake-derived motifs in the Tucson Basin (Jernigan 1978:65) as well as Snaketown (Haury 1937b:143). The use of geometrics to create a more stylized design increased over time, especially during the Sedentary and into the Classic period (Jernigan 1978:65).

The popularity of ring-pendants in the shell assemblages from sites dating to the Sedentary period is noted. According to Vokes (2006a:27) there appears to be a shift in popularity between zoomorphic pendants and geometric styles between the Colonial and Sedentary periods. In the latter, the geometric forms are equal to or more abundant than the zoomorphic forms. Although there were no identified geometric forms from the Marsh Station Road site, the edges on some of the worked fragments suggest that they may have originally been cut-shell geometrics, while one fragment appeared to be a stylized bird wing made from *Argopecten.* This trend toward the geometric and more abstract representations may also be seen in the incised decoration and low relief carving on bracelets. The current shell assemblage has two examples of this type of decoration on re-worked bracelet fragments. Jernigan (1978:65) noted that in the Rillito phase (early Sedentary period), the bands of the carved bracelets tended to depict snakes that had more of a sense of motion, while in the Rincon phase (late Sedentary period), the carved bands seem to be more static in appearance.

The style of ornamentation present on the cut-shell pendant manufactured from *L. elatum* is also known from other late Sedentary/Classic period sites, and is similar to those recovered from sites such as Hodges Ruin (Kanakoff and Hill 1978), Painted Rocks (Wasley and Johnson 1965), AZ AA:12:674 (ASM) (Virden-Lange 2005), Los Muertos (Jernigan 1978:56), and Los Morteros (Urban 1989:288).

CONCLUSIONS

The shell recovered from the Marsh Station Road site is similar to other assemblages from contemporary Hohokam collections in the Tucson Basin. Because of the lack of comparative material from other sites located near the Marsh Station Road site, Sedentary period sites of similar site type in the Tucson Basin were used for comparison. Although the collection is small, it is still somewhat diverse with the shell species and ornament forms that are present and is uniquely Hohokam by design. The presence of *Glycymeris* shell bracelets and rings, *Laevicardium* cut-shell zoomorphic pendant and the *Nassarius* whole shell bead are typical of what one would find in a Hohokam shell assemblage. Also, the occurrence of raw material, worked and in-process artifacts suggests that the inhabitants of this site may have been producing shell ornaments in order to supplement what they obtained through trade. Such production, however, probably occurred on a small scale. The reworking of *Glycymeris* bracelet fragments also suggests that the inhabitants highly prized the few shell ornaments that they had.

The shell material recovered from the Marsh Station Road site supports the idea that the local inhabitants in this area were in relatively close contact with Hohokam populations to the west. Not only does the composition of the assemblage appear to be similar to contemporary Hohokam collections, but many of the specific ornament forms and decorative motifs are known from other Hohokam assemblages. The most likely source of the marine shell recovered in the collection is the Gulf of California, suggesting that a network or exchange mechanism for procurement existed, and that occupants at the Marsh Station Road site par- ticipated in this exchange network. Most likely that network included the Tucson Basin, as the shell types and ornament forms are very similar to Sedentary period Hohokam sites along the Santa Cruz River.

Chapter 10
Macrobotanical Remains

Karen R. Adams

Numerous charred plant remains were recovered from the Marsh Station Road site, located at the confluence of Mescal Wash and Cienega Creek, just south of Tucson. The site is next to a riparian habitat at the intersection of Mescal Wash and Cienega Creek, and is located within the semidesert grassland biotic community, today characterized by mesquite, shrubs, cacti, and grasses, but formerly heavily dominated by grasses (Brown 1982:123–131). This biotic community includes a number of plants common to both the plains grassland and the Chihuahuan desert scrub biotic communities, among them: sotols (*Dasylirion* spp.), beargrasses (*Nolina* spp.), agaves (*Agave* spp.), yuccas (*Yucca* spp.), junipers (*Juniperus*), and a diversity of cacti and other perennial plants (Brown 1982:123-131).

FLOTATION SAMPLES

A total of 38 flotation samples, which represent a range of pre-Hispanic time periods from the Early Agricultural through the Formative periods, was examined from the site (Table 10.1). Flotation samples were individually processed by WSA laboratory staff by use of a simple system that consisted of pouring sediment into a large, 55-gallon drum of fresh water, and then immediately skimming/decanting the buoyant light fraction of floating materials into a cloth mesh for drying. All equipment was cleaned between samples to ensure no cross-contamination of plant specimens. During analysis, the light fraction portion of each flotation sample was first sorted through a set of graduated screens, and all particle sizes larger than .50 mm were then completely examined. Reproductive parts were segregated and identified, and up to 20 fragments of charred wood were identified if they had a broad enough cross section surface to view anatomical details. All items were examined under a Zeiss binocular microscope at magnifications ranging from 8x to 50x, and then identified in comparison to an extensive modern collection of regional plant materials backed by herbarium specimens deposited in the University of Arizona Herbarium (ARIZ). Criteria of identification of the taxa and parts recovered for this project have been previously reported (K. Adams 1994, 1997).

MACROBOTANICAL SAMPLES

In addition to the flotation samples noted, 32 macrobotanical samples collected from the Marsh Station Road site during excavation

Table 10.1. List of flotation samples analyzed from the Marsh Station Road site

Site No.	Feature No.	Feature Type	FN	Phase or Period
AZ EE:2:44	44.00	medium nonthermal pit	1651.01	San Pedro
AZ EE:2:44	98.00	bell pit	2791.01	
AZ EE:2:44	98.00	bell pit	2698.01	
AZ EE:2:44	12.00	medium nonthermal pit	1295.01	San Pedro?
AZ EE:2:44	16.00	bell pit	2835.01	
AZ EE:2:44	95.00	roasting pit	2679.01	
AZ EE:2:44	139.00	bell pit	2886.01	
AZ EE:2:44	139.00	bell pit	2812.01	
AZ EE:2:44	61.00	indeterminate thermal pit	1902.01	Early Formative
AZ EE:2:44	112.00	medium nonthermal pit	2509.01	
AZ EE:2:44	6.00	other extramural surface	1599.01	Late Middle Formative
AZ EE:2:44	6.00	other extramural surface	1428.01	
AZ EE:2:44	7.00	pit house	1300.01	
AZ EE:2:44	7.02	posthole	1716.01	
AZ EE:2:44	11.09	bell pit	2748.01	
AZ EE:2:44	17.00	pit house	2973.01	
AZ EE:2:44	17.01	indeterminate nonthermal pit	3627.01	
AZ EE:2:44	19.00	roasting pit	1196.01	
AZ EE:2:44	29.00	roasting pit	1110.01	
AZ EE:2:44	41.00	other extramural surface	1184.01	
AZ EE:2:44	41.00	other extramural surface	3656.01	
AZ EE:2:44	49.00	roasting pit (intrusive to F. 7)	1181.01	
AZ EE:2:44	54.00	large nonthermal pit	1368.01	
AZ EE:2:44	72.00	indeterminate thermal pit	2091.01	
AZ EE:2:44	109.00	bell pit	2411.01	
AZ EE:2:44	109.00	bell pit	2481.01	
AZ EE:2:44	136.00	medium nonthermal pit	2850.01	
AZ EE:2:44	152.00	pit house	3167.01	
AZ EE:2:44	152.03	posthole	3250.01	
AZ EE:2:44	152.11	firepit (unprepared hearth)	3504.01	
AZ EE:2:44	152.12	hearth	3631.01	
AZ EE:2:44	173.00	bell pit	3553.01	
AZ EE:2:44	206.00	pit house	3655.01	
AZ EE:2:44	15.00	medium nonthermal pit	1578.01	Early Agricultural–Formative
AZ EE:2:44	21.00	medium nonthermal pit	1627.01	
AZ EE:2:44	28.00	roasting pit	1130.01	
AZ EE:2:44	30.00	roasting pit	1137.01	
AZ EE:2:44	81.00	roasting pit	2196.01	

by archaeologists were also examined (Table 10.2). Macrobotanical samples generally represent visible plant parts picked from site sediment or during screening; as such they represent discretionary, rather than systematically, collected samples. Each of these larger samples was spread out on clean paper, and any reproductive parts present identified. Wood charcoal fragments were then analyzed in the same manner as for flotation samples, and criteria of identification of the plant taxa and parts identified can be found in the same publications listed immediately above.

RESULTS

A minimum of 13 different plant taxa/part(s) provided foods, fuels, and other resources to ancient groups at the Marsh Station Road site (Table 10.3). Evidence of domesticated maize (corn) was recovered as cob segments and fragments and smaller portions of cobs (cupules) that formerly held kernels on the cob. The plant parts discussed below were all charred or partially charred and are assumed to have become so due to actions of people in the past. A small number of uncharred fragments of juniper (Juniperus) wood from a historic fence post context are also included in this report.

The southern Arizona ethnographic record (Castetter 1935; Castetter and Bell 1942, 1951; Crosswhite 1980, 1981; Curtin 1984; Rea 1997; Russell 1908) is rich in information regarding historic uses of the plants and their parts recovered in this project. An assumption is made that plants used historically by groups living in southern Arizona were likely also of interest to ancient occupants of the same region. In addition, the regional archaeobotanical record supports this assumption by revealing many of these plants as routinely recovered from southern Arizona archaeological sites (K. Adams 2002a, 2002b; Bohrer 1970, 1971, 1987, 1991, 1992; Gasser and Kwiatkowski 1991a, 1991b).

Early Agricultural Period

The earliest evidence of charred plant parts from the Marsh Station Road site dates to the San Pedro phase of the Early Agricultural period (Table 10.4). Flotation samples from two San Pedro phase pits (Features 44 and 98) clearly indicate domesticated maize (Zea mays) was present during this time. A charred maize cob segment collected during excavation from bell pit Feature 98 reinforces this record. In addition, local groups gathered seeds in the cheno-am (Chenopodium-Amaranthus) group of weedy plants, grass (Gramineae) grains, and mesquite (Prosopis) and saltbush (Atriplex) wood. These same wild plants were recovered in four additional pits (Features 12, 16, 95, and 139) considered likely to also represent the San Pedro phase.

Early Formative and Late Middle Formative Periods

During the Early Formative period, charred plant remains in flotation samples from one thermal pit and one nonthermal pit (Features 61 and 112) indicate use of maize and weedy cheno-am plants, along with mesquite and juniper wood (Table 10.5). Twenty features from the late Middle Formative period represent extramural surfaces, pit houses, both thermal and nonthermal pits, and postholes (see Table 10.5). This time period is well-represented at the Marsh Station Road site, and the plant record contained within these diverse domestic features indicates frequent consumption of maize as a food, and the secondary use of left-over maize cobs as a fuel. Other likely foods during this time include grass grains and cheno-am seeds, broad-leaf yucca fruit, and possibly the carbohydrate-rich tissue of a mem-

Table 10.2. List of macrobotanical samples analyzed from the Marsh Station Road site

Feature No.	FN	Feature Type	Phase or Period
n/a	3010	no feature	–
98	2691	bell pit	San Pedro
5	1219	roasting pit	Late Middle Formative
5	1220	roasting pit	
5	1221	roasting pit	
6	1531	other extramural surface	
6	1532	other extramural surface	
6	1602	other extramural surface	
6	1673	other extramural surface	
6	1689	other extramural surface	
6	1705	other extramural surface	
7	1443	pit house	
7.29	3671	hearth	
11	2354	pit house	
41	1115	other extramural surface	
41	1116	other extramural surface	
41	1147	other extramural surface	
41	1187	other extramural surface	
41	1188	other extramural surface	
41.01	1348	posthole	
52	2172	bell pit	
97	2643	medium nonthermal pit	
109	2372	bell pit	
109	2484	bell pit	
118	2419	indeterminate thermal pit	
118	2474	indeterminate thermal pit	
152	3075	pit house	
152	3159	pit house	
152	3246	pit house	
20	1511	large nonthermal pit	Early Agricultural–Formative
107	2430	indeterminate nonthermal pit	
130	2795	medium nonthermal pit	

Table 10.3. List of all plant taxa and parts identified in all samples analyzed

Taxon	Common Name	Part(s)	Condition(s)
Acacia	acacia	wood	charred
Atriplex	saltbush	wood	charred
Celtis reticulata	hackberry	wood	charred
Cheno-am	cheno-am	seed	charred
Gramineae	grass	caryopsis, stem fragment	charred
Juniperus	juniper	wood	charred, partially charred, uncharred
Larrea	creostoe bush	wood	charred
Monocotyledon	monocot	tissue	charred
Phragmites	reedgrass	stem fragment	charred
Populus/Salix	cottonwood/willow	wood	charred
Prosopis	mesquite	seed fragment, wood	charred
Yucca baccata	broad-leaf yucca	seed, seed fragment	charred

Table 10.4. Charred plant remains from San Pedro phase and probable San Pedro phase flotation samples

Feature No.	Stripped Area	Feature Type	Period	FN	Taxon	ID Level	Part
44	3	medium nonthermal pit	San Pedro	1651.01	*Prosopis*	type	wood
44	3	medium nonthermal pit		1651.01	*Zea mays*		cupule
44	3	medium nonthermal pit		1651.01	*Atriplex*	type	wood
98	3	bell pit		2791.01	*Atriplex*	type	wood
98	3	bell pit		2791.01	*Gramineae*	type	caryopsis
98	3	bell pit		2791.01	*Cheno-am*		seed
98	3	bell pit		2791.01	*Prosopis*	type	wood
98	3	bell pit		2698.01	*Cheno-am*		seed
98	3	bell pit		2698.01	*Prosopis*	type	wood
12	4	medium nonthermal pit	San Pedro?	1295.01	*Prosopis*	type	wood
16	4	bell pit		2835.01	*Prosopis*	type	wood
95	4	roasting pit		2679.01	*Prosopis*	type	wood
95	4	roasting pit		2679.01	*Cheno-am*		seed
95	4	roasting pit		2679.01	*Gramineae*	type	stem fragment
139	5	bell pit		2812.01	*Prosopis*	type	wood
139	5	bell pit		2812.01	*Atriplex*	type	wood
139	5	bell pit		2886.01	*Prosopis*	type	wood

Table 10.5. Charred plant remains from Early Formative and late Middle Formative period flotation samples

Feature No.	Feature Type	Period	FN	Taxon	ID Level	Part
61	indeterminate thermal pit	Early Formative	1902.01	*Prosopis*	type	wood
61	indeterminate thermal pit		1902.01	*Juniperus*	type	wood
61	indeterminate thermal pit		1902.01	*Zea mays*		cupule
112	medium nonthermal pit		2509.01	Cheno-am		seed
112	medium nonthermal pit		2509.01	*Juniperus*	type	wood
112	medium nonthermal pit		2509.01	*Zea mays*		cupule
112	medium nonthermal pit		2509.01	*Prosopis*	type	wood
6	other extramural surface	Late Middle Formative	1599.01	*Celtis reticulata*	type	wood
6	other extramural surface		1428.01	*Phragmites*	type	stem fragment
6	other extramural surface		1428.01	*Populus/Salix*	type	wood
6	other extramural surface		1428.01	*Prosopis*	type	wood
6	other extramural surface		1428.01	*Zea mays*		cupule
6	other extramural surface		1599.01	*Phragmites*	type	stem fragment
19	roasting pit		1196.01	*Prosopis*	type	wood
19	roasting pit		1196.01	*Yucca baccata*	type	seed fragment
7	pit house		1300.01	*Prosopis*	type	wood
7	pit house		1300.01	*Zea mays*		cupule
7.02	posthole		1716.01	*Zea mays*		cupule
7.02	posthole		1716.01	*Phragmites*	type	stem fragment
11.09	bell pit		2748.01	*Populus/Salix*	type	wood
11.09	bell pit		2748.01	Monocotyledon	type	tissue
11.09	bell pit		2748.01	*Larrea*	type	wood
11.09	bell pit		2748.01	*Celtis reticulata*	type	wood
11.09	bell pit		2748.01	*Prosopis*	type	wood
11.09	bell pit		2748.01	*Zea mays*		cupule
17	pit house		2973.01	*Prosopis*	type	wood
17	pit house		2973.01	*Zea mays*		cupule fragment
17.01	indeterminate nonthermal pit		3627.01	*Zea mays*		cupule

Table 10.5. Charred plant remains from Early and late Middle Formative period flotation samples, cont'd

Feature No.	Feature Type	Period	FN	Taxon	ID Level	Part
17.01	indeterminate nonthermal pit		3627.01	*Prosopis*	type	wood
29	roasting pit		1110.01	*Prosopis*	type	wood
41	other extramural surface		3656.01	*Prosopis*	type	wood
41	other extramural surface		1184.01	*Juniperus*	type	wood
49	roasting pit (intrusive to f. 7)		1181.01	*Prosopis*	type	wood
49	roasting pit (intrusive to f. 7)		1181.01	*Zea mays*		cupule
54	large nonthermal pit		1368.01	*Prosopis*	type	wood
72	indeterminate thermal pit		2091.01	*Prosopis*	type	wood
72	indeterminate thermal pit		2091.01	*Zea mays*		cupule fragment
109	bell pit		2481.01	Cheno-am		seed
109	bell pit		2481.01	*Phragmites*	type	stem fragment
109	bell pit		2481.01	*Zea mays*		cupule
109	bell pit		2481.01	*Atriplex*	type	wood
109	bell pit		2481.01	*Prosopis*	type	wood
109	bell pit		2411.01	*Zea mays*		cupule
109	bell pit		2411.01	*Prosopis*	type	wood
136	medium nonthermal pit		2850.01	*Prosopis*	type	wood
136	medium nonthermal pit		2850.01	*Zea mays*		cupule
152	pit house		3167.01	*Zea mays*		cupule
152	pit house		3167.01	Cheno-am		seed
152	pit house		3167.01	*Prosopis*	type	wood
152.03	posthole		3250.01	Cheno-am		seed
152.03	posthole		3250.01	*Prosopis*	type	wood
152.03	posthole		3250.01	*Zea mays*		cupule
152.03	posthole		3250.01	*Yucca baccata*	type	seed
152.03	posthole		3250.01	Gramineae	type	caryopsis
152.03	posthole		3250.01	*Celtis reticulata*	type	wood
152.03	posthole		3250.01	Gramineae	type	stem fragment
152.11	firepit (unprepared hearth)		3504.01	Gramineae	type	stem fragment

Table 10.5. Charred plant remains from Early and late Middle Formative period flotation samples, cont'd

Feature No.	Feature Type	Period	FN	Taxon	ID Level	Part
152.11	firepit (unprepared hearth)		3504.01	*Prosopis*	type	wood
152.11	firepit (unprepared hearth)		3504.01	*Phragmites*	type	stem fragment
152.11	firepit (unprepared hearth)		3504.01	*Zea mays*		cupule
152.12	hearth		3631.01	*Zea mays*		cupule
152.12	hearth		3631.01	*Celtis reticulata*	type	wood
152.12	hearth		3631.01	Gramineae	type	stem fragment
173	bell pit		3553.01	*Celtis reticulata*	type	wood
173	bell pit		3553.01	*Zea mays*		cupule
173	bell pit		3553.01	*Prosopis*	type	wood
206	pit house		3655.01	*Prosopis*	type	wood

Table 10.6. Charred or partially charred plant remains within late Middle Formative period macrobotanical samples

Feature No.	Feature Type	FN	Taxon	ID Level	Part
5	roasting pit	1219	*Prosopis*	type	wood
5	roasting pit	1220	*Prosopis*	type	wood
5	roasting pit	1221	*Prosopis*	type	wood
6	other extramural surface	1532	*Celtis reticulata*	type	wood
6	other extramural surface	1531	*Populus/Salix*	type	wood
6	other extramural surface	1531	*Celtis reticulata*	type	wood
6	other extramural surface	1602	*Celtis reticulata*	type	wood
6	other extramural surface	1673	*Prosopis*	type	wood
6	other extramural surface	1689	*Acacia*	type	wood
6	other extramural surface	1705	*Celtis reticulata*	type	wood
6	other extramural surface	1531	*Prosopis*	type	wood
7	pit house	1443	*Populus/Salix*	type	wood
7.29	hearth	3671	not plant		
11	pit house	2354	*Prosopis*	type	wood
41	other extramural surface	1115	*Prosopis*	type	wood
41	other extramural surface	1188	*Juniperus*	type	wood
41	other extramural surface	1187	*Celtis reticulata*	type	wood
41	other extramural surface	1187	*Prosopis*	type	wood
41	other extramural surface	1147	*Prosopis*	type	wood
41	other extramural surface	1116	*Prosopis*	type	wood
41.01	posthole	1348	*Juniperus*	type	wood
52	bell pit	2172	*Juniperus*	type	wood
97	medium nonthermal pit	2643	*Prosopis*	type	wood
109	bell pit	2484	*Prosopis*	type	wood
109	bell pit	2372	*Zea mays*		cob segment
118	indeterminate thermal pit	2474	*Prosopis*	type	wood
118	indeterminate thermal pit	2419	*Atriplex*	type	wood
118	indeterminate thermal pit	2419	*Prosopis*	type	wood
152	pit house	3075	*Prosopis*	type	wood
152	pit house	3159	*Prosopis*	type	wood
152	pit house	3246	*Prosopis*	type	wood

ber of the Monocotyledon group. In addition, people regularly brought in mesquite wood for their fires. Less often they gathered and burned wood from hackberry, juniper, and cottonwood/willow trees, and from saltbush and creosote bush shrubs. Reedgrass and other grass stems served additional material culture needs.

The macrobotanical record from the Marsh Station Road site representing the late Middle Formative period (Table 10.6) reveals use of many of the same plants as preserved within the flotation samples just discussed. During the late Middle Formative period, charred macrobotanical plant parts that preserved within various pits, extramural surfaces, and other features together indicate heavy use of mesquite wood, as well as wood of hackberry, juniper and cottonwood/willow trees, and acacia and saltbush shrubs. A maize cob segment from bell pit Feature 109 is the only evidence of food recovered in this macrobotanical record.

Early Agricultural through Formative Periods

A limited number of flotation and macrobotanical samples from the broadly defined Early Agricultural through Formative time periods (Table 10.7) contained charred examples of the same plant taxa and parts already discussed, and simply add additional confirmation of the plants utilized at the Marsh Station Road site through time. Mesquite wood was clearly preferred, along with saltbush and juniper wood.

Historic Period

The Marsh Station Road site also yielded a number of uncharred juniper (*Juniperus*) wood fragments within a historic 1870s fence post (FN 44-3010). Juniper wood has often been sought for historic posts due to superior preservation qualities.

DISCUSSION

The following section provides a brief discussion of several research themes related to the macrobotanical assemblage that can be addressed with data from the Marsh Station Road site excavations.

Subsistence

The charred plant specimens considered indicative of ancient food use are generally limited in both diversity and frequency of recovery. Evidence from the Marsh Station Road site suggests maize was grown during the San Pedro phase of the Early Agricultural period. People also gathered grass grains and seeds of weedy plants in the cheno-am group; such plants could easily have occupied maize fields and other disturbed locations in the vicinity of dwellings. This record of reproductive parts implies groups in the area may not have spent a great deal of time preparing and eating meals. However, it is also possible that small sample size and poor preservation conditions have left little evidence for interpretation.

Evidence of maize use continued during the Middle Formative period at the Marsh Station Road site. Once kernels had been removed from cobs for preparation and consumption, the left-over cobs provided a fuel or tinder source. People also gathered grass grains and cheno-am seeds, and occasionally used broad-leaf yucca fruit and perhaps the hearts of some members of the Monocotyledon group of plants, such as *Agave*. It is interesting that sites in the vicinity of Mescal Wash and that currently host agave (also known as "mescal") plants did not produce more of a record of *Agave* use, but generally poor preservation conditions may in part explain such an anomaly.

Wood Use

Mesquite wood was utilized most often by the occupants of the Marsh Station Road site. The site was likely situated adjacent to mesquite bosques, similar to the current vegetation. In addition to serving as a fuel, the solid mesquite limbs and trunks also offer sturdy and long-lasting construction elements. Wood of juniper, cottonwood, willow, and hackberry trees also serves several purposes. Creosote bush, acacia, and saltbush wood primarily provide only quicker-burning fuels, due to their small size. Reedgrass stems can be used in construction of temporary structures such as ramadas, as room dividers, and as outdoor fences.

Plant Use through Time

Plant use displays little variability through time (Table 10.8). Although sampling intensity differs between time periods, maize provided food at the Marsh Station Road site during both the San Pedro phase of the Early Agricultural period and Formative period occupations. Grass grains and seeds of weedy plants were also gathered. On occasion broad-leaf yucca fruit and possibly Monocotyledon tissue may also have been eaten. People consistently preferred mesquite wood as a fuel and for other needs. They also occasionally sought wood from other locally available trees (hackberry, juniper) and shrubs (acacia, saltbush, and creosote bush). The well-sampled late Middle Formative period contained the longest list of plant taxa/parts gathered for both food and nonfood uses.

Spatial Variability in Plant Use

Archaeobotanical results are adequate to examine intrasite variability in plant use at the Marsh Station Road site. For the San Pedro phase, Stripped Area (SA) 3 features (Features 44 and 98) are spatially separated from SA 4 features (Features 12, 16, and 95), and from a feature in SA 5 (Feature 139). Features 44 and 98 have been definitively dated to the San Pedro phase through radiocarbon dating, while Features 12, 16, 95, and 139 are believed to date to the San Pedro phase based on spatial associations and artifact assemblages, but have not been absolutely dated to this phase.

Table 10.7. Charred plant remains recovered from Early Agricultural–Formative period flotation (F) and macrobotanical (M) samples

Feature No.	Feature Type	FN	Taxon	ID Level	Part	Sample Type
15	medium nonthermal pit	1578.01	*Atriplex*	type	wood	F
15	medium nonthermal pit	1578.01	*Juniperus*	type	wood	F
15	medium nonthermal pit	1578.01	*Prosopis*	type	wood	F
21	medium nonthermal pit	1627.01	*Prosopis*	type	wood	F
28	roasting pit	1130.01	*Prosopis*	type	wood	F
30	roasting pit	1137.01	*Prosopis*	type	wood	F
81	roasting pit	2196.01	*Prosopis*	type	wood	F
20	large nonthermal pit	1511.00	*Prosopis*	type	wood	M
107	indeterminate nonthermal pit	2430.00	*Prosopis*	type	wood	M
130	medium nonthermal pit	2795.00	*Prosopis*	type	wood	M

All features represent nonthermal and thermal pits. The widespread distribution of mesquite wood, grass and saltbush remains, and cheno-am seeds suggests that these same plants were being gathered and utilized regardless of activity location or group affiliation. Maize remains are associated only with SA 3, suggesting that maize was not fully integrated into the subsistence base at this time.

Early Formative period Features 61 and 112, two pits located in SA 4 of the Marsh Station Road site, have preserved some of the same charred plant remains as recovered in the preceding San Pedro phase. During the Early Formative period, occupants gathered and utilized mesquite wood and had access to cheno-am seeds and maize. They also added juniper wood to their list of useful resources.

Table 10.8. Presence of charred plant taxa/parts recovered within flotation and macrobotanical samples through time

	Phase or Period	San Pedro Phase	Early Formative Period	Late Middle Formative Period
Number of flotation (F) and macro-botanical (M) samples		8(F), 1(M)	2(F)	23(F), 27(M)

Taxon	Common Name	Part(s)			
Acacia	acacia	wood			X
Atriplex	saltbush	wood	X		X
Celtis reticulata	hackberry	wood			X
Cheno-am	cheno-am	seed	X	X	
Gramineae	grass	caryopsis	X		X
Gramineae	grass	stem fragment	X		X
Juniperus	juniper	wood		X	X
Larrea	creosote bush	wood			X
Monocotyledon	monocot	cissue			X
Phragmites	reedgrass	stem fragment			X
Populus/Salix	cottonwood/ willow	wood			X
Prosopis	mesquite	wood	X	X	X
Yucca baccata	broad-leaf yucca	seed, seed fragment			X
Zea mays	maize	cupule, cob fragment, cob segment	X	X	X

During the late Middle Formative period, activities involving plant resources were being carried out in different areas of the Marsh Station Road site. For this time period, features have been organized into spatially distinct groups located within archaeological stripped areas (Table 10.9). A pit house (Feature 17), a nonthermal pit (Feature 17.01), and a bell pit (Feature 173) within SA 1 preserved mesquite and hackberry wood and maize remains. It is likely the wood provided construction elements and fuel, and the maize cobs provided fuel or tinder. Some distance away, in SA 4, two groups of spatially separate features do not share the same record of plant use. A bell pit (Feature 11.09), a roasting pit (Feature 23), and a pit house (Feature 206) preserved a range of plant parts indicative of wood use, plus maize remains and possible harvest of a Monocotyledon plant such as agave. In contrast, two nonthermal pits (Features 54 and 136), an indeterminate thermal pit (Feature 72), and a roasting pit (Feature 19) to the west in the same stripped area preserved only mesquite wood, yucca seed, and maize remains. The differences in feature types between the two groups of SA 4 features might account for these plant record differences. Finally, two groups of features in or adjacent to the boundary between SAs 4 and 5 are well-represented by charred plant remains. One of these groups, including a pit house (Feature 152) and its associated posthole (Feature 152.03), firepit (Feature 152.11), and hearth (Feature 152.12), preserved a fairly good

Table 10.9. Presence of charred plant remains from flotation samples associated with spatially grouped late Middle Formative period features located within Stripped Areas 1, 4 and 5

Taxon	ID Level	Part(s)	Stripped Area[a]				
			1	4 (a)	4 (b)	4/5 (a)	4/5 (b)
Atriplex	type	wood					X
Celtis reticulata	type	wood	X	X		X	X
Cheno-am		seed				X	X
Gramineae	type	caryopsis				X	
Gramineae	type	stem fragment				X	
Juniperus	type	wood					X
Larrea	type	wood		X			
Monocotyledon	type	tissue		X			
Phragmites	type	stem fragment				X	X
Populus/Salix	type	wood		X			X
Prosopis	type	wood	X	X	X	X	X
Yucca baccata	type	seed			X	X	
Zea mays		cupule, cupule fragment	X	X	X	X	X

[a]Stripped Area 1 Features: 17, 17.01, 173. Stripped Area 4(a) Features: 11.09, 29, 206. Stripped Area 4(b) Features: 19, 54, 72, 136. Stripped Area 4/5 (a) Features: 7, 7.02, 49, 152, 152.03, 152.11, 152.12. Stripped Area 4/5 (b) Features: 6, 41, 109.

record of both food (maize, broad-leaf yucca fruit, grass grains, and cheno-am seeds), and nonfood (mesquite and hackberry wood, and grass and reedgrass stems) plant uses. The posthole contained many different plant taxa/ parts, suggestive of midden materials entering the empty hole. Finally, another grouping of features that also straddle the boundary of SAs 4 and 5 included two extramural surfaces (Features 6 and 41) and a bell pit (Feature 109). The list of plants identified from this group of features included saltbush, juniper, and cottonwood/willow wood, cheno-am seeds and maize remains, hackberry and mesquite wood, and reedgrass stems. The nature of the archaeobotanical records during the late Middle Formative period suggests differences in some of the activities involving plant resources within spatially distinct groups of features across the Marsh Station Road site. The fact that these feature groups do not all represent the same kinds of features from location to location may also contribute to the differences in plant records noted here.

Maize Varieties through Time

Two distinctive maize (*Zea mays*) varieties were recovered at the Marsh Station Road site, represented by charred maize cob segments (broken portions of cobs still complete around their circumference for at least a portion of their length). A very short and flattened maize cob segment (FN 44-2691) from Feature 98 and two charred maize cob segments (FN 44-2372, Specimens A and B) from Feature 109 are described here and then placed within a framework of known regional maize traits and archaeological periods.

After careful brushing and cleaning, traits commonly reported on maize fragments were recorded (Table 10.10). Cob row number is the number of rows of kernels around the circumference of the cob, and is only recorded on cob

segments to insure accuracy of this observation. Row number is always an even number, and can range from 8 to 22. Sometimes cob preservation permits an actual count of the individual kernel rows. However, row counts must often be made by multiplying the number of cupules visible around the cob circumference (preferably near the middle of the cob) by two. A cupule is a small pocket portion of the cob that previously held two kernels that sat side by side, and is often the smallest recognizable part of a maize cob that preserves. In some sites, cupules are the only maize fragments available to describe and measure.

The single short cob segment from Feature 98 once held 16 rows of maize kernels (Figure 10.1). It displayed a mean cupule width of 3.0 mm, mean cupule length of 1.9 mm, and a pith diameter of 5.76 mm. However, because of its post-use flattened condition, the pith diameter (located in the center of the cob) measurement may well be over-estimated.

The two maize cob segments preserved within Feature 109 were, in each case, composed of two pieces that clearly fit together. Both cobs are missing some (unknown) portion of their tops and bases. The two cob segments from Feature 109 are very similar to each other in traits observed. Both are quadrangular in cross section and formerly held 8 rows of kernels. Specimen A (Figure 10.2) appeared to exhibit more variability among the cupules measured (n = 36), when compared to specimen B cupules (n = 44). In both cobs, narrowing toward the top of the cob resulted in smaller cupule measurements on the top piece when compared to the bottom piece. By calculating a ratio of the cupule width to the cupule length (also referred to as height), an expression of kernel shape can be determined. Values closer to one indicate a square shape, and higher values indicate increasing rectangularity in kernels. However, a more accurate assessment of individual kernel shape is derived by

Table 10.10. Measurements and calculated ratios of three charred *Zea mays* cob segments from two features

Feature No.	Specimen	Row No.	Cob Length	Pith Diameter (mm)	Cupule Width Mean (mm)	Cupule Length Mean (mm)	Ratio of Cupule Width/ Cupule Length	Individual Kernel Shape Ratio[a]
98	–	16	8.0 mm	5.76	3.0	1.9	1.57	0.79
109	A	8	4.0 cm	4.50	6.6	1.5	4.37	2.20
109	Bottom	–	–	–	6.9	1.6	4.34	2.20
109	Top	–	–	–	6.2	1.5	4.41	2.10
109	B	8	5.5 cm	4.50	6.8	1.9	3.72	1.80
109	Bottom	–	–	–	7.1	1.9	3.69	1.90
109	Top	–	–	–	6.4	1.7	3.78	1.90

[a]To determine individual kernel shape ratios, cupule width means were first divided by two (to adjust for the fact that two kernels sit side by side within a single cupule), then divided by the cupule length mean.

first dividing the cupule mean width by two (because two kernels originally sat side by side within each cupule), then calculating the individual kernel shape ratio. The individual kernel shape ratio results suggest the kernels within the cupules of the Feature 98 cob were closer to being square, and those within the Feature 109 cobs were about twice as wide as long (high). This is in part related to the original cob row numbers, that is, Feature 109 cobs with 8 rows of kernels must fill the same space around the circumference as the Feature 98 cob fills with twice the number of kernels.

It is clear that the Feature 98 maize cob segment differs notably from the Feature 109 cob segments. Two recent publications on early maize collections provide perspective for these maize specimens (Diehl 2005a; L. Huckell 2006). In an examination of Early Agricultural maize collections from southern Arizona, Diehl (2005a) focused on cupule traits (cupule width, cupule length, cupule thickness) and pith diameter. Diehl reports mean cupule widths for San Pedro phase maize as 3.2 mm, and for late Cienega phase maize as 3.5 mm. For a limited number of cob segments complete enough

around their circumference to determine the original number of kernel rows, the mean row number was similar between San Pedro (11.58 rows) and Late Cienega phase maize (11.6 rows), and not statistically significant.

Lisa Huckell (2006) has also described charred collections of San Pedro phase and Cienega phase maize cob segments from southern Arizona sites. Her results suggest that San Pedro phase maize had fewer rows of kernels (approximately 10) than Cienega phase maize, which tended toward having 12 rows. No statistically significant differences existed between San Pedro and Cienega maize for cupule width, cupule height (also called length), and the ratio of cupule width to length (L. Huckell 2006). The actual cupule measurements reported by L. Huckell (2006: Figure 7.7) appear to average a little over or under 3.0 mm for cupule width, and between 1.5 mm and 1.9 mm for cupule height. The cupules of the Marsh Station Road site maize are illustrated in Figure 10.3.

In comparison to these two reports on Early Agricultural maize in southern Arizona, the maize cob segments from the Marsh Station Road site appear to represent two different vari-

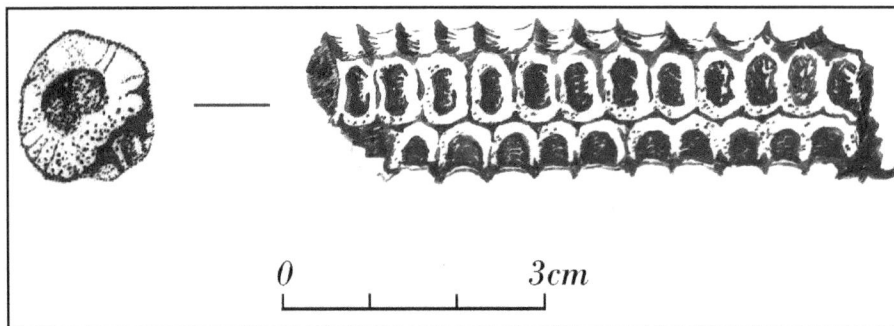

Figure 10.1 Sketch of the charred maize (Zea mays) cob segment (FN 44-2691) from Feature 98.

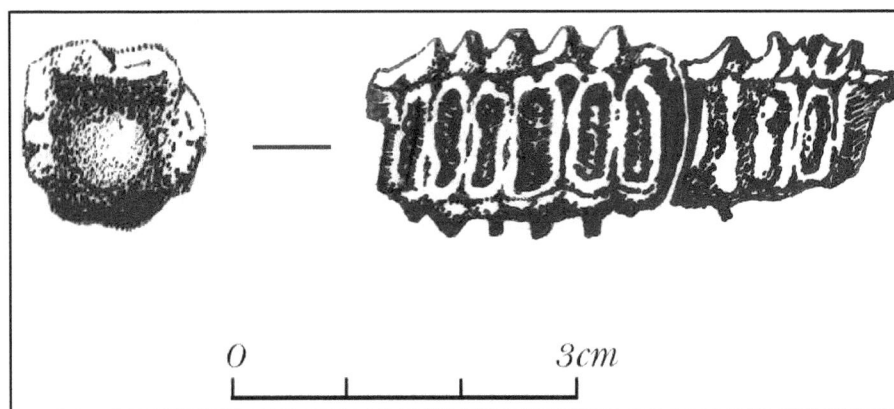

Figure 10.2 Sketch of the charred maize (Zea mays) cob segment (FN 44-2372, Specimen A) from Feature 109.

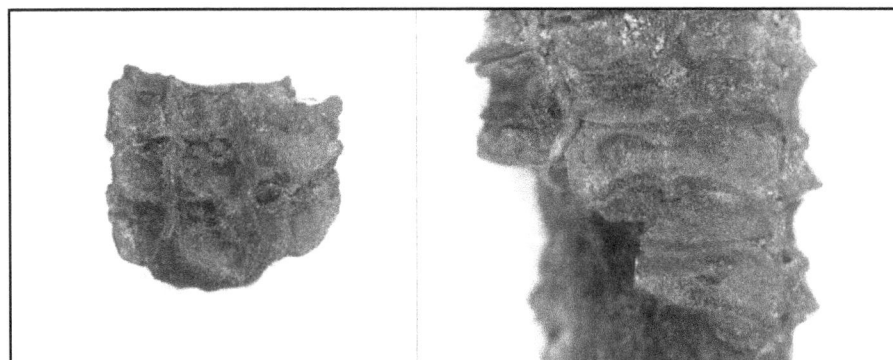

Figure 10.3. Charred maize (Zea mays) cob segments from the Marsh Station Road site. The cob on the left, from Feature 98 (FN 44-2691), and the cob on the right, from Feature 109 (FN 44-2372, Specimen B), were both photographed at 12x magnification. Note the relatively small and square shape of the cupules on the left, and the relatively rectangular shape of the very wide cupules on the right. Radiocarbon dates on the left cob indicate the San Pedro phase, and on the right cob they indicate the Formative period.

eties. However, the fact that only three specimens provide information requires caution in placing too much emphasis on these results. Also, the effects of different temperatures and lengths of burning on cupule traits is currently not well understood, although it is known from casual burning experiments that cob row number is not affected by burning. The Feature 98 maize cob is similar in most respects to Early Agricultural maize, with the exception of having a relatively high row number. However, L. Huckell does report a few 16-rowed cobs from this time period (2006). In contrast, the Feature 109 maize cobs have a lower mean row number (8) than reported for small Early Agricultural maize populations (10–12), some of which do, however, contain examples of 8-rowed maize. Cupule widths also vary notably, with the Feature 98 mean cupule width (3.0 mm) being less than half that of the Feature 109 mean cupule widths (6.6 to 6.8 mm). Diehl reports Early Agricultural maize cupule widths of 3.2 to 3.5 mm, and L. Huckell of about 3.0 mm. Both Diehl and L. Huckell report that mean cupule width becomes increasingly larger from the Early Agricultural through the Classic Hohokam (Diehl 2005a:370) periods and into modern times (L. Huckell 2006: Figure 7.7). The cupule width to cupule height ratios of the Feature 109 maize (3.72 to 4.37) are again nearly double those reported by L. Huckell for the Early Agricultural period (ratio means less than 2.0). And, the Feature 109 maize pith diameters (4.5 mm) are over twice those reported by Diehl for Early Agricultural maize (mean of 2.09 mm). Cupule length (height) for the Feature 109 maize ranges between 1.5 mm and 1.9 mm, and those reported by L. Huckell are quite similar (2006: Figure 7.7), and somewhat similar to those reported by Diehl (2005a:Figure 4).

Based on this limited number of specimens, the single cob segment from Feature 98 appears closer in all respects to San Pedro and Cienega phase maize, while the two Feature 109 maize cob segments appear much larger in most respects, suggesting a later date. Radiocarbon dates on these maize cobs in fact confirmed the ages of San Pedro phase (Feature 98) and Formative period (Feature 109) for these two features (see Chapter 4).

THE NATURE OF PAST PLANT COMMUNITIES

The plants recovered within both sites can still be found growing in the region at present. However, the plant record at the Marsh Station Road site clearly indicates a riparian habitat was present during the Formative period, and possibly earlier during the San Pedro phase. Together, the presence of mesquite, hackberry, and cottonwood/willow trees along with stands of reedgrass suggest available water close to the ground surface in Cienega Creek and/or Mescal Wash. It is likely that having access to surface or near surface water was a primary reason for settling the area in the first place. Other plants such as acacia, creosote bush, juniper, and broad-leaf yucca would have grown in nonriparian upland locations within the region.

SEASONALITY OF PLANT RESOURCE USE

The archaeological plant record reported here generally suggests use of the region during the summer through fall seasons. Wood can be acquired during any season and its presence sheds no light on seasonality of landscape use. However, maize requires at least three months of growth and development during the summer, and it generally matures in late summer/early fall. Likewise, *Chenopodium* and *Amaranthus* plants generally do not produce mature seeds until during the monsoon season, which generally starts in the month of July. Because the grass grains are not identified to taxon, they shed no particular light on their season(s) of maturity and availability. Both mesquite and broad-leaf yucca fruit generally ripen in mid- to late summer. The reproductive record presented here indicates the season(s) when groups most likely harvested the mature resources, but does not preclude that the resources may have been in storage for some months prior to actual use (Adams and Bohrer 1998).

Comparison to Archaeobotanical Records for the Region

Macrobotanical data from the Marsh Station Road site is discussed below in comparison to the archaeobotanical records from other contemporaneous sites in the Tucson Basin, the Cienega Valley, and the San Pedro River valley.

San Pedro Phase Subsistence

The San Pedro phase archaeobotanical record in southern Arizona includes a suite of tropical cultigens labeled the "Early Mesoamerican Crop Complex" by Mabry (2005b). Charred fragments of maize (*Zea mays*) have preserved in most excavated San Pedro phase sites, often in notable abundance. Other possible evidence of cultigens, including amaranth (*Amaranthus* sp.), squash (*Cucurbita* sp.), cotton (*Gossypium* sp.), and tobacco (*Nicotiana* sp.), may also have been a part of this complex (Mabry, ed. 2008). Mabry suggests that these early farmer-foragers not only collected, but also possibly protected, encouraged, and/or cultivated numerous leafy annual plants that thrive in the disturbed soil of active floodplains and cultivated fields and canals, such as goosefoot (*Chenopodium* sp.), amaranth (*Amaranthus* sp.), and tansy mustard (*Descurainia* sp.).

Within the general upland region, other excavated sites date to the Early Agricultural period. Not far from the Marsh Station Road

site project area, two San Pedro phase sites, the Donaldson Site (AZ EE:2:30 [ASM]) and Los Ojitos (AZ EE:2:137 [ASM]), are located less than 15 km upstream along Cienega Creek within adjacent Matty Canyon (B. Huckell 1995). A number of flotation samples from these two sites produced a rich record of the plants formerly utilized there (L. Huckell 1995). The plant inventory suggested a system of maize agriculture combined with gathering a broad range of wild resources, some of which may have required some travel to acquire. The groups occupying these Matty Canyon locations effectively integrated both foraging and farming and took advantage of the natural plant resources available in upland biotic communities.

A few other reports within the uplands are worthy of mention. Archaeologists excavating adjacent areas of the Mescal Wash site (AZ EE:2:51 [ASM]) consider their limited evidence of Late Archaic/Early Agricultural period occupation of the site to be quite similar to the contemporaneous Los Ojitos and Donaldson sites discussed above (Vanderpot 2001; Vanderpot and Altschul 2007). Farther south and west in the Santa Rita Mountains, a number of Archaic period archaeological sites in the Rosemont area excavated as part of the ANAMAX-Rosemont project yielded a few carbonized plant remains, among them walnuts (*Juglans*) and goosefoot (*Chenopodium*) seeds, both likely gathered for food (L. Huckell 1984).

In contrast to these upland sites, the Las Capas site (AZ AA:12:111 [ASM]) is a stratified Tucson Basin site buried in the former floodplain of the Santa Cruz River (Mabry, ed. 2008). Radiocarbon dates from numerous fragments of maize and other plant parts suggest almost continuous occupation of this site during the San Pedro phase (1200 to 800 B.C.). Increases in densities of charred plant remains during occupation of Las Capas suggested substantial population growth over time (Diehl 2005b). The occupants of Las Capas also practiced a fair amount of mobility over the calendar year as they traveled to and from their dwellings to harvest wild resources some distance away. Wild plants sought included plants in the cheno-am group, tansy mustard (*Descurainia* sp.) seeds, saguaro (*Carnegiea* sp.) and prickly pear (*Opuntia* sp.) fruit, mesquite (*Prosopis* sp.) pods, grass (Gramineae) grains, and small seeds of numerous other weedy plants. Maize (*Zea mays*) was commonly recovered in both early San Pedro and late San Pedro features at Las Capas (Diehl 2005b:80–81), suggesting it was an important crop. Evidence of domesticated beans (*Phaseolus* sp.) was rare, and no domesticated squash (*Cucurbita* sp.) or agave (*Agave* sp.) remains were found for these time periods.

The Las Capas plant assemblages indicate a broad diet breadth consistent with a mixed foraging and farming strategy. An apparent decrease in diet breadth occurred later in time during the Early Ceramic period (A.D. 50 to 650), as suggested by presence of low return-rate wild plant resources. This was presumably accompanied by increasing energetic returns from agricultural production that coincided with the ability to securely store seed stock within ceramic vessels. Based on a large dataset of archaeological sites, Diehl (2005b:84–86) noted that the mean number of plant taxa at sites by time period in the Tucson Basin decreased from the early San Pedro phase (n = 28.0) to the Late Cienega phase (n = 23.3) to the Sedentary period (n = 14.9). When all Early Agricultural period assemblages were compared to all Ceramic period assemblages, the differences in diet breadth were striking (21.3 taxa vs. 13.4 taxa) and statistically significant (Diehl 2005b:86).

The limited San Pedro phase deposits from the Marsh Station Road site preserved a subset of the subsistence resources described above from the Tucson Basin. In this upland setting, maize farmers supplemented their subsistence by gathering seeds of cheno-am plants and wild grass grains. The maize they grew is very similar in appearance to maize from other sites of this time period, suggesting many farmers had access to a very common maize variety. It is likely these farmers also utilized other wild foods, such as mesquite pods, because they lived adjacent to a mesquite bosque. The low diversity of foods reported here is likely due to both a low level of sampling and to the location of the Marsh Station Road site in an upper elevation semidesert grassland setting some distance from the botanically diverse Tucson Basin Sonoran Desert bajadas and river floodplains. It is also possible that the Mescal Wash region was not occupied year-round, but was visited primarily during the summer and early fall months.

Early Formative Period Subsistence

A number of Tucson Basin archaeobotanical reports on the Early Formative period have been summarized by Lisa Huckell (1998:342–344). The sites representing this time period include the Agua Caliente phase Houghton Road site (AZ BB:13:398 [ASM]), and the Tortolita phase components of El Arbolito (AZ EE:1:153 [ASM]), the Dairy Site (AZ AA:12:285 [ASM]), and Lonetree (AZ AA:12:120 [ASM]). This record indicates that cultigens (maize, domesticated beans, and squash) are an established dietary component during this time. In addition, cotton and agave evidence also preserved. The range of wild plants utilized reveals a broadly diverse strategy of gathering foods from upper elevations, bajadas, alluvial fans, and riparian areas. The three most prominent subsistence resources included legumes, cheno-ams, and cacti. Similarly, the Early Formative archaeobotanical record from the Marsh Station Road site reported here, although represented by a relatively small number of flotation samples, clearly indicates use of both maize and cheno-ams as food. The repeated use of mesquite wood for fuel and other needs implies the edible pods would have been available and likely utilized for food.

Late Middle Formative Period Subsistence

The record of subsistence and plant use for the Rillito–Rincon and Rincon phase components of the Formative period in the Tucson Basin have been summarized by Charles Miksicek (1988) for the Punta de Agua sites (AZ BB:13:16, AZ BB:13:41, AZ BB:13:43, AZ BB:13:49, and AZ BB:13:50 [ASM]), West Branch (AZ AA:16:3 [ASM]), Tanque Verde Wash (AZ BB:13:68 [ASM]), and Cienega sites (AZ EE:2:30, AZ EE:2:50, AZ EE:2:62, AZ EE:2:103, and AZ EE:2:137 [ASM]). Miksicek reports the presence of the following domesticates: maize, common beans (*Phaseolus vulgaris*), jack beans (*Canavalia ensiformis*), squash (*Cucurbita* spp.), bottle gourd (*Lagenaria siceraria*), cotton (*Gossypium hirsutum*), and tobacco (*Nicotiana rustica*). Maize presence ranges from 14 to 60 percent in these sites, and the domesticated beans reach over 30 percent in some locations. Miksicek also reports agave (*Agave*) and amaranth (*Amaranthus*) as cultivated plants, along with a number of encouraged wild plants (e.g., tansy mustard [*Descurainia*], goosefoot [*Chenopodium*]), agricultural field weeds, and perennial taxa. Farther to the west in the Avra Valley, two Rillito phase sites were occupied by maize farmers who supplemented their diet with wild plant foods, particularly cheno-ams and cacti (Kwiatkowski 1989).

In comparison, a number of late Middle Formative period features at the Marsh Station Road site preserved plant resources gathered in the past for food. These included maize, broad-leaf yucca fruit, grass grains, and a plant in the Monocotyledon group, possibly agave. These foods reflect resources available in the semidesert grassland setting, and therefore document different food choices from those available to groups living in the Tucson Basin.

SUMMARY

The archaeobotanical record from the Marsh Station Road site sheds light on subsistence and other uses for plants during the San Pedro phase of the Early Agricultural period, and during both the Early and late Middle portions of the Formative period. The site is located within the semidesert grassland biotic community, dominated by grasses, cacti, agaves, yuccas, and a range of upland plants. The site is also situated in a location adjacent to mesquite bosques and with access to water.

A total of 39 flotation samples and 32 macrobotanical samples comprises the sample base, with most of these samples dating to the San Pedro phase and the late Middle Formative period.

At the Marsh Station Road site, the plant remains indicative of subsistence include both maize and wild plants. Maize was grown during both the San Pedro phase and the early and late Middle Formative period, and left-over cobs were utilized as fuel/tinder. The maize varieties appear distinctly different in cob morphology between these two time periods, which was expected. The San Pedro phase maize conforms to descriptions of Early Agricultural period maize from the Tucson Basin. The later Formative period maize exhibits notably different traits suggesting that, in most respects, the ears were larger.

Farmers also gathered seeds from wild cheno-am plants that would have occupied their agricultural fields as weeds, and occasionally harvested grass grains. During the late Middle

Formative period they also occasionally sought broad-leaf yucca fruit and possibly the carbohydrate rich tissue of a plant such as agave. Wood use through time focused on mesquite, but also included branches and stems of hackberry, saltbush, creosote bush, juniper, and cottonwood/willow. In addition, grass stems and reedgrass stems offered raw materials for other material culture needs.

Plant use displays little variability through time. Maize and a limited number of wild plants provided subsistence resources during both the San Pedro phase and the Formative period. At the Marsh Station Road site, there does appear to be some intrasite variability in plant use, especially during the late Middle Formative. A comparison of features associated with a number of archaeological stripped areas revealed some differences in activities involving plant resources across space; however, the types of features varied from location to location and may be partly responsible for this patterning.

Plant communities available in the past hosted many of the same plants as occupy the modern landscape. However, one difference may have been better developed riparian communities during the pre-Hispanic period, evidenced by access not only to mesquite trees, but also to cottonwood and willow trees, hackberry trees, and reedgrass plants, based on the archaeobotanical record reported here.

The archaeological plant record generally indicates use of the region during the summer through fall seasons. Most reproductive parts identified ripen in the mid-to late summer through fall months. This does not preclude the possibility that people were also in the region at other times of the year, or that they prepared these resources after having stored them for some months.

Comparisons to other southern Arizona archaeobotanical records reveal some similarities and some differences. Generally, the Marsh Station Road site preserved a subset of San Pedro phase subsistence resources reported from Matty Canyon sites (south along Cienega Creek) and from some well-preserved Tucson Basin sites. During the Formative period, the site again preserved subsets of plant resources reported elsewhere for this period. Poor preservation and limited sampling may have in part contributed to these patterns. However, differences between semidesert grassland resources and Sonoran Desert resources may also affect the range of plants accessible to groups. The nature of occupation of the sites, whether as semi-permanent locations or occasionally visited locales during certain periods of the year, would also affect the availability and potential use of plants in the region.

Chapter 11
Pollen Results

Bruce G. Phillips

A total of 30 pollen samples from the Marsh Station Road site was analyzed. During the Early Agricultural period, the site probably was used for farming, procurement, and processing; the site may also have served as a habitation locus as it did during the Formative period, although, only one structure possibly dating to the Early Agricultural period was documented as part of the project.

At the Marsh Station Road site, maize pollen was not present in the few Early Agricultural period samples analyzed, potentially indicating that farming was not conducted at that time (but see Chapter 10 for the macrobotanical perspective). In contrast, maize pollen and aggregates were common to Formative period contexts; squash pollen also was present. Other resources include cacti, cheno-ams, members of the sunflower and grass families, and white mat. Cattail, wild buckwheat, and members of the mustard family also might have been used. Overall, pollen of economic resources was relatively well distributed; no evidence of specialized functions among feature types was discerned. Rather, repeated habitation might have blended sediments across the site, obscuring patterns of pollen distribution.

ENVIRONMENTAL SETTING

Elevation at the Marsh Station Road site is approximately 1,097 m (3,600 feet) above mean sea level. The site has been impacted by railroad construction, pipelines, fiber optic lines, and roads. The native biotic community of the site is semidesert grassland (Brown, ed. 1994). In its original state, perennial bunch grasses dominate the landscape. Conspicuous elements include stem and leaf succulents, such as sotol (*Dasylirion sp.*), beargrass (*Nolina sp.*), agave (*Agave sp.*), and yucca (*Yucca sp.*). Heavy cattle grazing in late 1800s and early 1900s greatly reduced grass cover, lowering the frequency of wildfires. This allowed the invasion of woody and shrubby species, such as mesquite (*Prosopis sp.*), juniper (*Juniperus sp.*), cacti (*especially Opuntia sp.*), burroweed (*Isocoma sp.*), and snakeweed (*Gutierrezia sp.*). Such vegetative communities are characterized as disjunct semidesert grassland (Brown 1994:126). Today the Marsh Station Road site is covered and surrounded by creosote bush (*Larrea tridentata*), mesquite, cacti, yucca, agave, ocotillo (*Fouqueria splendens*), and low grasses and forbs.

Currently, mesquite grows thick along the banks of the entrenched channel of Cienega Creek. Thick sedimentary layers and organic deposits exposed in arroyo walls reflect fluctuating conditions in the past. Prior to the late nineteenth century, Cienega Creek was a shallow, perennial stream, flowing slowly through an ill-defined channel (Eddy and Cooley 1983; Hastings and Turner 1965; B. Huckell 1995). Occasional marshes (ciénegas) were surrounded by willow (*Salix sp.*), cottonwood (*Populus sp.*), ash (*Fraxinus velutina*), and black walnut (*Juglans major*). Aquatic types included rushes (*Juncus sp.*), sedges (*Scirpus sp.*), and cattail (*Typha sp.*). By 1890, Cienega Creek was becoming a deep, narrow channel. Most wetlands dried up and mesquite forests replaced earlier riparian types. What caused the change remains a matter of debate, but a combination of climatic, geomorphic, and human factors are likely to blame (also see Chapter 3). Extant ciénegas can be found along Cienega Creek in Empire Valley, south of the site.

RESEARCH THEMES

The majority of features investigated are associated with the Hohokam culture. Others are associated with Early Agricultural peoples. Five general research themes are addressed for the Marsh Station Road site: site formation processes, chronology, cultural affiliation and interaction, diet and subsistence, and intrasite activity patterns. Diet and subsistence is the focal theme in the pollen analysis.

Environmental reconstruction is an important aspect of studies of prehistoric subsistence. As mentioned previously, investigations by Eddy and Cooley (1983) showed the environment of Cienega Creek varied through time. As conditions changed, the opportunities afforded to site residents also would have changed, potentially causing adjustments to subsistence

strategies. Reconstructing the paleoenvironment was a secondary goal of the current palynological study.

Pollen samples from archaeological features were selected, processed, and analyzed, creating an inventory of potential resources. Pollen data were compared to historic and modern analogues, identifying those elements that are common and those that are anomalous. Such anomalies might include the relative abundance of disturbance indicators (for example, weeds) and abundance of cultivated types. Cultigens were inventoried. Measures of abundance and concentration were used to analyze the pollen assemblage and identify those wild resources most important to the population and those plants that played lesser roles.

METHODS

Pollen grains are male cells carrying genetic material necessary for reproduction, and range in size from about 8 to 120 μm (0.008–0.12 mm). For pollination, pollen is carried by wind (anemophilous) and by animals (zoophilous). At any time, varying amounts of pollen are in the air (pollen rain). Pollen assemblages resulting from the pollen rain are expected to reflect surrounding plant communities. As pollen falls to the ground, it is incorporated into sediment. In a strict sense, most pollen recovered from unconsolidated sediment is not fossilized, but is nevertheless called fossil pollen. In cultural settings, pollen assemblages are affected by human activity, which obscured the natural pollen rain. Pollen is often found in contexts that would not happen naturally; in such cases, the pollen can be interpreted culturally. In a sense, fossil pollen grains are artifacts and can therefore be used to examine certain aspects of behavior, such as subsistence.

Sediment samples were sent to the Paleoecology Laboratory, Texas A&M University, for pollen extractions. Sample bag contents were mixed thoroughly, and 20 g subsamples were taken. Approximately 27,000 grains of *Lycopodium* were added to estimate pollen concentration. Samples were then treated with 10 percent hydrochloric acid to reduce carbonates, followed by a swirl-and-decant step (Mehringer 1967:136–137) to reduce the heavier matrix fraction (greater than 180 μm). Silicates were reduced by a hydrofluoric acid treatment over an approximately 20-hour period. Heavy liquid flotation in zinc bromide (with a specific gravity of 1.9) was followed by acetolysis to further reduce organics. The remaining residues were washed with water and alcohol, stained with saffranin, and suspended in glycerol.

At EcoPlan laboratories, Mesa, Arizona, extracts were mounted in a glycerol medium onto glass slides; they were then examined at a viewing power of 400x on an Olympus BHTU compound microscope. Subsequent percentage calculations were based on standard 200 grain counts. Identifications were aided by EcoPlan reference material and keys (Kapp 1969; Moore et al. 1991). Each fossil pollen grain was identified to the generic level when possible. If a grain could not be differentiated from similar genera, it was identified only to the family level. Pollen grains that were broken, corroded, or degraded beyond recognition were assigned to the indeterminate category.

Following standard examination, slides were scanned at 100x magnification to record cultigens and rare pollen types with possible cultural significance (such as cacti). Pollen aggregates (clumps) were recorded. Because aggregates are not efficiently transported by wind, they indicate either a source in the immediate sampling area (Fish 1995:661) or introduction to the site by humans (Gish 1991). Based on work by Gish (1993) and Smith (1995), the following aggregate size cutoffs were used: maize and cacti, none; cheno-am, 30

grains; others, 10 grains. Although cutoffs are subjective, they help filter out small aggregates resulting from natural processes or laboratory procedures (Smith 1995:171). Finally, the number of tracers per slide was determined. This allowed a concentration estimate for each category recorded in scanning.

Pollen concentrations were calculated with the following formula:

$$\text{Concentration} = \frac{\text{pollen grains counted}}{\text{tracers counted}} \times \frac{\text{tracer concentration}}{\text{sample volume}}$$

Pollen concentration values are estimates of the quantity of fossil pollen preserved in each gram of sediment. In natural settings, these values can indicate sedimentation rates, pollen production and dispersion rates, and the effects of differential preservation. In cultural settings, concentrations can indicate the intensity of site and/or feature use. Because many factors can influence pollen concentrations, they must be interpreted with discretion. Susan Smith, a palynologist at Northern Arizona University, has said that the figures are estimates; differences on an order of a magnitude or more are likely significant. Thus, while the data are presented as they were calculated, 20 grains/gram is not necessarily greater than 10 grains/gram; rather 200 grains/gram versus 20 grains/gram should be considered a significant difference.

Degraded pollen assemblages are not uncommon in the Southwest (Hall 1981, 1985; Holloway 1981). Many factors cause pollen deterioration, and the process is not well understood. Mechanical factors can cause grains to be crushed or torn apart, whereas chemical agents can affect their structural integrity. Chief among chemical agents is the cycle of wetting and drying (Holloway 1989), which commonly affects open-air sites. Another factor is heat, which can oxidize and destroy pollen grains. Also affecting the number and distribution of pollen types is the amount of sporopollenin in grains of different plants. Sporopollenin is a highly resistant organic compound that allows pollen to be preserved in sediments and other settings. Because cheno-ams and Asteraceae often have large amounts of the compound and hence preserve well, they are often over-represented in the pollen record. Degraded grains were tracked in the analysis.

RESULTS

All samples contained sufficient grains for valid 200 grain counts. Thirty-four taxa were seen in pollen samples (Table 11.1), including maize and squash. Of those types in the Trees category, only mesquite is a local, native type. Within the Herbs and Shrubs category, all types are local except for Mormon Tea, which grows at higher elevations. Filaree is generally interpreted as an exotic, introduced in early historic times. Nomenclature and plant ecology follow Kearney and Peebles (1960); plants are discussed using their common names, except for cheno-ams, and high- and low-spine Asteraceae. Other sources for flowering season are Gish (1989), Rea (1997), and Smith (1995).

Cheno-ams dominate the pollen assemblage, having the highest frequencies in all but three instances; grass pollen was most common in surface control samples from the Marsh Station Road Site. Subdominants of the assemblage were the Asteraceae and grasses. Other common types were cattail, mustards, members of the Pea family, and creosote bush. Wind-pollinated pine, juniper, oak, and Mormon tea grow at higher elevations and were likely blown or washed to the project area from the surrounding mountains. Pollen signatures of subsurface samples generally reflected the Sonoran vegetation of the lower bajada and floodplains (Schoenwetter and Doerschlag 1971). Surface samples were more typical of grasslands. High cheno-am frequencies were probably due to the site's proximity to the floodplain, and to ground disturbance, which allowed the opportunistic plants to thrive. Globemallow, spiderling, and Arizona poppy grains were rare; no sample had combined frequencies totaling 10 percent or greater, the level suggested by Fish (1984, 1998) as indicating agricultural intensity. Although this would suggest casual, nonintensive farming, edaphic factors could have caused the low frequencies. The riparian zone was represented by cattail and willow.

In scans, maize was found in 20 samples (66.6 percent) and squash was seen in 3 samples (10 percent). Of the cacti, cholla was most common, occurring in eight samples (26.6 percent). With a few exceptions, cultigen and cacti grain concentrations were relatively low, suggesting that in general, subsistence activities were not intensive. Cheno-ams were the most common aggregate type, found in 23 samples (76.6 percent). Overall, aggregate concentrations were low-to-moderate, further suggesting relatively low levels of activity. Collectively, the grain aggregate assemblage suggested spring through fall occupations.

Economic resources are those plants that played an important role in prehistoric subsistence. By default, all cultigens are considered economic resources and, based on ethnographic evidence (Castetter 1935; Castetter and Bell 1942; Rea 1997), cacti also are considered important. Identifying wild plants that were important to the diet can be difficult and somewhat subjective—essentially all of the taxa identified in the study have ethnographically documented uses. In this study, wild economic resources were considered those types occurring in greater than 75 percent of 200 grain counts and that also occurred as aggregates, which included cheno-ams, the Asteraceae, grasses, and white mat. Cattail, wild buckwheat, and the mustards fell short of

Table 11.1. Scientific names, common names, flowering seasons, and pollination modes of pollen types found at the Marsh Station Road site

Scientific Name	Common Name	Flowering Season	Pollination
Cultigens			
Zea mays	maize	summer	wind
Cucurbita	squash	summer	insect
Cacti			
Cylindropuntia	cholla	spring–early summer	insect
Platyopuntia	prickly pear	spring	insect
Cereus-type	saguaro, hedgehog	spring	insect
Riparian Types			
Typha	cattail	summer	wind
Salix	willow	spring	wind
Trees			
Pinus pondersosa-type	ponderosa pine	late spring	wind
Pinus edulis-type	pinyon pine	summer	wind
Juniperus	juniper	late winter–early	wind
Quercus	oak	spring	wind
Prosopis	mesquite	spring	insect
Herbs and Shrubs			
Cheno-Am	includes goosefoot, pigweed, and others	spring–fall	wind/insect
Low-spine Asteraceae	includes bursage, ragweed	summer–fall	wind
High-spine Asteraceae	includes sunflower, seepwillow, desert broom	spring–fall	wind/insect
Liguliflorae	liguliflorae	spring	insect
Poaceae	grass family	spring–fall	wind
Sphaeralcea-type	globemallow	spring–fall	insect
Boerhaavia-type	spiderling	summer–fall	insect
Kallstroemia	Arizona poppy	summer	insect
Eriogonum	wild buckwheat	spring–summer	insect
Euphorbia	spurge	spring–fall	insect
Ephedra	Mormon tea	spring	wind
Tidestromia	white mat	summer	insect
Erodium	crane's bill	spring	insect
Brassicaceae	Mustard family	spring	insect
Cf. Fabaceae	Pea family	spring–fall	insect
Solanaceae	Nightshade family	spring–fall	insect
Rosaceae	Rose family	spring–summer	insect
Liliaceae	Lily family	spring	insect
Apiaceae	Parsley family	spring	insect
Onagraceae	Evening primrose family	spring–summer	insect
Plantago	plantain	spring	insect
Larrea	creosote bush	spring	insect

the criteria, but were still relatively common and also occurred as aggregates; here, they are considered potential economic resources.

Discussion

Residential and extramural features were investigated at the Marsh Station Road site. The vast majority of features were thermal and nonthermal pits. Following is a review of potential economic plant resources in the project area, a discussion of the pollen data from the Marsh Station Road site, and a comparison of the current pollen assemblage with other studies in the region.

Ecology, Ethnobotany, and Taphonomy of Economic Resources

By reviewing plant ecology and how historic and modern groups have used them, we better understand how the remains recovered during excavation originally entered the archaeological record. The prehistoric residents likely were afforded similar opportunities and probably used similar subsistence strategies as the historic and present day Aikmel O'odham (Pima) and Tohono O'odham (Papago), taking advantage of agriculture on floodplains, while exploiting both riverine and upland resources (Castetter and Bell 1942). Economic resources identified in the current project were cultigens—maize and squash—and several wild resources—cacti, cheno-ams, the sunflower family (Asteraceae), grasses, and white mat. Wild plant use may have been governed more by geography than by cultural factors (Gasser and Kwiatkowski 1991a:432). Specifically, the Hohokam more likely exploited those plants in their neighborhoods rather than traveling long distances to gather resources. Cattail, wild buckwheat, and the mustard family (Brassicaceae) were also identified in the current

project and are here considered potential wild resources.

Maize

Maize was a staple of prehistoric groups in the Southwest, and is often the most abundant cultigen at archaeological sites (Gasser and Kwiatkowski 1991a). With origins in Mesoamerica, primitive chapalote-type maize entered the Southwest before 1500 B.C. (Wills 1988), and perhaps as early as 2100 B.C. (Mabry, ed. 1998, 2008). Recent research in southern Arizona shows maize farming was firmly established by 1000 B.C. (Mabry, ed. 1998). As Hohokam society developed, maize gained importance, its production bolstered by extensive irrigation systems in riverine locales. However, there is evidence that maize was also intensively grown at sites away from core areas using alternative techniques, such as *ak chin* (Gasser and Kwiatkowski 1991b) and floodwater farming (Phillips 1998).

Ethnographically, Piman groups along the Gila River had two growing seasons: a spring planting that produced a summer crop, and a summer planting that resulted in a mid-fall harvest. Summer planting, however, was more common (Castetter and Bell 1942), probably due to the reliability of summer rain. Initial processing involved roasting unhusked ears, which burned much of the husk away. Ears were then dried and stored in various ways for later use. Sometimes ears were completely husked prior to storage. Shelled kernels were often ground into meal. Maize was stored as whole cobs, seeds, and meal.

When desired, stalks and leaves could be dried and used (e.g., as fuel or matting) at nearly any time during the growing season. Once maize ears were harvested, the remainder of the plant was allowed to dry in the field, to be burned and mulched the following season. Maize pollen grains are large and do not fall far from flowering stalks. Therefore, significant amounts of pollen in nonfield areas implies introduction during transport and processing of mature ears. Pollen is progressively removed from maize as it is processed. For example, the most pollen is expected on fresh, unhusked ears with some tassel remaining. Maize stored in this form should also leave aggregates. After roasting, shelling, and processing, little pollen may remain with the fruit (Smith and Geib 1999). However, following a rich harvest, communal rituals, processing, and feasting could potentially spread pollen grains throughout a site.

Squash

Squash remains are sporadically found at Hohokam sites, usually as small bits of charred rind or occasional pollen grains (Gasser and Kwiatkowski 1991a:431). Pumpkin (*Cucurbita pepo*) has been recovered from cave deposits in New Mexico dating to 300 B.C. (Cutler and Whitaker 1961). Like maize, the Pima planted two crops of squash and pumpkins. Throughout the growing season, unproductive flowers could be plucked and fried or made into cakes. Fruits were prepared in a variety of ways, including roasting, frying, and boiling. Seeds were also roasted and eaten.

Several factors limit squash in the archaeological record. The fleshy nature of squash generally prohibits preservation, with an exceptional charred rind or seed recovered by flotation. Also, squash is insect-pollinated, produces relatively small amounts of pollen, and the large grains tend to remain in or near the flower. Furthermore, buds usually wither and fall off the fruits before maturity. Pollen may be introduced to features when a resistant bud remained on harvested fruit or when flowers were prepared for consumption.

Cacti

The seeds of various cacti are consistently recovered from Hohokam sites, often in substantial numbers. Evidence is also mounting that cholla was not only an important wild resource for the Hohokam, but was also cultivated (Bohrer 1991; Gasser and Kwiatkowski 1991a; Miksicek 1992). Cholla flower buds were an important component of the Piman diet (Castetter and Bell 1942); they collected the cactus buds during the spring. After roasting or baking the buds, the spines could be rubbed off (Kearney and Peebles 1960:581), and the buds could then be consumed or stored. The Pima collected fruits of both cholla and prickly pear in the summer. Other members of the cactus family were also important to native people. In fact, the Tohono O'odham calendar begins with the harvest of saguaro fruit and the annual saguaro wine ceremony (Castetter and Bell 1942; Crosswhite 1980). Cacti are insect-pollinated and grains are not expected far from the plant in natural settings. Understandably, the collection and processing of flower buds would introduce more pollen to cultural settings than would fruit. Conversely, mature fruits would be necessary to introduce seeds to thermal or other features.

Cheno-ams

The term cheno-ams refers to members of the family Chenopodiaceae and genus Amaranthus, whose pollen grains are indistinguishable. The seeds of some species also are virtually inseparable. Seeds from cultivated amaranths (e.g., *Amaranthus hypochondriacus* and *A. cruentus*) are occasionally found in archaeological contexts (e.g., Miksicek 1992). Cheno-ams are frequently the most commonly recovered remains from both pollen and flotation samples. Preferring disturbed areas, cheno-ams are found in and around habitation areas and in agricultural fields. Although commonly considered weed-types, the greens and seeds of cheno-ams were a food source (Castetter and Bell 1942; Curtin 1984; Greenhouse et. al. 1981). Roasting pits were lined with greens to protect other foods, produce steam, and add flavor. The seeds were also ground into meal. Seeds and flowers can be found on the same plant, and pollen can be introduced into a feature whether the cheno-ams were used for seeds or greens. As stated above, cheno-ams proliferate in disturbed soil, such as in and around habitations and in agricultural fields, concentrating the pollen type in the local pollen rain. Also, Cheno-ams naturally grow abundantly on floodplains, further increasing the amount of local pollen regardless of whether the plants have been culturally manipulated or not. In such settings, distinguishing cultural use of cheno-ams versus a natural signal can be difficult; the presence of pollen aggregates is important.

Sunflower Family

The sunflower family (Asteraceae; also known as Compositae) is one of the largest families in the plant kingdom and many members were used one way or another by native groups. Historically, composites served many purposes, mostly medicinal and utilitarian. The low-spine Asteraceae category mainly reflects the dominance of bursages (*Ambrosia spp.*) on the bajada. However, the bursages were not much used by the Gila River Pima (Rea 1997:125) and other low-spine types may be responsible for the elevated frequencies and aggregates in the current pollen assemblage. Plants contributing high-spine Asteraceae pollen to the assemblage include shrubby types that grow along rivers and ditches, such as desert broom (*Baccharis sarothroides*) and arrow-weed (*Pluchea sericea*), which served a number of primarily utilitarian purposes (Rea 1997:145–149).

Because members of the sunflower family are common constituents of pollen rain and many species make up the large family, discerning prehistoric use is difficult at best.

Grass Family

Charred grass remains are found often enough at Hohokam sites to be considered a regular food item (Gasser and Kwiatkowski 1991a: 439). Dropseed, brome, canary, panic, bristle, and other grass seeds have been identified. Additionally, little barley grass (*Hordeum pusillum*) has been identified as a cultigen. Different grass species flower and set fruit throughout the year. Unfortunately, many charred grass seeds are fragmented, limiting identification. Also, grass pollen grains are rarely distinguishable below the family level, the exceptions being maize and Old World cereals. Various methods were used to process grass grains, including fire-threshing (Wheat 1967:11), which could char some grains. The reduced fruit could be used in a number of ways, especially when ground into meal and added to other foods. Pollen could be introduced with immature flower spikes.

White Mat

White mat is a member of the pigweed family (Amaranthaceae). The low prostrate annual grows on sandy or rocky soils, flowers from July to October, and sets small seeds in the late summer and fall. White mat pollen has been considered an indicator of prehistoric ground disturbance (Gish 1991:243), and historically white mat has become a pest in agricultural fields (Parker 1972:122). Ethnographic use of white mat is lacking in local groups. In fact, Rea (1997:399) found that common wooly white mat (*Tidestromia lanuginosa*) was unnamed among the Gila River Pima. Prehistoric residents may have gathered the plant for its seeds or greens, unintentionally brought it from fields along with crops, or used it for some other unknown purpose.

Cattail

Cattail proliferates in Southwestern wetlands. Prior to river control, cattail was widespread. The O'odham primarily used the long slender stalks for basketry and thatching; occasionally the tender white stalks and roots were collected and eaten raw (Rea 1997:108). Other native groups added cattail pollen to meal or made pollen biscuits (Curtin 1984:64–65). Apache used cattail pollen in ceremonies. Plants gathered during flowering and used for utilitarian purposes may introduce some pollen to dwellings. Ceremony and consumption would introduce greater amounts.

Wild Buckwheat

Hopi used wild buckwheat as an analgesic; Hopi women used the plant as a gynecological aid and to expedite childbirth (Colton 1974:314). Some Navajo groups used the herb as a panacea, treating numerous ailments (Wyman and Harris 1951). No recorded uses are found among the Pima (Rea 1997). Wild buckwheat pollen could be introduced from flowering plants. The herb proliferates under favorable edaphic conditions, such as on well-watered floodplains and alluvial fans.

Mustard Family

There is evidence that mustards (family name Cruciferae) were used by the Salado in east-central Arizona (Fish 1998) and by the Hohokam of southern Arizona (Gish 1993). The O'odham used tansy mustard (*Descurainia pinnata*) to make a pinole from the roasted ground seeds (Rea 1997:224) and it also served medicinal purposes. Other mustards might have been used similarly in the past.

THE MARSH STATION ROAD SITE

From the Marsh Station Road site, 29 archaeological samples and 1 control sample from overburden were analyzed. The overburden sample was dominated by grass pollen. Apparently, not long after the site was abandoned, vegetation changed from an environment rich in cheno-ams to one covered in grasses.

The sample set from the Marsh Station Road site consisted of 3 securely identified Early Agricultural period (all San Pedro phase) contexts, 18 from Formative period (mostly Rincon phase) contexts, and 8 from contexts of unknown age, presumably either the Early Agricultural or Formative periods (Tables 11.2 and 11.3).

Maize pollen was absent from all Early Agricultural period samples, suggesting agriculture was not conducted in the immediate area at that time. Some of the samples from unknown temporal contexts, however, contained maize pollen and might actually date to the San Pedro phase. Cattail pollen was present in low percentages in all samples, reflecting riparian vegetation along Cienega Creek. No feature had exceptionally high percentages or concentrations of any particular taxa. Both samples from a bell pit (Feature 98) had higher cheno-am and grass pollen percentages than the nonthermal pit (Feature 44), possibly reflecting lining of the bell pit with greens or the wild resources stored there. Cheno-am and white mat aggregates were found in all samples, potentially indicating exploited wild resources or local abundance.

Maize pollen was found in 72 percent, and maize aggregates in 28 percent, of Formative Period samples; squash also was present. Both indices indicate that farming was conducted nearby and that fresh produce was brought to the site. In particular, a sample from Feature 152, a pit house, had an extremely high concentration of maize pollen and aggregates showing that fresh ears were initially stored in the structure and possibly processed there. Cholla, prickly pear, cheno-am, and wild buckwheat pollen aggregates suggested that other resources might also have been stored in Feature 152. Feature 109, a bell pit, had a somewhat high percentage of cattail pollen, potentially shed from stored resources or from pit lining. Feature 6, an extramural use surface, contained relatively high percentages of white mat and Mustard family pollen, suggesting the wild resources were processed on the surface or were abundant nearby. Otherwise, overall percentages of economic resources were not substantially different than those of Early Agricultural data, suggesting that similar resources were available in both times. Cattail appeared in one-third of samples, possibly indicating that the riparian zone was more reduced than in earlier times.

When the contexts of unknown age are included, summary statistics of both the 200 grain count and the scan do not change substantially, suggesting that general activities at the site remained relatively consistent through time. Therefore, an examination of the spatial distribution of resources included all contexts (Table 11.4). Ubiquities of economic resources identified in scans were used. All sizes of nonthermal pits were combined, as were thermal pits and roasting pits. Pit house samples include floor fill, floor, and subfeature contexts. Maize pollen and aggregate concentrations were most common to surfaces and nonthermal pits. It is possible produce was processed on use-surfaces and then stored in pits; it is also possible that pit samples included refuse. Cholla and prickly pear pollen were well distributed, indicating that they were commonly used. Similarly, cheno-ams were well distributed, but were ubiquitous to bell pits, possibly reflecting stored resources or greens lining the pits. White mat was well distributed, but rare in pit houses and might have been intentionally kept

out for unknown reasons. Overall, economic pollen was relatively well distributed and no distinct patterns were apparent that suggested specialized functions among feature types. While people might not have made such distinctions, it is possible that patterns of pollen distribution were obscured as sediments across the site blended over time.

Regional Comparisons

Early Agricultural period data were viewed in light of a recent synthesis of archaeobotanical data from the Tucson Basin (Diehl, ed. 2005). Formative period pollen results were compared with three projects—ANAMAX, Houghton Road, and Marana—in the region that were roughly contemporaneous and had similarly sized data sets.

Early Agricultural Communities in Southern Arizona

The sites of Las Capas (AZ AA:12:11 [ASM]) and Los Pozos (AZ AA:12:91 [ASM]) offer the finest spatial and temporal data available in southern Arizona for examining differences in the intensity and duration of site location during the Early Agricultural period (Diehl 2005b:73). In his synthesis of botanical data from these sites, Diehl (2005b:89) speculates that San Pedro phase people were both farmers and foragers pursuing a mixed subsistence strategy that relied heavily on cultivated goods along with a variety of wild resources. Maize, mesquite, and saguaro were the primary staples, and were substantially augmented by a wide variety of wild resources. To maintain their diet, occupants spent the spring living on the floodplain, maintaining irrigation canals, and preparing and planting fields of crops. With the ripening of cacti in the foothills in June and July, floodplain settlements were largely abandoned as people moved to harvest the

Table 11.2. Economic pollen types found in 200 grain counts comparing Early Agricultural versus Formative period contexts

	Maize	Cholla	Prickly Pear	Saguaro, Hedgehog	Cattail	Cheno-am	Low-spine Asteraceae	High-spine Asteraceae	Grass Family	Wild Buckwheat	White Mat	Mustard Family	Degraded	Types per Sample	Concentration (grains/gram)
						Early Agricultural									
Average (n=3)		0.2		0.8		59.3	9.7	4.8	10.3	1.5	1.7	1.8	7.7	11.7	47,048
Ubiquity (n=3)		33.3		100.0		100.0	100.0	100.0	100.0	100.0	100.0	100.0			
						Formative									
Average (n=18)	0.1	0.1		0.9		55.3	10.8	5.6	11.0	0.9	1.4	1.1	9.5	11.8	40,004
Ubiquity (n=18)	11.1	22.2	5.6	5.6	66.7	100.0	100.0	100.0	100.0	77.8	100.0	61.1			
						All Contexts									
Average (n=29)		0.1	0.0	0.9		56.9	10.4	5.3	11.0	0.9	1.3	1.3	8.7	11.7	39,570
Ubiquity (n=29)	6.9	17.2	3.4	3.4	75.9	100.0	100.0	100.0	100.0	72.4	96.6	72.4			

Table 11.3. Economic pollen types found in low-resolution scans comparing Early Agricultural versus Formative period contexts

	Grains/gram					Aggregates/gram									
	Maize	Squash	Cholla	Prickly Pear	Saguaro, Hedgehog	Maize	Prickly Pear	Cheno-am	Low-spine Asteraceae	High-spine Asteraceae	Grass Family	White Mat	Cattail	Wild Buckwheat	Mustard Family
						Early Agricultural									
Average (n=3)					1.3			9.7		1.3	5.5	8			
Ubiquity (n=3)					33.3			100.0		33.3	66.7	100.0			
						Formative									
Average (n=18)	27.5	0.3	4.0	2.2	0.9	4.6	1.5	9.4	1.1	0.7	0.8	2.3		0.6	0.3
Ubiquity (n=18)	72.2	5.6	33.3	16.7	11.1	27.8	5.6	66.7	11.1	16.7	11.1	27.8		5.6	5.6
						All Contexts									
Average (n=29)	18.7	0.6	2.7	2.3	0.7	3.0	0.9	13.6	0.7	0.8	2.2	2.7	0.1	0.3	0.4
Ubiquity (n=29)	65.5	10.3	27.6	20.7	10.3	20.7	3.4	79.3	6.9	20.7	20.7	37.9	3.4	3.4	6.9

Table 11.4. Average concentrations of economic pollen grains and aggregates according to feature types

Feature Type	Grains/gram						Aggregates/gram									
	Maize	Squash	Cholla	Prickly Pear	Saguaro, Hedgehog		Maize	Prickly Pear	Cheno-am	Low-spine Asteraceae	High-spine Asteraceae	Grass Family	White Mat	Cattail	Wild Buckwheat	Mustard Family
Bell pits (n=6)	33.3	16.7	16.7	16.7					100.0		16.7	16.7	66.7			16.7
Nonthermal pits (n=6)	83.3			33.3	16.7		50.0		66.7		33.3	16.7	50.0	16.7		16.7
Pit house contexts (n=9)	66.7		55.6	22.2	22.2		22.2	11.1	77.8	22.2			11.1		11.1	
Roasting and thermal pits (n=5)	60.0	20.0	20.0	20.0					80.0		40.0	20.0	40.0			
Use-surface contexts (n=3)	100.0	33.3	33.3				33.3		66.7		33.3		33.3			
All (n=29)	65.5	10.3	27.6	20.7	10.3		20.7	3.4	79.3	6.9	20.7	20.7	37.9	3.4	3.4	6.9

wild resource. As mesquite became available in August, groups returned to the floodplain. Maize matured from late August through October, requiring substantial labor to harvest and process. Both farmed and foraged goods were stored for the winter. While the small sample from confidently recognized San Pedro phase contexts in the current project did not contain maize pollen, other undated contexts potentially used at that time did have maize (see Chapter 10 for a discussion of maize recovered as macrobotanical remains). Otherwise, data from the current project suggested that early residents at the Marsh Station Road site were involved in collecting wild resources, possibly grasses, cheno-ams, and white mat. Mesquite might have been pursued but was not detected in the analysis (but see Chapter 10).

Formative Period Comparison: ANAMAX Project

The ANAMAX project was located on the slopes of the Santa Rita Mountains, southwest of the current project area. Twenty pollen samples from Archaic period contexts were analyzed (Thompkins 1984a:275). Of the six samples containing sufficient pollen from analysis, three were from archaeological contexts. With the exception of grass pollen, all other types fell within the range of variability of modern samples. The low representation of grass pollen from one sample suggested that grasslands were not as widespread as they now are. No cultural activity was evident.

A total of 101 sediment samples from Hohokam sites were analyzed, including seven surface control samples; 40 samples contained sufficient pollen for analysis (Thompkins 1984b). Archaeological samples were uniformly dominated by cheno-am pollen. It is possible that the abundance of cheno-ams was due to the removal of native taxa and replacement by field weeds, the encouragement of

cheno-ams as an edible green, or active cultivation. The data suggested that the Hohokam had a large-scale impact on the environment. Maize pollen was recovered from seven samples at three sites, indicating farming was conducted nearby.

Formative Period Comparison: Houghton Road

Thirty-seven pollen samples were analyzed, 17 of which came from a large communal structure; two Archaic-style pit houses were also examined (Scott-Cummings 1998:317). Mesquite, cheno-ams, and cholla were well represented, indicating local availability. The presence of maize pollen reflected local agriculture. A wide variety of other plants rounded the diet. Evidence from roasting pits suggested that cholla and maize were the most commonly processed foods, and that cheno-am greens were often used in the roasting process. Mesquite pods might also have been roasted or mesquite wood used for fuel, introducing pollen to the pits.

Formative Period Comparison: Marana Sites

Eighty-three pollen samples yielded adequate pollen for analysis (Fish 1987:161). Most samples were from late Sedentary and early Classic period contexts; the majority of those were from structure floors. The data showed that patterns of food production and consumption varied among the three sites excavated. Maize and cholla pollen were the most common economic types. Distribution of these resources suggested that activities at the sites were largely determined by opportunities of the surrounding landscape. That is, maize was most prevalent where floodwater farming could be conducted, while cacti pollen was more common on ridges. Levels of maize pollen were comparable to other small nonriverine sites at higher elevations in the Tucson Basin, but less than at larger sites along the Santa Cruz River.

Comparisons with the Marsh Station Road Site

The Marsh Station Road site Early Agricultural samples did not contain maize pollen, unlike the two sites located along the Santa Cruz River described above. A larger data set might find that maize was grown along Cienega Creek during that time. Formative period contexts differed from the other projects with respect to riparian types—cattail and willow were common at Marsh Station, indicating an established riparian environment. With respect to economic resources, the Hohokam pollen assemblage at the Marsh Station Road site was comparable to other sites. Maize was a staple, augmented by a variety of wild resources. The abundance of cheno-am pollen in all analyses reflects intensive ground disturbance and availability of a versatile herb.

Summary and Conclusion

Having analyzed and interpreted the pollen data, we can now review and address research questions. In summary, pollen from 30 sediment samples was analyzed, including 29 archaeological and 1 overburden samples. The majority of samples were from residential and extramural contexts at the Marsh Station Road site. All samples had sufficient pollen for analysis. Thirty-four taxa were indentified, including maize and squash. Cheno-ams dominated the project assemblage, likely reflecting widespread ground disturbance. With a few exceptions, cultigen and cacti grain concentrations were relatively low, suggesting that in general, subsistence activities were not intensive. Residents of the project area collected wild resources, and possibly also conducted casual farming.

Diet refers to food consumption while subsistence involves procurement of dietary items. Seven economic plant resources were conclusively determined to have been used by residents —maize, squash, cacti, cheno-ams, the Asteraceae, grasses, and white mat. Three other types—cattail, wild buckwheat, and mustards—might also have been a part of the diet.

The Marsh Station Road site was a relatively substantial settlement, with at least six structures in the project area and scores of extramural pits. The small sample of confidently identified contexts from the Early Agricultural period did not contain maize, potentially indicating that farming was not conducted at that time (but see Chapter 10 for the macrobotanical perspective). It is possible however, that some of the undated features containing maize were from this period. Data from the large Hohokam pollen data set indicated that the community took advantage of farming and gathering opportunities along Cienaga Creek and Mescal Wash.

Environmental reconstruction is an important aspect in studies of prehistoric subsistence. As mentioned previously, investigations by Eddy and Cooley (1983) showed the environment of Cienega Creek varied through time. As conditions changed, the opportunities afforded to site residents also would have changed, potentially causing adjustments to subsistence strategies. Within the current project assemblage, samples were largely confined to Formative period contexts, precluding a detailed evaluation of the paleoenvironment. Furthermore, samples from the Marsh Station Road site were from archaeological contexts; environmental data might have been obscured. In contrast, Eddy and Cooley (1983) used samples from a natural stratigraphic column of the Cienega Creek riverbank. Nevertheless, cattail pollen was present in all Early Agricultural samples, reflecting nearby riparian vegetation. In contrast, cattail appeared in one-third of Hohokam-aged samples, potentially indicating that the riparian environment had reduced over time.

Chapter 12
Synthesis and Interpretations

Melanie A. Medeiros, Brandon M. Gabler, Michael J. Boley, and John C. Ravesloot

The goal of the excavations at the Marsh Station Road site was to investigate the site in the light of five research themes: site formation processes, cultural affiliation and interaction, chronology and site development, diet and subsistence, and intrasite activity patterns. Our interpretations are necessarily limited by the sample of the site—only an estimated 4 percent of the total site area—that was investigated. Despite this, interpretation of the data generated through our investigations at the Marsh Station Road site suggests the site is important for understanding the prehistory of southern Arizona. Accordingly, we present a discussion of the research themes addressed by data recovered from the Marsh Station Road site, and attempt to situate the site in local and regional prehistory (also see Chapter 4).

SITE FORMATION PROCESSES

The Marsh Station Road site lies on Pleistocene and Holocene terraces, and on the Holocene floodplain. The portions of the site nearer Cienega Creek and Mescal Wash have seen considerable alluviation over the last several thousand years. The minimal deposition on the higher terraces is the result of slopewash.

The site has been impacted by historic and modern infrastructure development. Three Southern Pacific railroad grades have been built through the site area. The first of these seems to have had relatively little impact, being built onto the site deposits with minimal preparation. The tracks crossed Stripped Area 2/3, causing localized disturbance. The second railroad alignment was placed on a more substantial embankment created by berming site deposits, evidenced by artifacts found in the fill. The construction of this embankment probably resulted in some disturbance to site deposits and features at the eastern edge of SAs 2/3 and 4/5. The most significant disturbance to the site area, however, resulted from the construction of the third, most recent grade (AZ Z:2:40 [ASM]), which remains in use as the Union Pacific mainline. A substantial cutting was excavated to level the grade for this track, which cuts through the northeastern portion of the Marsh Station Road site. McConville and Holzkamper (1955) suggested the railroad cut through a trash mound. While no evidence of a trash mound remains today, artifact densities were quite high in the area. Trenches excavated outside the railroad right-of-way in 1955 suggested there was no depth of cultural material along much of the proposed pipeline alignment in this area. Trenches excavated in 2007 as part of data recovery largely support this finding.

Three phases of communications infrastructure have been built by AT&T through the northeastern portion of the site. The first was a coaxial telephone cable built just after World War II. This was followed by a fiber optic cable in the 1980s and additional fiber ducts installed in the early 2000s. The right-of-way for the most recent project was mitigated by WCRM, which surface-collected and excavated test units and several features (Kearns 2009).

The first petroleum pipeline across the site was built by Southern Pacific Pipeline in 1955. Limited archaeological mitigation was associated with this work (McConville and Holzkamper 1955). A second line was built in the 1960s without any cultural work. Investigations along the latest alignment suggest the impact of these earlier projects was not as severe as might have been expected; the pipelines appear to have been trenched from the ground surface with minimal right-of-way improvement. Construction of the latest pipeline, however, involved intense right-of-way improvement. As a result, no in situ deposits are likely to remain within the APE, area of probable effect, except in close proximity to the previously constructed lines.

Despite the impact of these construction projects, the great majority of the site has not been impacted. The distribution of artifacts on the modern ground surface largely corresponded to the locations of subsurface features within the construction corridor, which suggests reasonable site integrity. No significant impact to the central and southwestern portion of the site has been identified and it is extremely likely that subsurface deposits and features remain in situ.

CULTURAL AFFILIATION

Based on the rich cultural history of the Cienega Valley and the site's location in a cultural transition zone (see Sullivan and Bayman, eds. 2007), the expectation was to find diversity in the Formative-aged material culture and features. At the nearby Mescal Wash site (AZ EE:2:51 [ASM]), material culture and distinctive architectural traits suggested that various cultural groups—the Hohokam, Mogollon, and local indigenous populations (the "Dragoon culture")—all inhabited the site at various times, perhaps concurrently (Vanderpot and Altschul 2007: 65–66). In fact, Vanderpot and Altschul (2007:63) have suggested that the Mescal Wash site was located on the "fringes of the Hohokam regional system...east of the Tucson Basin 'heartland' and west of the Hohokam presence extending down the San Pedro River," an argument they largely based on the lack of a ballcourt as well as the presence of artifacts and features indicative of a mixed cultural (Hohokam, Mogollon, and "Dragoon") presence at the site. However, the data gathered at the Marsh Station Road site suggest that its inhabitants had a strong connection to the Hohokam of the Tucson Basin (Figure 12.1), and indeed, many scholars (e.g., Doyel 1991; Fish et al. 1992; Wilcox 1999) extend the Hohokam tradition to just east of the San Pedro River valley, and several contemporary Hohokam ballcourts have been found within 25 km of the Marsh Station Road site, in the Santa Rita Mountains and along the San Pedro River (Marshall 2001; Wilcox 1991; Wilcox and Sternberg 1983; also see Figure 12.1). In particular, the ceramics recovered from the Marsh Station Road site are primarily Tucson Basin wares. Ceramics indicative of contact with other cultural groups—the Phoenix Basin Hohokam, the Mogollon, the Dragoon, and groups in northern Mexico—were recovered in very small numbers. The eight projectile points dating to the Middle Formative period are morphologically similar to points recovered from other Hohokam sites, such as Hodges Ruin (Kelly et al. 1978) in the Tucson Basin

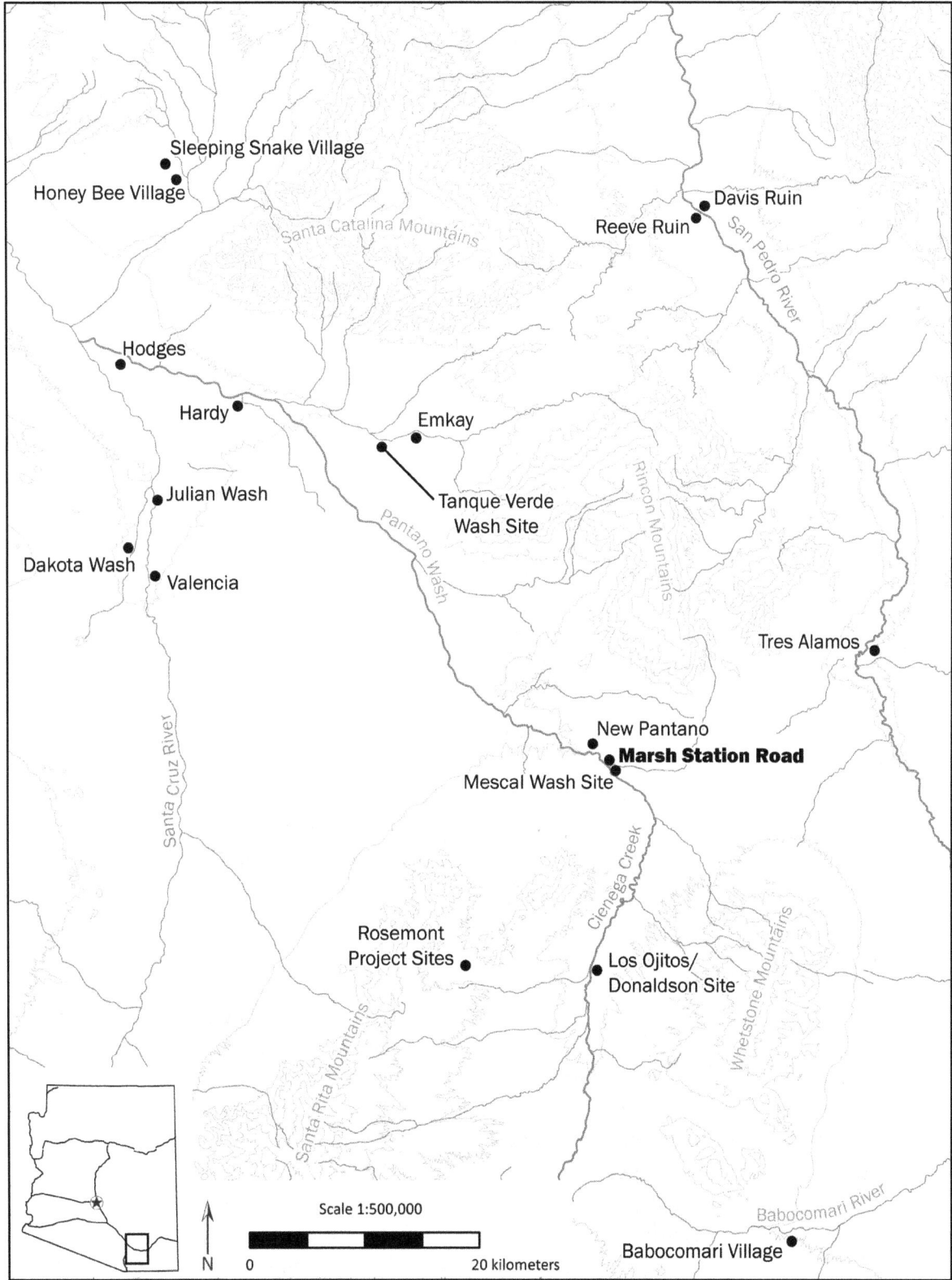

Figure 12.1. Location of the Marsh Station Road site in comparison to other contemporary sites in the region.

and Snaketown (Haury 1976) along the middle Gila River. Unlike at the Mescal Wash site, no architectural traits suggestive of the Mogollon or Dragoon were identified at the Marsh Station Road site. Rather, the structures that date to the Middle Formative share morphological characteristics of those excavated at Rincon phase sites in the Tucson Basin, like Valencia (Doelle, ed. 1985; Elson, ed. 1986; Huntington, ed. 1986). In addition, the majority of the burials documented at the Marsh Station Road site were cremations, a trait typical of the pre-Classic Hohokam (Crown and Fish 1996; McGuire 1992; Reid and Whittlesey 1997). Although several primary inhumations, which are characteristic of Mogllon and Anasazi cultures, were also excavated at the site, it should be noted that Hohokam burial practices began to include more inhumations during the Sedentary to Classic period transition (Crown and Fish 1996; Doelle and Wallace 1991). Finally, although the suite of food resources identified at the Marsh Station Road site reflect, both botanical and faunal resources, available near the Marsh Station Road site, and "therefore document different food choices from those available to groups living in the Tucson Basin" (Adams, Chapter 10), the identified suite is comparable to the types of resources documented in Hohokam sites in southern Arizona dating to the same periods (e.g., see Gasser and Kwiatkowski 1991a, 1991b).

CHRONOLOGY AND SITE DEVELOPMENT

One Gypsum projectile point and a number of Cortaro projectile points suggest a pre-San Pedro phase occupation of the site, but the earliest established occupation was during the San Pedro phase (1500 to 800 BC). The occupation continued over the next 2,500 years, although the Cienega phase of the Early Agricultural period and the Early Formative

(the Agua Caliente and Tortolita phases) period are not particularly well represented. The site witnessed another fairly intense occupation during the late Middle Formative (Rillito-Rincon Phases), and then the occupation seems to have tailed off again in latest prehistory (the Classic period). Several historic features—all Euroamerican, associated with railroad operations through the region, and dating from the late nineteenth through the twentieth century—were also documented. It should also be noted that the majority of the excavated features (n = 62) could not be assigned a temporal affiliation beyond that spanning the site's occupation history.

Early Agricultural Period

The earliest established occupation at the Marsh Station Road site dates to the San Pedro phase of the Early Agricultural period, and is represented by 37 San Pedro projectile points and two radiocarbon assays (1120–810 B.C. and 1250–1240/1220–980 B.C.), one of which is a maize cob segment containing characteristics similar to other San Pedro phase maize from southern Arizona (Diehl 2005a; L. Huckell 2006; also see Chapter 10). In addition, 37 aceramic extramural pits may also be associated with the San Pedro phase occupation of the site. Feature 11, a pit house, may date to this period. Other than possibly Feature 11, no Early Agricultural period habitation structures or occupation surfaces were documented at the site. The majority of the features associated with the San Pedro phase occupation of the site are located in SA 2/3 (see Figures 12.2 and 12.3). Only 8 of the 37 San Pedro phase features were located outside of this area, in SA 4/5 (see Figure 12.3); none were located in SA 1. Although only a few features potentially dating to this phase were excavated in SA 4/5, it is possible that additional evidence of this early occupation in SA 4/5 was destroyed by the later, more intense Middle Formative period occupation. Evidence for a Cienega phase occupation consists of one Cienega Flared projectile point.

Early Formative Period

Only a few features (two with supporting radiocarbon dates) and a very limited amount of material culture—primarily ceramic sherds—date to the Early Formative period, equivalent to the Agua Caliente and Tortolita phases in the Tucson Basin.

Middle Formative Period

The late Middle Formative/Rincon phase period occupation of the site is well-documented. A total of 64 features, including at least five of the six pit houses/structures, dates to the Middle Formative period, as indicated by 10 radiocarbon and 4 archaeomagnetic assays, and the presence of decorated ceramic wares dating to this period. In addition, eight projectile points and two maize cob segments indicative of this period were recovered. As mentioned above, only an estimated 4 percent of the total area of the site was investigated by the current project. Based on survey data, surface collection, and excavation results, which produced the densest cluster of artifacts and features in the southern-most portion of the excavations in SA 4/5 (Figure 12.4), it seems likely that the southeastern portion of the site, as one moves closer to the confluence of Cienega Creek and Mescal Wash, contains densely distributed features associated, at the very least, with the Middle Formative period occupation of the site. It is also possible that additional features associated with an Early Agricultural and/or Middle Formative period occupation of the site could be located in the northeastern portion of the site, near SA 1 and WCRM's 2002 excavations (see Kearns and McVickar 2009 for a discussion of the WCRM excavation results).

Protohistoric and Historic Periods

Although several features believed to be associated with historic Native use of the site area were recorded during the Class III survey, and ethnographic evidence suggests that the Cienega Valley was historically utilized by both the Sobaipuri and the Apache, no definitive evidence of a protohistoric and/or early historic use of the area by these groups was documented during excavations at the Marsh Station Road site. The lack of such evidence should not be taken to indicate that the site area was never used by historic native groups, but rather it suggests that any native historic occupation of the Marsh Station Road site was ephemeral and/or confined to unexcavated areas of the site.

Four historic features were also recorded during excavation. All four historic features date to the late nineteenth or twentieth century, are Euroamerican, and are associated with railroad operations through the region.

Site Development

The preponderance of data generated from excavations at the Marsh Station Road site suggests that occupations at the site differed in nature between the Early Agricultural period and late Middle Formative period. In general, based on the number and types of features dated to the Early Agricultural period as well as the results of artifact and environmental samples analyses, it seems that the occupation of the site during this period was likely less intense than the occupation of the site during the Middle Formative period. B. Huckell (1988, 1995) has previously suggested that during the Early Agricultural period, populations in southern Arizona lived in small hamlets and grew cultigens near resource-rich ciénega environments, and that the habitable areas along Cienega Creek, with the agricultural potential of nearby land (see Heilen and Homburg 2007) and the

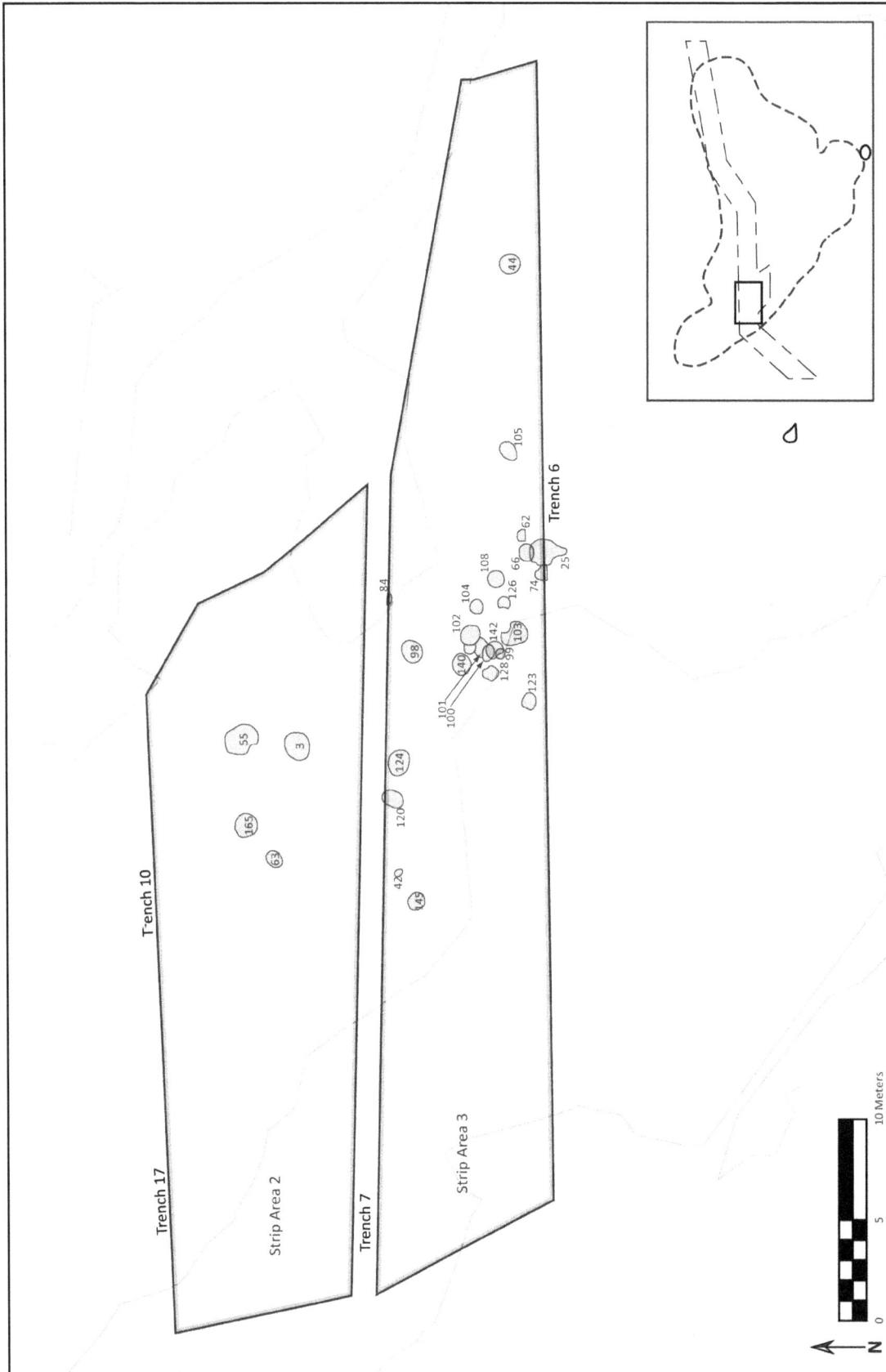

Figure 12.2. Features dating to the San Pedro phase (Early Agricultural period) in Stripped Area 2/3.

Figure 12.3. Features dating to the San Pedro phase (Early Agricultural period) in Stripped Area 4/5.

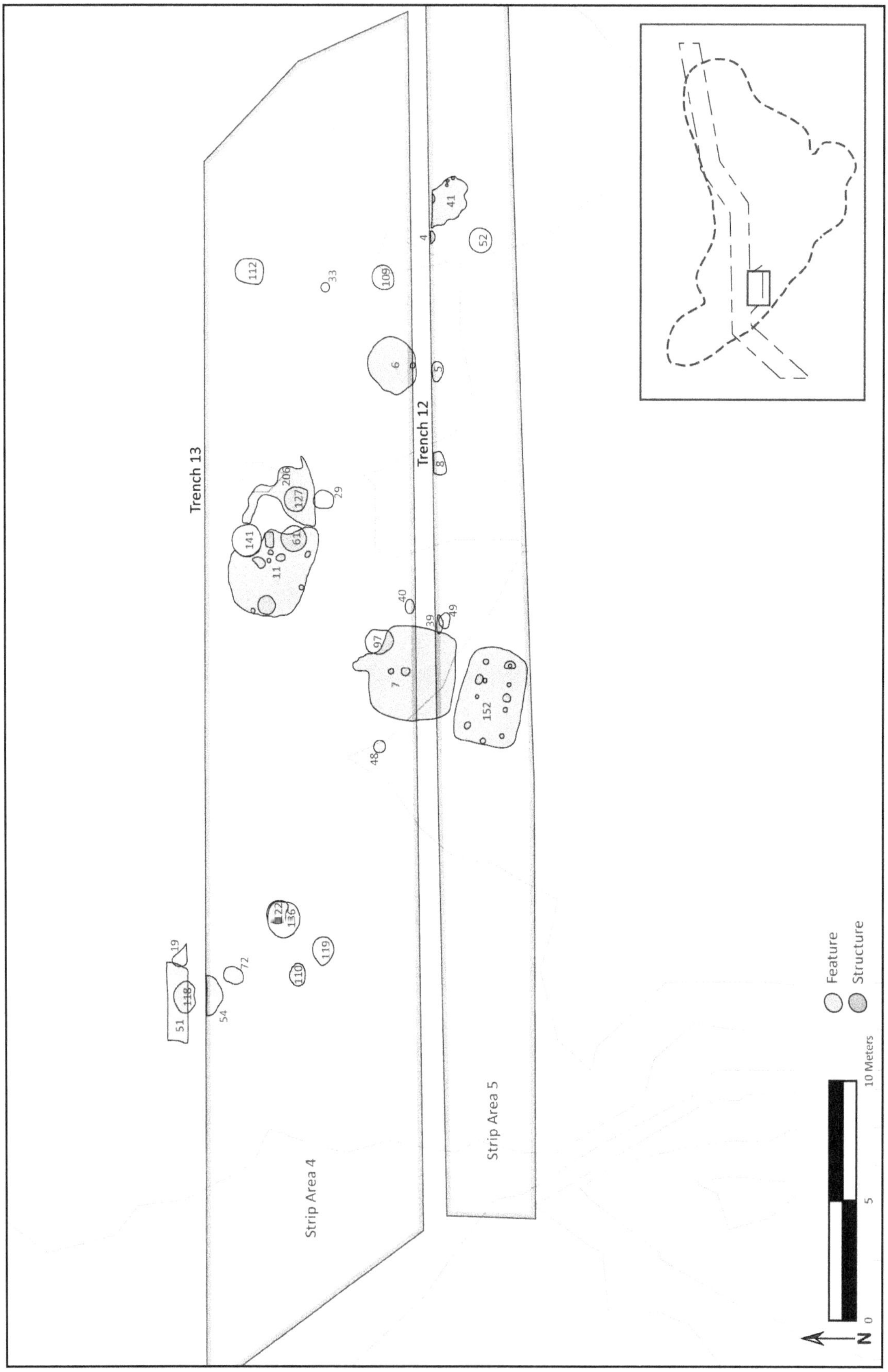

Figure 12.4. Features dating to the Formative period in Stripped Area 4/5.

availability of lithic raw materials as well as firewood and construction materials, made this area a desirable location. And in fact, the Early Agricultural occupation at the Marsh Station Road site is explained quite well by Mabry's (2005b) model of niche filling, although WSA's excavations did not produce definitive evidence of agriculture being conducted near the site during this period. However, the location of the site, in a ciénega environment just below the confluence of two significant drainages (Cienega Creek and Mescal Wash), would likely have allowed for the two of Mabry's cultivation techniques characterized by the lowest labor investment, lowest risk, highest yield, and highest efficiency: water-table farming and overbank flood farming. Indeed, Mabry's model would predict that evidence for the earliest farmers in the region should be found at sites like the Marsh Station Road site, and in fact this may explain the numerous Cortaro points recovered from the site, if these are truly indicative of a pre-San Pedro phase occupation. Mabry's model, however, is not as effective in explaining the lack of Cienega phase material from the site. Perhaps environmental data is not presently refined enough to speak to the efficacy of his model for this period.

The Middle Formative occupation of the site was likely more intense than that of the Early Agricultural period, as reflected by the presence of several pit houses and extramural occupation surfaces and the amount and diversity of cultural material associated with the later period. However, the archaeological evidence is more ambiguous when considering the level of residential mobility and/or sedentism of the Middle Formative period occupation of the site. Clearly, there is a persistence to the site, as has been suggested by both Vanderpot and Altschul (2007) for the Mescal Wash site, and more generally by B. Huckell (1995) for the Cienega Valley (see discussion below). However, as B. Huckell (1995:128) has also noted,

discussing previous studies by both Wills and Windes (1989) and Rafferty (1985), "there are no unambiguous [or single] archaeological indicators of sedentism," although an evaluation of multiple possible indicators of a sedentary occupation—more substantial houses; evidence of community planning; the presence of mounds or ceremonial structures or areas; reliance on agricultural subsistence; large, heavy artifacts; presence of storage facilities; development of deep, dark midden deposits; and flora or fauna indicative of multiseasonal occupation—can provide some clue as to the level of mobility or sedentism practiced at a particular site. In light of these possible indicators, an evaluation of the Middle Formative occupation of the Marsh Station Road site is presented.

As previously discussed, all the pit houses documented at the Marsh Station Road site date to the late Middle Formative period, with the possible exception of Feature 11. In addition, several of the pit houses contained evidence of labor-intensive preparation in the form of plaster and formal subfeatures, characteristics perhaps not likely to be found in houses intended for single and/or very short-term use. Storage features, including bell pits, were also present at the site. Yet, there were no courtyard groups or other features such as defined cemeteries or integrative/ceremonial structures indicative of true long-term, sedentary communities. The low number of burials found at the site suggests that the site population was very low, and/or that the occupation(s) may have been semipermanent or perhaps even seasonal. Additionally, no dense midden deposits were located at the site, and excavated feature deposits do not appear to be indicative of intentional trash deposition, but rather are more characteristic of general sheet trash deposited throughout the site over time. However, data addressing these indicators of sedentism at the site are necessarily limited both by the vertiable lack of stratigraphy at the site, wherein multitudes of features of different types are intrusive and/or superimposed over each other, "suggesting that occupation of the settlement was sufficiently intense and temporally extensive that the use of space changed over the course of its occupation" (B. Huckell 1995:125) and by the small portion of the site excavated by WSA.

While the macrobotanical and pollen data indicative of nearby agriculture for the Early Agricultural period are inconclusive, the same data suggest that casual (rather than intensive) maize agriculture was conducted near the Marsh Station Road site during the Middle Formative period. Wild flora and faunal resources, most of which were locally available but a few of which, such as bighorn sheep, would have required logistical forays to collect or, as with cholla and saguaro, could have been brought when its occupants traveled to the site during the spring, continued to play an important role in the diet. Although present in small quantities, large, heavy artifacts, such as metates, were also present at the site. Given that the metates at the site are signficantly outnumbered by manos and that very few compatible mano/metate sets were recovered, it seems likely that a greater number of metates likely once existed at the site and may have been removed by the occupants at abandonment or subsequently scavenged. Finally, both the macrobotanical and pollen data strongly indicate summer and fall occupation of the site and possible occupation during the spring, although the majority of the spring indicators occur either in very low quanities or in low enough quantities that they were considered only as potential economic resources by the analysts.

Even when taking these possible indicators into account, it is difficult to assess whether the late Middle Formative occupation(s) at the site were seasonal, year-round, or of a repeated nature. However, when considered in conjunction with each other, the available data

suggest that the Middle Formative occupation of the Marsh Station Road site was likely at least semi-permanent, with people living at the site for several seasons of the year. A possible scenario supported by the current data is that a group wintered in the Tucson Basin, and came to the Marsh Station Road site during the spring to plant agricultural fields. Perhaps the occupants remained at the site during the spring and into the early summer, or perhaps a portion of or even the entire population left on logistical foraging trips during this time. The group would have then returned to the site during the mid- to late summer and fall to harvest maize. While it is entirely possible, and perhaps even likely, that the occupation may have been more permanent and/or continuous, we can only speak to what our current data can definitively support. However, as discussed above, numerous features not investigated by the current project are likely located in the southern and eastern portions of the site, closer to the confluence of Cienega Creek and Mescal Wash. Documentation of this portion of the site could revise the assessment of the nature of occupation at the Marsh Station Road site.

DIET AND SUBSISTENCE

Data informing on the diet and subsistence practices of the occupants at the Marsh Station Road site is somewhat limited, despite the large number (n = 442) of macrobotanical, flotation, and pollen samples collected, approximately 22 percent of which were analyzed. These data indicate that people at the Marsh Station Road site were consuming maize, squash, cholla, prickly pear, grass grains, cheno-am seeds, broad-leaf yucca fruit, and perhaps the hearts of some members of the Monocotyledon group of plants, such as *Agave* sp. By the Middle Formative period, both maize and squash were likely casually, rather than intensively, grown near the site. Additionally, occupants exploited local and upland fauna including small birds, lagomorphs (including the eastern cottontail, an upland species that would have been brought to the site by humans), small mammals, and deer. Evidence for agave processing and roasting is notably absent from the Marsh Station Road site, even though nearby sites, such as Mescal Wash, contain abundant evidence of agave exploitation. The lack of small animal remains recovered from pits located within structures suggests that food storage may have occurred outside the pit houses. In addition, the population of extramural pits and subfeatures at the Marsh Station Road site, which includes thermal pits, such as roasting pits or hornos, and various types of nonthermal pits, were likely utilized for a wide range of subsistence-related activities including cooking, processing, and storage. However, none of the extramural pits contained abnormally high pollen concentrations of any plant or in-situ artifacts that might provide further evidence of diet and subsistence activities at the site.

Overall, the floral, faunal, and ground stone data suggest that the occupants relied on hunting and gathering of wild resources in addition to agricultural produce for their subsistence (see Diehl, ed. 2005). The data also indicate that the site was at least occupied during the warmer months (spring, summer, and/or fall), although the data are more ambiguous as to whether the occupation(s) were discontinuous and/or seasonal, or more continuous/year-round (see Adams, Chapter 10 and Phillips, Chapter 11). Very little variation in diet and subsistence practices over time was documented, although this is partially due to the paucity of data from Early Agricultural period features, and therefore may not be representative of subsistence practices throughout the site's occupation history.

INTRASITE ACTIVITY PATTERNS

No clear intrasite activity patterns were identified. Extramural pits dating to the same period did not appear to be clustered together, but rather were irregularly spread out across the area of the site that was investigated. Although six pit houses/structures were identified, none faced each other, and they were generally spaced out, indicating that no courtyard groups were present. Virtually all of the pit structures were cleaned out prior to their abandonment, leaving little evidence about activities that may have occurred within the structure. Very few artifacts were recovered from the two identified occupation surfaces (Features 6 and 41).

THE MARSH STATION ROAD SITE AS A PERSISTENT PLACE ON THE CULTURAL LANDSCAPE

According to Schlanger (1992:97), a persistent place is one that was "repeatedly used during long-term occupations of regions" and that represent, through associations with important environmental and/or cultural features, "the conjunction of particular human behaviors on a particular landscape." Although Schlanger uses the idea as a way to theoretically link shifting use of limited activity, seasonal, and habitation loci through an archaeological landscape model, the concept is applicable to a wide variety of cultural settings that experienced oscillations in the settlement system pattern over a long period of time, including occupation of the Marsh Station Road site.

Schlanger (1992:97) identified three types of persistent place: 1) those with desirable/unique environmental qualities that, such as suitable and nearby agricultural land, rich and locally available wild flora and faunal resources, and permanent water, that encourage and facilitate certain suites of activities, practices, or behaviors; 2) those whose features attract and reorient occupation and structure the activities associated with each occupation; and 3) those that provide an exploitable resource through the presence of cultural materials. Although these types of persistent places are described independent of one another, they are not mutually exclusive, and it is entirely plausible, and even expected, that a persistent place may cycle through these types over the course of its history. Thus, a residential site originally may have been established because of its location near permanent water. As time passed and the settlement grew, the village might have shifted locations, moving a short distance away to an area capable of supporting the larger population. However, some families likely retained ties or, perhaps, rights to arable land and wild resources near the former settlement, and therefore may have returned to that location season after season, using their previous habitation structures as seasonal field houses. Long after the residential abandonment of the area, perhaps for environmental or overpopulation reasons, religious specialists return to the area to pray at a shrine built by the original occupants or a hunting party passing through the area remembers that a village once existed nearby, and scavenges flaked stone material from the site's midden to replace some of their broken tools.

Vanderpot and Altschul (2007:69) have previously suggested that the Mescal Wash site represents a persistent place on the prehistoric landscape of southern Arizona, wherein "the function that [the site] originally served and the manner in which it entered the cultural geography of southeast Arizona...," as a 'free zone' accessible to and shared by various different cultures, "...shaped and oriented subsequent occupation." In this sense, the Mescal Wash site falls into Schlanger's second type of persistent place. Although the Marsh Station Road site appears to occupy a different place on the

cultural landscape than the Mescal Wash site, based on the results of WSA's investigations, it too can also be interpreted as a persistent place. From a site-specific perspective, the Marsh Station Road site, while not occupied continuously, has a long occupation history spanning more than 2,500 years. The site was likely originally settled because of its location in a rich riparian environment with access to abundant wild resources and arable land, and the availability of water for floodwater farming. These features likely encouraged repeated and continued use of the site area through time, whether as a seasonally occupied, semi-permanent, or more permanent locus. In addition, it seems clear that later occupants or visitors to the Marsh Station Road site utilized cultural materials from previous occupations, as is mostly readily apparent when considering that most of the Early Agricultural San Pedro projectile points were recovered from Middle Formative period features, some relatively close to the occupation surface, although the proposed post-occupation scavenging of metates from the site also may point to persistent knowledge of the site and its cultural materials. More in line with Schlanger's original conceptualization of persistent places, the Marsh Station Road site, in conjunction with the larger Mescal Wash settlement system (see Vanderpot and Altschul 2007:67), is a persistent cultural landscape, wherein various groups occupied and reoccupied the region over thousands of years, performing a variety of activities, practices, and behaviors at different site types throughout the region. However, a fuller understanding of this cultural landscape, including the Marsh Station Road site, as a persistent place in southern Arizona awaits full publication of SRI's work at the Mescal Wash site, the most thoroughly investigated site in the region, as well as additional archaeological work, both survey and excavation, in the region. In addition, examination of the regional landscape as a persistent place might shed light on the similarities and differences the occupation of the Marsh Station Road site and surrounding sites shared with other contemporaneous landscapes in the Tucson Basin and along the San Pedro River.

SUMMARY AND CONCLUSION

Our understanding of the occupational history of the Marsh Station Road site is necessarily limited by the sample of the site that was available for excavation, limited to the current project's area of potential effect and constituting less than 4 percent of the total site area. The interpretation of the site presented below, while taking this limitation into consideration, is based on multiple lines of evidence that suggest the multicomponent site was occupied repeatedly, most likely in a semi-permanent nature, for thousands of years spanning from at least the Early Agricultural period to the Classic/Late Formative period, with the most intense occupation occurring during the Rincon phase/late Middle Formative period.

The site's location provided its inhabitants with abundant and varied resources. Situated at the confluence of two prehistorically perennial washes, the residents had ready access to a rich riparian environment. Much of the length of Cienega Creek was, indeed, a ciénega, defined by Hendrickson and Minckley (1984:131) as "...wetlands characterized by permanently saturated, highly organic reducing soils" that functioned within the ecosystem as self-protecting reservoirs. Other nearby biotic communities included the desert grassland and the oak woodland on the slopes of the Rincon Mountains. The site occupants exploited all these communities, as evidenced by floral and faunal remains such as cattail pollen, Gramineae, and eastern cottontail.

While the washes were perennial, stream-flow during the Late Holocene varied (Eddy and Cooley 1983). Fairly wet and stable conditions from about 1500 B.C. to A.D. 300 allowed the ciénegas to reach their maximum extent. During the Middle Formative period, on the other hand, fluvial material was laid down on much of the floodplain, filling the ciénegas and likely increasing the effective farming area available to the site occupants.

Investigation of the site resulted in the documentation of 246 features and subfeatures, 148 of which were excavated, and the collection of over 50,000 artifacts, which provided evidence of substantial occupations during the San Pedro phase of the Early Agricultural period and the Rincon phase/late Middle Formative period at the site. Data concerning the San Pedro phase occupation contributes to the rapidly growing corpus of similar information from the larger Tucson Basin (Mabry 2005a, Mabry, ed. 2008; Merrill et al. 2009). Two assays on maize provided calibrated radiocarbon dates of 1120 to 810 B.C. and 1250 to 1240 B.C./1220 to 980 B.C. Both samples were recovered from pit features in association with San Pedro points. The maize cob segment from Feature 98 has 16 rows, a mean cupule width of 3.0 mm, a mean cupule length of 1.9 mm, and a pith diameter of 5.76 mm, all of which are similar to San Pedro phase maize from southern Arizona (Diehl 2005a; L. Huckell 2006). Additional evidence of this early occupation includes 37 San Pedro projectile points and a number of aceramic pits that also may be contemporaneous.

The Rincon phase/late Middle Formative period occupation is represented by 64 features, including at least five of the six pit houses/structures, as well as the presence of numerous decorated ceramic wares broadly dating to this period. In addition, eight projectile points diagnostic of the Middle Formative period as well as two maize cob segments with characteristics typical of later-dating maize were recovered from the site. The Middle Formative occupation was documented in all five stripped areas, although the largest number and densest concentration of features dating to this period were located in SA 4/5.

Our work at the Marsh Station Road site (AZ EE:2:44 [ASM]) is interesting in light of previous interpretations. Specifically, it has been suggested (see Vanderpot and Altschul 2007) that the Mescal Wash site, just across Mescal Wash from the Marsh Station Road site, is in a 'hinterland' between the better known Hohokam, Mogollon, Anasazi and Salado, and Casas Grandes cultural developments. The Mescal Wash site is characterized by elements of what has been labeled "Dragoon," including houses with distinctive recessed hearths, known only from a handful of sites, and a locally made pottery. These characteristics, combined with the lack of ballcourt at such a large site, led Vanderpot and Altschul (2007:63) to conclude that the Mescal Wash site "...was on the fringes of the Hohokam regional system." The Marsh Station Road site, however, presents a different picture. Here, the predominance of Tucson Basin Hohokam red-on-brown pottery and the lack of any "Dragoon" elements indicate a strong tie to the Tucson Basin. Indeed, the Tucson Basin Hohokam may be seen as extending at least as far east as the confluence of Cienega Creek and Mescal Wash (see Figure 12.1).

Where our results concord with what has been presented about the Mescal Wash site (Vanderpot and Altschul 2007) is that both sites were occupied persistently. The substantial Early Agricultural occupation at the site, particularly during the San Pedro phase, complements the picture of how these early farmers used the landscape, a picture that heretofore had been primarily colored by the extensively documented occupations along the Santa Cruz River, and in light of Mabry's (2005b) agricultural niche model, highlights the importance of investigating sites located in nonriverine settings, outside of the two major Hohokam population centers in the Phoenix and Tucson basins. However, because so little data is available from the area immediately surrounding the Marsh Station Road site, a fuller interpretation of the history of the site, including an assessment of both its place in Mabry's niche-filling model and its role as a persistent place on the cultural landscape, would be strengthened by additional studies in the surrounding region.

References Cited

Abbott, David R.

1983   A Technological Assessment of Ceramic Variation in the Salt-Gila Aqueduct Area: Toward a More Comprehensive Documentation of Hohokam Ceramics. In *Hohokam Archaeology along the Salt-Gila Aqueduct, Central Arizona Project: Vol. 8. Material Culture*, edited by Lynn S. Teague and Patricia L. Crown, pp. 3-118. Archaeological Series 150. Arizona State Museum, University of Arizona, Tucson.

2000   *Ceramics and Community Organization among the Hohokam.* University of Arizona Press, Tucson.

Abbott, David R., Alexa M. Smith, and Emiliano Gallaga

2007   Ballcourts and Ceramics: The Case for Hohokam Marketplaces in the Arizona Desert. *American Antiquity* 72:461–485.

Adams, Jenny L.

1979   *Groundstone from Walpi. In Walpi Archaeological Project, Phase II,* Vol. 4, edited by E. Charles Adams. Museum of Northern Arizona, Flagstaff.

1993   Technological Development of Manos and Metates on the Hopi Mesas. *Kiva* 58:331-344.

1997   *Manual for a Technological Approach to Ground Stone Analysis.* Center for Desert Archaeology, Tucson.

1999   Refocusing the Role of Food-grinding Tools as Correlates for Subsistence Strategies in the U.S. Southwest. *American Antiquity* 64:475–498.

2002   *Ground Stone Analysis: A Technological Approach.* University of Utah Press, Salt Lake City.

2005   Early Agricultural Period Grinding Technology. In *Material Cultures and Lifeways of Early Agricultural Period Communities in Southern Arizona*, edited by Jane R. Sliva, pp. 99–119. Anthropological Papers No. 35. Center for Desert Archaeology, Tucson.

2008   Beyond the Broken. In *New Approaches to Old Stones: Recent Studies of Ground Stone Artifacts*, edited by Yorke M. Rowan and Jennie R. Ebeling, pp. 213–229. Equinox Publishing, London.

Adams, Karen R.
　　1994　Macrobotanical Analyses. In *The Roosevelt Rural Sites Study, Changing Land Use in the Tonto Basin, 3*, edited by Richard Ciolek-Torrello and John R. Welch, pp. 167-187. Technical Series 28. Statistical Research, Tucson.

Adams, Karen R., cont'd
　　1997　Macrobotanical Analyses. In V*anishing River: Landscapes and Lives of the Lower Verde Valley: The Lower Verde Archaeological Project: Vol. 2. Agricultural, Subsistence, and Environmental Studies*, edited by Jeffrey A. Homburg and Richard Ciolek-Torrello, pp. 149-178. Statistical Research, Tucson. Accompanied by "Appendix H. Criteria for Identification of Archaeological Plant Specimens from Lower Verde Sites," with text descriptions of plant parts, measurement data (Tables H1.1, H1.2, and H1.3), and flotation (Table H.1) and macrofossil (Table H.2) databases.

　　2002a　Archaeobotanical Remains. In *Archaeological Investigations at the Sweetwater Site on the Gila River Indian Community*, edited by Kyle M. Woodson, pp. 199-205. CRMP Technical Report No. 2002-14. Cultural Resource Management Program, Gila River Indian Community, Sacaton, Arizona.

　　2002b　*Archaeobotanical Studies and Paleoenvironmental Reconstructions, Gila River Indian Community, Arizona*. P-MIP Technical Report No. 2002-03. Cultural Resource Management Program, Gila River Indian Community, Sacaton, Arizona.

Adams, Karen R., and Vorsila L. Bohrer
　　1998　*Archaeobotanical Indicators of Seasonality: Examples from the Arid Southwestern United States. In Seasonality and Sedentism: Archaeological Perspectives from Old and New World Sites*, edited by Thomas R. Rocek and Ofer Bar-Yosef, pp. 129-141. Bulletin 6. Peabody Museum of Archaeology and Ethnology, Harvard University, Cambridge, Massachusetts.

Agenbroad, Larry D.
　　1970　Cultural Implications from the Statistical Analysis of a Prehistoric Lithic Site in Arizona. Unpublished Master's thesis, Department of Anthropology, University of Arizona, Tucson.

Altschul, Jeffery H.
　　1997　From North to South: Shifting Sociopolitical Alliances during the Formative Period in the San Pedro Valley. In *Prehistory of the Borderlands: Recent Research in the Archaeology of Northern Mexico and the Southern Southwest*, edited by John Carpenter and Guadalupe Sanchez, pp. 57-69. Arizona State Museum Archaeological Series 186. Arizona State Museum, University of Arizona, Tucson.

Altschul, Jeffrey H., and Bruce A. Jones
　　1990　*Settlement Trends in the Middle San Pedro River Valley: A Cultural Resources Sample Survey of the Fort Huachuca Military Reservation*. Technical Series 19. Statistical Research, Tucson.

Altschul, Jeffrey H., César A. Quijada, and Robert A. Heckman
　　1999　Villa Verde and the Late Prehistoric Period along the San Pedro River. In *Sixty Years of Mogollon Ar-chaeology: Papers from the Ninth Mogollon Conference, Silver City, New Mexico, 1996*, edited by Stephanie M. Whittlesey, pp. 81–92. SRI Press, Tucson.

Andrefsky, William, Jr.
　　1998　*Lithics: Macroscopic Approaches to Analysis*. Cambridge University Press, Cambridge.

Antevs, Ernst V.
　　1983　Geologic Dating. In The Cochise Cultural Sequence in Southeastern Arizona, edited by Edwin B. Sayles, pp. 26-43. Anthropological Papers No. 42. University of Arizona Press, Tucson.

Archer, Gavin H.
1998   Extramural Pits. In *Archaeological Investigations on the Wetlands Site, AZ AA:12:90 (ASM)*, edited by Andrea K. Freeman, pp. 65-80. Technical Report No. 97-5. Desert Archaeology, Tucson.

Bahre, Conrad J.
1991   *Legacy of Change: Historic Human Impact on Vegetation in the Arizona Borderlands*. University of Arizona Press, Tucson.

Baker, Kathleen A., and Joshua Jones
2004   *Archaeological Survey of Link Two Arizona Ingress/Egress Routes: Addendum 4 to an Archaeological Survey of the Arizona Portion of Link Two of the AT&T NexGen/Core Project*. WCRM(F) Report No. 222. Western Cultural Resources Management, Farmington, New Mexico.

Basso, Keith H.
1983   Western Apache. In *Southwest*, edited by Alfonso Ortiz, pp. 462-488. Handbook of North American Indians, Vol. 10. William C. Sturtevant, general editor. Smithsonian Institution, Washington, D.C.

Bequaert, Joseph C., and Walter B. Miller
1973   *Mollusks of the Arid Southwest with an Arizona Check List*. University of Arizona Press, Tucson.

Berry, Claudia F., and Michael S. Berry
1986   Chronological and Conceptual Models of the Southwest Archaic. In *Anthropology of the Desert West: Essays in Honor of Jesse D. Jennings*, edited by Carol J. Condie and Don D. Fowler, pp. 253-327. Anthropological Papers No. 110. University of Utah Press, Salt Lake City.

Binford, Lewis R.
1979   Organization and Formation Processes: Looking at Curated Technologies. *Journal of Anthropological Research* 35:255–273.

Bohrer, Vorsila L.
1970   Ethnobotanical Aspects of Snaketown, a Hohokam Village in Southern Arizona. *American Antiquity* 35:413-430.

1971   Paleoecology of Snaketown. *The Kiva* 36(3):11-19.

1987   The Plant Remains from La Ciudad, a Hohokam Site in Phoenix. In *La Ciudad, Specialized Studies in the Economy, Environment, and Culture of La Ciudad, Part III*, edited by JoAnn E. Kisselburg, Glen E. Rice, and Brenda L. Shears, pp. 67-202. Anthropological Field Studies 20. Arizona State University, Tempe.

1991   Recently Recognized Cultivated and Encouraged Plants among the Hohokam. *Kiva* 56:227-235.

1992   New Life from Ashes II: A Tale of Burnt Brush. *Desert Plants* 19(3):122-125.

Bostwick, Todd W., and James H. Burton
1993   A Study in Sourcing Hohokam Basalt Ground Stone Implements. *Kiva* 58:357–372.

Bousman, C. Britt, Barry W. Baker, and Anne C. Kerr
2004   Paleoindian Archaeology in Texas. In *The Prehistory of Texas*, edited by Timothy K. Perttula, pp. 15–97. Texas, A & M University Press, College Station, Texas.

Brackenridge, R. G.
1984 Late Quaternary Geology and its Relation to Archaeological Resources. In *A Class III Survey of the Tucson Aqueduct Phase A Corridor, Central Arizona Project: An Intensive Archaeological Survey in the Lower Santa Cruz River Basin, Picacho Reservoir to Rillito, Arizona*, edited by Jon S. Czaplicki, pp. 6–16. Archaeological Series 165. Cultural Resource Management Division, Arizona State Museum, University of Arizona, Tucson.

Broderip, W. J. Esq.
1832 Characters of New Species of Mollusca and Conchifera, collected by Mr. Cuming. *Proceedings of the Committee of Science and Correspondence of the Zoological Society of London* 2:126.

Bronitsky, Gordon, and James D. Merritt
1986 *The Archaeology of Southeast Arizona: A Class I Cultural Resource Inventory*. Cultural Resource Series Monograph 2. Bureau of Land Management, Arizona State Office, Phoenix.

Brown, David E.
1982 143.1. Semidesert Grassland. In *Biotic Communities of the American Southwest--United States and Mexico*, edited by David E. Brown, pp. 123-131. Desert Plants 4(1-4). University of Utah Press, Salt Lake City.

1994 Semidesert Grassland. In *Biotic Communities: Southwestern United States and Northwestern Mexico*, edited by David E. Brown, pp. 123-131. University of Utah Press, Salt Lake City.

Brown, David E. (editor)
1994 *Biotic Communities–Southwestern United States and Northwestern Mexico*. University of Utah Press, Salt Lake City.

Brown, David E., and Charles H. Lowe
1980 *Biotic Communities of the Southwest*. A Supplementary Map to *Biotic Communities: Southwestern United States and Northwestern Mexico*, edited by David E. Brown. University of Utah Press, Salt Lake City.

Brusca, Richard C.
1980 *Common Intertidal Invertebrates of the Gulf of California*. 2nd ed. University of Arizona Press, Tucson.

Buikstra, Jane E., and Douglas H. Ubelaker (editors)
1994 *Standards for Data Collection from Human Skeletal Remains: Proceedings of a Seminar at The Field Museum of Natural History, Organized by Jonathan Haas*. Research Series No. 44. Arkansas Archaeological Survey, Fayetteville, Arkansas.

Bull, William B.
1991 *Geomorphic Responses to Climatic Change*. Oxford University Press, New York.

Casteel, Richard W.
1978 Faunal Assemblages and the "Wiegemethode" or Weight Method. *Journal of Field Archaeology* 5:71-77.

Castetter, Edward F.
1935 *Ethnobiological Studies in the American Southwest: I. Uncultivated Native Plants Used as Sources of Food*. UNM Bulletin, Whole Number 266, Biological Series Vol. 4, No. 1. University of New Mexico Press, Albuquerque.

Castetter, Edward F., and Willis H. Bell
1942 *Pima and Papago Indian Agriculture.* Inter-Americana Studies 1. University of New Mexico Press, Albuquerque.

1951 *Yuman Indian Agriculture.* University of New Mexico Press, Albuquerque.

Castetter, Edward F., and Ruth M. Underhill
1935 *The Ethnobiology of the Papago Indians.* Bulletin 275. University of New Mexico Press, Albuquerque.

Chapman, John
2000 *Fragmentation in Archaeology: People, Places, and Broken Objects in the Prehistory of South-eastern Europe.* Routledge, London.

Cheatum, Elmer P., and Richard W. Fullington
1971 *The Aquatic and Land Mollusca of Texas.* Bulletin 1, Parts I–III. Dallas Museum of Natural History, Dallas.

Christensen, G. E., and R. E. Purcell
1985 Correlation and Age of Quaternary Alluvial-Fan Sequences, Basin and Range Province, Southwestern United States. In *Soils and Quaternary Geology of the Southwestern United States*, edited by David L. Weide, pp. 115–122. Special Paper 203. Geological Society of America, Boulder, Colorado.

Chronic, Halka
1983 *Roadside Geology of Arizona.* Mountain Press, Missoula, Montana.

Colton, Harold S.
1974 Hopi History and Ethnobotany. In *Hopi Indians*, edited by D. A. Horr. Garland, New York.

Cordell, Linda S.
1997 *Archaeology of the Southwest.* 2nd ed. Academic Press, San Diego.

Cordell, Linda S., and George J. Gumerman
1989 Cultural Interaction in the Prehistoric Southwest. In *Dynamics of Southwest Prehistory*, edited by Linda S. Cordell and George J. Gumerman, pp. 1-18. Smithsonian Institution, Washington, D.C.

Craig, Douglas B. (editor)
2001 *The Grewe Archaeological Research Project.* Anthropological Papers 99-1. 4 vols. Northland Research, Flagstaff and Tempe.

Craig, Douglas B., and Mary-Ellen Walsh-Anduze
2001 Pits. In T*he Grewe Archaeological Research Project: I. Project Background and Feature Descriptions*, edited by Douglas B. Craig, pp. 125-135. Anthropological Papers No. 99-1. Northland Research, Flagstaff.

Crosswhite, Frank S.
1980 The Annual Saguaro Harvest and Crop Cycle of the Papago, with Reference to Ecology and Symbolism. *Desert Plants* 2(1):3-62.

1981 Desert Plants, Habitat, and Agriculture in Relation to the Major Pattern of Cultural Differentiation in the O'odham People of the Sonoran Desert. *Desert Plants* 3(3):47-76.

Crown, Patricia L.
1983   Field Houses and Farmsteads in South-Central Arizona. In *Hohokam Archaeology along the Salt-Gila Aqueduct, Central Arizona Project: Vol. 5. Small Habitation Sites on Queen Creek*, edited by Lynn S. Teague and Patricia L. Crown, pp. 3–22. Archaeological Series 150. 8 vols. Arizona State Museum, University of Arizona, Tucson.

Crown, Patricia L., cont'd.
1985   Morphology and Function of Hohokam Small Structures. *The Kiva* 52:209–228.

1991   The Hohokam: Current Views of Prehistory and the Regional System. In *Chaco and Hohokam: Prehistoric Regional Systems in the American Southwest*, edited by Patricia L. Crown and W. James Judge, pp. 135-157. School of American Research, Santa Fe.

1994   *Ceramics and Ideology: Salado Polychrome Pottery*. University of New Mexico Press, Albuquerque.

Crown, Patricia L., and Suzanne K. Fish
1996   Gender and Status in the Hohokam Pre-Classic to Classic Transition. *American Anthropologist* 98:803–817.

Culin, Stewart
1992   *Games of the North American Indians*. Bison Books and the University of Nebraska Press, Lincoln. Reprinted. Originally published, 1907, in the 24th Annual Report of the Bureau of American Ethnology [1902-1903], Smithsonian Institution, Washington, D.C.

Curtin, Leonora Scott Muse
1984   *By the Prophet of the Earth: Ethnobotany of the Pima*. University of Arizona Press, Tucson. Reprinted. Originally published, 1949, Santa Fe, San Vicente Foundation.

Cutler, Hugh C., and Thomas W. Whitaker
1961   The History and Distribution of the Cultivated Cucurbits in the Americas. *American Antiquity* 26:469-485.

da Costa, Emanuel Mendes
1778   *Historia Naturalis Testaceorum Britanniae, or the British Conchology:* i-xii, 1–254. Meffirs, Millan, B. White, Elmsley, and Robson, Booksellers, London.

Deal, Michael
1998   *Pottery Ethnoarchaeology in the Central Maya Highlands*. University of Utah Press, Salt Lake City.

Deal, Michael, and Melissa B. Hagstrum
1995   Ceramic Reuse Behavior among the Maya and Wanka: Implications for Archaeology. In *Expanding Archaeology*, edited by James M. Skibo, William H. Walker, and Axel E. Nielson, pp. 111-125. University of Utah Press, Salt Lake City.

Dean, Jeffrey S. (editor)
2000   *Salado*. Amerind Foundation New World Studies Series No. 4. University of New Mexico Press, Albuquerque.

Dean, Jeffrey S., Mark C. Slaughter, and Dennie O. Bowden, III
1996   Desert Dendrochronology: Tree-ring Dating Prehistoric Sites in the Tucson Basin. *Kiva* 62:7-26.

Deaver, William L.

1984   Pottery. In *Hohokam Habitation Sites in the Northern Santa Rita Mountains*, Vol. 2, Part 1, edited by Alan Ferg, Kenneth C. Rozen, William L. Deaver, Martyn D. Tagg, David A. Phillips, Jr., and David A. Gregory, pp. 237-419. Archaeological Series 147. Cultural Resource Management Division, Arizona State Museum, University of Arizona, Tucson.

2004   A Consideration of Style in Colonial and Sedentary Period Ceramics: Rincon Styles A and B Revisited. In *Pots, Potters, and Models: Archaeological Investigations at the SRI Locus of the West Branch Site, Tucson, Arizona: Vol. 2. Synthesis and Interpretations*, edited by Stephanie M. Whittlesey, pp. 377-432. Technical Series 80. Statistical Research, Tucson.

Di Peso, Charles

1956   *The Upper Pima of San Cayetano de Tumacacori: An Archaeological Reconstruction of the Ootam of the Pimeria Alta.* Archaeological Series No. 7. Amerind Foundation, Dragoon, Arizona.

Dickinson, William R.

1991   *Tectonic Setting of Faulted Tertiary Strata Associated with the Catalina Core Complex in Southern Arizona.* Special Paper 264. Geological Society of America, Boulder.

Diehl, Michael W.

2005a   Morphological Observations on Recently Recovered Early Agricultural Period Maize Cob Fragments from Southern Arizona. *American Antiquity* 70:361-375.

2005b   Early Agricultural Period Foraging and Horticulture in Southern Arizona: Implications from Plant Remains. In *Subsistence and Resource Use Strategies of Early Agricultural Communities in Southern Arizona*, edited by Michael W. Diehl, pp. 73-90. Anthropological Papers No. 34. Center for Desert Archaeology, Tucson.

Diehl, Michael W. (editor)

1997   *Archaeological Investigations of the Early Agricultural Period Settlement at the Base of A Mountain, Tucson, Arizona.* Technical Report No. 96-21. Desert Archaeology, Tucson.

2005   *Subsistence and Resource Use Strategies of Early Agricultural Communities in Southern Arizona.* Anthropological Papers No. 34. Center for Desert Archaeology, Tucson.

Dobres, Marcia-Anne, and Christopher R. Hoffman (editors)

1999   *The Social Dynamics of Technology: Practice, Politics, and World Views.* Smithsonian Institution, Washington, D.C.

Dobyns, Henry F.

1974   The Kohatk: Oasis and Ak-Chin Horticulturists. *Ethnohistory* 21:317-327.

Doelle, William H. (editor)

1985   *Excavations at the Valencia Site, a Preclassic Hohokam Village in the Southern Tucson Basin.* Anthropological Papers 3. Institute for American Research, Tucson.

Doelle, William H., Frederick W. Huntington, and Henry D. Wallace

1987   Rincon Phase Organization in the Tucson Basin. In *The Hohokam Village: Structure and Organization*, edited by David E. Doyel, pp. 71–95. AAAS Publication 87-15. American Association for the Advancement of Science, Southwest and Rocky Mountain Division, Glenwood Springs, Colorado.

Doelle, William H., and Henry D. Wallace
  1991 The Changing Role of the Tucson Basin in the Hohokam Regional System. In *Exploring the Hohokam: Prehistoric Desert Peoples of the American Southwest*, edited by George J. Gumerman, pp. 279–345. New World Studies Series No. 1. Amerind Foundation, Dragoon, Arizona, and University of New Mexico Press, Albuquerque.

  1997 A Classic Period Platform Mound System on the Lower San Pedro River, Southern Arizona. In *Prehistory of the Borderlands: Recent Research in the Archaeology of Northern Mexico and the Southern Southwest*, edited by John Carpenter and Guadalupe Sanchez, pp. 71-84. Archaeological Series 186. Arizona State Museum, University of Arizona, Tucson.

Dohrenwend, J. C.
  1987 Basin and Range. In *Geomorphic Systems of North America*, edited by William L. Graf, pp. 303–342. Centennial Special Volume 2. Geological Society of America, Boulder, Colorado.

Downum, Christian E., and Gregory Burrell Brown
  1998 The Reliability of Surface Artifact Assemblages as Predictors of Subsurface Remains. In *Surface Archaeology*, edited by Alan P. Sullivan III, pp. 111–123. University of New Mexico Press, Albuquerque.

Doyel, David E.
  1977 *Excavations in the Middle Santa Cruz Valley, Southeastern Arizona*. Contributions to Highway Salvage Archaeology in Arizona No. 44. Arizona State Museum, University of Arizona, Tucson.

  1991 Hohokam Exchange and Interaction. In *Chaco and Hohokam: Prehistoric Regional Systems in the American Southwest*, edited by Patricia L. Crown and W. James Judge, pp. 135-157. School of American Research, Santa Fe.

Doyel, David E. (editor)
  1987 *The Hohokam Village: Site Structure and Organization*. AAAS Publication 87-15. American Association for the Advancement of Science, Southwestern and Rocky Mountain Division, Glenwood Springs, Colorado.

Drake, R. J.
  1959 Nonmarine Molluscan Remains from Recent Sediments in Matty Canyon, Pima County, Arizona. *Southern California Academy of Sciences Bulletin* 58(3):146-154.

Eddy, Frank W.
  1958 A Sequence of Cultural and Alluvial Deposits in the Cienega Creek Basin, Southeastern Arizona. Unpublished Master's thesis, Department of Anthropology, University of Arizona, Tucson.

Eddy, Frank W., and Maurice E. Cooley
  1983 *Cultural and Environmental History of Cienega Valley, Southeastern Arizona*. Anthropological Papers No. 43. University of Arizona Press, Tucson.

Egloff, Brian J.
  1973 A Method for Counting Ceramic Rim Sherds. *American Antiquity* 38:351-353.

Eiselt, B. Sunday, and E. Christian Wells
  2003 *Chronology and Chronometric Dating on the Gila River Indian Community*. P-MIP Technical Report No. 2003-02. Cultural Resource Management Program, Gila River Indian Community, Sacaton, Arizona.

Elson, Mark D.
1998   *Expanding the View of Hohokam Platform Mounds: An Ethnographic Perspective.* Anthropological Papers of the University of Arizona No. 63. University of Arizona Press, Tucson.

Elson, Mark D. (editor)
1986   *Archaeological Investigations at the Tanque Verde Wash Site: A Middle Rincon Settlement in the Eastern Tucson Basin.* Anthropological Papers No. 7. Institute for American Research, Tucson.

Eppley, Lisa G.
1986   Lithic Analysis. In *Archaeological Investigations at the Tanque Verde Wash Site, a Middle Rincon Settlement in the Eastern Tucson Basin,* edited by Mark D. Elson, pp. 271-300. Anthropological Papers No. 7. Institute for American Research, Tucson.

1990   Lonetree Chipped and Ground Stone Analysis. In *Archaeological Investigations at the Lonetree Site, AA:12:120 (ASM), in the Northern Tucson Basin,* edited by Mary Bernard-Shaw, pp. 127-148. Technical Report No. 90-1. Center for Desert Archaeology, Tucson.

Erickson, Winston P.
1994   *Sharing the Desert: The Tohono O'odham in History.* University of Arizona Press, Tucson.

Euler, Robert C., and Henry F. Dobyns
1983   The Ethnoarchaeology of Pai Milling Stones. In *Collected Papers in Honor of Charlie Steen, Jr.,* edited by N. L. Fox, pp. 253-267. Papers of the Archaeological Society of New Mexico, No. 8. Albuquerque Archaeological Society Press, Albuquerque.

Fenneman, Nevin M.
1931   *Physiography of the Western United States.* Academic Press, New York.

Ferg, Alan
1980   Shell from Gu Achi. In *Excavations at Gu Achi: A Reappraisal of Hohokam Settlement and Subsistence in the Arizona Papagueria,* edited by W. Bruce Masse, pp. 371-394. Publications in Anthropology No. 12. Western Archaeological Center, National Park Service, Department of the Interior, Tucson.

Ferg, Alan, Kenneth C. Rozen, William L. Deaver, Martyn D. Tagg, David A. Phillips, Jr., and David A. Gregory (editors)
1984   *Hohokam Habitation Sites in the Northern Santa Rita Mountains.* Archaeological Series 147, Vol. 2. Cultural Resource Management Division, Arizona State Museum, University of Arizona, Tucson.

Ferguson, C. A., A. Youberg, W. G. Gilbert, T. R. Orr, S. M. Richard, and J. E. Spencer
2001   *Geologic Map of the Mount Fagan 7.5' Quadrangle, Eastern Pima County.* DGM 11, 1 sheet, 33 pages text, Scale 1:24,000. Arizona Geological Survey, Tucson.

Fewkes, Jesse B.
1896   Pacific Coast Shell from Prehistoric Tusayan Pueblos. *American Anthropologist* 9:359-367.

Field, John J.
2001   Channel Avulsion on Alluvial Fans in Southern Arizona. *Geomorphology* 37:93–104.

Fish, Paul R., Suzanne K. Fish, and John H Madsen
1990   Sedentism and Settlement Pattern Mobility Prior to A.D. 1000 in the Tucson Basin. In *Perspectives in Southwestern Prehistory,* edited by Paul Minnis and Charles L. Redman, pp. 26–91. Westview Press, Boulder.

Fish, Suzanne K.

    1984   Agriculture and Subsistence Implications of the Salt-Gila Aqueduct Pollen Analysis. In *Hohokam Archaeology along the Salt-Gila Aqueduct Central Arizona Project: Vol. 7. Environment and Subsistence*, edited by Lynn S. Teague and Patricia L. Crown, pp. 111-138. Archaeological Series 150. Arizona State Museum, University of Arizona, Tucson.

    1987   Marana Sites Pollen Analysis. In *Studies in the Hohokam Community of Marana*, edited by Glen E. Rice, pp. 161-170. Office of Cultural Resource Management, Department of Anthropology, Arizona State Museum, Tempe.

    1995   Pollen Results from Los Morteros. In *Archaeological Investigations at Los Morteros, a Prehistoric Settlement in the Northern Tucson Basin*, Part II, edited by Henry D. Wallace, pp. 661-671. Anthropological Papers No. 17. Center for Desert Archaeology, Tucson.

    1998   A Pollen Perspective on Variability and Stability in Tonto Basin Subsistence. In *Environment and Subsistence in the Classic Period Tonto Basin: The Roosevelt Archaeology Studies, 1989 to 1998*, edited by Katherine A. Spielmann. Anthropological Field Studies No. 10; Roosevelt Monograph Series 10. Department of Anthropology, Arizona State University, Tempe.

Fish, Suzanne K., Paul R. Fish, and John H. Madsen

    1992   Evolution and Structure of the Classic Period Marana Community. In *The Marana Community in the Hohokam World*, edited by Suzanne K. Fish, Paul R. Fish, and John H Madsen, pp. 20–40. University of Arizona Press, Tucson.

Fish, Suzanne K., Paul R. Fish, and John H. Madsen (editors)

    1992   *The Marana Community in the Hohokam World*. University of Arizona Press, Tucson.

Franklin, Hayward H.

    1978   *Excavations at Second Canyon Ruin, San Pedro Valley, Arizona*. Contributions to Highway Salvage Archaeology in Arizona No. 60. Arizona State Museum, University of Arizona, Tucson.

Fratt, Lee, and Maggie Biancaniello

    1993   Homol'ovi Ground Stone in the Raw: A Study of the Local Sandstone Used to Make Ground Stone Artifacts. *Kiva* 58:373–391.

Freeman, Andrea K.

    1998   *Archaeological Investigations at the Wetlands Site, AZ AA:12:90 (ASM)*. Technical Report 97-5. Desert Archaeology, Tucson.

Frick, Paul S.

    1954   An Archaeological Survey in the Central Santa Cruz Valley, Southern Arizona. Unpublished Master's Thesis, Department of Anthropology, University of Arizona, Tucson.

Fulton, William S.

    1938   *Archaeological Notes on Texas Canyon, Arizona*. Museum of the American Indian Contributions Vol. 12, No. 1-3. Heye Foundation, New York.

Fulton, William S., and Carr Tuthill

    1940   *An Archaeological Site near Gleason, Arizona*. Amerind Foundation Publications No. 1. Amerind Foundation, Dragoon, Arizona.

Gasser, Robert E., and Scott M. Kwiatkowski

1991a Food for Thought: Recognizing Patterns in Hohokam Subsistence. In *Exploring the Hohokam: Prehistoric Desert Peoples of the American Southwest*, edited by George J. Gumerman, pp. 417-459. Amerind Foundation, Dragoon, Arizona, and the University of New Mexico Press, Albuquerque.

1991b Regional Signatures of Hohokam Plant Use. *Kiva* 56:207-226.

Gasser, Robert E., Christine K. Robinson, and Cory Dale Breternitz

1990 *Archaeology of the Ak-Chin Indian Community West Side Farms Project: The Archaeological Data Recovery Plan*, Vol. 3. Publications in Archaeology No. 9. Soil Systems, Phoenix.

Gilbert, B. Miles

1973 *Mammalian Osteo-archaeology: North America*. Missouri Archaeological Society, Columbia.

Gile, Leland H., John W. Hawley, and Robert B. Grossman

1981 *Soils and Geomorphology in the Basin and Range Area of Southern New Mexico – Guide to the Desert Project*. Memoir 39. New Mexico Bureau of Mines and Mineral Resources, Socorro, New Mexico.

Gilman, Patricia A.

1997 *Wandering Villagers: Pit Structures, Mobility, and Agriculture in Southeastern Arizona*. Anthropological Research Paper No.49. Arizona State University, Tempe.

Gish, Jannifer W.

1989 Palynological Perspectives on La Cuenca del Sedimento. In *Prehistoric Agricultural Activities on the Lehi-Mesa Terrace: Vol. I. Excavations at La Cuenca del Sedimento*, edited by T. Kathleen Henderson, pp. 243-302. Northland Research. Submitted to Arizona Department of Transportation. Contract No. 86-102. Copies available from Northland Research, Flagstaff.

1991 Current Perceptions, Recent Discoveries, and Future Directions in Hohokam Palynology. *Kiva* 56:237-254.

1993 Shelltown and the Hind Site: A Pollen Study of Two Settlements, with an Overview of Hohokam Subsistence. In *Shelltown and the Hind Site: A Study of Two Hohokam Craftsman Communities in Southwestern Arizona*, Vol. I, edited by William S. Marmaduke, and Richard J. Martynec, pp. 449-562. Northland Research, Flagstaff.

Gladwin, Harold S.

1928 *Excavations at Casa Grande, Arizona, February 12- May 1, 1927*. Southwest Museum Papers No. 2. Southwest Museum, Los Angeles.

Gladwin, Harold S., and Winifred Gladwin

1929 *The Red-on-Buff Culture of Papagueria*. Medallion Papers No. 8. Gila Pueblo, Gila, Arizona.

Gladwin, Harold S., Emil W. Haury, Edwin B. Sayles, and Nora Gladwin

1937 *Excavations at Snaketown: Vol. I. Material Culture*. Medallion Papers No. 25. Gila Pueblo, Globe, Arizona.

Gladwin, Winifred, and Harold S. Gladwin

1934 *A Method for the Designation of Cultures and Their Variations*. Medallion Papers No. 15. Gila Pueblo, Globe, Arizona.

Goar, Toni R., Peter Condon, Amador Minjares, Michael Kennedy, and Matthew Dawson
  2010   *Data Recovery and Monitoring Results of Three Sites along the SFPP East Line Expansion Project, Texas Portion*. TRC. Submitted to the Bureau of Land Management, Las Cruces District Office, and SFPP, LP. Copies available from TRC, Albuquerque.

Goar, Toni R., Amador Minjares, Michael Kennedy, and Maria E. Hroncich
  2010a   *Data Recovery and Monitoring Results of Nine Sites along the SFPP El Paso to Phoenix Expansion Project, New Mexico Portion (draft)*. TRC. Submitted to the Bureau of Land Management, Las Cruces District Office, and SFPP LP, TRC Project No. 49194/110082. Copies available from TRC, Albuquerque.

  2010b   *Data Recovery and Monitoring Results of Seven Sites along the SFPP El Paso to Phoenix Expansion Project, Texas Portion (draft)*. TRC. Submitted to SFPP LP, TRC Project No. 49194/110082. Copies available from TRC, Albuquerque.

Goar, Toni R., Elia Perez, Matthew Dawson, Amandor Minjares, Michael Kennedy, Gwen Mohr, and Dawn Muecke
  2009   *Data Recovery and Monitoring Results of 35 Sites along the SFPP East Line Expansion Project, New Mexico Portion*. TRC. Submitted to the Bureau of Land Management, Las Cruces District Office, and SFPP, LP. Copies available from TRC, Albuquerque.

Goodman, Alan H., and Jerome C. Rose
  1990   Factors Affecting the Distribution of Enamel Hypoplasias within the Human Permanent Dentition. *American Journal of Physical Anthropology* 68:479–493.

Grayson, Donald K.
  1973   On the Methodology of Faunal Analysis. *American Antiquity* 38:432-439.

  1979   On the Quantification of Vertebrate Archaeofaunas. In *Advances in Archaeological Method and Theory, 2*, edited by Michael B. Schiffer, pp. 199-237. Academic Press, New York.

  1981   The Effects of Sample Size on Some Derived Measures in Vertebrate Faunal Analysis. *Journal of Archaeological Science* 8:77-88.

Greenleaf, J. Cameron
  1975   *Excavations at Punta de Agua in the Santa Cruz River Basin, Southeastern Arizona*. Anthropological Papers No. 26. University of Arizona Press, Tucson.

Greenwald, David H., and Richard Ciolek-Torrello
  1987   Picacho Pass Site, NA 18,030. In *Hohokam Settlement along the Slopes of the Picacho Mountains: The Picacho Area Sites*, edited by Richard Ciolek-Torrello, pp. 130–216. Museum of Northern Arizona, Flagstaff.

Gregory, David A.
  1991   Form and Variation in Hohokam Settlement Patterns. In *Chaco and Hohokam: Prehistoric Regional Systems in the American Southwest*, edited by Patricia L. Crown, and W. James Judge, pp. 159-193. School for American Research, Santa Fe.

Gregory, David A. (editor)
  2001   *Excavations in the Santa Cruz River Floodplain: The Early Agricultural Component at Los Pozos*. Anthropological Papers No. 21. Center for Desert Archaeology, Tucson.

Griffith, Carol
    1989   Analysis of the Shell Material from the AAPL. In *Cultural Resources Report for the All American Pipeline Project: Santa Barbara, California, to McCamey, Texas, and Additional Areas to the East Along the Central Pipeline Route in Texas*, pp. 773-796. Cultural Resources Management Division, Sociology and Anthropology Department, New Mexico State University, Las Cruces, New Mexico.

Hackbarth, Mark R.
    1993   Morphological and Functional Analysis of the SCFAP Pits. In *Classic Period Occupation of the Santa Cruz Flats: The Santa Cruz Flats Archaeological Project*, edited by T. Kathleen Henderson, and Richard J. Martynec, pp. 513-540. 2 vols. Northland Research, Flagstaff.

Halbirt, Carl D., Annick Kaler, and Kurt E. Dongoske
    1993   Pit Features from Coffee Camp: An Evaluation of Form and Function. In *Archaic Occupation on the Santa Cruz Flats: The Tator Hills Archaeological Project*, edited by Carl D. Hilbert, and T. Kathleen Henderson, pp. 129-171. Northland Research, Flagstaff.

Hall, Stephen A.
    1981   Deteriorated Pollen Grains and the Interpretation of Quaternary Pollen Diagrams. *Review of Paleobotany and Palynology* 32:193-206.

    1985   Bibliography of Quaternary Palynology in Arizona, Colorado, New Mexico, and Utah. In *Pollen Records of Late-Quaternary North American Sediments*, edited by Vaughn Bryant and Richard G. Holloway, pp. 407-423. American Association of Stratigraphic Palynologists, Dallas.

Hastings, James R., and Raymond M. Turner
    1965   *The Changing Mile: An Ecological Study of Vegetation Change with Time in the Lower Mile of an Arid and Semiarid Region.* University of Arizona Press, Tucson.

Haury, Emil W.
    1931   Minute Beads from Prehistoric Pueblos. *American Anthropologist* 33:80–87.

    1936   *The Mogollon Culture of Southwestern New Mexico.* Medallion Papers No. 20. Gila Pueblo, Globe, Arizona.

    1937a Pottery Types at Snaketown. In *Excavations at Snaketown: Vol. I. Material Culture*, edited by Harold S. Gladwin, Emil W. Haury, Edwin B. Sayles, and Nora Gladwin, pp. 169-229. Medallion Papers No. 25. Gila Pueblo, Globe, Arizona.

    1937b Shell. In *Excavations at Snaketown: Vol. I. Material Culture*, edited by Harold S. Gladwin, Emil W. Haury, Edwin B. Sayles, and Nora Gladwin, pp. 135–153. Medallion Papers No. 25. Gila Pueblo, Globe, Arizona.

    1950   *The Stratigraphy and Archaeology of Ventana Cave.* University of Arizona Press, Tucson.

    1953   Artifacts with Mammoth Remains, Naco, Arizona, I: Discovery of the Naco Mammoth and the Associated Projectile Points. *American Antiquity* 19:1-14.

    1957   An Alluvial Site on the San Carlos Indian Reservation, Arizona. *American Antiquity* 23:2–27.

    1975   Stone Palettes and Ornaments. In *Excavations at Snaketown: I. Material Culture*, edited by Harold S. Gladwin, Emil W. Haury, Edwin B. Sayles, and Nora Gladwin, pp. 121–134. Reprinted. Originally published, 1938, University of Arizona Press, Tucson.

Haury, Emil W., cont'd.

1976   *The Hohokam, Desert Farmers and Craftsmen: Excavations at Snaketown, 1964-1965.* University of Arizona Press, Tucson.

1985   *Mogollon Culture in the Forestdale Valley, East-Central Arizona.* University of Arizona Press, Tucson.

Haury, Emil W., Edwin B. Sayles, and William W. Wasley

1959   The Lehner Mammoth Site, Southeastern Arizona. *American Antiquity* 25:2-32.

Hawley, Fred G.

1947   The Use of Lead Mineral by the Hohokam in Cremation Ceremonials. *Southwestern Journal of Anthropology* 3:69–77.

Hayden, Julian D.

1957   *Excavations, 1940, at University Indian Ruin, Tucson, Arizona.* Southwestern Monuments Association, Technical Series, No. 5. Gila Pueblo, Globe.

1972   Hohokam Petroglyphs of the Sierra Pinacate, Sonora, and the Hohokam Shell Expeditions. *The Kiva* 37(2):74-83.

Haynes, Jr., C. Vance, and Bruce B. Huckell (editors)

2007   *Murray Springs: A Clovis Site with Multiple Activity Areas in the San Pedro Valley, Arizona.* University of Arizona Press, Tucson.

Heckman, Robert A.

2000a   The Tucson Basin Tradition. In *Prehistoric Painted Pottery of Southeastern Arizona*, edited by Robert A. Heckman, Barbara K. Montgomery, and Stephanie M. Whittlesey, pp. 83-94. Technical Series 77. Statistical Research, Tucson.

2000b   The Dragoon Tradition. In *Prehistoric Painted Pottery of Southeastern Arizona*, edited by Robert A. Heckman, Barbara K. Montgomery, and Stephanie M. Whittlesey, pp. 43-62. Technical Series 77. Statistical Research, Tucson.

2000c   The Trincheras Tradition. In *Prehistoric Painted Pottery of Southeastern Arizona*, edited by Robert A. Heckman, Barbara K. Montgomery, and Stephanie M. Whittlesey, pp. 75-82. Technical Series 77. Statistical Research, Tucson.

Heckman, Robert A., Barbara K. Montgomery, and Stephanie M. Whittlesey (editors)

2000   *Prehistoric Painted Pottery of Southeastern Arizona.* Technical Series 77. Statistical Research, Tucson.

Heidke, James M.

1986   Plainware Ceramics. In *Archaeological Investigations at the West Branch Site: Early and Middle Rincon Occupation in the Southern Tucson Basin*, edited by Frederick W. Huntington, pp. 165-196. Anthropological Papers No. 5. Institute for American Research, Tucson.

1995   Ceramic Analysis. In *Archaeological Investigations at Los Morteros, A Prehistoric Settlement in the Northern Tucson Basin*, edited by Henry D. Wallace, pp. 263-442. Anthropological Papers No. 17. Center for Desert Archaeology, Tucson.

Heidke, James M., cont'd.
2005   Early Agricultural Period Pottery from Las Capas and Los Pozos. In *Material Cultures and Lifeways of Early Agricultural Communities in Southern Arizona*, edited by R. Jane Sliva, pp. 171–206. Anthropological Papers No. 35. Center for Desert Archaeology, Tucson.

Heidke, James M., and Alan Ferg
2001   Ceramic Containers and Other Artifacts of Clay. In *Excavations in the Santa Cruz River Floodplain: The Early Agricultural Component at Los Pozos*, edited by David A. Gregory, pp. 163–194. Anthropological Papers No. 21. Center for Desert Archaeology, Tucson.

Heidke, James M., Elizabeth J. Miksa, and Michael K. Wiley
1998   Ceramic Artifacts. In *Archaeological Investigations of Early Village Sites in the Middle Santa Cruz Valley: Analysis and Synthesis*, Part II, edited by Jonathan B. Mabry, pp. 471–544. Anthropological Papers No. 19. Center for Desert Archaeology, Tucson.

Heilen, Michael P., and Jeffrey A. Homburg
2007   Assessing Soil Quality in Ancient Agricultural Landscapes of Southern Arizona. Poster presented at the session, "Ancient Cultures, Soil Genesis, and Landuse Management," at the ASA (American Society of Agronomy)-CSSA (Crop Science Society of America)-SSSA (Soil Science Society of America) International Annual Meeting, November 4–8, 2007, New Orleans.

Hemmings, E. Thomas, M. D. Robinson, and R. N. Rogers
1968   Field Report on the Pantano Site (Arizona EE:2:50). Manuscript on file, Arizona State Museum, University of Arizona, Tucson.

Henderson, T. Kathleen
1987   *Structure and Organization at La Ciudad*. Anthropological Field Studies No. 18; La Ciudad Monograph Series Vol. 3. Office of Cultural Resource Management, Department of Anthropology, Arizona State University, Tempe.

2001   Household Organization and Activity at Grewe. In *The Grewe Archaeological Research Project: Vol. 3. Synthesis*, edited by Douglas B. Craig, pp. 93-113. Anthropological Papers No. 99-1. Northland Research, Flagstaff.

Henderson, T. Kathleen, and Douglas B. Craig
2008   Houses, Households, and Household Organization. In *The Hohokam Millennium*, edited by Suzanne K. Fish and Paul R. Fish, pp. 31-37. School for Advanced Research, Santa Fe.

Hendricks, David M.
1985   *Arizona Soils*. College of Agriculture, University of Arizona, Tucson.

Hendrickson, Dean A., and W. L. Minckley
1984   Cienegas: Vanishing Climax Communities of the American Southwest. *Desert Plants* 6:131–175.

Hereford, Richard
1993   *Entrenchment and Widening of the Upper San Pedro River*. Special Paper 282. Geological Society of America, Boulder, Colorado.

Herr, Sarah

    1993   Broken Pots as Tools. In *Across the Colorado Plateau: Anthropological Studies for the Transwestern Pipeline Expansion Project: XVI. Interpretation of Ceramic Artifacts*, edited by Barbara J. Mills, Christine E. Goetze, and Maria Nieves Zedeño, pp. 347-376. Submitted to Transwestern Pipeline Company. UNM Project 185-461B. Copies available from the Office of Contract Archaeology and Maxwell Museum of Anthropology, University of New Mexico, Albuquerque.

Hesse, Jerome

    2010   Clovis Point Found Near Tucson. *Arizona Archaeological Council Newsletter* 34(1):8.

Hewitt, James E., and David V. M. Stephen

    1981   *Archaeological Investigations in the Tortolita Mountains Region, Southern Arizona.* Pima Community College Anthropology Series, Archaeological Field Report No. 10. Pima Community College, Tucson.

Hill, J. Brett, Jeffery L. Clark, William H. Doelle, and Patrick D. Lyons

    2004   Prehistoric Demography in the Southwest: Migration, Coalescence, and Hohokam Population Decline. *American Antiquity* 69:689-716.

Hodge, Frederick W.

    1950   Those Small Pottery Disks. *The Masterkey* 24:171-172. Southwest Museum, Los Angeles.

Hoffman, Christopher R.

    1999   Intentional Damage as Technological Agency: Breaking Metals in Late Prehistoric Spain. In *The Social Dynamics of Technology: Practice, Politics, and World View*, edited by Marcia-Anne Dobres and Christopher R. Hoffman, pp. 103–123. Smithsonian Institution, Washington, D.C.

Hoffmeister, Donald F.

    1986   *Mammals of Arizona.* University of Arizona Press and the Arizona Game and Fish Department, Tucson.

Holliday, Vance T.

    2000   The Evolution of Paleoindian Geochronology and Typology on the Great Plains. *Geoarchaeology: An International Journal* 15(3):227–290.

    2004   *Soils in Archaeological Research.* Oxford University Press, New York.

Holloway, Richard G.

    1981   Preservation and Experimental Diagenesis of the Pollen Exine. Unpublished Ph.D. dissertation, Department of Biology, Texas A&M University, College Station, Texas.

    1989   Experimental Mechanical Pollen Degradation and Its Application to Quaternary Age Deposits. *Texas Journal of Science* 41:131-145.

Horsfall, G. A.

    1987   Design Theory and Grinding Stones. In *Lithic Studies Among the Contemporary Highland Maya*, edited by Brian Hayden, pp. 332-377. University of Arizona Press, Tucson.

Howard, Ann Valado

    1993   Marine Shell Artifacts and Production Processes and Shelltown and the Hind Site. In *Shelltown and the Hind Site: Volume I. A Study of Two Hohokam Craftsman Communities in Southwestern Arizona*, edited by William S. Marmaduke, and Richard J. Martynec, pp. 321-423. Northland Research, Flagstaff.

Huckell, Bruce B.
 1984 The Paleo-Indian and Archaic Occupation of the Tucson Basin: An Overview. *The Kiva* 49(3-4):133-145.

 1988 Late Archaic Archaeology of the Tucson Basin: A Status Report. In *Recent Research on Tucson Basin Prehistory: Proceedings of the Second Tucson Basin Conference*, edited by William H. Doelle and Paul R. Fish, pp. 57–76. Anthropological Papers No. 10. Institute for American Research, Tucson.

 1989 Hohokam Flaked-Stone Analysis: Insights from the Phase B Data. In *Hohokam Archaeology along Phase B of the Tucson Aqueduct, Central Arizona Project*, Vol. 1, Part II, edited by Jon S. Czaplicki and John C. Ravesloot, pp. 417-438. Archaeological Series 178. Cultural Resource Management Division, Arizona State Museum, University of Arizona, Tucson.

 1990 *Late Preceramic Farmer-Foragers in Southeastern Arizona : A Cultural and Ecological Consideration of the Spread of Agriculture into the Arid Southwestern United States*. Ph.D. dissertation, University of Arizona, Tucson. University Microfilms, Ann Arbor, Michigan.

 1995 *Of Marshes and Maize: Preceramic Agricultural Settlements in the Cienega Valley, Southeastern Arizona*. Anthropological Papers No. 59. University of Arizona Press, Tucson.

 1996 The Archaic Prehistory of the North American Southwest. *Journal of World Prehistory* 10:305-373.

 1998 An Analysis of Flaked Stone Artifacts. In *Early Farmers of the Sonoran Desert: Archaeological Investigations at the Houghton Road Site, Tucson, Arizona*, edited by Richard Ciolek-Torrello, pp. 89-117. Technical Series 72. Statistical Research, Tucson.

Huckell, Bruce B., and Lisa W. Huckell
 1979 Marine Shell from AZ Y:8:3, The Largo Seco Site. In *The Coronet Real Project: Archaeological Investigations on the Luke Range, Southwestern Arizona*. Arizona State Museum, University of Arizona, Tucson.

Huckell, Lisa W.
 1981 Marine Shell. In *Test Excavations at Painted Rock Reservoir: Sites AZ Z:1:7, AZ Z:1:8, and AZ S:16:36*, edited by Lynn S. Teague, pp. 60-67. ASM Archaeological Series 143. Cultural Resource Management Division, Arizona State Museum, University of Arizona, Tucson.

 1984 Appendix A: Archaeobotanical Remains from Archaic Sites in the Rosemont Area, Santa Rita Mountains, Arizona. In *The Archaic Occupation of the Rosemont Area, Northern Santa Rita Mountains, Southeastern Arizona*, Vol. 1, edited by Bruce B. Huckell, pp. 267-274. Archaeological Series 147. Cultural Resource Management Division, Arizona State Museum, University of Arizona, Tucson.

 1995 Farming and Foraging in the Cienega Valley: Early Agricultural Period Paleoethnobotany. In *Of Marshes and Maize: Preceramic Agricultural Settlements in the Cienega Valley, Southeastern Arizona*, edited by Bruce B. Huckell, pp. 74-97. Anthropological Papers No. 59. University of Arizona Press, Tucson.

 1998 Paleoethnobotany. In *Early Farmers of the Sonoran Desert: Archaeological Investigations at the Houghton Road Site, Tucson, Arizona*, edited by Richard Ciolek-Torrello, pp. 327-344. Technical Series 72. Statistical Research, Tucson.

 2006 Ancient Maize in the American Southwest: What Does It Look Like and What Can It Tell Us? In *Histories of Maize: Multidisciplinary Approaches to the Prehistory, Linguistics, Biogeography, Domestication, and Evolution of Maize*, edited by John Staller, Robert Tykot, and Bruce Benz, pp. 97-107. Elsevier, Boston.

Huckleberry, Gary, S. Joy Lite, G. Katz, and P. A. Pearthree
2006   Fluvial Geomorphology. In *Riparian Area Conservation and Ecology in a Semi-Arid Region: The San Pedro River Example*, edited by J. Stromberg and B. Tellman. University of Arizona Press, Tucson; in press.

Hull, Frank W.
1984   Archaeological Evidence of Nonagricultural Subsistence. In *Hohokam Archaeology Along the Salt-Gila Aqueduct: VII. Environment and Subsistence*, edited by Lynn S. Teague, and Patricia L. Crown, pp. 171-? Archaeological Series No. 150. Cultural Resource Management Division, Arizona State Museum, University of Arizona, Tucson.

Huntington, Frederick W.
1988   Rincon Phase Community Organization. In *Recent Research in Tucson Basin Prehistory: Proceedings of the Second Tucson Basin Conference*, edited by William H. Doelle, and Paul R. Fish, pp. 207–224. Anthropological Papers 10. Institute for American Research, Tucson.

Huntington, Frederick W. (editor)
1986   *Archaeological Investigations at the West Branch Site, Early and Middle Rincon Occupation in the Southern Tucson Basin*. Anthropological Papers 5. Institute for American Research, Tucson.

Jacobs, David (editor)
1994   *Archaeology of the Salado in the Livingston Area of Tonto Basin, Roosevelt Platform Mound Study: Report on the Livingston Management Group, Pinto Creek Complex*. Anthropological Field Studies No. 26. Office of Cultural Resource Management, Department of Anthropology, Arizona State University, Tempe.

Jernigan, E. Wesley
1978   *Jewelry of the Prehistoric Southwest*. School of American Research Press, Santa Fe, and University of New Mexico Press, Albuquerque.

Jeske, Robert J.
1992   Energetic Efficiency and Lithic Technology: An Upper Mississippian Example. *American Antiquity* 57:467-481.

Johnson, Alfred E.
1960   The Place of the Trincheras Culture of Northern Sonora in Southwestern Archaeology. Unpublished Master's thesis, Department of Anthropology, University of Arizona, Tucson.

1965   The Development of Western Pueblo Culture. Unpublished Ph.D. dissertation, Department of Anthropology, University of Arizona, Tucson.

Johnson, Alfred E., and William W. Wasley
1966   Archaeological Excavations near Bylas, Arizona. *The Kiva* 31:205-253.

Johnson, N., N. D. Opdyke, and E. H. Lindsay
1975   Magnetic Polarity Stratigraphy of Pliocene-Pleistocene Terrestrial Deposits and Vertebrate Faunas San Pedro Valley, Arizona. *Geological Society of America Bulletin* 86:5–12.

Justice, Noel D.
2002   *Stone Age Spear and Arrow Points of the Southwestern United States*. University of Indiana Press, Bloomington and Indianapolis.

Kanakoff, George, and Howard Hill
    1978   Shell. In T*he Hodges Ruin, a Hohokam Community in the Tucson Basin*, edited by Isabel T. Kelly, James E. Officer, and Emil W. Haury. Anthropological Papers No. 30. University of Arizona Press, Tucson.

Kapp, Ronald O.
    1969   *Pollen and Spores*. W. C. Brown, Dubuque, Iowa.

Kearney, Thomas H., and Robert H. Peebles
    1960   *Arizona Flora*. University of California Press, Berkeley.

Kearns, Timothy M. (compiler)
    2009   *Archaeological Investigations for the AT&T NexGen/Core Project: Arizona Segment*. Report No. WCRM(F)218. 6 vols. Western Cultural Resource Management, Farmington, New Mexico.

Kearns, Timothy M., Thomas J. Lennon, Dorothy L. Webb, Joshua Jones, and Steven F. Mehls
    2001   *An Archaeological Survey of the Arizona Portion of Link Two of the AT&T NexGen/Core Project.* WCRM(F) Report 174. Western Cultural Resource Management, Farmington, New Mexico.

Kearns, Timothy M., and Janet L. McVickar
    2009   Investigations at a Hohokam Hamlet on Mescal Arroyo, AZ EE:2:44 (ASM). In *Archaeological Investigations for the AT&T NexGen/Core Project: Arizona Segment*, Vol 2, compiled by Timothy M. Kearns, pp. 330–415. Report No. WCRM(F)218. Western Cultural Resource Management, Farmington, New Mexico.

Keen, Myra A.
    1971   *Sea Shells of Tropical West America: Marine Mollusks from Baja California to Peru*. 2nd ed. Stanford University Press, Palo Alto, California.

Kelly, Isabel T., James E. Officer, and Emil W. Haury
    1978   *The Hodges Ruin: A Hohokam Community in the Tucson Basin*. Anthropological Papers No. 30. University of Arizona Press, Tucson.

Kelly, Robert L.
    1988   The Three Sides of a Biface. *American Antiquity* 53:717–734.

    2001   *Prehistory of the Carson Desert and Stillwater Mountains: Environment, Mobility, and Subsistence in a Great Basin Wetland*. Anthropological Papers No. 123. University of Utah Press, Salt Lake City.

Kent, Kate Peck
    1957   The Cultivation and Weaving of Cotton in the Prehistoric Southwestern United States. *Transactions of the American Philosophical Society* 47:457-732.

Kramer, Carol
    1997   *Pottery in Rajasthan: Ethnoarchaeology in Two Indian Cities*. Smithsonian Institution, Washington, D.C.

Kwiatkowski, Scott M.
    1989   Pre-Classic Hohokam Subsistence in the Tucson Aqueduct Project Phase B Area: The Macrofloral Evidence. In *Hohokam Archaeology along Phase B of the Tucson Aqueduct Central Arizona Project: Vol. I. Syntheses and Interpretations*, edited by Jon S. Czaplicki, and John C. Ravesloot, pp. 253-276. Archaeological Series 178. Arizona State Museum, University of Arizona, Tucson.

LaMotta, Vincent M., and Michael B. Schiffer
    1999   Formation Process of House Floor Assemblages. In *The Archaeology of Household Activities*, edited by Penelope M. Allison, pp. 19-29. Routledge, London and New York.

Lekson, Stephen H.
    1999   Great Towns in the Southwest. In *Great Towns and Regional Polities in the Prehistoric American Southwest and Southeast*, edited by Jill E. Neitzel, pp. 3-21. Amerind Foundation New World Studies Series No. 3. University of New Mexico Press, Albuquerque.

    2000   Salado in Chihuahua. In *Salado*, edited by Jeffrey S. Dean, pp. 275-294. University of New Mexico Press, Albuquerque.

Lindeman, Michael W.
    2003   Excavation Results. In *Roots of Sedentism: Archaeological Excavations at Valencia Vieja, a Founding Village in the Tucson Basin of Southern Arizona*, edited by Henry D. Wallace, pp. 35–121. Anthropological Papers No. 29. Center for Desert Archaeology, Tucson.

Lindsay, E. H., G. A. Smith, and C. Vance Haynes
    1990   Late Cenozoic Depositional History and Geoarchaeology, San Pedro Valley, Arizona. In *Geologic Excursions through the Sonoran Desert Region, Arizona and Sonora*, edited by George Gehrels and Jon E. Spencer, pp. 9–19. Special Paper 7. Arizona Geological Survey, Tucson.

Mabry, Jonathan B.
    1996   *A Rincon Phase Occupation at the Julian Wash Site, AZ BB:13:17 (ASM)*. Technical Report No. 96-7. Center for Desert Archaeology, Tucson.

    1998   *Paleoindian and Archaic Sites in Arizona: Historic Context Study*. Arizona State Historic Preservation Office, Arizona State Parks Board, Phoenix.

    2000   Radiocarbon Age Ranges of Paleoindian and Archaic Projectile Point Types in the Southwest. In *Rethinking the Peopling of the Americas*, compiled by Jonathan Mabry as a Supplement to Archaeology Southwest 14(2), Spring 2000. Electronic document, http://www.cdarc.org/what-we-do/exhibits/rethinking-the-peopling-of-the-americas/radiocarbon-age-ranges-of-paleoindian-and-archaic-projectile-point-types-in-the-southwest/, accessed December 22, 2010.

    2005a Changing Knowledge and Ideas about the First Farmers in Southeastern Arizona. In *The Late Archaic Across the Borderlands: From Foraging to Farming*, edited by Bradley J. Vierra, pp. 41-83. Texas Archaeology and Ethnohistory Series. University of Texas Press, Austin.

    2005b Diversity in Early Southwestern Farming Systems and Optimization Models of Transitions to Agriculture. In *Subsistence and Resource Use Strategies of Early Agricultural Communities in Southern Arizona*, edited by Michael W. Diehl, pp. 113-152. Anthropological Papers No. 34. Center for Desert Archaeology, Tucson.

    2005c Reading the Traces of Early Farming Villages. In *Material Cultures and Lifeways of Early Agricultural Communities in Southern Arizona*, edited by R. Jane Sliva, pp. 1-17. Anthropological Papers No. 35. Center for Desert Archaeology, Tucson.

    2008a Introduction. In *Las Capas: Early Irrigation and Sedentism in a Southwestern Floodplain*, edited by Jonathan B. Mabry, pp. 1-34. Anthropological Papers No. 28. Center for Desert Archaeology, Tucson.

Mabry, Jonathan B., cont'd.
2008b Irrigation, Short-Term Sedentism, and Corporate Organization during the San Pedro Phase. In *Las Capas: Early Irrigation and Sedentism in a Southwestern Floodplain*, edited by Jonathan B. Mabry, pp. 257–278. Anthropological Papers No. 28. Center for Desert Archaeology, Tucson.

Mabry, Jonathan B. (editor)
1998 *Archaeological Investigations of Early Village Sites in the Middle Santa Cruz Valley: Analyses and Synthesis*, Part I. Anthropological Papers No. 19. Center for Desert Archaeology, Tucson.

2008 *Las Capas: Early Irrigation and Sedentism in a Southwestern Floodplain*. Anthropological Papers No. 28. Center for Desert Archaeology, Tucson.

Mabry, Jonathan B., Deborah L. Schwartz, Helga Wöcherl, Jeffrey J. Clark, Gavin H. Archer, and Michael W. Lindeman
1997 *Archaeological Investigations at Early Village Sites in the Middle Santa Cruz Valley: Site and Feature Descriptions*. Anthropological Papers No. 18. Center for Desert Archaeology, Tucson.

Marshall, John T.
2001 Ballcourt. In *The Grewe Archaeological Research Project, Volume 1: Project Background and Feature Descriptions*, edited by Douglas B. Craig, pp. 109-124. Anthropological Papers No. 99-1. Northland Research, Tempe.

Martin, Paul S.
1943 *The SU Site: Excavations at a Mogollon Village, Western New Mexico, Second Season, 1941*. Anthropological Series Vol. 32, No. 2 Publication 526. Field Museum of Natural History, Chicago.

Martin, Paul S., John B. Rinaldo, E. A. Bluhm, and Hugh C. Cutler
1956 *Higgins Flat Pueblo, Western New Mexico*. Fieldiana: Anthropology 45. Field Museum of Natural History, Chicago.

Matson, Richard G.
1991 *The Origins of Southwestern Agriculture*. University of Arizona Press, Tucson.

1999 The Spread of Maize to the Colorado Plateau. *Archaeology Southwest* 13(1):10–11.

McConville, John T., and Frank M. Holzkamper
1955 Archaeological Survey of the Southern Pacific Pipeline Right-Of-Way in Southeastern Arizona. Manuscript on file, Arizona State Museum, University of Arizona, Tucson.

McGuire, Randall H.
1992 *Death, Ideology, and Society in a Hohokam Community*. Westview Press, Boulder.

McKee, Brian R.
2007 *Volcanism, Household Archaeology, and Formation Processes in the Zapotitán Valley, El Salvador*. Ph.D. Dissertation, University of Arizona, Tucson. University Microfilms, Ann Arbor.

Mehringer, Peter J.
1967 Pollen Analysis of the Tule Springs Area, Nevada. In *Pleistocene Studies in Southern Nevada*, edited by H. M. Wormington and Dorothy Ellis, pp. 130-200. Anthropological Papers 13. Nevada State Museum, Carson City, Nevada.

Meltzer, David J.
   2009   *First Peoples in a New World: Colonizing Ice Age America.* University of California Press, Berkeley.

Menges, C. M., and P. A. Pearthree
   1989   Late Cenozoic Tectonism in Arizona and Its Impact on Regional Landscape Evolution. In *Geologic Evolution of Arizona*, edited by J. P. Jenny, and S. J. Reynolds, pp. 649–680. Digest 17. Arizona Geological Survey, Tucson.

Merrill, William L., Robert J. Hard, Jonathan B. Mabry, Gayle J. Fritz, Karen R. Adams, John R. Roney, and A. C. MacWilliams
   2009   The Diffusion of Maize to the Southwestern United States and Its Impact. *Proceedings of the National Academy of Science* 106(50):21019–21026.

Miksa, Elizabeth J., and Charles Thompkins
   1998   Rock and Mineral Materials and Sources. In *Archaeological Investigations at Early Village Sites in the Middle Santa Cruz Valley: Analyses and Synthesis*, Part I, edited by Jonathan B. Mabry, pp. 655–696. Anthropological Papers No. 19. Center for Desert Archaeology, Tucson.

Miksicek, Charles H.
   1988   Rethinking Hohokam Paleoethnobotanical Assemblages: A Progress Report for the Tucson Basin. In Recent Research on Tucson Basin Prehistory: *Proceedings of the Second Tucson Basin Conference*, edited by William H. Doelle and Paul R. Fish, pp. 47-56. Anthropological Papers No. 10. Institute for American Research, Tucson.

   1992   The Verde Bridge Project: A View from the Float Tank. In *Prehistoric and Historic Occupation of the Lower Verde River Valley: The State Route 87 Verde Bridge Project*, edited by Mark R. Hackbarth, pp. 313-339. Northland Research. Submitted to the Arizona Department of Transportation, Contract No. 89-28. Copies available from Northland Research, Flagstaff.

Mills, Barbara J.
   1989   Integrating Functional Analyses of Vessels and Sherds through Models of Ceramic Assemblage Formation. *World Archaeology* 21:133-147.

Moore, Peter D., J. A. Webb, and Margaret E. Collinson
   1991   *Pollen Analysis.* Blackwell Scientific Publications, London.

Morrison, R. B.
   1985   Pliocene/Quaternary Geology, Geomorphology, and Tectonics of Arizona. In *Soils and Quaternary Geology of the Southwestern United States*, edited by David L. Weide, pp. 123–146. Special Paper 203. Geological Society of America, Boulder, Colorado.

Muenchrath, D. A., M. Kuratomi, J. A. Sandor, and Jeffrey A. Homburg
   2002   Observational Study of Maize Production Systems of Zuni Farmers in Semiarid New Mexico. *Journal of Ethnobiology* 22:1–33.

Nelson, Ben A., and Steven A. LeBlanc
   1986   *Short-term Sedentism in the American Southwest: The Mimbres Valley Salado.* Maxwell Museum of Anthropology and University of New Mexico Press, Albuquerque.

Nelson, Margaret C.
   1990   The Study of Technological Organization. *Journal of Archaeological Method and Theory* 3:57–100.

Nelson, Margaret C., and Heidi Lippmeier
1993   Grinding-Tool Design as Conditioned by Land-Use Patterns. *American Antiquity* 58:289–305.

Nelson, Richard S.
1991   *Hohokam Marine Shell Exchange and Artifacts*. Archaeological Series 179. University of Arizona, Arizona State Museum, University of Arizona, Tucson.

Nichols, K. K., P. R. Bierman, W. R. Foniri, A. R. Gillespie, M. Caffee, and R. Finkel
2006   Dates and Rates of Arid Region Geomorphic Processes. *GSA Today* 16:4–11.

Oppelt, Norman T.
1984   Worked Potsherds of the Prehistoric Southwest: Their Forms and Distribution. *Pottery Southwest* 11(1):1-6.

Parker, Kittie F.
1972   *An Illustrated Guide to Arizona Weeds*. University of Arizona Press, Tucson.

Parry, William J., and Robert L. Kelly
1987   Expedient Core Technology and Sedentism. In *The Organization of Core Technology*, edited by Jay K. Johnson and Carol A. Morrow, pp. 285-304. Westview, Boulder.

Pelletier, J. D., L. Mayer, P. A. Pearthree, P. K. House, K. A. Demsey, J. E. Klawon, and K. R. Vincent
2005   An Integrated Approach to Flood Hazard Assessment on Alluvial Fans Using Numerical Modeling, Field Mapping, and Remote Sensing. *Geological Society of America Bulletin* 117:1167–1180.

Perkins, Dexter, Jr., and Patricia Daly
1968   A Hunters' Neolithic Village in Turkey. *Scientific American* 219:96-106.

Peterson, Roger Troy
1990   *Western Birds*. Houghton Mifflin, New York.

Phillips, Bruce G. (preparer)
1998   *Prehistoric Floodwater Agriculture along Middle Cave Creek, Maricopa County, Arizona*. Cultural Resource Report No. 103. Archaeological Consulting Services, Tempe.

Pima Association of Governments (PAG)
2003   Geologic Influences on the Hydrology of Lower Cienega Creek. Electronic Report, http://www.pagnet.org/documents/Water/LIB/cienega_geology.pdf, accessed June 2008.

Plog, Stephen
1985   Estimating Vessel Orifice Diameters: Measurement Methods and Measurement Error. In *Decoding Prehistoric Ceramics*, edited by Ben A. Nelson, pp. 243-253. Southern Illinois University Press, Carbondale.

Purdue, James R.
1983   Epiphyseal Closure in White-Tailed Deer. *Journal of Wildlife Management* 47:1207-1213.

Rafferty, Janet E.
1985   The Archaeological Record on Sedentariness: Recognition, Development, and Implications. *Advances in Archaeological Method and Theory*, Vol. 8, edited by Michael B. Schiffer, pp. 113–156. Academic Press, New York.

Ramenofsky, Ann F., and James K. Feathers
2002 Documents, Ceramics, Tree Rings, and Luminescence: Estimating Final Native Abandonment of the Lower Rio Chama. *Journal of Anthropological Research* 58:121–159.

Ravesloot, John C., Michael J. Boley, and Melanie A. Medeiros (editors)
2010 *Results of Testing and Data Recovery, SFPP, LP, El Paso to Phoenix Expansion Project, Arizona Portion: Cochise and Pima Counties*. Technical Report No. 2008-49. 2 vols. William Self Associates, Tucson.

Ravesloot, John C., M. Kyle Woodson, and Michael J. Boley (editors)
2007 *Results of Testing and Data Recovery, SFPP, LP, East Line Expansion Project, Arizona Portion. Cochise, Pima, Pinal, and Maricopa Counties, Arizona*. Technical Report No. 2007-04. 4 vols. William Self Associates, Tucson, and Gila River Indian Community Cultural Resource Management Program, Sacaton, Arizona.

Rawson, Paul M., Morgan Rieder, and Michael J. Boley
2006 *Class III Cultural Resources Survey, SFPP, LP, El Paso to Phoenix Expansion Project, Arizona Portion: Addendum*. Technical Report No. 2006-12. William Self Associates, Tucson.

Rawson, Paul M., Trevor Self, and Tylia Varilek
2007 *Class III Cultural Resources Survey, SFPP, LP, El Paso to Phoenix Expansion Project, Arizona Portion: Cienega Creek Access Roads Addendum, Pima County, Arizona*. Technical Report No. 2007-01. William Self Associates, Tucson.

Rea, Amadeo M.
1997 *At The Desert's Green Edge: An Ethnobotany of the Gila River Pima*. University of Arizona Press, Tucson.

Reed, Erik K.
1948 The Western Pueblo Archaeological Complex. *El Palacio* 55:9–15.

Reeve, Lovell Augustus
1843 Monograph of the Genus Pectunculus. *Conchologia Iconica* 1:208–209, Plate 1.

Reid, J. Jefferson, and Stephanie M. Whittlesey
1997 *The Archaeology of Ancient Arizona*. University of Arizona Press, Tucson.

Reitz, Elizabeth J., and Dan Cordier
1983 Use of Allometry in Zooarchaeoloigcal Analysis. In *Animals in Archaeology: Vol. 2. Shell Middens, Fishes, and Birds*, edited by Caroline Grigson and Juliet Clutton-Brock, pp. 237-252. BAR International Series 183. Archaeopress, Oxford.

Reitz, Elizabeth J., Irvy R. Quitmyer, H. Stephen Hale, Sylvia J. Scudder, and Elizabeth S. Wing
1987 Application of Allometry to Zooarchaeology. *American Antiquity* 52:304-317.

Reitz, Elizabeth J., and Elizabeth S. Wing
2008 *Zooarchaeology*. 2nd ed. Cambridge University Press, New York.

Rice, Glen E.
1987 *A Spatial Analysis of the Hohokam Community of La Ciudad*. Anthropological Field Studies No. 16; La Ciudad Monograph Series Vol.1. Office of Cultural Resource Management, Department of Anthropology, Arizona State University, Tempe.

Rice, Glen E., cont'd.

1995   Special Artifacts and Evidence for the Differentiation of Residential and Ritual Rooms at the Bass Point Mound. In *Where the Rivers Converge, Roosevelt Platform Mound Study: Report on the Rock Island Complex*, edited by Owen Lindauer. Anthropological Field Studies No. 41; Roosevelt Monograph Series No. 4. Office of Cultural Resource Management, Department of Anthropology, Arizona State University, Tempe.

1998   Structuring the Temporal Dimension for Tonto Basin Prehistory. In *A Synthesis of Tonto Basin Prehistory: The Roosevelt Archaeology Studies, 1989-1998*, edited by Glen E. Rice, pp. 11-32. Anthropological Field Studies No. 41; Roosevelt Monograph Series No. 12. Office of Cultural Resource Management, Department of Anthropology, Arizona State University, Tempe.

2003   *A Research Design for the Study of Hohokam Houses and Households*. P-MIP Technical Report No. 2003-05. Cultural Resource Management Program, Gila River Indian Community, Sacaton, Arizona.

Rice, Glen E., and John C. Ravesloot

2001   *Who Used the Area Between the Villages? The Role of Camps, Activity Areas, and Fields in the Study of Prehistoric Landscapes*. P-MIP Technical Report No. 2001-09. Cultural Resource Management Program, Gila River Indian Community, Sacaton, Arizona.

Richard, Stephen M., and Raymond C. Harris

1996   *Geology and Geophysics of the Cienega Basin Area, Pima and Cochise Counties, Arizona*. Open-File Report No. 96-21. Arizona Geological Survey, Tucson.

Richard, Stephen M., J. E. Spencer, C. A. Ferguson, and A. Youberg

2002   *Geologic Map of the Southern Part of the Vail 7.5' Quadrangle*. DGM 12, 1 sheet, 2- pages text, Scale 1:24,000. Arizona Geological Survey, Tucson.

Rieder, Morgan, Paul M. Rawson, and Jennifer E. Epperson

2006   *Class III Cultural Resources Survey, SFPP, LP, El Paso to Phoenix Expansion Project, Arizona Portion: Cochise and Pima Counties, Arizona: Final Report*. Technical Report No. 2006-08. William Self Associates, Tucson.

Rinaldo, J. B.

1952   Specimens of Stone, Bone, and Clay. In *Mogollon Cultural Continuity and Change: The Stratigraphic Analysis of Tularoas and Cordova Caves*, edited by P.S. Martin, J. B. Rinaldo, E. A. Bluhm, H. C. Cutler, and R. Jr. Grange. Fieldiana: Anthropology 40:102–204. Field Museum of Natural History, Chicago.

Roberts, Heidi M.

1993   *An Archaeological Survey of the Marsh Station Traffic Interchange on U.S. Interstate 10 East of Tucson, Pima County, Arizona*. Archaeological Report 93-63. SWCA Environmental Consultants, Tucson.

Roth, Barbara J.

1989   Late Archaic Settlement and Subsistence in the Tucson Basin. Unpublished Ph.D. dissertation, Department of Anthropology, University of Arizona, Tucson.

1992   Sedentary Agriculturalists or Mobile Hunter-Gatherers? Recent Evidence for the Late Archaic Occupation of the Northern Tucson Basin. *Kiva* 57:291–314.

2000   Households at a Rincon Phase Hohokam Site in the Tucson Basin of Southern Arizona. *Journal of Field Archaeology* 27:285–294.

Roth, Barbara J., and Bruce B. Huckell
 1992   Cortaro Points and the Archaic of Southern Arizona. *Kiva* 57:353-367.

Russell, Frank
 1908   *The Pima Indians*. Twenty-sixth Annual Report of the Bureau of American Ethnology [1904–1905], pp. 3–389. Smithsonian Institution, Washington, D.C.

Sayles, Edwin B.
 1945   *The San Simon Branch: Excavations at Cave Creek and in the San Simon Valley: Vol. 1. Material Culture.* Medallion Papers No. 34. 2 vols. Gila Pueblo, Globe, Arizona.

 1983   *The Cochise Culture Sequence in Southeastern Arizona.* Anthropological Papers No. 42. University of Arizona Press, Tucson.

Sayles, Edwin B., and Ernst V. Antevs
 1941   *The Cochise Culture.* Medallion Papers No. 29. Gila Pueblo, Globe, Arizona.

Scantling, Frederick H.
 1939   Jackrabbit Ruin. *The Kiva* 5(3):9-12.

 1940   Excavations at the Jackrabbit Ruin, Papago Indian Reservation, Arizona. Unpublished Master's thesis, Department of Anthropology, University of Arizona, Tucson.

Schelberg, J. D.
 1997   The Metates of Chaco Canyon, New Mexico. In *Ceramics, Lithics, and Ornaments of Chaco Canyon*, Vol. 3, edited by J. Mathien, pp. 1013–1117. Publications in Arhcaeology 18G, Chaco Canyon Studies. National Park Service, Santa Fe.

Schiffer, Michael B.
 1972   Archaeological Context and Systemic Context. *American Antiquity* 37:156-165.

 1987   *Formation Processes of the Archaeological Record.* University of New Mexico Press, Albuquerque.

 1992   *Technological Perspectives on Behavioral Change.* University of Arizona Press, Tucson.

Schiffer, Michael B., and James M. Skibo
 1987   Theory and Experiment in the Study of Technological Change. *American Antiquity* 28:595-622.

Schlanger, Sarah
 1992   Recognizing Persistent Places in Anasazi Settlement Systems. In *Space, Time, and Archaeological Landscapes*, edited by Jacqueline Rossignol and LuAnn Wandsnider, pp. 91–112. Plenum Press, New York.

Schmid, Elisabeth
 1972   *Atlas of Animal Bones for Prehistorians, Archaeologists, and Quaternary Geologists.* Elsevier, Amsterdam.

Schoenwetter, James, and Larry A. Doerschlag
 1971   Surficial Pollen Records from Central Arizona, I: Desert Scrub. *Journal of the Arizona Academy of Science* 6:216-221.

Schroeder, K, J., and Christine H. Virden
    1994   Shell Remains. In *The Pioneer & Military Memorial Park Archaeological Project, Phoenix, Arizona 1990-1992*, edited by K. J. Schroeder, pp. 189-209. Publications in Anthropology No. 3. Roadrunner Archaeology, Phoenix.

Schuster, J. E., and Kevin Katzer
    1984   The Quaternary Geology of the Northern Tucson Basin, Arizona, and its Archaeological Implications. Unpublished Master's thesis, Department of Geosciences, University of Arizona, Tucson.

Scott-Cummings, L.
    1998   Pollen Analysis. In *Early Farmers of the Sonoran Desert: Archaeological Investigations at the Houghton Road Site, Tucson, Arizona*, edited by Richard Ciolek-Torrello, pp. 317-325. Technical Series 72. Statistical Research, Tucson.

Sellers, William D., and Richard D. Hill
    1974   *Arizona Climate*, 1931–1972. University of Arizona Press, Tucson.

Severinghaus, C. W.
    1949   Tooth Development and Wear as Criteria of Age in White-Tailed Deer. *Journal of Wildlife Management* 13:195-216.

Seymour, Deni J.
    1990   Sobaipuri-Pima Settlement along the Upper San Pedro River: A Thematic Survey between Fairbank and Aravaipa Canyon. Report prepared for the Bureau of Land Management. Manuscript on file, Arizona State Museum, University of Arizona, Tucson.

    2003   Sobaipuri-Pima Occupation in the Upper San Pedro Valley: San Pablo de Quiburi. *New Mexico Historical Review* 78(2):147–166.

Shackley, M. Steven
    1990   The Stone Tool Technology of Ishi and the Yana of North Central California: Inferences for Hunter-Gatherer Cultural Identity in Historic California. *American Anthropologist* 102:696–712.

    1996a Range and Mobility in the Early Hunter-Gatherer Southwest. In *Early Formative Adaptations in the Southern Southwest*, edited by Barbara J. Roth, pp. 5–16. Monographs in World Archaeology No. 25. Prehistory Press, Madison, Wisconsin.

    1996b Elko or San Pedro? A Quantitative Analysis of Late Archaic Projectile Points from White Tanks, Yuma County, Arizona. *Kiva* 61:416-432.

Shepard, Anna O.
    1976   *Ceramics for the Archaeologist*. 9th ed. Publication No. 609. Carnegie Institution, Washington, D.C.
    Sheridan, Thomas E.

    1995   *Arizona: A History*. University of Arizona Press, Tucson.

Shott, Michael
    1986   Technological Organization and Settlement Mobility: An Ethnographic Examination. *Journal of Anthropological Research* 42:15–51.

Silver, I. A.
1969   The Ageing of Domestic Animals. In *Science and Archaeology: A Survey of Progress and Research*, edited by D. R. Brothwell and E. S. Higgs, pp. 283-302. Praeger, New York.

Simpson, George Gaylord, Anne Roe, and Richard C. Lewontin
1960   *Quantitative Zoology*. Harcourt, Brace, and Co., New York.

Sires, Earl W., Jr.
1987   Hohokam Architectural Variability and Site Structure during the Sedentary-Classic Transition. In *The Hohokam Village: Site Structure and Organization*, edited by David E. Doyel, pp. 171-182. AAAS Publication 87-15. American Association for the Advancement of Science, Southwestern and Rocky Mountain Division, Glenwood Springs.

Sliva, R. Jane
1998   Flaked Stone Artifacts. In *Archaeological Investigations at Early Village Sites in the Middle Santa Cruz Valley: Analyses and Synthesis*, edited by Jonathan B. Mabry, pp. 299-355. Anthropological Papers No. 19. Center for Desert Archaeology, Tucson.

1999   Flaked Stone Artifacts. In *Excavations in the Santa Cruz River Floodplain: The Middle Archaic Component at Los Pozos*, edited by David A. Gregory, pp. 33–45. Anthropological Papers No. 20. Center for Desert Archaeology, Tucson.

2001   Flaked Stone Artifacts. In *Excavations in the Santa Cruz River Floodplain: The Early Agricultural Period Component at Los Pozos*, edited by David A. Gregory, pp. 91–106. Anthropological Papers No. 21. Center for Desert Archaeology, Tucson.

2003   Valencia Vieja and Changing Perspectives on Early Ceramic and Early Pioneer Period Flaked Stone Technology. In *Roots of Sedentism: Archaeological Excavations at Valencia Vieja, a Founding Village in the Tucson Basin of Southern Arizona*, edited by Henry D. Wallace, pp. 227-251. Anthropological Papers No. 29. Center for Desert Archaeology, Tucson.

2005   Developments in Flaked Stone Technology during the Transition to Agriculture. In *Material Cultures and Lifeways of Early Agricultural Communities in Southern Arizona*, edited by Jane R. Silva, pp. 47-98. Anthropological Papers No. 35. Center for Desert Archaeology, Tucson.

Sliva, R. Jane (editor)
2005   *Material Cultures and Lifeways of Early Agricultural Communities in Southern Arizona*. Anthropological Papers No. 35. Center for Desert Archaeology, Tucson.

2009   Common Middle Archaic and Early Agricultural Period Points in Southern Arizona. *Archaeology Southwest* 23(1), Supplemental Information.

Smith, Alexa, Barbara K. Montgomery, and Stephanie M. Whittlesey
2004   Whole, Reconstructible, and Partial Vessels and Additional Observations on Painted Rim Sherds. In *Pots, Potters, and Models: Archaeological Investigations at the SRI Locus of the West Branch Site, Tucson, Arizona: Vol. I. Feature Descriptions, Material Culture, and Specialized Analyzes*, edited by Karen G. Harry and Stephanie M. Whittlesey, pp. 156-166. Technical Series 80. Statistical Research, Tucson.

Smith, Susan J.
1995   McDowell-to-Shea Pollen Analysis. In *Archaeology at the Head of the Scottsdale Canal System: Vol. 2. Studies of Artifacts and Biological Remains*, edited by T. Kathleen Henderson and David R. Abbott, pp. 165-184. Anthropological Papers No. 95-1. Northland Research, Flagstaff.

Smith, Susan J., and P. R. Geib
  1999   An Experimental Study of Grinding Tool Pollen Washes: Bridging the Inferential Gap between Pollen Counts and Past Behavior. Poster presented at the 64th Annual Meeting of the Society of American Archaeology, Chicago.

Spencer, J. E., C. A. Ferguson, S. M. Richard, T. R. Orr, P. A. Pearthree, W. G. Gilbert, and R. W. Krantz
  2002   *Geologic Map of the Narrows 7.5' Quadrangle and the Southern Part of the Rincon Peak 7.5' Quadrangle, Eastern Pima County, Arizona.* DGM 10, 1 sheet, 33 pages text, Scale 1:24,000. Arizona Geological Survey, Tucson.

Stark, Miriam T., Jeffrey J. Clark, and Mark D. Elson
  1995   Causes and Consequences of Migration in the 13th Century Tonto Basin. *Journal of Anthropological Archaeology* 14:212–246.

Stevens, Michelle N.
  2001a Archaic and Early Agricultural Period Land Use in Cienega Valley, Southeastern Arizona. Unpublished Ph.D. dissertation, Department of Anthropology, University of Arizona, Tucson.

  2001b Archaic and Early Agricultural Period Land Use in the Cienega Valley. *Archaeology Southwest* 15(4):3-5.

Stevens, Michelle N., and Jane R. Silva
  2002   Empire Points: An Addition to the San Pedro Phase Lithic Assemblage. *Kiva* 67:297-326.

Stinson, Susan L.
  2005   Remembering the Ancestors: Ceramic Figurines from Las Capas and Los Pozos. In *Material Cultures and Lifeways of Early Agricultural Communities in Southern Arizona*, edited by R. Jane Sliva, pp. 207–216. Anthropological Papers No. 35. Center for Desert Archaeology, Tucson.

Stone, Tammy
  1994   The Impact of Raw Material Scarcity on Ground-Stone Manufacture and Use: An Example from the Phoenix Basin Hohokam. *American Antiquity* 59:680–694.

Sullivan, Alan P. III, and James M. Bayman (editors)
  2007   *Hinterlands and Regional Dynamics in the Ancient Southwest.* University of Arizona Press, Tucson.

Sullivan, Alan P. III, and Kenneth C. Rozen
  1985   Debitage Analysis and Archaeological Interpretation. *American Antiquity* 50:755-779.

Thomas, David Hurst
  1971   On Distinguishing Natural from Cultural Bone in Archaeological Sites. *American Antiquity* 36:366-371.

Thompkins, R. S.
  1984a Appendix B. Pollen Analysis of Archaeological Contexts from Archaic Sites in the ANAMAX-Rosemont Project Area. In *The Archaic Occupation of the Rosemont Area, Northern Santa Rita Mountains, Southeastern Arizona*, Vol. I, edited by Bruce B. Huckell, pp. 275-278. Archaeological Series 147. Cultural Resource Management Division, Arizona State Museum, University of Arizona, Tucson.

Thompkins, R. S., cont'd.

1984b   Appendix C. Pollen Analysis from Hohokam Sites in the Rosemont Project Area. In *Hohokam Habitation Sites in the Northern Santa Rita Mountains*, Vol. 2, Part 2, edited by Alan Ferg, Kenneth C. Rozen, William L. Deaver, Martyn D. Tagg, David A. Phillips, Jr., and David A. Gregory, pp. 921-934. Archaeological Series 147. Cultural Resource Management Division, Arizona State Museum, University of Arizona, Tucson.

Tuthill, Carr

1947   *The Tres Alamos Sites on the San Pedro River, Southeastern Arizona*. Publication No. 4. Amerind Foundation, Dragoon, Arizona.

Urban, Sharon F.

1989   Shell from Los Morteros. In *The 1979–1983 Testing at Los Morteros (AZ AA:12:57 ASM), A Large Hohokam Village Site in the Tucson Basin*, edited by Richard C. Lange and William L. Deaver, pp. 285-297. Archaeological Series 177. Arizona State Museum, University of Arizona, Tucson.

Van West, Carla, and Jeffrey H. Altschul

1994   Agricultural Productivity Estimates for the Tonto Basin, A.D. 740–1370. In *Proceedings of the Second Salado Conference*, edited by Richard C. Lange and Stephen Germick, pp. 172–181. Arizona Archaeological Society, Phoenix.

Vanderpot, Rein

1997   From Foraging to Farming: Prehistoric Settlement and Subsistence Dynamics in the San Pedro Valley. In *Prehistory of the Borderlands: Recent Research in the Archaeology of Northern Mexico and the Southern Southwest*, edited by John Carpenter and Guadalupe Sanchez, pp. 33-45. Archaeological Series 186. Arizona State Museum, University of Arizona, Tucson.

2001   The Mescal Wash Site: A Persistent Place along Cienega Creek. *Archaeology Southwest* 15(4):10-11.

Vanderpot, Rein, and Jeffrey H. Altschul

2007   The Mescal Wash Site. In *Hinterlands and Regional Dynamics in the Ancient Southwest*, edited by Alan P. Sullivan III and James M. Bayman, pp. 50-69. University of Arizona Press, Tucson.

Virden-Lange, Christine H.

2005   Shell and Faunal. In *Archaeological Identification and Eligibility Testing for a Portion of AZ AA:12:674 (ASM) in the Town of Marana, Pima County, Arizona*, edited by Ingrid Klune, Marie-Blanche Roudant, and Christine H. Virden-Lange, pp. 29-30. Tierra Archaeological Report No. 2005-21. Tierra Right of Way Services, Tucson.

Vokes, Arthur W.

1987   Shell Artifacts. In *The Archaeology of the San Xavier Bridge Site (AZ BB:13:14) Tucson Basin, Southern Arizona*, edited by John C. Ravesloot, pp. 215-269. Archaeological Series 171. Arizona State Museum, University of Arizona, Tucson.

1988   Shell Artifacts. In *The 1982–1984 Excavations at Los Colinas: 4. Material Culture*, edited by Carol Ann Heathington and David A. Gregory, pp. 319-384. Archaeological Series 162. Cultural Resource Management Division, Arizona State Museum, University of Arizona, Tucson.

1989   Late Pioneer and Colonial Period Shell. In *Hohokam Archaeology along Phase B of the Tucson Aqueduct, Central Arizona Project: Vol. 1. Interpretation and Synthesis*, edited by Jon S. Czaplicki and John C. Ravesloot, pp. 477–488. Archaeological Series 178. Arizona State Museum, University of Arizona, Tucson.

Vokes, Arthur W., cont'd.

2001a Shell (from the Yuma Wash Site). Manuscript on file, Old Pueblo Archaeology Center, Tucson.

2001b The Shell Ornament Assemblage. In *Tonto Creek Archaeological Project: Life and Death along Tonto Creek*, edited by Jeffrey J. Clark and Penny Dufoe Minturn, pp. 353-419. Anthropological Papers No. 24. Center for Desert Archaeology, Tucson.

2004 Shell Artifacts. In *Pots, Potters, and Models: Archaeological Investigations at the SRI Locus of the West Branch Site, Tucson, Arizona: Vol. 1. Feature Descriptions, Material Culture, and Specialized Analyses*, edited by Karen G. Harry and Stephanie M. Whittlesey, pp. 285-301. Technical Series 80. Statistical Research, Tucson.

2006a The Julian Wash Shell Assemblage. In *Craft Specialization in the Southern Tucson Basin: Archaeological Excavations at the Julian Wash Site, AZ BB:13:17 (ASM): Part I. Introduction, Excavation Results, and Artifact Investigations*, edited by Henry D. Wallace. Anthropological Papers No. 40. Center for Desert Archaeology, Tucson.

2006b Shell Analysis. In *The Cultural Resources of Quail Creek: Vol. 1. Archaeological Excavations at AZ EE:1:317 (ShellMan), AZ EE:1:275, AZ EE:1:175, AZ EE:1:176, and AZ EE:1:302 (ASM)*, edited by Michael D. Cook, pp. 4.1-4.16. Cultural Resources Report No. 2006-42. WestLand Cultural Resources, Tucson.

Waguespack, Nicole M., and Todd L. Surovell

2003 Clovis Hunting Strategies, or How to Make Out on Plentiful Resources. *American Antiquity* 68:333–352.

Wallace, Henry D.

1985 Decorated Ceramics. In *Excavations at the Valencia Site, A Preclassic Hohokam Village in the Southern Tucson Basin*, edited by William H. Doelle, pp. 81–135. Anthropological Papers 3. Institute for American Research, Tucson.

1986a Decorated Ceramics. In *Archaeological Investigations at the Tanque Verde Wash Site, a Middle Rincon Settlement in the Eastern Tucson Basin*, edited by Mark D. Elson, pp. 125–180. Anthropological Papers 7. Institute for American Research, Tucson.

1986b Decorated Ceramics: Introduction, Methods, and Rincon Phase Seriation. In *Archaeological Investigations at the West Branch Site, Early and Middle Rincon Phase Occupation in the Southern Tucson Basin*, edited by Frederick W. Huntington, pp. 127–164. Anthropological Papers 5. Institute for American Research, Tucson.

1986c *Rincon Phase Decorated Ceramics in the Tucson Basin: A Focus on the West Branch Site*. Anthropological Papers No. 1. Institute for American Research, Tucson.

Wallace, Henry D. (editor)

2003 *Roots of Sedentism: Archaeological Investigations at Valencia Vieja, a Founding Village in the Tucson Basin of Southern Arizona*. Anthropological Papers No. 29. Center for Desert Archaeology, Tucson.

Wallace, Henry D., and Michael W. Lindeman

2003 Valencia Vieja and the Origins of Hohokam Culture. In *Roots of Sedentism: Archaeological Excavations at Valencia Vieja, a Founding Village in the Tucson Basin of Southern Arizona*, edited by Henry D. Wallace, pp. 371-405. Anthropological Papers No. 29. Center for Desert Archaeology, Tucson.

Wasley, William W., and Alfred E. Johnson
1965   *Salvage Archaeology in Painted Rocks Reservoir, Western Arizona.* Anthropological Papers No. 9. University of Arizona Press, Tucson.

Waters, Michael R.
1987   Holocene Alluvial Geology and Geoarchaeology of AZ BB:13:14 and the San Xavier Reach of the Santa Cruz. In T*he Archaeology of the San Xavier Bridge Site (AZ BB:13:14), Tucson Basin, Southern Arizona,* edited by John C. Ravesloot, pp. 39–60. Archaeological Series 170. Arizona State Museum, University of Arizona, Tucson.

1989   Late Quaternary Lacustrine History and Paleoclimatic Significance of Pluvial Lake Cochise, Southeastern Arizona. *Quaternary Research* 32:1–11.

1992   *Principles of Geoarchaeology: A North American Perspective.* University of Arizona Press, Tucson.

Waters, Michael R., and John J. Field
1986   Geomorphic Analysis of Hohokam Settlement Patterns on Alluvial Fans along the Western Flank of the Tortolita Mountains, Arizona. *Geoarchaeology: An International Journal* 1:329–345.

Waters, Michael R., and C. Vance Haynes
2001   Late-Quaternary Arroyo Formation and Climate Change in the American Southwest. *Geology* 29:399–402.
Waters, Michael R., and John C. Ravesloot
2001   Landscape Change and the Cultural Evolution of the Hohokam along the Middle Gila River and Other River Valleys in South-Central Arizona. *American Antiquity* 66:285-299.

Waterworth, Robert M. R., and Eric Blinman
1986   Modified Sherds, Unidirectional Abrasion, and Pottery Scrapers. *Pottery Southwest* 13(2):4-6.

Watson, J. P. N.
1978   The Interpretation of Epiphyseal Fusion Data. In *Research Problems in Zooarchaeology*, edited by D. R. Brothwell, K.D. Thomas, and Juliet Clutton-Brock, pp. 97-102. Occasional Publications 3. Institute of Archaeology, London.

Webb, Dorothy L., Chad Burt, and Jennifer Searles
2000   Site Card, AZ EE:2:44 (ASM). On file, Arizona State Museum, University of Arizona, Tucson.

Wells, E. Christian, Glen E. Rice, and John C. Ravesloot
2004   Peopling Landscapes Between Villages in the Middle Gila River Valley of Central Arizona. *American Antiquity* 69:627-652.

Western Regional Climate Center
2009   Arizona Climate Summaries. Electronic document, http://www.wrcc.dri.edu/summary/climsmaz.html, accessed November 30, 2009.

Whalen, Michael E.
1996   Ceramic Technology and the Seriation of El Paso Plain Brown Pottery. *Kiva* 62:171-184.

Whalen, Norman M.
1971   Cochise Cultural Sites in the Central San Pedro Drainage, Arizona. Unpublished Ph.D. dissertation, Department of Anthropology, University of Arizona, Tucson.

Wheat, Margaret M.
  1967 *Survival Arts of the Primitive Paiutes.* University of Nevada Press, Reno.

White, Devin Alan
  2004 *Hohokam Palettes.* Archaeological Series 196. Arizona State Museum, University of Arizona, Tucson.

White, Theodore E.
  1953 A Method of Calculating the Dietary Percentages of Various Food Animals Utilized by Aboriginal Peoples. *American Antiquity* 19:396-398.

Whittaker, John C.
  1994 *Flintknapping: Making and Understanding Stone Tools.* University of Texas Press, Austin.

Whittlesey, Stephanie M.
  1986 The Ceramic Assemblage. In *The 1985 Excavations at the Hodges Site, Pima County, Arizona*, edited by Robert W. Layhe, pp. 61-126. Archaeological Series 170. Cultural Resource Management Division, Arizona State Museum, University of Arizona, Tucson.

  1992 Ceramics. In *On the Frontier: A Trincheras-Hohokam Farmstead, Arivaca, Arizona*, edited by Stephanie M. Whittlesey and Richard Ciolek-Torrello, pp. 39-51. Technical Series 30. Statistical Research, Tucson.

  1998 Toward a Unified Theory of Ceramic Production and Distribution: Examples from the Central Arizona Deserts. In *Vanishing River: Landscapes of the Lower Verde Valley: The Lower Verde Valley Archaeological Project. Overview, Synthesis, and Conclusions*, edited by Stephanie M. Whittlesey, Richard Ciolek-Torrello, and Jeffrey H. Altschul, pp. 417-446. Statistical Research. Submitted to the United States Department of the Interior, Bureau of Reclamation, Phoenix Area Office. Contract No. 1425-2-CS-01870. Copies available from SRI Press, Tucson.

  2004a The Archaeological Context. In *Pots, Potters, and Models: Archaeological Investigations at the SRI Locus of the West Branch Site, Tucson, Arizona: Vol. 2. Synthesis and Interpretations*, edited by Stephanie M. Whittlesey, pp. 37–58. Technical Series 80. Statistical Research, Tucson.

  2004b Ceramic Containers. In *Pots, Potters, and Models: Archaeological Investigations at the SRI Locus of the West Branch Site, Tucson, Arizona: 2. Synthesis and Interpretations*, edited by Stephanie M. Whittlesey, pp. 283-322. SRI Technical Series 80. Statistical Research, Tucson.

  2004c Figurines and Other Modeled-Ceramic Artifacts. In *Pots, Potters, and Models: Archaeological Investigations at the SRI Locus of the West Branch Site, Tucson, Arizona: Vol. 2. Synthesis and Interpretations*, edited by Stephanie M. Whittlesey, pp. 323–332. Technical Series 80. Statistical Research, Tucson.

Whittlesey, Stephanie M. (editor)
  2004 *Pots, Potters, and Models: Archaeological Investigations at the SRI Locus of the West Branch Site, Tucson, Arizona.* Technical Series 80. 2 vols. Statistical Research, Tucson.

Whittlesey, Stephanie M., Richard S. Ciolek-Torrello, and Matthew A. Sterner
  1994 *Southern Arizona, the Last 12,000 Years: A Cultural-Historic Overview for the Western Army National Guard Aviation Training Site.* Technical Series 48. Statistical Research, Tucson.

Whittlesey, Stephanie M., and Robert A. Heckman
  2000 Culture History and Research Background. In *Prehistoric Painted Pottery of Southeastern Arizona*, edited by Robert A. Heckman, Barbara K. Montgomery, and Stephanie M. Whittlesey, pp. 1-22. Technical Series 77. Statistical Research, Tucson.

Wiessner, Polly
    1983   Style and Social Information in Kalahari San Projectile Points. *American Antiquity* 48:253–276.

Wilcox, David R.
    1979   The Hohokam Regional System. In *An Archaeological Test of Sites in the Gila Butte-Santan Region, South Central Arizona*, edited by Glen E. Rice, David R. Wilcox, Kevin Rafferty, and James Schoenwetter, pp. 77-116. Anthropological Research Papers No. 18. Arizona State University, Tempe.

    1991   The Mesoamerican Ballgame in the American Southwest. In *The Mesoamerican Ballgame*, edited by Vernon L. Scarborough and David R. Wilcox, pp. 101–125. University of Arizona Press, Tucson.

    1999   A Peregrine View of Macroregional Systems in the North American Southwest. In *Great Towns and Regional Polities in the Prehistoric Southwest and Southeast*, edited by Jill E. Neitzel, pp. 115–142. University of New Mexico Press, Albuquerque.

Wilcox, David R., Thomas R. McGuire, and Charles D. Sternberg
    1981   *Snaketown Revisited: A Partial Cultural Resource Survey, Analysis of Site Structure, and an Ethnohistoric Study of the Proposed Hohokam-Pima National Monument*. Archaeological Series 155. Cultural Resource Management Division, Arizona State Museum, University of Arizona, Tucson.

Wilcox, David R., and Charles D. Sternberg
    1983   *Hohokam Ballcourts and Their Interpretation*. Archaeological Series 160. Cultural Resource Management EArizona State Museum, University of Arizona, Tucson.

Wills, Wirt H.
    1988   *Early Prehistoric Agriculture in the American Southwest*. School of American Research, Santa Fe.

Wills, Wirt H., and Thomas C. Windes
    1989   Evidence for Population Aggregation and Dispersal during the Basketmaker III Period in Chaco Canyon, New Mexico. *American Antiquity* 54:347–369.

Windmiller, Ric
    1973   The Late Cochise Culture in the Sulphur Spring Valley, Southeastern Arizona. *The Kiva* 39(2):131-169.

Wing, Elizabeth S., and Antoinette B. Brown
    1979   *Paleonutrition: Method and Theory in Prehistoric Foodways*. Academic Press, New York.

Wöcherl, Helga
    2005   Pits and the Use of Extramural Space in Early Farming Communities. In *Material Cultures and Lifeways of Early Agricultural Communities in Southern Arizona*, edited by R. Jane Sliva, pp. 19-46. Anthropological Papers No. 35. Desert Archaeology, Tucson.

Woodson, M. Kyle
    2002   *Archaeological Investigations at the Sweetwater Site along State Route 587 on the Gila River Indian Community*. Technical Report No. 2002-14. Cultural Resource Management Division, Gila River Indian Community, Sacaton, Arizona.

Woodson, M. Kyle, John C. Ravesloot, Michael J. Boley, and Steve L. Forman
    2007   Chronology. In *Results of Testing and Data Recovery, SFPP, LP, East Line Expansion Project, Arizona Portion, Cochise, Pima, Pinal, and Maricopa Counties, Arizona*, Vol. 2, edited by John C. Ravesloot, M. Kyle Woodson, and Michael J. Boley, pp. 10.1–10.29. 2 vols. William Self Associates, Tucson.

Wright, Elizabeth
　　2002　*Ecological Site Description: Rangeland.* Database compiled and maintained by the United States Depart-
　　　　ment of Agriculture, Natural Resources Conservation Service. Electronic database, http://esis.egov.usda.gov/
　　　　esis_report/fsReport.aspx?id=R041XA001NM&rptLevel=all&approved=no, accessed February 10, 2009.

Wright, Katherine I.
　　1994　Ground-stone Tools and Hunter-Gatherer Subsistence in Southwest Asia: Implications for the Transition
　　　　to Farming. *American Antiquity* 59:238-263.

Wyman, Leland C., and Stuart K. Harris
　　1951　*The Ethnobotany of the Kayneta Navajo.* University of New Mexico Press, Albuquerque.

Appendix I

Artifact and Feature Summary Oversized Data Tables for Chapter 4

Table I.A. Distribution of artifacts collected from the surface of the Marsh Station Road site

Collection Unit	Debitage	Cores	Unifaces	Bifaces	Hammerstones	Ground Stone	Ceramics--Painted	Ceramics--Unpainted	Ceramics--Special	Ceramics--Other	Worked Shell	Total*
15	1											1
25	2											2
26	2											2
27	22											22
28	8											8
29	5	1										6
30	3	1										4
31	1											1
32	3	1										4
33	14	2					1					17
35								1				1
36								1				1
37								1				1
38	1											1
40								1				1
43	2											2
46	2											2
47	1											1
49		1										1
51	2											2
55	1									1		2
58	5							1				6
59	4							1				5
60	7											7

Table I.A. Distribution of artifacts collected from the surface of the Marsh Station Road site, cont'd.

Collection Unit	Debitage	Cores	Unifaces	Bifaces	Hammerstones	Ground Stone	Ceramics-- Painted	Ceramics-- Unpainted	Ceramics-- Special	Ceramics-- Other	Worked Shell	Total*
61	6											6
62	15	2										17
63	8	1										9
64	6		1									7
65	13							1		2		16
66	2							1				3
67	7	1										8
68	5	1										6
69	3	3										6
71	7	2	1				2					12
72	6											6
73	4	1										5
74	5											5
80									1			1
81	1						1					1
82	1											1
83		1							1			2
84									1			1
87		1										1
88	2											2
90	4											4
91	31	3				1			2			37
92	6											6
93	4	1							1			6

Table I.A. Distribution of artifacts collected from the surface of the Marsh Station Road site, cont'd.

Collection Unit	Debitage	Cores	Unifaces	Bifaces	Hammerstones	Ground Stone	Ceramics-- Painted	Ceramics-- Unpainted	Ceramics-- Special	Ceramics-- Other	Worked Shell	Total*
94	2											2
95	1											1
97								1				1
98								1				1
99	2											2
100	1											1
101	2	2										4
102	5	2	1									8
103	5	1										6
104	11											11
105	3	1										4
106	1	2										3
107	1	1										2
108	29		1					1		2		33
109	6	3				1						10
110	16	2	1									19
111	12											12
112	12											12
114	2											2
115	16		1				1	2				20
116	20	2						1		1		24
117	32	1	1					1				35
118	24	1		2								27
119	64	3		3								70

Table I.A. Distribution of artifacts collected from the surface of the Marsh Station Road site, cont'd.

Collection Unit	Debitage	Cores	Unifaces	Bifaces	Hammerstones	Ground Stone	Ceramics--Painted	Ceramics--Unpainted	Ceramics--Special	Ceramics--Other	Worked Shell	Total*
120	54	12			1			1				68
121	17	3										20
122	3	2										5
123	85	9	2				1	2				99
124	43	4				1	2	3			1	54
125	4	4										8
126		1										1
127	3											3
128	2	1										3
129	1											1
130	5											5
131	4	3										7
135	1											1
138	4											4
139	14							2	1			17
140	4	3					1	3				11
141	12						3	16		11		42
142	4	1					1	4				10
143	6	1				1	1	3		4		16
144	46		1				10	32		20		109
145	101	3	1			1	11	29	1	10	1	158
146	68	6					3	28		45		150
147	19	2					2	3		8		34
148	14	5						1				20

Table I.A. Distribution of artifacts collected from the surface of the Marsh Station Road site, cont'd.

Collection Unit	Debitage	Cores	Unifaces	Bifaces	Hammerstones	Ground Stone	Ceramics-- Painted	Ceramics-- Unpainted	Ceramics-- Special	Ceramics-- Other	Worked Shell	Total*
149	10	1				1						12
151	7	4										11
152	2	1										3
153	1										1	2
154	5											5
156	4											4
157	6	1										7
158	3	1										4
159	6											6
160	39	5						2			1	47
161	27	3	1		1	1	5	2			3	43
162	63	9	3				2	1			1	79
163	59	13	2				8	9			4	95
164	52	5		1				3				61
165	15	1					2					18
166	25											25
167	27	2	1	1			1	3			2	37
168	14	6		2								22
169	1					1						2
170	7		1									8
171	13		1									14
172	18	3						2			1	24
173	25	2	2					4			9	42
174	9							2				11

Table I.A. Distribution of artifacts collected from the surface of the Marsh Station Road site, cont'd.

Collection Unit	Debitage	Cores	Unifaces	Bifaces	Hammerstones	Ground Stone	Ceramics--Painted	Ceramics--Unpainted	Ceramics--Special	Ceramics--Other	Worked Shell	Total*
175	7	3										10
176	29	2	1				2					34
177	19	11										30
178	12	1										13
179	5	1										6
180	3							1				4
181	7	4						1				12
182	5	1										6
183	12	2								1		15
184	5	1										6
185	8	1										9
186	2	4						1				7
188	3							4				7
189	9	2					1	5				17
190	103	8					3	33			12	159
191	87	3	1				1	13			8	113
192	17		1					13				31
193	52	4				1	17	16			4	94
194	10							9				19
195	7						1					8
196	5	1										6
197	3											3
198	9	3	1									13
199	14	7						2			1	24

Table I.A. Distribution of artifacts collected from the surface of the Marsh Station Road site, cont'd.

Collection Unit	Debitage	Cores	Unifaces	Bifaces	Hammerstones	Ground Stone	Ceramics-- Painted	Ceramics-- Unpainted	Ceramics-- Special	Ceramics-- Other	Worked Shell	Total*
200	24	6		1			1	1	1			33
201	143	9	2				1	17		7		179
202	168	1	1	1		1	2	7		5		186
203	232	8	3				4	11		9		267
204	275	21	5	4			5	16		3		329
205	73	8	5	1	2			1				90
206	22		1	2				4				29
207	9	3					1					13
208	5											5
212	518	16	3	4		1	1	5		2		550
213	509	23	8	3			12	37		20		612
214	189	8	3	2			3	15		8		228
215	346	13	4	2	2		10	38		24		439
216	242	22	5	5	1		10	23		11		319
217	185	9	3	2			8	29		10		246
218	59	16	4				1	1				81
219	13		1									14
220	24	6	1									31
221	14	1	1									16
227	2											2
228	1											1
229	4						1					5
230	2											2
231	6						1					7

Table I.A. Distribution of artifacts collected from the surface of the Marsh Station Road site, cont'd.

Collection Unit	Debitage	Cores	Unifaces	Bifaces	Hammerstones	Ground Stone	Ceramics--Painted	Ceramics--Unpainted	Ceramics--Special	Ceramics--Other	Worked Shell	Total*
232	2						1					3
233	2	2										4
234	3							5		3		11
235	4											4
236	5							1				6
237	6						2					8
238	9						3	3				15
239	8						4	7		3		22
240	5	2						1				8
241	7	1				1						9
242	4											4
243	5											5
244	1	1										2
245	1							1				2
246	1	1					1	1				4
247	4											4
248	4											4
249	3											3
250	5											5
252	1											1
253	4						1	8				13
256							2	1				3
257							1	1				2
258	7	1										8

406

Table I.A. Distribution of artifacts collected from the surface of the Marsh Station Road site, cont'd.

Collection Unit	Debitage	Cores	Unifaces	Bifaces	Hammerstones	Ground Stone	Ceramics-- Painted	Ceramics-- Unpainted	Ceramics-- Special	Ceramics-- Other	Worked Shell	Total*
259	18	1										19
260	2							1				3
261	3	2										5
262	11											11
263	9	1		2								12
264	2											2
265	2	1										3
266	7											7
267	8	2					1	1				12
268	8	2					1	1				12
269	3											3
270	13	1					1	4				19
271	8							1				9
272	11							6				17
273	1											1
274	2											2
275	3	3										6
276	2											2
277	2	2										4
278	1	1						3				5
279	3										1	4
280	4							3				7
281	11	2						1				14
282	14	1					1					16

Table I.A. Distribution of artifacts collected from the surface of the Marsh Station Road site, cont'd.

Collection Unit	Debitage	Cores	Unifaces	Bifaces	Hammerstones	Ground Stone	Ceramics-- Painted	Ceramics-- Unpainted	Ceramics-- Special	Ceramics-- Other	Worked Shell	Total*
283	24						1	4				29
284	25	1	1				7	25		12		71
285	17							5				22
286	3							3				6
287	17	1					2	4				24
288	5	1						1				7
289	30	7	1					3				41
290	1											1
291	2											2
292	1											1
293	11	1										12
294	35	1					2	10				48
295	13	5						1				19
296	134	50	1			3	21	43		4		267
297	34	5				10	1	14				54
299	59	7					6	10				82
300	1											1
302	3											3
304	12	1										13
305	8	1										9
306	1											1
307	10	1										11
308	23	2				1						26
309	5							1		2		8

Table I.A. Distribution of artifacts collected from the surface of the Marsh Station Road site, cont'd.

Collection Unit	Debitage	Cores	Unifaces	Bifaces	Hammerstones	Ground Stone	Ceramics-- Painted	Ceramics-- Unpainted	Ceramics-- Special	Ceramics-- Other	Worked Shell	Total*
310								3				3
311	78	3	1	1			3	11				97
312	268	10	5	2			5	21				311
313	411	16	4				9	26		37		503
314	199	13	1	3			7	20	1	14		258
315	25							1		5		31
316	19	2	1					2				24
317	1											1
319	1	1	1					26				29
320	121	5	2				3	12		17		160
321	30	4	2	2	1							39
322	249	1	1	1			15	45		42	1	355
323	240	7	2	1		1	19	57		8		335
324	33	2	3				3	10		3		54
325	3			1								4
Totals	7329	565	104	48	12	22	267	887	4	402	3	9643

*Nine pieces of historic glass recovered from the site's surface are not included in this table

Table I.B. Distribution of artifacts collected from test units

Collection Unit	Debitage	Cores	Unifaces	Bifaces	Hammerstones	Ground Stone	Ceramics-- Painted	Ceramics-- Unpainted	Ceramics-- Special	Ceramics-- Other	Worked Shell	Total
15	1											1
25	2											2
26	2											2
27	22											22
28	8											8
29	5	1										6
30	3	1										4
31	1											1
32	3	1										4
33	14	2					1					17
35								1				1
36								1				1
37								1				1
38	1											1
40								1				1
43	2											2
46	2											2
47	1											1
49		1										1
51	2											2
55	1										1	2
58	5							1				6
59	4							1				5
60	7											7

Table I.B. Distribution of artifacts collected from test units, cont'd.

Collection Unit	Debitage	Cores	Unifaces	Bifaces	Hammerstones	Ground Stone	Ceramics--Painted	Ceramics--Unpainted	Ceramics--Special	Ceramics--Other	Worked Shell	Total
61	6											6
62	15	2										17
63	8	1										9
64	6		1									7
65	13							1			2	16
66	2							1				3
67	7	1										8
68	5	1										6
69	3	3										6
71	7	2	1				2					12
72	6											6
73	4	1										5
74	5											5
80								1				1
81							1					1
82	1											1
83		1						1				2
84								1				1
87		1										1
88	2											2
90	4											4
91	31	3				1		2				37
92	6											6
93	4	1						1				6

Table I.B. Distribution of artifacts collected from test units, cont'd.

Collection Unit	Debitage	Cores	Unifaces	Bifaces	Hammerstones	Ground Stone	Ceramics-- Painted	Ceramics-- Unpainted	Ceramics-- Special	Ceramics-- Other	Worked Shell	Total
94	2											2
95	1											1
97									1			1
98									1			1
99	2											2
100	1											1
101	2	2										4
102	5	2	1									8
103	5	1										6
104	11											11
105	3	1										4
106	1	2										3
107	1	1										2
108	29		1						1		2	33
109	6	3				1						10
110	16	2	1									19
111	12											12
112	12											12
114	2											2
115	16		1				1		2			20
116	20	2							1		1	24
117	32	1	1						1			35
118	24	1		2								27
119	64	3		3								70

Table I.B. Distribution of artifacts collected from test units, cont'd...

Collection Unit	Debitage	Cores	Unifaces	Bifaces	Hammerstones	Ground Stone	Ceramics--Painted	Ceramics--Unpainted	Ceramics--Special	Ceramics--Other	Worked Shell	Total
120	54	12		1					1			68
121	17	3										20
122	3	2										5
123	85	9	2				1		2			99
124	43	4				1	2		3		1	54
125	4	4										8
126		1										1
127	3											3
128	2	1										3
129	1											1
130	5											5
131	4	3										7
135	1											1
138	4											4
139	14							2		1		17
140	4	3					1	3				11
141	12						3	16			11	42
142	4	1					1	4				10
143	6	1				1	1	3			4	16
144	46		1				10	32			20	109
145	101	3	1			1	11	29	1	1	10	158
146	68	6					3	28			45	150
147	19	2					2	3			8	34
148	14	5						1				20

Table I.B. Distribution of artifacts collected from test units, cont'd.

Collection Unit	Debitage	Cores	Unifaces	Bifaces	Hammerstones	Ground Stone	Ceramics--Painted	Ceramics--Unpainted	Ceramics--Special	Ceramics--Other	Worked Shell	Total
149	10	1				1						12
151	7	4										11
152	2	1										3
153	1									1		2
154	5											5
156	4											4
157	6	1										7
158	3	1										4
159	6											6
160	39	5						2		1		47
161	27	3	1		1	1	5	2		3		43
162	63	9	3				2	1		1		79
163	59	13	2				8	9		4		95
164	52	5		1				3				61
165	15	1					2					18
166	25											25
167	27	2	1	1			1	3		2		37
168	14	6		2								22
169	1					1						2
170	7		1									8
171	13		1									14
172	18	3						2		1		24
173	25	2	2					4		9		42
174	9							2				11

Table I.B. Distribution of artifacts collected from test units, cont'd.

Collection Unit	Debitage	Cores	Unifaces	Bifaces	Hammerstones	Ground Stone	Ceramics--Painted	Ceramics--Unpainted	Ceramics--Special	Ceramics--Other	Worked Shell	Total
175	7	3										10
176	29	2	1				2					34
177	19	11										30
178	12	1										13
179	5	1										6
180	3							1				4
181	7	4						1				12
182	5	1										6
183	12	2								1		15
184	5	1										6
185	8	1										9
186	2	4						1				7
188	3							4				7
189	9	2					1	5				17
190	103	8					3	33		12		159
191	87	3	1				1	13		8		113
192	17		1					13				31
193	52	4				1	17	16		4		94
194	10							9				19
195	7						1					8
196	5	1										6
197	3											3
198	9	3	1									13
199	14	7						2			1	24

Table I.B. Distribution of artifacts collected from test units, cont'd.

Collection Unit	Debitage	Cores	Unifaces	Bifaces	Hammerstones	Ground Stone	Ceramics--Painted	Ceramics--Unpainted	Ceramics--Special	Ceramics--Other	Worked Shell	Total
200	24	6		1			1	1	1			33
201	143	9	2				1	17		7		179
202	168	1	1	1		1	2	7		5		186
203	232	8	3				4	11		9		267
204	275	21	5	4			5	16		3		329
205	73	8	5	1	2			1				90
206	22		1	2				4				29
207	9	3					1					13
208	5											5
212	518	16	3	4		1	1	5		2		550
213	509	23	8	3			12	37		20		612
214	189	8	3	2			3	15		8		228
215	346	13	4	2	2		10	38		24		439
216	242	22	5	5	1		10	23		11		319
217	185	9	3	2			8	29		10		246
218	59	16	4				1	1				81
219	13		1									14
220	24	6	1									31
221	14	1	1									16
227	2											2
228	1											1
229	4						1					5
230	2											2
231	6						1					7

416

Table I.B. Distribution of artifacts collected from test units, cont'd.

Collection Unit	Debitage	Cores	Unifaces	Bifaces	Hammerstones	Ground Stone	Ceramics--Painted	Ceramics--Unpainted	Ceramics--Special	Ceramics--Other	Worked Shell	Total
232	2						1					3
233	2	2										4
234	3							5		3		11
235	4											4
236	5							1				6
237	6						2					8
238	9						3	3				15
239	8						4	7		3		22
240	5	2						1				8
241	7	1				1						9
242	4											4
243	5											5
244	1	1										2
245	1							1				2
246	1	1					1	1				4
247	4											4
248	4											4
249	3											3
250	5											5
252	1											1
253	4						1	8				13
256							2	1				3
257							1	1				2
258	7	1										8

Table I.B. Distribution of artifacts collected from test units, cont'd.

Collection Unit	Debitage	Cores	Unifaces	Bifaces	Hammerstones	Ground Stone	Ceramics-- Painted	Ceramics-- Unpainted	Ceramics-- Special	Ceramics-- Other	Worked Shell	Total
259	18	1										19
260	2								1			3
261	3	2										5
262	11											11
263	9	1	2									12
264	2											2
265	2	1										3
266	7											7
267	8	2					1		1			12
268	8	2					1		1			12
269	3											3
270	13	1					1		4			19
271	8								1			9
272	11								6			17
273	1											1
274	2											2
275	3	3										6
276	2											2
277	2	2										4
278	1	1							3			5
279	3										1	4
280	4								3			7
281	11	2							1			14
282	14	1					1					16

Table I.B. Distribution of artifacts collected from test units, cont'd.

Collection Unit	Debitage	Cores	Unifaces	Bifaces	Hammerstones	Ground Stone	Ceramics--Painted	Ceramics--Unpainted	Ceramics--Special	Ceramics--Other	Worked Shell	Total
283	24						1	4				29
284	25	1	1				7	25		12		71
285	17							5				22
286	3							3				6
287	17	1					2	4				24
288	5	1						1				7
289	30	7	1					3				41
290	1											1
291	2											2
292	1											1
293	11	1										12
294	35	1					2	10				48
295	13	5						1				19
296	134	50	1		3	10	21	43		1	4	267
297	34	5					1	14				54
299	59	7					6	10				82
300	1											1
302	3											3
304	12	1										13
305	8	1										9
306	1											1
307	10	1										11
308	23	2				1						26
309	5							1			2	8

Table I.B. Distribution of artifacts collected from test units, cont'd.

Collection Unit	Debitage	Cores	Unifaces	Bifaces	Hammerstones	Ground Stone	Ceramics--Painted	Ceramics--Unpainted	Ceramics--Special	Ceramics--Other	Worked Shell	Total
310									3			3
311	78	3	1	1			3	11				97
312	268	10	5	2			5	21				311
313	411	16	4				9	26		37		503
314	199	13	1	3			7	20	1	14		258
315	25							1		5		31
316	19	2	1					2				24
317	1											1
319	1	1	1					26				29
320	121	5	2	2			3	12		17		160
321	30	4	2	2	1							39
322	249	1	1	1			15	45		42	1	355
323	240	7	2	1		1	19	57		8		335
324	33	2	3				3	10		3		54
325	3			1								4
Totals	7329	565	104	48	12	22	267	887	4	402	3	9643

Table I.C. Summary of feature characteristics

Feature	Feature Type	Feature Type Code[1]	Wöcherl Pit Class[2]	Locus[3]	Excavated	Screened[4]	Chronological Range	Best Guess: Tucson Basin-specific	Best Guess: Formative Terminology
1	*Voided*	*VOID*	*VOID*	*VOID*	*VOID*	*VOID*	*VOID*	*VOID*	*VOID*
2	Historic hearth	21	N/A	SA 4	Y	1	Historic	Historic	Historic
3	Indeterminate thermal pit	20	7	SA 2	Y	1	Early Agricultural-Formative	San Pedro?	San Pedro?
4	Indeterminate thermal pit	20	7	SA 5	Y	1	Early Agricultural-Formative	Rincon	late Middle Formative
5	Roasting pit	23	3	SA 5	Y	1	Middle Formative	Rincon	late Middle Formative
6	Occupation surface	17	N/A	SA 4	Y	1	Middle Formative	Rincon	late Middle Formative
6.01	Hearth	21		SA 4	Y	0	Middle Formative	Rincon	late Middle Formative
7	Pit house	1	N/A	SA 4/5	Y	1	Rillito-Middle Rincon	Early-Middle Rincon	late Middle Formative
7.01	Hearth	21		SA 4/5	Y	0	Rillito-Protohistoric	Early-Middle Rincon	late Middle Formative
7.02	Posthole	35	N/A	SA 4/5	Y	2	Early Rincon-Late Rincon	Early-Middle Rincon	late Middle Formative
8	Secondary cremation	53	N/A	SA 5	Y	4	Formative	Tortolita-Rincon	Formative
9	Medium nonthermal pit	32	4	SA 4	Y	1	Early Agricultural-Formative	Early Agricultural-Formative	Early Agricultural-Formative
10	Medium nonthermal pit	32	1	SA 4	Y	1	Early Agricultural-Formative	Early Agricultural-Formative	Early Agricultural-Formative
11	Pit house	1	N/A	SA 4	Y	2	Early Rincon-Late Rincon	Rincon	late Middle Formative
11.01	Firepit (unprepared hearth)	22		SA 4	Y	0	Early Rincon-Late Rincon	Rincon	late Middle Formative
11.02	Indeterminate nonthermal pit	30	3	SA 4	Y	1	Early Rincon-Late Rincon	Rincon	late Middle Formative
11.03	Posthole	35	N/A	SA 4	Y	1	Early Rincon-Late Rincon	Rincon	late Middle Formative

Table I.C. Summary of feature characteristics, cont'd.

Feature	Feature Type	Feature Type Code[1]	Wöcherl Pit Class[2]	Locus[3]	Excavated	Screened[4]	Chronological Range	Best Guess: Tucson Basin-specific	Best Guess: Formative Terminology
11.04	Medium nonthermal pit	32	5	SA 4	Y	1	Early Rincon-Late Rincon	Rincon	late Middle Formative
11.05	Posthole	35	N/A	SA 4	Y	4	Early Rincon-Late Rincon	Rincon	late Middle Formative
11.06	Posthole	35	N/A	SA 4	Y	4	Early Rincon-Late Rincon	Rincon	late Middle Formative
11.07	Posthole	35	N/A	SA 4	Y	4	Early Rincon-Late Rincon	Rincon	late Middle Formative
11.08	Posthole	35	N/A	SA 4	Y	4	Early Rincon-Late Rincon	Rincon	late Middle Formative
11.09	Bell Pit	34	5	SA 4	Y	1	Early Rincon-Late Rincon	Rincon	late Middle Formative
12	Medium nonthermal pit	32	7	SA 4	Y	1	Early Agricultural-Formative	San Pedro?	San Pedro?
13	Medium nonthermal pit	32	2	TR 13	Y	1	Early Agricultural-Formative	Early Agricultural-Formative	Early Agricultural-Formative
14	Medium nonthermal pit	32	2	TR 13	Y	0	Early Agricultural-Formative	Early Agricultural-Formative	Early Agricultural-Formative
15	Medium nonthermal pit	32	7	SA 4	Y	1	Early Agricultural-Formative	Early Agricultural-Formative	Early Agricultural-Formative
16	Bell Pit	34	5	SA 4	Y	1	Early Agricultural-Formative	San Pedro?	San Pedro?
17	Pit house	1	N/A	SA 1	Y	2	Rillito-Middle Rincon	Early-Middle Rincon	late Middle Formative
17.01	Indeterminate nonthermal pit	30	1	SA 1	Y	2	Rillito-Middle Rincon	Early-Middle Rincon	late Middle Formative
17.02	Posthole	35	N/A	SA 1	Y	1	Rillito-Middle Rincon	Early-Middle Rincon	late Middle Formative
17.03	Non-feature	99	N/A	SA 1	Y	1	N/A	N/A	N/A
17.04	Non-feature	99	N/A	SA 1	Y	1	N/A	N/A	N/A
17.05	Posthole	35	N/A	SA 1	Y	1	Rillito-Middle Rincon	Early-Middle Rincon	late Middle Formative

Table I.C. Summary of feature characteristics, cont'd.

Feature	Feature Type	Feature Type Code[1]	Wöcherl Pit Class[2]	Locus[3]	Excavated	Screened[4]	Chronological Range	Best Guess: Tucson Basin-specific	Best Guess: Formative Terminology
18	Secondary cremation	53	N/A	SA 1	Y	2	Formative	Rincon	Middle Formative
19	Roasting pit	23	7	SA 4	Y	4	Formative	Rincon	late Middle Formative
20	Bell Pit	34	5	TR 6	Y	1	Early Agricultural-Formative	Early Agricultural-Formative	Early Agricultural-Formative
21	Medium nonthermal pit	32	2	SA 3	Y	1	Early Agricultural-Formative	Early Agricultural-Formative	Early Agricultural-Formative
22	Medium nonthermal pit	32	4	SA 3	Y	1	Early Agricultural-Formative	Early Agricultural-Formative	Early Agricultural-Formative
23	Medium nonthermal pit	32	3	TR 6	Y	1	Early Agricultural-Formative	Early Agricultural-Formative	Early Agricultural-Formative
24	Voided	VOID	VOID	VOID	VOID	VOID	VOID	VOID	VOID
25	Large nonthermal pit	33	7	SA 3	Y	1	Early Agricultural-Formative	San Pedro?	San Pedro?
26	Medium nonthermal pit	32	7	SA 4	Y	1	Early Agricultural-Formative	Early Agricultural-Formative	Early Agricultural-Formative
27	Non-feature	99	N/A	SA 3	Y	1	NA	NA	NA
28	Roasting pit	23	1	SA 4	Y	1	Early Agricultural-Formative	Early Agricultural-Formative	Early Agricultural-Formative
29	Roasting pit	23	1	SA 4	Y	1	Early Agricultural-Formative	Rincon	late Middle Formative
30	Roasting pit	23	1	SA 4	Y	1	Early Agricultural-Formative	Early Agricultural-Formative	Early Agricultural-Formative
31	Medium nonthermal pit	32	1	SA 4	Y	1	Early Agricultural-Formative	Early Agricultural-Formative	Early Agricultural-Formative
32	Non-feature	99	N/A	SA 4	Y	1	NA	NA	NA
33	Roasting pit	23	1	SA 4	Y	1	Formative	Rincon	late Middle Formative
34	Non-feature	99	N/A	SA 1	Y	1	NA	NA	NA
35	Non-feature	99	N/A	SA 1	Y	4	NA	NA	NA
36	Non-feature	99	N/A	SA 1	Y	1	NA	NA	NA

Table I.C. Summary of feature characteristics, cont'd.

Feature	Feature Type	Feature Type Code[1]	Wöcherl Pit Class[2]	Locus[3]	Excavated	Screened[4]	Chronological Range	Best Guess: Tucson Basin-specific	Best Guess: Formative Terminology
37	*Voided*	*VOID*	*VOID*	*VOID*	*VOID*	*VOID*	*VOID*	*VOID*	*VOID*
38	Medium nonthermal pit	32	4	SA 4	Y	1	Early Agricultural-Formative	Early Agricultural-Formative	Early Agricultural-Formative
39	Roasting pit	23	3	SA 5	Y	1	Early Agricultural-Formative	Rincon	late Middle Formative
40	Roasting pit	23	7	SA 4	Y	1	Early Agricultural-Formative	Rincon?	late Middle Formative?
41	Occupation surface	17	N/A	SA 5	Y	1	Tortolita (Early Formative)-Historic	Rincon	late Middle Formative
41.01	Posthole	35	N/A	SA 5	Y	1	Formative	Rincon	late Middle Formative
41.02	Posthole	35	N/A	SA 5	Y	1	Formative	Rincon	late Middle Formative
41.03	Posthole	35	N/A	SA 5	Y	1	Formative	Rincon	late Middle Formative
41.04	Posthole	35	N/A	SA 5	Y	1	Formative	Rincon	late Middle Formative
42	Medium nonthermal pit	32	7	SA 3	Y	1	Early Agricultural-Formative	San Pedro?	San Pedro?
43	*Non-feature*	*99*	*N/A*	*SA 3*	*Y*	*1*	*N/A*	*N/A*	*N/A*
44	Medium nonthermal pit	32	4	SA 3	Y	1	San Pedro	San Pedro	San Pedro
45	*Non-feature*	*99*	*N/A*	*SA 3*	*Y*	*1*	*N/A*	*N/A*	*N/A*
46	*Non-feature*	*99*	*N/A*	*SA 3*	*Y*	*1*	*N/A*	*N/A*	*N/A*
47	*Non-feature*	*99*	*N/A*	*SA 4*	*Y*	*1*	*N/A*	*N/A*	*N/A*
48	Medium nonthermal pit	32	7	SA 4	Y	1	Formative	Rincon	late Middle Formative
49	Medium nonthermal pit	32	1	SA 4	Y	1	Middle-Late Rincon	Middle-Late Rincon	late Middle Formative
50	Indeterminate nonthermal pit	30	7	TR 13	Y	1	Early Agricultural-Formative	Early Agricultural-Formative	Early Agricultural-Formative
51	Pit house	1	N/A	SA 4	Y	2	Formative	Rincon	late Middle Formative
51.01	Indeterminate thermal pit	20		SA 4	Y	2	Formative	Rincon?	late Middle Formative

Table I.C. Summary of feature characteristics, cont'd.

Feature	Feature Type	Feature Type Code[1]	Wöcherl Pit Class[2]	Locus[3]	Excavated	Screened[4]	Chronological Range	Best Guess: Tucson Basin-specific	Best Guess: Formative Terminology
52	Bell Pit	34	5	SA5	Y	1	Formative	Rincon	late Middle Formative
53	Medium nonthermal pit	32	1	SA5	Y	2	Early Agricultural-Formative	Early Agricultural-Formative	Early Agricultural-Formative
54	Large nonthermal pit	33	2	SA4	Y	1	Early Agricultural-Formative	Rincon	late Middle Formative
55	Indeterminate thermal pit	20	7	SA2	Y	1	Early Agricultural-Formative	San Pedro?	San Pedro?
56	Roasting pit	23	7	SA4	Y	1	Early Agricultural-Formative	Early Agricultural-Formative	Early Agricultural-Formative
57	Medium nonthermal pit	32	2	TR 13	Y	1	Early Agricultural-Formative	Early Agricultural-Formative	Early Agricultural-Formative
58	Bell Pit	34	5	SA4	Y	1	Early Agricultural-Formative	San Pedro?	San Pedro?
59	Bell Pit	34	5	SA4	Y	1	Early Agricultural-Formative	San Pedro?	San Pedro?
60	Roasting pit	23	3	SA4	Y	1	Early Agricultural-Formative	Early Agricultural-Formative	Early Agricultural-Formative
61	Indeterminate thermal pit	20	1	SA4	Y	1	Early Formative?	Tortolita?	late Early Formative?
62	Medium nonthermal pit	32	7	SA3	Y	1	Early Agricultural-Formative	San Pedro?	San Pedro?
63	Medium nonthermal pit	32	7	SA2	Y	1	Early Agricultural-Formative	San Pedro?	San Pedro?
64	Medium nonthermal pit	32	1	SA4	Y	1	Early Agricultural-Formative	Early Agricultural-Formative	Early Agricultural-Formative
65	Large nonthermal pit	33	7	SA5	Y	1	Early Agricultural-Formative	Early Agricultural-Formative	Early Agricultural-Formative
66	Indeterminate nonthermal pit	30	7	SA3	Y	1	Early Agricultural-Formative	San Pedro?	San Pedro?
67	Bell Pit	34	5	SA4	Y	1	Early Agricultural-Formative	Early Agricultural-Formative	Early Agricultural-Formative
68	Indeterminate nonthermal pit	30	7	SA4	Y	1	Early Agricultural-Formative	Early Agricultural-Formative	Early Agricultural-Formative

Table I.C. Summary of feature characteristics, cont'd.

Feature	Feature Type	Feature Type Code[1]	Wöcherl Pit Class[2]	Locus[3]	Excavated	Screened[4]	Chronological Range	Best Guess: Tucson Basin-specific	Best Guess: Formative Terminology
69	Hearth	21		SA 5	Y	0	Early Agricultural-Formative	Early Agricultural-Formative	Early Agricultural-Formative
70	Medium nonthermal pit	32	7	SA 5	Y	1	Early Agricultural-Formative	Early Agricultural-Formative	Early Agricultural-Formative
71	Medium nonthermal pit	32	7	SA 5	Y	1	Early Agricultural-Formative	Early Agricultural-Formative	Early Agricultural-Formative
72	Indeterminate thermal pit	20	7	SA 4	Y	1	Rillito-Middle Rincon	Rillito-Middle Rincon	late Middle Formative
73	Indeterminate nonthermal pit	30	3	SA 4	Y	1	Early Agricultural-Formative	Early Agricultural-Formative	Early Agricultural-Formative
74	Indeterminate nonthermal pit	30	4	SA 3	Y	1	Early Agricultural-Formative	San Pedro?	San Pedro?
75	Medium nonthermal pit	32	2	SA 4	Y	1	Early Agricultural-Formative	Early Agricultural-Formative	Early Agricultural-Formative
76	Bell Pit	34	5	SA 4	Y	1	Early Agricultural-Formative	Early Agricultural-Formative	Early Agricultural-Formative
77	*Non-feature*	*99*	*N/A*	*NTR 13*	*Y*	*1*	*N/A*	*N/A*	*N/A*
78	Medium nonthermal pit	32	3	SA 4	Y	1	Early Agricultural-Formative	Early Agricultural-Formative	Early Agricultural-Formative
79	Medium nonthermal pit	32	4	SA 4	Y	1	Early Agricultural-Formative	Early Agricultural-Formative	Early Agricultural-Formative
80	Small nonthermal pit	31	7	SA 5	Y	1	Early Agricultural-Formative	Early Agricultural-Formative	Early Agricultural-Formative
81	Roasting pit	23	1	SA 4	Y	1	Early Agricultural-Formative	Early Agricultural-Formative	Early Agricultural-Formative
82	Indeterminate nonthermal pit	30	7	SA 4	Y	1	Early Agricultural-Formative	Early Agricultural-Formative	Early Agricultural-Formative
83	Indeterminate nonthermal pit	30	7	SA 4	Y	1	Early Agricultural-Formative	Early Agricultural-Formative	Early Agricultural-Formative
84	Indeterminate nonthermal pit	30	7	SA 3	Y	1	Early Agricultural-Formative	San Pedro?	San Pedro?

426

Table I.C. Summary of feature characteristics, cont'd.

Feature	Feature Type	Feature Type Code[1]	Wöcherl Pit Class[2]	Locus[3]	Excavated	Screened[4]	Chronological Range	Best Guess: Tucson Basin-specific	Best Guess: Formative Terminology
85	Medium nonthermal pit	32	1	SA 5	Y	1	Early Agricultural-Formative	Early Agricultural-Formative	Early Agricultural-Formative
86	Medium nonthermal pit	32	7	SA 5	Y	1	Early Agricultural-Formative	Early Agricultural-Formative	Early Agricultural-Formative
87	Primary inhumation	50	N/A	SA 3	Y	2	Early Agricultural-Formative	Early Agricultural-Formative	Early Agricultural-Formative
88	*Non-feature*	*99*	*N/A*	*SA 5*	*Y*	*1*	*N/A*	*N/A*	*N/A*
89	Small nonthermal pit	31	1	SA 5	Y	0	Early Agricultural-Formative	Early Agricultural-Formative	Early Agricultural-Formative
90	Indeterminate nonthermal pit	30	1	TR 13	Y	1	Early Agricultural-Formative	Early Agricultural-Formative	Early Agricultural-Formative
91	Medium nonthermal pit	32	7	SA 5	Y	1	Early Agricultural-Formative	Early Agricultural-Formative	Early Agricultural-Formative
92	Primary inhumation	50	N/A	SA 4	Y	2	Early Agricultural-Formative	Early Agricultural-Formative	Early Agricultural-Formative
93	Indeterminate nonthermal pit	30	4	SA 4	Y	1	Early Agricultural-Formative	Early Agricultural-Formative	Early Agricultural-Formative
94	Medium nonthermal pit	32	1	SA 5	Y	1	Early Agricultural-Formative	Early Agricultural-Formative	Early Agricultural-Formative
95	Roasting pit	23	7	SA 4	Y	1	Early Agricultural-Formative	San Pedro?	San Pedro?
96	Medium nonthermal pit	32	1	SA 4	Y	1	Early Agricultural-Formative	San Pedro?	San Pedro?
97	Medium nonthermal pit	32	2	SA 4	Y	1	Rillito–Late Rincon	Rincon	late Middle Formative
98	Bell Pit	34	5	SA 3	Y	1	San Pedro	San Pedro	San Pedro
99	Small nonthermal pit	31	1	SA 3	Y	1	Early Agricultural-Formative	San Pedro?	San Pedro?
100	Medium nonthermal pit	32	2	SA 3	Y	1	Early Agricultural-Formative	San Pedro?	San Pedro?
101	Medium nonthermal pit	32	1	SA 3	Y	1	Early Agricultural-Formative	San Pedro?	San Pedro?

Table I.C. Summary of feature characteristics, cont'd.

Feature	Feature Type	Feature Type Code[1]	Wöcherl Pit Class[2]	Locus[3]	Excavated	Screened[4]	Chronological Range	Best Guess: Tucson Basin-specific	Best Guess: Formative Terminology
102	Bell Pit	34	5	SA 3	Y	1	Early Agricultural-Formative	San Pedro?	San Pedro?
103	Medium nonthermal pit	32	3	SA 3	Y	1	Early Agricultural-Formative	San Pedro?	San Pedro?
104	Small nonthermal pit	31	3	SA 3	Y	1	Early Agricultural-Formative	San Pedro?	San Pedro?
105	Medium nonthermal pit	32	7	SA 3	Y	1	Early Agricultural-Formative	San Pedro?	San Pedro?
106	Medium nonthermal pit	32	1	SA 4	Y	1	Early Agricultural-Formative	Early Agricultural-Formative	Early Agricultural-Formative
107	Indeterminate nonthermal pit	30	3	SA 4	Y	1	Early Agricultural-Formative	Early Agricultural-Formative	Early Agricultural-Formative
108	Medium nonthermal pit	32	2	SA 3	Y	1	Early Agricultural-Formative	San Pedro?	San Pedro?
109	Bell Pit	34	5	SA 4	Y	1	Early Rincon-Tanque Verde	Late Rincon	late Middle Formative
110	Medium nonthermal pit	32	2	SA 4	Y	1	Formative	Rincon?	Middle Formative?
111	Medium nonthermal pit	32	1	SA 4	Y	1	Early Agricultural-Formative	Early Agricultural-Formative	Early Agricultural-Formative
112	Medium nonthermal pit	32	7	SA 4	Y	1	Late Agua Caliente-Tortolita	Late Agua Caliente-Tortolita	Early Formative
113	Medium nonthermal pit	32	2	SA 5	Y	1	Early Agricultural-Formative	Early Agricultural-Formative	Early Agricultural-Formative
114	Medium nonthermal pit	32	3	SA 5	Y	1	Early Agricultural-Formative	Early Agricultural-Formative	Early Agricultural-Formative
115	Medium nonthermal pit	32	1	SA 4	Y	1	Early Agricultural-Formative	Early Agricultural-Formative	Early Agricultural-Formative
116	Medium nonthermal pit	32	1	SA 4	Y	1	Early Agricultural-Formative	Early Agricultural-Formative	Early Agricultural-Formative
117	Medium nonthermal pit	32	1	SA 4	Y	1	Early Agricultural-Formative	Early Agricultural-Formative	Early Agricultural-Formative

Table I.C. Summary of feature characteristics, cont'd.

Feature	Feature Type	Feature Type Code[1]	Wöcherl Pit Class[2]	Locus[3]	Excavated	Screened[4]	Chronological Range	Best Guess: Tucson Basin-specific	Best Guess: Formative Terminology
118	Indeterminate thermal pit	20	1	SA4	Y	1	Early Agricultural-Formative	Rincon	late Middle Formative
119	Medium nonthermal pit	32	7	SA4	Y	1	Early Agricultural-Formative	Rincon?	Middle Formative
120	Medium nonthermal pit	32	3	SA3	Y	1	Early Agricultural-Formative	San Pedro?	San Pedro?
121	*Nonthermal*	*32*	*Unk.*	*SA3*	*N*	*0*	*Unknown*	*Unknown*	*Unknown*
122	Medium nonthermal pit	32	7	SA4	Y	1	Rillito-Rincon	Rillito-Rincon	Middle Formative
123	Medium nonthermal pit	32	1	SA3	Y	1	Early Agricultural-Formative	San Pedro?	San Pedro?
124	Indeterminate nonthermal pit	30	1	SA3	Y	1	Early Agricultural-Formative	San Pedro?	San Pedro?
125	*Voided*	*VOID*	*VOID*	*VOID*	*VOID*	*VOID*	*VOID*	*VOID*	*VOID*
126	Medium nonthermal pit	32	2	SA3	Y	1	Early Agricultural-Formative	San Pedro?	San Pedro?
127	Medium nonthermal pit	32	1	SA4	Y	1	Early Agricultural-Formative	Rincon	late Middle Formative
128	Medium nonthermal pit	32	7	SA3	Y	1	Early Agricultural-Formative	San Pedro?	San Pedro?
129	Bell Pit	34	5	SA4	Y	1	Early Agricultural-Formative	San Pedro?	San Pedro?
130	Medium nonthermal pit	32	3	SA4	Y	1	Early Agricultural-Formative	Early Agricultural-Formative	Early Agricultural-Formative
131	Small nonthermal pit	31	1	SA4	Y	1	Early Agricultural-Formative	Early Agricultural-Formative	Early Agricultural-Formative
132	Medium nonthermal pit	32	7	SA4	Y	1	Early Agricultural-Formative	Early Agricultural-Formative	Early Agricultural-Formative
133	Medium nonthermal pit	32	7	SA4	Y	1	Early Agricultural-Formative	Early Agricultural-Formative	Early Agricultural-Formative
134	Bell Pit	34	5	SA4	Y	1	Early Agricultural-Formative	Early Agricultural-Formative	Early Agricultural-Formative

Table I.C. Summary of feature characteristics, cont'd.

Feature	Feature Type	Feature Type Code[1]	Wöcherl Pit Class[2]	Locus[3]	Excavated	Screened[4]	Chronological Range	Best Guess: Tucson Basin-specific	Best Guess: Formative Terminology
135	Historic	99	N/A	SA 2	N		Historic	Historic	Historic
136	Medium nonthermal pit	32	7	SA 4	Y	1	Rillito-Middle Rincon	Rillito-Middle Rincon	Middle Formative
137	Medium nonthermal pit	32	7	SA 5	Y	1	Early Agricultural-Formative	Early Agricultural-Formative	Early Agricultural-Formative
138	*Non-feature*	*99*	*N/A*	*SA 4*	*Y*	*1*	*N/A*	*N/A*	*N/A*
139	Bell Pit	34	5	SA 5	Y	1	Early Agricultural-Formative	San Pedro?	San Pedro?
140	Medium nonthermal pit	32	2	SA 3	Y	1	Early Agricultural-Formative	San Pedro?	San Pedro?
141	Medium nonthermal pit	32	2	SA 4	Y	1	Early Rincon-Late Rincon	Rincon	late Middle Formative
142	Medium nonthermal pit	32	3	SA 3	Y	1	Early Agricultural-Formative	San Pedro?	San Pedro?
143	*Thermal*	*22*		*SA 5*	*N*	*0*	*Unknown*	*Unknown*	*Unknown*
144	*Thermal*	*23*		*SA 3*	*N*	*0*	*Unknown*	*Unknown*	*Unknown*
145	Medium nonthermal pit	32	1	SA 3	Y	1	Early Agricultural-Formative	San Pedro?	San Pedro?
146	*Nonthermal*	*32*	*Unk.*	*SA 3*	*N*	*0*	*Unknown*	*Unknown*	*Unknown*
147	*Nonthermal*	*32*	*Unk.*	*SA 3*	*N*	*0*	*Unknown*	*Unknown*	*Unknown*
148	*Nonthermal*	*32*	*Unk.*	*SA 3*	*N*	*0*	*Unknown*	*Unknown*	*Unknown*
149	Medium nonthermal pit	32	1	SA 4	Y	1	Early Agricultural-Formative	Early Agricultural-Formative	Early Agricultural-Formative
150	*Nonthermal*	*32*	*Unk.*	*SA 4*	*N*	*0*	*Unknown*	*Unknown*	*Unknown*
151	*Non-feature*	*99*	*N/A*	*SA 5*	*Y*	*1*	*N/A*	*N/A*	*N/A*
152	Pit house	1	N/A	SA 5	Y	1	Rillito-Historic	Middle-Late Rincon	late Middle Formative
152.01	Posthole	35	N/A	SA 5	Y	1	Early Rincon-Tanque Verde	Middle-Late Rincon	late Middle Formative

Table I.C. Summary of feature characteristics, cont'd.

Feature	Feature Type	Feature Type Code[1]	Wöcherl Pit Class[2]	Locus[3]	Excavated	Screened[4]	Chronological Range	Best Guess: Tucson Basin-specific	Best Guess: Formative Terminology
152.02	Posthole	35	N/A	SA 5	Y	1	Early Rincon-Tanque Verde	Middle-Late Rincon	late Middle Formative
152.03	Posthole	35	N/A	SA 5	Y	1	Early Rincon-Tanque Verde	Middle-Late Rincon	late Middle Formative
152.04	Posthole	35	N/A	SA 5	Y	1	Early Rincon-Tanque Verde	Middle-Late Rincon	late Middle Formative
152.05	Posthole	35	N/A	SA 5	Y	1	Early Rincon-Tanque Verde	Middle-Late Rincon	late Middle Formative
152.06	Posthole	35	N/A	SA 5	Y	1	Early Rincon-Tanque Verde	Middle-Late Rincon	late Middle Formative
152.07	Posthole	35	N/A	SA 5	Y	1	Early Rincon-Tanque Verde	Middle-Late Rincon	late Middle Formative
152.08	Posthole	35	N/A	SA 5	Y	1	Early Rincon-Tanque Verde	Middle-Late Rincon	late Middle Formative
152.09	*Non-feature*	*99*	*N/A*	*SA 5*	*Y*	*1*	*N/A*	*N/A*	*N/A*
152.10	Posthole	35	N/A	SA 5	Y	1	Early Rincon-Tanque Verde	Middle-Late Rincon	late Middle Formative
152.11	Firepit (unprepared hearth)	22		SA 5	Y	0	Early Rincon-Tanque Verde	Middle-Late Rincon	late Middle Formative
152.12	Hearth	21		SA 5	Y	0	Early Rincon-Tanque Verde	Middle-Late Rincon	late Middle Formative
153	*Thermal*	*20*		*SA 4*	*N*	*0*	*Unknown*	*Unknown*	*Unknown*
154	*Nonthermal*	*32*	*Unk.*	*SA 4*	*N*	*0*	*Unknown*	*Unknown*	*Unknown*
155	*Nonthermal*	*32*	*Unk.*	*SA 4*	*N*	*0*	*Unknown*	*Unknown*	*Unknown*
156	*Nonthermal*	*32*	*Unk.*	*SA 4*	*N*	*0*	*Unknown*	*Unknown*	*Unknown*
157	Bell Pit	34	5	SA 3	Y	1	Early Agricultural-Formative	San Pedro?	San Pedro?
158	Secondary cremation	53	N/A	SA 1	Y	0	Early Agricultural-Formative	Rincon?	Middle Formative?
159	*Nonthermal*	*32*	*Unk.*	*SA 5*	*N*	*0*	*Unknown*	*Unknown*	*Unknown*

Table I.C. Summary of feature characteristics, cont'd.

Feature	Feature Type	Feature Type Code[1]	Wöcherl Pit Class[2]	Locus[3]	Excavated	Screened[4]	Chronological Range	Best Guess: Tucson Basin-specific	Best Guess: Formative Terminology
160	Nonthermal	32	Unk.	SA 5	N	0	Unknown	Unknown	Unknown
161	Thermal	26		SA 5	N	0	Unknown	Unknown	Unknown
162	Nonthermal	31	Unk.	SA 5	N	0	Unknown	Unknown	Unknown
163	Nonthermal	32	Unk.	SA 4	N	0	Unknown	Unknown	Unknown
164	Thermal	20		SA 4	N	0	Unknown	Unknown	Unknown
165	Bell Pit	34	5	SA 2	Y	1	Early Agricultural-Formative	San Pedro?	San Pedro?
166	Nonthermal	32	Unk.	SA 3	N	0	Unknown	Unknown	Unknown
167	Nonthermal	32	Unk.	SA 3	N	0	Unknown	Unknown	Unknown
168	Thermal	23		SA 3	N	0	Unknown	Unknown	Unknown
169	Other Prehis	32	Unk.	SA 3	N	0	Unknown	Unknown	Unknown
170	Nonthermal	32	Unk.	SA 3	N	0	Unknown	Unknown	Unknown
171	Nonthermal	32	Unk.	SA 3	N	0	Unknown	Unknown	Unknown
172	Nonthermal	32	Unk.	SA 3	N	0	Unknown	Unknown	Unknown
173	Bell Pit	34	5	SA 1	Y	1	Middle Rincon-Tanque Verde	Late Rincon	late Middle Formative
174	Nonthermal	32	Unk.	SA 3	N	0	Unknown	Unknown	Unknown
175	Nonthermal	32	Unk.	SA 3	N	0	Unknown	Unknown	Unknown
176	Nonthermal	32	Unk.	SA 3	N	0	Unknown	Unknown	Unknown
177	Nonthermal	32	Unk.	SA 3	N	0	Unknown	Unknown	Unknown
178	Nonthermal	32	Unk.	SA 3	N	0	Unknown	Unknown	Unknown
179	Nonthermal	32	Unk.	SA 3	N	0	Unknown	Unknown	Unknown
180	Nonthermal	32	Unk.	SA 3	N	0	Unknown	Unknown	Unknown
181	Nonthermal	32	Unk.	SA 3	N	0	Unknown	Unknown	Unknown

Table I.C. Summary of feature characteristics, cont'd.

Feature	Feature Type	Feature Type Code[1]	Wöcherl Pit Class[2]	Locus[3]	Excavated	Screened[4]	Chronological Range	Best Guess: Tucson Basin-specific	Best Guess: Formative Terminology
182	Secondary cremation	53	N/A	TR 1	Y	2	Early Agricultural-Formative	Rincon?	Middle Formative?
183	Nonthermal	32	Unk.	SA 3	N	0	Unknown	Unknown	Unknown
184	Nonthermal	32	Unk.	SA 3	N	0	Unknown	Unknown	Unknown
185	Nonthermal	32	Unk.	SA 2	N	0	Unknown	Unknown	Unknown
186	Nonthermal	32	Unk.	SA 2	N	0	Unknown	Unknown	Unknown
187	Nonthermal	32	Unk.	SA 3	N	0	Unknown	Unknown	Unknown
188	Nonthermal	32	Unk.	SA 3	N	0	Unknown	Unknown	Unknown
189	Nonthermal	32	Unk.	SA 5	N	0	Unknown	Unknown	Unknown
190	Nonthermal	31	Unk.	SA 5	N	0	Unknown	Unknown	Unknown
191	Nonthermal	33	Unk.	SA 2	N	0	Unknown	Unknown	Unknown
192	Nonthermal	32	Unk.	SA 3	N	0	Unknown	Unknown	Unknown
193	Nonthermal	32	Unk.	SA 3	N	0	Unknown	Unknown	Unknown
194	Nonthermal	32	Unk.	SA 3	N	0	Unknown	Unknown	Unknown
195	Nonthermal	32	Unk.	SA 3	N	0	Unknown	Unknown	Unknown
196	Nonthermal	32	Unk.	SA 2	N	0	Unknown	Unknown	Unknown
197	Nonthermal	32	Unk.	SA 2	N	0	Unknown	Unknown	Unknown
198	Nonthermal	32	Unk.	SA 5	N	0	Unknown	Unknown	Unknown
199	Nonthermal	32	Unk.	SA 5	N	0	Unknown	Unknown	Unknown
200	Primary inhumation	50	N/A	SA 4	Y	2	Early Agricultural-Formative	Early Agricultural-Formative	Early Agricultural-Formative
201	Nonthermal	32	Unk.	SA 4	N	0	Unknown	Unknown	Unknown
202	Nonthermal	32	Unk.	SA 4	N	0	Unknown	Unknown	Unknown
203	Nonthermal	32	Unk.	SA 4	N	0	Unknown	Unknown	Unknown

Table I.C. Summary of feature characteristics, cont'd.

Feature	Feature Type	Feature Type Code[1]	Wöcherl Pit Class[2]	Locus[3]	Excavated	Screened[4]	Chronological Range	Best Guess: Tucson Basin-specific	Best Guess: Formative Terminology
204	*Nonthermal*	*32*	*Unk.*	*SA4*	*N*	*0*	*Unknown*	*Unknown*	*Unknown*
205	*Thermal*	*20*	*Unk.*	*SA4*	*N*	*0*	*Unknown*	*Unknown*	*Unknown*
206	Pit house	1	N/A	SA4	Y	1	Early Agricultural-Formative	Rincon	late Middle Formative
207	Roasting pit	23		-	N	0	Early Agricultural-Formative	Early Agricultural-Formative	Early Agricultural-Formative
208	Roasting pit	23		-	N	0	Early Agricultural-Formative	Early Agricultural-Formative	Early Agricultural-Formative
209	Historic	99	N/A	-	N		Historic	Historic	Historic

[1]Feature Type: Assign appropriate feature code (WSA)

[2]Pit Class: Assign appropriate pit classification code, 1-7 (based on Wocherl 2005, Desert Arch.)

[3]Size Gradient: Small (<0.5 m diameter), Medium (0.5-1.5 m diameter), Large (1.5 m> diameter)

[4]Locus: Assign appropriate code (SA, TR, TU, etc.) and number

[5]Screened: 0 = Not screened; 1 = 1/4"; 2 = 1/8"; 3 = point provenienced; 4 = unknown

[6]Prep: *Wall/Base* 1 = unlined; 2 = plastered; 3 = stone-lined; *Rim* 1 = unplastered; 2 = plastered; 3 = raised coping

[7]Diagnostics: List diagnostic artifacts by type (flaked stone) or ware (ceramics)

[8]Date: Relative dates based on diagnostic artifacts; Absolute dates based on C-14 and OSL dates

Table I.D. Distribution of artifacts recovered from excavated features[a] and subfeatures

Feature	*Flaked Stone*					Ground Stone	*Ceramics*				Faunal	Worked Shell	Unworked Shell	Total
	Debitage	Core	Uniface	Biface	Hammerstone		Painted Intrusive	RV Unpainted	Special	Other				
2	2										8			10
3	14			1										15
4	5							3						8
5	11						1	2			5			19
6	1447	8	2	12		1	42	235	4	70	86	2		1909
7	897	4	4	9		3	45	173	1	35	66	2		1239
7.02							1							1
7.03	2													2
7.05	1													1
7.19	5										1			6
7.21											5			5
8				3							7			10
9	25						1		1		1			28
10	105	1		1		1					2			110
11	1348	5	1	7		3	10	207	3	41	146			1771
11.02	9						1	8		1				19
11.03	3							1		1				5
11.04	228	2						5			2			237
11.09	15										7			22
12	191	3	2	2			2	3		1	23			227
13	53							2	1		2			58
14											9			9
15	11							2						13

Table I.D. Distribution of artifacts recovered from excavated features[a] and subfeatures, cont'd.

	Flaked Stone						*Ceramics*									
Feature	Debitage	Core	Uniface	Biface	Hammerstone	Ground Stone	Painted	Intrusive	RV	Unpainted	Special	Other	Faunal	Worked Shell	Unworked Shell	Total
16	201	2		1			1			2			1			208
17	101	1		2		6	24		1	92		67	89	4		387
17.01										1		1				2
17.02	1															1
17.03	*1*											*1*				*2*
18										4			6			10
19	111	1		2			5			36		18	6	1		180
20	48	1	1	1									1			52
21	40												2			42
22	18															18
23	107	1								1		1	2			112
25	61	3		2	1		1			1		1	229			299
26	126	4		1						5						136
28						1	1			1			61			64
29							1			4		3	14			22
30										1			21			22
31	12												53			65
32	2															2
33	1	1					2			1		1				6
34	*1*															*1*
35										*1*						*1*
36	*34*		*1*	*2*		*1*				*3*						*41*
38	15						1			2						18

Table I.D. Distribution of artifacts recovered from excavated features[a] and subfeatures, cont'd.

Feature	Flaked Stone					Ground Stone	Ceramics					Other	Faunal	Worked Shell	Unworked Shell	Total
	Debitage	Core	Uniface	Biface	Hammerstone		Painted	Intrusive	RV	Unpainted	Special					
39	2						1			2			2			7
40	1						1			3						5
41	451	6	2	1	1	3	9			36		6	20			535
41.01	3									3						6
42	26					4										30
43	7															7
44	146	3		1			1			9		7	27		1	195
45	27	1								3		5				36
46	6															6
47	3									3		1				7
48	108	1					2			10		5				126
50	16											2				18
51	549	7	1	4			36			133	2	19	73	1	1	826
51.01	7									1	1	1	2			11
51.02	2									1		1				4
52	504	10	2	2		1	23			61	1	89	1			694
53	31	2					1			6			5			45
54	68	2		2			12			20		30	18			152
55	17															17
56	7									1						8
57	149	10	2	2		1				2		2	12			180
58	94	1	1	1						1			12			110
59	379	1	1	2								2	6			391

Table I.D. Distribution of artifacts recovered from excavated features[a] and subfeatures, cont'd.

Feature	Flaked Stone					Ground Stone	Ceramics					Other	Faunal	Worked Shell	Unworked Shell	Total
	Debitage	Core	Uniface	Biface	Hammerstone		Painted	Intrusive	RV	Unpainted	Special					
60	28			1		1				2			2			34
61	58	3	1							10	3		3			78
62	1															1
63	11	1														12
64	37									1						38
65	48					1				2						51
66	20	1	1	1									1			24
67	26	2	1				4			3		1	6			43
68	3									1						4
70	9					1				1						11
71													1			1
72	165			2		1	6			14			7			195
73	28		1			1										30
74	30	2		1												33
75	30	1					1									32
76	37	1		1									154			193
77	2									2						4
78	4			1						1						6
79										1			25			26
80						1										1
81	36					1				8		2				47
82	1															1
83	20						1									21

Table I.D. Distribution of artifacts recovered from excavated features[a] and subfeatures, cont'd.

Feature	Flaked Stone					Ground Stone	Ceramics					Other	Faunal	Worked Shell	Unworked Shell	Total
	Debitage	Core	Uniface	Biface	Hammerstone		Painted	Intrusive	RV	Unpainted	Special					
84	2															2
85	21															21
86	10									6						16
87	18												1			19
88							*1*			*1*						*2*
90	27					2				4		4				37
91	20									4						24
92	123			1			1			4		3	1			133
93	109	5		1			1			1			10			127
94	10					1										11
95	128			1			3			2			27			161
96	37			1												38
97	74			3						2		1	3			83
98	364	5	2	7		2							77			457
99	3															3
101	22															22
102	152	3								1			31			187
103	40						1									41
104	7			1												8
105	94			2									3			99
106	16															16
107	110					3	2			3		2	11			131
108	84															84

Table I.D. Distribution of artifacts recovered from excavated features[a] and subfeatures, cont'd.

Feature	Flaked Stone					Ground Stone	Ceramics					Other	Faunal	Worked Shell	Unworked Shell	Total
	Debitage	Core	Uniface	Biface	Hammerstone		Painted	Intrusive	RV	Unpainted	Special					
109	265			1		1	54			50	1	37	139	1	1	549
110	7						1			8		3		1		20
111	15												1			16
112	147	4			1	3				4		7	22			188
113	12	1											1			14
114	67			1												68
115	3															3
116	8															8
117	11	1		1						2		2	5			22
118	25		1				1			8			8			43
119	45	2				1	3			5		1	8			65
120	52	1		1												54
122	36					2				3						41
123	17															17
124	35					2										37
126	13															13
127	8			1												9
129	607	4		3			1			3		2	22			642
130	5	1								1						7
131										1						1
132	15		3							1						19
134	2															2
136	99	1		1		1	2			4	1		3			112

Table I.D. Distribution of artifacts recovered from excavated features[a] and subfeatures, cont'd.

Feature	Flaked Stone					Ground Stone	Ceramics					Other	Faunal	Worked Shell	Unworked Shell	Total
	Debitage	Core	Uniface	Biface	Hammerstone		Painted	Intrusive	RV	Unpainted	Special					
137	10															10
138	*7*						*1*			*3*						*11*
139	166	1		2		3	2			2			58			234
140	12									1		1				14
141	132			2			1			1			1			137
142	10															10
145	15									1						16
149	55					2	1			1			4			63
151	*18*															*18*
152	1809	2	3	13		18	114			343	7	325	314	3	2	2953
152.01	2	1														3
152.02	5															5
152.03	1															1
152.06	2															2
152.08	3															3
152.1	4		1													5
152.11	7															7
152.12	6												1			7
157	24			1												25
158	1															1
165	209		1										2			212
173	21					3	14	1		17	1	3	30			90
182	1															1

Table I.D. Distribution of artifacts recovered from excavated features[a] and subfeatures, cont'd.

	Flaked Stone					Ground Stone	Ceramics							Worked Shell	Unworked Shell	Total
Feature	Debitage	Core	Uniface	Biface	Hammerstone	Stone	Painted	Intrusive	RV	Unpainted	Special	Other	Faunal			
200	108									5			4			117
202						1										1
206	33	2		1						3			1			40
208										1						1
Totals	14075	126	35	113	3	77	441	1	1	1634	24	812	2015	15	4	

[a]Listed features include all excavated features that contained artifacts, as well as nonfeatures excavated as features that contained artifacts; nonfeatures are in italics. Voided features (1, 24, 37, and 125) are not listed in this table; no artifacts were associated with these features.